24

The Road to Nunavut

ᐊᖅᑯᑎ ᓄᓇᕗᒻᒧ

By Keith Crowe, with files from Marion Soublière and Greg Coleman

ᑎᑎᕋᖅᑕᐅᔪᖅ ᑮᑦ ᑯᕉᓐ, ᐃᓚᖃᐅᑎᖃᕐᓂ ᐸᐸᑕᐅᓯᒪᔪᓂᑦ ᒥᐊᓇᐊᓐ ᓲᐱᓕᐃᒥ ᐊᒻᒪ ᒍᕆᒡ ᑰᓪᒪᓐ

With a land claim agreement and now, a territory, the Inuit of Canada's central and eastern Arctic are back in the driver's seat. Also, in "What Price Nunavut?," John Amagoalik examines the personal toll that negotiations took, while Jimi Onalik envisions the challenges that lie ahead in "The Next Generation"

ᓄᓇᑖᕋᓰᑎᒧᓐ ᐊᖏᕈᑎᑕᖃᕐᓯᑎᓪᓗᒍ ᐊᒻᒪ ᒫᓐᓇ, ᐃᒻᒥᒃᑰᖅᑐᒥ ᐊᕕᒃᓯᒪᔪᒥᓐ ᓄᓇᖃᕐᓱᑎᒃ, ᐃᓄᐃᑦ ᑲᓇᑕᐅᑉ ᖃᑎᒃᐊᓃᑦᑐᑦ ᐊᒻᒪ ᑲᓇᖕᓇᖓᓂ ᐅᑭᐅᖅᑕᖅᑐᖅᒥ ᐊᐅᓚᑦᑎᔨᐅᒃᑲᓂᕈᓐᓇᖅᓯᔪᑦ. ᐊᒻᒪᑦᑕᐅᖅ, ᐅᑦᓇ "ᖃᓄᖅ ᐊᑭᖃᖅᓯᒪᕙ ᓄᓇᕗᑦ?," ᔮᓐ ᐊᒪᒍᐊᓗᒃ ᖃᐅᔨᓴᖅᓯᒪᔪᖅ ᐃᒻᒥᓂᒃ ᑕᒪᓐᓇ ᖃᓄᖅ ᐊᒃᑐᐃᓂᖃᖅᓯᒪᒻᒪᖔᑦ ᐊᖏᖃᑎᒌᒃᓯᒪᓪᓗᓂᒃ, ᐊᒻᒪ ᐅᓇ ᔨᒥ ᐅᓈᓕᒃ ᑕᐅᑐᙱᓯᐅᖅ ᖃᓄᐃᓕᐅᕆᐊᖃᕐᓂᖏᑦ ᑐᕌᒐᖃᕐᕕᖓᓐᓂᑦ ᐅᑯᓇ "ᑭᖑᕚᒃᓴᓄᑦ"

Arthur Boutilier; oval inset: Nunavut Tourism

A SURGE OF PRIDE

ᐱᒃᑯᓕᓂᕐᒥᒃ ᓴᖅᑭᑦᑎᓂᖅ

Ever since the heady days of Confederation, Canada has been growing and changing, so that the nation we know today bears very little resemblance to the one that was conceived in 1867. Since those days, Manitoba, British Columbia, Prince Edward Island, and ultimately, Newfoundland, have helped flesh out the unfinished nation.

The biggest change came in the opening years of the century, when the old North West Territories (as the future prairie provinces were called) became a Mecca for one million immigrants who settled the empty land between the Shield and the Rockies. Thus was created a nation within a nation peopled by a new kind of Canadian we call the westerner.

I call this to mind because we are now witnessing a similar transformation in what I once dubbed "The Mysterious North." We like to think or boast about our country as stretching from sea to sea — from Atlantic to Pacific — but when we use that slogan we forget the presence of another sea at the top of the continent.

The white explorers who claimed dominion over this frozen world never understood it any more than they understood the indigenous people who had learned how to survive and even to prosper in the arctic clime.

How arrogant we whites have been in our dealings with the Inuit — how blind in our refusals to learn from them and to adapt to their world! And how patronizing have we been to assume that these remarkable people, who have managed to come to terms with a hostile environment, cannot be trusted to run their own affairs!

Now, at last, we are starting to redress the balance. The formation of a vast, new, self-governing territory, stretching from the tip of Ellesmere Island to the northern border of Manitoba, has been as significant as was the opening of the West after the turn of the century. It marks an about-turn in Canada's official attitude to the original peoples within its borders — not just

ᐱᒋᐊᕐᕕᖅᑲᖅᑯᓂ ᐱᒋᐊᓕᓵᓚᐅᖅᑎᑦᑐᒍ ᑲᓇᑕᐅᑉ ᒐᕙᒪᕐᑯᐅᓯᐊ, ᑲᓇᑕ ᐱᕈᖅᐸᓪᓕᐊᕐᒋᓐᓇᖅᓯᒪᔪᖅ ᐊᒻᒪ, ᐊᓯᔾᔨᖅᐸᓪᓕᐊᑦᑐᓂ. ᑕᐃᒪᓐᓇᒥ ᐅᓪᓗᒥᐅᔪᖅ ᑲᓇᑕ ᑕᐃᑦᓯᒪᓂᒥᑦ ᐱᒋᐊᕐᕕᓕᓚᐅᖅᑕᕆᕗᖏᑦ ᐃᓕᑕᕆᔭᐅᒐᔭᙱᑦᑐᖅ ᑕᑯᔭᐅᒐᔭᕈᓂ ᑕᐃᑦᓯᒪᓂ 1867-ᖑᓚᐅᖅᑐᒥ. ᑕᐃᑲᓂᑦ ᐱᒋᐊᖅᑐᓂ, ᒫᓂᑑᐸ, ᐳᕆᑎᔅ ᑲᓚᒻᐱᐊ, ᐳᕆᓐᔅ ᐃᑦᐅᑦ ᕿᑭᖅᑕᖅ, ᐊᒻᒪᓗ ᑭᖑᓪᓖᑦᑐᒥᒃ ᐃᓚᔭᐅᓪᓗᓂ ᓂᐅᕚᓐᓛᓐ ᐃᓗᐃᑦᑐᕐᖑᕈᑕᐅᓚᐅᕐᒪᑕ ᑲᓇᑕ ᐱᒋᐊᓕᖅᑎᑕᐅᑎᓪᓗᒍ.

ᐊᓯᕐᖑᕐᓂᖅᐸᐅᔪᖅ ᐱᒋᐊᓚᐅᖅᑐᖅ ᐊᕐᕋᒍᒋᔭᒃ ᐱᒋᐊᓕᖅᑎᓪᓗᒋᑦ, ᑕᐃᑦᓯᒪᓂ ᑕᐃᔭᐅᑦᑕᓚᐅᖅᑐᖅ North West Territories – ᖑᓂᕐᖅᑕᐅᓪᓗᓂ (ᑲᓇᑕᒥ ᓄᓇᐃᓐᓇᖑ ᑭᕐᖑᖃᖕᒋᑦᑐᖅ ᑕᐃᒪᓐᓇ ᑕᐃᔭᐅᓚᐅᖅᑎᓪᓗᒍ) ᑎᑭᑦᑕᕐᕕᐅᓕᓚᐅᖅᑎᓪᓗᒍ ᒥᓕᐊᓐᓄᑦ ᐃᓅᖕᓄᑦ ᑎᑭᓖᖅᑐᓄᑦ. ᑖᓂ ᓄᓇ ᐃᓅᖃᖕᒋᑦᑐᖅ ᕿᑎᖑᓂ ᐅᔭᕋᒡᔭᐊᑉ ᑲᓇᑕᒥ ᐊᒻᒪᓗ ᑭᕐᖑᕐᔭᐊᖑᓂ. ᑕᐃᒪᓕ ᐃᓅᖃᓕᓚᐅᖅᑐᖅ ᑲᓇᑕᐅᑉ ᐃᓗᐊᓂ ᐃᓘᒃᑯᖅᑐᓂᒃ ᑕᐃᔭᐅᔪᓂᒃ ᐅᐊᓕᓂᕐᒥᐅᓂᒃ.

ᑕᒪᓐᓇ ᐃᖅᑲᖅᑕᖅ ᐃᒪᓐᓇ ᐱᔾᔪᑎᒋᓪᓗᒍ ᐅᓪᓗᒥᐅᔪᖅ ᑕᑯᔪᓐᓇᕐᒥᒐᑦ ᐊᓯᔾᔨᕈᑕᐅᓕᕐᔪᒥᒃ ᑕᐃᓚᐅᖅᓯᒪᔪᓐᓃᑦᑐᒥ ᐃᒪᓐᓇ "ᖃᐅᔨᒪᓐᓇᖕᒋᑦᑐᒥ ᐅᑭᐅᖅᑕᖅᑐᒥ." ᓄᓇᕐᑯᑎᒋᔭᕗᑦ ᐃᓯᒪᒋᓯᕐᑎᒍ ᐅᕙᑦᓘᓐᓕᑦ ᐅᐱᒋᔪᑎᒋᓗᐳ ᑕᕆᐅᒥᑦ ᑕᕆᐅᒧᑦ ᐊᖕᒋᑎᒋᓯᒪᓂᕐᓗᒍ – ᐊᑦᓛᓐᑎᒃᒥᑦ ᑕᕆᐅᕐᔪᐊᒥᑦ ᐸᓯᕕᒃ ᑕᕆᐅᕐᔪᐊᒧᑦ – ᑭᓯᐊᓂᓕ ᑕᒪᑐᒪᓂ ᐅᖃᕈᓯᐅᑲᔾᔪᒥ ᐳᐃᒍᖅᐸᒃᑕᕗᑦ ᑕᕆᐅᕐᔪᐊᖅᑕᐅᖅ ᖁᓕᑦᑎᓐᓕᑦᑐᖅ ᓄᓇᕐᔪᐊᑉ ᖁᓖᖑᓂ.

ᑎᑭᓵᖅᑐᑦ ᖃᑦᓗᓈᑦ ᐊᖓᔪᖄᖅᑲᖅᕕᓕᐅᓚᐅᖅᑐᑦ ᓄᓇᐅᔪᒥ ᖁᐊᖅᓯᒪᔪᒥ ᑐᑭᓯᓚᐅᖕᒋᑦᑐᑦ ᖃᐅᔨᑦᑐᓂᖑᓂᒃ ᐊᒻᒪᓗ ᐃᓅᖁᑎᒋᔭᑐᖃᖕᒋᑦ ᖃᐅᔨᒪᓚᐅᖕᒋᑕᖕᒋᑦᑕᐅᖅ ᐅᑭᐅᖅᑕᖅᑐᒥᐅᑕᐅᔪᑦ ᐊᓐᓇᐅᒪᒍᓐᓇᑐᖅᑲᓚᐅᖅᑐᑦ ᐃᓅᒍᓐᓇᑦᑎᐊᖅᓱᑎᓗ ᑕᐃᑲᓂ.

ᐅᕙᒍᑦ ᖃᑦᓗᓈᖑᔪᒍᑦ ᓇᓗᑦᑕ ᖃᐅᔨᓇᖅ ᐱᓂᕐᓗᐃᓯᒪᔪᒍᑦ ᐃᓅᖑᓂᒃ – ᐃᓕᒍᒪᙱᓐᓂᑦᑎᓐᓄᑦ ᐃᓕᖅᑯᓯᖕᒋᓐᓂᑦ ᐊᒻᒪᓗ ᐊᓯᔾᔨᒪᒃᑕᙱᓐᓂᑦᑎᓐᓂᒃ ᐊᑐᖅᓯᒪᑎᓪᓗᑕ ᐃᓕᓐᓇᓚᐅᕐᓗᐊᖅᑎᓪᓗᑕ ᐃᓅᓯᓇᔾᔭᖕᒋᓐᓂᒃ ᖃᐅᔨᓇᖅᓗ ᓯᓚᕐᔪᐊᖕᒋᓐᓕᑦᑐᓂᒃ! ᐊᖑᔭᖅᑳᖑᔪᒪᓗᐊᕐᓂᕐᒧᑦ ᐱᐅᓂᖅᓴᐅᓇᓯᒋᓪᓗᑕ ᑖᒃᑯᐊ ᐊᔾᔨᒋᔭᖅᑲᖕᒋᑦᑐᑦ ᓯᓚᕐᔪᐊᕐᒥ, ᐊᔪᓐᖕᒋᓂᕐᒥᖕᓂᒃ ᒪᓕᒃᓱᑎᒃ ᐃᓅᒍᓐᓇᖅᓯᒪᔪᑦ ᐊᕙᑎᒥᖕᓂ ᑲᑉᐱᐊᓇᖅᑐᖅᑲᖅᑐᓂ, ᐃᓯᒪᒋᔭ-ᐅᑦᑕᖕᒋᒻᒪᑖᓐᓕᑦ ᐃᖕᒥᖕᓂᒃ ᐃᖕᒋᕐᖃᔪᓐᓇᓂᐊᖕᒋᓐᓂᑦ!

ᐅᓪᓗᒥᐅᔪᖅ, ᐊᓯᐊᑕᐃᓐᓇᖅ, ᐱᒋᐊᓕᖅᑐᒍᑦ ᑕᒪᑐᒥᖑ ᐋᖅᑭᒃᓯᓇᓯᒋᐊᒃᓴᖅ. ᐱᓇᓱᒃᑕᐅᓯᒪᑎᓪᓗᒍ ᐱᒋᐊᖅᑎᑕᐅᓪᓗᓂ ᐊᖕᒋᔪᒥᒃ, ᓇᖕᒥᓂᖅ ᒐᕙᒪᒃᑲᖅᑐᒥᒃ ᓄᓇᒋᔭᐅᔪᒥᒃ, ᐱᒋᐊᖅᑐᒥᒃ ᐊᐅᓯᐃᑦᑐᒥᐅᑦ ᕿᑭᖅᑕᖕᒋᓐᓂᑦ ᒫᓂᑑᐸᐅᑉ ᐃᓯᖑᓐᓄᑦ, ᐱᓪᒪᓇᐅᔪᖅ. ᐱᓪᒪᓇᐅᑎᒋᔪᖅ ᐅᐊᓕᓂᐅᑉ ᒪᑐᐃᓐᓇᐅᓂᖑᓐᓄ ᑲᓇᑕ ᓄᓇᖕᒍᖅᐸᓪᓕᐊᓂᖑᓐᓂᑦ. ᑭᓪᓕᒋᔭᐅᔪᖅ ᑲᓇᑕᐅᑉ ᒐᕙᓚᓕᓇᓂᖑᑕ ᓵᖏᐊᕐᓂᖑᓂᒃ ᓄᓇᖅᑲᖅᑳᖅᑐᓄᑦ

Greg Coleman

the Inuit of Nunavut, but to all the rich and varied communities whose common ancestry goes back to the days of the last great ice sheet.

These were the first to set foot on what was to become a land of immigrants; it is ironic that they should be the last to achieve their due. The Inuit are a stubborn people, as their environment and their history make clear. It took a quarter-century of stubborn negotiations for them to receive their dream. In making that dream come true, in gaining control of their land and their lives, they have done much more than maintain dominion over a sizable chunk of northern real estate. The creation of Nunavut has returned to them the two things that were lost when the white invaders arrived — a new sense of hope for the future, and a new surge of pride in themselves and their accomplishments.

ᐃᓕᖅᑯᓯᒥᓂᖔᓄᑦ. ᐅᑯᐊᑐᐃᓐᓇᐅᓐᖏᑦᑐᖅ ᓄᓇᕗᒥᐅᑦ, ᑭᓯᐊᓂᓕ ᑕᐃᒃᑯᓄᖓᑦ ᐊᒥᓲᔪᓄᑦ ᓇᖕᒥᓂᖅ ᐃᓕᖅᑯᓯᖃᐅᖅᑐᓄᑦ ᓯᕗᓪᓕᐱᓂᖃᑎᒋᒃᑐᑦ ᐃᑦᓴᖏᓂᑕᒥᐅᓚᐅᖅᑐᓂᒃ ᓯᑯᕐᔪᐊᑉ ᑭᖑᓪᓖᑦᑐᑉ ᐅᓪᓗᕆᐋᓚᐅᖅᑕᖏᓐᓂ.

ᑖᒃᑯᐊ ᓯᕗᓪᓖᑦᑑᓪᓗᑎᒃ ᑎᑭᖅᑳᓚᐅᖅᓯᒪᔪᑦ ᑭᖑᓂᐊᒍᑦ ᓄᓇᒋᔭᐅᓕᖁᔭᖅᑐᒧᑦ ᑎᑭᓕᕗᓄᑦ; ᐅᐊᑲᓪᓚᖒᓕ ᑭᖑᓪᓖᑦᑑᓪᓗᑎᒃ ᐃᓕᑕᕆᔭᐅᓕᖁᔭᖅᑐᑦ ᐱᔪᓐᓇᐅᑎᒋᒍᓐᓇᖁᔭᖅᑕᒥᓂᒃ. ᐃᓄᐃᑦ ᓴᐱᓕᖅᓴᖃᐃᑦᑑᓐᓇᖏᑦᑐᑦ, ᐊᕙᑎᒥᖕᓂ ᐊᒻᒪᓗ ᓯᕗᓂᕆᓚᐅᖅᑕᒥᖕᓂ ᓄᖅᑲᖅᓴᖃᐃᑦᑑᓐᓇᖏᓪᓗᑎᒃ ᐅᔾᔨᖅᓇᖅᓯᒪᖕᒪᑕ. ᐊᕐᕌᒍᐃᑦ ᕼᐊᓐᑕᓪᓚᑦ ᓯᑕᒪᖕᖓᓐᓂᒃ ᐊᒃᓯᕈᕐᑎᖃᖅᓯᒪᓪᓗᑎᒃ ᐊᖏᖃᑎᒌᓕᓯᐊᕈᑎᖃᖅᓯᒪᔪᑦ ᐱᓇᓱᐊᖅᑕᒥᖕᓂᒃ ᓇᖕᒥᓂᖏᓐᓂᐊᖅᑕᒥᖕᓄᑦ ᑎᑭᓐᓇᓱᒃᓗᑎᒃ. ᑕᒪᓐᓇ ᑐᕌᖅᑕᐅᓇᓱᒃᑎᓪᓗᒍ, ᓇᖕᒥᓂᖅ ᐊᐅᓚᑦᑎᓐᓇᖁᔭᕐᓂᕐᒥᒃ ᓄᓇᒥᖕᓂᒃ ᐊᒻᒪᓗ ᐃᓅᓯᕐᒥᖕᓂᒃ, ᓄᓇᖌᓯᑐᐃᓐᓇᕐᓂᕐᒥᒃ ᑎᑐᓯᓯᒪᔪᑐᐊᖃᓐᖏᓪᓚᑕ. ᓄᓇᕗᑖᕐᓂᖅ ᐅᑎᖅᓯᓯᒪᓗᑎᑕᐅᔪᖅ ᒪᕐᕉᖕᓂᒃ ᐊᓯᐅᔨᔭᐅᓚᐅᖅᑐᓂᒃ ᖃᓪᓗᓈᓄᑦ ᐊᖅᑲᖅᑕᐅᓯᒪᓚᐅᖅᑐᓂᒃ – ᓯᕗᓂᕐᒥ ᓂᕆᐅᖕᓂᖅᑲᕐᓇᐅᑎᒥᒃ, ᐊᒻᒪᓗ ᓄᑖᒥᒃ ᓇᖕᒥᓂᖅ ᐅᐱᒋᔪᑎᖃᕐᓇᖅᓂᕐᒥᒃ ᐱᔭᕇᖅᓯᒪᔭᒥᖕᓂᓪᓗ.

PIERRE BERTON • ᐱᐅᕐ ᐆᕐᑕᓐ

Nunavut Tourism ᓄᓇᕗᑦ ᐳᓛᕆᐊᕐᕕᖓ

LOOKING BACK

ᑭᖕᒍᒧᑦ ᕿᒥᕿᑦᑐᓂ

Thinking back to my childhood and about all the things that have happened between then and now, it feels as though I have been watching a revolution in slow motion. Profound changes have taken place in our lives and our society. From the almost total isolation from the outside world of my early years in Resolute Bay in the High Arctic, to the computer space age when the world is at my fingertips, has been a journey of sorrow, joy and adventure.

Speaking to a group of young people a while ago, I realized that some of the things I was saying to them were not connecting. I then realized that the reason was that I was assuming that they knew about the experiences of my generation and could easily understand why we were pursuing land claims and Nunavut. But I was wrong. Our recent history, the last 30 years, has not been adequately recorded yet.

ᑭᖕᒍᒧᑦ ᐃᖅᑲᐅᒪᓪᓗᒍ ᓱᕈᓯᐅᓂᕆᓚᐅᖅᑕᕋ ᐊᒻᒪᓗ ᐊᑐᖅᓯᒪᔪᒃ ᐃᓅᓯᕆᔭᓐᓂ ᑕᐃᑦᓯᒪᓂᒥᑦ ᒫᓐᓇᐅᔪᒧᑦ, ᑕᐅᑐᙵᔪᐊᖅᑑᔭᖅᖢᖓ ᐊᔾᔨᖅᐸᓪᓕᐊᔪᓂᒃ ᓱᒃᑲᐃᑦᑐᓂᒃ ᐃᓯᒪᒋᓯᖃᕋ. ᐊᔾᔨᒋᔭᐅᙱᑦᑐᓂᒃ ᐊᔾᔨᕈᑎᐅᔪᓂᒃ ᐃᓅᓯᑦᑎᓐᓂ ᑕᑯᓯᒪᓕᖅᑕ ᖃᓄᐃᓕᓯᒪᔪᓂᒃ. ᐱᒋᐊᖅᑐᓂ ᐃᓄᑭᑦᑐᓃᑉᐸᓪᓗᐊᖅᑎᓪᓗᑕ ᖃᐅᓯᐃᑦᑐᒥ ᐅᑭᐅᖅᑕᖅᑐᑉ ᐳᖅᑐᔪᙳᓂ, ᒫᓐᓇᓕᖅᑐᖅ ᖃᓂᑕᐅᔭᒃᑯᑦ ᓴᓇᖃᑦᑕᓕᖅᑎᓪᓗᑕ ᓯᓚᕐᔪᐊᓕᒫᒥᑦᑐᑦ ᐊᑐᐃᓐᓇᐅᓕᖅᑎᓪᓗᒋᑦ ᐊᒃᑐᐃᓐᓇᕐᓗᒋᑦ ᓇᕿᑦᑕᐅᑎᑦ, ᐊᖅᑯᑎᒋᓯᒪᔭᕋ ᕿᒃᒌᓐᓇᖅᑐᒃᑯᑦ, ᖁᕕᐊᓇᖅᑐᒃᑯᑦ ᐊᒻᒪᓗ ᐊᑐᕋᔦᒃᑕᐅᙱᑦᑐᒃᑯᑦ ᖃᓄᐃᓕᐅᕈᓘᔭᕐᓇᖅᑐᒃᑯᑦ.

ᐅᖃᓕᐊᖅᑐᖅᓯᒪᑎᑕᐅᓚᐅᕋᒪ ᒪᒃᑯᒃᑐᓄᑦ ᖃᐅᔨᓚᐅᖅᑐᖅ, ᐅᖃᐅᓯᕆᔭᖃᓚᐅᕋᒪ ᐅᖃᐅᓯᕆᔭᒪ ᐃᓕᑦᑎᓐᓂᒃ ᐊᑐᓚᐅᙱᓐᓂᖏᓐᓂᒃ. ᐱᔪᑕᐅᓚᐅᕋᒪ ᐊᕿᒍᖅᑎᕆᔭᒪ ᐊᑐᓚᐅᖅᑕᖏᑦ ᓱᓇᐅᑉ ᒫᓐᓇ ᐊᑐᖅᑕᐅᙱᓐᓂᖓᓄᑦ. ᐊᒻᒪᓗ ᔫᖅ ᐱᓇᓱᒻᒪᕆᑦᑕ ᓄᓇᕗᑖᕐᓂᕐᒥᒃ ᑐᑭᓯᔭᐅᑲᐅᑎᒋᓇᓱᒐᔭᕐᓂᕐᒥᑦ. ᓱᓇᐅᑉᐸᓕ ᑕᒪᕐᓂᖅᒪ. ᐊᕿᒍᐃᑦ ᐊᑐᖅᓯᒪᔭᕗᑦ, ᐊᕿᒍᐃᑦ ᑖᒃᑯᐊ ᕿᖑᕐᖅᓯᒪᓕᖅᑐᑦ 30, ᓱᓕ ᓇᓗᓇᐃᖅᑕᐅᓪᓗᑎᒃ ᑎᑎᕋᖅᑕᐅᑎᐊᖅᓯᒪᙱᓚᑕ.

It seems like a thousand years ago when we had to struggle for the very basics of life like food, shelter and clothing. Today, some kids get very upset when they don't have the television remote control. It seems like another world when I think back to Inuit children being taken from their families for their assimilation into another culture. Today, such government policy would be unthinkable. The relocations and forced movements of my generation seem like plots from a movie. Today's children need not worry about such things.

Living under conditions of colonialism is something our children, thankfully, will not know. Our fathers experienced a time when their independence and human rights were stolen from them. Through the settlement of our land claims and the rebirth of Nunavut, our generation has won back our right to determine our political future.

There was a time when many of my generation did not have pride in our Inuit identity and were not sure if they wanted to be Canadian citizens. Today, there is a resurgence of Inuit pride and we have become loyal Canadians. Even though our people have encountered racial discrimination in the past, we want reconciliation and we want all to feel welcome in our homeland. Our patience and our willingness to share continue to be cornerstones of our society.

There are some important dates in our recent history: 1971, when the Inuit Tapirisat of Canada was formed. The spring of 1982, when the people of the Northwest Territories voted to divide the NWT and create Nunavut. 1992, when the boundaries of Nunavut were established. June of 1993, when the *Nunavut Act* was passed by Parliament. February 15, 1999, when we had our first election for the first Nunavut legislative assembly.

There are other dates that a lot of people may not remember too well. Like the spring of 1979 when Peter Ittinuar, our first Inuk member of Parliament, stood up in the House of Commons and spoke Inuktitut. It may not have seemed like very much at the time, but to us it was another milestone in our epic journey.

ᑕᐃᑦᓯᒪᓂᕕᓂᐅᔮᕐᑐᖅ ᐊᒃᓯᕈᓇᐊᖅᑲᖅᑲᑦᑕᓚᐅᖅᑦᑕ ᐃᓅᓯᑦᑎᓐᓄᑦ ᐊᑐᓇᐊᖅᑲᖅᑕᑦᑎᓐᓄᑦ ᐱᓇᓱᒃᑎᓪᓗᑕ, ᒪᑯᓂᖓᓕᖅᓗᒃ ᓂᕿᒃᓴᑦᑎᓐᓂᒃ, ᐃᒡᓗᒃᓴᑦᑎᓐᓂᒃ ᐊᒻᒪᓗ ᐊᓐᓄᕌᒃᓴᑦᑎᓐᓂᒃ. ᐅᓪᓗᒥᐅᔪᖅ, ᐃᓚᖏᑦ ᓄᑕᖅᑲᐃᑦ ᓂᖕᒐᓯᕐᒪᑕ ᑕᓚᕖᓴᒧᑦ ᑕᑯᓐᓇᕈᓐᓇᐅᑎᒥᒃ ᑎᒃᑯᐊᕈᑎᖓᓂᒃ ᑎᒍᒥᐊᕈᓐᓇᓐᖏᒃᑳᖓᒥᒃ. ᐊᓯᖓᐅᔫᖅᑐᒥᒃ ᐃᓅᓯᖃᖅᓯᒪᖓᒪᑕ ᑕᐃᒃᑯᐊ ᐃᓄᐃᑦ ᕿᑐᕐᖓᖏᑦ ᐊᖅᑰᖅᑕᐅᕙᓚᐅᖅᑎᓪᓗᒋᑦ ᐃᓚᒥᓂᒃ ᐊᓯᖓᓄᑦ ᐃᓕᖅᑯᓯᓕᐅᔭᓄᑦ ᐃᓚᒋᔭᐅᓕᖅᑎᑕᐅᓇᓯᖕᓂᐊᖅᑎᓪᓗᒋᑦ ᐊᓯᒋᔭᐅᔦᒥᒃ. ᐅᓪᓗᒥᓕ, ᑲᕙᒪᒋᔭᐅᔪᖅ ᑕᐃᒪᐃᑦᑐᒥᒃ ᐊᑐᐊᒐᖅᑲᖅᓯᕐᓂᖓᓂᒃ ᐃᓯᒪᓇᖅᓯᙱᓚᑦ. ᓄᓇᒥᙵᖏᑕᒧᑦ ᓅᑎᖅᑕᐅᕙᓚᐅᖅᑐᑦ ᐊᒻᒪᓗ ᐊᔭᐅᖅᑕᐅᓪᓗᑎᒃ ᓅᑎᕐᑯᐊᖅᐸᓚᐅᖅᑐᑦ ᐅᓂᒃᑳᐅᓯᐅᔫᖅᓚᑦ. ᐅᓪᓗᒥᒧᑦᑐᖅᓯ ᓄᑕᖅᑲᑦ ᑕᒪᒃᑯᐊ ᐃᓯᒫᓘᑎᒋᔭᐅᒋᐊᖅᑲᓐᖏᓚᑦ.

ᐃᓅᓯᖅᑲᖅᓯᒋᐊᒃᓴᖅ ᐃᓕᖅᑯᓯᖅᑎᒋᓐᖏᑦᑕᒥᓄᑦ ᐊᐅᓚᑕᐅᓗᑎᒃ ᐅᓪᓗᒥᐅᔪᖅ ᓱᕈᓯᕗᑦ ᐊᑐᓇᐊᖅᑲᓐᖏᓚᑦ, ᖁᔭᓈᒥᒃ, ᖃᐅᔨᒪᒋᐊᖅᑲᓐᖏᓚᑦ ᑕᐃᒪᐃᑦᑐᒥᒃ. ᐊᖓᔪᖅᑳᕋᔭᕗᑦ ᐊᑐᓚᐅᖅᓯᒪᖓᑦ ᓇᖕᒥᓂᖅ ᐊᐅᓚᓂᐊᕐᓂᖏᑦ ᐃᓯᒪᖅᓯᕈᓐᓇᕐᓂᖏᑦ ᐊᒻᒪᓗ ᐱᔪᓐᓇᕐᓂᓗᓐᖏᑦ ᐊᖅᑰᖅᑕᐅᓯᒪᓯᒪᓂᖏᓐᓂᒃ. ᓄᓇᕗᑖᕐᓂᒃᑯᑦ ᐊᒻᒪ ᓇᖕᒥᓂᑖᕐᓂᕗᑦ ᓄᓇᒥᒃ, ᐅᑭᐅᑦ ᐊᕐᕌᒍᖅᑎᒋᔭᒃᑲᓗ ᓇᖕᒥᓂᖅ ᑎᒍᓯᒃᑲᓂᖅᓯᒪᓚᑳᑦ ᓇᖕᒥᓂᖅ ᐊᐅᓚᑦᓯᔪᓐᓇᕐᓂᕐᒥᒃ ᑲᕙᒪᓕᕆᓂᕐᒥᒃ ᓯᕗᓂᒃᓴᓇᐊᖅᑕᑦᑎᓐᓄᑦ.

ᑕᐃᑦᓯᒪᓂ ᐊᒥᓱᑦ ᐅᑯᓇ ᐊᖅᑰᖅᑲᖅᑎᒋᔭᓐᓂ ᐅᐱᒋᓐᖄᓚᐅᓐᖏᓚᑦ ᐃᓄᒻᒪᕆᐅᓂᕐᒥᓐᓂᒃ ᐊᒻᒪᓗ ᐃᓯᒪᓚᐅᖅᓚᑦ ᐊᒥᓱᑦ ᑲᓇᑕᒥᐅᑕᐅᔪᒪᓗᐊᖅᒪᖔᕐᒥᒃ ᓇᓗᓪᓗᑎᒃ. ᐅᓪᓗᒥᓕ, ᐃᓄᐃᑦ ᓇᖕᒥᓂᖅ ᐅᐱᒋᓐᖏᑦ ᐱᕙᓪᓕᐊᓕᕐᓚᑦ ᐊᒻᒪᓗ ᑲᓇᑕᒥᐅᑕᐅᓂᕐᒥᖕᓂᒃ ᐊᓕᐊᓇᐃᒋᔭᖅᑲᖅᓯᒪᓕᕐᒪᑕ. ᐃᓄᖕᓄᑎᒋᔭᐅᔪᑦ ᓇᓕᒃᑎᑕᐅᖕᖏᓐᓂᕐᒥᒃ ᑭᓇᐅᓂᕐᒥᓄᑦ ᐱᔾᔪᑎᖃᖅᑐᑎᒃ ᐊᑐᖅᓯᒪᓚᐅᖅᑎᓪᓗᒋᑦ, ᐅᓪᓗᒥᐅᔪᖅ ᐊᑕᐅᓯᕐᖑᓂᕐᒥᒃ ᐊᑐᕈᒪᓕᖅᑐᒍᑦ ᐊᒻᒪᓗ ᑭᓇᐅᓐᓇᐅᔪᓂᒃ ᑐᕐᖓᓯᖁᔨᔪᒍᑦ ᓄᓇᖁᑎᓯᒪᔭᑦᑎᓐᓂ ᐊᖏᖅᖃᓇᔭᑦᑎᓐᓂ. ᕿᓄᐃᖅᓯᓇᔭᒍᑦ ᐊᒻᒪᓗ ᐃᑲᔪᖅᑲᑦᑕᐅᑎᒍᓐᓇᖅᓯᓇᔭᒍᑦ ᓯᓚ ᐃᓅᓯᑦᑎᓐᓂ ᓴᓐᖏᓂᓇᑦᑎᒍ.

ᓯᕗᓂᓯᒪᔭᑦᑎᓐᓂ ᐳᐃᒍᑕᐅᕆᐊᖃᖅᑐᑦᑐᓂᒃ ᐅᓪᓗᖃᖅᑐᖅ: 1971, ᐃᓄᐃᑦ ᑕᐱᕇᑦ ᑲᓇᑕᒥ ᐱᕆᐊᖅᑎᑕᐅᓚᐅᖅᑎᓪᓗᒍ. ᐅᐱᕐᖔᒥ 1982-ᒥ, ᓄᓇᑦᓯᐊᕐᒥᐅᑦ ᓂᕈᐊᓚᐅᖅᑎᓪᓗᒋᑦ ᐊᕕᒃᑕᐅᓴᓇᕐᓂᖓᓂᒃ ᓄᓇᑦᓯᐊᑉ ᐊᒻᒪᓗ ᓄᓇᕗᑦ ᐱᕐᖑᖅᑎᑕᐅᕐᒍᓪᓗᒍ. 1992-ᒥ, ᓄᓇᕗᑦ ᑭᒡᓕᖓ ᐋᖅᑭᒃᑕᐅᓚᐅᖅᑎᓪᓗᒍ. ᔫᓂ 1993-ᒥ, ᓄᓇᕗᑦ ᒪᓕᒐᕐᔭᐊᖓ ᖃᖏᖅᑕᐅᓚᐅᖅᑎᓪᓗᒍ ᑲᓇᑕᐅᑉ ᒪᓕᒐᓕᐅᕐᕕᖓᓐᓂ. ᕖᕝᕗᐊᕆ 15, 1999-ᒥ, ᓂᕈᐊᕐᕕᖃᓚᐅᖅᑎᓪᓗᑕ ᓯᕗᓪᓕᖅᐹᖅᑦᑐᒥᒃ ᓄᓇᕗᒥ ᒪᓕᒐᓕᐅᖅᑏᑦ ᑲᑎᒪᕕᒡᔪᐊᓗᓂᐊᖅᑕᖓᓐᓂᒃ.

ᑕᒪᑦᑕᐅᖅ ᐅᓪᓗᖅᒥᔪᖅ ᐊᒥᓱᓄᑦ ᐃᖅᑲᐅᒪᔭᐅᓗᐊᖃᓐᖏᑦᑐᓄᑦ. ᔫᓗ ᑕᐃᑦᓯᒪᓂ ᐅᐱᕐᖔᖑᓚᐅᖅᑐᒥ 1979-ᖑᑎᓪᓗᒍ ᐲᑕ ᐃᑎᓄᐊᖅ Peter Ittinuar, ᓯᕗᓪᓕᖅᐹᖅᑦᑐᓂ ᐃᓄᒃᑐᓂ ᐃᓚᒋᔭᐅᔪᖅ ᒪᓕᒐᓕᐅᕐᕕᒡᔪᐊᒥ, ᓇᖏᖅᓯᓪᓗᓂ ᑲᓇᑕᐅᑉ ᑲᑎᒪᔨᕐᔪᐊᖓᓂ ᐅᖃᓪᓚᖕᓂᖓ ᐃᓄᒃᑎᑐᑦ. ᓱᓪᓗᐊᖑᓚᐅᖅᑑᔭᕆᓪᓗ ᑕᐃᑦᓯᒪᓂ, ᑭᓯᐊᓂᓕ ᐅᑯᑦᑎᓐᓄᑦ ᐊᖅᑯᑎᓯᔪᑦ ᑎᑭᓪᓚᐃᓐᓇᖅᑑᔭᖅᑕᑦᑎᓐᓂ ᓇᓗᓇᐃᒃᑯᑕᓚᐅᖅᓚᑦ. ᐊᒻᒪᓗ ᑕᐃᒪ ᐊᖅᑯᑎᒥᓂᐊᖅᑕᕗᑦ ᐱᕆᐊᓕᖅᓵᖅᑐᖅ.

JOHN AMAGOALIK • ᔫᓐ ᐊᒪᒍᐊᓚᒃ

NWT Dept. of Information / NWT Archives ᓄᓇᑦᓯᐊᑉ ᑐᓴᐅᑎᓕᕆᔨᖏᑦ / ᓄᓇᑦᓯᐊᒥ ᐸᐸᑕᐅᔦᑦ

Left: Arctic Ocean ice pans – a timeless feature of the new territory. Right: Joseph Idlouk, a resident of Baffin Island's Eclipse Sound area, sights through a telescope, 1951

ᓴᐅᒥᐊᓂᑦ: ᐅᑭᐅᖅᑕᖅᑐᐅᑉ ᐃᓖᓗᐊᑕ ᓯᑯᖏᑦ - ᑕᐃᒪᓐᓇ ᐱᑕᖅᑐᑦ ᑖᓂ ᓄᑖᒥ ᐃᒻᒥᒍᖅᑐᖅ ᐊᕕᒃᓯᒪᔪᖅ ᓄᓇ. ᑕᓕᖅᐱᐊᓂ: ᔫᓯᐱ ᐃᓪᓚᐅᖅ, ᕿᑭᖅᑖᓗᑉ ᑕᓯᐅᔭᖓᓂ ᓄᓇᖅᑐᖅ, ᕿᖑᒥᒐᖅᑐᖅ, 1951

ᓇᓪᓚᐅᓐᓂᕐᓯᐅᕐᓂᖅ ᑲᑐᔾᔨᖃᑎᒌᖕᓂᒃᑯᑦ
A celebration of co-operative spirit

ᐃᓚᒌᔅᑦᑯᑦ ᐱᒃᑯᓕᖃᑎᖃᕈᒪᔪᑦ ᓄᓇᕗᒻᒥ ᓄᓇᖃᖅᑐᓂ ᓴᖅᑭᒪᓃᓐᓂᐊᓕᖅᑐᒥᓐ ᓄᓇᕗᒥᓐ. ᖃᐅᔨᒪᔪᒍᑦ ᐱᓕᕆᓂᐅᔪᓂᑦ ᐊᒻᒪᓗ ᖃᓄᐃᒍᓐᓇᖅᑐᓂᑦ ᐊᑕᐅᑦᑎᒃᑯᑦ ᐱᓕᕆᖃᑎᒌᖕᒑᑦᑕ ᐊᑕᐅᓯᕐᒥᓐ ᐱᓇᓱᐊᕐᑎᓪᓗᑕ.

Arctic Co-operatives Limited would like to congratulate all Nunavut residents on the reality of their new territory. We recognize the challenges and the rewards that can result when we all work together for a common goal.

ᓴᐅᒥᐊᓂ ᑕᓕᕐᐱᐊᓄᑦ: ᓈᒪᓐ ᓂᖕᒋᐅᑦᓯᐊᖅ, ᐊᐃᐱᓕᒃ ᐊᕐᓇᐃᑦᑐᖅ (ᐃᓅᔪᓐᓂᕐᓯᒪᔪᖅ), ᑲᓈᖕᒋᓐᓇᖅ ᐳᑐᒍᖅ, ᒫᒃ ᐃᕙᓗᐊᕐᔪᒃ, ᒪᐃᒃ ᓇᓯᓴ, ᑑᓂ ᐄᓯᒃ, ᐱᐅᓪ ᓚᐃᐅᓪ ᐊᒻᒪ ᓴᐃᒪᓐ ᑲᑐᐊᔭᒃ, ᐃᒃᓯᕕᐅᑉᑐᑦ: ᒨᕆᓯ ᐊᕐᓇᑦᓯᐊᖅ, ᓗᐃ ᑕᐹᕐᔪᒃ ᐊᒻᒪ ᓴᓂᑐ ᐅᐃᓕ ᐋᑕᒻᔅ. ᓇᓗᓇᐃᒃᑯᑎᒃᓴᒥᓐ ᓴᖅᑭᑦᑎᓪᒪᓂᒃᑎᓪᓗᒋᑦ.

Arctic Co-operatives Limited begins. Left to right: Raymond Ningoecheak, late Ipeelie Arnaitook, Kanaanginaq Pootoogook, Mark Evaloarjuk, Mike Nasiza, Tony Eecherk, Bill Lyall and Simon Katoayak. Seated front: Maurice Arnatsiaq, Louis Tapardjuk and Sen. Willie Adams with the corporate seal.

ᐅᓂᒃᑳ ᐱᒋᐊᕐᑭᑖᓄᑦ • A BRIEF HISTORY

ᐃᓄᐃᑦ ᐅᑭᐅᕐᑕᖅᑐᖅᒥ ᓄᓇᓕᖕᓃᑦᑐᑦ ᑯᐊᐸᓂᑦ ᐱᒋᐊᕐᑎᑦᑎᓅᓪᓚᐊᓕᓚᐅᕐᓯᒪᔫᑦ 1960 ᐱᒋᐊᓕᕌᕐᓯᒪᑎᓪᓗᒍ ᐱᕕᖃᕈᒪᒧᓐ ᓄᓇᓕᖕᓂᑦᑐᓂ, ᐃᓚᒋᔭᐅᔪᓂ ᐱᓕᕆᕝᕕᖕᒥ ᐃᑲᔪᕐᖁᔭᕐᑐᒥᓐ ᐱᓅᓪᓚᐊᓂᕐᒥᓐ ᓄᓇᓕᖕᓂᑦ. ᐃᓱᒪᒋᔭᐅᓚᐅᕐᓯᒪᔪᖅ ᑕᒪᓐᓇ ᐱᒋᐊᓕᕌᕐᑎᓪᓗᒍ ᐱᔾᑎᖁᖃᑦᑕᕈᒪᓂᕐᒥ ᐊᒻᒪ ᐃᖅᑲᓇᐃᔮᓂᑦ ᓴᖅᑭᑦᑎᓂᕐᒧ ᓄᓇᖃᕐᑐᓄᑦ ᐊᑑᕐᑕᐅᔪᓐᓇᕐᓗᓂ.

ᐊᕐᖂᒍᑦ ᐊᓂᒍᕐᐸᓪᓕᐊᑎᓪᓗᒋ, ᐃᓚᒌᔅᑯ ᐱᓅᓪᓚᐊᒻᒪᕆᓚᐅᕐᐳᑦ ᐱᕈᕐᐸᓪᓕᐊᓪᓗᑎᒃ, ᐊᒻᒪᓗ ᑭᖑᓂᐊᒍᑦ ᒪᕐᕈᖕᒍᕐᑎᑕᐅᓪᓗᓂ ᓇᖕᒥᓂᕆᔭᐅᔪᑦ ᐱᔾᔪᑎᖃᕐᓂᕐᒧᓐ ᑲᑐᔾᔨᖃᑎᒌᑦ: ᐃᓚᒌᔅᑯᑦ (ACL) ᐊᒻᒪᓗ ᓄᓇᕐᓯᐊᕐᒥ ᑲᑐᔾᔨᖃᑎᒌᖕᓂᒃᑯ ᐊᐅᓚᑦᑎᓂᕐᒧᓐ ᐱᓅᓪᓚᐅᔪᓕᕆᓂᕐᒧᓐ ᑮᓇᐅᔭᖃᕐᑎᑦᑎᔩᑦ *(NWT Co-operative Business Development Fund)*. ᐅᓪᓗᒥᓕ, ᓄᓇᓕᖕᓂ ᑯᐊᐸᐃᑦ ᐅᓄᒪᕆᓕᕐᐳᑦ ᓇᓂᑐᐃᓐᓇᖅ. ᐃᓄᖕᓂ ᐱᔾᑎᖁᖃᑦᑕᖁᔪᐊᖁᒥᒃ ᐊᒻᒪᑦᑕᐅ ᐊᓯᖕᒋᓐᓂ ᐊᑐᕐᑐᓂᑦ ᐱᔾᑎᖁᐅᑎᖃᓇᒐᑦ ᐊᒻᒪ ᓴᖅᑭᑎᓯᒪᓯᒪᓕᕐᑐᑦ ᐃᓄᖕᓄ ᐱᑯᓕᓂᕐᒥᓐ ᑕᒪᓐᓇ ᑕᐅᑐᒃᑕᐅᓪᓗᓂ ᓇᖕᒥᓂᖅᑲᕐᓂᐅᔪᑦ ᐊᒻᒪ ᐃᖕᒥᖕᓂ ᐃᑲᔪᖅᑲᑦᑕᐅᑎᓂᒃᑯᑦ.

People in arctic communities began forming Co-operatives in the early 1960s to provide ourselves with community-based, member-owned businesses that would help stimulate our local economies. The concept was to provide services and employment opportunities that would benefit the entire community.

Over the years, the arctic Co-operatives thrived and, ultimately, affiliated to become two co-operatively owned service organizations: Arctic Co-operatives Limited (ACL) and the NWT Co-operative Business Development Fund (CBDF). Today, community Co-ops are everywhere. Not only do they provide Inuit with countless essential services, but they also create a special sense of Inuit pride that results from ownership and greater self-reliance.

ᐃᓱᒪᒋᔭᐅᓂᒃᑯ ᐅᓪᓗᒥᒧᓐ ᐊᒻᒪ ᖃᐅᒃᐸᒧᓐ • A vision for today and tomorrow

ᑯᐊᐸᒃᑯ ᐱᓕᕆᓂᖕᒐ ᐊᒃᑐᐃᓂᖅᑲᒪᕆᒃᐳᑦ ᐃᓄᐃᑦ ᓄᓇᖕᒋᓐᓂᑦ ᐅᑭᐅᕐᑕᖅᑐᖅᒥ. ᓇᒧᖕᒐᐅᓂᓕᒫ ᑯᐊᐸᐅᔪᑦ ᑕᑯᔭᒃᓴᐅᕗᑦ. ᖃᐅᔨᔪᓐᓇᕐᐳᑎ ᑯᐊᐸᒃᑯ ᐱᓕᕆᖃᑕᐅᔪᑦ ᐱᓕᕆᓂᕐᓂ ᐱᓅᓪᓚᐊᓂᒃᑯ ᓇᐅᒃᑯᑐᐃᓐᓇᖅ – ᓴᓇᖑᐊᒐᕐᓂᑦ ᓂᐅᕈᑎᖃᕐᓂᕐᒧᓐ ᓴᖅᑭᑎᓂᕐᒧᓐ ᐱᓕᕆᔾᔪᑎᓄᑦ.

ᐅᑯᐊ ᐃᓚᖃᕐᑐᑦ ᐱᒋᐊᕐᓯᒪᓂᕐᒥᓐ ᓴᖅᑭᑎᓂᕐᒥᓗ ᑲᑐᔾᔨᖃᑎᒌᖕᓂᒃᑯᑦ ᐱᓕᕆᐊᒃᓴᓂᑦ. ᒦᖕᒐ ᑲᑐᔾᔨᖃᑎᒌᖕᓂᒃᑯ ᓂᕿᓂᑦ ᓂᐅᕕᐊᒃᓴᖃᕐᓂᕐᒥᓐ ᒪᐅᖕᒐᓅᓐᓂ ᐱᓕᕆᖃᑕᐅᓂᕐᒧᓐ ᐊᑦᑕᑦᑕᐅᓂᒃᑯ ARDICOM-ᒥᓐ, ᑖᓐᓇ ᑐᓴᐅᒪᖃᑦᑕᐅᑎᓕᕆᓂᖅ ᓄᑖᖑᓛᒃᑯ ᐅᑭᐅᕐᑕᖅᑐᖅᒧᓐ. ᓄᓇᓕᖕᓂ ᑯᐊᐸ ᐱᕈᕐᐸᓪᓕᐊᖕᒋᓐᓇᕐᐳᑦ ᐱᔾᔨᑎᖃᓗᐊᕐᓗᑎᒃ ᐱᓇᓱᖕᓂᕐᒥᓐ ᐱᓕᕆᐊᒃᓴᓂᑦ ᐊᑐᐃᓐᓇᐅᓭᒃᑐᓂᑦ ᐱᓕᕆᓂᒃᑯ ᐊᒻᒪᓗ ᓴᖅᑭᑎᓭᓪᓕᐊᔪᑦ ᐊᑐᐃᓐᓇᐅᑎᑉᐸᒃᑕᖕᒋᑦᑎᒍᑦ.

The Co-operative System plays a major role in Inuit communities across the North. Virtually everywhere you go, Co-ops can be found. You'll find Co-ops involved in many business ventures in all areas of the economy – from the marketing of arts and crafts to the development of leading-edge technology.

These include fostering and promoting joint ventures – whether it's a strategic partnership with an internationally known food service company or hooking up with ARDICOM, a communications company bringing high-speed digital communications to the North. The community Co-op continues to expand its realm and capitalize on the challenges and opportunities contemporary business and industries have to offer.

ᓂᐅᕕᖅᕖᑦ – ᐱᓕᕆᓂᖅᓚᕇᑦ ᓄᓇᓕᖕᓂ ᑕᒪᐃᓐᓂᑦ • Retail – a vital part of every community

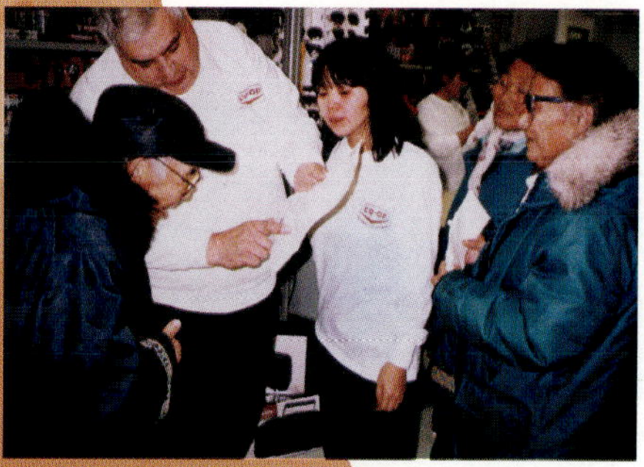

ᑯᐊᐸᒃᑯ ᐅᑭᐅᖅᑕᖅᑐᖅᒥ ᐱᔨᑦᑎᖅᑲᑦᑕᖅᐳᑦ ᐊᑐᖅᑐᒻᒪᕆᖕᓂᑦ ᐊᒻᒪᓗ ᐃᖅᑲᓇᐃᔮᒃᓴᓂ ᓴᖅᑭᑦᑎᓯᒪᓪᓗᑎᒃ ᓄᓇᓕᖕᓂ 42-ᓂᑦ.

ᐃᓚᖅᑲᒃᑲᓐᓂᖅᓱᓂ, ᑯᐊᐸᒃᑯᑦ ᐊᐅᓚᑕᖕᒋ ᐃᑲᔪᖅᑐᐃᓯᒪᔪᑦ ᐃᓚᒋᔭᐅᔪᓂᑦ: ᐃᓚᒋᔭᐅᔾᔪᑎᑎᒍᑦ – ᐊᒡᓚᖅᑐᓐᓂᑦ, $20ᒥᓕᐊᓐᑖᓚᓂᑦ ᐃᓚᒋᔭᐅᔾᔪᑎᓕᖕᓄᑦ ᐅᑎᖅᑎᑦᑎᓯᒪᓕᖅᑐᑦ. ᐊᒻᒪᑦᑕᐅᖅ, ᑮᓇᐅᔭᓕᐅᖅᓂᖅ ᐱᕈᖅᐸᓪᓕᐊᓂᖓᓄ, ᐱᕕᖃᖅᑎᑦᑎᓯᒪᒍᑦ ᑯᐊᐸᓂ ᓄᓇᓕᖕᓄᑦ ᐅᑎᖅᑎᑦᑎᕙᒃᓱᑎᒃ ᐱᕙᓪᓕᐊᓂᐅᔪᒥᓐ ᒪᑯᑎᒎᓇᖅ ᓴᖅᑭᑎᕙᓪᓕᐊᓂᒃᑯᑦ ᐱᓕᕆᕝᕕᒃᓴᓂᑦ ᐊᒻᒪᓗ ᓄᑖᖑᖅᑎᑦᑎᕙᓪᓕᐊᓪᓗᑎᒃ ᐱᓕᕆᕝᕕᐅᖄᓂᒃᑐᓂᑦ. ᑕᐃᒪᓐᓇ, ᐅᓪᓗᒥ ᑯᐊᐸᐅᔪᑦ ᐅᑎᖅᑎᖅᑎᓐᓇᖅᑲᑦᑕᖅᐳᑦ ᓄᓇᓕᖕᓄᑦ ᐊᒻᒪᓗ ᐱᕙᓪᓕᐊᓂᖅ ᓴᖅᑮᔭᖅᑎᑦᑎᖅᑲᑦᑕᖅᓱᑎᒃ ᑕᒪᓐᓇ ᑮᓇᐅᔭ ᓄᓇᓕᖕᓃᑏᓐᓇᖅᓱᓂᔾᔪᒃ.

The Co-op System in the North provides much-needed services and employment in 42 communities.

In addition, our Co-op businesses provide a unique benefit to our member owners: *member dividends*. In fact, over 20 million dollars have been paid back to member owners in this way. Also, equity built up allows Co-ops to invest back in the community through the development of new facilities and by upgrading existing ones. In this manner, today's Co-ops continue to give back to the community and provide economic sustainability by keeping the money in the community.

ᑯᐊᐸᒃᑯᑦ ᖃᓄᐃᓕᐅᕐᓂᕈᓘᔭᖏᑦ • The many faces of Co-operatives

ᑕᑯᓯᒪᔪᒃᓴᐅᒋᔪᓯ ᑯᐊᐸᒃᑯ ᐊᑐᒻᒪᕆᒃᑐᓂᑦ ᐱᔨᑦᑎᕋᐅᑎᓂ ᐊᑐᖅᑕᑦᑕᕐᐳᑦ ᐃᓄᖕᓄ ᐃᑲᔪᕐᓂᐅᔪᓂᑦ ᓄᓇᓕᖕᓄᓪᓗ. ᑕᒪᓐᓇ ᐱᒋᐊᕈᑎᖃᓚᐅᕐᓯᒪᑎᓪᓗᒍ ᓴᓇᖑᐊᒐᕐᓂ ᓂᐅᕕᖃᑦᑕᕐᓂᐅᓂᒃ ᐊᒻᒪ ᑯᐊᐸᓂᑦ ᐱᕈᕐᐸᓪᓕᐊᑎᑦᑎᓂᖅ, ᒫᓐᓇ ᐃᓕᓴᕆᔭᐅᓯᒪᒻᒪᕆᓪᓚᕐᐳᖅ ᓯᕗᓕᐅᕐᑎᐅᓂᖏᓐᓂ ᐃᓄᐃᑦ ᓴᓇᖑᐊᒐᖏᓐᓂ ᓂᐅᕕᐊᒃᓴᖃᕐᓂᖓ ᓴᓇᐅᒐᕐᓂᓪᓗ, ᐱᖃᓯᐅᑎᓪᓗᑎᒃ ᐋᖅᑭᒃᓯᐃᓂᖓ ᑕᑯᔭᒐᒃᓴᓂᑦ ᑲᓇᑕᐅᑉ ᐃᓗᐊᓂ ᐊᒻᒪ ᓄᓇᕐᔪᐊᓕᒦᒥᓐ. ᓯᕗᓕᐅᕐᑎᐅᒋᕗᒍᑦ ᓴᖅᑭᑦᑎᓂᒃᑯᑦ ᐃᓄᐃᑦ ᓴᓇᖑᐊᒐᖏᓐᓂ ᓴᓇᐅᒐᖏᓐᓂᓪᓗ ᓂᐅᕕᐊᒃᓴᓪᓗᑎᒍᑦ. ᐅᓪᓗᒥ ᑯᐊᐸᒃᑯᑦ ᐱᔨᑦᑎᕋᐅᑎᖏ ᐃᓚᖃᓕᕐᐳᑦ ᐅᕐᓱᐊᓗᖕᒥᓐ ᑲᒪᔨᐅᓂᕐᒥᓐ, ᑐᔪᕐᒥᕕᖕᓂᑦ, ᐃᓪᓗᓕᐅᕐᓂᕐᒥᓐ, ᐳᓚᕋᖅᑐᓕᕆᓂᕐᒥᓐ, ᑏᕖᓄᑦ ᐊᑦᑕᑦᑕᕐᑕᐅᑎᑦᑎᓯᒪᓂᕐᒥᓐ ᐊᒻᒪᓗ ᐊᓯᖏᓐᓂᑦ ᐅᓄᕐᑐᒻᒪᕆᖕᓂᑦ.

You'll also find that Co-operatives have a part in many essential services benefiting Inuit and our communities. What started as small arts and Co-op establishments have today become recognized industry leaders in the marketing of Inuit arts and crafts, including organizing many shows within Canada and internationally. We are also leaders in promoting our unique art through wholesale and retail marketing. Today's Co-op services also include petroleum distribution, hotels, construction, tourism, cable TV and more.

ᖁᐊᖅᓵᖅᓇᖏᑦᑐᒃᑯᑦ ᓯᕗᓂᒃᓵᖅ • A solid future

ᓯᕗᓂᒃᓴᖅ ᐱᐅᒻᒪᕆᒃᐳᖅ ᑯᐊᐸᒃᑯᑦ ᐱᕚᓪᓕᐊᓂᖏᓐᓄᑦ ᑲᓇᑕᐅᑉ ᐅᑭᐅᖅᑕᖅᑐᖓᓂ. ᐱᓗᐊᕐᑐᖅ ᐱᓯᕐᐸᓪᓕᐊᓂᒃᑯ. ᐱᓇᓱᐃᓐᓇᕐᓂᕐᑎᒍᑦ, ᓇᒍᓇᖏᓚᖅ ᓯᕗᓚᒃᓵᑎᓐᓄ ᐃᑲᔪᖅᓂᐊᖅᑐᒍᑦ ᐱᕚᓪᓕᐊᓂᒃᑯ ᐊᓂᒍᐃᑦᑎᐊᖅᓂᒃᑯᓪᓗ.

ᐊᒥᓱᑦ ᓄᓇᓖᑦ ᐃᓱᒪᒋᔭᖃᖅᓯᒪᖕᒪᑕ ᑲᑐᔾᔨᖃᑎᒌᖕᓂᒃᑯ ᐊᐅᓚᑦᑎᔨᒪᓂᖅᒥᓐ. ᐊᒻᒪᓗ ᒫᓐᓇ ᑕᐃᒪᐃᑦᑐᒪᔪᑦ ᐱᓇᓱᐃᓐᓇᕈᑎᒃ, ᐃᓱᒪᒋᔭᐅᒐᖅ ᑯᐊᐸᒃᑯᑦ ᑲᓇᑕᐅᑉ ᐅᑭᐅᖅᑕᖅᑐᖓᓂ ᐱᕈᖅᐸᓪᓕᐊᓂᐊᖅᑐᑦ ᓴᒃᑲᔪᒃᑯᑦ.

The future certainly looks bright for the Co-operative movement in Northern Canada. Especially if we continue our present expansion trends. Through our ongoing efforts, we are certain to benefit future generations of Inuit in gaining greater self-reliance and further success.

Many communities are interested in forming Co-operative businesses. And if current levels of interest are any indication, it is expected that the Co-operative movement in Northern Canada will continue to grow by leaps and bounds.

ᑯᐊᐸᒃᑯᑦ – ᐱᕙᓪᓕᐊᓂᕐᒧᑦ ᐊᓂᒍᐃᑦᑎᐊᓂᕐᒨᑐᐃᓐᓇᕐᒋᓚᑦ • Co-operatives – more than an economic success

ᑕᒪᕐᑕᐃᓕᒋᑦᑎ, ᑯᐊᐸᒃᑯ ᐊᐅᓚᑦᑎᓂᕐᒧ ᐱᑐᐃᓐᓇᕐᒋᓚᑦ. ᐊᔾᔨᐅᙱᑉᐳᑦ ᐊᒻᒪᓗ ᓄᓇᖃᖅᑳᖅᑐᓄᑦ ᓇᖕᒥᓂᕆᔭᐅᕗᑦ. ᑯᐊᐸᒃᑯᑦ ᐱᓇᓱᖕᓂᖕᒋᓐᓄᑦ, ᐃᓚᒋᔭᐅᔪᑦ, ᐊᕐᕌᒍᓗᓴᐅᓕᕐᑐᓂᑦ, ᐊᑐᕐᓯᒪᓕᕐᐳᑦ ᓄᓇᓕᖕᓂ ᐱᓇᓱᖕᓂᕐᓂᑦ ᐊᒻᒪᓗ ᐃᖕᒥᖕᓂᑦ ᐱᓇᓱᖕᓂᕐᒥᓐ ᓴᖅᑭᑦᑎᓯᒪᓂᒃᑯᑦ ᓄᓇᓕᖕᓂ ᐱᓕᕆᐊᓂᑦ.

1960 ᐱᒋᐊᓕᕌᕐᑎᓪᓗᒍ, ᐅᑭᐅᕐᑕᖅᑐᖅ ᐱᕙᓪᓕᐊᓂᒃᑯ ᐊᓯᖕᒍᕐᐸᓪᓕᐊᓕᒻᒪᓇᒃᑎᓪᓗᒍ, ᑯᐊᐸᒃᑯ ᐃᓕᓴᕐᓯᓯᒪᐃᓐᓇᕐᐳᑦ ᓄᓇᓕᖕᓂ ᐱᒋᔭᐅᔪᓂᑦ ᐊᐅᓚᑕ-ᐅᔪᓂᑦ ᓴᖅᑭᔮᖅᑐᕐᑲᓇᐊᕐᑲᕐᓂᕐᒥᑦ. ᑲᑐᔾᔨᕐᑲᑎᒌᖕᓂᐅᔪᖅ ᐃᓄᐃᑦ ᐃᓕᕐᑯᓯᖕᒋᑦᑎᑐᑦ ᐊᐅᓚᑕᐅᕐᑲᑦᑕᐃᓐᓇᕐᐳᑦ ᐊᕐᕌᒍᓗᓴᒻᒪᓇᐊᓗᖕᓂᑦ.

ᓄᓇᓕᖕᓂ ᑯᐊᐸᒃᑯᑎᒍᑦ, ᐃᓄᐃᑦ ᐃᓕᕐᑯᓯᖕᒥᖕᓂ ᐱᑯᓕᓯᒪᓪᓗᐊᕐᐳᑦ ᑕᒪᓐᓇ ᐊᓯᐅᖕᒌᓐᓇᕐᒪᓐ ᓄᓇᓕᖕᓂ ᐱᕙᓪᓕᐊᓂᖅ ᐊᑐᕐᐸᓪᓕᐊᓚᓗᐊᕐᑎᓪᓗᒍ.

ᓄᓇᓕᖕᓂ ᑯᐊᐸᒃᑯᑦ – ᓇᓪᓕᐅᓐᓂᕐᓯᐅᑎᒻᒪᕆᒃ ᐃᓄᐃᑦ ᐱᕙᓪᓕᐊ-ᔪᓐᓇᕐᓂᖕᒋᓐᓄ ᑲᑐᔾᔨᕐᑲᑎᒌᖕᓂᒃᑯᑦ.

Make no mistake, Co-ops are no ordinary businesses. They are unique and aboriginally owned. Through our Co-op ventures, members have, for many years, practised community empowerment and self-reliance through the establishment of our community-owned businesses.

Since the early '60s, when the North was going through rapid development, Co-ops have recognized the need for community-owned businesses. The Co-operative way was in harmony with the way the people of the North have been living for thousands of years.

Through community Co-ops, Inuit can embrace our traditional values without ever having to sacrifice economic development in our communities.

Community Co-ops – truly a celebration of Inuit entrepreneurship and co-operative spirit.

Arctic Co-operatives Limited

NWT Co-operative Business Development Fund

CO-OP

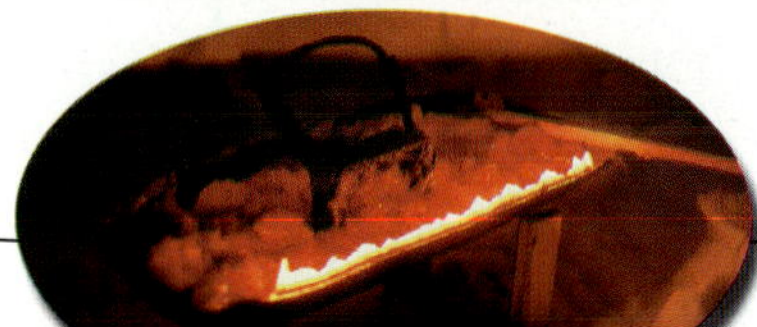

THE EARLY YEARS
ᐊᖅᖂᒧᐃᑦ ᐱᒋᐊᕆᑎᐅᔪᑦ

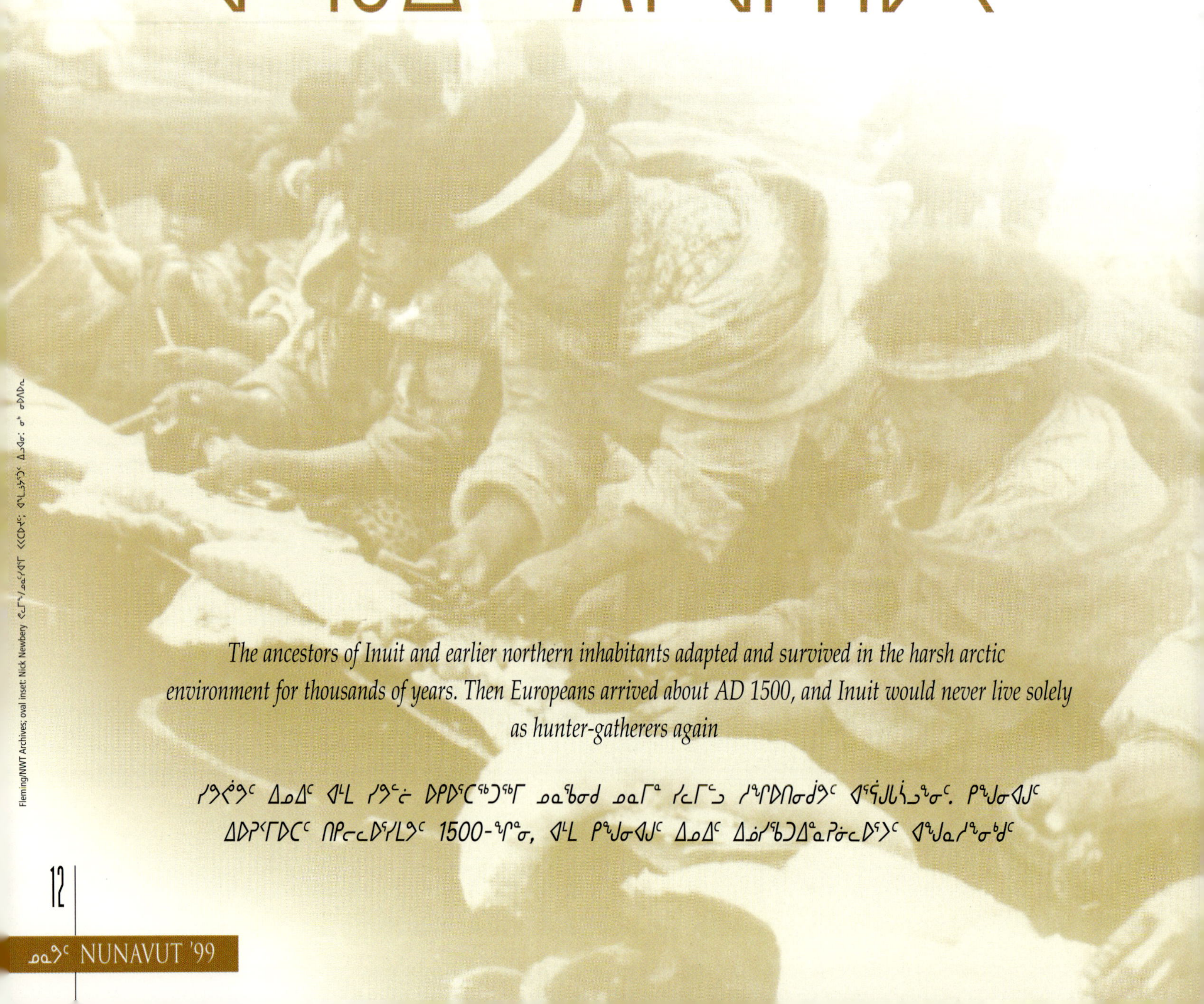

The ancestors of Inuit and earlier northern inhabitants adapted and survived in the harsh arctic environment for thousands of years. Then Europeans arrived about AD 1500, and Inuit would never live solely as hunter-gatherers again

ᓯᕗᐹᒍᑦ ᐃᓄᐃᑦ ᐊᒻᒪ ᓯᕗᓪᓖ ᐅᑭᐅᖅᑕᖅᑐᖅᒥ ᓄᓇᖅᑲᓂᑯ ᓄᓇᒥᓐ ᓯᓚᒥᓪᓗ ᓱᖕᒋᐅᑎᓂᒎᕗᑦ ᐊᖅᖁᒧᒐᔮᓗᖕᓂᖅ. ᑭᖕᒍᓂᐊᒍᑦ ᐃᐅᕈᑉᒥᐅᑕᑦ ᑎᑭᓕᓚᐅᖅᓯᒪᒍᑦ 1500-ᖕᒋᓐᓂ, ᐊᒻᒪ ᑭᖕᒍᓂᐊᒍᑦ ᐃᓄᐃᑦ ᐃᓅᓯᖅᑐᐃᓐᓇᕈᓃᓚᐅᕐᐳᑦ ᐊᖕᒍᓇᓱᖕᓂᒃᑯᑦ

Fleming/NWT Archives; oval inset: Nick Newbery

Ancient History

There was once a world before this, and in it lived people who were not of our tribe. But the pillars of the earth collapsed, and all were destroyed. And the world was emptiness. Then two men grew up from a hummock of earth. They were born and fully grown all at once. And they wished to have children. A magic song changed one of them into a woman, and they had children. These were our earliest forefathers, and from them all the lands were peopled.

— Tuglik, Igloolik area, 1922

Nunavut Tourism ᓄᓇᕗᑦ ᐳᓚᕋᕐᑐᓕᕆᔨᒃᑯ

By Robert McGhee

This traditional Inuit story tells of the origins of humans. Other traditions relate that when ancestral Inuit first arrived in Nunavut, they found the country occupied by a strange people whom they called *Tuniit*. These historical records tell us two important things about early Inuit history: that ancestral Inuit originally came to Nunavut from another homeland, and that they were not the first people to occupy the country that is now Nunavut. During the past few decades, archeology has confirmed both of these interpretations of the past, and has filled in many details of the early history of arctic North America.

ᑕᐃᑦᓯᒪᓂᑐᕐᖃᖅ

ᓯᓚᕐᔪᐊᖃᓪᓚᐅᖅᓯᒪᔪᖅ ᑕᒪᑐᒪ ᓯᕗᐊᓂ, ᐊᒻᒪ ᐃᓄᖃᖅᑐᓂ ᐅᐸᑦᑎᓐᓂᐅᙱᑦᑐᖅ. ᑭᓯᐊᓂᓕ ᓯᓚᕐᔪᐊᑉ ᓇᑉᐸᖅᑯᑎᖏᑦ ᐅᖅᑮᖕᒪᑕ, ᐊᒻᒪ ᓱᓇᑐᐃᓐᓇᐃᑦ ᓱᖁᒃᑐᑎᒃ. ᑕᐃᒪᓕ ᓯᓚᕐᔪᐊᖅ ᐃᓗᓕᖃᓐᖏᓕᓕᓚᐅᖅᑐᖅ. ᒪᖅᑮᓪᓕ ᐊᖑᑎᒃ ᐱᕈᓚᐅᖅᑐᒃ ᓇᒥᒃᑭᐊᖅ ᓄᓇᒥᑦ. ᐃᖅᓂᐊᕆᔭᐅᓪᓗᑎᒃ ᐃᓅᓕᕈᖅᑐᑎᒃ ᐊᒻᒪ ᐃᓐᓇᐅᓪᓗᑎᒃ ᐊᑕᐅᑦᑎᒃᑯᑦ. ᓄᑕᖃᕈᒪᓕᖅᑐᒃ. ᐱᓯᖅᒧᑦ ᐊᑕᐅᓯᖅ ᐊᕐᓇᙳᖅᑎᑕᐅᓪᓗᓂ, ᐊᒻᒪ ᓄᑕᖅᑲᖅᑐᑎᒃ. ᑕᐃᒃᑯᐊ ᓯᕗᓪᓕᕕᓂᖅᓴᓕᖅᑕᕗᑦ, ᐊᒻᒪ ᑕᐃᒃᑯᖕᖓᑦ ᐃᓄᒃᑖᑦ ᐱᕆᐊᓪᓚᐅᖅᓯᒪᔪᑦ.

- ᑐᒡᓕᒃ, ᐃᒡᓗᓕᖕᒥ, 1922

ᑎᑎᖅᑐᖅ ᕈᐹᑦ ᒪᒌ

ᑕᒪᓐᓇ ᐅᓂᒃᑳᖅᑐᐊᖅ ᐅᓂᒃᑲᐅᓯᓕᒃ ᐃᓄᐃᑦ ᐱᕆᐊᕐᓂᓇᓚᐅᖅᑕᖓᓂᒃ. ᐊᓯᖏᑦ ᐅᓂᒃᑲᓂᔭᐅᓯᒪᔪᑦ ᐅᖃᐅᓯᖃᖅᑐᑦ ᐃᓄᐃᑦ ᓯᕗᓕᕕᓂᖏᑦ ᑎᑭᓪᓛᖅᑎᓪᓗᒋᑦ ᐃᓄᐃᑦ ᓄᓇᕗᒻᒨᑦ, ᓱᓇᐅᕙ ᐃᓅᑲᓂᓚᐅᖅᑐᖅ ᑐᓂᖅᑯᑦ ᑕᐃᔭᐅᔪᓂᒃ. ᑖᒃᑯᐊ ᓯᕗᓂᖅᒥᒃ ᐅᓂᒃᑲᐅᓯᖏᑦ ᒪᖅᑮᖕᓂᒃ ᑐᑭᓯᓈᖅᑐᒃ: ᐃᓄᐃᑦ ᓯᕗᓖᖏᑦ ᑎᑭᓪᓚᕐᓯᒪᖕᒪᑕ ᓄᓇᕗᒧᑦ ᐊᓯᖕᖓᓂᒃ ᐊᖏᖅᑲᓇᓪᓚᐅᖅᑕᒥᖕᓂᒃ, ᐊᒻᒪ ᓯᕗᓪᓖᑦᑐᓪᓚᕆᐅᙱᑦ ᑖᒃᑯᐊ ᑎᑭᑦᑐᑦ ᓖᓐᓇᐅᔪᖅ ᓄᓇᕗᒥᒃ ᑕᐃᔭᐅᓕᖅᑐᒥᒃ. ᐊᕐᕌᒎᔪᓂ ᖁᓖᑦ ᐅᖓᑖᓃᑦᑐᓂ ᖃᐅᔨᒪᔾᔪᐊᑦ ᑕᒪᒃᑯᓂᖓ ᓇᓗᓇᐃᖅᓯᓯᒪᓕᖅᑕᐅᔪᑦ ᓱᓕᓂᖓᓂᒃ ᑐᑭᓯᓈᖅᑐᑎᒃ ᐅᖃᐅᓯᖃᖅᐳᖅ. ᐊᒻᒪ ᖃᐅᔨᓯᒪᓕᖅᑐᑎᒃ ᖃᓄᖅ ᐱᑕᖃᓚᐅᕐᓂᖏᓐᓂᒃ ᓯᕗᓂᐊᒎᑦ ᖃᐅᔨᒪᔭᐅᓚᐅᖏᑦᑐᓂᒃ ᐅᑭᐅᖅᑕᖅᑐᒥ ᓯᕗᓂᓕᐅᖅᑕᐅᕙᓐᓂ.

Left: Pangnirtung women cut whale blubber and collect the oil in kettles, 1935. Above: Tent rings, like this one near Bathurst Inlet, dot Nunavut's landscape and attest to the passage of several unique cultures

ᓴᐅᒥᐊᓂ: ᐸᖕᓂᖅᑑᒥᐅᑕᑦ ᐊᕐᓇᑦ ᐊᖅᕕᐅᑉ ᐅᖅᓱᖓᓂ ᐲᔭᐃᔪᑦ ᐊᒻᒪ ᐆᖅᑲᐃᓪᓗᑎᒃ ᖃᑦᑕᕐᓄ, 1935. ᖁᓛᓂ: ᑐᐱᖅᕕᕖᑦ, ᐆᑐᓇᖅ ᑭᖕᒐᐅᑉᒥ, ᓴᖅᑮᔅᓯᑦ ᓄᓇᕗᒻᒥ ᐊᒻᒪ ᓇᓗᓇᐃᒃᑯᑎᐅᓪᓗᑎᒃ ᐃᓕᖁᓯᕕᓂᖕᓂᑦ

Nunavut Tourism

The Glacial Period

(35,000 to 10,000 years ago)

During the last Ice Age, almost all of Nunavut was covered by glacial ice, in places up to several kilometres thick. There was so much water locked into continent-wide glaciers that the sea levels dropped, and the bottoms of shallow seas became dry land. What is now the Bering Sea, separating Siberia from Alaska, was a wide and ice-free plain across which ancestral American Indians moved to North America, and then down the Pacific coast to the areas south of the ice sheets.

When the glaciers covering Nunavut melted between about 15,000 and 10,000 years ago, they revealed a landscape which was empty of life. By shortly after 10,000 years ago, however, Nunavut looked very much as it does today, with caribou and muskoxen grazing the tundra, and walrus, seals, and whales — including bowhead whales — feeding in the channels between the Arctic islands.

ᓯᑯᕐᔪᐊᖑᓚᐅᖅᑐᑉ ᐃᓚᖓ

(35,000-ᒥᑦ 10,000-ᒧᑦ ᐊᕐᕌᒎᓚᐅᖅᑐᓂ ᑕᐃᑦᓱᒪᓂ)

ᑭᖑᓪᓖᑦᑐᒥ ᓯᑯᕐᔪᐊᖅᓱᒪᓂᐅᓚᐅᖅᑐᒥ, ᑕᒪᕐᒥᑲᓴᒃ ᓄᓇᕗᑦ ᓴᐅᓯᒪᓚᐅᖅᐳᖅ ᓯᑯᕐᔪᐊᒧᑦ ᐊᐅᓱᐃᑦᑐᒧᑦ, ᐃᓚᖓᓂ ᐳᖅᑐᓂᖕᓂᒃ ᖃᑦᓯᒐᓕᖕᓂᒃ ᑭᓗᒥᑕᓂᒃ. ᓯᑯᔪᐊᒃᑲᖏᓪᓗᒍ ᐃᒪᖅᒪᓪᓇᐊᓘᑦᑐᕕᓂᖅ ᓯᑯᕐᔪᐊᖅᓱᒪᔪᓂᒃ ᐊᐅᔨᑦᑐᓂ ᑕᓂᐅᑉ ᐳᖅᑐᓂᖓ, ᖃᑦᓯᓐᓂᒃᑎᑕᐅᓪᓗᓂ. ᐊᒻᒪᓗ ᑕᓇᐅᑉ ᐃᒃᑳᑦᑐᑦ ᒪᓂᕋᖕᒋᑦ ᐸᓂᒻᒪᖓᓚᐅᖅᑐᑦ. ᑕᐃᒪᓐᓇ ᐱᕐᖑᕈᑎᒋᓚᐅᖅᑕᖓ ᐃᖏᕕᒃᓴᐅᒍᓐᓇᖅᑐᖅ ᑕᓇᐅᖑᓚᐅᖅᑐᖅ Bering Sea-ᖑᓂᖅᑕᐅᔪᖅ, Siberia-ᒥᑦ ᐊᕕᒃᓯᓯᒪᓪᓗᓂ ᐊᓛᓯᑲᒥᑦ. ᐊᒻᒪᓗ ᓯᑯᖃᓐᖏᑦᑐᒃᑯᑦ ᒪᓂᖅᑲᒃᑯᑦ ᐃᖅᑭᓖᓯᑦ ᓯᕗᓪᓕᖏᑦ ᐃᖏᕋᓐᓇᓚᐅᖅᑐᑦ North America-ᒧᑦ. ᐊᒻᒪᓗ ᑕᐅᓄᖓ ᑎᑭᑉᐸᓪᓕᐊᓪᓗᑎᒃ ᐸᓯᕕᒃ ᑕᓇᐅᕐᔪᐊᑉ ᓯᓂᖓᓐᖓᓄᑦ ᑲᓇᖕᓇᖓᓄᑦ ᓯᑯᕐᔪᐊᖅᓱᒪᔪᑉ.

ᓯᑯᕐᔪᐊᖑᓚᐅᖅᑐᑦ ᐊᐅᔨᑦᑐᑦ ᖃᓇᐅᔭᐅᔪᑦ ᓄᓇᕗᒥ ᐊᐅᓚᐅᖅᑎᓪᓗᒋᑦ ᐊᕐᕋᒍᐃᑦ ᖃᓂᒋᔭᖓᓂ 15,000-ᒥᑦ 10,000-ᒧᑦ ᐊᕐᕌᒎᓚᐅᖅᑐᓂ ᑕᐃᑦᓱᒪᓂ, ᓴᖅᑮᓚᐅᖅᑐᖅ ᓄᓇᐃᓐᓇᕐᒥᒃ ᐆᒪᔪᖃᙱᑦᑐᒥᒃ. ᑭᓯᐊᓂᓕ, 10,000-ᐃᑦ ᐊᕐᕌᒎᓚᐅᖅᑐᑦ ᖄᖏᕐᒪᑕ, ᓄᓇᕗᑦ ᐅᓪᓗᒥᑎᑐᑦ ᑕᐅᑦᑐᖃᓚᐅᖅᑐᖅ, ᑐᒃᑐᖃᐅᖅᓱᓂ ᐅᒥᖕᒪᒃᑲᐅᖅᓱᓂᓗ ᓂᕆᐅᔭᖅᑐᓂᒃ ᓄᓇᐃᓐᓇᕐᒥ. ᐊᒻᒪᓗ ᐊᐃᕖᑦ, ᓇᑦᓯᑦ ᕿᓚᓗᒐᐃᓪᓗ ᓂᕆᔪᑦ - ᐃᓚᒋᔭᐅᓪᓗᑎᒃ ᐊᕐᕖᑦ - ᓂᕆᔪᑦ ᐃᑭᖅᓴᖏᓐᓂ ᐅᑭᐅᖅᑕᖅᑐᒥ ᕿᑭᖅᑕᖏᑕ ᖃᓂᒋᔭᖏᓐᓂ. ᐃᖅᑭᓖᑦ ᒪᒃᑲᐃᑎᑦ ᒪᓖᒃᓯᓚᐅᖅᑐᑦ ᑐᒃᑐᓂᒃ ᐅᑭᐅᖅᑕᖅᑐᑉ ᒥᒃᓵᓄᖓᐅᔪᓂᒃ ᓄᓇᐃᓐᓇᒃᑰᖅᓱᑎᒃ,

Movement of Peoples
ᐃᓄᐃᑦ ᐊᖅᑯᑎᕕᖏᑦ

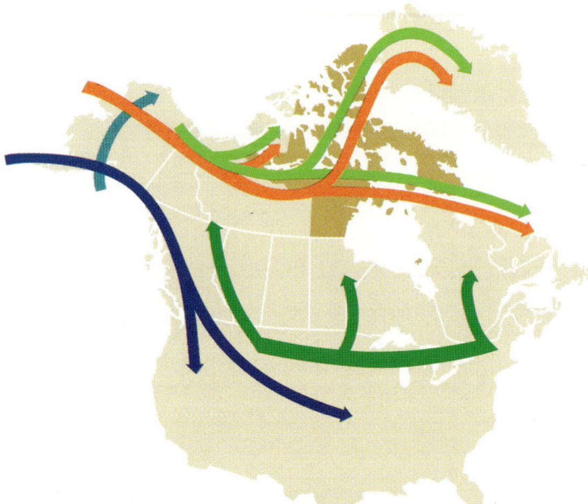

35,000–10,000 years ago **Ancestral American Indians** cross land bridge from Asia
ᐊᕐᕌᒎᓚᐅᖅᑐᓂ **ᐃᖅᑭᓖᑦ ᓯᕗᓪᓕᖏᑦ** ᐃᖄᖅᑐᑦ ᓄᓇᒃᑯᑦ ᐁᓴᒥᑦ

10,000–5,000 years ago **North American Indians** move northward to tree line with retreat of glaciers
ᐊᕐᕌᒎᓚᐅᖅᑐᓂ **ᐅᓪᓗᒥᐅᓕᖅᑐᑦ ᐃᖅᑭᓕᐅᔪᑦ** ᑲᓇᖕᓇᒧᑦ ᐃᖕᒋᕐᕆᔪᑦ ᓯᑯᔪᐊᑉ ᐊᐅᒃᐸᓪᓕᐊᓂᖓᓂᒃ ᒪᓕᒃᖢᑎᒃ ᓇᐸᖅᑐᓕᕐᒧᑦ

5,000–4,000 years ago **Tuniit (Dorset Culture people)** cross Bering Strait and move eastward
ᐊᕐᕌᒎᓚᐅᖅᑐᓂ **ᑐᓃᑦ, (Dorset-ᖑᓂᖅᑕᐅᔪᖅ)** ᐃᖄᖅᑐᑦ Bering Strait-ᒥᒃ ᐊᒻᒪᓗ ᓂᒋᕐᒧᑦ ᐃᖏᕐᕋᓪᓗᑎᒃ

3,000–2,000 years ago **South Bering Sea and North Pacific peoples** become North Alaska Inuit
ᐊᕐᕌᒎᓚᐅᖅᑐᓂ **South Bering Sea ᐃᓄᖏᑦ ᐊᒻᒪᓗ North Pacific ᐃᓄᖏᑦ** ᐋᓛᓯᑲᒥᐅᑕᐅᓕᖅᑐᑦ ᑲᓇᖕᓇᒥ ᐃᓄᖕᖑᖕᓂᒃ

1,000 years ago **Thule (North Alaska Inuit)** move eastward, displacing Tuniit
ᐊᕐᕌᒎᓚᐅᖅᑐᓂ **ᐃᓄᐃᑦ ᓯᕗᓪᓕᕕᓂᖏᑦ (ᐋᓛᓯᑲᒥᐅᑦ ᑲᓇᖕᓇᒥᙶ)** ᓅᑉᐸᓪᓕᐊᔪᑦ ᓂᒋᕐᒧᑦ ᐃᓇᖏᖅᓯᓪᓗᑎᒃ ᑐᓃᓂᒃ

Fleming/NWT Archives

"The government of Canada has agreed in principle to the division of the Northwest Territories and is ready to give favorable consideration to those Inuit proposals."

– Prime Minister Pierre Trudeau at the First Ministers Conference on Aboriginal Constitutional Matters, March 1984

Indian hunters followed the migrating caribou northwards across the barren grounds, much as the Dene did in more recent times, but never reached the Arctic coast or islands. For the following 5,000 years, the parts of Nunavut that were more than a few days' walk north of the tree line remained empty of human occupation.

The Tuniit, or Dorset Culture

(5,000 to 1,000 years ago)

The first people to arrive were the Tuniit. The archeological remains of their camps begin to appear in Alaska shortly after 5,000 years ago, and they quickly spread across the western Arctic, Nunavut, and down the coasts of Greenland and Labrador. The tools and weapons which we find in their North American camps resemble very closely those used by northern Siberian peoples of the time, and the foundations of their tents were also arranged in a typically Siberian pattern, marked by a mid-passage of stones flanking a central fire-box. We think that the earliest Tuniit brought with them two items of technology which allowed them to quickly occupy arctic North America: the bow and arrow, which may have reached America for the first time in their hands, and finely tailored skin clothing similar to that still used by the Inuit and northern Siberian peoples. Until about 1,000 years ago, the Tuniit (or as archeologists call them, the Dorset Culture people) were the sole occupants of most of arctic Canada.

The history of the Inuit can be traced to a much different part of the arctic world — not Siberia, but the southern Bering Sea or North Pacific. The central genius of ancient Inuit culture was adapting their maritime hunting life to the seasonally ice-covered waters of the Bering Sea. This adaptation was accomplished between about 3,000 and 2,000 years ago, and by the latter date large permanent settlements of ancestral Inuit were scattered around the coasts of the Bering and Chukchi seas. The

ᓵᕐᓗ ᐅᓪᓗᒥᒥᐅᑎᑐᑦ ᐃᖅᑭᓕᑐᑦ ᐱᕙᓐᓂᕐᓚᑐᑦ, ᑎᑭᑉᐸᓚᑎᑉ ᑕᕆᐅᑉ ᓯᓪᓭᖕᒐᓄᑦ ᕿᑭᖅᑕᓅᓐᓂᑦ. ᐊᕐᕌᒍᔪᓂ ᖃᐃᔪᓂ 5000-ᓂᒃ, ᓄᓇᕗᑦ ᐃᓚᖏᖕᒐ ᐱᓱᒃᑕᐅᒍᓐᓇᖅᑐᖅ ᐅᓪᓗᒧᑦ ᐊᑕᐅᓯᕐᒧᑦ ᐅᖕᒐᑖᓂ ᑎᑭᑕᐅᕙᓪᓚᐅᓐᖏᑦᑐᖅ ᓇᐸᖅᑐᕐᖃᕐᓇᖅᑐᑉ ᖃᓂᒋᔭᖕᒐᓂ ᐊᒻᒪ ᐃᓅᕐᑲᓚᐅᕐᕿᓂ ᑲᓇᒥᓐᓂᑦ.

ᑐᓃᑦ, Dorset-ᖑᓂᖅᑕᐅᔪᑦ

(5,000-ᒥᑦ 1,000-ᒧᑦ ᐊᕐᕋᒎᓚᐅᖅᑐᓂ ᑕᐃᑦᓯᒪᓂ)

ᐃᓄᐃᑦ ᑎᑭᕐᖓᓚᐅᖅᑐᑦ ᑐᓃ-ᖑᓂᖅᑕᐅᔪᑦ. ᐃᑦᑕᕐᓂᑕᐃᑦ ᓄᓇᕐᑲᕐᕕᕕᓃᑦ ᑕᑯᔭᐅᔪᓐᓇᖅᓯᓚᐅᖅᑐᑦ ᑖᒪᓂ 5,000 ᐊᕐᕋᒍᐃᑦ ᖄᖏᖅᓯᒪᓕᖅᑐᑦ ᖃᓂᒋᔭᖕᒑᓂ ᑕᐃᑲᓂ Siberia-ᒥ. ᐊᒻᒪᓗ ᓯᐊᒥᑉᐸᓪᓕᐊᓪᓗᑎᒃ ᓯᑲᔪᒥᒃ ᐅᐊᓕᓂᕐᒥ ᐅᑭᐅᖅᑕᖅᑐᒥ, ᓄᓇᕗᒥ, ᐊᒻᒪᓗ ᐊᑯᑭᑦᑐᒥ ᓯᓪᓭᖏᑎᖕᒑᓂ ᙯᐸᑐᐊᙵᒥᓗ. ᓴᓇᕆᑎᖏᑦ ᓇᓂᔭᐅᓯᒪᔪᑦ North America-ᒥ ᖃᓂᒋᔭᖏᓐᓂᒃ ᐊᔾᔨᖄᕈᔭᖅᑐᑦ ᓇᓂᔭᐅᓯᒪᔪᓂ ᐃᑦᓴᕐᓂᑕᓂ Siberia-ᒥᑦ, ᐊᒻᒪᓗ ᑐᐱᖕᕕᕕᓂᖏᑦ ᓯᓚᑦᑕᐅᖅ ᐊᔾᔨᒋᔭᖄᕐᒥᔪᑦ ᐳᓂᑕᕿᑭᓂᖑ-ᒥᐅᓂᒃ. ᐅᔭᖃᐃᑦ ᐋᖅᑭᒃᓯᒪᓂᖏᑦ ᐊᔾᔨᒋᔭᐅᔪᑦ Siberia-ᒥᐅᓂᒃ ᐃᒪᓐᓇ ᕿᑎᖕᒐᒍᑦ ᐃᓪᓕᕐᕖᖃᐅᖅᑐᑎᒃ ᐊᒻᒪᓗ ᕿᑎᖕᒐᓂᑦᑕᐅᖅ ᐃᑯᒪᖃᕐᕖᖅᖄᖅᑎᒃ. ᐃᓯᒪᔪᑦ ᑕᐃᒃᑯᐊ ᑎᑭᓛᓚᐅᖅᑐᑦ ᑐᓃᑦ ᐊᓪᓚᖅᓯᓚᐅᕐᒪᑕ ᐊᓴᓯᑲᐅᑉ ᑲᓇᖕᓇᖕᒐᓄᑦ ᒫᕿᖕᓂᒃ ᐊᑐᖅᐸᒃᑕᒥᖕᓂᒃ ᐊᓐᓇᐅᒪᔾᔪᑎᒋᓚᐅᖅᑕᒥᖕᓂᒃ: ᐱᑎᔫᒃ ᐊᒻᒪᓗ ᐊᓐᓄᕋᓂᒃ ᓴᓇᑦᓯᐊᖅᓯᒪᔪᓂᒃ. ᐊᓐᓄᕌᖏᑦ ᒥᖅᑯᓚᖕᓂᒃ ᓴᓇᓯᒪᓪᓗᑎᒃ ᑕᐃᒃᑯᓂᖕᒐᕐᒥᐅᑦ Siberia-ᒥᐅᑎᑐᑦ ᓴᓇᓯᒪᓂᕐᑲᖅᑐᓂᒃ ᐊᒻᒪᓗ ᐅᓪᓗᒥᒧᑦ ᓯᓚ ᐊᑐᖅᑕᐅᕙᒃᓗᑎᒃ. ᑎᑭᓪᓗᒍ 1,000 ᐊᕐᕋᒍᐃᑦ, ᑐᓃᑦ, (Dorset-ᖑᓂᖅᑕᐅᔪᑦ ᐃᑦᑕᕐᓂᑕᓕᓴᐦᓄᑦ) ᐃᓄᑐᐊᖑᓚᐅᖅᑐᑦ ᑕᐃᑲᓃᑦᑐᖁᖃᐅᓪᓗᑎᒃ ᑲᓇᑕᐅᑉ ᐅᑭᐅᖅᑕᖅᑐᖓᓂ.

ᐃᓄᐃᑦ ᓯᕗᓂᕕᓂᖓᑦ ᐊᓯᖓᓅᑦ ᑭᖑᒧᑦ ᓇᓗᓇᐃᔭᖅᑕᐅᔪᓐᓇᖅᑐᖅ ᐅᑭᐅᖅᑕᖅᑐᒥ — ᐅᕙᖓᐅᓐᖏᑦᑐᖅ Siberia-ᒥᐅᓂᒃ, ᑭᓯᐊᓂᓕ ᐱᖓᖓᓐᖓᓄᑦ Bering Sea-ᖑᓂᖅᑕᐅᔪᑉ

Above left: Metal tools and weapons were introduced to Nunavut by the Tuniit, or Dorset Culture people, nearly 5,000 years ago. Left: The Thule hunted enormous bowhead whales, but, beginning some 500 years ago, the Little Ice Age led Inuit to focus on smaller whales, such as these in Cumberland Sound in the mid-1930s. Right: The inuksuk *– "like a human" – has long been used to point the way along a route, or to help drive caribou toward hunters*

ᖁᓖᓂ ᓴᐅᒥᖕᒥ: ᓴᕕᖃᔾᔪᑦ ᓯᓇᒃᑯᑖᑦ ᐊᒻᒪ ᐊᖕᒐᓯᒌᑎ ᓵᖅᑭᑕᐅᓂᑰᕗᑦ ᓄᓇᕗᒻᒧ ᑐᓂᕐᓂ, ᑕᐃᔭᐅᖕᒥᔪᓂᑦ Dorset Culture People, ᐊᕐᕋᒍᑦ 5000 ᓯᕗᓂᑦᑎᓐᓂ. ᓴᐅᒥᐊᓂ: ᑑᓕᑦ ᐊᖑᓇᓱᒃᑲᑦᑕᓚᐅᕐᓯᒪᕗᑦ ᐊᖏᔪᕐᔪᖕᓂ ᐊᕐᕕᖕᓂ, ᑭᓯᐊᓂ, ᐱᒋᐊᕐᑎᓪᓗᒍ 500 ᐊᕐᕋᒍ ᓯᕗᓂᑦᑎᓐᓂ, ᓯᑯᐃᓐᓇᐅᑎᓪᓗᒍ ᐃᓄᐃᑦ ᐊᖑᓇᓱᖕᓂᕐᓴᐅᓕᓚᐅᕐᓯᒪᔪᑦ ᒥᑭᓐᓂᕐᓴᓂ ᐊᕐᕕᖕᓂ, ᒪᑯᑎᑐᓇᖅ ᑖᓪᓗᕈᑎᐅᑉ ᐃᒪᖕᒐᓂᑦ 1930 ᐊᑯᓐᓂᖕᒐᓂᑦ. ᑕᓕᖅᐱᐊᓂ: ᐃᓄᒃᓱᒃ - ᐊᑐᕐᑕᐅᓯᒪᔪᑦ ᓇᓗᓇᐃᒃᑯᑕᐅᓪᓗᑎᒃ ᐊᕐᖁᑎᒃᓴᒧᓐ, ᐅᕙᓗᓐᓂ ᑐᒃᑐᓂ ᐊᖑᓇᓯᒃᑎᓄᖕᒐᐅᑎᑦᑎᔾᔪᑕᐅᓪᓗᑎᒃ

Nunavut Tourism

Fleming/NWT Archives ᕖᓚᒥᖕ/ᓄᓇᑦᓯᐊᖅ ᐊᑦᑕᕐᓯ

splendid and fantastic carvings found in the remains of these settlements hint at a rich social and spiritual life. Metal tools had largely replaced stone implements, and the massive deposits of sea mammal bones associated with the villages tell of a secure economic base.

Thule Culture

(1,000 to 500 years ago)

Between 1,500 and 1,000 years ago, some of these Inuit groups learned to hunt bowhead whales, the largest animals in the arctic seas. Large communities were established on points of land along the northern coast of Alaska, where whales could be easily hunted as they migrated through narrow leads in the spring ice. Then, about 1,000 years ago, some of these North Alaska Inuit spread rapidly eastwards across arctic Canada and Greenland, quickly displacing the previous Tuniit occupants of the region and establishing the first Inuit occupation of Nunavut.

These early Inuit are called the Thule people by archeologists, since the remains of their settlements were first recognized near Thule in northwestern Greenland. The Thule people brought with them from Alaska most elements of their complex maritime hunting culture: kayaks with throwing-harpoons attached to floats; large *umiat* (skin-covered boats) that could transport an entire camp or be used as a platform from which to hunt bowhead whales; equipment for hunting and travelling on the ice; strong sinew-backed bows for hunting on land; and heavily insulated winter houses built from boulders and turf, raftered with whalebones. Within a very short time, the Inuit had adapted their Alaskan maritime hunting culture to most regions of Nunavut. They very soon came into contact with the Norse, who were establishing farming communities in southwestern Greenland at the same time, and traded with the Norse for the metal tools that were basic to Inuit technology.

Inuit and the Little Ice Age

(after 500 years ago)

About 500 years ago, Inuit culture in many parts of Nunavut underwent a significant change. Most regions of the High Arctic were abandoned, and

ᐅᕝᕙᓃᑦ ᐸᓯᕕᒃ ᑕᓄᐅᖓᑕ ᑲᓐᓂᖕᖓᓂᑦ. ᐃᓄᐃᑦ ᓯᕗᓪᓕᖏᑕ ᐃᓯᒪᑦᑎᐊᖅᐸᖕᓂᖓᑦ ᑕᑯᔭᐅᔪᓐᓇᖅᑐᖅ ᒪᓕᒃᑲᓪᓚᐅᕐᓂᖏᓐᓂᒃ ᐊᕐᕋᒍᑦ ᓯᓚᖓᑕ ᖃᓄᐱᓐᓂᖓᓂᒃ ᐊᖓᓇᔅᐸᖕᓂᖏᓐᓂᑦ. ᑕᐱᑲᓂ Bering Sea-ᖑᓂᖅᑕᐅᔪᑉ ᑕᓇᐅᖓᓂ. ᑕᒪᓐᓇ ᐊᕐᕋᒍᒥᒃ ᒪᓕᒃᑲᕐᓂᖅ ᐊᑐᓕᖅᑕᐅᓚᐅᖅᑐᖅ 3000-ᒥᑦ 2000-ᒧ ᐊᕐᕌᒍᔪᓂ ᖄᖏᖅᑐᓂ. ᐊᒻᒪ ᑭᖑᓪᓕᕐᒥ ᐅᓪᓗᒋᔭᐅᔪᒥ, ᐃᓄᒋᐊᒃᑐᓂᒃ ᓄᓇᖃᕐᕕᖃᖃᑦᑕᓚᐅᖅᑐᑦ ᓯᕗᓪᓖᑦ ᓯᓪᔭᓇᔭᐅᔪᓂ ᓇᒥᑐᐃᓐᓇᖅ Bering Sea-ᖑᓂᖅᑕᐅᔪᑉ ᑕᓇᐅᖓᓂ ᐊᒻᒪ Chukchi-ᖑᓂᖅᑕᐅᔪᑉ ᑕᓇᐅᖏᓐᓂ. ᓴᓐᖑᐊᓚᑦ ᒥᑭᑦᑐᑯᓗᐃᑦ ᓇᓂᔭᐅᓂᖁᑦᑕᓚᐅᖅᑐᑦ ᓄᓇᒋᔭᐅᕙᖕᓂᖓᑯᓂ. ᓯᓇᐅᕝᕙᕘᖅ ᑐᑭᓯᒍᑕᐅᓯᒪᔪᑦ ᐃᓅᓯᖃᓚᐅᕐᓂᖏᑦ ᐱᐅᔪᓂᒃ ᐊᒻᒪ ᐊᒃᓯᐃᓪᓗᑎᒃ ᐃᓚᖅᑯᓯᖏᓐᓄ ᐅᒃᐱᕐᓂᖃᖅᐳᑎᒃ. ᓴᕕᖕᓂᒃ ᐊᑐᖃᑦᑕᓚᕐᓂᖅᑎᓪᓗᒋᑦ ᐅᔭᕐᖏᓐᖑᒃ ᓴᓇᓯᒪᔪᓂᒃ ᐱᔪᓇᐅᑎᓂᒃ ᐊᑐᖅᑲᑦᑕᖕᖏᓕᖅᑎᓪᓗᒋᑦ ᓯᓇᑐᐃᓐᓇᕕᓂᖏᑦ ᓇᓂᔭᐅᓯᒪᔪᑦ, ᐊᒻᒪ ᐊᖏᔪᓂᒃ ᐳᐃᔨᓂᒃ ᐃᒪᕐᒥᐅᑕᓂᒃ ᓴᐅᓂᖏᑦᑕᐅᖅ ᓇᓂᔭᐅᓯᒪᖕᒥᔪᑦ ᓂᕿᒋᕙᓪᓚᐅᖅᑕᕕᓂᖏᑦ ᐃᓯᒪᒋᔭᐅᔪᓪᓗ ᑕᐃᒃᑯᐊ ᓄᓇᓕᖕᒥᐅᑕᐅᕙᓪᓚᐅᖅᑐᑦ ᐊᔪᖅᓴᖅᐸᓐᖏᓪᓚᐅᕐᓂᖏᑦ.

Arthur Boutilier ᐋᑐᖅ ᐴᑎᓕᐅᖅ

ᑐᓃᑦ ᐃᓕᖅᑯᓯᖓᑦ

(1,000-ᒥᑦ 500-ᒧᑦ ᐊᕐᕋᒎᓚᐅᖅᑐᓂ ᑕᐃᑦᓯᒪᓂ)

ᕿᑎᖓᓂ 1500-ᒥᑦ 1000-ᒧ ᐊᕐᕋᒎᔪᓂ ᖀᖏᖅᑐᓂ ᐃᓚᖏᑦ ᐃᓄᐃᑦ ᖃᐅᔨᓚᐅᖅᑐᑦ ᖃᓄᖅ ᐊᖑᓇᓱᖕᑲᑕᓗᐊᒃᓴᖅ ᐊᐃᕕᕐᓂᒃ, ᐊᖏᓂᖅᐸᐅᔪᖅ ᐳᐃᔨ ᐅᑭᐅᖅᑕᖅᑐᑉ ᑕᕆᐅᖏᓐᓂ. ᐃᓄᒋᐊᒃᑐᓂᒃ ᓄᓇᓕᕐᑲᐅᓚᐅᖅᑐᑦ ᓄᕗᖓᓂ ᐊᓛᓯᑲᐅᑉ ᓯᓪᔭᖏᓐᓂ, ᐊᐃᕖᑦ ᐊᖑᓇᓯᒃᑕᐅᕙᓚᐅᖅᑎᓪᓗᒋᑦ. ᐅᐱᕐᖔᒥ ᐋᔪᖅᑯᑦ ᐊᐅᓪᓛᓕᖅᑎᓪᓗᒋᑦ. ᖃᓂᒋᔭᖓᓂ ᑕᒫᓂ, 1000 ᐊᕐᕌᒍᓂ, ᐃᓚᖏᑦ ᑕᒪᒃᑯᐊ ᐃᓄᐃᑦ ᐊᓛᓯᑲᒥᐅᑦ ᐊᐃᓯᓕᕙᓪᓕᐊᓚᐅᖅᑐᑦ ᑲᓇᑕᐅᑉ ᐅᑭᐅᖅᑕᖅᑐᖓᒍᑦ ᐊᒻᒪ ᐊᑯᑭᑦᑐᒧᑦ. ᐃᓇᖏᖅᓯᓪᓗᑎᒃ ᑐᓂᕐᓂᒃ ᑕᐃᑲᓂ ᓄᓇᖃᖅᑐᓂᒃ ᐊᒻᒪ ᐃᓄᒃᑲᓪᓚᑎᑎᕙᓪᓕᐊᓪᓗᑎᒃ ᓄᓇᕗᒻᒥᒃ.

ᑖᒃᑯᐊ ᐃᓄᐃᑦ ᓯᕗᓪᓕᖏᑦ ᑕᐃᔭᐅᔪᑦ Thule ᖁᓪᓕᖅᑎᑐᑦ ᐱᑦᑕᕐᕕᑦᑕᓂ ᓱᖏᓐᓂᑦ, ᒪᓕᒃᓱᑎᒃ ᕿᒪᓚᐱᓂᖏᑕ ᓇᓂᔭᐅᖃᑦᑕᐅᕐᓂᖏᓐᓄᑦ Thule-ᒥ ᐊᑯᑭᑦᑐᑉ ᑲᓇᖕᓇᖓᓂ ᐅᐊᖕᓇᖓᓂᓗ. ᐃᓄᐃᑦ ᓯᕗᕚᖏᑦ ᓇᒃᓴᓚᐅᖅᑐᑦ ᐊᓛᓯᑲᒥᑦ ᐱᓇᓱᑎᒋᕙᓚᐅᖅᑕᒥᖕᓂᒃ ᐊᖑᓇᓱᑎᓂᒃ ᐳᐃᔨᓂᒃ: ᖃᔭᓂᒃ ᐅᓈᓕᖕᓂᒃ ᐊᑕᓯᒪᓪᓗᑎᒃ ᐳᒃᑕᓄᑦ; ᐅᒥᐊᓂᒃ ᐊᖏᔪᓂᒃ ᐊᐅᖅᑕᐅᔪᓐᓇᖅᑐᓂᒃ ᓄᓇᖅᑲᑎᒌᓗᒃᑖᖅᑐᓂᒃ. ᐅᕝᕙᓃᑦ ᐊᕕᖅᓯᐅᕐᕕᐅᔪᓐᓇᖅᑐᓂᒃ; ᐊᖑᓇᓱᑦᓇᐅᑎᓂᒃ ᓯᑯᒥ ᐊᒻᒪ ᐃᖏᕐᕋᕈᑎᓂᒃ; ᓴᐅᓐᖏᔪᓂᒃ ᐱᑎᒃᓯᓂᒃ ᐃᕙᓗᓄᑦ ᓴᐅᓐᖏᖅᑎᓯᒪᔪᓂᒃ ᐊᖑᓇᓱᑦᑕᐅᑐᑎᓂᒃ ᓄᓇᒥ; ᐊᒻᒪ ᐅᑭᐅᒥ ᖃᒪᓂᒃ ᓴᓇᓯᒪᔪᓂᒃ ᐅᔭᖅᑲᓂᒃ ᐃᔾᔪᒥᓗ. ᓴᐅᓂᖏᓐᓂᒃ ᐊᕐᕕᑦ ᐊᕙᓗᓕᐅᖅᓯᒪᓪᓗᑎᒃ. ᓱᑲᔪᒥᒃ, ᐃᓄᐃᑦ ᐊᑐᖅᑲᑦᑕᕐᓂᖁᓕᐅᖅᑐᓂᒃ ᐊᓛᓯᑲᒥ ᐊᑐᓕᖅᑕᐅᑎᑎᓕᐅᖅᑐᑦ ᓄᓇᕗᒥ. ᕿᓚᒥᒃᑯᑦᑕᐅᖅ ᓄᓇᓕᖅᑲᑎᖅᑲᕙᓕᐅᖅᑐᑦ Norse-ᖑᔪᓂᒃ, ᐱᕈᖅᓲᕆᐅᔪᓂᒃ ᐊᑯᑭᑦᑑᑉ ᐱᖓᖓᓐᖓᓂ ᑕᐃᑦᓯᒪᓂ ᐊᒻᒪ ᓂᐅᕕᖅᑲᑦᑕᐅᑎᓪᓗᑎᒃ ᓴᕕᖅᓯᖕᓂᒃ ᐊᑐᕐᓗᑎᒃ ᓴᓇᕈᑎᓂᒃ ᐃᓄᖕᓄᑦ ᐊᑐᕐᐅᓕᖅᓯᒪᔪᕕᓂᕐᓂᒃ.

ᓯᑯᕐᔪᐊᖑᓚᐅᖅᑐᖅ ᒥᑭᑦᑐᖅ ᐊᒻᒪ ᐃᓄᐃᑦ

(500-ᑦ ᐊᕐᕌᒎᓚᐅᖅᑐᓂ ᑭᖑᓂᐊᓂ)

500-ᒥᑦ ᐊᕐᕌᒎᓚᐅᖅᑐᓂ ᑭᖑᓂᐊᓂ ᖃᓂᒋᔭᖓᓂ, ᐃᓄᐃᑦ ᐃᓕᖅᑯᓯᖓᑦ ᐊᒥᓱᓂ ᓄᓇᕗᒥ ᐊᓯᔾᔨᓚᐅᖅᑐᖅ ᐊᖏᔪᒥᒃ. ᐊᒥᓱᑦ ᖁᑦᑎᒃᑐᒥ ᓄᓇᒋᔭᐅᓂᖁᑦ ᕿᒪᒃᑕᐅᓚᐅᖅᑐᑦ, ᐊᒻᒪ ᐊᒥᓱᑦ ᕿᑎᕐᒥᐅᑦ ᓄᓇᕗᒥ ᐊᖑᓇᓱᒃᐸᓐᖏᓕᓚᐅᖅᑐᑦ ᕿᓚᓗᒃᑲᓂᒃ ᐊᒻᒪ ᐱᓇᓱᒃᐸᓕᖅᓱᑎᒃ ᒥᑭᓐᓂᖅᓴᓂᒃ ᐳᐃᔨᓂᒃ, ᑐᒃᑐᓂᒃ ᐃᖃᓗᖕᓂᓪᓗ. ᓂᕿᒃᓴᖃᐃᓐᓇᕈᓐᓇᖏᓐᓇᒥᒃ ᐅᕿᒍᑎᔭᓐᓇᖅᑕᒥᖕᓂᒃ ᖃᒪᓕᐅᖅᐸᖏᓕᓚᐅᖅᑐᑦ ᓄᓇᖃᖏᓕᖅᓱᑎᒃ ᔫᕐᓗ ᓯᕗᓪᓕᑎᑐᑦ. ᐅᕿᐸᓕᓚᐅᖅᑐᑦ ᐃᒡᓗᓂ ᑲᑎᕐᖓᓪᓗᑎᒃ ᐊᖑᓇᓱᖕᓇᕐᓂᐊᖅᑎᒃ ᓇᑦᓯᓂᒃ ᓯᑯᒥ.

ᑕᒪᓐᓇ ᐊᓯᔾᔨᕈᑕᐅᔪᖅ ᑕᐃᒪᐃᑐᐃᓐᓇᕆᐊᖅᑲᓚᐅᖅᑐᖅ ᓯᓚᐅᑉ ᐃᒃᕿᓇᖅᐸᓪᓕᐊᓂᖓᓄᑦ. ᐃᓛᓂᒃᑯᑦ ᑕᐃᔭᐅᓯᖅᑐᖅ ᓯᑯᕐᔪᐊᖑᓚᐅᖅᑐᖅ ᒥᑭᑦᑐᖅ, ᑕᒥᓂ ᖃᓂᒋᔭᖓᓂ 1500-ᒥᑦ ᐊᒻᒪ 1850-ᑦ A.D., ᐊᒻᒪ ᐱᔭᓐᓇᕈᑕᐅᓚᐅᖅᓱᓂ

"ᑳᓇᑕᐅᑉ ᒐᕙᒪᖓᑦ ᐊᖏᖅᐳᑦ ᐊᕕᒍᓂᐅᔪᒥᓐ ᓄᓇᕐᓯᐊᖅᒥᓐ ᐊᒻᒪᓗ ᐸᕐᓇᒃᓯᒪᓂᖅᐳᑦ ᐊᖏᕐᖃᑎᒌᖕᓂᕐᒥ ᐃᓄᐃᑦ ᒪᓂᓴᐅᑎᖏᓐᓂᑦ."

– ᑳᓇᑕᐅᑉ ᐊᖓᔪᖅᖄᖅᔪᐊᖓ ᐱᐊᕐ ᑐᕉᑐ ᒥᓂᔅᑕ ᑲᑎᒪᕕᒃᔪᐊᖓᓂ ᓄᓇᖅᖄᖅᑐᑦ ᒦᑦᓱᓐ, ᒫᔾ 1984

many groups throughout the central portions of Nunavut gave up whaling and began to concentrate on hunting smaller sea mammals, caribou and fish. Unable to accumulate enough food to survive the winter in the permanent villages of their ancestors, they began to winter in snowhouse communities from which they could efficiently hunt ringed seals through the ice.

This change may have been caused by a cooling climate, sometimes referred to as the Little Ice Age, which occurred between approximately AD 1500 and 1850, and which may have made the traditional Thule economy impossible in many areas. The same period saw the advance of European fishermen, explorers, whalers and traders into the Inuit homelands, and a growing European influence on traditional Inuit ways of life.

The ancient history of Nunavut, and of the Inuit, is not a simple story of isolation and adaptation to an arctic environment. Rather, it is a complex tale involving great movements of populations, marvellous achievements, and encounters with strange peoples. In these terms, it is very much like the histories of any other people of the world.

Robert McGhee is curator of arctic archeology with the Canadian Museum of Civilization.

ᐃᓄᐃᑦ ᓯᕗᓕᖅᑎᑕ ᐱᕙᓪᓕᐊᒍᓐᓇᕐᓂᖏᓐᓄᑦ. ᐊᒻᒪᓗᑦᑕᐅᖅ ᐃᑲᔪᕈᑕᐅᓚᐅᕐᒥᔪᖅ ᐃᓄᐃᑦ ᐅᖅᑯᓂᖅᓴᓄᑦ ᓅᑉᐸᖕᓂᖏᓐᓄᑦ ᖃᓪᓗᓈᑦ ᑎᑭᒻᒪᑕ ᓯᑲᓂᖅᓴᐅᔪᒥᒃ ᐱᕙᓪᓕᐊᑎᑕᐅᓂᖏᓐᓂᒃ. ᒪᑯᐊ ᑎᑭᑎᓪᓗᒋᑦ ᖃᓪᓗᓈᓂᑦ ᐃᖃᓗᒃᓯᐅᖅᑏᑦ, ᕿᓂᖅᑏᑦ, ᕿᐅᓪᓗᒐᖅᓯᐅᖅᑏᑦ ᐊᒻᒪᓗ ᓂᐅᕕᖅᑏᑦ. ᐃᓄᐃᑦ ᐃᓅᓯᖏᓐᓂ ᐃᓚᐅᒍᓐᓇᕈᑕᐅᓚᐅᖅᒪᑦ.

ᓄᓇᕗᑦ ᓯᕗᓂᐱᓂᕆᓚᐅᖅᑕᖓ, ᐊᒻᒪᓗ ᐃᓄᐃᓐᓄᑦ, ᐅᓂᒃᑳᓯᐅᓐᖏᑦᑐᖅ ᐃᓄᖅᑳᓐᖏᑦᑐ-ᒦᓚᐅᕐᓂᕐᒥ ᐊᒻᒪᓗ ᐊᕙᑎᒧᑦ ᐊᓐᓄᓐᓇᐅ-ᑎᖅᑲᖅᓂᐅᓚᐅᖅᑐᒥᒃ. ᑭᓯᐊᓂᓕ, ᖃᓄᐃᓐᓇᕈᓘᔭᖅ ᓅᑉᐸᓕᐊᓂᐅᑦᑕᓚᐅᖅᑐᓂᒃ ᐊᒥᓱᓂᒃ ᓄᓇᖅ-ᑎᑭᒃᑐᓂᒃ, ᐊᒥᓱᒻᒪᕆᖕᓂᒃ ᑲᒪᓇᖅᑐᓂᒃ ᐊᔪᓐᖏᓐᓂᖅᑲᖅᓂᐅᓚᐅᖅᑐᓂᒃ, ᐊᒻᒪᓗ ᐊᔾᔨᒌᓐᖏᑦᑐᓂᒃ ᐅᓐᖏᑦᑐᓂᒃ ᐃᓅᖕᓂᒃ ᑕᑯᖃᑦᑕᓚᐅᖅᑎᓪᓗᒋᑦ. ᑕᐃᒪᓐᓇ ᐅᓂᒃᑳᓯᐅᑎᓪᓗᒍ, ᔫᒃᓗ ᐊᒥᓱᑎᑦ ᐊᓯᖏᓐᓂ ᓯᓚᕐᔪᐊᒥ ᖃᓄᐃᓕᖓᓐᓂᖅ ᐃᓄᖁᑎᖏᑎᑐᑦ ᐊᔾᔨᒋᔭᐅᔪᖅ.

ᕌᐳᑦ ᒪᒋ ᑲᒪᔨᐅᔪᖅ ᐅᑭᐅᖅᑕᖅᑐᒥ ᐃᑦᓯᕐᓂᖁᑎᖏᓐᓂᒃ ᑕᑯᓐᓇᒐᖅᑲᕕᖕᒥ Canadian Museum of Civilization-ᒥ.

NWT Dept. of Information/NWT Archives

Top left: The Thule introduced the qajaq *(kayak) to Nunavut beginning about 1,000 years ago. The* qajaq *was still key to hunting seals and other sea mammals when this picture was taken in 1942. Left: The* qarmaq *(sod house) helped the Thule survive Nunavut's harsh climate, and was used by Inuit until the 1960s. This* qarmaq *was built as an exhibit near Pond Inlet in 1991. Right: Taqulik, father of James Eetoolook, one of the land-claim negotiators, carries fox furs past the Taloyoak HBC post, 1963. Below: Hunter Joseph Idlouk trades Pond Inlet HBC clerk Bren Halloran arctic fox furs for aluminum tokens, April 1954. HBC tokens were used to purchase goods in the unheated store*

ᖁᓕᓂ ᑕᓕᕐᐱᐊᓂ: ᑑᓖ ᖃᔭᖅ ᓴᖅᑭᑎᑕᐅᓯᒪᒍᑦ ᓄᓇᕗᒻᒧᑦ 1,000 ᐊᕐᕌᒍ ᐊᓂᒍᖅᓯᒪᓕᖅᑐᓂ ᓯᕗᓂᖅᑎᓐᓂᑦ. ᖃᔭᐃ ᓇᑎᕐᓯᐅᑎᓗᐊᑕᐅᓚᐅᖅᐳᑦ ᐊᒻᒪᓗ ᐊᓯᖏᓐᓄ ᐃᒪᕐᒥᐅᑕᕐᓄ ᑕᐃᓯᒪᓂ ᑖᓇ ᐊᔾᔨᓕᐅᕆᔭᐅᑎᓪᓗᒍ 1942ᒥ. ᓴᐅᒥᐊᓂ: ᖃᕐᒪᑦ ᑑᓕᓂ ᐆᒪᑎᑦᑎᓚᐅᕐᓯᒪᒐᑦ ᓄᓇᕗᑦ ᓯᓚᖓ ᓂᓪᓕᓯᒃᑲ-ᐅᑎᓪᓗᒍ, ᐊᒻᒪᓗ ᐃᓄᖕᓄᑦ ᐊᑐᖅᑕᐅᖃᑦᑕᓚᐅᖅᓯᒪᔪᖅ 1960 ᑎᑭᓪᓗᒍ. ᐅᓇ ᖃᕐᒪᖅ ᓴᓇᔭᐅᓂᑯ ᑕᑯᔭᒃᓴᐅᑎᓪᓗᓂ ᒥᑦᒪᑕᓕᐅᑉ ᖃᓂᒋᔭᓂ 1991ᒥ. ᑕᓕᕐᐱᐊᓂ: ᑕᖁᓕᒃ, ᔭᐃᒥᓯ ᐃᑐᓘ ᐊᑖᑕᖓ, ᓄᓇᕗᑖᖅᓯᒃᑐᓂ ᐋᖅᑭᑎᐅᖃᑕᐅᔪᖅ, ᑎᓴᒐᓂᐊᖅᑰᑎᓂ ᐊᑯᖅᓯᔪᖅ ᑕᓗᕐᔪᐊᑉ ᓂᐅᕕᕐᕕᐊᓂ ᖃᖏᖅᓯᓪᓗᓂ, 1963. ᐊᑖᓂ: ᐊᖑᓇᓱᒃᑎ ᔫᓯᐱ ᐃᓪᓗᐅᖅ ᑕᐅᓯᖃᑎᒌᖅᑐᖅ ᒥᑦᒪᑕᓕᖕᒥ ᓂᐅᕕᖅᑎᒥᓐ ᐳᕆᓐ ᕼᐋᓗᕌᓐ ᑎᓴᒐᓂᐊᕐᔪᖕᓂ ᓴᕕᕆᔭᖕᓂ ᑮᓇᐅᔭᐅ-ᓚᐅᖅᓯᒪᔪᓂᑦ, ᐄᐳᕆ 1954. ᓂᐅᕕᖅᑎᑯ ᑮᓇᐅᔭᖏ ᐊᑐᖅᑕᐅᖃᓚᐅᖅᐳᑦ ᓂᐅᕕᐅᑕᐅᓚᐅᖅᑎᑦ ᓂᐅᕕᐊᕐᕕᖕᓂ ᐅᖅᖁᓴᐅᑎᖃᖏᑦᑐᒥ ᓂᐅᕕᕐᕕᖕᒥ

Wilkinson/NWT Archives

Early History

ᐱᒋᐊᓕᓵᕆᑎᑦ ᐊᓂᒍᖅᓯᒪᓂᑯᐃᑦ

By Keith Crowe

The first meeting between Inuit and Europeans likely occurred about AD 1500, when Basque or Portuguese fishermen and whalers reached southern Labrador. The Inuit called the strangers *qallunaat* because of their comparatively bushy eyebrows.

At that time, the Inuit of what is now Canada comprised nine main groups, distinguishable by region, dialect, clothing and adaptation to regional conditions. All Inuit, however, shared a common language, legends and spiritual beliefs.

Fleming/NWT Archives ᕝᓕᒥᓐ/ᓄᓇᑦᓯᐊᕐᒥ ᐸᐸᑦᑐᔪᑦ

Whalers, explorers and fur traders

During the next four centuries, European and American whalers hunted bowhead whales for their oil and baleen in arctic waters, while explorers sailed the same channels in search of a Northwest Passage to the Orient. The explorers also travelled overland, and along the Mackenzie River.

Both groups of intruders brought to the Inuit guns, cloth, metal, tools and utensils, musical instruments and dances, alcohol and tobacco, disease and new genes. Some whalers, particularly in Hudson Bay and Cumberland Sound, employed Inuit families in the industry, creating a new seasonal way of life that blended two cultures.

The old system of barter between Inuit was expanded to include European goods, and furs became an important item. As whaling declined, the fur trade became a paramount influence, with posts throughout the Arctic.

Catholic and Protestant missionaries became the fourth element of change, sometimes competing for converts. Some bizarre cults emerged among Inuit caught in a conflict of beliefs. One of the most notable led to a string of murders on the Belcher Islands in 1941.

By about 1920, the main thrust of exploration was over, and few bowhead whales remained in arctic waters. In the Mackenzie Delta, the Inuit had been decimated by epidemic disease, and their places taken by Alaskan Inuit. Qallunaat were moving into the region.

In the less accessible central Arctic, there were Inuit who even as late as 1900 had not seen a *qallunaaq*, while in Labrador, European settlers had displaced the Inuit from the coast, or mingled with them, everywhere except the Far North.

ᑎᑎᕋᖅᑐᖅ ᑮᑦ ᑯᕉ

ᓯᕗᓪᓕᖅᐹᒥᒃ ᐃᓄᐃᑦ ᖃᓪᓗᓈᓗ ᑕᑯᔭᕆᐅᕆᑎᓪᓗᑎᕐᓂᓚᐅᕐ ᐱᔪᓐᓇᐅᓪᓗᐅᓐᓂᕈᓐ ᖃᓂᒡᒋᓚᐅᕐᓂ 1500 AD-ᒥ, ᑎᑭᓪᓚᐅᕐᒪᑕ-ᐅᓪᓗᐅᓐᓂᕐᒪᑕ ᐃᖃᓗᓯᐅᓐᓂᑦ ᕿᓚᓗᒐᓯᐅᓐᓂᑦᓗ Basque ᐅᕙᓃᑦ ᐳᐊᑐᕆᑦ (Portuguese). ᑎᑭᓪᓗᐅᖅᑎᓪᓗᒋᑦ ᑲᐸᑐᐊᓇᕐ ᐱᖑᓚᖓᓚᐅᑦ. ᐃᓄᐃᑦ ᑎᑭᓪᓕᐅᖅᑐᓂᒃ ᐊᑦᑏᓪᓗᐅᖅᑐᑦ ᖃᓪᓗᓈᓂᒃ ᖃᓪᓗᖏᑦ ᑐᕿᓂᖅᓴᐅᔪᑦ ᐱᔪᑎᒋᓪᓗᒋᑦ.

ᑕᐃᑦᓯᒪᓂᐅᔪᖅ ᐃᓄᐃᑦ ᒫᓇᐅᓕᖅᑐᖅ ᑲᓇᑕᒥᒃ ᑕᐃᔭᐅᖃᑦᑕᓕᖅᑐᒥᑦᑐᑦ ᐃᓕᑦᑐᓂ 9-ᖑᔪᓂ ᑲᑎᖕᒐᓪᓗᐅᖅᑐᑦ. ᐊᕕᒃᑐᖅᓯᒪᔪᓃᑦᑐᓂ ᐊᔾᔨᐅᖏᑦᑐᓂ ᐊᒻᒪᓗ ᐅᖃᐅᓯᖏᑦ, ᐊᓄᕌᖏᓪᓗ ᐃᓵᒃᑯᖅᑐᒃᑯᑦ ᐃᓕᑕᖅᓇᖅᓱᑎᒃ ᐊᒻᒪᓗ ᖃᓄᑎᒌ ᓱᖏᐅᑎᓯᒪᓂᖏᑦ ᐊᔾᔨᐅᖏᑦᑐᓂ ᓄᓇᐅᑉ ᖃᓄᐃᓐᓂᖏᓐᓂ. ᐃᓄᒃᑕᑦ, ᑭᓯᐊᓂᓕ, ᐅᖃᐅᓯᖃᑎᒌᒃᑐᑦ, ᐅᓂᒃᑲᐅᓯᖃᑎᒌᒃᓱᑎᓪᓗ ᐊᒻᒪᓗ ᐅᒃᐱᕐᓂᖃᐅᖅᓱᑎᒃ ᐊᔾᔨᒥᒃ.

ᕿᓚᓗᒐᓂᐊᖅᑎᑦ, ᕿᓂᖅᑎᑦ ᐊᒻᒪᓗ ᓂᐅᕕᖅᑎᑦ

ᑎᑭᑉᐸᓪᓕᐊᔪᓂ ᐊᕐᕌᒍᐃᑦ 100 ᓯᑕᒪᐃᖅᓱᓯᑦ, ᖃᓪᓗᓈᑦ ᑕᓇᐅᑉ ᐊᑭᐊᓂᒥᖕᖏᓛᖅᑐᑦ ᐊᒻᒪᓗ ᐊᒥᐊᓇᒃᑲᑦ ᕿᓚᓗᒐᓂᐊᖅᑎᑦ ᐱᓇᓱᒃᐸᓪᓗᖅᑐᑦ ᐊᕐᕕᖕᓂᒃ ᐱᔪᒪᓪᓗᑎᒃ ᐅᖅᓱᖕᒐᓂᒃ ᐊᒻᒪᓗ ᐃᓗᓕᐊᑭᓯᖕᒐᓂᒃ. ᐅᑭᐅᖅᑕᖅᑐᐸ ᑕᕆᐅᖕᒋᓐᓂ ᐊᕐᕕᖅᓯᐅᖅᓱᑎᒃ ᐊᒻᒪᓗ ᕿᓂᖅᑎᑦ ᐃᑭᖁᓯᖕᒋᓐᓂ ᕿᓂᖅᑎᓪᓗᒋᑦ ᐊᖅᑯᑎᒥᒃ ᓱᓪᓗᐊᓗᖕᒥᒃ ᐅᐊᓕᓂᕐᒥᑦ ᕿᑭᖅᑖᓗᖕᒍᑦ ᐃᖕᒋᖅᑐᒥᒃ. ᕿᓂᖅᑎᑦ ᐃᖕᒋᖅᑭᕙᓪᓕᐅᖅᒥᔪᑦ ᓄᓇᒃᑯᑦ, ᐊᒻᒪᓗ ᐅᐊᓕᓂᕐᒥᐅᑦ ᑰᖕᒐᒍᑦ (Mackenzie River).

ᑕᒪᒃᑭᖕᓂᒃ ᐃᑖᖅᑏᑦ ᑎᑭᑦᔾᔨᓪᓗᐅᖅᑐᑦ ᐃᓄᖕᓂᒃ ᒪᑯᓂᖕᒐᖃᓗᒃ ᖁᑭᐅᑎᓂᒃ, ᖃᓪᓗᓈᖅᑕᓂᒃ, ᓴᕕᒃ, ᓴᓇᕿᑎᑦ ᐊᒻᒪᓗ ᐊᑐᐊᒐᐃᑦ, ᑐᓴᕐᓇᐅᑎᑦ ᒧᒥᕐᓂᕐᓗ, ᐃᒥᐊᓗᒃ ᑎᕘᑭᓗ, ᐋᓐᓂᐊᓂᒃ ᓄᑖᓂᓪᓗ ᑕᐅᑦᑐᓂᒃ. ᐃᓚᖏᑦ ᕿᓚᓗᒐᓂᐊᖅᑎᑦ, ᐱᓗᐊᖅᑐᒥᒃ Hᐊᑦᓴᓐ ᐲᒥ ᐊᒻᒪᓗ ᑎᓄᔾᔭᕕᖕᒥ, ᐃᖅᑲᓇᐃᔭᖅᑎᑎᕚᓪᓗᐅᖅᑐᑦ ᐃᓄᐃᑦ ᐃᓚᒌᓂᒃ. ᐊᕐᕌᒍᑕᓖᑦ ᓴᓇᕕᒃᓴᐅᓇᔭᖅᑐᒥᒃ ᓄᑖᒥᒃ ᒪᓕᒃᓱᑎᒃ ᒪᕿᖕᓂᒃ ᐃᓕᖅᑯᓯᖕᓂᒃ ᑲᑐᑎᓪᓗᒋᑦ.

ᐃᓄᐃᑦ ᐊᑐᖅᑕᐅᖃᑦᑕᓚᐅᖅᑕᖕᒐ ᓂᐅᕕ-ᖃᑦᑕᕐᓂᖅ ᐱᔪᓇᐅᑕᐅᓪᓚᐅᖅᑐᖅ ᖃᓪᓗᓈᖅᑕᓂᒃ ᐊᑐᖕᒐᓕᖅᑐᑎᒃ, ᐊᒻᒪᓗ ᒥᖅᑯᓖᑦ ᐊᒃᓯᕆᑕ-ᐅᓕᓪᓚᐅᖅᑐᑎᒃ. ᐊᕕᖅᓯᐅᓂᖅ ᑲᑕᒃᐸᓪᓕᐊᑎᓪᓗᒍ, ᒥᖅᑯᓕᖕᓂᒃ ᓂᐅᕕᐅᑎᖃᖅᐸᖕᓂᖅ ᐱᑯᖅᐸᓪᓕ-ᐊᓪᓚᐅᖅᑐᖅ, ᓂᐅᕕᕕᒃᑲᓪᓚᖅᑐᓂ ᓇᒥᑐᐃᓐᓇᖅ ᐅᑭᐅᖅᑕᖅᑐᒥ.

ᐃᒃᓯᕿᔭᐊᑦ ᐊᒻᒪᓗ ᐊᔭᖅᓯᐃᔾᔨᑦ ᐊᓯᔾᔨᖅᑎᐅᔭᓂ ᓯᑕᒥᕆᔭᐅᓯᒪᔪᑦ. ᐃᓚᓐᓂᒃᑯᑦ ᓵᓪᓚᖅᑲᖅᑲᓯᐊᖅᓱᑎᒃ ᓇᓕᐊᒃ ᒪᓕᒃᑎᒃᓴᓂᒃ ᐊᒥᓱᓂᖅᓴᓂᒃ ᐱᓇᔪᕐᒪᖕᒐᕐᒥᒃ. ᖃᓄᕿᓱᔭᖅ ᑐᑭᓯᓂᕐᓗᒃᑐᓂᒃ ᐱᑕᖃᓕᕐᓗᑎᒃ ᐅᒃᐱᕆᓯᓂᒃ ᐃᓄᖕᓂ. ᐊᑕᐅᓯᖅ ᐃᖅᑲᐅᒪᔭᒃᓴᐅᔪᖅ

ᐃᓄᐊᖅᑐᖅᑲᖅᑎᓪᓗᒍ ᐊᑕᐅᓯᕐᒪᖕᒋᑦᑐᒥᒃ ᓴᓂᑭᓗᐊᒥ 1941-ᖑᑎᓪᓗᒍ.

ᑕᒪᓐᓇ ᐊᑐᓕᖅᑎᓪᓗᒍ 1920, ᕿᓂᖅᑎᑦ ᑎᑭᑉᐸᓪᓕᐊᑦᑕᕐᓂᖏᑦ ᐊᓂᒍᓪᓗᐅᖅᑐᖅ, ᐊᒻᒪᓗ ᐊᕐᕖᑦ ᓄᖑᖅᑕᐅᓪᓗᑎᒃ ᐅᑭᐅᖅᑕᖅᑐᑉ ᑕᕆᐅᖕᒋᓐᓂ. ᐅᐊᓕᓂᕐᒥ, ᐃᓄᐃᑦ ᓱᒃᑯᑕ-ᐅᓐᓂᖅᑎᓪᓗᒋᑦ ᐋᓐᓂᐊᓄᑦ, ᐊᒻᒪᓗ ᐃᓄᖕᓄᑦ ᐊᓛᓯᑲᒥᐅᓄᑦ ᐃᓇᖏᖅᑕᐅᓪᓗᑎᒃ. ᖃᓪᓗᓈᑦ ᑕᐃᑯᖕᒐ ᑎᑭᓪᓕᐅᓕᖅᑎᓪᓗᒋᑦ.

ᑎᑭᒍᓐᓇᖅᑕᐅᔾᔮᖏᓐᓂᖅᓴᒥ ᕿᑎᕐᒥᐅᓂ, ᖃᓂᒋᔭᖓᓂᓐᓃᑦ 1900 ᐃᓄᖃᓪᓚᖅᑐᖅ ᑕᑯᓪᓚᐅᖏᑦᑐᓂᒃ ᖃᓪᓗᓈᓂᒃ. ᐊᒻᒪᓕ ᓛᐸᑐ-ᐊᓇᒥ, ᖃᓪᓗᓈᑦ ᑎᑭᓪᓕᐅᖅᑐᑦ ᐃᓇᖏᖅᓯᓯᒪᓪᓗᐅᖅᑐᑦ ᐃᓄᖕᓂᒃ ᓯᓐᔨᓂᑦ, ᑲᑎᖅᑕᐅᓪᓗᑎᓪᓚᓃᑦ, ᐅᑭᐅᖅᑕᖅᑐᒥ ᐳᖅᑐᔪᒥ ᓄᓇᖃᕆᐊᖏᑦᑐ-ᑐᐊᖑᓪᓗᑎᒃ.

ᐃᓕᕆᑦᑕᐅᖅ ᖃᓪᓗᓈᑦ ᑎᑭᓪᓗᐅᖅᑐᑦ ᐅᑭᐅᖅᑕᖅᑐᒧᑦ ᐅᑯᐊᖑᔪᑦ ᑲᓇᒥ ᐸᓖᓯᐅᔪᑦ, ᐳᑭᖅᑖᓪ (RCMP). ᑲᓇᑕᐅᑉ ᒐᕙᒪᖓ, ᐃᓱᒪᑎᖃᖅᑐᑎᒃ ᐊᒥᐊᓇᒃᑲᒥᐅᓂᒃ ᕿᓚᓗᒐᓂᐊᖅᑎᑦ ᖃᓄᐃᓕᐅᕐᓂᖏᓐᓂᒃ Hᐊᑦᓴᓐ ᐲᒥ ᐊᒻᒪᓗ ᕿᓂᖅᑎᑦ ᐊᓯᒥᐅᑕᐃᑦ ᐅᑭᐅᖅᑕᖅᑐᖅ ᐳᖅᑐᔪᖓᓂ,

Wilkinson/NWT Archives ᕕᐊᑭᓐᓴᓐ/ᓄᓇᑦᓯᐊᕐᒥ ᐸᐸᑦᑐᔪᑦ

Another group of qallunaat to enter the Arctic around this time was Canada's federal police force, the North West Mounted Police, or NWMP (later called the Royal Canadian Mounted Police). The Canadian government, concerned by the presence of American whalers in Hudson Bay and by the activities of foreign explorers in the High Arctic, began to set up NWMP posts in order to enforce Canadian laws and exert control.

Nunavut Tourism ᓄᓇᕗᑦ ᐳᓚᕋᖅᑐᓕᕆᔨᒃᑯ

The unsung role of Inuit

Written histories of the Arctic during the 19th century often comment on the contrast between the Inuit, who had long before adapted superbly to their environment, and the ill-equipped Europeans, who starved, froze, sickened and sank their way around the Arctic.

Little attention, however, has been paid to the role of Inuit who helped the newcomers as hunters, guides and interpreters. To name a few, Ipilgvik (Joe) and his wife Taqalikitaq (Hannah) of Cumberland Sound saved the lives of a ship's crew, and advanced the careers of several explorers at great cost to themselves. Ouligbuk of Hudson Bay and his son William spoke many languages, and made the hazardous crossing of the continent several times in the service of Europeans.

During the 1920s and 1930s, most Inuit were troubled by fluctuating fur prices, epidemics and shortages of wildlife. A further burden was the establishment of five residential schools that removed Inuit children as young as five from their families and the whole context of Inuit culture, sometimes for years. Incidents of physical and sexual abuse also took place at some church-run residential schools. In general, however, the Inuit retained their language and sense of independence, within or despite the ill-defined authority of the "Big Three": policeman, trader and missionary. This equilibrium continued until the outbreak of the Second World War.

Keith Crowe is the author of A History of the Original Peoples of Northern Canada.

ᐱᒋᐊᓕᓚᐅᖅᑐᑦ ᐸᓖᓯᖃᕐᑎᑎᓂᕐᒥᒃ. ᑲᓇᑕᐅᑉ ᒪᓕᒐᖏᓐᓂᒃ ᐊᑐᕐᑎᑎᖁᑦᑐᒋᑦ ᐊᒻᒪ ᐊᐅᓚᑦᑎᓂᖃᖁᑦᑐᒋᑦ.

ᐃᓄᐃᑦ ᐃᓕᑕᕐᔭ-ᐅᙱᓐᓂᖏᑦ

ᑎᑎᖅᑕᐅᓯᒪᔪᑦ ᐊᓂᒍᖅᓯᒪᓂᑯᓂᒃ ᐱᔾᔪᑎᖃᖅᑐᑎᒃ ᐊᑐᖅᑎᑦᑐᒍ 19-ᒥᔭᐅᔪᖅ ᐊᕐᕌᒍᖓᑦ ᐊᒥᓱᐃᖅᑐᑎᒃ ᐅᖃᖅᓯᒪᔪᖃᖅᑐᑦ ᐊᔾᔨᒋᙱᓚᐅᕐᓂᖏᓐᓂᒃ ᐃᓄᐃᑦ ᖃᓄᐃᓐᓂᖏᑦ ᐊᒻᒪ ᖃᑦᑐᓈᑦ. ᐃᓄᐃᑦ ᐊᕙᑎ-ᒥᐅᑕᑦ ᐊᔪᙱᓪᓗᑎᒃ ᐊᓇᐅᒪᒍᓐᓇᑦᑎᐊᕐᓂᕐᒥᒃ ᐊᒻᒪ ᑯᑦᑕᖑᔪᑦ ᖃᑦᑐᓈᑦ, ᐊᕿᐊᕈᐊᖅᐸᓚᐅᖅᑐᑦ, ᖁᐊᖅᐸᒃᑐᑎᒃ, ᐋᓐᓂᐊᓕᖅᐸᒃᑐᑎᒡᒎ ᐊᒻᒪ ᑭᕕᕙᒃᑐᑎᒃ ᐅᑭᐅᖅᑕᖅᑐᒥ.

ᐃᓕᑕᕐᔭᐅᔪᐃᑦᑐᑦ, ᑭᓯᐊᓂᐅᒐᓗᐊᖅ, ᐃᓄᐃᑦ ᐃᑲᔪᖅᑎᐅᕙᓚᐅᖅᓂᖏᑦ ᑎᑭᓕᕈᖅᑐᓄᑦ. ᒪᖃᐃᑎ-ᐅᕙᒃᑐᑎᒃ, ᑕᓯᐅᖅᑎᐅᑦᑐᑎᒃ ᐅᖃᖅᑎᐅᑦᑐᑎᒡᒎ. ᑕᐃᒍᒋᑦ ᐊᒥᓲᓐᖏᑦᑐᑦ, ᐃᐱᖕᕕᒃ (Joe) ᐊᒻᒪ ᓄᓕᐊᖓ, ᑕᖃᓕᑭᑖᖅ (Hannah) ᑎᓈᔾᔭᕐᕕᖕᒥᐅᑕᒃ. ᓴᐳᔾᔨᓚᐅᖅᑐᒃ ᐅᒥᐊᕐᔪ-ᐊᕐᒥᐅᓂᒃ ᓴᓇᔾᔨᖕᒋᓐᓂᒃ, ᐊᒻᒪ ᖁᓂᖅᑎᓄᑦ ᖃᑦᓯᑲᓪᓚᖕᓄᑦ ᐃᑲᔪᖅᑎᐅᓚᐅᖅᑐᒃ ᓯᓚᓇᐊᖕᖏᓐᓂᒃ ᓯᕗᒻᒧᐃᓚᐅᖅᑐᒃ ᐃᖕᒥᖕᓂᒃ ᐃᓯᒪᒐᑎᒃ ᐊᒃᓯᕈᕐᓇᖅᑐᒃᑯᓪᓗᑎᒃ. ᐅᓕᕝᐸᖅ ᕼᐊᑦᓴᓐ ᐲᒥᐅᑕᖅ ᐊᒻᒪ ᐃᕐᓂᖓ ᐅᐃᓕᐊᒻ ᐊᒥᓱᓂᒃ ᐅᖃᐅᓯᓂᒃ ᓇᓗᓐᖏᑦᑐᖅ, ᐊᒻᒪ ᑲᖑᐊᓐᓇᖅᑐᒃᑯᑦ ᐃᑳᖅᓯᕙᒃᖢᑎᒃ ᖃᑦᓯᓪᓚᑲᓐᓂᒃ ᐃᑲᔪᖅᑎᐅᒃᖢᑎᒃ ᖃᑦᑐᓈᓄᑦ.

ᐊᑐᓕᖅᑎᓪᓗᒋᑦ 1920 ᐊᒻᒪ 1930, ᐃᓄᐃᑦ ᐊᔪᖅᓴᕐᑎᖃᓕᓚᐅᖅᑐᑦ ᒥᖅᑯᓖᑦ ᐊᑭᖏᑦ ᑲᑕᒃᑎᓪᓗᒋᑦ, ᐋᓐᓂᐊᕐᓃᓪᓗ ᑎᑭᑎᓪᓗᒋᑦ ᐆᒪᔪᐃᓪᓗ ᐊᔪᕐᓇᓕᖅᑎᓪᓗᒋᑦ. ᐊᒃᓯᕈᕈᑕᐅᓚᐅᕐᒥᔪᖅ ᑕᓪᓕᒪᓂᒃ ᐃᓕᓐᓂᐊᕐᕖᖕᓂᒃ ᐱᑕᖃᓕᖅᑎᓪᓗᒍ ᓄᑕᖄᑦ ᑕᓪᓕᒪᓂᒃ ᒫᒃᑯᖕᓂᓖᓐᓅᓐᓃᑦ ᐊᖕᖏᕐᖏᒥᖕᓂᒃ ᐲᖅᑕᐅᑦᑐᑎᒃ ᐊᐅᓪᓚᖅᑎᑕᐅᕝᕕᑎᓪᓗᒋᑦ. ᐃᓚᒥᖕᓂᒃ ᓇᔾᔮᖖᒋᓕᖅᑐᑎᒃ ᐊᒻᒪ ᐃᓕᖅᑯᓯᕐᒥᖕᓂᒃ, ᐃᒫᓐᓂᒃᑯᑦ ᐊᕐᕋᒎᓂᒃ ᐊᕐᒥᓂᒃ. ᐃᓚᖏᑦ ᑐᒃᓯᐊᕐᕕᖕᓄᑦ ᐊᐅᓚᑕᐅᔪᓄᑦ ᐃᓕᓐᓂᐊᕐᕕᖕᓂ ᓯᓕᓇᐊᓇᔭᐅᑦᑕᓚᐅᖅᑐᑦ ᓄᑦᑖᖅᑲᓂᒃ ᖁᓄᔪᖕᓂ-ᐊᖅᑐᓂᒃ ᐊᒻᒪ ᐋᓐᓂᖅᑎᓇᕐᕋᒃᑐᒃ. ᑕᒪᐃᓐᓂᒃ, ᑭᓯᐊᓂ, ᐃᓄᐃᑦ ᓇᖕᒥᓂᖅ ᐅᖃᐅᓯᕐᒥᖕᓂᒃ ᐊᓯᐅᔨᓚᐅᙱᑦᑐᑦ ᐊᒻᒪ ᐃᓱᒪᖅᓱᕐᓇᕐᓂᕐᒥᖕᓂᒃ, ᑖᒃᑯᐊ ᐊᓯᔾᔨᕆᑎᐅᔪᑦ ᐊᐅᓚᑦᑎᓂᖕᒋᑦ ᐊᔭᐅᖅᓯᒪᒍᓐᓇᖅᑎᓪᓗᒋᑦ "ᐱᖓᓱᑦ ᐊᖏᔫᔪᑦ": ᐸᓖᓯᒃᑯᑦ, ᓂᐅᕕᖅᑎᒃᑯᑦ ᐊᒻᒪ ᑐᒃᓯᐊᖅᑏᒃᑯᑦ. ᑕᒪᓐᓇ ᓱᓇᓗᐅᙱᑦᑐᖅ ᓯᓚᕐᔪᐊᓗᒃᑖᒥ ᐅᓇᑕᕝᕕᐊᓗᐊᕐᓂᖅ ᑐᓕᐊ ᑎᑭᑦᑐᒍ.

ᑮᑦ ᑯᕈ ᑎᑎᕋᖅᑎᐅᔪᖅ ᐅᖃᓕᒫᒐᒥᒃ *A History of the Original Peoples of Northern Canada.*

Left: The RCMP has maintained detachments in present-day Nunavut since 1903, including the Pond Inlet detachment, seen here in the 1950s. Above: David Kaniak, Moses Koihok, Paul Omilgoetok, and Bessie Omilgoetok, Cambridge Bay. Christianity remains a strong element in Inuit culture, despite overly zealous beginnings by early missionaries. Right: Grey Nuns of the Chesterfield Inlet convent, established in 1931, watch Inuit cut meat and maktaaq *from beluga whales, 1950*

ᓴᐅᒥᐊᓂᑦ: ᐸᓖᓯᒃᑯ ᐱᓕᕆᕝᕕᖃᓕᖅᐳᑦ ᓅᓇᕗᒻ 1903ᒥ, ᐱᖃᓯᐅᑎᓪᓗᓂ ᒥᑦᑎᒪᑕᓕᖕᒥ, ᑖᓐᓇ ᑕᑯᒃᓴᐅᔪᖅ 1950ᖏᓐᓂ. ᖁᓖᓂ: ᑕᐃᕕᑦ ᑲᓂᐊᒃ, ᒨᓯᓯ ᑯᐃᓯᒃ, ᐹᓪ ᐅᒥᐊᒍᐃᑦᑐᒃ, ᐊᒻᒪ ᐱᓯ ᐅᒥᐊᒍᐃᑦᑐᒃ, ᐃᖃᓗᒃᑑᑦᑎᐊᖅ. ᐅᒃᐱᕐᓂᖅ ᓴᙱᓂᕐᔭᐅᒐᖅ ᓯᓚ ᐃᓄᐃᑦ ᐃᓕᖅᑯᓯᖏᑦᑎᒍᑦ, ᐱᒋᐊᓕᕼᕐᓂᖅ ᐊᑲᐅᓗᐊᓚᐅᖕᒥᒃᑲᓗᐊᕐᑎᓪᓗᒍ ᑐᒃᓯᐊᕐᑎᓂ. ᑕᓕᕐᐱᐊᓂ: ᓇᔭᑦ ᐃᒡᓗᓕᒡᓯᔪᖕᒥ, ᓴᖅᑭᑕᐅᓂᒍ 1931ᒥ, ᑕᐅᑐᒃᑐᑦ ᐃᓄᖕᓂ ᕿᓚᓗᒐᐅᑉ ᓂᕿᖓᓂᑦ ᐊᒻᒪ ᒪᒃᑖᖓᓂ ᐱᓕᕆᑦᑐᓕ, 1950

Wilkinson/NWT Archives

Roméo LeBlanc
Governor General of Canada

Roméo LeBlanc
gouverneur général du Canada

ᕈᒥᐅ ᓚᑉᓛᖕᒃ
ᒐᕙᓇᐅᔪᖅ ᑲᓇᑕᒥ

NUNAVUT
ᓄᓇᕗᑦ

A new territory in Northern Canada has been created. Its name is Nunavut and nature has given all its blessings to this spacious land. It is a place of vast untapped resources, diverse wildlife, unspoiled wilderness and haunting beauty. For all the benefits of the land, Nunavut's greatest asset is its people. They are strong and resourceful and determined.

While Nunavut is a new political reality, the majority of the people who live there have ties to the land that reach back thousands of years. Inuit have worked hard to bring into being a territory where their beliefs, culture and traditions could find a home. Although Nunavut will reflect their unique aspirations, it will continue to be welcoming and hospitable — like all places where Inuit live.

As Governor General of Canada, I send my congratulations and best wishes to the people of Nunavut as they begin life in their new home. The determination of Nunavut's people has overcome the obstacles of the past and I am sure it will triumph over the challenges of the future.

Un nouveau territoire vient d'être créé dans le Nord canadien. Cette vaste étendue, appelée Nunavut, a été comblée par la nature. Elle est riche d'une multitude de ressources inexploitées, d'une faune diversifiée, d'un milieu sauvage intact et d'une beauté envoûtante. Au-delà de tous ces avantages naturels, le plus grand atout que possède le Nunavut est sans nul doute sa population, vigoureuse, ingénieuse et déterminée.

Le Nunavut est certes une nouvelle réalité sur le plan politique, mais la majorité de ses résidants ont tissé des liens avec ce territoire depuis des milliers d'années. Les Inuits ont travaillé avec acharnement à l'établissement d'un territoire où leurs croyances, leur culture et leurs traditions trouveraient place. Le Nunavut sera à l'image de leurs aspirations uniques, mais continuera d'être accueillant et hospitalier— comme il en est de tous les endroits où vivent les Inuits.

À titre de Gouverneur général du Canada, je transmets mes félicitations et mes meilleurs vœux à la population du Nunavut, qui entame une autre étape de sa vie dans son nouveau foyer. Grâce à leur détermination, les résidants du Nunavut ont surmonté les obstacles du passé, et je suis convaincu qu'ils relèveront avec brio les défis du futur.

ᓄᓇᑖᕐᑐᖅᑲᕐᑐᖅ ᑲᓇᑕᐅᑉ ᐅᑭᐅᖅᑕᖅᑐᖓᓂ ᐱᙳᕐᑎᑕᐅᔪᒥᒃ. ᓄᓇᕗᒥ ᐊᑎᖅᑲᕐᑐᖅ ᐊᒻᒪᓗ ᓯᓚᐅᑉ ᐊᐅᓚᓂᖓ ᐋᖅᑭᒃᓱᐃᑦᑎᐊᖅᓯᒪᓪᓗᓂ ᓄᓇᕐᔪᐊᕆᔭᐅᔪᒥᒃ. ᐃᓂᕆᔭᐅᒍᖅ ᐊᒃᑐᖅᑕᐅᓯᒪᙱᑦᑎᐊᖅᑐᓂᒃ ᓄᓇᒥᐅᑕᓂᒃ, ᐆᒪᔪᕈᓘᔭᖏᑦ, ᓱᕈᖅᑕᐅᓯᒪᙱᑦᑐᒥᒃ ᓯᓚᓚᒃ ᐊᒻᒪᓗ ᑲᔫᔾᓇᖅᑐᒪᕆᐅᓪᓗᓂ. ᐃᑲᔫᑕᐅᔪᓕᒫᑦ ᓄᓇᒥ, ᓄᓇᕗᑦ ᑐᓐᓂᕿᑎᒋᓂᖅᐹᖅᑲᖅᐳᖅ ᐃᓄᖏᓐᓂᒃ. ᓵᙱᔫᔪᑦ ᐊᑑᑎᑦᑎᐊᖅᓱᑎᒃ ᐊᒻᒪᓗ ᐱᓂᐊᕈᒪᓂᖅᑦᑎᐊᖅᓱᑎᒃ.

ᓄᓇᕗᑦ ᓄᑖᖑᑎᓪᓗᒍ ᒐᕙᒪᒃᑯᑎᒍᑦ ᐱᓪᓚᑦᑖᓐᖑᖅᑎᓪᓗᒍ, ᐃᓅᖏᑦ ᐅᓄᕐᓂᖅᓴᐃᑦ ᐊᒃᑐᐊᓂᖅᑲᖅᑐᑦ ᓄᓇᒥᙵᑦ ᑕᐃᔅᓯᒪᓂᑐᕿᓘᖕᓂᓂᑦ ᐊᕐᕌᒍᓚᔅᓴᐅᔪᓂᒃ. ᐃᓄᐃᑦ ᐊᒃᓯᕈᖅᓯᒪᔪᑦ ᓄᓇᒋᔭᖕᒐᑦ ᐅᒃᐱᕈᓲᑎᖕᒋ, ᐃᓕᖅᑯᓯᖕᒋᑦ ᐱᖅᑯᓯᖕᒋᓪᓗ ᐊᖕᒋᕐᕿᖅᑲᓕᖁᓪᓗᒋᑦ. ᓄᓇᕗᑦ ᐊᔾᔨᐅᖕᒋᑦᑐᓂᒃ ᑎᑭᑕᐅᔪᒪᓂᐅᔪᓂᒃ ᑕᑯᒃᓴᐅᑎᑦᑎᓂᐊᕐᓗᐊᖅᑎᓪᓗᒍ, ᑐᙵᓇᐃᓐᓇᕐᓂᐊᖅᑐᖅ ᑐᔪᕐᒥᓇᕐᑎᐊᕐᓗᓂ -- ᓇᒥᓕᒫᑦᑎᐊᖅ ᐃᓄᐃᑦ ᑕᐃᒪᐃᖅᑲᑦᑕᕐᒪᑕ ᓄᓇᒋᔭᕐᒥᓂᒃ.

ᒐᕙᓅᓪᓗᐊᑕᐅᓪᓗᖓ ᑲᓇᑕᒥ, ᖁᕕᐊᓱᒋᑦᑎᕙᒪᕙᔭ ᐊᒻᒪᓗ ᓂᕆᐅᒋᔭᒃᓴᖅᑎᐊᖁᓪᓗᒋᑦ ᐃᓅᔪᑦ ᓄᓇᕗᒥ ᐊᖏᕐᕿᑖᕆᐊᓕᖅᑎᓪᓗᒋᑦ. ᓄᓇᕗᑦ ᐃᓅᖏᑕ ᐱᓂᐊᕈᒪᔭᖏᑦ ᐋᕐᕿᓐᖅᑐᒃᑯᖅᑕᖅᓯᒪᕙᒥᒃ ᑮᓇᒍᓂᑦᑎᓐᓂ ᓯᓚᕗᖓᑦᑕᐅᖅ ᑲᔪᓯᑦᑎᐊᕐᓂᐊᕐᓂᖏᓐᓂᒃ ᐊᒃᓯᕈᕐᓇᑦᑎᐊᖅᑐᒃᑯᕐᓂᐊᓕᖅᑎᓪᓗᒋᑦ ᓯᕗᓂᑦᑎᓐᓂ.

NUNAVUT
ᓄᓇᕗᑦ

On behalf of all Canadians, I would like to welcome Nunavut to the Canadian federation. The creation of Nunavut represents history in the making as we change the map of our country for the first time in 50 years. The eyes of the world are upon us as Nunavut comes into being peacefully and democratically.

The creation of Nunavut is the culmination of more than twenty years of hard work by individuals and governments alike. As we move into the 21st century, we honour the past by building upon the ancient traditions of the Inuit to forge a public government which represents all residents of the territory equally and fairly.

The creation of the territory of Nunavut marks the beginning of an exciting new chapter in the history of Canada. In celebrating the new territory, we recognize that there are challenges ahead to realize the full potential of Nunavut and its people. The solid record of achievements to date will provide a strong foundation on which to move forward and build effective partnerships.

I look forward to new partnerships between the Government of Canada and Nunavut and sharing the great pride and happiness that April 1 brings for all Canadians.

Au nom de tous les Canadiens et Canadiennes, je désire souhaiter la bienvenue au Nunavut dans la fédération canadienne. La création de ce nouveau territoire est un événement historique. En effet, nous modifions la carte de notre pays pour la première fois depuis 50 ans, et nous le faisons d'une manière paisible et démocratique qui attire l'attention du monde entier.

Les personnes et les gouvernements qui travaillent d'arrache-pied depuis plus de 20 ans à la création du Nunavut voient aujourd'hui leurs efforts récompensés. À l'aube du 21e siècle, nous faisons honneur à notre passé en nous appuyant sur les traditions ancestrales des Inuits pour constituer une administration publique qui représente tous les résidants et résidantes du territoire de manière juste et équitable.

La création du Nunavut marque le commencement d'un nouveau chapitre captivant de l'histoire du Canada. Nous célébrons l'établissement du nouveau territoire, mais nous sommes tout de même conscients qu'il reste encore beaucoup de défis à relever pour que le Nunavut et sa population soient en mesure de réaliser tout leur potentiel. Heureusement, nous pourrons nous inspirer de plusieurs réalisations pour aller de l'avant et créer des partenariats fructueux.

Il me tarde de voir à l'œuvre les nouveaux partenariats qui lieront le gouvernement du Canada et celui du Nunavut, et de partager les sentiments de fierté et de joie que le 1er avril fera naître chez tous les Canadiens et Canadiennes.

ᑲᓇᑕᒥᐅᑦ ᑭᓪᓕᖅᑐᕐᓗᒋᑦ, ᑐᙵᓱᒃᑎᑦᑐᒪᕚᕋ ᓄᓇᕗᑦ ᑲᓇᑕᒥ ᐃᓚᒌᒃᑐᖁᑎᖏᓐᓄᑦ. ᓯᕗᓪᓕᖅᐹᒥ ᐊᕐᕌᒍᓂ 50-ᓂᒃ ᓄᓇᙳᐊᕗᑦ ᓄᓇᑦᑎᓐᓂ ᐊᓯᔾᔨᕐᓂᐊᓕᖅᑐᖅ. ᑕᐃᒪᐃᑉᐳᒍᑦ ᓄᓇᕐᔪᐊᑉ ᑕᑯᑦᑐᖏᓐᓂᒃ ᑕᒪᓐᓇ ᐊᓯᔾᔨᑦᑎᐊᕐᓂᐊᓕᖅᑎᓪᓗᒍ ᑕᐃᒪᐃᓚᔪᖏᑦᑐᒥ - ᓴᐃᒪᓪᓗᓂ ᐊᖏᖅᑲᑎᒌᖕᓂᒃᑯᓪᓗ.

ᐱᙳᖅᑎᑕᐅᓂᖓ ᓄᓇᕗᑦ ᐸᕐᓇᐃᓐᓚᐅᖅᑐᑦ ᓄᐊᑎᑕᐅᓯᒪᓂᖏᓐᓂᒃ ᐱᒋᐊᖅᓯᒪᕙᖅ 20 ᐊᕐᕌᒍᐃᑦ ᐅᖓᑖᓂ ᐊᒻᒪᓗ ᐊᕐᕌᒍᓚᖀᓗᓂᐊᖅᑐᓄᑦ. ᐱᒋᐊᓕᖅᑎᓪᓗᒍ 21-ᖑᓂᖅᑕᐅᔪᖅ ᕼᐋᓐᓇᓚᐃᑦ ᐊᕐᕌᒍᐃᑦ ᑲᑎᖅᓱᖅᑕᐅᓯᒪᑎᓪᓗᒋᑦ, ᐃᓄᐃᑦ ᐱᖁᓯᑐᖄᓗᕆᑦ ᑐᙵᕝᕕᒋᓪᓗᒋᑦ ᐋᖅᑭᒃᓱᐃᓂᐊᖅᑎᓪᓗᑕ ᒐᕙᒪᐅᔪᒥᒃ ᐊᐅᓚᑕᐅᔪᒥᒃ ᐃᓄᖕᓄᑦ ᐱᒋᐊᖅᑎᑕᐅᔪᖅ ᑭᒡᓕᖅᑐᐃᖁᓪᓗᒋᑦ ᐃᓄᓕᒫᖏᓐᓂᒃ ᓇᓕᒧᑦᑐᒥᒃ ᓈᒻᒪᒃᑐᒥᒡᓗ.

ᐱᙳᖅᑎᑕᐅᓂᖓ ᓄᓇᕗᑦ ᓄᓇᕘᑎᒋᓂᐊᖅᑕᖓ ᐃᓱᓕᕝᕕᐅᙱᓚᖅ, ᑭᓯᐊᓂᓕ ᓄᑖᖑᕗᖅ ᕿᒥᕐᕈᐊᕙᐅᓂᐊᖅᑎᓪᓗᒍ ᒫᑉᐱᖅᑐᖅᑎᑐᑦ ᑕᐅᑐᒡᓗᒍ ᑲᓇᑕᒥ ᐊᑐᖅᐸᓪᓕᐊᓯᒪᔪᓂᒃ. ᖁᕝᕙᐊᓵᑎᖅᑲᖅᑎᓪᓗᑕ ᓄᓇᑖᙳᖅᑐᒥᒃ, ᐱᔾᔭᒃᓴᖅᑲᒻᒪᕆᒃᐳᑦ ᓱᓕ ᐱᕈᖅᓯᓪᓗᒍ ᓄᓇᕗᑦ ᐃᓗᐃᑦᑐᙳᖅᓯᓪᓗᒍ.

ᓱᔪᕐᓕ, ᑎᑎᕋᖅᑕᐅᓯᒪᔪᓂᒃ ᑎᑭᓐᓂᐅᔪᓂᒃ ᐊᑯᖅᓯᒪᓪᓚᑦᑎᐊᕐᑕᑦ ᑐᙵᕝᕕᕆᔭᕐᓇᖅᑕᑦᑎᓐᓂᒃ ᑲᑐᔾᔨᑦᑎᐊᖁᓪᓗᑕ ᑲᔪᓯᓇᓱᐊᖅᑎᓪᓗᑕ.

ᓂᕆᐅᒃᑐᖓ ᑲᑐᔾᔨᖅᑲᑎᒌᖕᓂᖓᖁᓪᓗᑕ ᒐᕙᒪᐅᔪᑦ ᑲᓇᑕᒥ ᓄᓇᕗᒻᒥ ᐅᐱᒋᖅᑲᑎᒌᑦᑎᐊᖁᓪᓗᑕ ᖁᕝᕙᐊᓯᖅᑲᑎᒌᖁᓪᓗᑕᓗ ᑲᓇᑕᓕᒫᒥ ᐄᐳᕈ 1 ᑐᖔᕈᑎᖃᖅᑎᓪᓗᒍ.

Jean Chrétien
Prime Minister

Jean Chrétien,
premier ministre

ᔫᓐ ᑯᕆᑦᑎᐊᓐ
ᐊᖏᔪᖅᑲᖅ ᒥᓂᔅᑕᑦ

Canada

ᓄᓇᕗᑦ ᐱᓪᓗᐊᕆᑦ

ᑭᒡᒐᖅᑐᐃᓪᓗᖓ ᑲᓛᓪᓚᖅᒥᐅᓂ ᐊᒻᒪᓗ ᐊᑯᑭᑦᑑᑉ ᒐᕙᒪᖏᓐᓂ, ᖁᕕᐊᓱᖅᑲᑎᖅᑲᕈᒪᕗᖓ ᑲᓇᑕᒥᐅᓂᑦ ᐃᓄᖕᓂᑦ ᓄᓇᕗᑦ ᓴᖅᑭᖕᓂᐊᓕᖅᑎᓪᓗᒍ. ᐊᒻᒪᑦᑕᐅᖅ ᐱᕕᖅᑳᖅᓂᖕᓂ ᐱᒃᑯᒥᒻᒪᕆᒃᐸᒃᑲ ᐱᓕᕆᔩᐅᓚᐅᖅᑐᑦ ᑕᒪᓐᓇ ᓄᓇᕗᑦ ᓴᖅᑭᑎᓐᓇᓱᓕᖅᖢᒍ.

ᓄᓇᕗᑦ ᐃᓄᖕᓄ ᓇᖕᒥᓂᕆᔭᐅᓂᐊᖅᑎᓪᓗᒍ ᑕᒪᓐᓇ ᐅᕙᑦᑎᓐᓄ ᐃᒃᐱᖕᓇᒻᒪᕆᒃᐳᖅ. ᑕᐃᒪᐃᓐᓂᖓᓄᑦ ᐃᓚᑦᑎᓐᓄ ᐱᖕᒐᓇᑦᑎᓐᓃᑦᑐᓄᑦ ᑲᑎᖅᑲᑎᖅᑲᕈᓐᓇᖅᓯᓂᐊᓕᖅᐳᒍᑦ. ᑕᐃᒪᐃᒻᒪᑦ ᖁᕕᐊᓱᒃᐳᖓ ᐊᑯᑭᑦᑑᑉ ᒐᕙᒪᖓ ᐱᓕᕆᓂᖅᒥᓐ ᓴᖅᑭᑦᑎᖅᑲᑎᖅᑲᕈᓐᓇᖅᓂᐊᓕᖅᒪᑕ. ᒫᓐᓵᖕᒍᓚᐅᖅᑐᖅ ᒪᑐᐃᖅᑕᐅᓚᐅᖅᑐᖅ ᑭᒡᒐᖅᑐᐃᕝᕕᖅ ᐊᑯᑭᑦᑑᑉ ᒐᕙᒪᖓᓄ ᐋᑐᕚᒥ ᓴᖅᑭᑎᑦᓯᒪᓕᖅᐳᖅ ᐱᓕᕆᖅᑲᑎᖅᑲᕈᒪᓂᑦᑎᓐᓂᒃ.

ᐱᒃᑯᒋᑐᐃᓐᓇᖅᑎᓪᓗᒍ ᓄᓇᕗᑦ ᓴᖅᑭᓐᓂᐊᖅᓂᖓ, ᑕᒪᓐᓇ ᐊᕐᕌᒍ ᓇᓗᓇᐃᒃᑯᑕᐅᓂᐊᖅᒪᑦ ᐊᕐᕌᒍᓂ ᐊᕙᑎᓂ ᐊᑯᑭᑦᑐᒥᐅᑕᑦ ᓇᖕᒥᓂᖅ ᒐᕙᒪᖅᑲᖅᓂᖓᓐᓂᑦ. ᑕᒪᓐᓇ ᑕᐅᑐᖕᒍᐊᖅᑲᑦᑕᖅᑯ ᓱᕐᓗ ᓄᓇᕗᑦ ᓂᕕᐊᕐᓵᖅ ᐊᕐᕌᒍᖅᑲᓕᖅᑐᖅ ᐊᕙᑎᓂᑦ. ᑕᐃᒪᐃᓐᓂᖓᓄ ᐱᒃᑯᓕᒻᒪᕆᒃᐳᖓ ᐃᓄᖕᓂ ᑲᓇᑕᒥᐅᓂᑦ, ᒫᓐᓇ ᑖᒃᑯᐊ – ᓇᓗᓇᐃᒃᑯᑎᒻᒪᕆᐅᓕᖅᓂᖏᓐᓂ ᐊᕐᕌᒍ 2000ᒧᓐ – ᑲᒪᔨᐅᓂᐊᓕᖅᓂᖏᓐᓂ ᐱᕈᖅᓴᐃᓂᖅᒥᓐ ᓄᓇᕗᑦ ᓵᕆᓯᖓᓂᑦ.

ᐃᓱᒋᓕᖅᓗᓂᐅ, ᑐᓐᖓᓱᖅᑯᔨᕗᖓ ᓄᓇᕗᒻᒥ, ᐊᒻᒪᓗ ᓂᕆᐅᖕᓂᖅᑲᖅᑯᓪᓗᓯ ᓈᒻᒪᓈᖅᓯᒪᓂᖅᒥᓐ ᐱᓕᕆᐊᕆᓂᐊᓕᖅᑕᔅᓯᓐᓄᑦ. ᖃᒪᓐᖓ ᐱᓱᒥᒃ ᐱᓪᓗᐊᕆᑦᓯ.

ᔫᓇᑕᓐ ᒫᑦᔅᕕᐅᑦ, ᓯᕗᓕᐅᖅᑎ

Nunavut pilluarit

On behalf of the people of Greenland and the Government of Greenland, I would like to extend our greetings to our Canadian Inuit friends on the inauguration of Nunavut. I would also like to take this opportunity to congratulate everyone who has played a part in making the Nunavut dream a reality.

As an Inuit nation, the establishment of Nunavut means a lot to us. It means that we can now reach out to our brothers and sisters in the west. It is therefore an honor for me to reaffirm the will of the Government of Greenland to develop our relationship with Nunavut on many fronts. The recent opening of the Office of the Representative of the Government of Greenland, at the Royal Danish Embassy in Ottawa, is testament to such aspirations on our part.

Besides heralding the birth of Nunavut, this year marks the 20th anniversary of the introduction of home rule in Greenland. I usually compare our home rule settlement with a *niviarsiaq* (maiden), now turning twenty years old. I am therefore very proud to extend my greetings to our Canadian Inuit friends, who now – at this, the very threshold to a new millennium – will take on the responsibility of bringing up the Nunavut child.

In conclusion, I would welcome Nunavut once again, and wish you all the best of luck with your endeavour. *Qamannga pisumik pilluaritsi.*

HON. JONATHAN MOTZFELDT, PREMIER

Info Design aps · Nuuk · Greenland

Minister
of National Defence

Ministre
de la Défense nationale

The Department of National Defence and the Canadian Forces welcome the birth of Nunavut as Canada's newest territory. This is a truly historic moment for all Canadians.

The Canadian Forces has been present in the Eastern Arctic for almost a century and will continue to contribute to the development of the North well into the foreseeable future. Canadian Rangers patrols and periodic deployments of military elements ensure that the Canadian Forces will always be there to support the Nunavut people. We will also continue to support the Canadian Cadet Organizations and the Junior Canadian Rangers in Nunavut.

We congratulate you, the people of Nunavut, and thank you for welcoming us into your community.

Le ministère de la Défense nationale et les Forces canadiennes se réjouissent de l'arrivée du dernier-né des territoires du Canada, le Nunavut. Il s'agit véritablement d'un moment historique pour tous les Canadiens.

Depuis près d'un siècle, les Forces canadiennes sont présentes dans la région est de l'Arctique et elles continueront, dans un avenir prévisible, de participer au développement du Nord. Les patrouilles de Rangers canadiens et les déploiements périodiques d'éléments militaires garantissent que nous serons toujours là pour servir les intérêts de la population du Nunavut. Nous continuerons également d'appuyer les organisations de cadets du Canada et les Rangers junior canadiens du Nunavut.

Nous tenons à vous féliciter, vous, habitants du Nunavut, et à vous remercier de l'accueil que vous nous faites au sein de votre communauté.

ᑲᓇᑕᐅᑉ ᐅᓇᓯᒃᓯᓂᕆᔨᖏ ᐊᒻᒪᓗ ᐅᓇᑕᖅᑐᒃᓯᑦ ᑐᓐᖓᓱᒃᑎᑦᑎᕗᑦ ᓄᓇᕗᑦ ᓴᖅᑭᓐᓂᕆᔭᖓᓂ ᑕᒫᓂ ᓄᑖᖑᓛᒥᓐ ᐊᕕᒃᑐᖅᓂᒃᑯᑦ ᓴᖅᑮᖅᑐᒥᓐ. ᐅᓇᓂ ᐅᓪᓗᖅ ᐳᐃᒍᓐᓇᔾᔮᖕᖏᓪᒪᕆᓐᓂᖅᑐᖅ ᑲᓇᑕᒥᐅᑕᓕᒫᓄᑦ.

ᐅᓇᑕᖅᑐᒃᓯᑦ ᓴᖅᑭᔮᖅᑕᐃᓐᓇᖅᓯᒪᒍᑦ ᑲᓇᑕᐅᑉ ᐅᑭᐅᖅᑕᖅᑐᖓᑕ ᑲᓇᖕᓇᖓᓂ ᐊᕐᕌᒍ 100-ᖏᓐᓂᑉᐸᓗᒃ ᐊᒻᒪᓗ ᐃᑲᔪᖅᑕᐃᓐᓇᕐᓂᐊᕐᓗᑎᒃ ᐱᕙᓪᓕᐊᓂᕐᒥᓐ ᐅᑭᐅᖅᑕᖅᑐᒥᓐ ᓯᕗᓂᒃᓴᑦᑎᓐᓂ. ᑲᓃᑎᐊᓐ ᐅᓇᑕᖅᑐᒃᓴᖑᐊᑦ ᖃᐅᔨᓴᖅᑎᐅᕗᑦ ᐊᒻᒪᓗ ᐱᓕᕆᔾᔪᑎᓂ ᖃᐅᔨᓴᕈᑎᓂ ᐱᓕᕆᐊᖃᖃᑦᑕᖅᐳᑦ ᑕᐃᒪᐃᓐᓂᖓᓄᑦ ᐅᓇᑕᖅᑐᒃᓯᑦ ᐃᑲᔪᖅᑐᐃᖏᓐᓇᕐᓂᐊᕐᓗᑎᒃ ᓄᓇᕗᒻᒥᐅᓂᑦ. ᐃᑲᔪᖅᑐᐃᖅᑕᐃᓐᓇᕐᓂᐊᕆᕗᒍᑦ ᐅᓇᓯᒃᓴᔾᔪᐊᓂᑦ (ᑲᑕᑦᔅ) ᐊᒻᒪᓗ ᐃᓅᓯᒃᑐᓂᑦ ᐅᓇᑕᖅᑐᒃᓴᖑᐊᓂᑦ ᓄᓇᕗᒻᒥ.

ᐱᒃᑯᒋᓪᒪᕆᒃᐸᑦᑎᒋᑦ, ᓄᓇᕗᒻᒥᐅᖑᔪᓯ, ᐊᒻᒪ ᖁᔭᓐᓇᒦᒃ ᑐᓐᖓᓱᒃᑎᑕᐅᑉᐸᑦᑕ ᓄᓇᓯᓐᓂ.

Arthur C. Eggleton • ᐋᑐ ᓯ. ᐊᒍᑕᓐ

National Defence
Défense nationale

Canada

THE ROAD

One era ends, another begins. Before he died in his mid-90s in 1995, Pangnirtung's Aksayuk Etuangat, right, the last of the whalemen, witnessed a blizzard of change that has taken industrialized countries at least 5,000 years to make. But he did not live to see the most gratifying achievement by his fellow Inuit – the creation of the new territory of Nunavut. Far right: That new journey belongs to a new generation

ᐊᑕᐅᓯᖅ ᐃᓕᕐᖁᓯ ᐃᓯᓕᑉᐳᖅ, ᐊᓯᖓᓗ ᐱᒋᐊᓕᕐᓗᓂ. ᑐᖁᓚᐅᕐᓂ 90ᖏᓐ ᐊᕐᕋᒍᖃᓕᕐᓗᓂ 1995ᒥ, ᐸᖕᓂᕐᑑᕐᒥᐅᑕᖅ ᐊᒃᓴᔪᒃ ᐃᑐᐊᖕᖓᑦ, ᑕᓕᕐᐱᐊᓂ, ᑭᖑᓪᓕᕐᐋᖑᓚᐅᕐᑐᖅ ᐊᕐᕙᓯᒃᑎᓂ, ᑕᐅᑐᒃᓯᒪᔪᖅ ᐊᓯᖑᕐᐸᓪᓕᐊᒻᒪᕆᒃᑐᒥᓐ ᐱᕚᓪᓕᐊᒻᒪᕆᒃᑐᓂ ᓄᓇᓂ ᐊᑐᕐᑕᐅᔪᒥᓐ ᐊᕐᕌᒍᓂ 5000-ᓗᐊᐸᓘᕐᓂ ᐱᕚᓪᓕᐊᓂᒃᑯᑦ. ᑭᓯᐊᓂᓕ ᑕᑯᖏᓐᑐᖅ ᖁᕕᐊᓇᕐᑐᒥᓐ ᐱᓇᓱᒃᑕᐅᓯᒪᔪᒥᓐ ᐃᓅᖃ-ᑎᖏᓐᓂᑦ – ᓄᓇᕗᑦ ᓴᖅᑭᓐᓂᖅᑲᓂᑦ. ᑕᓕᕐᐱᖏᒥ: ᑕᒪᓐ ᐃᖏᕐᕋᓂᖅ ᓄᑖᓄᑦ ᑭᖑᕚᕈ ᐊᑐᕐᑕᐅᓂᐊᓯᒐᖅ

Nunavut Tourism; oval inset: Nunavut Tourism ᓄᓇᕗᑦ ᐳᓚᕋᖅᑐᓕᕆᔨᒃᑯ; ᐊᖓᒧᔭᕐᑐᑦ ᐃᓗᐊᓂ: ᓄᓇᕗᑦ ᐳᓚᕋᖅᑐᓕᕆᔨᒃᑯ

"When Inuit are determined to get something, they go out and get it."

– Bob Kadlun, a chief negotiator for Inuit on the land claim

TO NUNAVUT

ᐊᕐᑯᑎ ᓄᓇᕗᒻᒧᑦ

A land claim settlement was just half of the Inuit plan for self-determination — full control would only come through a hard-won territory and government

ᓄᓇᑖᕋᓱᖕᓂᐅᔪᖅ ᐃᓚᐃᓐᓇᓚᐅᕐᐹ ᐃᓄᐃᑦ ᐃᓱᒪᒋᔭᖏᓐᓂᑦ - ᐊᐅᓚᑦᑎᓂᒻᒪᕆᒃ ᑭᖑᓂᐊᒍ ᐊᑐᕐᓂᐊᕐᓗᓂ ᐊᒃᓯᕉᓐᓇᕐᑐᒥᓐ-ᓵᓚᒃᕿᓂᒃᑯᑦ ᐃᒻᒥᒃᑰᖓᔪᒥᓐ ᐊᕚᒃᓯᒪᔪᒥᓐ ᐊᒻᒪ ᒐᕙᒪᓕᕆᓂᕐᒥᓐ

By Keith Crowe, with files from Marion Soublière and Greg Coleman

The Second World War brought massive change to the North, as airbases were built. During the Cold War that followed, several east-west lines of radar stations were built for a Distant Early Warning system, and military manoeuvres were held. In 1950, a new patrol ship, the *CD Howe*, was launched, expanding the range of annual patrols, and dispensing medical and administrative services in the eastern Arctic. Tuberculosis patients were brought south, often for long periods; the children forgot their language and had a hard time returning to northern life.

In addition to the migration of Inuit between hunting and trapping areas, governments began to move families to places of supposed economic opportunity, such as Churchill, Manitoba, and the new town of Inuvik, Northwest Territories (NWT). In 1953, the federal government also moved 17 families from Pond Inlet and the northern Quebec community of Inukjuak to Resolute Bay and Grise Fiord in the High Arctic. That same year, a new federal Department of Northern Affairs and National Resources was created, and soon northern service officers from this department were posted to Inuit communities to administer a variety of programs. Starvation among Inuit of the

ᑎᑎᕋᖅᑐᖅ ᑮᑦ ᑯᕈ, ᐃᓚᖃᕐᓗᓂ ᐱᔾᔪᓯᒪᓂᑯᓂᑦ ᒥᐅᕆᐊᓐ ᓲᐱᓕᐅᕐ ᐊᒻᒪ ᒍᕆ ᑰᓪᒪᓐᒧᓐ

ᑭᓇᕐᔪᐊᓕᒫᒥᓐ ᐅᓇᑕᕖᔭᐊᕐᓇᕐᑕᖅᑳᕐᑎᓪᓗᒍ ᐊᐃᑉᐸᖓᓂ ᐊᓯᖑᖅᑎᑦᑎᒻᒪᕆᓚᐅᕐᐳᖅ ᐅᑭᐅᕐᑕᖅᑐᕐᒥ, ᑕᒪᒃᑯᐊ ᒥᑦᑕᕐᕖ ᓴᓇᔭᐅᑲᑕᓕᕐᑎᓪᓗᒋᑦ. ᑭᖑᓂᐊᒍᑦ ᐊᑭᕋᖅᑐᖃᑦᑕᐅᑎᓂᕐᑕᖅᑳᕐᑎᓪᓗᒍ, ᐊᒥᓱᑦ ᑲᓇᖕᓇᕐᒥᐱᖓᖕᓇᕐᒧ ᖃᐅᔨᓴᕐᑎᓂᑦ ᓴᓇᔭᐅᓕᓚᐅᕐᓯᒪᔫ ᑑᓚᐄᖑᓂᖅᑕᐅᔪᑦ (Dew Line) ᑕᒪᒃᑯᐊ ᖃᐅᔨᓴᕐᑕᐅᓪᓗᑎᒃ ᐅᓇᑕᖅᑐᒃᓴᓄᑦ. 1950-ᒥ, ᓄᑖᒥᓐ ᐅᒥᐊᕐᔪᐊᕐᒥ ᖃᐅᔨᓴᕐᑕᐅᓂᐊᕐᑐᒥᓐ, *ᓯᑏ ᕼᐊᐅ (CD Howe)* ᓵᖅᑭᑕᐅᓕᓚᐅᕐᓯᒪᕗᖅ, ᖃᐅᔨᓴᕐᑎᓂᑦ ᐅᓄᕐᓯᕆᐊᕐᑎᑦᑎᒃᑳᓐᓂᕐᓗᑎᒃ, ᐊᒻᒪ ᑖᓐᓇ ᐋᓐᓂᐊᕐᑐᓂᑦ ᖃᐅᔨᓴᕐᑕᐅᓪᓗᓂ ᐊᒻᒪ ᐊᐅᓚᑦᑎᓂᕐᒧᓐ ᐊᑐᕐᑕᐅᓕᓪᓗᓂ ᐅᑭᐅᕐᑕᖅᑑᑉ ᑲᓇᖕᓇᖖᒍᓄᑦ. ᐳᕿᒡᓗᒃᑐᑦ ᖃᓪᓗᓈᓄᑦ ᐊᐅᓪᓚᕐᑎᑕᐅᖃᑦᑕᓚᐅᕐᐳᑦ, ᐃᑖᓐᓂᒃᑯ ᐊᑯᓂᐊᓘᕐᐸᒃᓗᑎᒃ ᐊᐅᓪᓚᕐᓯᒪᓪᓗᑎᒃ; ᓄᑕᕋᑦ ᐳᐃᒍᕐᐸᕶᖅᐸᒃᓗᑎᒃ ᐅᖃᐅᓯᑐᖃᒥᖕᓂ ᐊᒻᒪ ᐊᒃᓯᕉᖅᓗᑎᒃ ᑭᓯᐊᓂ ᐃᓅᓯᕐᒥᓂᑦ ᐅᑭᐅᕐᑕᖅᑐᕐᒥ ᐅᑎᕐᑎᕆᓚᐅᕐᐳᑦ.

ᐃᓚᖃᓯᐅᑎᓯᒪᓪᓗᓂ ᐃᓄᐃᑦ ᓅᖃᑦᑕᕐᓂᖏᓐᓂ ᐊᖑᔭᒃᓴᓂ ᒪᓕᒃᓗᑎ ᑮᔭᖃᑦᑕᓕᓪᓗᑎᓪᓗ, ᒐᕙᒪᒃᑯ ᐃᓚᒌᓂ

Nunavut Tourism

Keewatin barren lands resulted in more relocation, the creation of a new community (Rankin Inlet), and the opening of two mines to employ Inuit. Meanwhile, the Canadian Broadcasting Corporation initiated Inuktitut broadcasts during the 1950s, and later assisted in the creation of Inuit radio networks.

The 1960s rocked the world, with the Vietnam War, hippies, satellites, transistors, the Beatles and snowmobiles. The mix of social revolution, innovation and better communications set the stage for change in Northern Canada, too.

David Roberts ᑕᐃᕕᑦ ᕈᐹᑦᔅ

A series of adult-education newsletters, edited by young Inuit, became a forum for political development in the eastern Arctic, and in the Mackenzie Delta, a Committee for the Original Peoples Entitlement (COPE) was formed, first representing a variety of ethnic groups and later, the Inuvialuit only. During the mid-1960s, a federal public housing program, complete with an orientation phase, created instant villages using prefabricated units. This ended the old scattered camp distribution of Inuit.

In response to a growing call for redress of native grievances, a Commissioner of Native Claims was appointed in December 1969, and the federal government provided funding to emerging aboriginal associations to help them prepare their cases. Next door to Northern Canada, a pivotal achievement was reached in 1971: the Alaska Native Claims Settlement. The first settlement of its kind, it gave Alaskan native peoples 180,000 square kilometres of land and $962 million US.

> *"The history of the relationship between governments and native peoples is a tragic one. We do not want to dwell on these past failings. We are here today because we look to the future. We are seeking to develop a new relationship with government; one based on trust and mutual respect"*
>
> **John Amagoalik**
> **Speaking at the First Ministers Conference on Aboriginal Constitutional Matters, March 1984**

ᓅᑎᓇᓕᓚᐅᕐᐳᑦ ᓄᓇᓄ ᐱᕙᓪᓕᐊᓂᕐᒧᓐ ᐃᒃᓯᕚᑕᐅᒐᓴᓇᓴᐅᔭᓄᑦ, ᓲᕐᓗ ᐅᕗᖓ ᑰᓪᔭᐊᕐᔪᙳᓐ, ᒫᓂᑑᐸᒥ, ᐊᒻᒪᓗ ᐃᓅᕕᖕᒧᓐ ᑖᓇ ᓄᑖᖑᖁᑎᓪᓗᒍ ᓄᓇ, ᓄᓇᑦᓯᐊᕐᒥ. 1953-ᒥ, ᒐᕙᒪᒃᑯᑦ ᓄᒃᑎᖅᑎᑦᑎᓚᐅᕐᐳᑦ 17-ᓂ ᐃᓚᒌᓂ ᒥᑦᑎᒪᑕᓕᖕᒥ ᐊᒻᒪᓗ ᑯᐸᐃᒃ ᐅᐊᖕᓇᖕᒐᓂ ᐃᓄᒃᔭᐊᕐᒥ ᖃᐅᓯᐃᑦᑐᒧᓐ ᐊᒻᒪ ᐊᐅᓯᐃᑦᑐᒧᓐ ᖁᑎᒃᑐᕐᒥᑦ. ᑕᕝᕙᓂ ᐊᕐᖁᒧᑦᑕᐃᓐᓇᕐᒥ, ᒐᕙᒪᒃᑯᑦ ᓴᖅᑭᑎᓕᓚᐅᕐᐳᑦ ᓄᑖᒥᓐ ᐃᓄᓕᕆᔾᔪᑎᒃᑰᓂᐊᕐᑐᒥᓐ, ᐊᒻᒪ ᑭᖑᓂᑦᑎᐊᖕᒐᒍ ᑖᒃᑯᐊ ᐱᓕᕆᔾᔭᖕᖏᓐᓂ ᐃᓄᐃᑦ ᓄᓇᖕᒐᓄᑦ ᐊᐅᓪᓚᕐᑎᑦᑎᖃᑦᑕᓕᒪᐅᕐᓯᒪᔪᑦ ᑲᒪᔨᐅᓂᐊᕐᑐᓂᑦ ᐱᓕᓇᐊᓇᔾᔪᖕᖏᓐᓂᑦ. ᐱᕐᓕᕐᓂᕐᒧᓐ ᑐᖁᑲᑕᓕᓚᐅᕐᓯᒪᔪᑦ ᓅᑎᓇᑲᑕᖕᓂᕐᒧᓐ ᑭᕙᓪᓕᕐᒥ, ᓄᑖᒥᓐ ᓄᓇᒥ ᓴᖅᑭᑎᓂᕐᒥᓐ (ᑲᖏᖅᖢᓂᖅᒥ), ᐊᒻᒪ ᐅᔭᕋᒃᓴᖅᓯᐅᕐᕕᖕᒥᓐ ᒪᕿᐃᓂ ᐃᖅᑲᓇᐃᔭᖅᕕᒃᖅᑎᑦᑎᒐᓯᒧᓐ ᐃᓄᖕᓂ. ᑕᓖᓂᑦᑕᐃᓐᓇᖅ, ᔩᐱᔩᑯ ᐃᓄᒃᑎᑑᖕᒐᔪᒥᓐ ᓈᓚᐅᑎᒃᑯᑦ ᓴᖅᑭᑎᑎᓕᓚᐅᕐᓯᒪᔪᑦ 1950-ᖏᓐᓂ, ᐊᒻᒪ ᑭᖑᓂᐊᒍᑦ ᐃᑲᔪᕐᓗᑎᒃ ᓴᖅᑭᑎᓂᕐᒥᓐ ᐃᓄᒃᑎᑐᑦ ᓈᓚᐅᓯᓇᓂᕐᒥᓐ.

1960-ᖏᓐᓕᓕᕐᑎᓪᓗᒍ ᓄᓇᕐᔭᐊᖅ ᑎᒃᓴᕐᓚᓕᓚᐅᕐᓯᒪᔪᖅ, ᕕᐊᑦᓈᒻᒥᓐ ᐅᓇᑕᕕᒡᔭᐊᕐᓂᖅᑲᕐᓗᓂ, ᖃᓪᓗᓈᓪᓗ ᓄᔭᖅᑯᖅᑐᔭᐊᓘᓕᕐᓗᑎᒃ Hᐃᐱᐅᓂᕋᕐᑕᐅᓪᓗᑎᒃ, ᖃᖕᒐᑦᑕᖅᑎᑦᑎᑲᑕᒃᓱᑎᒡᓗ ᓯᓚᐃᓐᓇᕐᒧᓐ, ᓈᓚᐅᑎᕋᓃᓂ ᓴᓇᓕᕐᓱᑎᒃ, ᐲᑐᔅ (Beatles) ᐊᒻᒪ ᓯᑭᑑᓪᓗ. ᐃᓕᕐᑯᓯᕐᑲᑎᒋᖕᖏᓐᓂᖅ, ᐱᓕᕆᐊᕐᑲᕋᓯᖕᓂᖅ ᐊᒻᒪ ᑐᓴᐅᑎᓕᕆᓂᖅ ᐱᐅᓯᑉᐹᓪᓕᕐᓂᐅᔭᖅ ᑲᓇᑕᐅᑉ ᐅᑭᐅᕐᑕᖅᑐᖕᒐᓂᑦ ᐊᓯᖑᐃᑎᑦᑎᓗᐊᓕᕐᓂᑰᖅᑕᐅᕙᑦ.

ᑐᓴᒃᓴᓕᐅᕈᑎᕈᔫᔭᑦ ᐃᓐᓇᕐᓂ ᐃᓕᓐᓂᐊᕐᑐᓂᑦ ᓴᖅᑭᑕᐅᑲᑕᓕᓚᐅᕐᓯᒪᔪᑦ, ᓴᓇᔭᐅᕙᒃᓱᑎᒃ ᒫᒃᑯᒃᑐᓄᑦ, ᐊᒻᒪᓗ ᑕᒪᓐᓇ ᒪᓕᒐᓕᕆᓂᕐᒥᓐ ᐱᒋᐊᕈᑕᐅᓕᓚᐅᕐᓯᒪᔪᖅ ᐅᑭᐅᕐᑕᖅᑑᑉ ᑲᓇᖕᓇᖕᒐᓂ, ᐊᒻᒪᓗ ᒪᑳᕐ ᑎᐊᑕᒥᓐ, ᑲᑎᒪᔩᑦ ᐃᓄᐃᑦ ᐱᔭᕐᓇᐅᑎᖏᓐᓄ ᓴᖅᑭᔾᔭᑕᐅᓕᓚᐅᕐᓯᒪᔪᖅ, ᓯᕗᓪᓕᕐᒥ ᑭᓪᓕᕐᑐᐃᓪᓗᑎᒃ ᐊᔾᔨᖏᖏᑦᑐᓂᑦ ᐃᓕᕐᑯᓯᓕᖕᓄᑦ ᐊᒻᒪ ᑭᖑᓂᐊᒍ, ᐃᓅᕕᐊᓗᖕᓄ ᑐᕐᖓᓗᑐᐃᓐᓇᓕᕐᓗᓂ. 1960 ᐊᑯᓐᓂᖓᓂ, ᒐᕙᒪᒃᑯᑦ ᐃᓪᓗᓕᓇᓂᕐᒧᓐ ᐱᓕᕆᓂᕐᒥᓐ, ᐱᒋᐊᕐᑎᒥᓐ ᐱᑕᖅᑲᕐᓗᓂ, ᓴᖅᑭᑎᓂᐅᓕᓚᐅᕐᓯᒪᔪᖅ ᓄᓇᓕᖕᓂᑦ ᐃᓪᓗᑕᖅᑲᓕᕐᑐᓂᑦ. ᑕᒪᓐᓇᓗ ᓄᓇᓕᕐᖁᓂᑦ ᓄᖑᕐᕋᐃᓕᓚᐅᕐᐳᖅ.

ᓄᓇᖃᖅᑳᖅᑐᑦ ᐱᔪᒪᔾᔪᖕᖏᓐᓄ, ᑲᒥᓯᓇᒥᓐ ᓄᓇᖃᖅᑳᖅᑐᓄᑦ ᑎᒃᑯᐊᕐᑕᐅᔭᖅᑲᓕᓚᐅᕐᓯᒪᔪᖅ ᑎᓯᐱᓇ 1969-ᒥᓐ, ᐊᒻᒪᓗ ᒐᕙᒪᒃᑯᑦ ᕿᓇᐅᔭᓂ ᐊᑐᐃᓐᓇᐅᑎᑦᑎᓕᓚᐅᕐᓯᒪᔪᑦ ᓄᓇᖃᖅᑳᖅᑐᑦ ᑲᑐᔾᔨᖃᑎᒌᖏᓐᖏᓐᓄᑦ ᐱᓇᓱᒃᑕᖏᓐᖏᓐᓄᑦ ᑐᕌᖓᔪᓂᑦ. ᑲᓇᑕᐸ ᐅᑭᐅᕐᑕᖅᑐᖓᑕ ᓴᓂᑦᑎᐊᖓᓕᑦᑐᑦᓕ ᐱᓇᓱᐊᕐᑕᖏᓐᓂ 1971-ᒥ ᐊᑐᓕᓚᐅᕐᓯᒪᔪᑦ: ᐊᓛᔅᑲᒥ ᓄᓇᖃᖅᑳᖅᑐᑦ ᓄᓇᑖᖅᓱᑎᒃ. ᑖᓇ ᓯᕗᓪᓕᕐᐸᐅᓚᐅᕐᓯᒪᔪᖅ ᑕᐃᒪᐃᓐᓇᓱᒃᑐᓂᑦ. ᑕᒪᓐᓇ ᐊᓛᔅᑲᒥᐅᑦ ᐃᓄᖏᓐᓂ ᓄᓈᕈᑕᐅᓕᓚᐅᕐᓯᒪᔪᖅ 180,000 ᑭᓗᒥᑕᓂᒃ ᐊᖏᑎᒋᔭᒥᓐ ᐊᒻᒪᓗ ᕿᓇᐅᔭᖃᕈᑕᐅᓪᓗᓂ $962 ᒥᓕᐊᓐ ᑖᓚᓂᑦ.

Nortext ᓄᐊᑦᑕᒃᔅ

Top: Inuit Tapirisat of Canada's first president, Tagak Curley. Left: Anxiously awaiting the outcome of the April 1982 territory-wide plebiscite on dividing the NWT. Seated are, left to right, Andy Theriault, Aimo Nookiguaq, John Amagoalik. Behind them stand Dave Monteith and Kenn Harper

ᖁᓛᓂ: ᐃᓄᐃᑦ ᑕᐱᕇᒃᓴᑦᑯ ᓯᕗᓕᖅᐹ ᐊᖓᔪᖅᑳᖓ, ᑕᒑᖅ ᑰᓕ. ᓴᐅᒥᐊᓂ: ᐅᑕᕿᔪᑦ ᓂᓇᐅᒪᓇᓱᒃᖢᑎᒃ 1982ᒥ ᓄᓇᑦᓯᐊᓕᒫᒥ ᓂᕈᐊᕐᓂᕐᑕᖅᑎᓪᓗᒍ ᐊᕕᖕᓂᐊᕐᓂᕐᒧᓐ ᓄᓇᑦᓯᐊᕐᒥᓐ. ᐃᒃᓯᕚᕐᑐᑦ, ᓴᐅᒥᖕᒐᓂ ᑕᓕᕐᐱᐊᓄ, ᐋᓐᑎ ᑎᐅᕆᐅᑦ, ᐊᐃᒧ ᓄᑭᒋᐊᖅ, ᔮᓐ ᐊᒪᒋᐊᓕᒃ. ᑐᓄᖓᖕᒐᓂ ᓇᖏᕐᑐᑦ ᑕᐃᕙ ᒫᓐᑎᑦ ᐊᒻᒪ ᑭᐊᓐ Hᐋᐳ (ᐃᓕᓴᐃᔨᑰᒃ)

Nortext

Left to right: Paul Okalik, David Aglukark and Allen Maghagak pause during negotiations. Pressing for a Nunavut government was essential, says former chief negotiator Maghagak, "to make sure that our claims settlements covered everything. Past land claims agreements dealt only with real estate and cash"
ᓴᐅᒥᖕᒐᓂ ᑕᓕᖅᐱᐊᓄᑦ: ᐹᓪ ᐅᑲᓕᖅ, ᑕᐃᑲᑦ ᐊᒡᓘᑲᖅ ᐊᒻᒪ ᐋᓚᓐ ᒪᒃᕚᖅ ᓄᖅᑲᖓᓚᐅᒃᐳᑦ ᐋᓐᑲᑕᖓᓂᒥᓐ. ᓄᓇᕗᑦ ᒐᕙᒪᑖᖅᑎᑕᓲᖑᓂᖓᑦ ᐱᒪᕆᐅᓚᐅᖅᐳᖅ, ᐅᖃᖅᑐᖅ ᐊᖓᔪᖅᖄᖑᓂᑯ ᐋᓐᓂᐅ ᒪᒃᕚᖅ, "ᓄᓇᑖᖅᓯᓂᐸᑦ ᑕᒪᐃᓐᓂ ᐱᑕᖃᖅᑎᒐᓱᒃᖢᑎᒍ. ᓄᓇᑖᖅᓯᓃᑉᐱᓐ ᓄᓇᑦᑕᐃᓐᓇᖅᒥᓐ ᑮᓇᐅᔭᓂᓪᓗ ᐱᔾᔪᑎᖃᕈᑎᖃᓚᐅᖅᓯᒪᖕᒪᑕ"

In that year, too, the Inuit Tapirisat of Canada (ITC) was formed to pursue land claims in the NWT. The Northern Quebec Inuit Association was formed the following year and began negotiations for the James Bay claim.

Aboriginal claims and self-government gained crucial headway in 1973 with three court decisions supporting aboriginal title, a right that stems from the long-term use and occupation of lands by Aboriginal Peoples prior to European colonization. ITC began talks with government officials about Inuit hunting rights, and received federal assistance for a study of land use and occupancy to support the claims of Inuit throughout the NWT. Meanwhile, the Inuit of Quebec joined the Cree in negotiation concerning the James Bay hydro-electric project, and achieved a final agreement in November 1975.

Early in 1976, ITC presented its Nunavut claim to the federal government, including a proposal for a new territory. It was a strategic move, says founding ITC president Tagak Curley, because the whole concept of settling land claims was new and "as a single issue, it was very rough going. We felt at that time that it was important that we get a little broader base to pursue the whole two issues: aboriginal Inuit settlement and the outstanding land claims, and political development."

The land claim was accepted for negotiation, but not the idea of dividing the existing Northwest Territories.

"The Liberal government, back in the very early '80s, absolutely refused to include political change for the creation of Nunavut," says a former chief negotiator for the Inuit, Bob Kadlun. "But we kept chipping away at it."

ᑕᐸᕐᓂᑦᑕᐃᓐᓇᖅ ᐊᕿᒍᒥ, ᐃᓄᐃᑦ ᑕᐱᕇᒃᓯᑦᑯ ᑲᓇᑕᒥ ᐋᖅᑭᒃᑕᐅᓚᐅᖅᐳᖅ ᓄᓇᑖᖅᓯᖕᓂᕐᒥ ᐱᓕᕆᐊᕐᒪᑕ. ᐊᒻᒪᓗ ᑯᐸᐃᒃ ᑕᕿᖕᖓᓂ ᐃᓄᐃᑦ ᑲᑐᔾᔨᖅᑲᑎᒌᑦ ᓴᖅᑭᓪᓚᐅᖅᓯᒪᔭᑦ ᐊᕿᒍ ᐊᓂᒍᖅᑎᓪᓗᒍ ᐊᒻᒪᓗ ᓯᐃᒻᔅ ᐸᐃᒥ ᓄᓇᑖᖅᓯᖕᓂᕐᒥ ᐱᓕᕆᓯᕆᐊᖅᓱᑎᒃ

ᓄᓇᖃᖅᑳᖅᑐᑦ ᐱᓇᓱᒃᑕᖕᕆ ᐊᒻᒪ ᓇᖕᒥᓂᖅ ᒐᕙᒪᖃᖅᓂᖅ ᐱᕆᐊᒻᒪᓕᕐᓕᐅᖅᓯᒪᔪᖅ 1973-ᒥ ᐱᖓᓱᓂ ᐃᖅᑲᖅᑐᐃᕖᖕᓂ ᑕᑉᐱᖅᑕᐅᓚᐅᖅᑎᒃ ᓄᓇᖃᖅᑳᖅᓂᕐᒧᑦ, ᑕᒪᓐᓇ ᐱᔪᓐᓇᕐᓂᐅᔪᖅ ᐱᕆᐊᖅᓯᒪᓚᐅᖅᓂ ᐊᑯᓂᐊᓗᒃ ᓄᓇᖃᖅᓯᒪᓂᕐᒧᑦ ᐊᑐᓕᖅᑕᐅᓪᓗ ᓄᓇᖃᖅᑳᖅᑐᓄᑦ ᐊᓯᐊᕐᒥᐅᑦ ᑎᑭᓚᐅᖅᑎᓐᓇᒋᑦ. ᐃᓄᐃᑦ ᑕᐱᕇᒃᓯᑦᑯ ᒐᕙᒪᑯᓐᓄᑦ ᐅᖃᖃᑎᖃᖅᑲᑦᑕᓕᓚᐅᖅᐳᑦ ᐊᖑᓇᓱᒃᑲᓐᓂ-ᐅᔪᓐᓇᖅᑐᑦ ᒥᒃᓵᓄᑦ, ᐊᒻᒪᓗ ᑮᓇᐅᔭᓂ ᑐᓂᔭᐅᓚᐅᖅᓱᑎᒃ ᖃᐅᔨᓴᕐᑎᒃᓴᒥᓐ ᓄᓇᒥ ᐊᑐᖅᑕᐅᓂᐅᔪᒥᓐ ᐊᒻᒪ ᓄᓇᖃᖅᑐᖅᑕᖅᑐᓂᖅᑕᐅᕙᓪᓕᐊᖅᑐᒥᓐ ᐃᓄᖕᓂ ᓄᓇᑦᓯᐊᕐᒥᑦᑐᓂᑦ. ᑕᐃᒪᐃᑎᓪᓗᒋᑦ, ᐃᓄᐃᑦ ᑯᐸᐃᒃᒥ ᐊᓪᓚᓂᑦ ᐱᓕᕆᖃᑎᖃᖅᑕᓕᖅᐳᑦ ᐱᔪᑕᐅᓪᓗᓂ ᓯᐃᒻᔅ ᐸᐃ ᐃᒪᕐᒧᑦ ᖃᐅᒻᒪᖅᑎᕆᓇᓂᕐᒥᒃ, ᐊᒻᒪᓗ ᐊᖏᕈᑎᒥᒃ ᓵᓚᒃᓴᕐᓗᑎᒃ ᓄᕕᐱᕆ 1975-ᒥ.

1976 ᐱᒋᐊᓕᖅᑎᓪᓗᒍ, ᐃᓄᐃᑦ ᑕᐱᕇᒃᓯᑦᑯ ᓴᖅᑭᑎᓕᐅᖅᐳᑦ ᓄᓇᕗᑦᑖᕈᑎᒃᓴᒥᓐ ᒐᕙᒪᒧᖕᒃᑯᓐᓄᑦ, ᐱᖃᓯᐅᑎᓪᓗᒍ ᐃᒪᒃᑯᖕᒐᔪᒥᓐ ᐊᕕᒃᑐᖅᓯᒪᓂᒃᑯ ᓄᓇᑖᖅᓯᔨᒥᓐ.

ᑕᒪᓐᓇ ᐱᓕᕆᓂᖅ ᐸᓇᓯᒍᑕᐅᓪᓗᐊᑕᓚᐅᖅᐳᖅ, ᐅᖃᖅᑐᖅ ᐃᓄᐃᑦ ᑕᐱᕇᒃᓯᑦᑯ ᐱᒋᐊᖅᑎᑦᑎᔪᖅ ᐊᖓᔪᖅᖄᖑᓚᐅᖅᑐᖅ ᑕᒐᖅ ᑰᓕ, ᓱᖅᑲᐃᒻᒪ ᓄᓇᑖᖅᓯᒃᑐᕆᐊᖅᑎᖏᑦ ᖃᓯᖕᓂᖅ ᓄᑖᖑᓚᐅᖅᑐᖅ ᐊᒻᒪᓗ "ᐃᒻᒥᓂᑦᑑᖓᓂ, ᐊᔪᕐᓇᒻᒪᕆᖕᓚᐅᖅᑐᖅ. ᐃᓱᒪᓚᐅᖅᐳᒍ ᑕᐃᓯᒪᓂ ᐱᒪᕆᐅᔪᖅᑰᕐᓯᒪᓕᖅᑐᖅᑎᑐᖅ ᐊᖏᓂᖅᓴᒥ ᐸᓇᓯᒍ-ᑎᖃᕆᑦᑕ ᒪᕿᐃᓂᑦ: ᓄᓇᖃᖅᑳᖅᑐᑦ ᐃᓄᐃᑦ ᓄᓇᒋᔭᖓ ᐊᒻᒪ ᓄᓇᑖᖅᓯᖕᓂᖅ ᐱᔭᐅᓯᒪᔾᔭᓯᒪᓂᖓ, ᐊᒻᒪᓗ ᒐᕙᒪᓕᕆᓂᒃᑯᓐᓂ ᐱᕙᓪᓕᐊᓂᐅᔪᖅ."

ᓄᓇᑖᖅᓯᖕᓂ ᐊᖏᖅᑕᐅᓚᐅᖅᓯᒪᔪᖅ ᑭᓯᐊᓂ ᐋᓐᓂᖅᑎᕆᓂᖅᑯ, ᑭᓯᐊᓂᓕ ᐊᕕᖕᓂᐅᔪᖅ ᓄᓇᓯᐊᖅ ᐅᖃᐅᓯᐅᖏᓐᓂ.

"ᓕᐳᕈ ᒐᕙᒪᒃᑯ, 1980 ᐱᒋᐊᓕᖅᑎᓪᓗᒍ, ᐊᖏᖏᓪᓗᓐᓇᓕᐅᖅᓯᒪᓚᐅᖅᑐᑦ ᒪᓕᒐᓕᕆᓂᕐᒥ ᑕᒪᓐᓇ ᓄᓇᕗᑦ ᓴᖅᑭᓐᓂᐊᕐᓂᖓ ᐃᓚᐅᓂᐊᕐᓂ," ᐊᓂᖅᑎ-ᐅᖃᑕᐅᓂᑯ ᐃᓄᖕᓄ ᓄᓇᑖᖅᓯᖕᓂᕐᒧᑦ ᐸᑉ ᑲᓪᓗᓐ ᐅᖃᖅᑐᖅ. "ᑭᓯᐊᓂᓕ ᑕᒪᓐᓇ ᐱᓕᕆᐊᕆᓐᓇ-ᓚᐅᖅᐸᒍᑦ."

ᐊᕿᒍᒪᓴᖕᓂᑦ ᐱᓕᕆᓐᓇᖅᓱᑎᒃ ᐊᒃᓯᕋᖅᓂᒃᑯ, ᓄᓇᕗᑦ ᐃᓱᒪᒋᔭᐅᓂᖓ ᒐᕙᒪᑐᖅᑲᒃᑯᓐᓂ ᐊᖏᖅᑕᐅᓕᖅᑎᓪᓗᒋᑦ ᐊᒻᒪᓗ ᓄᓇᖅᓯᐊᑉ ᒐᕙᒪᒃᑯᖏᓐᓂᑦ, ᑭᓯᐊᓂᓕ ᐊᓯᐊᒍᑦ ᐋᓐᓂᖅᑯ ᐱᓕᕆᐊᕆᖅᑯᔭᐅᓪᓗᓂ ᓴᓂᑦᑎᐊᖓᔪᒃᑯᑦ ᓄᓇᑖᖅ-ᓯᖕᓂᐅᑉ.

“ ᐊᑐᖅᑯ ᐱᓕᕆᖅᑎᕆᖕᓂᒃᑯ ᒐᕙᒪᒃᑯᑦ ᐊᒻᒪᓗ ᓄᓇᖃᖅᑳᖅᑐᑦ ᐱᐅᖕᖏᑦᑐᒪ. ᑭᓯᐊᓂᓕ ᐊᑲᐅᖕᖏᑦᑐᑦ ᐃᓯᒪᒋᔭᒪᕐᒋᖕᓇᖅᑎᑦᑐᒍ. ᐅᑦᓗᒥ ᐅᕙᖓᓕᖅᐳᒍ ᓯᕗᓂᒃᓴᕋ ᐃᓯᒪᒐᓯᒃᑲᑦᑕ. ᖁᓂᖅᓯᒃᐳᒍᑦ ᐱᓕᕆᐊᕐᑎᒍᓐᓇᐅᑎᒥᓐ ᒐᕙᒪᒃᑯᓐᓂᑦ; ᐱᓕᕆᐊᕐᑎᕆᖕᓂᕐᒥᓐ ᐅᒃᐱᕆᖅᑕᐅᑎᓂᒃᑯ ᐊᒻᒪ ᐃᓕᓴᖅᓯᓯᒪᓂᕐᒥ ᐃᒃᐱᒋᔭᒥᓐ. ”

ᔫᓐ ᐊᒪᕈᐊᓕᒃ
ᐅᖃᓪᓚᒃᑎᓪᓗᒍ ᒥᓂᔅᑕ ᑲᑎᒪᕕᖕᔪᐊᖅᓂᖕᒐᓂ
ᓄᓇᖃᖅᑳᖅᑐᑦ ᐱᔪᑎᒋᓪᓗᒋ, ᒫᔾ 1984

The Inuit: a maritime people ᐃᓄᐃᑦ: ᓯᒃᔭᒥᐅᑕᑦ

> **"** *Sixty years ago, Inuit were not able to vote. . . . We were controlled so much from the outside, to a point where our parents didn't know how to control things. From that point on, we wanted to get back in controlling our own selves. . . . And 60 years later, here we have a new territory that the federal government agreed to give us.* **"**

Paul Quassa
Chief negotiator and member of Inuit negotiating team in other roles, 1985–1993

After several years of struggle, the concept of Nunavut was accepted by the federal and NWT governments, but was to be negotiated in a separate process, parallel with the land claim.

Over the next 16 years the two processes went ahead, in spite of international, national, organizational and personal crises. The same group of Inuit leaders and their consultants dealt with it all. Although it is impossible to name everyone, some of the key players included Curley, Kadlun, David Aglukark, Allen Maghagak, Jack Kupeuna, John Amagoalik, James Eetoolook, Solomon Kugak, Eric Tagoona, Donat Milortuk, Thomas Suluk, Louis Tapardjuk, Mark Evaloarjuk, Paul Quassa, Paul Okalik, Simon Taipana, Louis Pilakapsi, Meeka Kilabuk, Ollie Ittinuar, John Merritt, Randy Ames, Bruce Gillies, Terry Fenge, and Mary Crnkovich. The federal team was headed first by John Naismith, then Keith Crowe, in the early years, followed by Bob Mitchell and Tom Molloy. Angus MacKay, and then Ross MacKinnon took the helm of the NWT government's negotiating team.

The largest claim settlement in Canada's history

Some members of ITC disagreed with the 1976 *Nunavut* proposal on the grounds that it was written by consultants and did not reflect the goals and feelings of the Inuit. A new document was prepared and endorsed by a majority vote of an ITC assembly. This one listed 11 principles for self-government, and retained the concept of a new territory.

Negotiation on the Nunavut claim began with fruitless wrangling over the territory issue. Talks were alternately threatened and stimulated by intense exploration and development of oil, gas and mining in the Northwest Territories. At the same time, Canada's First Ministers were staging discussions on the national Constitution. The small group of Inuit and consultants who had to attend constitutional meetings, court sessions and public hearings relevant to their claim acquitted themselves well.

continued on page 30

ᐊᕐᕌᒍ 16 ᐃᓗᐊᓂ ᑖᒃᑯᐊ ᒪᕐᕉ ᐱᓕᕆᐊᖑᔫ ᐱᓕᕆᐊᖑᒻᒪᕆᓕᓚᐅᕐᓯᒪᕘ, ᑕᒪᒃᑯᐊ ᓄᓇᕐᔪᐊᕐᒥ, ᑲᓇᑕᒥ, ᑲᑐᔾᔨᖅᑎᕆᖕᓂᒃᑯ ᐊᒻᒪ ᐃᒻᒥᒃᑯ ᐊᑲᐅᖏᓕᐅᕈᑎᓂᑦ ᓴᖅᑮᔭᖅᑐᖃᓗᐊᕐᑎᓪᓗᒍ. ᑖᒃᑯᐊᑦᑕᐃᓐᓇᖅ ᐱᓕᕆᔩᑦ ᓯᕗᓕᐅᕐᑏ ᐅᖃᐅᓯᖃᐃᔩᖏᓪᓗ ᑕᒪᑐᒥᖓ ᐱᓕᕚᓐᓇᓚᐅᕐᐳᑦ. ᐊᔾᔨᕐᓇᖃᓗᐊᕐᑎᓪᓗᒍ ᑕᒪᐃᓐᓂ ᑕᐃᓯᔭᕆᐊᒃᓴᖅ, ᐅᑯᐊᓕ ᐱᓕᕆᓪᓗᐊᑕᓚᐅᕐᐳᑦ ᑖᓚᖅ ᑰᓕ, ᑲᓪᓗᓐ, ᑕᐃᕕᑦ ᐊᒡᓗᒃᑲᖅ, ᒫᒃᕼᐋᒐᖅ, ᔮᒃ ᑰᐱᐅᓇ, ᔮᓐ ᐊᒪᑰᐊᓕᒃ, ᐃᓚᒃ ᑕᑰᓈᖅ, ᔭᐃᒻᔅ ᐃᑦᑐᓗᒃ, ᓵᓚᒪᓐ ᑯᒐᒃ, ᑑᓇᑦ ᒥᓗᕐᑐᖅ, ᑖᒪᔅ ᓱᓗᒃ, ᓗᐃ ᑕᐹᕐᔪᒃ, ᒫᒃ ᐃᕙᓗᐊᕐᔪᒃ, ᐹᓪ ᖁᐊᓴ, ᐹᓪ ᐅᑲᓕᖅ, ᓴᐃᒪᓐ ᑕᐃᐸᓇ, ᓗᐃ ᐱᓚᑲᑉᓯ, ᒦᑲ ᕿᓚᑉᐸᖅ, ᐆᓕ ᐃᑎᓐᓇᖅ, ᔮᓐ ᒥᐅᕆᑦ, ᕌᓐᑎ ᐁᒥᔅ, ᐳᕈᔅ ᒋᓕᔅ, ᑎᐅᕆ ᕕᐊᓐᔾ, ᐊᒻᒪ ᒥᐊᕆ ᑯᖃᑯᕕᑦᔅ. ᑲᕙᒪᒃᑯᓐᓂ ᐱᓕᕆᔩᑦ ᓯᕗᓕᐅᕐᑎᖅᑲᓪᓚᐅᕐᐳᑦ ᓯᕗᓪᓕᖅᒥᓐ ᔮᓐ ᓇᐃᔅᒥᑦᒥᓐ, ᐊᒻᒪ ᑮᑦ ᑯᕌ, ᐊᕐᕌᒍᑦ ᐱᒋᐊᓕᕋᓂᖏᓐᓂ, ᑭᖑᓂᐊᒍᓪᓕ ᐹᑉ ᒥᑦᓯᓪ ᐊᒻᒪ ᑖᒻ ᒪᓗᐊᐃ. ᐋᖓᔅ ᒪᒃᑲᐃ, ᐊᒻᒪ ᑭᖑᓂᐊᒍᑦ ᕉᔅ ᒪᑭᓐᓇᓐ ᓯᕗᓕᐅᕐᑎᐅᓕᓪᓚᐅᕐᐳᖅ ᓄᓇᑦᓯᐊᑉ ᑲᕙᒪᒃᑯᖏᓐᓂ ᐋᖅᑎᖏᓐᓂ ᑭᒡᒐᖅᑐᐃᓪᓗᓂ.

ᐊᖏᓛᒻᒪᕆᒃ ᓄᓇᑖᕆᔭᐅᔪᖅ ᑲᓇᑕᒥ ᓇᓗᓇᐃᕐᓯᒪᔪᓂᑦ

ᐃᓚᖏ ᐃᓚᒋᔭᐅᔪᑦ ᐃᓄᐃᑦ ᑕᐱᕇᒃᓴᒃᑯᖓᓂ 1976-ᒥ ᓄᓇᕘᑦᑖᕆᔫᑎ ᐱᐅᒋᓚᐅᕐᓯᒪᖏᓚᖓ ᐅᖃᕋᒥᒃ ᑖᓐᓇ ᐊᖏᕈᑎ ᑎᑎᕋᕐᑕᐅᓯᒪᓂᕋᕐᓂᔾᔪᒃ ᐅᖃᓪᓚᐅᔾᔨᐃᔨᓂ ᐊᒻᒪᓗ ᑐᕌᒐᓕᐅᕐᔪᐊᕐᒥᓐ ᐃᓱᒪᒋᔭᐅᔪᓂᓪᓗ ᐃᓄᖕᓄ ᐱᓯᒪᖕᒋᓐᓂᖕᖓᓂᑦ. ᓄᑖᒥ ᑎᑎᖅᓯᒪᔪᒥᓐ ᐋᖅᑮᒃᓯᓕᓪᓗᑎᒃ ᐊᒻᒪᓗ ᓴᖅᑭᑎᑕᐅᒻᒪᕆᒃᑐᓂ ᐃᓄᐃᑦ ᑕᐱᕇᒃᓯᑯ ᑲᑎᒪᓂᕐᔪᐊᖕᒐᓂᑦ ᐃᓚᒋᔭᐅᔪᓄᓪᓗ ᐊᖏᕐᑕᐅᓪᓗᓂ ᐅᓄᕐᓂᖅᓴᓂᑦ. ᐅᓇᓕ ᑎᑎᖅᑲᖅ ᓇᓗᓇᐃᕐᓯᓯᒪᓪᓚᐅᕐᐳᖅ 11-ᓂ ᐱᔾᔪᑕᐅᓗᐊᕐᑐᓂᑦ ᑲᒪᑖᕋᓯᖕᓂᕐᒧᓐ ᓇᖕᒥᓂᖅ, ᐊᒻᒪᓗ ᑎᑎᕋᐅᓯᖅᑲᖅᓯᓂ ᓄᓇᒥ ᐃᒥᒍᕐᑐᒃᓴᒥᓐ ᐊᕕᒃᓯᒪᓂᒃᑯᑦ.

ᐊᑏᕐᓂᐅᔪᑦ ᓄᓇᕗᑦᑖᕋᔫᑎ ᐱᒋᐊᓯᓚᐅᕐᐳᖅ ᑕᒻᒪᓗ ᓇᓗᖕᖓᐅᓇᓂ ᐊᕕᖕᓂᐅᔪᖅ. ᑕᒪᒃᑯᐊ ᐅᖃᓪᓚᖕᓂᐅᔪᑦ ᐅᓚᕕᑕᐅᖃᑦᑕᕐᓗᑎᒃ ᖃᐅᔨᓴᕐᓂᐅᔪᓂᑦ ᐱᕙᓪᓕᐊᓂᐅᔪᒥᓪᓗ ᐅᖅᓱᐊᓗᓕᕆᓂᕐᒧᑦ, ᐅᔭᓕᕆᓂᕐᒧᑦ ᐊᒻᒪ ᐅᔭᖅᑲᖅᓯᐅᕐᓂᕐᒧᑦ ᓄᓇᓯᐊᕐᒥ. ᑕᕙᓂᑦᑕᐃᓐᓇᖅ, ᑲᓇᑕᐅᑉ ᒥᓂᔅᑕᖏ ᐅᖃᐅᓯᖅᑲᑕᓚᐅᕐᓯᒪᔪᑦ ᑲᓇᑕᐅᑉ ᒪᓕᒐᕐᔪᐊᖓᓂ. ᐅᓄᖏᑦᑐᑦ ᐃᓄᐃᑦ ᐱᓕᕆᔩᑦ ᐅᖃᐅᓯᖃᐃᔩᖏᓪᓗ ᐅᑲᐅᑎᒋᐊᖅᑲᖅᑲᑦᑕᓚᐅᕐᐳᑦ, ᐃᖅᑲᖅᑐᐃᕕᓕᕆᔨᓂᓪᓗ ᐊᒻᒪ ᐃᓄᒋᐊᓄᑦ ᐅᖃᓪᓚᒋᐊᖅᑐᓇᐊᖅᑲᖅᐸᒃᓱᑎᒃ ᓄᓇᑖᖅᓯᕐᓂᖅᔫᖕᒐᔪᓂ ᐊᒻᒪᓗ ᐃᖕᒥᖕᓂ ᑭᒡᒐᖅᑐᖅᑎᐊᖅᓱᑎᒃ.

ᑲᔪᓯᔪᖅ ᒫᒃᐱᒐᖅ 30

> **"** *ᓯᕗᓂᑦᑎᓐᓂ ᐊᕐᕌᒍᑦ 60, ᐃᓄᐃᑦ ᓂᕈᐊᕈᓐᓇᓚᐅᕐᓯᒪᖏᑦᑐᑦ... ᐊᐅᓚᑕᐅᓚᐅᕐᓯᒪᒐᑦ ᓯᓚᑎᒥᐅᑦᑎᓐᓂ, ᐊᖏᓛᓗᓐᓂᑦ ᐊᖓᔪᖅᑳᒐᑦ ᐊᐅᓚᑦᑎᔾᔪᓐᓇᓚᐅᕐᓯᒪᖏᑦᑐᑦ ᖃᓄᐃᓕᐅᕐᓂᐅᔪᓂᑦ. ᑕᐃᒪᓐᖓᓂ, ᐃᓅᓯᑦᑎᓐᓂ ᐊᐅᓚᑦᑎᔪᒪᓕᓚᐅᕐᓯᒪᒐᒍᑦ... ᐊᒻᒪ ᐊᕐᕌᒍᑦ 60 ᐱᐊᓂᒃᓯᒪᓕᕐᑎᓪᓗᒍ, ᑎᑭᐅᑎᒐᒍᑦ ᓇᖕᒥᓂᖅ ᐃᒥᒃᑯᕐᑐᒥ ᐊᕕᒃᓯᒪᔪᒥᓐ ᓄᓇᕗᓯᒐᒍ ᑲᕙᒪᑐᖃᒃᑯ ᐊᖏᕐᓗᑎ ᐅᐸᑦᑎᓐᓄ ᑐᓂᓯᓪᓗᑎᒃ.* **"**

ᐹᓪ ᖁᐊᓴ
ᐊᖓᔪᖅᑳᖅ ᐋᖅᑮᖅᑎᓄᑦ ᐊᒻᒪ ᐃᓚᒋᔭᐅᑦᓗᓂ
ᐃᓄᖕᓂ ᐋᖅᑮᑎᐅᔪᓂᑦ ᐊᓯᖏᓐᓄᑦ, 1985–1993

Nunatsiaq News

What Price Nunavut?
ᖃᓄᖅ ᐊᑭᖃᖅᓯᒪᕙ ᓄᓇᕗᑦ?

By John Amagoalik

The last 30 years have seen incredible changes for the Inuit of Nunavut. These changes, mostly for the better, have been the result of pioneering work by Inuit leaders who were determined to improve the lives of their people. This work has demanded the dedication and sacrifice of these people as they struggled to secure land and political rights for their children.

In the early 1970s, being an Inuk leader working in land claims was sometimes a lonely feeling. Explaining to the older generation why it was necessary to "claim" our homeland was not an easy task. Trying to explain what a modern treaty might contain was just as difficult.

The Inuit leadership also had to face hostile governments and a Canadian population largely ignorant of Inuit, their homeland, and their history. Inuit negotiators also had to break new ground in their land claim talks. Governments did not have any policy in many areas that Inuit felt had to be part of any final deal. The negotiations were stalled many times as governments struggled with things like royalties, offshore rights, self-government institutions with real legal powers, and new political entities. The process was grindingly slow and frustrating.

The weight of responsibility and the amount of effort it took to make progress took its toll on Inuit leaders. Many experienced burnout under the pressure of intense negotiations, long periods of absence from family and community, and unfamiliar environments in big cities. Alcohol abuse became a serious problem that contributed to other problems, like family breakups and run-ins with the law. It was the demand by ordinary Inuit that their leaders clean up their acts that has resulted in a more stable leadership in recent years.

To all those who sacrificed for the benefit of future generations, your loneliness and struggle will not go unrecognized.

John Amagoalik is chief commissioner of the Nunavut Implementation Commission. Involved in negotiations to secure a land claim agreement and territory for Nunavut since 1975, he served as the negotiator for the Inuit of Nunavut on the political accord for the creation of Nunavut.

ᑎᑎᕿᖅᑐᖅ ᔫᓐ ᐊᒪᕈᐊᓕᒃ

ᐊᕐᕌᒍᐃᑦ 30-ᐅᔪᑦ ᖄᖏᖅᓯᒪᓕᖅᑐᑦ ᑲᒪᓐᒪᕆᒃᑐᓂᒃ ᐊᓯᔾᔨᕈᑕᐅᔪᓂᒃ ᐃᓄᖕᓄᑦ ᓄᓇᕗᒥᐅᓄᑦ ᐊᑐᖅᑕᐅᓂᖃᖅᓯᒪᓕᕐᒪᑕ. ᑕᒪᒃᑯᐊ ᐊᓯᔾᔨᕈᑕᐅᔪᐃᑦ, ᐊᒥᓱᑦ ᐱᐅᔪᑦ, ᐱᕆᐊᓕᖅᑎᑕᐅᓯᒪᔪᑦ ᓯᕗᓕᖅᑎᐅᔪᓄᑦ ᐃᓄᖕᓄᑦ ᐊᒃᓱᕈᖅᓯᒪᓂᖃᖅᑐᓄᑦ ᐃᓄᐃᑦ ᐃᓅᓯᖏᑦ ᐊᑲᐅᓯᕚᓪᓕᐊᑎᑕᐅᖁᓪᓗᒋᑦ. ᑕᒪᓐᓇ ᓴᓇᓂᑐᖃᐅᔪᖅ ᓄᖅᑲᔪᐃᑦᑐᓄᑦ ᑲᒪᒋᔭᐅᓯᒪᑐᖃᓕᖅᑐᖅ ᐊᒻᒪᓗ ᐊᑭᖃᓕᖅᑎᑕᐅᓯᒪᓪᓗᓂ ᐱᓇᓱᒃᑎᐅᔪᓄᑦ ᓄᓇᒥᒃ ᓇᖕᒥᓂᖅᑖᕐᓂᕐᒥᒃ ᐊᒻᒪᓗ ᒐᕙᒪᓕᕆᓂᕐᒥᒃ ᐱᔪᓐᓇᐅᑕᐅᔪᓂᒃ ᐃᓄᖕᓄᑦ. ᑕᒪᐃᑕ ᓱᕈᓰᑦ ᑭᖑᕚᖏᓪᓗ ᓇᖕᒥᓂᖃᕐᓗᑎᒃ ᐱᔪᓐᓇᐅᑎᖃᕐᖁᓪᓗᒋᑦ.

ᐱᕆᐊᓕᕌᖅᑎᓪᓗᒋᑦ 1970-ᒥᑦ, ᐃᓅᓪᓗᓂ ᓯᕗᓕᖅᑎᐅᓪᓗᓂ ᐃᖅᑲᓇᐃᔮᓯᔭᖅᑲᖅᓗᓂ ᓄᓇᕗᑖᕆᓯᐊᕐᓂᕐᒥᒃ ᐃᓅᓗᐊᕐᓇᓚᐅᖅᓯᒪᔪᖅ. ᐃᓐᓇᒪᕆᐅᓂᖅᓴᐅᔪᑦ ᑐᑭᓯᑎᑕᐅᓇᓱᒃᐸᓚᐅᖅᑎᓪᓗᒋᑦ "ᓇᖕᒥᓂᖃᕐᓂᕐᒥᒃ" ᓄᓇᒥᒃ ᐊᒻᒪᓗ ᓱᓇᐅᑎᖕᒪᖔᑦ ᖃᐅᔨᒃᑲᐃᓇᓱᒃᑎᐅᓪᓗᓂ. ᑕᒪᓐᓇ ᐊᔪᕐᓇᖕᖏᑦᑐᐊᖕᖏᑦᑐᓚᐅᖅᑐᖅ. ᑐᑭᓯᑦᓯᓇᓱᓪᓗᓂ ᖃᓄᖅ ᑐᑭᖃᕐᒪᖔᑦ ᐊᖏᕈᑎᓕᐅᕐᓂᕐᒥᒃ ᓄᓇ ᐱᔪᑎᒋᓪᓗᒍ ᐊᒻᒪᑦᑕᐅᖅ ᐊᔪᕐᓇᕈᔪᖃᑦᑕᓚᐅᕐᒥᔪᖅ.

ᐊᒻᒪᑦᑕᐅᖅ ᐃᓄᐃᑦ ᓯᕗᓕᖅᑎᐅᔪᑦ ᓵᖓᔭᕆᐊᖃᖃᑦᑕᓚᐅᕐᒪᑕ ᒐᕙᒪᓂᒃ ᐊᑭᖃᖅᑐᖅᐸᒃᑎᐅᔪᓂᒃ ᐊᒻᒪᓗ ᑲᓇᑕᒥᐅᓂᒃ ᖃᐅᔨᒪᖕᖏᓗᐊᖅᑐᓂᒃ ᐃᓄᖕᓂᒃ, ᓄᓇᖓᔪᖃᖕᓂᒃ ᐊᒻᒪᓗ ᓯᕗᓂᓴᓚᐅᖅᑕᖕᖓᓂᒃ. ᐃᓄᐃᑦ ᐊᖏᖃᓱᒃᑎᐅᔪᑦ ᓄᑖᓂᒃ ᐊᖅᑯᑎᓕᐅᖅᐸᓪᓕᐊᕆᐊᖃᖅᐸᓪᓚᐅᕐᒪᑕ. ᒐᕙᒪᐃᑦ ᒪᓕᒐᒃᓴᖃᓚᐅᓐᖏᓚᑦ ᐊᑐᐊᒐᒃᓴᓂᒃ ᐃᓄᐃᑦ ᐱᑕᖃᖁᔭᖏᓐᓂᒃ ᐃᓚᒋᔭᐅᖁᔭᐅᔪᓂᒃ ᐊᖏᖃᑎᒌᒍᑕᐅᓂᐊᖅᑐᒥ ᑭᖑᓪᓕᖅᐹᖅᑐᒥ. ᓄᖅᑲᖅᑲᓚᐅᖅᑐᑦ ᐊᒥᓱᐃᖅᓗᑎᒃ ᒐᕙᒪᐅᔪᑦ ᑐᑭᓯᑕᐃᓐᓇᖅᐸᒃᑎᓪᓗᒋᑦ ᒪᑯᓂᖓ ᓄᓇᒥᒃ ᐊᑐᒐᖅᓴᖏᓐᓄᑦ ᐊᑭᓕᐅᑎᓂᒃ, ᑕᓄᐅᕐᒥᐅᑕᓂᒃ ᐱᔪᓐᓇᐅᓯᖃᖅᓯᓂᒃ, ᓇᖕᒥᓂᖅ ᒐᕙᒪᖃᖅᓯᒪᔪᑦ ᓴᓇᒃᑯᑖᖑᔪᓕᖓᔪᓂᒃ ᒪᓕᒐᑎᒍᑦ ᓴᓐᖏᓂᖃᖅᓯᒪᖅᑐᓂᒃ, ᐊᒻᒪᓗ ᓄᑖᑦ ᑎᒥᖁᑎᐅᔪᑦ ᒐᕙᒪᓕᕆᓂᕐᒧᑦ. ᐊᖅᑯᑎᒋᓴᐅᔪᖅ ᓯᒃᑲᐃᑦᑐᒻᒪᕆᐊᖃᓪᓚᐅᖅᑐᖅ ᐊᒻᒪᓗ ᐱᓴᓇᑐᑦᑐᓂ.

ᐅᖁᒪᐃᒃᓴᖅᐸᓪᓕᐊᒍᑎᖃᖅᑐᐊᓘᑎᒃ ᐊᒻᒪᓗ ᓴᓇᓪᓗᐊᕐᓇᖅᑎᓪᓗᒍ ᓯᕗᒻᒧᓕᓯᐊᕐᓂᖅ ᑕᖃᒍᑕᐅᑦᑕᓪᓚᐅᖅᑐᖅ ᓯᕗᓕᖅᑎᐅᔪᓄᑦ ᐃᓄᖕᓄᑦ. ᐊᒥᓱᑦ ᓱᒃᑯᓕᓪᓚᐅᖅᑐᑦ ᐅᖁᒪᐃᒃᓴᓗᐊᕐᓂᕐᒧᑦ ᐊᒃᓱᕈᕐᓇᖅᐸᒃᑎᓪᓗᒍ ᐊᒃᓯᐊᓗᒃ ᐊᖏᖃᑎᒌᒃᑕᓯᐊᕐᓂᖅ. ᐊᒻᒪᓗ ᐊᑯᓂᐊᓗᒃ ᐊᐅᓪᓚᖅᓯᒪᒋᐊᖃᖃᑦᑕᖅᑎᓪᓗᒋᑦ ᑕᑯᑕᖕᖏᓪᓗᒋᑦ ᐃᓚᒥᖕᓂᒃ ᓄᓇᓕᖕᓂᓪᓗ. ᐅᐸᐃᓯᒪᒋᐊᖃᖃᑦᑕᖅᑐᓂᒃ ᐃᓄᒋᐊᒃᑐᓂᒃ ᓱᖏᐅᑎᓯᒪᓐᖏᑕᒥᖕᓂᒃ. ᐃᒥᐊᓗᒃ ᐊᔪᕐᓇᕈᑎᐅᕙᓪᓗᓂ ᐊᒻᒪᓗ ᓱᓕᒃᑲᓐᓂᖅ ᑲᑕᖕᓂᕐᒧᑦ ᓵᓕᕈᐅᔾᔪᑎᑐᐃᓐᓇᐅᕙᓪᓚᐅᖅᑐᖅ ᐊᓯᖏᓐᓄᓪᓗ ᖁᕕᐊᓇᖕᖏᑦᑐᓄᑦ ᐊᑐᓕᕈᑎᑐᐃᓐᓇᐅᒍᑕᐅᓪᓗᓂ, ᔫᓯ ᐃᓚᒌᑦ ᐊᐱᑦᑕᕐᓂᖏᑦ ᐊᒻᒪᓗ ᐊᓯᔾᔭᐅᖕᖑᖅᑎᑕᐅᕙᒃᓗᑎᒃ ᒪᓕᒐᕐᓂᒃ ᓯᖁᐃᓂᒃᑯᑦ. ᐃᓄᐃᓪᓕ ᓵᓚᔪᓂᒃ ᓯᕗᓕᖅᑎᖃᕈᒪᓂᖏᓐᓄᑦ ᑕᐃᒃᑯᐊ ᐱᐅᓂᖅᓵᒃᑯᑦ ᐊᖅᑯᑎᖃᓕᖅᑎᑕᐅᓚᐅᖅᑐᑦ ᐊᒻᒪᓗ ᓯᕗᓕᖅᑎᐅᔪᑦ ᖁᓚᕐᓇᖏᓐᓂᖅᓴᐅᓕᕐᒪᑕ ᐊᕐᕌᒍᓂ ᖃᓂᑦᑐᓂ ᖄᖏᖅᓯᒪᓕᖅᑐᓂ.

ᑕᐃᒃᑯᓄᖓᓗᒃᑖᖅ ᓴᐃᒥᓂᖅᑲᓚᐅᖅᑐᖅ ᖃᓄᑐᐃᓐᓇᖅ ᓯᕗᓂᖓᓂᑦ ᐋᖅᑮᓱᕐᓂᕐᒥᑦ, ᐃᓅᓗᐊᕈᑎᐅᓂᑦ ᐊᒻᒪᓗ ᐊᒃᓱᕈᖅᐸᓪᓚᐅᕐᓂᑦ ᐃᓕᑕᕆᔭᐅᔪᑦ.

ᔫᓐ ᐊᒪᕈᐊᓕᒃ (John Amagoalik) ᐋᖅᑭᒃᑎᕆᓕᓯᐊᖅᑎᐅᔪᖅ ᓄᓇᕗᑦ ᑲᒪᔨᖏᓐᓂᖓᓐᓂ. ᐃᓚᐅᓚᐅᖅᑐᖅ ᓄᓇᕗᑖᖑᓯᐊᕐᓂᕐᒥ ᐊᖏᖃᑎᒌᒃᓯᐊᖅᑐᓂ ᐊᒻᒪᓗ ᓄᓇᕗᑦ ᐱᕋᔭᖅᑎᑕᐅᓂᖓᓂ ᐱᒋᐊᖅᓱᓂ 1975-ᒥ. ᐊᖓᔪᖅᑳᖑᓪᓗᓂ ᐊᖏᖃᑎᒌᒃᓯᐊᖅᑐᓂ ᓄᓇᕗᒥᐅᓂᒥ ᐃᓄᖕᓄᑦ ᐱᔨᑦᑎᕋᖅᑐᓂ ᐊᒻᒪᓗ ᒐᕙᒪᓕᕆᓂᕐᒧᑦ ᐊᖏᕈᑎᒥ ᓄᓇᕗᑦ ᐱᕋᔭᖅᑎᑕᐅᓂᖓᓄᑦ.

continued from page 28

The Inuit tried hard to get a freeze on industrial development during negotiation, without much success. Other controversial issues loomed as well, such as the powers of a wildlife management board, Inuit rights to the offshore, and the boundary between Dene and Inuit claims, a point still contested today by Manitoba Dene in an ongoing Federal Court case.

David Roberts CAAC

In balance, there were events that aided Inuit, too. The Baker Lake court case was decided by the Federal Court in 1979, recognizing an aboriginal right to occupy and harvest land. When American ships sailed without permission through Canadian waters in 1970 (the *Manhattan*) and 1985 (the *Polar Sea*), their intrusions highlighted the crucial role of Inuit in defining Canadian sovereignty. Another blessing was Section 35 of the newly repatriated *Constitution Act, 1982*, which confirmed the status of claim settlements.

Over the years, federal and territorial governments changed, and so did policies and procedures. The organization of the Inuit shifted several times. In 1982, the Tungavik Federation of Nunavut (TFN) was created to pursue negotiations on behalf of Inuit of Nunavut. Although emotions inevitably ran high at times, there was mutual respect and humor

continued on page 32

ᐃᓚᖓ ᒪᒃᐱᒐᐅᑉ 28

ᐃᓄᐃᑦ ᐊᒃᓱᕈᕐᒪᕆᓚᐅᕐᐳᑦ ᓄᖅᑲᖓᕿᖅᑎᑦᑎ-ᓇᓱᖕᓂᕐᒥᓐ ᐱᕙᓪᓕᐊᓂᐅᔪᒥᓐ ᐋᖅᑭᒃᑕᐅᑎᓪᓗᒋᑦ, ᑭᓯᐊᓂ ᑕᒪᓐᓇ ᐊᓂᒍᑦᑎᐊᖏᓐᓂ. ᐊᓯᖏᑦ ᐊᑲᐅᖏᑦᑐᓕᐅᕈᑏ ᓴᖅᑮᔭᖏᓐᓇᕐᐸᒃᓱᑎᒃ, ᒪᑯᑎᑐᓇᖅ ᐊᐳᓪᓕᕆᔨᒥᓐ ᐆᒪᔪᓂ ᑲᑎᒪᔨᓂᑦ, ᐃᓄᐃᑦ ᐱᔪᓐᓇᐅᑎᖏᓐᓂᑦ ᐃᒪᕐᒥᐅᑕᑦ ᒥᒃᓵᓄᑦ, ᐊᒻᒪᓗ ᓄᓇᐅᑉ ᐊᕝᕕᒃᓯᒪᓂᖓᓂᐊᕐᑕᖓ ᐊᑲᐅᖏᓐᓂᕐᖃᕐᓗᓂ ᐊᓪᓚᓄᑦ ᐃᓄᖕᓄᓪᓗ, ᑕᓐᓇᓗ ᒫᓇ ᐃᖅᑲᖅᑐᐃᔨᒃᑯ ᐱᓕᕆᐊᖑᕗᖅ.

ᐊᒻᒪᑦᑕᐅᖅ ᐃᓄᐃᑦ ᐃᑲᔪᖅᑕᐅᕙᓪᓚᐅᓇᔾᔪᑦ. ᖃᒪᓂᑦᑐᐊᕐᒥ ᐃᖅᑲᖅᑐᐃᔨᓪᓚᕆᓐᓂᐅᔪᖅ ᐋᖅᑭᑕ-ᐅᓪᓚᐅᕐᓯᒪᔪᖅ ᒐᕙᒪᒃᑯᑦ ᐃᖅᑲᖅᑐᐃ-ᕕᓪᓚᓴᖑᕐᖏᓐᓄᑦ 1979-ᒥ, ᐃᓕᓯᖅᓯᓂᖃᓕᕐᓗᑎᒃ ᓄᓇᖃᖅᑳᖅᑐᑦ ᓄᓇᒥ ᐱᔪᓐᓇᐅᑎᖃᕐᓂᖏᓐᓂᑦ ᓂᕆᔪᑎᓄᓪᓗ. ᒥᐊᓕᒐᒃᑯ ᐅᒥᐊᕐᔪᐊᖏᑦ ᒫᕐᑭ ᑲᓇᑕᐅᑉ ᐃᒪᖓᓕᓕᕐᒪᑕ ᐊᖏᕐᓴᑕᐅᓯᒪᓇᑎᒃ 1970-ᒥ (the Manhattan) ᐊᒻᒪ 1985-ᒥ (the Polar Sea), ᑕᒪᐅᓈᕐᓂᖏᑦ ᓴᖅᑭᑎᑦᑎᓪᓗᐅᕐᓯᒪᕗᖅ ᐃᓄᐃᑦ ᐊᑐᕐᓂᖃᕐᓂᖏᓐᓂᑦ ᑲᓇᑕᐅᑉ ᐱᔪᓐᓇᐅᑎᖓᓄᑦ. ᐊᑲᐅᓈᓗᐅᕐᒥᔪᖅ ᐃᓅᖅ ᐃᓚᒍᑕᖅ 35 ᐋᖅᑭᑦᑭᐊᕐᓯᒪᓕᕐᑐᒥ *ᑲᓇᑕᐅᒻ ᒪᓕᒐᕐᔪᐊᖓ, 1982 ᐅᖅᑲᓯᒪᓂᖅᑲᕐᓂᖓᓄᑦ ᓄᓇᑖᕐᓯᖕᓂᕐᒥ.*

ᐊᕐᕌᒍᓗᓴᑦ ᐊᓂᒍᕐᐸᓪᓕᐊᔪᑎᒍᑦ, ᒐᕙᒪᒃᑯᑦ ᐊᒻᒪ ᓄᓇᓯᐊᑉ ᒐᕙᒪᒃᑯᖏᑦ ᐊᓯᖑᕈᓪᓚᕐᐳᑦ, ᐊᒻᒪᓗ ᑕᒪᒃᑯᐊ ᐊᑐᐊᒐᑦ ᐊᒻᒪ ᒪᓕᒐᑦ. ᑲᑐᔾᔨᖃᑎᒌᖕᓂᖓᑦ ᐃᓅᖅ ᐊᓯᖑᕐᓯᒪᓚᐅᕐᐳᑦ ᐅᓄᕐᑐᐃᔾᔨᒪᓇᖅᑐᑎᒃ. 1982-ᒥ, ᑐᙵᕙᒃᑯᑦ ᑲᑐᔾᔨᖃᑎᒌᖕᖓ ᓄᓇᕗᒻᒧ ᓴᖅᑭᑕᐅᓕᓪᓚᕆᒪᕗᖅ ᐋᖅᑭᒃᑕᖕᓂᕐᒧᓐ ᑐᕌᖓᑎᑕᐅᓪᓗᓂ ᐃᓄᖏᓐᓂ ᑭᒡᒐᖅᑐᐃᓪᓗᑎᒃ ᓄᓇᕗᒻᒥᐅᓂᑦ. ᐃᓐᓇᓂᒃᑯ ᓂᖓᓂᖅ ᓴᖅᑭᑉᐸᒃᓚᐅᕐᑎᓪᓗᒍ, ᐃᓱᓕᕐᓯᖓᕐᑎᐊᕐᓗᖅ ᖁᐱᐊᓱᖕᓂᓪᓗ ᓴᖅᑭᔮᕐᓇᖅᑲᑦᑕᐅᓯᒪᔪᑦ ᑕᒪᐃᑎᒍᑦ ᐱᖓᓱᐃᓕᖅᑲᖓᔪᓂᑦ ᐋᖅᑎᐅᔪᓂᑦ, ᐋᒡᒐᒃᑕᓕᐊᓪᓚᒃᐸᒃᓗᑎᒃ ᐊᖅᑭᑐᖓᖓᒃᓯᓕ-ᐊᓪᓚᒃᐸᒃᓗᑎᒃ.

ᐊᖏᕈᑎᒥ-ᐱᔪᑎᒻᒪᓇᐅᔪᒧᓐ ᓴᖅᑭᑦᑐᖃ-ᓕᓚᐅᖅᐳᖅ 1990-ᒥ. ᑭᖑᓂᐊᒍᑦ ᐊᖁᒃ ᒫᕐᑭ ᐱᓕᓇᓂᐅᓕᓚᐅᖅᐳᑦ ᐋᖅᑭᒃᓯᐃᑲᓐᓂᕈᑕᐅᓪᓗᓂ ᓇᓗᓇᐃᖅᓯᒃᑲᓐᓂᕈᑎᓂᑦ, ᐱᖃᓯᐅᔾᔭᐅᓪᓗᓂ ᓂᕈᐊᕐᓂᖅ ᓄᓇᒥ ᑲᒪᒋᔭᐅᓪᓗᓂ ᐋᖅᑐᐅᔪᓂᑦ ᓄᓇᓕᖕᓄᑦ ᑕᒪᐃᓐᓄᑦ ᐳᓚᖅᖢᑎᒃ.

ᑭᖑᓪᓕᖅᐸ ᐊᖏᕈᑎ ᐋᖅᑭᒃᑕᓕᐅᕐᓯᒪᔪᖅ ᓯᑎᐱᕆ 1992-ᒥ, ᐊᒻᒪᓗ ᑕᒪᓐᓇ ᐊᖏᖅᑕᐅᓪᓗᓂ ᓄᓇᖅᑐᓄᑦ ᐃᓄᖕᓄᑦ ᓂᕈᐊᕐᓂᒃᑯᑦ ᓄᕕᐱᕆ 3-ᒥ 5-ᒧ, 1992. ᐃᓚᖏᓐᓄᑦ ᓂᕈᐊᕐᑎᓄᑦ ᑕᒪᓐᓇ ᓈᒻᒪᓗᐊᓚᐅᖏᓛᖅ ᐊᔭᕐᓇᕈ-ᑕᐅᕈᔭᕐᓗᓂ ᓲᖅᑲᐃᒻᒪ ᐱᔪᓐᓇᐅᑎᓂ ᐃᓚᖏᓐᓂ ᓴᒃᑯᐃᒐᔭᕐᓂᖏᓐᓄᑦ ᓄᓈᖑᓚᔪᓂᑦ ᐊᒻᒪ ᐃᒪᕐᒥᐅᑕᕐᓄᑦ ᑖᓂ ᓄᓇᒋᑦᑐᕐᓂᐊᕐᑐᒧ, ᑭᓯᐊᓂᓕ ᑕᒪᓐᓇ ᐊᖏᓂᖅᑐᖅ 355,842 ᑭᓘᒥᑕᓂᒃ ᐃᓄᐃᑦ ᓄᓇᖏᓐᔅᑕᖓ. ᐃᓱᐊᓂᓕ, 84.7 ᐳᓴᓐᑦ ᓂᕈᐊᖑᐊᕐᑐᑦ ᑕᒪᑐᒥᖓ ᐊᖏᓕᓚᐅᕐᐳᑦ ᐊᖏᕈᑎᒥ.

"ᐃᓄᐃᑦ ᓂᕈᐊᕐᓂᖓ ᑕᒪᑐᒥᖓ ᓴᖅᑭᑎᑦᑎᒪ-ᓇᓕᓚᐅᕐᐳᖅ. ᐊᓯᖏᓐᓅᓚᐅᖏᑦᑐᕐᓕ," ᐅᖃᕐᑐᖅ ᐊᖓᔪᒃᖄᖅ ᐋᕐᕿ ᓚᐸᒪᒃᑯᖕᓄ ᐱᐅᓇ ᑑᒐ, ᑖᓐᓇ ᑎᓴᒐᓇ ᑐᔪᕐᒥᕝᕆᓚᐅᕐᑐᖅ ᐃᖃᓗᖕᓂ

ᑲᔪᓯᔪᖅ ᒪᒃᐱᒐᖅ 32

Nunavut Tourism ᓄᓇᕗᑦ ᐳᓚᕋᑦᑕᓂᖅ

Left: Life in an outpost camp. Top: Thomas Suluk. Until now, Nunavut has garnered little attention within Canada. Globally, though, it's a different story. "I remember I had to go to Moscow the next day," recalls Jack Stagg, after the federal government guaranteed a territory in the land claims agreement in December 1991. "I turned on CNN and there it was. Within basically 24 hours of that decision, it was a world event"

ᓴᐅᒥᐊᓂ: ᐃᓅᓯᖅ ᓄᓇᓕᕐᕆᒥ. ᖁᓖᓂ: ᑖᒪᔅ ᓱᓗᒃ. ᓄᓇᕗᑦ ᐱᓇᓱᐊᕈᐊᖏᓚᑦ ᑲᓇᑕᐅᑉ ᐃᓗᐊᓂ. ᓄᓇᕐᔪᐊᓕᒫᒥᓪᓕ, ᑭᓯᐊᓂ ᑕᑯᔅᓴᐅᕗ ᐊᓯᐊᒍᑦ. "ᐃᖅᑲᐅᒪᕗᖓ ᖃᐅᑉᐸᒍᑐᐊᕐᒪ ᒨᔅᑲᐅᒧᐊᓇᐊᖅᑐᖓ," ᐃᖅᑲᐅᒪᔪᖅ ᔮᒃ ᔅᑖᒡ, ᒐᕙᒪᒃᑯᑦ ᓇᓗᓇᐃᓚᐅᕐᑎᓪᓗᒋ ᓄᓇᑖᕐᑎᑦᑎᓂᕐᒥ ᐃᒻᒥᒃᑯᕐᑐᒥ ᐊᖏᕈᑎᑎᒍ ᑎᓯᐱᓇ 1991. "ᑕᓚᕖᓴ ᐃᑯᓪᓗᒍ ᓰᐊᓐᐊᓐᓄᓐ ᐅᖃᐅᓯᐅᔪ ᓴᖅᑮᔪᓂ. ᐃᖅᑲᖅᑲᑦ 24 ᐃᓗᐊᓂ ᓄᓇᕐᔪᐊᓕᒫᒥ ᑐᓴᐅᒪᔭᐅᓕᓚᐅᕐᐳᖅ"

Milestones ᐊᑐᕐᑐᕕᓃᑦ ᐃᖅᑲᐅᒪᓇᕐᑐᑦ

1971 Inuit Tapirisat of Canada (ITC) forms
ᐃᓄᐃᑦ ᑕᐱᕇᒃᓴᑦᑯ ᑲᓇᑕᒥᓐ ᐱᒋᐊᓯᕗᑦ

1973 Three landmark court decisions, including the Nishga Indians' Calder Case, support aboriginal rights for the first time
ᐱᖓᓱᑦ ᐃᖅᑲᖅᑐᐃᕕᒃᑎᒍᑦ ᐋᖅᑭᒃᑕᐅᔪᑦ, ᐱᒃᓯᐅᑎᓪᓗᓂ ᐃᖅᑭᓖᑦ ᓂᔅᒐᒃᑯ ᐱᓕᕆᐊᖓ ᑕᐃᔭᐅᔪᖅ Nishga Indians' Calder Case,
ᐃᑲᔪᖅᑐᐃᓂᒃᑯᑦ ᓄᓇᖃᖅᑳᖅᑐᑦ ᐱᔪᓐᓇᐅᑎᖏᓐᓂᑦ ᓯᕗᓪᓕᖅᐹᓪᒪᕆᖕᒥ

1976 Inuit present the *Nunavut* proposal to Ottawa, and negotiations for a land claim agreement and territory begin in earnest
ᐃᓄᐃᑦ ᓴᖅᑭᑦᑎᕗᑦ ᓄᓇᕗᑖᕐᓯᑎᓂᑦ ᐋᑐᕚᒧᑦ, ᐊᒻᒪ ᐋᕐᑲᑎᕆᖕᓂᖅ ᓄᓇᑖᕐᓯᐅᖕᓂᕐᒧᑦ ᐊᖏᕈᑎᓕᐅᕐᓂᕐᒧᑦ ᐱᒋᐊᓪᒪᕆᓯᕗᖅ

April ᐄᐳᕆ 1982 Most NWT residents vote "yes" to division in a territory-wide plebiscite
ᐅᓄᕐᓂᖅᓴᑦ ᓄᓇᑦᓯᐊᕐᒥᐅᑕᑦ "ᐊᖏᕐᐳᑦ" ᐊᕕᖕᓂᕐᒧᑦ ᓄᓇᑦᓯᐊᓕᒫᒥ ᓂᕈᐊᕐᓂᒃᑯᑦ

November ᓄᕕᐱᕆ 1982 The federal government conditionally agrees to the creation of Nunavut
ᒐᕙᒪᒃᑯᑦ ᑭᓯᐊᓂᖅᑲᕐᓗᑎᒃ ᐊᖏᕐᐳᑦ ᓄᓇᕗᑦ ᓴᖅᑭᑎᑕᐅᓯᖕᓂᖓᓂᑦ

May ᒪᐃ 1992 Buoyed by high voter turnout in the east, residents endorse a boundary splitting the NWT into two
ᓯᕗᓕᐅᕐᑕᐅᓪᓗᑎᒃ ᐊᒥᓱᓄᑦ ᓂᕈᐊᕆᐊᕐᑐᓄᑦ ᑲᓇᖕᓇᒥ, ᓄᓇᑦᓯᐊᕐᒥᐅᑕᑦ ᓴᖅᑭᑦᑎᕗᑦ ᐊᕕᒃᕕᐅᓂᐊᕐᑐᒥᓐ ᒪᕐᕈᐃᖕᒍᕐᑎᕐᑎᓂᕐᒥᓐ ᓄᓇᑦᓯᐊᕐᒥᓐ

September ᓯᑎᐱᕆ 1992 Inuit and government negotiators reach a final land claim agreement
ᐃᓄᐃᑦ ᐊᒻᒪ ᒐᕙᒪᒃᑯ ᐋᕐᑎᖏ ᐋᖅᑭᒃᓯᔪᑦ ᓄᓇᑖᕐᓯᑎᒥᓐ

November ᓄᕕᐱᕆ 1992 84.7 per cent of voters ratify the land claim agreement
84.7% ᐃᓄᐃᑦ ᓄᓇᕗᒻᒥ ᐊᖏᕐᐳᑦ ᓄᓇᑖᕐᓯᑎᒧᓐ

June ᔫᓂ 1993 Canadian Parliament passes the *Nunavut Land Claims Agreement Act* and the *Nunavut Act*
ᑲᓇᑕᒥ ᒪᓕᒐᓕᐅᕐᕕᒃ ᐊᓂᒍᐃᑎᑦᑎᕗᑦ ᓄᓇᕗᑦᒥ ᓄᓇᑖᕐᓂᕐᒧᓐ ᐊᖏᕈᑎᐅᑉ ᒪᓕᒐᖓᓂᑦ ᐊᒻᒪ ᓄᓇᕗᑦ ᒪᓕᒐᖓᓂᑦ

April 1, ᐄᐳᕆ 1, 1999

The territory of Nunavut legally joins the federation of Canada
ᓄᓇᕗᑦ ᐃᓚᐅᓪᓚᓇᓕᕐᐳᖅ ᑲᓇᑕᐅᑉ ᒪᓕᒐᕐᔪᐊᖏᑦᑎᒍᑦ

> *"Inuit achieved their near-lifetime goal of getting Nunavut without needing to resort to civil disobedience or litigations. . . . These kinds of things can be achieved by negotiation."*

Tom Molloy
Chief federal negotiator on the land claim, 1982–1993

> *"ᐃᓄᐃᑦ ᐱᓇᓱᐊᕐᑕᖏᓐᓂ ᐱᓕᓚᐅᕐᐳᑦ ᐃᓅᓯᓕᒫᑉᓗᖏᓐᓂ ᓄᓇᕗᑦᑖᕐᓯᐅᖕᓂᕐᒧᓐ ᒪᓕᒐᕐᓂᒃ ᓯᕐᐃᓚᐅᕐᑎᒃ ᐅᕝᕙᓘᓐᓃᑦ ᐃᖅᑲᖅᑐᐃ-ᕕᒎᖅᑎᑦᑎᓚᐅᕐᑎᒃ... ᑕᐃᒪᐃᓕᐅᕐᓃᑦ ᐱᔭᐅᔪᓐᓇᕐᑐᑦ ᐋᕐᓂᒃᑯᑦ."*

ᑖᒻ ᒪᓗᐊᐃ
ᐊᖓᔪᖅᑳᖅ ᒐᕙᒪᒃᑯᑦ ᐋᕐᑎᖏᓐᓄᑦ ᓄᓇᑖᕐᓯᐅᖕᓂᕐᒧᑦ, 1982–1993

continued from page 30

among the three negotiating teams at the table, with an occasional arctic baseball game, and practical joking.

An agreement-in-principle was reached in 1990. The next two years were spent in hammering out final details, including the selection of Inuit lands by negotiators who visited each community.

A final agreement was reached in September 1992, and ratified by Inuit beneficiaries in a plebiscite held Nov. 3–5, 1992. For some voters, the choice was made difficult because voting for the land claim agreement meant they would have to exchange aboriginal rights and title to all land and water in the Nunavut Settlement Area, save for the 355,842 square kilometres of Inuit-owned land. In the end, 84.7 per cent of voters still endorsed the agreement.

"It was the Inuit vote that made the deal. It wasn't all the other symbolic acts," says senior federal negotiator Barry Dewar, who was at the Discovery Lodge Hotel in Iqaluit when the ratification committee announced the results. Surrounded by members of the Inuit negotiating team — Paul Quassa, James Eetoolook, Jack Kupeuna, Bob Kadlun — it was a uniquely emotional moment.

"The mixture of joy, relief, validation — all encapsulated in faces in one minute."

On May 25, 1993, the final agreement was signed in Iqaluit. It was the largest claims settlement in Canada in terms of financial compensation and land: $1.1 billion to be paid out between 1993 and 2007, and 1.9 million square kilometres of land and water, including mineral rights to 35,257 square kilometres within the Inuit-owned land portion.

ᐃᓚᖓ ᒫᑉᐱᒐᐅᑉ 30

ᓂᕈᐊᕐᓂᐅᔪᖅ ᖃᓄᐃᓐᓂᖓ ᐅᖃᐅᓯᐅᑎᓪᓗᒍ. ᐱᖃᑎᖃᐅᕐᓗᓂ ᐋᐃᕐᑎᐅᔪᓂ ᐃᓄᖕᓂ — ᐹᓪ ᖁᐊᓴ, ᔭᐃᒻᔅ ᐃᑦᑐᓗᒃ, ᔮᒃ ᑯᐱᐅᓇ, ᐹᑉ ᑲᓪᓗᓐ — ᑕᒪᓐᓇ ᐃᑉᐱᓐᓇᒻᒪᕆᓪᓗᐊᕐᐳᖅ ᐊᑐᕐᑎᓪᓗᒍ.

"ᖁᕕᐊᓱᖕᓂᖅ, ᖃᔅᓱᕐᒥᖅ, ᓴᖅᑭᑦᑎᓐᓂᒪᕆᐅᔪᖅ–ᐊᑕᐅᑦᑎᒃᑯ ᑲᑎᓯᒪᓪᓗᐅᕐᐳᑦ ᑖᒃᑯᐊ ᕿᓇᐃ ᑕᑯᓪᓗᒋ."

ᒣ 25 1993-ᒥ ᑭᖑᓪᓕᕐᐹᖅ ᐊᖏᕈᑎ ᐊᑎᓕᐅᖅᑕᐅᓕᓪᓗᐅᕐᓯᒪᕗᖅ ᐃᖃᓗᖕᓂ, ᐊᖏᓂᕐᐹᖅ ᐊᖏᕈᓯᐊᕆᔭᐅᔪᖅ ᑲᓇᑕᒥ ᑕᐅᑐᒃᓱᒍ ᕿᓇᐅᔭᕐᑖᕆᔭᐅᓂᐊᕐᑐᖅ ᐊᒻᒪ ᓄᓇ: $1.1 ᐱᓕᐊᓐ ᑕᒪᓐᓇ ᑐᓐᓂᖁᑕᐅᕙᓐᓂᐊᕐᓗᓂ ᐊᕐᕌᒍᑦ 1993-ᒧ 2007-ᒧ ᐊᑯᓐᓂᖓᓂ, ᐊᒻᒪ 1.9 ᒥᓕᐊᓐ ᑭᓗᒥᑕ ᐊᖏᓂᖃᕐᑐᖅ ᓄᓇ ᐊᒻᒪ ᐃᒪᖅ, ᐱᖃᓯᐅᑎᓯᒪᓪᓗᓂ ᐅᔭᕋᐅᔭᓄᑦ ᐱᔪᓐᓇᐅᑎᓂᑦ ᐊᖏᓂᓕᖕᒥᑦ 35,257 ᑕᒫᒪ ᓄᓇᑖᕆᔭᐅᔪᖕ ᐃᓗᐊᓂ.

> *At the end of the day we always said we've got to deal with the creation of a Nunavut territory or political institution in Nunavut. Otherwise, we cannot convince our membership to ratify the land claims.*
>
> **Allen Maghagak**
> **Chief negotiator for Inuit negotiating team, 1980–1985**

> *ᐅᓪᓗᖅ ᐱᐊᓂᒃᑳᖓ ᐅᖃᖃᑦᑕᓚᐅᕐᐳᒍ ᐱᓕᕆᐊᖃᖅᓂᑦᑎᓐᓂ ᓴᖅᑭᑦᑎᓂᕐᒥ ᓄᓇᕗᒻᒥ ᐃᒥᒃᑰᓕᕐᓗᓂ ᐅᑉᐱᓗᓐᓂ ᒪᓕᒐᓕᕆᔨᖏᓐᓂ ᓄᓇᕗᒻᒥ. ᑕᐃᒪᐃᖏᒃᑯᑦᑕ, ᓄᓇᖃᑎᒋᔅ ᐊᖏᕐᑎᒍᓐᓇᖁᔭᓪᓗᐊᕆᓐᓇᑎᒍ ᓄᓇᑖᕋᔾᔪᑎᓂᕐ.*
>
> **ᐋᓚᓐ ᒫᒃᕼᐋᒐᖅ**
> **ᐊᖓᔪᖅᑳᖅ ᐋᐃᖅᑎᓄᑦ ᐃᓄᖕᓄ,**
> **1980–1985**

Nunavut Tourism ᓄᓇᕗᑦ

The turning point: Dec. 14, 1991, West Block, Parliament Hill, Ottawa

> *The most striking moment involved negotiating (for) Article 4 — whether the land claim agreement would include provision for a government. We'd been playing chicken (on this point) since '79. It had come to the moment of truth. I remember it was in one of those nice rooms. We had ordered Kentucky Fried Chicken for dinner. The KFC arrived. Just after the KFC feast, wording came back from the government side. Essentially, the federal minister had agreed. It was sort of a euphoric moment, a sort of 'pinch me, is it true?' feeling. But we had to be sure not to act too elated because we were still out for bargaining for everything we could get into the agreement.*

John Merritt
Legal counsel to Inuit negotiating team on the land claim and political accord, 1979–1984 and 1989–1993

> *It was one question that a bureaucrat asked about the future of Nunavut. And we think that's where the whole claim moved and shifted. But it was all done behind closed doors (in caucus) . . . the very last night of the agreement-in-principle.*

Ross MacKinnon
Chief negotiator for the government of the Northwest Territories on the land claim, 1983–1992

ᐊᓯᐊᒍᑦ ᐱᓕᐊᕐᕕᑦ: ᑎᓯᐱᕆ 14, 1991, ᐱᖕᒪᖕᒪᓂ, ᒪᓕᒐᓕᕆᕕᒃᔪᐊᕐᒥ, ᐋᑐᕚ

> *ᐃᖅᑲᐅᒪᓇᓖᖑᓚᐅᕐᑐᕐᓕ ᐋᔩᕐᓂᐅᔭᓂᑦ ᐃᓚᒍᑕᕐᒥᓐ 4 – ᑕᒪᓐᓇ ᐊᖕᒋᕈᑎᑎᒍᑦ ᐃᓚᐅᕆᐊᖅᑲᕆᐊᒃᓴᖕᒐᓂᑦ ᒐᕙᒪᖅᑲᖅᓂᐅᔪᖅ. ᐅᓗᕆᐊᖅᓵᕆᖅᑕᐅᑎᔫᓚᐅᖅᑕ 1979-ᒥ ᐱᒋᐊᕐᓗᓂ. ᑭᓯᐊᓂᓕ ᑕᒪᓐᓇ ᓱᓕᓂᕐᒧᓐ ᑎᑭᓕᓚᐅᖅᐳᖅ. ᐃᖅᑲᐅᒪᒐᖕᒐ ᐃᓗᐱᓯᖅᒦᕐᓗᑕ ᐱᐅᔫᓗᖕᒥ. ᑎᑭᓵᓪᓗᑕ ᐊᖏᓪᒋᖅᔭᐊᕐᓂᑦ ᐸᓚᐅᓖᓕᕐᓂ ᓂᕆᓂᐊᕐᑕᕐᑎᓐᓂ. ᑳᑕᑭ ᑯᖅᐃᑦ ᓯᑲ ᖃᐃᑕᐅᓪᓗᓂ. ᓂᕆᐊᓪᓚᓚᐅᕐᓗᑕ, ᑐᓴᖅᑎᑕᐅᓕᓚᐅᖅᐳᒍ ᒐᕙᒪᒃᑯᓐᓂᖕᒍᖅᑐᒥᓐ. ᒐᕙᒪᑐᖅᑲᒃᑯ ᒥᓂᔅᑕᖕᒐ ᐊᖏᕐᓂᕐᓗᓂ. ᑐᓴᕐᑕ ᐊᒃᓯᐋᓗ ᖁᕕᐊᓇᕐᑐᒥᓐ ᐃᒃᐱᖕᓇᕐᓂᖅᑲᓚᐅᖅᐳᒍᑦ, ᓲᖅᓗ 'ᐳᒃᔭᓚᐅᖕᒐ, ᓱᓕᒐᓗᐊᖅᒪᖔ?' ᑕᐃᒪᓐᓇ ᐃᒃᐱᒍᓯᒃᑎᕆᓚᐅᖅᐳᒍᑦ. ᑭᓯᐊᓂᓕ ᖁᕕᐊᓯᖕᓂᖅᐳᑦ ᓴᖅᑭᑦᑐᐊᖅᑕᐃᓕᓚᐅᖅᐸᒋᑦ ᓲᖅᑲᐃᒻᒪ ᓱᓕ ᐱᓕᕆᐊᒃᓴᖅᑲᓚᐅᖅᑕ ᐱᓇᓱᖕᓂᕐᒥ ᐊᖕᒋᕈᑎᒦᑦᑐᒃᓴᓂᑦ ᖃᓄᐃᑦᑐᑐᐃᓐᓇᓂᑦ.*

ᔫᓐ ᒥᐊᕆᑦ
ᒪᓕᒐᓕᕆᔨ ᐃᓄᖕᓄ ᐋᔩᖅᑎᓂ ᑭᒡᒐᖅᑐᐃᔨ ᓄᓇᑖᖅᓯᕐᓂᕐᒧᓐ ᐊᒻᒪᓗ ᒪᓕᒐᖅᔭᐊᓕᕆᓂᕐᒧᓐ, 1979-1984 ᐊᒻᒪ 1989-1993

Nortext ᓄᑎᑦ

Left: Bob Kadlun, in hat, and Donat Milortuk
ᓴᐅᒥᐃᓂ: ᐹᑉ ᑲᓪᓗᓐ, ᓇᓴᖅᓯᒪᔪᖅ ᐊᒻᒪ ᑐᓇᑦ ᒥᓗᖅᑐᒃᓃ

Towards a Nunavut territory

Before division in 1999, the NWT stretched across one-third of Canada's land mass and comprised two main regions — the partly forested Mackenzie Valley in the west, with an ethnically mixed population of Dene, Métis, Inuit and non-aboriginal people; and the almost treeless east, where 85 per cent of residents are Inuit.

Gold was discovered in the west, then petroleum. Even 40 years ago, some residents were advocating division of the NWT so as to let the west progress. In 1963, the Diefenbaker federal government almost passed legislation for division, but the matter died after an electoral defeat. In 1966, the Carrothers Commission, a federal commission that had been formed to study the question, recommended against division. It felt the split would have unfairly manoeuvred "the indigenous peoples of the North out of participation in self-government."

ᓄᓇᕗᑦ ᑎᑭᑉᐸᓪᓕᐊᓪᓗᒍ

ᐊᕕᖕᓂᓪᓚᖓᒃ ᐊᑐᓚᐅᖅᑎᓐᓇᒍ 1999-ᒥ, ᓄᓇᑦᓯᐊᖅ ᑲᓇᑕᐅᑉ ᐅᑭᐅᖅᑕᖅᑐᖕᒑᓂ ᐱᖕᒐᓲᓕᖅᑲᖕᒐᓗᓂ ᐊᑕᐅᓯᖅ ᓄᓇᑦᓯᐊᖑᖃᔭᖅᑐᖅ ᐊᒻᒪᓗ ᑖᓇ ᒪᖐᐃᖕᒍᖅᑎᓯᒪᓪᓗᓂ ᐃᒻᒥᒃᑰᖅᑐᓂ ᐊᕕᒃᓯᒪᓂᒃᑯᑦ – ᓈᑉᐹᖅᑐᖅᑲᐅᖅᑐᖅ ᒪᒃᑳᓃ ᐹᓕ ᐱᖕᒐᕐᓇᖅᒦᑦᑐᖅ ᐊᒻᒪᓗ ᐃᓄᖅᑲᐅᖅᓱᓂ ᐊᓪᓚᓂᑦ ᐃᓕᖅᑯᓯᖅᑲᑎᕆᖕᖏᑦᑐᓂ ᐊᒻᒪ ᐊᓪᓚᖕᒐᔪᓂ, ᐃᓄᖕᓂ ᐅᑭᐅᖅᑕᖅᑐᖅᒦᑦᑐᓂ ᐊᒻᒪᓗ ᓄᓇᖅᑲᖅᑰᖅᑯᓂᖕᖏᑦᑐᓂᑦ; ᐊᒻᒪᓗ ᑲᓇᖕᓇᖅ ᑕᒪᓇᓂ ᓈᑉᐹᖅᑐᖅᑲᔫᖕᖏᑦᑐᖅ, ᐊᒻᒪᓗ 85 ᐳᓴᓐᑦ ᐃᓅᓪᓚᕆᐅᓪᓗᑎᒃ.

ᔫᓗᒥ ᐱᖕᒐᖕᓇᒥᓐ ᓇᓂᓯᔭᖅᑲᓚᐅᖅᓯᒪᒐᖅ, ᐊᒻᒪ ᑭᖑᓂᐊᒍᑦ ᐅᖅᓯᐊᓗᒃᓴᒥᓐ. ᐊᕐᕌᒍᑦ 40 ᓯᒐᓂᑦᑎᓐᓂ, ᐃᓚᖏ ᓄᓇᖅᑲᖅᑐᑦ ᐊᕕᖕᓂᕐᒥᓐ ᐃᓱᒪᒋᔭᖅᑲᖅᑲᑦᑕᓕᓚᐅᖅᓯᒪᒐᓪ ᓄᓇᑦᓯᐊᕐᒥ ᑕᒪᓐᓇ ᐱᖕᒐᖕᓇᖅ ᐱᕙᓪᓕᐊᔪᓐᓇᕐᓂᐊᕐᒪᓐ. 1963-ᒥ ᑏᕝᐸᐃᑯ ᒐᕙᒪᖓ ᐊᓂᒍᐃᑎᑦᑎᑲᓴᑦᑎᐊᓚᐅᖅᓯᒪᒐᑦ ᐊᕕᖕᓂᕐᒥᓐ, ᑭᓯᐊᓂᓕ ᑕᒪᓐᓇ ᓄᖅᑲᐅᔾᔭᐅᓕᓚᐅᖅᓯᒪᔪᖅ ᓵᓚᐅᖕᒪᑕ ᓂᕈᐊᕐᓂᒃᑯ. 1966-ᒥ, ᑯᕌᑐ'ᔅ ᑲᐅᒥᔅᓂᓴᖕᒐ, ᒐᕙᒪᑐᖅᑲᒃᑯᑦ ᖃᐅᒥᔅᓯᑕᐅᑎᑕᖕᒐ ᖃᐅᒥᒐᔅᓗᑎ ᑖᔅᓱᒥᖕᒐ ᐊᐱᖅᑯᑎᒥᓐ, ᐃᓱᒪᒋᔭᐅᔪᖅ ᐊᕕᖕᓂᐅᔪᒥᓐ. ᐃᓱᒪᒋᔭᐅᓚᐅᖅᐳᖅᓕ ᑕᒪᓐᓇ ᐊᕕᖕᓂᐅᔪᖅ ᐃᓚᐃᓐᓇᖅᓯᐅᖅᓂᐊᖅᓯᒋᔭᐅᓪᓗᓂ "ᓄᓇᖅᑲᖅᑳᖅᑐᑦ ᐅᑭᐅᖅᑕᖅᑐᒥ ᓇᖕᒥᓂᖅ ᒐᕙᒪᖅᑲᖅᓂᖅᒧᓐ ᐃᓚᐅᖕᒋᑐᐃᓐᓇᕆᐊᖅᑲᖅᓴᐅᓪᓗᑎᒃ."

ᑲᑎᒪᔩᑦ ᓄᓇᑦᓯᐊᕐᒧᓐ, ᐃᖅᑲᓇᐃᔭᖅᑏ ᒐᕙᒪᑐᖅᑲᒃᑯᓐ ᐋᑐᕚᒥ, ᐃᓚᑖᖅᐸᓪᓕᐊᓕᓚᐅᖅᐳᑦ ᐊᓪᓚᓂᑦ, ᐊᓪᓚᖕᒐᔪᓂᑦ ᐊᒻᒪ ᐃᓄᖕᓂ, ᐱᖅᑲᓯᐅᑎᓪᓗᑎᒃ ᐊᐃᑉ ᐅᒃᐱᒃᒥ ᐊᒻᒪ ᓴᐃᒨᓂ

> *ᐊᑕᐅᓯᖅ ᐊᐱᖅᑯᑕᐅᓚᐅᖅᐳᖅ ᒐᕙᒪᓕᕆᔨᒥᓐ ᓄᓇᕗᑦ ᓯᕗᓂᒃᓴᖓᑕ ᒥᒃᓵᓄ. ᐊᒻᒪ ᐃᓱᒪᓕᕐᓗᑎᒃ ᑖᔅᓱᒪᖓ ᓄᓇᑖᖅᓯᓂᐅᔪᖅ ᐊᐅᓚᔾᔭᓚᐅᓇᐊᒃᓴᖕᒐᓂ. ᑭᓯᐊᓂᓕ ᑕᒪᓐᓇ ᐅᖅᑲᓪᓚᖕᓂᐅᔪᖅ ᑐᓵᓐᓇᖕᒋᑦᑐᒥᓐ ᐅᖅᑲᐅᓯᐅᓚᐅᖅᓯᒪᓐ... ᑭᖑᓪᓕᖅᐹᖕᒐᓂ ᐊᖕᒋᕈᓯᐅᖃᓯᒃᑎᓪᓗᒋᑦ.*

ᕌᔅ ᒪᒃᑭᓐᓇᓐ
ᐋᔩᖅᑎᓄᑦ ᓄᓇᑦᓯᐊᑉ ᒐᕙᒪᒃᑯᖏᓐᓄᑦ ᑭᒡᒐᖅᑐᐃᔨ ᓄᓇᑖᖅᓯᕐᓂᕐᒧᓐ, 1983-1992

Nunatsiaq News ᓄᓇᑦᓯᐊᕐᒥ ᐱᕙᓪᓕᐊᔪᑦ

ᒪᐃᑯᓪᒥᓐ 1960 ᐊᑯᓐᓂᖓᓂᑦ. 1967ᒥ, ᑲᒥᓯᓇᐅᑉ ᐊᓪᓚᕝᕕᖓ ᓄᓇᑦᓯᐊᕐᒥ, ᑲᑎᒪᔩᓪᓗ ᓅᑎᓪᓚᐅᕐᓯᒪᕗᑦ ᔭᓗᓇᐃᕝᒧᓐ, ᐊᒻᒪᓗ 1975 ᑎᑭᑦᓱᒍ, ᑲᑎᒪᔩ ᓂᕈᐊᕐᑕᐅᓂᒃᑯ ᒪᓕᒐᓕᐅᕐᑎᐅᓕᓚᐅᕐᓯᒪᕗᑦ. 1980ᒥ, ᑲᓇᑕᐅᑉ ᐊᖓᔪᖅᑳᖅᑯᖓ ᐱᐅᕐ ᑐᕈᑑ ᑭᒡᒐᕐᑐᐃᔨᖓ, ᓯ. ᐊᒻ. ᑐᕈᕆ (C.M. Drury), ᓴᖅᑭᑦᑎᓕᓚᐅᕐᓯᒪᕗᖅ ᑲᑎᒪᔨᕋᓃᓂ ᓴᖅᑭᑦᑐᖅᑲᖁᔨᓪᓗᓂ ᑕᒪᑐᒥᖓ, ᐊᕕᖓᓂᕐᒥ ᖃᐅᔨᓴᕐᓂᐊᕐᑐᓂᑦ. ᑖᒃᑯᐊᓕ ᑲᑎᒪᔨᕋᓛᑦ ᐊᕕᖓᓂᕐᒥ ᐃᓯᒪᒋᔭᖃᓕᓚᐅᕐᓯᒪᕗᑦ, ᓂᕈᐊᕐᓂᕐᒥᓐ ᓴᖅᑭᑦᑐᖃᓚᐅᕐᑎᓪᓗᒍ ᓄᓇᖃᕐᑐᑦ ᐃᓚᐅᓪᓗᑎᒃ.

ᐃᐳᕆ 1982ᒥ, ᓄᓇᑦᓯᐊᓕᒫᒥ ᓂᕈᐊᕐᓂᖅᑕᖃᓚᐅᕐᐳᖅ "ᐊᖏᕐᑐ" ᐊᒥᓲᓂᕐᓴᐅᒪᓇᒃᑯᑎᒃ; ᐊᒻᒪ ᓅᕕᐱᓇ ᑕᕝᕙᓂ ᐊᕐᖒᑦᑕᐃᓐᓇᕐᒥ, ᑲᓇᑕᐅᑉ ᒐᕙᒪᖏ ᑐᓴᕐᑎᑦᑎᓕᓚᐅᕐᐳᑦ ᐊᖏᕐᓂᕐᒥᖕᓂ ᓄᓇᕗᑦ ᓴᖅᑭᑦᑐᕐᓴᐅᓂᖓᓂ, ᑭᓯᐊᓂ ᓂᕈᐊᕐᓂᕐᑕᖃᓚᐅᕐᑎᓪᓗᒍ ᐊᒻᒪᓗ ᐊᓯᖏᓐᓂ ᐱᕐᑯᔭᐅᔪᓂ ᐊᑐᕐᓂᐊᕈᑎᒃ. ᑭᖑᓂᑦᑎᐊᖓᒍ, ᑲᓇᖕᓇᕐᒧ ᑭᒡᒐᕐᑐᐃᔨᒥ ᐱᕆᐊᕐᑐᖃᓚᐅᕐᓯᒪᕗᑦ ᓄᓇᑦᓯᐊᕐᒧᑦ, ᐊᒻᒪᓗ ᑭᒡᒐᕐᑐᐃᔨᖃᓕᕐᓗᑎᒃ ᓯᕗᓪᓕᖅᐹᒥᓐ ᐃᓅᓪᓚᖑᒥ ᒪᓕᒐᓕᐅᕐᑎᒥᓐ, ᐲᑕ ᐃᑎᓐᓄᐊᕐ.

ᒐᕙᒪᒃᑯ ᓄᓇᑦᓯᐊᕐᒧ ᓴᖅᑭᑦᑎᓚᐅᕐᐳᑦ ᒪᓕᒐᕐᔪᐊᖅᒨᕐᑐᒃᓴᒥᓐ ᑕᐃᔭᐅᔪᖅ Constitutional Alliance, ᐊᒻᒪ ᒪᕐᕈᐃᓂ ᖃᐅᔨᓴᕐᑎᓂ ᓴᖅᑭᑦᑐᖃᓇᓪᓗᓂ: ᐱᖓᖓᓇᕐᒥ ᒪᓕᒐᓕᕆᔩᒃᓴᑦ ᐊᒻᒪᓗ ᓄᓇᕗᒻᒧ ᒪᓕᒐᓕᕆᔩᒃᓴᑦ. ᐊᕐᖒᒍᓚᓵᓗᐃᑦ ᐊᑐᕐᑕᐅᓚᐅᕐᐳᑦ ᖃᐅᔨᓴᕐᓂᕐᒧᓐ, ᒐᕙᒪᑐᖅᑲᒃᑯ ᒪᓕᒐᓕᕆᓂᒐᓗᐊᕐᑎᓪᓗᒋᑦ ᐊᒻᒪ ᐅᑭᐅᕐᑕᖅᑐᕐᒥ ᓄᓇᑖᕐᓯᒃᑲᓗᐊᕐᑎᓪᓗᒋᑦ. 1984ᒥ, ᐱᓃᕕᐊᓗᐱᑦ ᒪᑲᓃ ᑎᐊᑕᒥ, ᑖᒃᑯᐊᑦᑕᐅᖅ ᐃᒻᒥᒃᑯ ᓄᓇᑕᕐᓯᒃᑎᓪᓗᒋ, ᐊᑎᓕᐅᓚᐅᕐᓯᒪᕗᑦ ᐊᖏᕈᑎᒥᓐ ᑲᓇᖕᓇᕐᒥᐅᑦ ᐃᓄᖏᓐᓂ ᐃᓅᖃᑎᒌᖓᓂᖏᓐᓄᑦ, ᐊᒻᒪᓗ ᐊᕕᒃᕕᐅᓚᔪᕐᑐᒥᓐ ᐱᑖᓇᓚᓯᒃᑕᖏᓐᓂᑦ. 1987ᒥ, ᑖᒃᑯᐊ ᒪᕐᕉᒃ ᐱᓕᕆᔩ ᐊᖏᕈᑎᒥᓐ ᐊᑎᓕᐅᓚᐅᕐᐳᑦ ᐊᕕᒃᕕᐅᓚᔪᕐᑐᒥᓐ ᓄᓇᕗᒻᒥ ᐊᒻᒪ ᐱᖓᖓᓇᕐᒥ ᓄᓇᑦᓯᐊᕐᒥ (ᐊᒻᒪᓗ ᐊᑎᕐᒥ ᐅᕐᑲᐅᖏᓐᓂᖏᓐᓂᑦ, ᑖᒃᑯᐊ ᓯᓕ ᓇᓗᓇᐃᕐᑕᐅᕙᒃᐳᑦ ᓄᓇᑦᓯᐊᕐᒥᓐ).

The Council of the NWT, originally a small group of federal officials based in Ottawa, began to acquire Indian, Métis and Inuit members, including Abe Okpik and Simeonie Michael in the mid-1960s. In 1967, the office of the Commissioner of the NWT, with the Council, moved to Yellowknife, and by 1975, the Council was a fully elected legislative assembly. In 1980, Prime Minister Pierre Trudeau's special representative, C.M. Drury, proposed a special committee of the assembly to study the matter of dividing the NWT. The resulting Unity Committee recommended division, subject to a plebiscite involving the inhabitants.

In April 1982, a territory-wide plebiscite on division yielded a resounding "yes"; on Nov. 26 of the same year, the Canadian government announced its assent to the creation of Nunavut, provided a plebiscite was held and other conditions met. Shortly after, the new eastern federal riding of Nunatsiaq was created, soon represented by Canada's first Inuk MP, Peter Ittinuar.

Nunatsiaq News ᓄᓇᑦᓯᐊᕐᒥ ᐱᕙᓪᓕᐊᔪᑦ

The government of the NWT formed a Constitutional Alliance, and two study groups emerged: a Western Constitutional Forum and a Nunavut Constitutional Forum. Several years were spent on studies, in light of federal constitutional matters and

> *All the parties should be sitting on the same side of the table when implementing the agreement. Parties still tend to sit on opposite sides of the table with suspicions of interpretations.*
>
> **Jose Kusugak**
> **President of Nunavut Tunngavik Incorporated**
> **(established in 1993 to ensure promises made in the Nunavut Land Claims Agreement are carried out)**

Above: The numbers said it as Meeka Kilabuk added votes, and the jubilant faces of Pauloosie Keyootak, Simatuk Michael and Dennis Patterson said it as voters agreed on a boundary to divide the NWT, May 4, 1992. The headline, far top right, across the front page of the Nov. 13, 1992 issue of Nunatsiaq News *said it once more: "The answer is Yes." The Inuit of Nunavut had ratified the land claim agreement*

ᖁᓛᓂ: ᓇᐃᓴᐅᑏ ᓇᓗᓇᐃᕐᓯᓚᐅᕐᐳᑦ ᒦᑲ ᕿᓚᐸᒃ ᑲᑎᕐᓯᐃᑦᓱᓂ ᓂᕈᐊᕈᑕᐅᔪᓂᑦ, ᖁᕕᐊᓱᒻᒪᓇᒃᑐᑦ ᐸᐅᓗᓯ ᕿᔪᒃᑖᖅ, ᓯᐃᒪᑕᖅ ᒪᐃᑯᓪ ᐊᒻᒪ ᑕᓂᔅ ᐹᑐᓴᓐ ᓇᓗᓇᐃᕈᑕᐅᖁᖅ ᓂᕈᐊᕐᑐᑦ ᐊᖏᕐᓂᖏᖕᓄ ᐊᕕᖓᓂᐅᓂᐊᕐᑐᒥᓐ ᓄᓇᑦᓯᐊᕐᒥ, ᒪᐃ 4, 1992. ᐅᓂᒃᑲᐅᓯᐅᑉ ᓇᓗᓇᐃᕈᑎᖓ, ᖁᓛᓂ ᑕᓕᕝᕙᓂ, ᓅᕕᐱᓇ 13, 1992ᒥ ᓄᓇᑦᓯᐊᕐᒥ ᐱᕙᓪᓕᐊᔪᑦ ᐅᖃᐅᓯᖃᒃᑲᓂᕐᐳᑦ ᑕᒪᑐᒥᖓ: "ᐊᓕᐊᓇᐃᑦᑐᖅ" ᐃᓄᐃᑦ ᓄᓇᕗᒻᒥ ᐱᒻᒪᕆᐅᕐᑎᕐᑎᕗᑦ ᓄᓇᑖᕐᓯᓃᑎᐅᑉ ᐊᖏᕈᑎᖓᓂᑦ

northern land claims. In 1984, the Inuvialuit of the Mackenzie Delta, who had been pursuing their own claim, signed an agreement with the Inuit of the east concerning the relationship between them, and the boundary of their respective land claim areas. In 1987, the two forums signed an agreement on the boundary between Nunavut and a western territory (until a decision on a new name is made, the latter still goes by the name "Northwest Territories").

In a quiet moment devoid of fanfare, in an office tower high above a plush downtown Ottawa hotel, the Nunavut political accord that would lead to Canada's newest territory was initialled by John Amagoalik of TFN, the chief negotiator for Inuit; Jack Stagg, the federal chief negotiator; and Liz Snider, the NWT chief negotiator. The plebiscite would determine whether residents of the NWT agreed.

In a May 1992 plebiscite, a majority of NWT residents endorsed a divisional boundary. The accord was signed on Oct. 30, 1992 by ministers of the federal and territorial governments and the president of TFN. Parliament subsequently gave its assent to the *Nunavut Act*, calling for the creation of Nunavut by April 1, 1999.

ᓂᐱᖃᖕᕿᐅᔾᔪᕐᑐᒥᓐ, ᐊᓪᓚᕝᕕᖕᒥ ᐃᒡᓗᐊᓗᖕᒥ ᐋᑐᕚ ᑐᔪᕐᒥᕝᕕᖕᖔᑦᑕ ᐃᓚᖓᓂ, ᓄᓇᕗᑦ ᒪᓕᒐᓕᕆᓂᕐᒧ ᐃᓚᓕᐅᔾᔨᐅᓂᖓᓂ ᑕᒪᓐᓇ ᐱᕆᐊᕈᑎᒻᒪᕆᐅᑦᑐᓂ ᑲᓇᑕᐅᑉ ᓄᑖᖑᒍᖅ ᐃᒥᒃᑰᕐᑐᖅ ᐊᕝᕚᒪᓂᒃᑯ ᐊᑎᓕᐅᕐᑕᐅᓕᓚᐅᕐᔪᖅ ᔮᓐ ᐊᒪᑯᐊᓕᖕᒧᓐ ᑐᓐᖓᕕᒃᑯᓐᓂᖕᖏᕐᓗᓂ, ᐋᕆᐅᕐᑎᓪᓚᒃ ᐃᓄᖕᓄᑦ; ᔮᒃ ᓴᑖᒃ, ᒐᕙᒪᑐᖃᒃᑯ ᐋᕆᐅᕐᑎᖕᖓ; ᐊᒻᒪᓗ ᓕᔅ ᓯᓇᐃᑐ, ᓄᓇᕐᓯᐊᑉ ᐋᕆᐅᕐᑎᖕᖓ. ᓂᕈᐊᕐᓂᖅᓯ ᖃᐅᔨᔪᕐᑕᐅᓕᓚᐅᕐᓗᓂ ᓄᓇᕐᓯᐊᕐᒥᐅᑦ ᐊᖏᕋᓗᐊᓇᐊᒃᓴᖕᖏᓐᓂᑦ.

ᒪᐃ 1992 ᓂᕈᐊᕐᓂᒃᑯ, ᐅᓄᕐᓂᖅᓴᐃᑦ ᓄᓇᕐᓯᐊᕐᒥ ᐊᕕᖕᓂᐅᓂᐊᕐᑐᒥᓐ ᐊᖏᓚᐅᕐᓯᒪᔪᑦ. ᐊᖏᕈᑎ ᐊᑎᓕᐅᕐᑕᐅᓪᓗᓂ ᐅᒃᑐ 30, 1992ᒥ ᒥᓂᔅᑕᓄᑦ ᒐᕙᒪᑐᖃᒃᑯᓐᓄ ᐊᒻᒪᓗ ᓄᓇᕐᓯᐊᕐᒧᓐ ᐊᒻᒪᓗ ᐊᖓᔪᖅᑳᕐᒧᓐ ᑐᓐᖓᕕᒃᑯᓐᓄᑦ. ᒪᓕᒐᓕᐅᕕᐊᓗ ᐊᖏᓕᓪᓕᐅᕐᓯᒪᔪᑦ ᓄᓇᕗ ᒪᓕᒐᖓᓂᑦ, ᑕᒪᓐᓇ ᓴᖅᑭᑎᑦᓯᑕᐅᓕᕐᓗᓂ ᓄᓇᕗᒥᓐ ᐄᐳᕆ 1, 1999ᒥᓐ.

> “ᑲᑎᒪᔩᑦ ᑕᒪᕐᒥ ᐃᒡᓗᐊᓂ ᑮᐳ ᐃᒃᓯᕚᓐᓇᐊᖅᑐᑦ ᐋᖅᑭᒃᓯᓂᐊᓕᖁᖓᑕ ᐊᖏᕈᑎᒥᓐ. ᓯᓚ ᑕᐃᒪᐃᔾᔪᑦ ᑐᑭᓯᑎᐊᔾᔮᕐᓯᒪᓂᑉ ᐅᖃᐅᓯᐅᕙᒥᓐ.”
>
> **ᔩᓯ ᑯᓯᒐᖅ**
> **ᐃᓯᒪᑕᖅ ᓄᓇᕗᑦ ᑐᓐᖓᕕᒃ ᑎᒥᖓᓄᑦ (ᓴᖅᑭᑕᐅᓂᖓ 1993ᒥ ᑕᒪᒃᑯᐊ ᐊᖏᕈᑏ ᓴᖅᑭᑎᑕᐅᑎᐊᕐᖁᔨᐅᑦᑐᑎᒃ)**

Nunatsiaq News ᓄᓇᑦᓯᐊᕐᒥ ᐱᕐᓕᕆᐊᓯᐊᑦ

Left: Inuit negotiators Jack Kupeuna (foreground) and, behind him, Sam Omik, shake hands with well-wishers after the public signing ceremony of the Nunavut accord in Iqaluit, October 1992
ᓴᐅᒥᐊᓂ: ᐃᓄᐃᑦ ᐋᕆᐅᕐᑏ, ᔮᒃ ᑯᐱᐅᓇ (ᓯᕗᓂᐊᓂ) ᐊᒻᒪ, ᑭᖑᓂᕐᑎᐊᖓᓂ, ᓵᒻ ᐅᒥᒃ, ᑕᓯᐅᖃᑦᑳᑲᑕᒃᑐᑦ ᖁᕕᐊᓱᒃᑐᓂᑦᑕᐅᖅ ᐊᑎᓕᐅᕐᓂᖃᓚᐅᕐᑎᑦᑐᒍ ᓄᓇᕗᑦ ᒪᓕᒐᖓᓂᑦ ᐃᖃᓗᖕᓂ, ᐆᒃᑐ 1992

Nick Newbery

ᐃᓄᐃᑦ ᓇᓂᓯᓚᐅᕐᐳᑦ ᓯᕗᓕᐅᕐᑎᓂ ᓴᖅᑭᑎᔨᓐᓇᕐᑐᓂᑦ

ᐊᕐᕌᒍᑦ 100 ᐃᓗᐊᓂ, ᐃᓄᐃᑦ ᓯᑰᒃᑲᒥᙵ ᐊᑯᑭᑦᑐᓄᑦ ᐊᓯᖑᐃᓂᕐᒥ ᖃᐅᔨᓯᒪᕗᑦ ᐊᒻᒪᓗ ᑕᒪᓐᓇ ᐱᕙᓪᓕᐊᑎᑦᑎᔾᔪᑕᐅᒃᑐᓂᑦ ᐊᑐᕐᑕᐅᓚᕿᓕᐅᕐᑐᖅ ᐊᕐᕌᒍᓂ 5000ᓂ. ᐅᓇ ᐊᓯᖑᐃᓂᖅ ᐅᖁᒪᐃᒃᓴᕈᑕᐅᓯᒪᕗᖅ ᐃᓄᖕᓂ, ᐃᒻᒥᒃᑯᕐᓂᒃᑯ ᐊᑕᐅᑦᑎᒃᑯᓪᓗᓐᓇᓪᓚᑦ, ᑭᓯᐊᓂᓪᓕ ᐊᔪᕆᓐᓕᕆᑕᐅᓯᒪᔪᑦ ᐊᖑᓇᓱᖕᓂᒃᑯ ᐊᔪᙱᔾᔨᑕᐅᒪᓇᓕᐅᕐᐳᖅ ᐊᓯᖑᕐᐸᓪᓕᐊᔪᒥᙵ ᐃᓪᓕᐅᑎᔨᓐᓇᕐᓂᕐᒥᙵ ᓄᓇᖅᔪᐊᒥᙵ.

ᐃᓄᐃᑦ ᑲᑎᖅᑲᑎᕆᓯᒪᕗᑦ ᓄᓇᕐᔪᐊᒥ ᐃᓄᐃᑦ ᑲᑎᒪᓂᖏᑦᑎᒍᑦ, ᑕᐱᕇᒃᓴᑯᑎᒍᑦ, ᐊᒻᒪᓗ ᐊᕐᓇᐃᑦ ᑲᑐᔾᔨᖃᑎᒋᖏᑦᑎᒍ, ᐸᐅᒃᑑᑎᑦ. ᐊᕕᒃᑐᕐᓯᒪᓂᒃᑯ ᐊᒻᒪᓗ ᓄᓇᓕᖕᓄ ᑐᕌᖓᔪᓂ ᑲᑐᔾᔨᖅᑲᑎᒋᖕᓂᕐᑕᖅᐅᕐᐳᖅ ᐊᔾᔨᒌᖏᑉᐳᔭᕐᑐᓂᑦ, ᐱᖃᓯᐅᑎᓪᓗᒍ ᑯᐊᐸᒃᑯᑦ ᐊᒻᒪ ᒐᕙᒪᒃᑯ. ᑖᒃᑯᓇ ᐱᓕᕆᖃᑎᒌᖕᓂᒃᑯ ᐃᒻᒪ ᐃᓚᓯᓐᓂᖅᑳᕐᑕᐅᑎᓂᒃᑯ, ᐃᓄᐃᑦ ᑲᓇᑕᒥᐅᑦᑕᑦ ᐋᖅᑭᕐᓂᒃᑯ ᑎᓴᒪᓂ ᓄᓇᑖᕈᓯᕐᓂ ᐱᓯᒪᓕᕐᐳᑦ. ᑖᓐᓇᓕ ᓄᑖᖑᓕᖅ ᐃᒻᒥᒃᑯᕐᑐᖅ ᐊᕕᒃᓯᒪᓂᒃᑯ, ᓄᓇᕗᑦ ᐊᖏᕈᑎᖓ ᐊᖏᓛᒻᒪᓇᐅᕗᖅ ᑕᒪᐃᑦᑐᓂᑦ ᓄᓇᕐᔪᐊᓕᒥᓐ.

ᐃᓄᐃᑦ ᓵᓚᖃᓕᐅᕐᓯᒪᕗᑦ 1976ᒥ ᓄᓇᑖᕈᓯᑎᐅᓚᐅᖅᐊᕐᒥ ᓴᖅᑭᑎᖖᓚᖕᖑᑎᒃ ᓄᑖᖑᓇᐊᕐᓯᒪᔪᒥ ᓄᓇᑖᕈᓯᑎᒥ ᓴᖅᑮᔭᕐᑎᑦᑎᓂᖅᓴᒥᙵ ᐃᓄᐃᑦ ᐃᓕᖅᑯᓯᖏᓐᓂ. ᑕᒪᓐᓇ ᑕᐅᑐᒃᑯᒍ ᐊᔾᔨᒌᖏᓗᐊᓚᐅᕐᓯᒪᖕᒪᑕ ᐱᓕᕆᔨᐃᑦ ᑕᐃᒪᓕ ᑕᒪᓐᓇ ᓵᓚᒋᔭᐅᑐᐃᓐᓇᓕᓚᐅᕐᓯᒪᕗᖅ. ᓄᓇᑖᕈᓯᖕᓂᕐᔪᓐᓇ ᐊᒻᒪᓗ ᓄᑖᒥ ᐃᒻᒥᒃᑰᕐᑐᒥ ᓄᓇᒥ ᓴᖅᑭᑎᓇᓯᖕᓂᐅᔨᖅ ᓴᖅᑭᑎᓕᓚᐅᕐᐳᖅ ᓚᕿᒪᓕᕆᓂᐅᔨᒥᙵ, ᖁᓇᐅᔭᕐᑐᔨᓕᕆᓂᕐᒥᙵ ᐊᒻᒪ ᐃᖅᑲᖅᑐᐃᕕᓕᕆᓂᕐᒥᙵ.

ᐃᓄᐃᑦ ᐱᓕᕆᔾᔨᑎᖕᒐ ᓵᒃᓴᓕᓚᐅᕐᐳᖅ ᑭᖑᓂᐊᒍᑦ, ᑭᓯᐊᓂᓕ, ᐋᖓᔮᖅᑲᑎᒌᒍᑖᖕᓂᕐᑕᖅᑯᓐᓂ ᑲᑎᒪᕕᖕᓂ ᐊᒻᒪ ᓯᓚᑖᓂᑦ. ᐃᓄᐃᑦ ᐋᖓᔮᖅᑎᖕᒥ ᐃᓅᖅᑲᑎᒥ ᐃᓯᒪᑭᔭᖅᑎᑦᑎᐊᖕᒋᓇᓚᐅᕐᐳᑦ, ᓂᕆᐊᕐᓂᓴᐅᑦᓗᑎ ᑐᑭᓯᐅᒪᓂᕐᒥᙵ ᒪᑯᓇᖕᒐ ᐱᐅᖁᔮᔾᔨᑎᓂ ᐊᒻᒪ ᑭᐅᒻᒪᓂᑦᑎᐊᕈᓐᓇᕐᓂᕐᒥᙵ. ᑕᒪᐅᓇ, ᐋᖓᔮᖅᑎᒌᖕᓂᖅ ᐱᓕᕆᐊᖅᑎᒌᖕᓂᕐᒥ ᓴᖅᑭᑎᓚᐅᕐᐳᖅ ᐋᖅᑭᒃᓯᐃᕙᓪᓕᐊᓂᒃᑯ ᐱᓗᐊᕐᑐᒥ ᐊᕙᑎᓕᓐᓂᕐᒥ ᐊᐅᓚᑦᑎᓂᕐᒥ.

ᐊᒥᓯᕈᖅᓴᐅᕙᒃᑲᓗᐊᕐᑎᓪᓗᒋ ᐱᓕᕆᖃᑎᒋ ᐊᓯᖑᕐᐸᓪᓕᐊᓂᖕᒋ ᐃᓄᐃᑦ ᓄᓇᖕᒋᓐᓂ, ᐱᓕᕆᖃᑎᒋ ᓯᕗᓕᐅᕐᑏ ᐊᒻᒪᓗ ᐱᓕᕆᐊᒥ ᐸᓇᓯᒻᒪᕆᒃᑐᑦ ᐊᑐᐃᓐᓇᓕᐅᕐᐳᑦ ᐃᓕᖁᓯᒥᙵ ᐱᔾᔨᑕᐅᒐᓱᒃᑐᒥᓪᓗ ᐊᕐᕌᒍ ᐊᒥᓱᑦ ᐊᑐᖅᓗᐊᕐᑎᓪᓗᒋ. ᒐᕙᒪᒃᑯᓪᓚ, ᒐᕙᒪᑐᖅᑲᒃᑯ ᐊᒻᒪ ᓄᓇᓯᐊᕐᒥ, ᑭᐅᖅᑳᑦᑕᓚᐅᓇᕗᑦ ᑕᐃᒪᓐᓇᑦᑕᐃᓐᓇᖅ ᐃᓄᐃᑦ ᐱᓕᕆᔾᔨᓯᖕᒋᑦᑎᑐᑦ.

ᐊᒥᓱᑦ ᐃᓄᐃᑦ ᖃᐅᔨᒪᕗᑦ ᐊᑲᐅᖕᒋᓕᐅᕆᑎᓂᑦ ᐊᐳᑎᓂᐊᕐᓂᖕᒋᓐᓂ ᓄᓇᕗᒥ — ᐱᖃᓯᐅᑎᓪᓗᒍ ᐱᕙᓪᓕᐊᓂᖅ ᐱᑕᖃᓗᐊᖕᒋᓐᓂᖕᒐ, ᓂᐅᕕᖅᐸᒐᓛᑦ ᐅᖕᒐᓯᖕᓂᖕᒋ, ᓯᓚ ᐊᑲᐅᖕᒋᓪᓚᐅᒃᐸᖕᓂᖕᒐᓂᑦ, ᐊᒻᒪᓗ ᐸᓐᓇᒃᓯᒪᓗᐊᖕᒋᑦᑐᓂᑦ ᓄᓇᖅᑐᓂᑦ.

ᑲᔪᓯᔪᖅ ᒪᒃᐱᒐᖅ 39

Inuit found the leaders to make things happen

During the past century, Inuit from Chukotka to Greenland have undergone change that took the industrial peoples of the world at least 5,000 years to make. This blizzard of change has taken a heavy toll on Inuit, individually and collectively, but some of the qualities that sustained the old hunting culture have enabled Inuit to adapt remarkably well to an invasive, unstable modern world.

Canadian Inuit have united within an Inuit Circumpolar Conference, in ITC, and the women's organization, Pauktuutit. There are regional and local organizations of many kinds, including co-operatives and governments. Under this canopy of unity and identity, the Inuit of Canada have negotiated four major land claim treaties. If the new territory is included, the Nunavut agreement is the most extensive of its kind in the world.

Those Inuit who repudiated the original 1976 claim submission envisaged a revised claim that embodied the simplicity, humanity and common sense of traditional Inuit society. Given the vast difference between the

continued on page 39

> *When I look back at it now and think that I participated — I can travel, take business risks or risks of any kind. I don't worry about it because it's a lot easier than what I was going through.*

Thomas Suluk
Chief negotiator and member of Inuit negotiating team on and off between 1979 and 1992

Top: Chief negotiator Paul Quassa and Prime Minister Brian Mulroney at the May 1993 signing ceremony in Iqaluit. Canada's largest-ever aboriginal land claim agreement calls for Inuit impact and benefit agreements on upcoming developments, the right to harvest wildlife throughout the Nunavut Settlement Area, and other provisions that give the agreement room to grow

ᖁᓛᓂ: ᐊᖓᔪᖅᑳᖅ ᐋᔩᖅᑎᓄᑦ ᐹᓪ ᖁᐊᓴ ᐊᒻᒪ ᑲᓇᑕᐅᑉ ᐊᖓᔪᖅᑳᖓ ᐳᕋᐃᐊᓐ ᒪᕈᓂ ᒪᐃ 1993ᒥ ᐊᑎᓕᐅᕐᓂᐅᔪᒥ ᐃᖃᓗᖕᓂ. ᑲᓇᑕᐅᑉ ᐊᖏᓂᕐᐹᖓ ᓄᓇᖃᖅᑳᖅᑐᑦ ᓄᓇᑖᕈᓯᖓᓄᑦ ᐊᖏᕈᑎ ᐱᔪᑎᓕ ᐃᓄᖕᓄ ᐊᒻᒪ ᖃᓄᐃᓕᖓᓂᐊᕐᑕᖏᖕᓄ, ᐱᕙᓪᓕᐊᓂᕐᒧᑦ, ᐱᔪᓇᐅᑎ ᐊᐅᓚᑦᑎᓂᕐᒥ ᓄᓇᕗᑦᑖᕈᓯᐅᔪᒥ, ᐊᒻᒪᓗ ᐊᓯᖏᓐᓂ ᐱᕕᖃᖅᑳᕐᓂ ᐱᒋᐅᕐᐸᓪᓕᐊᓂᕐᒧᑦ ᑕᕝᕙ

> *ᑭᖑᒧᒻᒧ ᑕᒪᓐᓇ ᐃᓱᒪᒋᓕᖅᖓᒃᑯ ᐃᓚᐅᓂᓇᓚᐅᕐᑕᖅ — ᓄᑦᑕᕈᓐᓇᕐᐳᖓ, ᐱᓕᕆᐊᓂᓪᓗ ᐱᓯᓂᓯᐅᔨᓂ ᐱᓕᕆᐊᓐᓇᕐᐸᖕᖓ. ᐃᓱᒫᓗᑎᒋᖅᑕᕐᑕᖏᓚᖅ ᓱᖅᑯᐃᒻᒪ ᐊᔪᕐᓇᖏᓐᓂᖅᓴᐅᓕᕐᑐ ᑕᐃᓯᒪᓂᐅᓚᐅᕐᑐᒥ.*

ᑖᒪᔅ ᓱᓗᒃ
ᐋᔩᖅᑎᓄᑦ ᐊᖓᔪᖅᑳᖅ ᐃᓚᒋᔭᐅᑦᑐᓂᓗ ᐃᓄᖕᓂ ᐋᔩᖅᑎᓐ ᐃᓚᐅᓕᖅᐸᒃᓱᓂ ᐃᓚᐅᔪᓐᓃᖅᐸᒃᓱᓂ 1979ᒧ 1992ᒧ ᐊᑯᓐᓂᖓᓂ

The Next Generation
ᑭᖑᕚᒃᓴᓇᔭᕗᑦ

Nunatsiaq News

By Jimi Onalik

In my mind's eye, I can imagine those hectic and crazy days when the negotiations began. I like to picture smoky community halls, hot from body heat, filled with passionate debate and confusion — children running around as a group of young leaders work towards rallying their community in support of new ideas. Ideas that they felt would deal with the vast problems facing the people of Nunavut. Ideas that would provide hope at a time when it was quickly fading.

This is how I like to picture it. I was born almost four years after negotiations for Nunavut began, so I do not really know if this is how it was. But it is painfully clear where we are today.

As clocks across Nunavut struck midnight on March 31, 1999, a couple of things happened. One was the widespread celebration to mark the major accomplishment of the creation of the government of Nunavut. A quarter-century of work is about to finally bear fruit, and we will finally have the government we have been working towards for so long.

Another much more quiet event came in the form of a question collectively whispered by young people in Nunavut. "What does this all mean?"

At a time when the youth of Nunavut are hurting and cynical, we are all wondering how this new government will act as a vehicle for change. Will our friends and family members stop committing suicide? Will we have jobs? Will our children have better futures?

These are crucial questions, with life-and-death answers. If the creation of the government of Nunavut does not help us answer "yes" to these questions, then it was not worth pursuing. We cannot afford to waste time on a political exercise.

But on April 1, 1999, amidst the self-congratulatory speeches, and the pomp and circumstance, there will be a hidden challenge to a new generation of leadership. A generation that brought us the structure and framework of a democracy will say: "This is our legacy. This is what we present to you. What will you do with it? What will you make it become?"

Today, as the generation that brought us the Nunavut government approaches retirement and, too often, removal from power, there is enormous pressure on the youth of

Arthur Boutilier

ᑎᑎᕋᖅᑐᖅ ᔩᒥ ᐅᓇᓕᒃ

ᐃᓱᒪᒋᔭᓐᓂ ᑕᐅᑐᓐᖑᒍ ᐊᕐᓗᒍ, ᐊᖏᖃᑎᒌᒐᓯᐊᕐᓂᐅᑉ ᓄᓇᕗᑖᕐᓂᕐᒥᒃ ᐱᒋᐊᕐᕕᒋᓚᐅᖅᑕᖓ ᖃᓄᐃᓚᐅᕐᓂᖓ ᐃᓱᒪᒋᔫᖑᔪᕐ ᐃᒪᐃᓐᓇᓯᒋᓚᐅᕐᓗᒍ, ᐃᓄᒋᐊᒃᑐᑦ ᑲᑎᒪᑎᓪᓗᒋᑦ ᐱᕐᖑᔪᐊᕐᕕᖓᓂ, ᐃᓄᒋᐊᒃᑲᒥᒃ ᐅᖅᑰᑎᓪᓗᒍ ᐊᖏᖃᑎᒌᒐᓯᐊᖅᑐᑦ ᐅᖃᖃᑎᒌᒃᑎᓪᓗᒋᑦ ᐊᒻᒪᓗ ᐃᓄᒋᐊᒃᑲᒥ ᐃᓛᖏᑦ ᓄᑕᖅᑲᑦ ᐅᐃᒪᔫᕐᓇᖅᑎᓪᓗᒋᑦ ᓇᒥᑐᐃᓐᓈᓗ ᐸᕝᕕᓐᓇᐅᓪᓗᓂ ᓯᒻᒪᓪᓕᐊᖅᑐᖅᑐᓄᑦ. ᓄᑕᖅᑲᐃᑦ ᐅᓪᓚᐅᒪᓪᓗᑎᒃ ᒪᒃᑯᖕᓂᖅᓴᐅᑎᓪᓗᒋᑦ ᓯᕗᓪᓕᖅᑎᒋᔭᐅᕙᑦ ᓄᓇᓕᖕᒥᐅᓂᒃ ᐃᑲᔪᖅᑕᐅᔪᒪᓂᕐᒥᒃ ᑐᒃᓯᕋᖅᑎᓪᓗᒋᑦ ᐃᓱᒪᒋᔭᑎᒃ ᓵᓐᖏᒍᑎᖃᒃᑯᓪᓗᒋᑦ. ᐃᓱᒪᒋᔭᐅᔪᑦ ᐋᖅᑭᒃᓯᕈᑎᒋᔭᐅᔪᒪᔪᑦ ᐃᓄᐃᑦ ᓄᓇᕗᒥᐅᑦ ᐊᔪᕐᓵᕈᑎᒋᐸᒃᑕᖏᑦ ᑲᒪᒋᔭᐅᒐᓪᓗᒋᑦ ᐅᖃᓕᒫᒋᔭᐅᓯᖅᑐᑦ. ᐃᓱᒪᒋᔭᐅᔪᑦ ᓂᕆᐅᒋᔭᐅᓪᓗᑎᒃ ᐊᑲᐅᓯᒍᑎᐅᓂᐊᕐᓂᕐᒥᒃ ᓱᓇᑐᐃᓐᓇᐃᑦ ᐃᖏᕐᕋᑎᓪᓗᒋᑦ ᖁᓪᓕᕐᓇᖅᐸᓪᓕᐊᓪᓗᑎᒃ.

ᑕᐃᒻᓇ ᑕᐅᑐᖕᖑᐊᓰᓐᓇᕙᒃᑯ ᑕᐃᒻᓇᐃᓚᐅᕋᓯᒋᓪᓗᒍ. ᐃᓅᓕᐅᖅᓯᒪᕙᕋ ᓯᑕᒪᑦ ᐊᕐᕌᒍᐃᑦ ᖄᖏᖅᓯᒪᑎᓗᒋᑦ ᐊᖏᖃᑎᒌᒍᑕᐅᓇᓯᐊᖅᑐᑦ ᐃᖏᕐᕋᑎᑕᐅᓂᖓᓂ. ᑕᐃᒻᓇ ᕿᖅᑲᐃᓪᓚ ᐱᔭᕆᑦᓯᒍᑦ ᑕᐃᒪᐃᓪᓕᓇᓕᐅᕐᓗᐊᕐᓂᖓ ᖃᐅᔨᒪᓕᓐᖏᑦᑕᕐ. ᑭᓯᐊᓂᓕ ᐅᖃᕈᓐᓇᖁᑎᐊᖅᑐᖓ ᐅᓪᓗᒥ ᖃᓄᐃᓯᒪᓕᕐᓂᖓᓂᒃ.

ᓯᕿᕐᖑᔭᐃᑦ/ᖃᐅᔨᓴᐅᑎᑦ ᖁᓛᓅᖅᑎᓪᓗᒍ ᓄᓇᕗᓕᒥ ᒫᔅᓴᐅᓕᖅᑎᓪᓗᒍ 31, 1999-ᒥ, ᒪᕐᕉᒃ ᐊᑐᓕᓚᐅᕐᐳᑦ. ᓯᕗᓪᓕᖅ ᖁᕕᐊᓱᒍᑕᐅᓂᐅᔪᖅ ᐱᒋᐊᕐᓗᓂ ᓇᓗᓇᐃᒃᑕᓇᓗᓂᐅᒃ ᐱᔭᓐᓂᖅᑕᐅᓂᖓ ᓄᓇᕗᑦ ᒐᕙᒪᒃᓴᓇᓂᐊᖅᑕᖓ. ᐊᕐᕋᒍᐃᑦ 25-ᖑᔪᑦ ᐊᒃᓯᕈᕈᑕᐅᓯᒪᓚᐅᖅᑐᑦ ᓄᐃᑎᑎᑲᔭᕐᒪᑕ ᓯᕗᓂᕐᒧᑦ ᐸᕐᓇᒍᑕᐅᓚᐅᖅᑐᓂᒃ. ᑕᐃᒪᓗ ᐊᒃᓯᕈᕈᑎᒋᓚᐅᖅᑕᑦᑎᓐᓂᒃ ᒐᕙᒪᖅᑲᓕᕐᔪᕐᓗᑕ ᑕᒪᓐᓇ ᐊᑯᓂ ᓯᓚᓇᐊᓇᔭᐅᓯᒪᑎᓪᓗᒍ.

ᐊᐃᑉᐸᖑᓪᓚᑦᑕᐅᖅ, ᓂᐱᖃᓐᖏᓐᓂᖅᓴᐅᔪᕐᓕ ᐊᑐᓚᐅᕐᐳᖅ ᐃᓱᒪᒋᔭᐅᓂᒃᑯᑦ ᐊᐱᖅᑯᓯᐅᓗᓂ. ᒪᒃᑯᑦᑐᓄᑦ ᓄᓇᕗᒥ ᑕᒻᒥᕐᓗᑎᒃ ᐊᐱᓇᓪᓚᖑᓚᔪᖓᑦ, "ᖃᓄᕐᓕ ᑕᒪᓐᓇ ᑐᑭᖃᖅᐸ?"

ᐅᓗᒥᐅᔪᖅ ᒪᒃᑯᑦᑐᐃᑦ ᐋᓐᓂᕐᓯᒪᓂᖃᖅᑎᓪᓗᒋᑦ ᐊᒻᒪᓗ ᓯᕗᓂᒃᓴᒥᒃ ᓂᓇᐅᖕᓂᖃᓗᐊᓐᖏᑎᓪᓗᒋᑦ, ᖃᓄᕐᓕ ᑕᒪᓐᓇ ᓴᕿᒪᔭᐅᓂᐊᓕᖅᑐᖅ ᐃᑲᔪᕐᓂᐊᖃ ᐊᓯᔾᔨᕈᑕᐅᓗᓂ. ᐃᒪᐃᓐᓂᐊᕐᓗᐊᖅᐸ ᐅᕙᒍᑦ ᐃᓚᒋᔭᕗᑦ ᐃᖕᒥᓃᖅᐸᓐᖏᓕᕐᔪᕐᓗᑎᒃ? ᐅᕙᒍᓪᓕ ᐃᖅᑲᓇᐃᔭᖃᓕᖕᖓᕕᑕ? ᕿᑐᕐᖓᕗᑦ ᓯᕗᓂᒃᓴᖅᑎᐊᕐᔪᕐᓗᐊᖅᐸᑦ?

Top: Looking ahead. For young adults like Baker Lake's Karen Kabloona, left, who now assume the responsibility of making a new territory and government work, the future of Nunavut is filled with personal challenges

ᖁᓛᓂ: ᓯᕗᒧᑦ ᑕᐅᑐᖕᓂᖅ. ᐃᓐᓇᕆᕐᐸᓪᓕᐊᓕᖅᑐᓄᑦ ᐆᑐᓇᖅ ᖃᒪᓂᑦᑐᐊᕐᒥᐅᑎᑐ ᑭᐅᕋ ᑲᑉᓗᓇ, ᑕᓕᖅᐱᐊᓂ, ᑲᒪᔩᑦᑐᓂᐊᓯᕗᑦ ᑕᒪᑐᒧᖓ ᓄᓇᑖᖑᔪᒧᓐ ᐃᓕᑯᕐᓂᐊᕐᓕᕐᑐᒥ ᐊᒻᒪ ᒐᕙᒪᐅᓂᐊᕐᑐᒥᓐ ᐊᑐᕐᑎᑦᑎᓂᐊᕐᓂᕐᒥ, ᓄᓇᕗᑦ ᓯᕗᓂᒃᓴᖓ ᐱᔭᒃᓴᓕᐊᖑᓂᐊᕐᐳᑦ

Nunavut. We have been promised a government staffed largely by Inuit. We have been promised a government that will better respond to the social ills of Nunavut's society. We have been promised a more creative and better government.

These promises, however, can only be fulfilled if young people in Nunavut work towards fulfilling them. If there is to be a majority of Inuit in government, it will be a majority of young Inuit. Our government of Nunavut will be a catalyst for social change only if young people are ready and willing to take a risk and embrace that change. Our government will only be creative if we foster innovation throughout our communities. Our government will only be open if young people throw off the blanket of apathy and demand to see inside it. Our government will only be ours if we are constantly laying claim to it.

This is a huge burden of responsibility that many of us are taking on grudgingly. If we are to come close to fulfilling the ideals outlined in the creation of the government, then we will need a huge amount of support from all people in Nunavut. We will need to be allowed to make mistakes, allowed to be idealistic, and most of all, allowed to be ourselves. Without this support, we will fail.

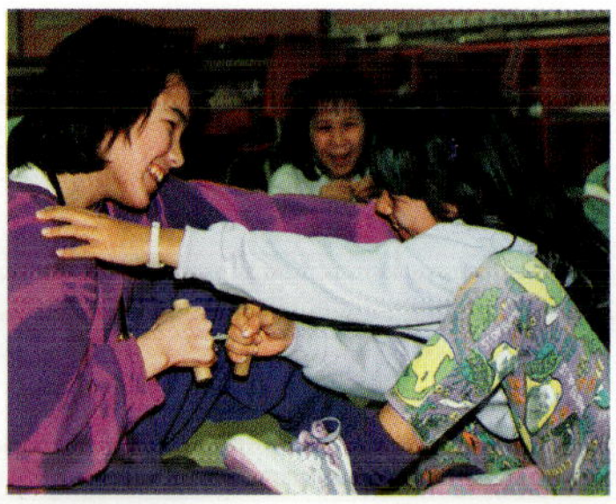
Nunatsiaq News ᓄᓇᑦᓯᐊᖅ ᐱᕙᓪᓕᐊᔪᑦ

It will be interesting to see how those of us who were playing street hockey when the early meetings took place react in the coming years. I have to believe that we, too, will be out there in community halls, getting involved in the government, holding it accountable, and bringing it closer. I have to believe that we will be gathered in living rooms and in tents on the land, seriously discussing the issues we face and finding new ideas to bring back hope at a time when hope is still fading. And for me, that hope is on the rise.

Jimi Onalik of Iqaluit works in policy development with the government of Nunavut.

ᑕᒪᒃᑯᐊ ᐊᐱᕆᔭᐅᔪᑦ ᐱᓪᓗᐊᕕᐅᔪᑦ ᐊᑐᕐᓂᖃᖅᑕᕆᒃᑐᖅ. ᑭᐅᔭᐅᓂᕐᒋᑦᓗ ᐃᓅᓯᖃᕐᓂᕐᒧᑦ ᑐᕌᓂᖃᖅᑕᕆᒃᓗᑎᒃ. ᓄᓇᕗᑦ ᒐᕙᒪᖃᕐᓂᕌᑕ ᑕᒪᑐᒥᖓ ᑭᐅᔪᓐᓂᕋᖅᐸᑕ ᐊᕐᕆᕐᓗᑎᒃ, ᓯᕗᓂᕐᒧᑦ ᓯᕗᒻᒨᑎᕆᓂᐊᕐᓗᕆᑦ ᓱᕙᓕᑭᐊᖅ ᐊᑐᕐᓂᖃᓐᖏᑦᑐᖅ. ᐱᕙᒃᓴᐅᓇᔭᖅᑐᑦ ᔭᕙᐃᔭᐅᓇᔭᖅᐸᑕ ᒐᕙᒪᓕᕆᓂᒃᑯᑦ ᐃᓚᐅᑐᐃᓐᓇᕈᓐᓇᕐᓂᓐᓇᑦᑕ.

ᑭᓯᐊᓂᓕ ᐄᑉᑭ 1, 1999-ᒥ, ᓇᒻᒥᓂᖅ ᐅᐱᒍᓱᖕᓂᕐᒧᑦ ᐅᖃᓕᐊᖅᑐᖅᓯᒪᔪᖅᑲᖅᑎᓪᓗᒋᑦ, ᐊᒻᒪᓗ ᑕᑯᓐᓇᕋᒃᓴᒃᑯᑦ ᖄᖓᒍᑦ ᑭᓯᐊᓂ ᑐᑭᖃᖅᑐᑎᒍᑦ ᐱᕕᒡᔭᐊᖅᑐᖃᖅᑎᓪᓗᒍ, ᓄᑖᒥᒃ ᓵᕐᖓᔪᐅᒥᐊᓕᖕᓂᒃ ᓴᖅᑭᖅᑐᖃᖅᓯᒪᖅᑐᖅ ᓯᕗᓕᖅᑎᐅᔪᓄᑦ ᕿᓄᐃᓵᖅᑎᐅᓇᔭᖅᑐᓂᒃ. ᑎᑭᑎᑎᓯᒪᔪᑦ ᒐᕙᒪᐃᑦ ᐋᖅᑭᒃᓯᒪᓇᔭᖅᓯᒪᓂᖏᓐᓂᒃ ᐃᒪᓐᓇ ᐅᖃᖅᓯᒪᖅᑐᓂᒃ: "ᑖᓐᓇᕙ ᑕᒪᓐᓇ ᐃᖅᑲᐅᒪᔾᔪᑕᐅᒍᑎᒃᓴᖑᑦ. ᑕᒪᑐᒥᖓ ᐃᓕᑦᓯᓐᓄᑦ ᑐᓂᕐᕿᓯᖅᓯᒪᒐᓗᑦ. ᖃᓄᐃᓐᓂᐊᖅᐱᓯᓕ ᑖᓐᓇᕙ? ᓱᓇᕐᖑᖅᑎᓐᓇᔭᖅᐱᓯᐅᒃ?"

ᐅᓪᓗᒥᐅᔪᖅ, ᑕᐃᒃᑯᐊ ᓯᕗᓕᖅᑎᐅᓚᐅᖅᑐᑦ ᐃᓄᑐᖃᕐᖑᖅᐸᓪᓕᐊᑎᓪᓗᒋᑦ ᒐᕙᒪᓕᐅᖅᑕᐅᓚᐅᖅᑐᑦ, ᐊᒻᒪᓗ ᐃᓇᖏᖅᑕᐅᖃᑦᑕᖅᑎᓪᓗᒋᑦ, ᓄᓇᕗᑦ ᒪᒃᑯᒃᑐᕐᑎᖏᑦ ᐊᒃᓯᕐᕿᑎᑕᐅᓯᒪᓂᖃᓕᕐᒪᑕ. ᐃᒪᓐᓇᓐᓃᑦ ᓱᓇ ᐅᖃᐅᓯᖅ ᐊᑐᖅᑕᐅᒐᔪᕐᓂᖓ ᒪᒃᑯᒃᑐᓄᑦ ᐃᓯᒪᒃᓴᖅᓯᐅᕈᑕᐅᕆᐊᖃᓕᖅᑐᖅ ᐊᕐᖁᐃᑦ ᖁᓕᑦ ᑳᖏᖅᐸᑕ ᐊᑐᖅᑕᐅᓇᔭᖅᑐᖅ. ᐊᖏᖅᑕᐅᓯᒪᓕᑦᑕ ᒐᕙᒪᖃᕐᓂᐊᕐᓂᑦᑎᓐᓂᒃ ᐃᖅᑲᓇᐃᔭᖅᑎᖃᕐᓂᐊᖅᑐᓂᒃ ᐃᓄᖕᓂᒃ ᐊᒥᓲᓂᖅᓴᐅᔪᖃᖅᑐᓂᒃ. ᐊᖏᖅᑕᐅᓯᒪᔪᒍᑦ ᒐᕙᒪᒃᓴᐅᓂᐊᖅᑐᓂᒃ ᐃᒃᐱᒋᔭᖃᕐᓂᖅᓴᐅᔪᒥᒃ ᐃᓄᐃᑦ ᐃᓅᑎᐊᕐᓂᖕᒐᑕ ᖃᓄᐃᓐᓂᖏᓐᓄᑦ. ᐊᖏᖅᑕᐅᓯᒪᓪᓚᑕ ᐱᐅᓂᖅᓴᐅᓇᔭᖅᑐᒥᒃ ᒐᕙᒪᖃᕐᓂᕐᒥᒃ ᐋᖅᑭᑦᑎᐊᖅᓯᒪᓂᖅᓴᐅᔪᒥᒃ ᐃᓱᒪᒋᔭᐅᑦᑎᐊᖅᑐᒥᓪᓗ.

ᑕᒪᒃᑯᐊ ᐊᖏᖅᑕᐅᓯᒪᔪᑦ ᐱᕙᓪᓕᐊᓕᕈᓐᓇᖅᑐᑦ ᑭᓯᐊᓂ ᒪᒃᑯᑎᑦ ᓯᕗᓂᕐᒧᑦ ᐊᒃᓯᕈᕐᓂᖅᑲᖅᑐᑎᒃ ᑲᒪᒋᔭᖅᑲᖅᐸᑕ ᑕᒪᒃᑯᓂᖓ. ᑕᐃᒃᑯᐊ ᓯᕗᓂᕆᓚᐅᖅᑕᕗᑦ ᒐᕙᒪᓕᕆᕝᕕᐅᓚᐅᖅᑐᑦ ᐊᒻᒪᓗ ᐱᕆᐊᖅᑎᑎᓚᐅᖅᑐᑦ ᓄᓇᕗᑖᕐᓂᒃ ᐃᓂᖅᐃᓐᓃᕐᓇᓂᓪᓗᑕ ᐊᖓᔪᖅᑳᖅᑲᕕᖕᒥᓂ. ᐊᒥᓲᓂᖅᓴᐅᓚᖕᒐᒃᑲᑦ ᐃᓄᐃᑦ ᒐᕙᒪᒥᒃᓴᐅᔪᒥ, ᐊᒥᓲᓂᖅᓴᐃᑦ ᒪᒃᑯᑦ ᒐᕙᒪᖁᑎᒥᓂᒃ ᓄᓇᕗᒥ ᐊᓯᔾᔨᖅᐸᓪᓕᐊᑐᑕᐅᔪᓐᓇᖅᑐᖅ ᑭᓯᐊᓂ ᐃᓚᐅᖃᑕᐅᒃᐸᑕ ᐱᕙᓪᓕᐊᖃᑕᐅᒃᐸᑕᓗ ᐊᓯᔾᔨᖅᐸᓪᓕᐊᔪᓂᒃ. ᒐᕙᒪᖁᑎᒋᓚᖓᔪᒐᑦ ᓄᑖᓂᒃ ᐊᑐᓕᖅᐸᓪᓕᐊᒍᓐᓇᖅᑐᑦ ᑭᓯᐊᓂ ᓄᓇᓕᖁᑎᒋᔭᑎᓐᓂ ᓯᕗᒻᒧᑦ ᐊᔪᖅᑕᐅᓂᖅᐸᑕ. ᒐᕙᒪᖁᑎᒋᔭᒐᑦ ᒪᑐᐃᖓᓚᖓᔪᖅ ᒪᒃᑯᑦᑐᐃᑦ ᐊᒃᓯᕈᖅᐸᓪᓕᐊᒃᐸᑕ ᐃᓚᐅᖃᑕᐅᒍᓐᓇᕐᓂᕐᒥᒃ ᓴᒃᑯᐃᓗᑎᒃ ᑲᒪᒍᒪᓐᓂᕐᓂᕐᒥᖕᓂᒃ. ᒐᕙᒥᓚᖓᔪᖅ ᓇᒻᒥᓂᓗᒍ ᑭᓯᐊᓂ ᑎᒍᐃᓐᓇᕈᑎᒍ ᐅᑯᒍᑦ.

ᑕᒪᓐᓇ ᐅᖁᒪᐃᒻᒪᓂᒃᑐᖅ ᒪᒃᑯᑦᑐᓄᑦ ᑎᒍᔭᐅᕙᓪᓕᐊᔪᖅ. ᐊᒥᓱᓄᑦ ᑎᒍᔭᐅᕙᓪᓕᐊᔪᖅ ᓴᐱᓇᔭᐅᓚᐅᖅᓱᓂ. ᑕᐃᒃᑯᐊ ᑐᕌᖅᑕᐅᓇᓱᒃᑐᑦ ᐱᔭᓅᖅᑕᐅᔪᒪᔪᑦ ᒐᕙᒪᓕᐅᕐᓂᒃᑯᑦ ᓈᔭᐅᓇᓱᒐᓐᖅᐸᑕ, ᐃᑲᔪᖅᑕᐅᕆᐊᖃᕐᓂᖅᑐᑦ ᐃᓄᓕᒫᓄᑦ ᓄᓇᕗᒦᑦᑐᓂᑦ. ᓯᕗᓂᕐᒪᓂ ᑖᒻᒪᖅᑦᑕᓕᐅᖁᔪᐊᕐᔪᑕ, ᖃᓄᑐᐃᓐᓇᖅ ᐃᓱᒪᒋᔭᑦᑎᓐᓂᒃ ᑐᖅᑭᒪᔭᑦᑎᓐᓂᒃ ᐃᓄᖅᓴᖅᑎᑕᐅᓐᖏᑦᑐᑕ, ᐊᒻᒪᓗ ᐱᔪᐊᖅᑐᒥᒃ, ᓇᒻᒥᓂᖅ ᐃᓕᖅᑯᓯᑦᑎᓐᓂᒃ ᐊᑐᕈᓐᓇᖅᑎᑕᐅᓗᑕ. ᑕᒪᓐᓇ ᐃᑲᔪᕐᓂᖅ ᐱᑕᖃᕆᐊᖃᖅᐸᑦ, ᑲᑐᐃᓐᓇᕆᔭᖅᑐᒍᑦ.

ᑕᑯᔪᒥᓇᖅᑐᖅ ᖃᓄᖅ ᑕᐃᒃᑯᐊ Hᐋᑭᖕᒍᐊᖅᐸᓪᓚᐅᖅᑐᑦ ᓄᑕᖅᐅᓪᓗᑎᒃ ᐊᖏᖅᑲᑎᒌᓕᓯᐊᕿᑕᐅᑎᓪᓗᒍ ᓄᓇᕗᑦ ᖃᓄᐃᓐᓂᐊᖅᑲᓯᓂᖏᑦ ᐊᖅᑰᒍᐸᓪᓕᐊᓚᖓᔪᓂ. ᐅᒃᐱᕈᓱᒃᑐᖓᓕ ᑕᐃᑲᓃᖅᑕᐅᓂᐊᕐᒪᑕ ᑲᑎᒪᕕᐅᔪᓂ ᐱᖅᑯᐊᖅᕕᖕᓂ ᓄᓇᓕᖕᓂ, ᐃᓚᐅᖃᑕᐅᓪᓗᑎᒃ ᒐᕙᒪᖁᑎᒥᓂᒃᐅᔪᓂ, ᐃᖏᕐᖅᑎᐊᖃᓗᐊᖅᓂᕐᒐᓂᒃ ᖃᐅᔨᓴᖅᑕᐅᓪᓗᑎᒃᑕᐅᖅ, ᐊᒻᒪᓗ ᐃᓅᖕᓄᑦ ᖃᓐᓂᖅᓴᐅᓂᕐᒐᓂᒃ ᐃᑲᔪᖅᑐᐃᓗᑎᒃ. ᐅᒃᐱᕈᓱᒃᑐᖓᓕ ᑲᑎᓐᓇᔭᖅᑕ ᐊᖏᖅᑲᓇᔪᐊᓂ ᐊᒻᒪᓗ ᑐᐱᕐᓂ ᓄᓇᐃᓐᓇᕐᒥ, ᐅᖃᖅᑎᕐᕋᖅᑕᐅᓗᑕ ᑲᒪᒋᔪᐅᕆᐊᖃᖅᑐᓂᒃ ᓯᕗᓂᑦᑎᓐᓂ. ᓄᑖᓂᓪᓗ ᓇᓂᓯᖅᑕᐅᓗᑕ ᐃᓱᒪᒋᔭᐅᓯᒪᓐᖏᑦᑐᓂᒃ ᓂᖏᐅᕐᓂᖅᑕᐊᓕᖅᑯᓪᓗᒋᑦ ᑕᐃᒃᑯᐊ ᖁᓚᓕᖅᐸᓪᓕᐊᔪᑦ. ᐅᐸᓐᓂᓕ ᑐᑭᓯᒪᓂᕐᓴᓐᓇᑦ ᑖᓐᓇ ᓂᕆᐅᓐᓂᐅᔪᖅ ᐱᕈᖅᐸᓪᓕᐊᐸᓪᓕᐊᓕᖅᑐᖅ.

ᔩᒥ ᐅᓇᓕᒃ (Jimi Onalik) ᐃᖃᓗᖕᒦᑦᑐᖅ ᐃᖅᑲᓇᐃᔭᖅᑕᐅᑦᓗᓂ ᐊᑐᐊᒐᓕᐅᔪᑦᑎᑦ ᐱᕙᓪᓕᐊᑎᑕᐅᓂᖏᓐᓂ (ᒪᓕᒐᓕᐅᓕᐅᖅᑎᓂ) ᓄᓇᕗᑦ ᒐᕙᒪᒃᑯᖓᓂ.

Nunavut Tourism ᓄᓇᕗᑦ ᐳᓚᕋᑦᑕᓂᓕᕆᔨᑦ

"People assume that the day you sign these deals that they're going to start working as though there are no problems on the first day," muses Liz Snider, who helped negotiate the Nunavut political accord. "There will be glitches, and that doesn't mean that it was the wrong thing to do – it's just that it's part of a process"

"ᐃᓄᐃᑦ ᐃᓱᒪᓕᒪᑕ ᐊᑎᓕᐅᖅᑕᐅᑐᐊᖅᐸᑦ ᐊᑐᓕᕐᓂᐊᕋᓱᒋᓪᓗᓂᔾᔪ ᓲᕐᓗ ᐊᑲᐅᖏᓕᐅᕈᑎᖃᖏᓪᓗᑎᑦ ᐅᓪᓗᖅ ᓯᕗᓪᓕᖅᐹᖓᓂ," ᐅᖃᖅᑐᖅ ᓕᔅ ᓴᐃᑐᕐ, ᐃᑲᔪᖅᑕᐅᓂᑯ ᓄᓇᕗᑦ ᒪᓕᒐᓕᐅᖓᓂᑦ ᐋᖅᑭᒃᓯᐃᓂᕐᒥᓐ." ᐊᑲᐅᖏᓕᐅᕈᑎᖃᕐᓂᐊᖅᑐᖅ, ᑕᐃᒪᐃᓐᓂᖓᓗᓪᓗ ᐃᓱᒪᓇᖏᓪᓗᖅ ᑕᒪᓐᓇ ᑕᒻᒪᖅᓯᒪᑎᐊᒃᓴᖓᓂᑦ – ᑭᓯᐊᓂᓕ ᑕᒪᓐᓇ ᐱᓕᕆᓂᕐᒧᖓ ᐊᑕᐃᓐᓇᐅᔪᕐᒪᖓ"

continued from page 36

two bargaining cultures, that goal was inevitably lost. Both thc claim agreement and the new territory create bureaucracy, complex financing, and legalities.

The Inuit way did succeed, however, during the long negotiation period, both at the table and away. The Inuit negotiators maintained an atmosphere of respect and courtesy, preferring pragmatism and reason to posturing and rhetoric. In this climate, bargaining led to joint planning, particularly in the field of environmental management.

Although there were numerous reorganizations within the Inuit camp, a core group of leaders and dedicated consultants kept continuity of style and purpose throughout the years of negotiation. The government side, both federal and territorial, responded in kind to the Inuit approach.

Most people are aware of the problems that Nunavut faces — among them sparse resources, distant markets, climate, and an ill-prepared population, all in a volatile global setting.

But to the pessimists, we can pose the question, "How many people, in

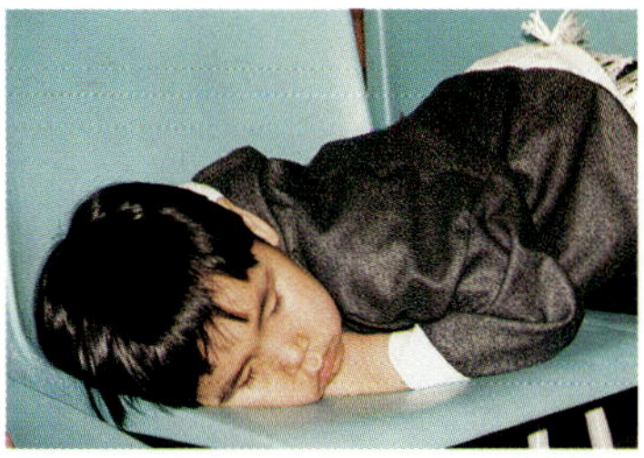

Nunatsiaq News ᓄᓇᑦᓯᐊᕐᒥ ᐱᕙᓪᓕᐊᑦ

1950, would have believed that half a century later, Canadian Inuit would own and direct several multi-million-dollar corporations, in addition to being the majority participants in local, regional and territorial government?" No one could have foreseen the full spectrum of change, but Inuit knew the need to survive and to regain control of their lives and lands. They found leaders to make it happen. If the other parties fulfil their obligations, and perhaps a little more, the Inuit will make Nunavut work.

Keith Crowe has extensive experience in Inuit affairs, beginning as a northern service officer in 1959. He was the chief negotiator for the Inuit of Quebec (James Bay and Northern Quebec Agreement) 1974/75, and senior federal negotiator during the first decade of the Nunavut claim. Marion Soublière and Greg Coleman, both from Ottawa, are the co-editors of *Nunavut '99*.

Nunatsiaq News ᓄᓇᑦᓯᐊᕐᒥ ᐱᕙᓪᓕᐊᑦ

Top left: The road was long, and community meetings were tiring. But as people like David Alagalak, above, in hat, and George Qulaut envision the days to come in this first administration of the new government of Nunavut, it is in the knowledge that, for Inuit, the footsteps still to be taken will be in a direction of their own choosing

ᖁᓛᓂᑦ ᓴᐅᒥᖕᒐᓂᑦ: ᐊᖅᑯᑎ ᑕᑭᔪᐋᓗᓚᐅᕐᐳᖅ, ᐊᒻᒪᓗ ᓄᓇᓕᖕᓂ ᑲᑎᒪᓂᐅᔪᑦ ᑕᖃᓈᕐᓗᑎᒃ. ᑭᓯᐊᓂᓕ ᐆᑐᓇᖅ ᑕᐃᑲ ᐊᓚᒐᓚᒃᑎᑐᑦ, ᖁᓛᓂ, ᓇᓴᓯᒪᔪᖅ, ᐊᒻᒪ ᔪᐊᔾ ᖁᓚᐅᑦᑎᑐᑦ ᓯᕗᓂᒃᓴᑦ ᐅᓪᓗᑦ ᓂᕆᐅᓇᕐᓯᕗᑦ ᐊᐅᓚᑦᑎᓂᓕᕆᓂᖅ ᐱᓕᕆᐊᖑᓂᐊᓕᕐᑎᓪᓗᒍ ᓄᓇᕗᒻᒥ, ᖃᐅᔨᒪᔭᐅᔪᖅ, ᐃᓅᖕᓄᑦ, ᐊᖅᑯᑎᐅᓂᐊᕐᑐᖅ ᐋᖅᑭᒃᓯᕐᓂᐊᕐᑕᖓᑦ ᐃᓄᐃᑦ ᓂᕈᐊᕆᔭᖓᑦᑎᒍᑦ

ᐃᓚᖓ ᒪᒃᐱᒐᐅᑉ 36

ᑕᒪᒃᑯᓄᖓᓕ ᓇᓗᕐᑯᑎᒃᑐᔪᓄ, ᐊᐱᕆᔪᓐᓇᕐᐳᒍᑦ, "ᖃᔅᓯᑦᑎᑭᐊᖅ ᐃᓄᐃᑦ ᖃᐅᔨᒪᓚᐅᕐᐸᑦ ᐊᕐᕌᒍ 50 ᐊᓂᒍᕐᓯᒪᓕᕐᐸ, ᑲᓇᑕᒥᐅᑕᑦ ᐃᓄᐃᑦ ᓇᖕᒥᓂᖃᕐᓂᐊᕐᓂᖏᓐᓂ ᐊᐅᓚᑦᑎᔾᔪᑎᓂᐊᕐᓂᖏᓐᓂ ᑮᓇᐅᔭᕐᑐᔪᕐᔪᐊᕐᕋᓗᖕᓂ ᑯᐊᐳᕇᓴᓂᑦ, ᐊᒻᒪ ᐅᓇ ᐃᓚᓕᐅᑎᓪᓗᒍ ᐅᖃᕐᓂᕐᓴᑦ ᓄᓇᖅᑲᕐᑐᑦ ᐃᓚᐅᓇᔭᕐᓂᖏᓐᓂᑦ ᓄᓇᖏᓐᓂ, ᐊᕕᒃᑐᕐᓯᒪᓂᕐᑯᓪᓗ ᒐᕙᒪᓕᕆᔩᓐᓂ?" ᑭᓇᑐᐃᓐᓇᖅ ᑕᐃᒪᓐᓇ ᓂᕆᐅᒃᑐᒃᓴᐅᓚᐅᖏᓚᖅ ᐊᓯᔾᔨᕐᑐᒃᓴᒥᓐ, ᑭᓯᐊᓂᓕ ᐃᓄᐃᑦ ᖃᐅᔨᒪᖕᒪᑕ ᐆᒪᕆᐊᖃᕐᓂᕐᒥᓐ ᐊᒻᒪᓗ ᐃᓅᓯᕐᒥᖕᓂ ᐊᐅᓚᑦᑎᕆᐊᖃᕐᓂᕐᒥ ᐊᒻᒪ ᓄᓇᓂᑦ. ᓇᓂᓯᓚᐅᕐᐳᑦ ᓯᕗᓕᐅᕐᑎᓂ ᑕᒪᑐᒥᖓ ᓴᖅᑭᑦᑎᔪᓐᓇᕐᑐᓂᑦ. ᑕᐃᒃᑯᐊ ᐊᓯᖏ ᐱᔭᕆᐊᖃᕐᑕᒥᖕᓂ ᐊᑐᕈᑎ, ᐃᓚᒃᑲᓐᓂᐊᕐᔪᓪᓗᒍᓘᓐᓕ, ᐃᓄᐃᑦ ᓄᓇᕗᒻᒥ ᑲᔪᓯᑎᑦᑎᑦᑎᐊᕈᓐᓇᕐᑐᑦ.

ᑮᑦ ᑯᕈ ᖃᐅᔨᒪᒻᒪᕆᒃᑐᖅ ᐃᓄᐃᑦ ᒥᒃᓵᓄᑦ, ᐱᒋᐊᕐᓯᒪᓪᓗᓂ ᐅᑭᐅᕐᑕᖅᑐᒥ ᐱᓯᑦᑎᕐᑎᐅᓂᕐᒥ 1959ᒥ. ᐊᖓᔪᕐᑎᓂ ᐊᖏᕐᖃᒃᑲᖕᒍᓚᐅᕐᐳᖅ ᑭᐅᕐᑐᐃᓪᓗᓂ ᐃᓄᖕᓂ ᑯᐸᐃᒃᒥᓐ (ᔭᐃᒻᔅ ᐸᐃᒥ ᐊᒻᒪ ᑯᐸᐃᒃ ᑕᕐᕆᖓᓂ ᐊᖏᕈᑎᓂᑦ) 1974/75, ᐊᒻᒪᓗ ᐊᖓᔪᒃᑲᐅᓪᓗᓂ ᐊᖓᔪᕐᑎᓂ ᐱᒋᐊᓖᕐᑎᓪᓗᒍ ᓄᓈᕗᑦᑕᕐᓯᖓᓂᖅ. ᒥᐅᕆᐊᓐ ᓲᓖᐃ ᐊᒻᒪ ᒍᕆ ᑰᓪᒪᓐ, ᑕᒪᕐᒥᒃ ᐋᑐᕚᒥᐅᑖᒃ, ᐋᖅᑭᒃᓱᐃᔨᐅᖄᒃ ᓄᓇᕘᑦ *'99ᒥᓐ*.

"We did our best."

Paul Okalik
Assistant chief negotiator and member of the Inuit negotiating team in other roles, 1985–1991

"ᐱᔪᓐᓇᕐᓂᑦᑎᒍᑦ ᐱᓇᓱᒪᕆᓚᐅᕐᐳᒍᑦ."

ᐹᓪ ᐅᑲᓕᖅ
ᐃᑲᔪᖅᑎᐅᓚᐅᕐᑐᖅ ᐊᖓᔪᖅᑳᖅ ᐊᒻᒪᓗ ᐃᓚᒋᔭᐅᓚᐅᕐᑐᓂ ᐃᓄᖕᓂ ᐊᓯᖏᓐᓂ ᐱᓕᕆᑦᑐᒋᑦ, 1985 - 1991

Our future has a name.
ᓯᕗᓂᑦᓴᕗᑦ ᐊᑎᖅᑲᓕᖅᐳᖅ.

In 1993, the Inuit, the government of Canada and the government of the Northwest Territories signed the Nunavut Land Claims Agreement (NLCA)—the largest aboriginal land claim agreement in Canadian history.

The claim could have gone many different ways, but the Inuit negotiators always said a separate territory with our own government must be part of it. They were even, at several crucial points in the 1980s, willing to sacrifice the claim rather than give up and sign an agreement which did not include this crucial point.

It took 20 long years to finalize this agreement. It was an exhausting process that wore out dozens of bureaucrats and negotiators and spanned the terms of four prime ministers. But finally, the NLCA was ratified by the Inuit of Nunavut in November of 1992 and became part of Canadian law in July 1993. Today, Inuit hopes and aspirations for the future hinge on the successful implementation of all provisions contained in the agreement.

- Total population of Nunavut: 28,000 (est.)
- Inuit population of Nunavut: 24,000 (est.)
- Inuit population as ratio of overall population: 85%
- Population per square kilometre in Nunavut area: 0.01
- Languages spoken: Inuktitut, Inuinnaqtun, English, French
- 28 communities in Nunavut
  - — Northernmost community: Grise Fiord
  - — Southernmost community: Sanikiluaq (geographically situated south of Ontario's northern border)
  - — Largest community: Iqaluit, pop.: 4,300
  - — Smallest community: Bathurst Inlet, pop.: 18
- Land mass: 1,900,000 sq. kilometres

- ᓄᓇᖃᖅᑐᓕᒫᑦ ᐅᓄᕐᓂᖏᑦ ᓄᓇᕗᒻᒥ: 28,000 (ᖃᓂᖕᓚᐃᓯᒪᑐᐃᓐᓇᕐᑐᖅ)
- ᐃᓄᒃᑕᓖᑦ ᐅᓄᕐᓂᖏᑦ ᓄᓇᕗᒻᒥ: 24,000 (ᖃᓂᖕᓚᐃᓯᒪᑐᐃᓐᓇᕐᑐᖅ)
- ᐃᓄᐃᑦ ᓄᓇᖃᖅᑐᓕᒫᓂ ᑕᒪᐃᑎᒍᑦ ᐅᓄᕐᓂᕈᑦ ᐳᓴᓐᑎᒍᑦ: 85%
- ᐊᑕᐅᓯᖅ ᐹᓚᒥᑕ ᑕᐅᑐᒃᓱᒍ ᐃᓄᐃᑦ ᐃᓗᐊᓃᖕᒍᐊᖅᓱᕐᑐᑦ ᓄᓇᕗᓕᒫᒥᓐ: 0.01
- ᐅᖃᐅᓰᑦ ᐅᖃᓪᓚᒃᑕᐅᕙᒃᑐᑦ: ᐃᓄᒃᑎᑐᑦ, ᐃᓄᐃᓐᓇᖅᑐᓐ, ᖃᑦᓗᓈᑐᑦ, ᐅᐃᕖᑎᑐᑦ
- 28 ᓄᓇᓖᑦ ᓄᓇᕗᒻᒥ
  - — ᐅᐊᖕᓇᖕᓚᓕᓖᑦ ᓄᓇᓖᑦ: ᐊᐅᔪᐃᑦᑐᖅ
  - — ᓂᒋᖅᐸᓯᖕᒦᓖᑦ ᓄᓇᓖᑦ: ᓴᓂᑭᓗᐊᖅ
  - — ᐊᖏᓂᖅᐹᖅ ᓄᓇᓕᖕᓂ: ᐃᖃᓗᐃᑦ, ᐃᓄᒋᐊᖕᓂᓕᒃ: 4,300
  - — ᒥᑭᓂᖅᐹᖅ ᓄᓇᓕᖕᓂ: ᕿᓐᖕᓚᐅᑦ, ᐃᓄᒋᐊᖕᓂᓕᒃ: 18
- ᓄᓇᐅᑉ ᐆᒃᑐᕋᐅᑎᒃᑯ ᐊᖏᓂᖓ: 1,900,000 ᑭᓛᒥᑐᕐᑯᑦ

It's called *Nunavut.*

ᑕᐃᔭᐅᔪᖅ ᓄᓇᕗᑦ.

1993-ᒥ, ᐃᓄᐃᑦ, ᑲᓇᑕᐅᑉ ᒐᕙᒪᖓ ᐊᒻᒪᓗ ᓄᓇᕐᔪᐊᑉ ᒐᕙᒪᖓ ᐊᑎᓕᐅᕆᐅᕐᓯᒪᖕᒪᑕ ᓄᓇᕗᑦ ᓄᓇᒥ ᓇᖕᒥᓂᖃᕐᓂᕐᒧᑦ ᐊᖏᕈᑎᒥᓐ (NLCA) – ᐊᖏᓂᕐᐹᖅ ᓄᓇᖃᖅᑳᖅᑐᑦ ᓄᓇᑖᕐᔫᑎᖕᒐᓄᑦ ᐊᖏᕈᑎ ᑲᓇᑕᒥ ᑕᐃᒪᓐᓇ ᑎᑎᕋᐅᓯᐅᖃᑕᓕᕐᒪᑕ.

ᓄᓇᑖᕐᔫᑎ ᐊᓯᐊᒎᕿᓖᔾᔨᓐᓇᓕᐅᕐᑑᒐᓗᐊᖅ, ᑭᓯᐊᓂᓕ ᐋᖅᑭᐅᔪᑦ ᐃᓄᐃᑦ ᐅᖃᖃᑕᐅᓇᓕᐅᕐᐳᑦ ᐃᒻᒥᒃᑯᕐᑐᒥᓐ ᐊᕖᒃᓯᒪᓂᒃᑯ ᐊᒻᒪ ᓇᖕᒥᓂᖅ ᒐᕙᒪᖃᕐᓂᐅᔪᖅ ᐃᓚᓕᐅᑎᓯᒪᔨᐊᖃᕐᓂᖕᒐᓂᑦ. ᐃᓛᓐᓂᒎᑦᑐᓐᓂ, ᖃᔾᔩᒃᑖᕐᒃᑎᒃ 1980ᖏᓐᓂ ᑕᒪᓐᓇ ᓄᓇᑖᕐᔫᑎᖕᓂᐅᓚᐅᕐᑐᖅ ᖁᔭᓈᕈᒪᖃᑕᓚᐅᕐᑕᖕᒐ ᐊᖏᕈᒪᓇᑎᒃ ᑕᒪᑐᒥᖕᒐ ᐃᓗᓕᖅᑲᖏᑦᑐᒥᓐ.

ᐊᕐᕌᒍᓂ ᐊᕙᑎᓂ ᑕᒪᓐᓇ ᐊᑐᕐᑕᐅᓚᐅᕐᐳᖅ ᐊᖏᕈᑎ ᐊᑎᓕᐅᕐᑕᐅᑕᐃᓐᓇᕐᑎᑦᑐᒍ. ᑕᒪᓐᓇ ᑕᖃᓇᒻᒪᓇᒃᐸᓚᐅᕐᐳᖅ ᐊᒻᒪ ᐊᒥᓯᓂᑦ ᒪᓕᒐᓕᓇᕈᓂ ᑕᑯᓯᒪᕚᓯᒃᓱᓂ ᐋᖅᑭᓐᓂᓗ ᐊᒻᒪᓗ ᑎᓴᒻᒪᓇᖕᓂ ᑲᓇᑕᐅᑉ ᐊᖕᒐᔭᖅᑳᒻᒪᓇᖏᓐᓂ ᑕᑯᓯᒪᓪᓗᓂ. ᑭᓯᐊᓂᓕ, ᑕᒪᓐᓇ ᓄᓇᕗᑦ ᓄᓇᒥ ᓇᖕᒥᓂᖃᕐᓂᕐᒧᑦ ᐊᖏᕈᑎ ᓴᖅᑭᑎᑕᐅᒻᒪᓇᓕᓚᐅᕐᓯᒪᔪᖅ ᐃᓄᖕᓄᑦ ᓄᓇᕗᒻᒥ ᓈᓚᒍ 1992ᒥ ᐊᒻᒪᓗ ᑕᒪᓐᓇ ᑲᓇᑕᐅᑉ ᒐᓚᖏᓐᓂ ᐃᓚᓕᐅᔾᔭᐅᓕᖅᓱᓂ ᔪᓚᐃ 1993ᒥ. ᐅᓪᓗᒥ, ᐃᓄᐃᑦ ᓂᓇᐅᒋᓯᒪᔭᕋ ᐊᒻᒪ ᑕᑯᔪᒪᔭᖏᑦ ᓯᕗᓂᒃᓴᒥᓐ, ᐊᑐᕈᓐᓇᖅᓯᓂᐊᕐᑐᑦ ᐊᑐᖅᔭᐅᓯᒪᔪᓂ ᐊᖏᕈᑎᐅᑉ ᐃᓗᐊᓃᑦᑐᓂᑦ.

Keeping the promise of Nunavut

In July 1993, Nunavut Tunngavik Incorporated (NTI) was set up to ensure the promises made in the NLCA are carried out. NTI is headed by a four-person Executive Committee elected at large by all Inuit 16 years of age or over and it speaks with an authority that is unmatched by any other organization in Nunavut.

By upholding the provisions of the NLCA, NTI touches nearly every aspect of life in Nunavut—from social well-being to economics, to wildlife and land management. It is our responsibility to safeguard the hard-won rights of the Inuit of Nunavut: to manage our own land and our own affairs consistent with Inuit values and traditions.

Turning words into action

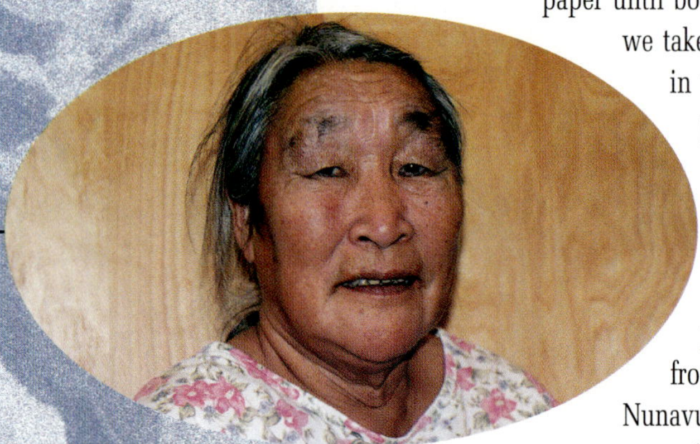

A land claims agreement, like any contract, is just a piece of paper until both parties agree to implement it. At NTI, we take the obligations, principles and policies in the claim and turn them into real-world programs, services and organizations. In addition to the financial settlement, NTI negotiated funding from the federal government which ensures the articles of the NLCA can be implemented. Every year, the organization receives interest from the settlement, which is invested by Nunavut Trust. This money is used to fund programs, projects and operations that uphold the land claim and benefit Inuit.

NTI DEPARTMENTS The day-to-day operations of NTI are managed through offices in Iqaluit, Rankin Inlet, Cambridge Bay and Ottawa.

ADMINISTRATION centrally controls NTI operations and manages executive affairs.

BUSINESS DEVELOPMENT promotes the Nunavut economy and works with Inuit-owned businesses to provide jobs and income in the North.

LAND AND RESOURCES manages and monitors all Inuit-owned lands, contributes to the conservation and development of all Nunavut surface and subsurface lands and resources, and operates a Geographic Information System for mapping.

ENROLLMENT AND ELIGIBILITY works to enroll all Inuit with NTI, in order that Inuit can benefit from the Nunavut Land Claims Agreement.

FINANCE manages NTI finances and ensures that each department spends money according to directives of the NTI board.

HUMAN RESOURCES recruits staff, manages staff benefits, annual leave, staff appraisals, and actively promotes training and Inuit employment goals.

HUNTER SUPPORT PROGRAM manages hunter support benefits and represents NTI wildlife management interests with the Nunavut Wildlife Management Board.

ELDERS BENEFIT PROGRAM provides income support to all elders 55 years of age and older.

IMPLEMENTATION ensures the promises in the Nunavut Land Claims Agreement are carried out according to legislation and defended according to law.

COMMUNICATIONS informs the public and the media about NTI policies, programs and activities; publishes *Ittuaqtuut Magazine*, an annual report, brochures and posters; maintains the www.tunngavik.com web site.

ᓄᓇᕗ ᓯᖅᑭᑎᑕᐅᓂᐊᕐᓂᖓ ᐊᑐᕐᑕᐅᓪᓚᓇᒃᐳᖅ

ᔪᓚᐃ 1993ᒥ, ᓄᓇᕗᑦ ᑐᓐᖓᕕᒃ ᑎᒥᖓ ᓯᖅᑭᑎᑕᐅᓕᓚᐅᕐᓯᒪᕗᖅ ᑕᒪᒃᑯᐊ ᐊᑐᕐᓂᐊᓂᕋᖅᑕᐅᔪᑦ ᓄᓇᕗᒻᒥ ᓄᓇᑖᖅᓂᕐᒧ ᐊᖏᕈᑎᓃᑦᑐᑦ ᓯᖅᑭᑎᑕᐅᓂᐊᕐᒪᑕ. ᓄᓇᕗᑦ ᑐᓐᖓᕕᒃᑯ ᐊᐅᓚᑕᐅᕗᖅ ᑎᓴᒪᓄ ᐊᐅᓪᓚᑎᓂᕐᒧᑦ ᑲᑎᒪᔨᓂ ᓂᕈᐊᕐᑕᐅᓯᒪᔪᓂ ᐃᓄᖕᓄ ᐊᕐᕌᒍᓕᖕᓄ 16 ᐅᖓᑖᓂᓪᓗ ᐊᒻᒪ ᐅᖃᕐᑕᖏ ᓵᓚᐅᔪᓐᓇᖏᓪᓗᑎᒃ ᐊᓯᖏᓐᓄ ᑲᑐᔾᔨᖅᑎᒋᓄᑦ ᓄᓇᕗᒻᒥ.

ᑕᒪᑐᒥᖓ ᓄᓇᕗᒻᒥ ᓄᓇᑖᖅᓂᕐᒧ ᐊᖏᕈᑎᐅ ᐃᓗᐊᓃᑦᑐᓂ ᐊᑐᕐᑎᑦᑎᓪᓚᕆᐊᓪᓗᑎᒃ, ᓄᓇᕗᑦ ᑐᓐᖓᕕᒃ ᐊᒃᑐᐃᓂᖅᑲᖅᐳᑦ ᑕᒪᐃᓐᓂᐸᓗᒃ ᐃᓅᓯᕐᒧᓐ ᐊᒃᑐᐊᔪᓂ ᓄᓇᕗᒻᒥ – ᐃᓅᓯᖃᑦᑎᐊᕐᓂᕐᒥ ᐱᕙᓪᓕᐊᔪᓚᕆᓂᕐᒧ, ᓂᕐᔪᑎᓕᕆᓂᕐᒧᓐ ᐊᒻᒪ ᓄᓇᒥ ᐊᐅᓪᓚᑎᓂᕐᒧ. ᐱᓕᕆᐊᕆᔭᐊᖃᖅᐸᒃᑲ ᑕᒪᓐᓇ ᐊᒃᓱᕈᑎᒃᑯ-ᓵᓚᒃᓴᖅᑕᐅᓂᒃᑯ ᐱᔪᓐᓇᕐᓂᖅ ᓄᓇᕗᑦ ᐃᓄᖏᓐᓄᑦ: ᓄᓇᑦᑎᓐᓂ ᐊᐅᓪᓚᑎᔪᓐᓇᕐᓂ ᐊᒻᒪ ᐅᐸᑦᑎᓐᓄ ᑐᕌᖓᔪᑦ ᐃᓄᐃᑦ ᐅᒃᐱᓇᔾᔭᖏᑦᑎᑐ ᐃᓕᑦᑯᓯᖏᑦᑎᑐᓪᓗ.

ᐅᖃᐅᓰ ᓯᖅᑭᑎᑕᐅᓂᖏᑦ

ᓄᓇᕗᒻᒥ ᓄᓇᑖᖅᓂᕐᒧ ᐊᖏᕈᑎ, ᒪᑯᑎᑐᓇᖅ ᑳᓐᑐᕋᖑᓯᑎᑐ, ᐸᐃᑉᐹᑐᐃᓐᓇᐅᕗᖅ ᑭᓯᐊᓂ ᑕᒪᕐᒥ ᐱᓕᕆᔾᔪ ᐊᖏᕐᑐᐃᓐᓇᐅᒍᑎ. ᓄᓇᕗᑦ ᑐᓐᖓᕕᒃᑯᑎᒍᑦ, ᐱᓕᕆᐊᕆᐊᖃᖅᑕᕗᑦ, ᐱᔾᔪᑎᒋᔭᕗᑦ ᐊᒻᒪ ᐊᑐᐊᒐᑦ ᓄᓇᑖᖅᓂᕐᒧ ᓯᖅᑭᑎᓯᒪᓂᕗᑦ ᐱᓕᕆᐊᒃᓯᓪᓚᕈᓕᕐᑎᓗᑎᒍᑦ, ᐱᔨᑦᑎᕆᐅᑎᒋᓕᕐᓗᑎᒍ ᐊᒻᒪ ᑲᑐᔾᔨᖅᑎᒋᖕᒍᕐᑎᓗᑎᒍᑦ. ᐃᓚᖃᒃᑲᓂᕐᓗᓂ ᕿᓇᐅᔭᑦ ᐊᖏᕐᑕᐅᓂᖏ, ᓄᓇᕗᑦ ᑐᓐᖓᕕᒃ ᐋᔩᓂᒃᑯ ᕿᓇᐅᔭᓂ ᐊᑐᕐᑐᒃᓴᓂ ᓄᓇᑖᕋᓯᑎᐅᑉ ᐃᓗᐊᓂᑦᑐᓂ ᓯᖅᑭᑎᑦᑎᔾᔨᑎᒃᓴᓂ ᐱᔪᓐᓇᖅᓯᓯᒪᓕᕗᑦ. ᐊᕐᕌᒍᑕᒫᓐ, ᑐᓐᖓᕕᒃᑯ ᓄᓇᑖᕐᓂᕐᒧᓐ ᕿᓇᐅᔭᕐᑖᕕᓂᖏᓐᓂᑦ ᖁᑦᓯᖏᑦᑐᕈᑎᖏᓐᓂᑦ ᐱᑖᖅᑕᕐᕆᕗᑦ, ᑕᓐᓇᓗ ᓄᓇᕗᑦ ᐸᐸᑦᑎᕙᖓᓐᓂ (Nunavut Trust) ᖁᑦᓯᖏᑦᑐᕐᑎᑕᐅᕙᒃᖢᓂ. ᐅᓇ ᕿᓇᐅᔭᖅ ᐊᑐᕐᑕᐅᖃᑦᑕᖅᐳᖅ ᐱᓕᕆᐊᒃᓴᓄᑦ ᐊᑭᓕᐅᑕᐅᕙᒃᐳᖅ, ᐱᓕᕆᔾᔪᑎᓄᓪᓗ ᐊᒻᒪ ᐊᐅᓪᓚᑎᓂᕐᒧ ᑕᒪᒃᑯᐊ ᓄᓇᑖᕐᓯᒪᓂᕐᒧᓐ ᐱᓕᕆᔾᔪᑕᐅᔪᑦ ᐃᓄᖕᓄ ᐃᑲᔪᖅᑕᐅᓂᖏᓐᓄᑦ.

ᓄᓇᕗᑦ ᑐᓐᖓᕕᒃ ᑎᒥᖓ ᐱᓕᕆᕖᖏᑦ – ᖃᐅᑕᒻᒫ ᐱᓕᕆᓂᐅᔪᑦ ᓄᓇᕗᑦ ᑐᓐᖓᕕᒃᑯᓐᓂ ᐊᐅᓚᑕᐅᖃᑦᑕᖅᐳᑦ ᐊᓪᓚᕕᖓᓂ ᐃᖃᓗᖕᓂ, ᑲᖏᖅᖠᓂᖅᒥ, ᐃᖃᓗᒃᑑᑎᐊᕐᒥ ᐊᒻᒪ ᐋᑐᕚᒥ.

ᐊᐅᓚᑦᑎᔩ – ᐱᓕᕆᕕᖕᒪᕆᒃ ᐊᐅᓚᑦᑎᔩᑦ ᓄᓇᕗᑦ ᑐᓐᖓᕕᒃᑯ ᐱᓕᕆᐊᖏᓐᓂᑦ ᐊᒻᒪᓗ ᐊᐅᓚᑦᑎᔩᑦ ᐱᓕᕆᐊᖏᓐᓂᑦ.

ᓈᒻᒥᓂᖃᖅᓯᓂᕐᒧᑦ ᐱᕙᓪᓕᐊᑎᑦᑎᓂᖅ – ᓯᖅᑭᑎᑦᑎᔩ ᓄᓇᕗᑦ ᐱᕙᓪᓕᐊᓂᖏᓐᓂ ᐊᒻᒪᓗ ᐱᓕᕆᐸᒃᐳᑦ ᐃᓄᐃᑦ ᓈᒻᒥᓂᕐᓱᖏᓐᓂ ᐱᓕᕆᕝᕕᖓᓂ ᓯᖅᑭᑎᑦᑎᓯᒪᔾᔪᓂᖅᒧᑦ ᐃᖅᑲᓇᐃᔮᖅᑐᓂᑦ ᐊᒻᒪ ᕿᓇᐅᔭᑦᑖᕈᑎᖅᑐᓂᑦ ᐅᑭᐅᑦᑕᖅᑐᖅᒥ.

ᓄᓇ ᐊᒻᒪ ᐊᑐᒃᑲᓂᕈᓇᖅᑐᑦ – ᐊᐅᓚᑦᑎᔨ ᐊᒻᒪ ᖃᐅᔨᒪᔩᑦ ᐃᓄᐃᑦ ᓄᓇᖁᑎᓕᒫᖏᓐᓂ, ᐃᑲᔪᖅᑕᖅᓱᑎᒃ ᓄᓇᒥ ᓱᖅᑕᐅᑦᑕᐃᓕᓂᖓᓂ ᐊᒻᒪ ᐱᕙᓪᓕᐊᓂᕐᒥ ᓄᓇᕗᑦ ᖄᖓᓕᓂᑦᑐᓂ ᐊᒻᒪ ᐊᑎᑦᑎᐊᖓᓕᓂᑦᑐᓂ ᓄᓇᓂᑦ ᐊᑐᖅᑐᒃᓴᓂᓪᓗ, ᐊᒻᒪᓗ ᐊᐅᓚᑦᑎᔾᔪᑎᑦ ᓄᓇᖁᐊᕆᓂᕐᒧ ᑐᓴᐊᒪᔭᐅᕆᐊᓕᖕᓂ ᓄᓇᖁᐊᓕᐅᕐᓂᒃᑯᑦ.

ᐃᓚᐅᑎᑦᑎᔩᑦ ᐊᒻᒪ ᐊᔪᖏᑎᑦᑎᔩᑦ – ᐱᓇᓱᒃᑕᕐᑐᑦ ᐃᓄᓕᒫᓂ ᑎᑎᕋᖅᑕᐅᑎᑦᑎᓂᕐᒧ ᓄᓇᕗᑦ ᑐᓐᖓᕕᒃᑯᓐᓄ, ᑕᒪᒃᑯᐊ ᐃᓄᐃᑦ ᐃᑲᔫᒪᓪᓗᑎ ᑕᕝᕗᓇ ᓄᓇᕗᑦ ᓄᓇᒥ ᓈᒻᒥᓂᖅᑲᖅᓯᓂᕐᒧᑦ ᐊᖏᕈᑎᒃᑯᑦ.

ᕿᓇᐅᔭᓕᕆᔩᑦ – ᐊᐅᓚᑦᑎᔨᐅᕗᑦ ᓄᓇᕗᑦ ᑐᓐᖓᕕᒃᑯ ᕿᓇᐅᔭᖃᕐᓂᖏᓐᓂᑦ ᐊᒻᒪᓗ ᑲᒪᔨᐅᓪᓗᑎᒃ ᑕᒪᕐᒥᒃ ᐱᓕᕆᐊᒥ ᕿᓇᐅᔭᓂᑦ ᐊᑐᖅᑕᐅᓂᖏᓐᓂᑦ ᒪᓕᒃᖢᑎᒃ ᓄᓇᕗᑦ ᑐᓐᖓᕕᒃᑯ ᑲᑎᒪᔨᖏᑦᑕ ᐱᖁᔭᖏᓐᓂᑦ.

ᐃᖅᑲᓇᐃᔭᕐᑐᓕᕆᓂᖅ – ᐃᖅᑲᓇᐃᔭᕐᑎᑖᕐᓂᒥ ᐱᓕᕆᔨᐅᔪᑦ, ᐊᐅᓚᑦᑎᔨᐅᓪᓗᑎᒃ ᐃᖅᑲᓇᐃᔭᕐᑎ ᕿᓇᐅᔭᕐᑖᓚᖅᑕᖅᑕᖏᓐᓂᑦ, ᐊᕐᕌᒍᑕᒫᓐ ᖃᒃᓴᓇᐅᕙᒃᑐᓂᑦ, ᐃᖅᑲᓇᐃᔭᕐᑎ ᐱᕙᓪᓕᐊᓂᖏᓐᓄᑦ ᖃᐅᔨᓴᕐᑎᑦ, ᓯᖅᑭᑎᑦᑎᔩᑦ ᐃᓕᓐᓂᐊᕙᒃᓯᓂᑦ ᐊᒻᒪᓗ ᐃᓄᐃᑦ ᐃᖅᑲᓇᐃᔮᒃᓴᖅᑲᑎᓯᒪᔾᔪᓂᖅᔪᒃ.

ᐊᖑᓇᓯᒃᑎᑦ ᐃᑲᔫᓯᐊᓇᖅᑕᖅᑕᖏᑦ – ᐊᐅᓚᑦᑎᔨ ᐊᖑᓇᓯᒃᑎᑦ ᐃᑲᔫᓯᐊᓇᖅᑕᖅᑕᖏᓐᓂᑦ ᐊᒻᒪᓗ ᑭᖑᕐᑐᐃᔨᐅᓪᓗᑎᒃ ᓄᓇᕗᑦ ᑐᓐᖓᕕᒃᑯ ᐆᒪᔪᓕᕆᔨᖏᓐᓂ ᐱᓇᖅᑎᖅᑕᖅᖢᑎᒃ ᓄᓇᕗᑦ ᐆᒪᔪᓕᕆᔨᒋᔭᐅᔪᓄ ᑲᑎᒪᔨᖏᓐᓂᑦ.

ᐃᓐᓇᑐᖅᑦ ᐃᑲᔫᓯᐊᓇᖅᑕᖅᑕᖏᑦ – ᐃᓐᓇᑐᖅᑲᓂ ᕿᓇᐅᔭᓂᑦ ᐃᑲᔪᖅᑎᐅᔪᑦ ᐃᓐᓇᑐᖅᑲᓄᑦ ᐊᕐᕌᒍᓕᖕᓄᑦ 55ᓂ ᐅᖓᑖᓂᓪᓗ.

ᓯᖅᑭᑎᑦᑎᔩᑦ – ᓯᖅᑭᑎᑕᐅᒥᐊᖅᑐᓂᑦ ᐅᖃᖅᓯᒪᔪᓂᑦ ᓄᓇᕗᑦ ᓄᓇᒥ ᓇᖕᒥᓂᖃᖅᓯᓂᕐᒧᑦ ᐊᖏᕈᑎᓂᑦ ᑎᑎᕋᖅᓯᒪᔪᓂᑦ ᐊᒻᒪᓗ ᑕᒪᒃᑯᐊ ᓴᐳᔾᔨᓯᒪᓗᒋᑦ ᑕᒪᒃᑯᓂᖓ ᒪᓕᒃᑎᒍᑦ.

ᑐᓴᐅᒪᑎᑦᑎᔩᑦ – ᐃᓄᓕᒫᓂᑦ ᑐᓴᐅᒪᑎᑦᑎᓯᒪᒋᐊᕐᑎᓗᑎᒃ ᐊᒻᒪᓗ ᑐᓴᐅᑎᓕᕆᓂᑦ ᐱᓕᕆᐅᔪᓂ ᓄᓇᕗᑦ ᑐᓐᖓᕕᒃᑯ ᐊᑐᐊᒐᖏᓐᓂᑦ, ᐱᓕᕆᐊᖏᓐᓂ ᐊᒻᒪᓗ ᐊᑐᕐᓚᖅᑐᐊᔭᖏᓐᓂᑦ, ᓯᖅᑭᑎᑦᑎᔩᑦ ᐅᖃᓪᓚᒃᑕᖅᑐᓂᑦ ᐃᑦᑐᐊᖅᑐᑦ, ᑖᓐᓇ ᐊᕐᕌᒍᑕᒫᓐ ᐅᓂᒃᑲᐊᖑᓯᖅ ᐱᓇᓄᑦ ᒥᒃᓵᓄᑦ, ᐅᖃᓪᓚᒃᑎᕈᓐᓂ ᓯᖅᑭᑎᑦᑎᔩᑦ ᐊᒻᒪ ᐊᑭᓐᓇᒥᐅᑕᖏᑦ: ᐋᖅᑭᒃᓯᐊᕐᓚᐃᔩᑦ ᖃᓇᓯᐅᔭᒃᑯ ᓯᖅᑭᔭᕐᑎᑕᐅᔪᒥᓐ.
www.tunngavik.com

Mining and exploration development

One of the most important and complex of our direct responsibilities is the management of surface and subsurface development. NTI is the only organization that can issue licences to companies who wish to explore for subsurface minerals on Inuit-owned lands. We're working with the mining sector to build a healthy industry—one that promotes the Nunavut economy, and is efficient and profitable for the operators, while at the same time, is respectful to the environment, wildlife, and the values and culture of the Inuit.

Helping business succeed

We're also extremely proactive in promoting a healthy Inuit business sector. The NTI Business Development department oversees all the economic development aspects of the NLCA, including government contracting. This does not mean Inuit firms are guaranteed to win government contracts. But it does mean that Inuit do have some special considerations when bidding on those contracts—for job training, in learning how to bid for government work, and in finding employment. We have also set up a process for registering qualified Inuit firms. This up-to-date list of Inuit-owned firms must be used by government or any interested party in finding an Inuit firm with any needed expertise when seeking either federal or territorial government contracts.

Grassroots assistance

NTI's involvement doesn't concentrate solely on large projects. We believe small, community-based businesses offer Inuit entrepreneurs their best introduction to the private sector. That's why NTI provides $2.1 million every year to help support small Inuit businesses. This money is distributed through a network of Inuit agencies in the three regions of Nunavut, and is used for loans, grants, and business training programs. Questions can be addressed to: ntiecdev@nunanet.com

Elders Benefit Program

The work of our elders, the living libraries of our rich oral tradition, was crucial to the success of the land claim negotiations. While rich in knowledge and wisdom, many, like older people elsewhere, depend on others for their everyday needs. To this end, NTI's Nunavut Elders Benefit Program provides income support to all elders 55 years of age and older.

Maintaining a proud tradition

Hunting is the mainstay of Inuit culture. Many Nunavut families maintain their tradition of hunting caribou, muskoxen, fish and sea mammals for meat and furs. It has enabled us to make

ᐅᔾᔪᒃᓴᓯᐅᕐᓂᖅ ᐊᒻᒪ ᖃᐅᔨᓴᕐᓂᕐᒧᑦ ᐱᓕᕆᐊᓂᖅ

ᐱᒻᒪᕆᐅᖅᑕᐅᓛᖑᔪᕐᓕ ᐱᑐᐃᓐᓇᐅᓪᓚᕐᓂᖓ ᐊᒻᒪ ᑲᒪᒋᓪᓗᐊᑕᕆᖅᑲᓯᐅᑎᓪᓗᒍ ᒫᓐᓇ ᐊᐅᓚᑦᑎᓂᐅᔪᖅ ᓄᓇᐅᑉ ᖄᖓ ᐊᒻᒪ ᐊᑎᑦᑎᐊᖓᓂ ᐱᓕᕆᐊᓂᐅᔪᖅ. ᓄᓇᕗᑦ ᑐᓐᖓᕕᒃ ᑲᑐᔾᔨᖃᑎᒌᖑᔪᓂᑦ ᐱᕕᖃᕐᑐᑑᕗᑦ ᑐᓂᓯᔪᓐᓇᕐᓂᑦ ᐱᔪᓐᓇᐅᑎᓂᑦ (ᓚᐃᓴᓐᔅ) ᑲᒻᐸᓂᓄᑦ ᖃᐅᔨᓴᕈᒪᔪᓄᑦ ᐅᔾᔪᕐᐅᔾᔭᕐᓂ ᑖᒃᑯᓂ ᐃᓄᐃᑦ ᓄᓇᖏᓐᓂ. ᐱᓕᕆᖃᑎᖃᕐᐳᒍᑦ ᐅᔾᔪᒃᓴᓯᐅᕐᑎᓕᕆᔾᔨᓂ ᑕᒪᓐᓇ ᐱᓕᕆᐊᓕᕆᒃᑐᒥ ᐱᓕᕆᔪᒪᔪᒧᓐ–ᓄᓇᕗᒻᒥ ᐱᓕᕆᐊᓂᕐᒥ ᓴᖅᑭᖁᔨᒧᓐ, ᐊᒻᒪ ᐊᑲᐅᓈᖅᓯᒪᔪᒃᑯᕐᑎᑦᑎᕙᓯᓐᓂᕐᒧᓐ ᖃᓄᐅᔾᔭᓕᐅᕐᓇᕐᓗᓂᓗ ᐱᓕᕆᔾᔪᒪᓕᕈᔪᓅᑦ, ᑕᐻᓂᑦᑕᐃᓐᓇᕐᓗ ᐊᕝᕙᑎᐅᔪᒥᓐ ᓂᕐᔪᑎᓂᓪᓗ ᐊᒻᒪ ᐃᓄᐃᑦ ᐃᓕᕐᖁᓯᖏᑦᑎᒍ ᐊᑐᕐᑕᐅᔪᓂ ᓱᕋᐃᖏᑦᑐᓂᑦ.

ᐃᑲᔪᕐᓂᖅ ᐱᓕᕆᕝᕕᖕᓂ ᐊᓂᒍᐃᑦᑎᐊᕐᑎᑦᑎᓂᕐᒥᑦ

ᐱᓇᓱᒪᓂᒃᑭᕗᒍ ᓴᖅᑭᑦᑎᑦᓯᓯᖕᓂᕐᒥ ᐃᓅᓯᕐᒧᓐ ᐅᓗᓇᐊᓈᖏᑦᑐᒥ ᐃᓄᐃᑦ ᐱᓕᕆᕝᕙᖅᓚᕐᑎᓯᒃᓱᒋᑦ. ᓄᓇᕗᑦ ᑐᓐᖓᕕᒃᑯ ᓈᒥᓂᖅᑲᕐᓂᕐᒧᑦ ᐱᓕᕆᐊᑎᑦᑎᓂᖅ ᐱᓕᕆᕝᕕᖓ ᑲᒪᔨᐅᕗᑦ ᐱᓕᕆᐊᓂᐅᔪᓂᑦ ᑕᒪᐃᑎᒍᑦ ᓄᓇᕗᑦ ᓄᓇᒥ ᓈᒥᓂᖅᑲᕐᓂᕐᒧᑦ ᐊᖏᕈᑎᑎᒎᖓᔪᓂᑦ, ᐱᖃᓯᐅᑎᓪᓗᓂ ᓴᓪᓕᒃᑯᓐᓂ ᑳᓐᑐᕐᖅᑎᑦᑎᕙᖕᓂᖅ. ᑕᒪᐃᓐᓂᖓᓄ ᐅᖃᓯᒪᖏᓪᓕ ᐃᓄᐃᑦ ᐊᐅᓚᑕᓪᓖᖏ ᐊᖏᑦᑕᐅᖃᑦᑕᕐᔭᕐᓂᖏᓐᓂᑦ ᓴᓪᓕᒃᑯ ᑳᓐᑐᕐᓯᔾᔪᑎᖏᓐᓂᑦ. ᑭᓯᐊᓂᓪᓚ ᑐᑭᖃᕐᑐᖅ ᐃᓄᐃᑦ ᐃᓯᒪᒋᔭᐅᖃᓇᐊᖃᕐᓂᖏᓐᓂᑦ ᑳᓐᑐᕐᓂᑦ ᐱᑕᖃᓪᓗᖕᒐ – ᐃᖅᑲᓇᐃᔮᒃᓴᓄᑦ ᐃᓪᓗᓂᐊᑭᑕᐅᔪᓈᕐᑐᓄᑦ, ᐃᓚᑎᓯᒪᔪᓂᕐᒧᓐ ᖃᓄᖅ ᑳᓐᑐᕐᓂ ᐱᓇᓯᒍᓈᕐᓂᕐᒧᓐ ᓴᓪᓕᒃᑯ ᐱᔭᒃᓴᐅᑎᑕᖏᓐᓈᓄᑦ, ᐊᒻᒪᓗ ᐃᖅᑲᓇᐃᔮᒃᓴᓂ ᐱᓇᓱᖕᓂᒃᑯᑦ. ᐋᖅᑭᔅᓯᒪᒋᐊᓪᓗᒍᑦ ᑲᑎᖅᓯᐃᔾᔪᑎᒥᓐ ᐃᓅᖕᓂ ᓈᒥᓂᕆᐅᔪᓂᑦ ᓇᓗᓇᐃᖅᓯᔾᔪᑎᒥᓐ ᐃᓕᓴᕆᐅᓯᒪᔪᓂᑦ. ᐅᓇ ᑲᑎᖅᓯᓪᓗᓂ ᐃᓄᐃᑦ ᐱᓕᕆᐊᖑᕆᓐᓄ ᐊᑐᕐᑕᐅᒃᑕᕆᐊᖃᖅᓯᒪᔪᖅ ᓴᓪᓕᒃᑯᓐᓂᑦ ᐅᑭᐅᖑᓐᓂ ᑭᒃᑯᐃᓐᓇᓐᓄ ᖃᓂᖅᑐᓂᑦ ᐃᓅᖕᓂ ᐊᐅᓚᑕᐅᔪᓂᑦ ᐱᔪᓐᓇᕐᓂᖅᑐᓂᑦ ᐊᑐᕐᑕᐅᔪᒪᔪᓂᑦ ᐱᓕᕆᔪᑎᓄᑦ ᐱᓇᓱᖕᖑᑕ ᓴᓪᓕᑐᖅᑯ ᓄᓇᖓᐊᓪᓘᓐᓃᑦ ᓴᓪᓕᖏᓐᓄᑦ ᑳᓐᑐᕐᒃᓴᐅᑎᑕᐅᔪᓄᑦ.

ᓄᓇᒥᓪᓚᕝᑕᒧᓐ ᐃᑲᔫᓯᐊᕈᑎᑦ

ᓄᓇᕗᑦ ᑐᓐᖓᕕᒃᑯ ᐱᓕᕆᓂᖏ ᐱᓇᓱᐃᓐᓇᕈᑕᐅᖏᓪᓚᑦ ᐊᖏᔪᓂᑦ ᐱᓕᕆᐊᒃᓴᓂᑦ. ᐅᒃᐱᕈᓱᒃᐳᒍᑦ ᒥᑭᑦᑐᑦ, ᓄᓇᓕᖕᓂᖖᒍᕐᓯᒪᔪ ᐱᓕᕆᕖ ᓴᖅᑭᑎᑦᑎᔪᓐᓇᕐᓂᖏᓐᓂ ᐃᓅᖖᓄᑦ ᐱᓇᓯᒃᑐᓂ ᑕᒪᓐᓇ ᐊᑲᐅᓛᖑᔪᒥᐊᒃᓴᖕᖓᓂ ᓴᖅᑭᑎᓂᖅ ᐱᓕᕆᕝᕕᒃᓴᓂ ᐱᓕᕆᐊᔾᔪᑎᒃᓴᓄᑦ. ᑕᒪᐃᓐᓂᖕᖓᓄᑦ ᓄᓇᕗᑦ ᑐᓐᖓᕕᒃᑯ ᐊᑐᐃᓐᓇᐅᑎᑦᑎᖅᑕᕐᑕᕗᑦ $2.1-ᒥᐊᓕᓐᑖᓪᓚᓂ ᐊᕐᕌᒍᑕᒫᓐ, ᐃᑲᔪᕐᓯᒃᑰᑎᒃ ᐃᓅᖕᓄᑦ ᓈᒥᓂᖅᓴᐅᔪᓂᑦ ᐱᓕᕆᕝᕕᖕᓂᑦ. ᐅᓇ ᑮᓇᐅᔭᖅ ᓯᐊᕐᒥᒃᑕᐅᕙᒃᐳᖅ ᐃᓅᖕᓄᑦ ᐊᐅᓚᑕᐅᔪᓄᑦ ᐱᖕᖓᓱᓄᑦ ᐊᕕᒃᓯᒪᓂᒃᑯ ᑲᑐᔾᔨᖃᑎᒌᖕᓄ ᑖᒥᓂ ᓄᓇᕗᒻᒥ, ᐊᒻᒪᓗ ᐊᑐᕐᑕᐅᑎᑕᐅᓪᓚᕙᒃᐸᓂ ᐊᑐᕐᑐᐊᕐᑕᐅᑎᓂᒃᑯ, ᐃᑲᔫᓯᐊᒃᑯᑦ ᐊᒻᒪ ᓈᒥᓂᖅᓂᖅᑯᓐ ᐃᓕᓐᓂᐊᕈᑎᑎᒍᑦ. ᐊᐱᖅᑯᑏ ᑖᔅᓯᒧᖓ ᑐᕌᖅᑎᑕᐅᔪᓐᓇᕐᐳᑦ ᐅᕙᖓ: ntiecdev@nunanet.com

ᐃᓐᓇᑐᖃᑦ ᑮᓇᐅᔾᔮᖃᕐᑲᑦᑕᕐᑕᖏᓐᖓ ᐱᓕᕆᓂᖅ

ᐃᓐᓇᑐᖃᑦ ᐱᓕᕆᖃᑦᑕᓂᖏ, ᑖᒃᑯᐊ ᖃᐅᔨᒪᔩᑦ ᐅᖃᓪᓚᖖᓂᒃᑯ, ᐱᒻᒪᕆᐅᓚᐅᕐᓯᒪᔪᖅ ᑕᒪᓐᓇ ᓄᓇᑖᕐᓯᒪᖖᓂᕐᒧᓐ ᖃᖏᐅᑎᑦᑎᑦᑎᐊᕐᓂᕐᒧᓐ. ᑕᒃᑯᐊ ᖃᐅᔨᒪᑎᓪᓗᒋ ᓯᓚᑐᓂᖏᓪᓗ, ᐊᒥᓱᒃ, ᑕᒃᑯᑎᑐᓇᖅ ᐃᓐᓇᑐᖄᖅᑐᑦ ᓇᓂᑐᐃᓐᓇᖅ ᐃᑲᔪᖅᑕᐅᖃᑦᑕᓇᕐᖄᖅᐳᑦ ᖃᐅᑕᒫ ᐊᑐᓇᕐᑲᑦᑕᖏᓐᓄᑦ. ᑕᒪᐃᓐᓂᖕᖓᓄᑦ, ᓄᓇᕗᑦ ᑐᓐᖓᕕᒃᑯ ᐃᓐᓇᑐᖃᓄᑦ ᐃᑲᔫᓯᐊᕐᑎᑦᑎᓂᖅ ᐱᓕᕆᓂᖕᖓ ᐃᑲᔪᖃᑦᑕᕐᐳᑦ ᑮᓇᐅᔭᓂ ᐃᑲᔫᒃᑲᓂᖅᓯᒧᓐ ᐃᓐᓇᑐᖃᓂᑦ ᐊᕐᕌᒍᓕᖕᓂ 55 ᐅᖓᑖᓂᑦ.

ᐃᓕᖅᑯᓯᑐᖃᖅᒥᓐ ᓴᖅᑮᖅᑎᑦᑏᓐᓇᕐᓂᖅ

ᐊᖑᓇᓯᖕᓂᖅ ᐃᓄᐃᑦ ᐃᓕᖅᑯᓯᖓᓂᑦ ᓴᖅᑮᖅᑎᑎᒪᓂᖕᓂᐅᕗᖅ. ᐊᒥᓱᑦ ᓄᓇᕗᑦ ᐃᓚᕇᖕᒥ ᓯᓚ ᐊᑐᕐᐸᒃᐳᑦ ᐊᖑᓇᓯᖕᓂᕐᒥᓐ ᑑᑐᓂᑦ, ᐅᒥᖕᒪᖕᓂᑦ, ᐃᖃᓗᓯᖕᓂᒃᑯ ᐊᒻᒪ ᐃᒪᕐᒥᐅᑕᕐᓂᑦ ᓂᕿᔅᓴᓂᑦ ᐊᒻᒪᓗ ᐊᒥᖏᓐᓄᑦ. ᑕᒪᓐᓇ ᐅᑯᑦᑎᓐᓄ ᓄᓇᒥᓐ ᐊᑐᕐᑎᑦᑎᓯᒪᔪᖅ ᐊᓯᑦᑎᓐᓄ ᐃᓯᒪᕆᔭᐅᓯᒪᔪᒥᓐ ᑐᓐᖓᕙᓇᔭᐅᖏᕈᓐᓂ ᑭᓯᐊᓂᓕ ᐅᑯᑦᑎᓐᓄ ᓂᕿᖃᖅᑎᑦᑎᑦᑎᐊᕐᓯᒪᔪᖅ ᐊᒻᒪ ᐊᓄᕌᖅᑎᑦᑎᓯᒪᔪᖅ ᑕᒪᑐᒥᖓ ᓄᓇᒥ ᖃᓄᐃᒃᓴᖏᔾᔪᑎᒃᓴᓂᑦ.

ᐊᑭᑭᒃᑲᓗᐊᕐᑎᓪᓗᓯ ᒥᖅᑯᓕᑦ, ᐅᓇ ᐃᓕᖅᑯᓯᖅ ᐱᓕᕆᐊᓂᐅᒻᒪᕆᒃᐳᖅ ᐃᓅᖕᓄᑦ ᐱᓕᕆᐊᔾᔪᑕᐅᓪᓗᓂ. ᑭᓯᐊᓂᓕ, ᐃᓅᓯᖅᑲᕐᓯᒪᔪᓂᖅ ᐊᖑᓇᓯᖕᓂᑐᐃᓐᓇᒃᑯ ᐊᒃᓯᕿᕐᓇᓕᐅᔾᔪᒍᖅ – ᓖᓐᓇ ᕿᔫ ᐊᒻᒪ ᒥᖅᑯᓕᑦ ᐊᑭᑰᖕᒪᑕ ᐊᒻᒪᓗ ᐊᑭᓕᐅᑕᐅᕐᓂᒍᓐᓇᕐᑎᒃ ᐊᖑᓇᓰᑎᓄᑦ. ᑕᒪᐃᓐᓂᖕᖓᓄᑦ ᓄᓇᕗᑦ ᑐᓐᖓᕕᒃ ᓴᖅᑭᑎᓯᒪᔪᖅ ᓄᓇᕗᑦ ᐊᖑᓇᓯᒃᑏᑦ ᐃᑲᔫᓯᐊᖏᓐᓂᑦ – ᐃᑲᔪᕐᓯᒧᓐ ᐃᓚᒋᓂ ᐃᖃᓗᓯᒃᑎᐅᔪᓂᑦ, ᐊᖑᓇᓯᒃᑎᐅᔪᓂᑦ ᐊᒻᒪᓗ ᒥᑭᑭᐊᕐᑎᐅᔪᓂᑦ ᐅᒻᒥᐊᑎᖅᑲᕐᑐᓂᑦ. ᑕᒪᓐᓇ ᐱᓕᕆᓂᖅ ᐃᑲᔪᖅᑲᑦᑕᖅᐳᖅ $12,000ᑖᓪᓚᑦ ᑎᑭᓪᓗᒍ ᐊᖑᓇᓰᑎᓄᑦ. ᑮᓇᐅᔾᔭᑦ ᑖᔅᓱᒧᖓ

ourselves comfortable in a land others consider inhospitable, with a diet rich in healthy country foods and clothing that helps us withstand the harsh elements.

Despite low fur prices, this traditional way of life is a thriving part of the Inuit modern economy. However, making a living as a hunter can be a challenge—current sealskin and fur prices are low and do not always offset the cost of hunting equipment.

That is why NTI created the Nunavut Hunter Support Program—to assist families who fish, hunt and trap for a living. The program provides up to $12,000 for equipment. Money for this program comes from a trust jointly created by NTI and the GNWT. As well as managing hunter support benefits, the program also manages NTI's wildlife management interests, working alongside the Nunavut Wildlife Management Board.

Working together for the common good

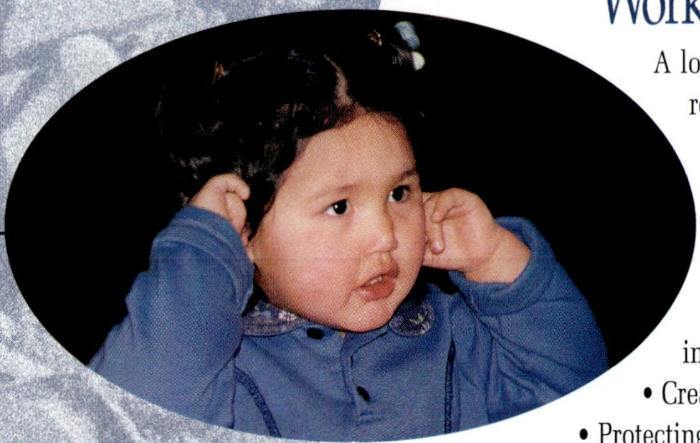

A lot of our work is shared with other Inuit organizations. We work closely with regional Inuit organizations and others in creating a thorough structure of policies, systems and procedures needed to manage a territory one-fifth the size of Canada.

Other organizations include the Nunavut Planning Commission, the Nunavut Impact Review Board, the Nunavut Water Board and the Nunavut Surface Rights Tribunal. We're working together, with responsibilities that include:

- Creating national and territorial parks
- Protecting conservation areas
- Promoting the use of Inuit contractors
- Promoting responsible exploration and development of Inuit-owned lands
- Changing the boundaries of municipal lands
- Protecting deposits of carving stone
- Monitoring water quality
- Regulating public access to Inuit-owned lands ... and much more.

The Nunavut government

NTI, as one of the three signatories of the Nunavut Accord, has the responsibility of reviewing and participating in the design of the new territorial government. Our goal has been to ensure that the government's form and functions reflect the spirit and letter of the claim—to ensure there is a territorial public government in place that will be chosen by, and serve, all the citizens of Nunavut.

Into the future

With Nunavut finally a reality, NTI continues to work hard in fulfilling the dream of Nunavut as a vibrant, beneficial and equally respected part of the Canadian mosaic. In the words of NTI President Jose Kusugak, "We want to level the playing field, to participate like any other Canadian. We're all in this together to develop a good Canada."

ᐱᓕᕆᓂᖅᒧᓐ ᐱᔭᐅᕙᒃᐳᖅ ᐸᐸᑦᑎᕕᖕᒥ ᓴᖅᑭᑕᐅᓯᒪᔪᒥᓐ ᓄᓇᕗᑦ ᑐᓐᖓᕕᒃᑯᓐᓂ ᐊᒻᒪ ᓄᓇᑦᓯᐊᑉ ᑲᒪᒃᑯᖏᓐᓂᑦ. ᐊᐅᓚᑦᑎᔨᐅᓪᓗᑎ ᑕᒪᑐᒥᖓ ᐱᓕᕆᐊᒥ ᐱᓕᕆᕙᓪᓗᐊᕐᒥ ᐊᒻᒪᑦᑕᐅᖅ, ᐱᓕᕆᓂᖅ ᑲᒪᔨᐅᓲᖑᔪᖅ ᐊᐅᓚᑦᑎᓂᕐᒥ ᓄᓇᕗᑦ ᑐᓐᖓᕕᒃᑯ ᓂᕈᐊᖅᑎᖏᓐᓂ ᐱᓕᕆᐊᖃᕈᒪᔪᓂᑦ, ᐱᓕᕆᖃᑎᖃᖅᑐᑎᒃ ᓄᓇᕗᑦ ᐆᒪᔪᓕᕆᔨᖅᔪᐊᒃᑯᖏᑦᑕ ᑲᑎᒪᔨᖏᓐᓂᑦ.

ᐱᓕᕆᖃᑎᒌᖕᓂᖅ ᐱᐅᔪᒧᓐ

ᐱᓕᕆᐊᕆᖃᑦᑕᕗᑦ ᐃᓚᖏ ᑲᑐᔾᔨᓂᒃᑯᑦ ᐱᓕᕆᐊᕆᔭᐅᖃᑦᑕᖅᐳᑦ ᐊᓯᖏᑦᑎᒍᑦ ᐃᓄᐃᑦ ᑲᑐᔾᔨᖃᑎᒌᖕᓂᖏᑦᑎᒍᑦ. ᐱᓕᕆᖃᑎᖃᖃᑦᑕᖅᐳᒍᑦ ᐃᓄᐃᑦ ᑲᑐᔾᔨᖃᑎᒌᖏᓐᓂ ᐊᐅᓪᓚᖓᔪᓂ ᐊᕕᒃᑐᖅᓯᒪᓂᒃᑯᑦ ᐊᒻᒪ ᐊᓯᖏᑦᑎᒍ ᓴᖅᑭᑎᑕᐅᔪᑦ ᐊᑐᐊᒐᖅᓂᑦ, ᒪᓕᒃᓴᓂᑦ ᐊᒻᒪ ᐊᑐᕆᐊᖅᑐᓂ ᐊᐅᓚᑦᑎᓂᖅᒧᓐ ᓄᓇᒥᓐ ᑲᓇᑕ ᑕᓯᒪᐃᖅᓯᕈᓂ ᐃᓚᖓᓂ ᐊᖏᑎᕆᔪᒥᓐ.

ᐊᓯᖓ ᑲᑐᔾᔨᖅᑎᕆᑦ ᐃᓚᖅᑲᖅᐳᑦ ᓄᓇᕗᑦ ᐸᕐᓇᐃᔾᔨᖏᓐᓂᑦ, ᓄᓇᕗᑦ ᐊᒃᑐᐊᑕᐅᔪᓐᓂᖏᑦᑕ ᖃᐅᔨᓴᖅᑎᖏᓐᓄᑦ ᑲᑎᒪᔨᓂ, ᓄᓇᕗᑦ ᐃᒪᓕᕆᔨᖏᑦᑕ ᑲᑎᒪᔨᖅᔪᐊᖏᓐᓂ, ᐊᒻᒪ ᓄᓇᓕᕆᓂᕐᒧᓐ ᐋᖅᑭᐊᒃᑲᐃᔨᓂᑦ. ᐱᓕᕆᖃᑎᒌᒃᐳᒍᑦ, ᐅᑯᓂᖓ ᐱᓕᕆᐊᒃᓴᖃᖅᑐᑎ:

- ᓴᖅᑭᑦᑎᓂᖅ ᑲᓇᑕᒥ ᓄᓇᑦᓯᐊᖅᒥᑦᑐ ᒥᖅᑯᐃᖅᓯᕖᖕᓂ
- ᓴᐳᔾᔨᓯᒪᓂᖅᒥᓐ ᓄᓇᓂᑦ ᐊᒃᑐᖅᑕᐅᑦᑕᐃᓕᓯᒪᑎᑕᐅᔪᓂᑦ
- ᐃᓕᓐᓂᐊᖅᑎᑦᑎᑕᐅᓯᒪᔪᓂᖅᒥᓐ ᐃᓄᖕᓂ ᑳᓐᑐᖅᓰᖅᑎᑕᐅᔪᓂᑦ
- ᐃᓕᓐᓂᐊᖅᑎᑦᑎᑕᐅᓯᒪᔪᓂᖅᒥᓐ ᖃᐅᔨᓴᖅᑎᓂᑦ ᐅᔾᔨᕈᓱᑦᑎᐊᖅᓂᖅᒥᓐ ᐊᒻᒪ ᐱᕙᓪᓕᐊᓂᖅᒥᓐ ᐃᓄᐃᑦ ᓄᓇᖁᑎᖏᓐᓂᑦ
- ᐊᓯᐅᔫᖅᑎᑦᑎᕙᖕᓂᖅᒥᓐ ᓄᓇᓖᑦ ᓇᑯᓇᐃᒃᑯᑎᖏᓐᓂᑦ
- ᓴᐳᔾᔨᓯᒪᓂᖅᒥᓐ ᐅᒃᑯᓯᒃᓴᖅᑐᓂᑦ ᓄᓇᓂᑦ
- ᖃᐅᔨᓴᖅᑎᐅᓂᖅᒥᓐ ᐃᒪᖅᓂᑦ
- ᒪᓕᒐᓕᐅᖅᑎᐅᓂᖅᒥᓐ ᑭᒃᑯᐃᓐᓇᖅᓄᑦ ᐊᑐᖅᑕᐅᔪᓐᓇᖅᑐᓂ ᐃᓄᐃᑦ ᓄᓇᖏᓐᓃᑦᑐᓂᑦ … ᐊᒻᒪ ᐊᓯᖏᓐᓂ ᐅᓄᖅᒪᕆᒃᑐᓂᑦ.

ᓄᓇᕗᑦ ᒐᕙᒪᖓ

ᓄᓇᕗᑦ ᑐᓐᖓᕕᒃ, ᐃᓚᒋᔭᐅᑎᓪᓗᒋ ᐱᖓᓱᓂ ᐊᑎᓕᐅᖅᑎᐅᔪᓂ ᓄᓇᕗᑦ ᒪᓕᒐᖓᓂ, ᑲᒪᔨᐅᓕᖅᓯᒪᕗᑦ ᖃᐅᔨᓴᖅᓂᒥ ᐊᒻᒪ ᐃᓚᐅᔪᓐᓇᖅᓂᒥ ᐋᖅᑭᒃᓱᐃᓂᖅᒧᓐ ᓄᑖᒥ ᐃᒻᒥᒃᑰᖅᑐᒥ ᐊᕕᒃᓯᒪᓂᒃᑯ ᒐᕙᒪᖓᓂᑦ. ᑎᑭᓯᒃᑕᕗᑦ ᑕᒪᓐᓇ ᒐᕙᒪᐅᓂᐊᖅᑐᖅ ᖃᓄᐃᓕᖓᓂᖓ ᐱᓕᕆᐊᒃᓴᖏᓐᓗ ᓴᖅᑭᑎᓯᒃᓱᒥ ᐃᓯᒪᕆᔭᐅᔪᖅ ᐊᒻᒪ ᑎᑎᖅᑲᑕᐅᓯᒪᔪᑎᒍᑦ ᒪᓕᒃᑎᓯᒃᓱᑎᒍᑦ ᓄᓇᑖᖅᓯᑎᒥᑦᑐᒃ — ᓴᖅᑭᑎᓯᒃᓱᑕ ᐃᓅᓐᓄ ᒐᕙᒪᐅᓂᐊᖅᑐᒥ ᐃᓅᓐᓄ ᓂᕈᐊᕆᔭᐅᔪᓂᑦ, ᐊᒻᒪ ᐱᔾᔪᑎᖃᖅᑎᐅᓂᐊᖅᑐᒥ ᓄᓇᕗᒻᒥᐅᑕᓕᒫᓄᑦ.

ᓯᕗᓂᑦᑎᓐᓄᖕᒐᐅᕙᓪᓕᐊᓂᖅ

ᓄᓇᕗᑦ ᑕᕝᕙᒪᓂᐅᓕᖅᑎᓪᓗ, ᓄᓇᕗᑦ ᑐᓐᖓᕕᒃ ᐱᓕᕆᓐᓇᖅᐳᑦ ᐊᒃᓯᕈᖅᓱᑎ ᓴᖅᑭᑎᓯᖕᓂᒃᑯ ᓄᓇᕗᒻᒥ ᐱᔪᓐᓇᒪᓕᒃᑐᒥ, ᐱᑖᕈᑕᐅᔪᓐᓇᖅᑐᒥ ᐊᒻᒪ ᐃᓕᓐᓂᐊᖅᓯᒪᔪᒥ ᑲᓇᑕᐅ ᐃᓚᒋᓐᖓᓄᑦ. ᐅᖃᐅᓯᐅᓂᖅᑯᖓ ᓄᓇᕗᑦ ᑐᓐᖓᕕᒃᑯ ᐃᓯᒪᑕᖓᑕ, ᔫᓯ ᑯᓯᒐᐅᑉ, "ᐱᓕᕆᕐᕕᒃᐳᑦ ᒪᓂᒃᓴᖃᕈᑦ ᓇᓕᒨᒃᑎᓪᓗᒍ, ᑲᓇᑕᒥᐅᑕᑎᑦ ᐃᓚᐅᔪᒪ. ᑕᒪᑦᑕ ᑕᒪᑐᒥᖓ ᐱᓕᕆᐊᒃᓴᖅᐳᒍᑦ ᓴᖅᑭᑎᓂᖅᒥ ᑲᓇᑕᑎᐊᕙᖕᒥᓐ."

For more information, including the entire text of the Nunavut Land Claims Agreement, our annual report, and other information about NTI, please visit our Internet web site at: www.tunngavik.com

ᖃᐅᔨᒃᑲᓐᓂᕈᒪᒍᕕᑦ ᐅᕙᓗᓐᓂᑦ ᓄᓇᕗᑦ ᓄᓇᒥ ᓇᖕᒥᓂᖅᑲᖅᓂᖅᒧᑦ ᐊᖏᕈᑎᐅᑉ ᐃᓗᓕᖏᓐᓂ, ᐊᖅᖁᓕᓖᖅᓯᐅᑎᓂ ᐅᓂᒃᑳᓂ, ᐊᒻᒪ ᐊᓯᖏᓐᓂ ᓄᓇᕗᑦ ᑐᓐᖓᕕᒃᑯ ᑎᒥᖓᑕ ᒥᒃᓵᓄ, ᑕᑯᒋᐊᕈᓐᓇᖅᐳᓯ ᖃᕆᓴᐅᔭᒃᑯ ᓴᖅᑮᔭᖅᑎ-ᑕᑦᑎᓐᓂᑦ ᐅᕙᓂ: www.tunngavik.com

Nunavut Tunngavik Incorporated
ᓄᓇᕗᑦ ᑐᓐᖓᕕᒃᑯ ᑎᒥᖓ

IQALUIT ᐃᖃᓗᐃᑦ
Parnaivik Building
Box 638
Iqaluit, NT X0A 0H0
Tel. / ᐅᖄᓚᐅᑎᖓ: (867) 979-3232
Fax / ᓱᒃᑲᔪᒃᑯ: (867) 979-3240

CAMBRIDGE BAY ᑲᖏᖅᖠᓂᖅ
Box 1041
Cambridge Bay, NT X0E 0C0
Tel. / ᐅᖄᓚᐅᑎᖓ: (867) 983-2517
Fax / ᓱᒃᑲᔪᒃᑯ: (867) 983-2723

RANKIN INLET ᐃᖃᓗᒃᑑᑦᑎᐊᖅ
Sakku Building
Box 280
Rankin Inlet, NT X0C 0G0
Tel. / ᐅᖄᓚᐅᑎᖓ: (867) 645-5400
Fax / ᓱᒃᑲᔪᒃᑯ: (867) 645-3451

OTTAWA ᐋᑐᕚ
130 Albert Street
Suite 1108
Ottawa, ON K1P 5G4
Tel. / ᐅᖄᓚᐅᑎᖓ: (613) 238-1096
Fax / ᓱᒃᑲᔪᒃᑯ: (613) 238-4131

INUIT AND THE LAND AS ONE

ᐃᓄᐃᑦ ᓄᓇᓗ ᐊᑕᐅᓯᐅᔪᑦ

The bond between Inuit and the land and wildlife was weakened when settlements replaced their nomadic lifestyle. The Nunavut Land Claims Agreement aims to change that

ᐃᓄᐃᑦ ᐆᒪᔪᐃᓪᓗ ᓄᓇᒧᓪᓗ ᐊᒃᑐᐊᓂᖓᑦ ᓵᓐᖏᓕᕐᑎᑕᐅᓯᒪᔪᖅ ᐃᓄᐃᑦ ᓄᓇᓕᖃᐅᓕᖅᑎᓪᓗᒋᑦ ᓇᒧᑐᐃᓈᖅᐸᓪᓚᐅᕐᓂᖏᑦ ᐊᑐᖅᑕᐅᓐᖏᓕᕐᒪᑕ. ᑮᓯᐊᓂᓕ ᓯᒃᓂᕐᕌᔪᒧᑦ ᓄᓇᐅᑉ ᑲᒪᒋᔭᐅᓂᖓ ᑎᒍᒥᐊᖅᑕᐅᓕᖅᑎᓪᓗᒍ ᐃᓄᖕᓄᑦ, ᓯᕗᒻᒧᒃᑕᐅᒍᓐᓇᖅᑯᖅᑐᖅ ᐊᑯᓂᑦ ᐊᑐᖃᔭᖅᑐᒥᒃ ᓵᑭᖅᑎᑕᐅᓂᖓ ᓄᓇᐅᑉ ᐃᓄᐃᑦ ᐊᒃᑐᐊᕈᓪᓚᐅᕐᓂᖏᑦ ᑕᐃᒪᒃᑳᓂᒥᑦ

By Brian Aglukark

The snow was melting on the streets of Arviat. I got excited whenever the school bell rang, in hopes that my father was preparing the sleds for a goose hunt. Sometimes, through the window of your classroom, you would watch the geese sailing through the clear, blue sky. As usual, the teacher couldn't understand your love for the season at hand, or your inner voice screaming at you to be out on the land as the geese cried out, flying in perfect formation in their annual migration north for the summer.

An unexpected visitor walked into our classroom. Looking behind me, I recognized my father speaking ever so quietly to the teacher. To my surprise, the teacher excused me from class for the rest of the day. I raced back to my desk, cleaned up, and rushed to our little house at the end of town to prepare for the hunt. This wasn't an unusual turn of events. Many of my classmates had not attended school for the last week because they were out on the land, enjoying the spring weather with their whole family. This was, and still is, a yearly spring tradition.

The next morning I woke up to the hum of wings flapping and the ever distinct sound of the geese as they flew over our tent.

ᑎᑎᖅᑐᖅ ᐸᕋᐃᐊᓐ ᐊᓪᓘᒃᑲᖅ

ᐊᕐᕕᐊᒥ ᐊᖅᑯᑎᖏᑦ ᐊᐳᑏᖅᐸᓪᓕᐊᓪᓚᐅᖅᑐᑦ. ᓂᕆᐅᒃᐸᓪᓕᐊᓪᓗᖓ ᐃᓕᓐᓂᐊᕐᕕᖕᒥ ᓯᕙᓂᐅᑦ ᓯᕙᓂᓕᖅᖓᑦ, ᐊᑖᑕᒐᒃᑲᐃ ᐸᕐᓇᐃᓕᖅᑐᖅ ᖃᒧᑏᖕᓂᒃ ᑎᖕᒥᐊᖅᓯᐅᕐᓂᐊᕐᓂᕐᒧᑦ ᑲᖑᕐᓂᒃ. ᐃᓛᓐᓂᒃᑯᑦ, ᐃᓚᖏᒃᑯᑦ ᑲᖑᐃᑦ ᑎᒋᐸᓪᓕᐊᔪᑦ ᑕᑯᒃᓴᐅᑉᐸᓪᓕᐅᖅᑐᑦ, ᓯᓚᑦᑎᐊᑉᐅᑎᓪᓗᒍ ᓄᕗᔭᖕᓈᖕᒋᑎᓪᓗᒍ, ᑐᖑᔪᕈᔪᑦᑎᐊᖅᓗᓂ ᓯᓚ. ᒌᖅᑲᐃᒻᒪᐅᓚᓗᐊᖅ ᐃᓕᓐᓂᐊᖅᑎᐅᔪᖅ ᑐᑭᓯᓐᓇᓪᓚᐅᖕᖏᑦᑐᖅ ᐊᐅᓪᓚᖅᑕᐅᔪᒪᓂᕐᓂᒃ ᔫᖅ ᓄᓇᐃᓐᓇᕐᒧᑦ ᐃᓚᐅᖅᑲᑕᐅᔪᒪᓂᕐᓂᒃ. ᑐᓴᓐᓇᖅᑎᓪᓗᒋᑦ ᑲᖑᐃᑦ ᑎᒋᐸᓪᓕᐊᔪᑦ ᐃᓯᖅᓯᒪᔪᒪᓐᓇᕐᓂᐅᓪᓗᐊᖅ, ᓴᓂᓕᓈᒃᓗᑎᒃ ᑎᖕᒥᔪᑦ ᓄᓇᒋᔭᒥᖕᓄᑦ ᐅᑭᐅᖅᑕᖅᑐᒧᑦ ᐅᑎᖅᐸᓪᓕᐊᓪᓕᖅᑎᓪᓗᒋᑦ ᐊᐅᔭᓕᒫᖅ ᑕᐃᑲᓐᓂᐊᖅᓗᑎᒃ.

ᓂᓪᓗᖕᓇᕐᓂ ᐃᓯᖅᑐᖅᑲᕐᓂᖅᑎᓪᓗᒍ ᐃᓕᓐᓂᐊᕐᕕᒋᔭᑦᑎᓐᓄᑦ. ᑐᓄᒻᒧᑦ ᑕᑯᒥᐊᕐᒪ, ᐊᑖᑕᒐ ᐃᓕᑕᕆᓪᓗᒍ ᓂᐱᖅᑯᖅᑐᐊᕐᓂ ᐅᖃᖅᑎᖃᖅᑐᖅ ᐃᓕᓐᓂᐊᖅᑎᑎᔨᒥᓂᒃ. ᐅᐸᑎᐊᒃᑯᓐᒪ ᐃᓕᓐᓂᐊᖅᑎᑎᔨᒪ ᖃᐃᖁᓪᓗᓂᖓ, ᐊᓂᖃᓕᒍᓐᓇᖅᑐᖓᒥᒃ ᐃᓚᐅᖅᑲᑕᐅᓂᐊᕐᒪ ᑎᖕᒥᐊᖅᓯᐅᕐᓂᐊᖅᑐᓂ. ᑕᒪᐃᓚᔪᓪᓗᑐᖅ ᐃᓕᓐᓂᐊᖅᑎᒃ ᐊᒥᓯᑦ ᖃᐃᖕᖏᖅᑲᑦᑕᓕᖅᑎᓪᓗᒋᑦ ᐱᓇᓱᐊᕈᓯᕐᒥ ᑲᖑᐃᑦ ᑎᒋᐸᓪᓕᐊᓂᖏᓐᓂ. ᐅᐱᕐᖔᒥ ᓄᓇᒥᓯᐅᖅᑐᑦ ᐃᓚᒌᑦ. ᑕᒪᐃᐸᓪᓕᐅᖅᑐᖅ, ᐊᒪᓗ ᓯᓕᔪᖅ ᓯᓕ ᐅᓪᓗᒥᒧᑦ, ᐅᐱᕐᖔᖅᕿᖓᑦ ᐊᑐᖅᑕᐅᕙᓪᓕᐅᖅᑐᖅ.

ᖃᐅᖕᒪᑦ ᑐᐸᒃᑐᖓ ᐃᖃᕈᖅᓯᕐᓂᖕᒋᓐᓂᒃ ᑐᖅᓱᓪᓗᖓ ᐊᒪᓗ ᓂᓪᓕᐊᓂᖕᒋᓐᓂᒃ ᑐᐱᑦᑕ ᖁᓖᓄᑦ ᑎᖕᒥᑎᓪᓗᒋᑦ.

Nunavut Tourism; oval inset: Nunavut Tourism ᓄᓇᕗᑦ ᐳᓚᕋᖅᑐᓕᕆᔨᑦ; ᐊᖏᒪᔅᓯᐅᑦ ᐃᓗᐊᓂ: ᓄᓇᕗᑦ ᐳᓚᕋᖅᑐᓕᕆᔨᑦ

"Like a newborn to her mother"

Historically, the survival of Inuit depended solely on the land and waters and the wildlife that they provide. The relationship between the Inuit and the land was one, like a newborn baby to her mother. Inuit lived as nomads, moving from place to place in order to follow the migration routes of caribou, seals, fish and birds. The land also offered shelter from freezing winter temperatures of –30° C to –40° C with *igluit* (igloos) built from snow, or from summer rains by way of caribou-skin tents or huts constructed either from stone, or stone and dirt.

In this century, the white man has ushered in a new lifestyle in which Inuit must not only live away from the land, but also in comfort and ease, having been introduced to instant foods, rifles, snowmobiles, wooden houses and formal education. Today, the connection between Inuit and the land has weakened, and Inuit struggle with their identity: the Inuit's latest challenge in a land that has always been challenging.

Nunavut — "our land" — is divided into three administrative regions: Kitikmeot, Kivalliq (also known by its former name, Keewatin) and Baffin (Qikiqtaaluk). The Inuit in each region faced different hunting challenges, because each region includes several distinct ecosystems in which certain animals played a key role in the survival of the Inuit.

In the west Kitikmeot Region, the Inuit depended on the migration of the caribou. The Inuit in the east Kitikmeot (the *Nattilingmiut*) depended on the seal. In coastal areas of the Kivalliq, Inuit relied mainly on seal, caribou and arctic char, whereas Inuit on the mainland hunted caribou, geese and ptarmigan, and fished lake trout. In the northern tip of the Kivalliq Region, walruses were also hunted. The people of Baffin Island sought walruses, seals and arctic char. Caribou, Canada geese, ptarmigan, seals, whales and arctic char are all found throughout Nunavut and are part of the diet of all Inuit.

“ᓱᕐᓗ ᐃᓅᓕᕿᖅᑐᖅ ᐊᓈᓇᒥᓄᑦ”

ᑕᐃᑦᓱᒪᓂᐅᕙᓪᓕᐅᖅᑐᖅ ᓯᕗᓕᑦᑎᓐᓂ, ᐃᓄᐃᑦ ᐊᓈᓇᐅᒪᕙᓪᓕᐅᕐᒪᑕ ᓄᓇᐃᓐᓇᒦᓪᓗᑎᒃ ᐊᒻᒪᓗ ᐃᒪᖕᖏᓐᓂ ᐆᒪᔪᓂᒃ ᓂᕿᖃᕈᕐᒥᒃ ᐱᔪᓐᓇᖅᑕᒥᖕᓂᒃ. ᐊᒃᑐᐊᓂᖕᖏᑦ ᓄᓇᒧᑦ ᐊᑕᐅᓯᐅᓪᓕᐅᖅᑐᒃ, ᓄᑕᕋᓛᑐᑦ ᐃᓅᓕᕿᖅᑐᑦ ᐊᓈᓇᒥᓄᑦ. ᐃᓄᐃᑦ ᐃᖕᖏᕐᕋᑕᖅᓱᑎᒃ ᐃᓅᕙᓪᓕᐅᕐᒪᑕ, ᓅᑉᐸᓪᓕᐊᕙᒃᓱᑎᒃ ᐆᒪᔪᓂᒃ ᒪᓕᒃᓱᑎᒃ ᓂᕿᖏᔅᒥᖕᓂᒃ ᒪᑯᓂᖓ ᑐᒃᑐᓂᒃ, ᓇᑦᓯᓂᒃ, ᐃᖃᓗᖕᓂᒃ ᑎᖕᒥᐊᓂᓗ. ᓄᓇ ᐃᓂᖏᔭᐅᕙᓪᓕᐅᖅᑐᖅ ᐊᖕᖏᕐᕿᓕᐅᖅᓱᑎᒃ ᐃᒃᐱᓈᓗᖕᒥ ᐅᑭᐅᒥ ᑖᒥᓂ ᖃᓂᒋᔭᖕᖓᓂ -30°-ᒥᑦ -40°-ᒧᑦ. ᐃᒡᓗᐱᒐᓕᐅᖅᓱᑎᒃ, ᐅᕙᓗᓐᓕᑦ ᐊᐅᔭᒥ ᑐᒃᑐᓂᑦ ᑐᐱᓕᐅᖅᓱᑎᒃ ᖃᒻᒪᓕᐅᖅᓱᑎᒡᓗᓐᓕᑦ ᐅᔭᖅᑲᓂᒃ, ᐅᕙᓗᓐᓕᑦ ᐅᔭᖅᑲᓂᒃ ᐊᒻᒪᓗ ᓄᓇᐃᓐᓇᕐᒥᒃ.

ᑕᒪᑐᒪᓂ ᐊᕐᕿᓘᔪᓂ ᐊᑐᓕᖅᑕᑦᑎᓐᓂ, ᖃᑦᓗᓈᓂᖕᖖᒑᖅᑐᓂᒃ ᑎᑭᕙᐅᓯᒪᓕᕐᑕ. ᐃᓄᐃᑦ ᓄᓇᓕᑐᕐᑲᕐᒥᖕᓂᑦ ᓅᓯᒪᓕᕐᒪᑕ ᓄᓇᐃᓐᓇᕐᒦᓐᖏᓕᖅᓱᑎᒃ, ᐊᒻᒪᓗ ᐅᑦᓗᒥᐅᔪᖅ ᐊᔪᕐᓇᓐᖏᑦᑐᓂᒃ ᐊᑐᓕᕐᒪᑕ, ᓯᓇᑐᐃᓐᓇᐃᑦ ᐊᑐᐃᓐᓇᐅᓕᖅᑐᑦ ᐊᑐᖅᑕᐅᔪᓐᓇᓕᕐᒪᑕ ᒪᑯᐊᕋᓗᐃᑦ ᓂᕿᑦ ᓴᓇᑲᐅᑎᒋᔭᐅᔪᓐᓇᖅᑐᑦ, ᖁᑭᐅᑏᑦ, ᖃᒧᑕᐅᔭᐃᑦ, ᐃᒡᓗᐃᑦ ᕿᔪᖕᒥᒃ ᓴᓇᓯᒪᔪᑦ ᐊᒻᒪᓗ ᐃᓕᓐᓂᐊᕐᓂᖅ ᐃᓄᖅᓵᖅᑕᐅᓐᖏᓕᖅᓱᓂ. ᐅᓪᓗᒥ, ᐃᓄᐃᑦ ᐊᒃᑐᐊᓂᖕᖏᑦ ᓄᓇᒧᑦ ᓵᓐᖑᓕᖅᑎᑕᐅᓯᒪᔪᖅ, ᐊᒻᒪᓗ ᐃᓄᐃᑦ ᑭᓇᐅᖕᒪᖖᒋᕐᒥᒃ ᐅᔾᔨᕆᔭᖃᕈᓐᓇᓕᕐᒪᑕ: ᐃᓄᐃᑦ ᐊᒃᓱᕈᕐᓂᕐᒥᒃ ᐊᑐᐃᒐᔪᒃᓯᒪᖕᒪᑕ ᓄᓇᖃᖅᓯᒪᑐᖃᕐᒥᒃ ᐊᒃᓱᕈᕐᓇᖅᑐᒥ.

Nunavut - “ᓄᓇᕗᑦ” - ᐊᕕᒃᑐᖅᓯᒪᔪᖅ ᐱᖕᖓᓱᓕᖅᑎᑕᐅᓪᓗᑎ ᐊᐅᓚᑦᑎᕕᖃᐅᖅᑐᓂᒃ: ᕿᑎᕐᒥᐅᑦ, ᑭᕙᓪᓕᖅ (ᖃᐅᔨᒪᔭᐅᖕᒥᔪᖅ ᐊᑎᖓᑐᖃᓪᓚᐅᖅᑕᖕᖓᓄᑦ, ᑮᕙᑎᓐ) ᐊᒻᒪᓗ ᕿᑭᖅᑖᓗᒃ. ᐃᓄᐃᑦ ᐊᔾᔨᒋᓐᖏᑦᑐᓂ ᐊᕕᒃᑐᖅᓯᒪᔪᓂᒥᐅᑕᐃᑦ ᐊᔾᔨᒋᓐᖏᑦᑐᓂᒃ ᐆᒪᔪᓕᕆᓂᐅᔪᓂᒃ ᓵᖕᖓᔪᑦ. ᑕᒪᐃᑕ ᐊᔾᔨᒋᓐᖏᑦᑐᑦ ᐊᕕᒃᑐᖅᓯᒪᔪᐃᑦ ᐊᔾᔨᒋᓐᖏᑦᑐᓂᒃ ᐆᒪᔪᖃᕐᕕᖃᕐᒪᑕ. ᓄᓇᕗᑦ ᐊᔾᔨᒋᓐᖏᑦᑐᓂᒃ ᐆᒪᔪᕐᑯᑎᖃᕐᓂᕐᒧᑦ ᐊᔾᔨᒋᓐᖏᑦᑐᑎᒍᑦ ᐊᒃᑐᐃᓂᖃᓪᓕᐅᖅᑐᑦ ᐃᓄᐃᑦ ᐊᓈᓇᒪᔪᓐᓇᕐᓂᖕᖏᓐᓂᒃ.

ᐅᐊᓕᓂᕐᒥ ᕿᑎᕐᒥᐅᓂ, ᐃᓄᐃᑦ ᐃᓅᒍᑎᖃᕈᓐᓇᓪᓚᐅᕐᒪᑕ ᑐᒃᑐᐃᑦ ᓇᒨᖅᑕᕐᓂᖕᖓᓐᓂᒃ ᒪᓕᒃᓱᑎᒃ. ᕿᑎᕐᒥᐅᑦ ᐅᖅᑯᖕᖓᓂ (ᓇᑦᓯᓕᖕᒥᐅᑕᐃ) ᓂᕿᖃᖃᑦᑕᖅᑎᓪᓗᒋᑦ ᐊᓈᓇᒫᔪᑎᖃᖅᑎᓪᓗᒋᓪᓗ ᓇᑦᓯᕐᓂᒃ. ᑭᕙᓪᓕᕐᒥᐅᑦ ᓯᒡᔭᖃᐅᕐᓂᖕᖓᓂ, ᐃᓄᐃᑦ ᐊᖑᓇᓱᒃᐸᓪᓕᐅᖅᑐᑦ ᓇᑦᓯᕐᓂᒃ, ᑐᒃᑐᓂᒃ ᐃᖃᓗᒃᐱᖕᓂᓗ, ᓄᓇᐃᓐᓇᕐᒥᐅᑕᐃᑦ ᐊᖑᓇᓱᖕᓂᖅᓴᐅᕙᒃᑎᓪᓗᒋᑦ ᑐᒃᑐᓂᒃ, ᑎᖕᒥᐊᓂᒃ/ᑲᖑᕐᓂᒃ ᐊᒻᒪᓗ ᐊᖅᑭᒡᒋᕐᓂᒃ, ᐃᖃᓗᒃᓯᐅᖅᐸᒃᓱᑎᒡᓗ ᐃᓗᕐᖁᔪᖕᓂᒃ. ᑲᓇᖕᓇᖕᖓᓂ ᑭᕙᓪᓕᕐᒥ, ᐊᐃᕖᑦ ᐱᓇᓱᒃᑕᐅᕙᓪᓚᐅᕐᒥᔪᑦ. ᕿᑭᖅᑖᓗᖕᒥᓕ ᐊᐃᕕᖅᓯᐅᖅᐸᓪᓕᐅᖅᑐᑦ, ᓇᑦᓯᖅᓯᐅᖅᓱᑎᒃ ᐃᖃᓗᒃᓯᐅᖅᓱᑎᒡᓗ. ᑐᒃᑐᐃᑦ, ᐅᓗᐊᒍᓪᓖᑦ (ᑲᖑᐃᑦ), ᐊᖅᑭᒡᒌᑦ, ᓇᑦᓰᑦ, ᕿᓪᓗᒐᐃᑦ ᐃᖃᓗᒃᐲᓪᓗ ᓇᒥᑐᐃᓐᓇᖅ ᓄᓇᕗᒥ ᐱᑕᖃᖅᑐᑦ ᐊᒻᒪᓗ ᐃᓄᖕᓄᑦ ᓂᕿᒋᔭᐅᔪᑦ.

Nunavut Tourism ᓄᓇᕗᑦ ᐳᓚᕋᖅᑐᓕᕆᔨᒃᑯᑦ

Wilkinson/NWT Archives

Left: In 1957, Inuit at a Baker Lake Christmas party were given canned goods as presents, but over the years, costly imported foods have never replaced nutritious "country food." Above: John Kaunak provides a maktaaq *(whale skin) snack in Repulse Bay. Far left: Managing the land's resources so that generations of Inuit can continue to hunt is a key land claim victory*

ᓴᐅᒥᐊᓂ: 1957ᒥ, ᐃᓄᐃᑦ ᖃᒪᓂᑦᑐᐊᕐᒥ ᖁᕕᐊᓲᓯᐊᕐᑖᖅᑎᑕᐅᓪᓚᐅᕐᒪᑦ ᐃᐳᐃᑦᑐᓂ ᓂᕿᓂ, ᑭᓯᐊᓂᓕ ᐊᕐᕌᒍᑦ ᐊᓂᒍᕐᐸᓪᓕᐊᑎᓪᓗᒍ, ᐊᑭᑐᔪᑦ ᑎᑭᑎᑕᐅᓯᒪᔪᑦ ᓂᕿᓪᓚᖕᖑᓂ ᓵᓚᖃᕐᖏᓪᓚᑦ. ᖁᓛᓂᑦ: ᔫᓐ ᖃᐅᓇᖅ ᒫᒃᑖᕐᑐᖅᑎᑦᑎᕗᖅ ᓇᐅᔾᔮᓂ. ᓴᐅᒥᒐᓐᓂᐊᓂᑦ: ᓄᓇᒥᓐ ᐊᐅᓚᑦᑎᓂᖅ ᐱᓪᒪᕆᐅᕗᖅ ᐃᓄᐃᑦ ᐊᖑᓇᓱᒐᑦᑕᐃᓐᓇᕈᓐᓇᕐᓂᑦ

Nunavut Tourism ᓄᓇᕗᑦ

ᓄᓇᕗᑦ NUNAVUT

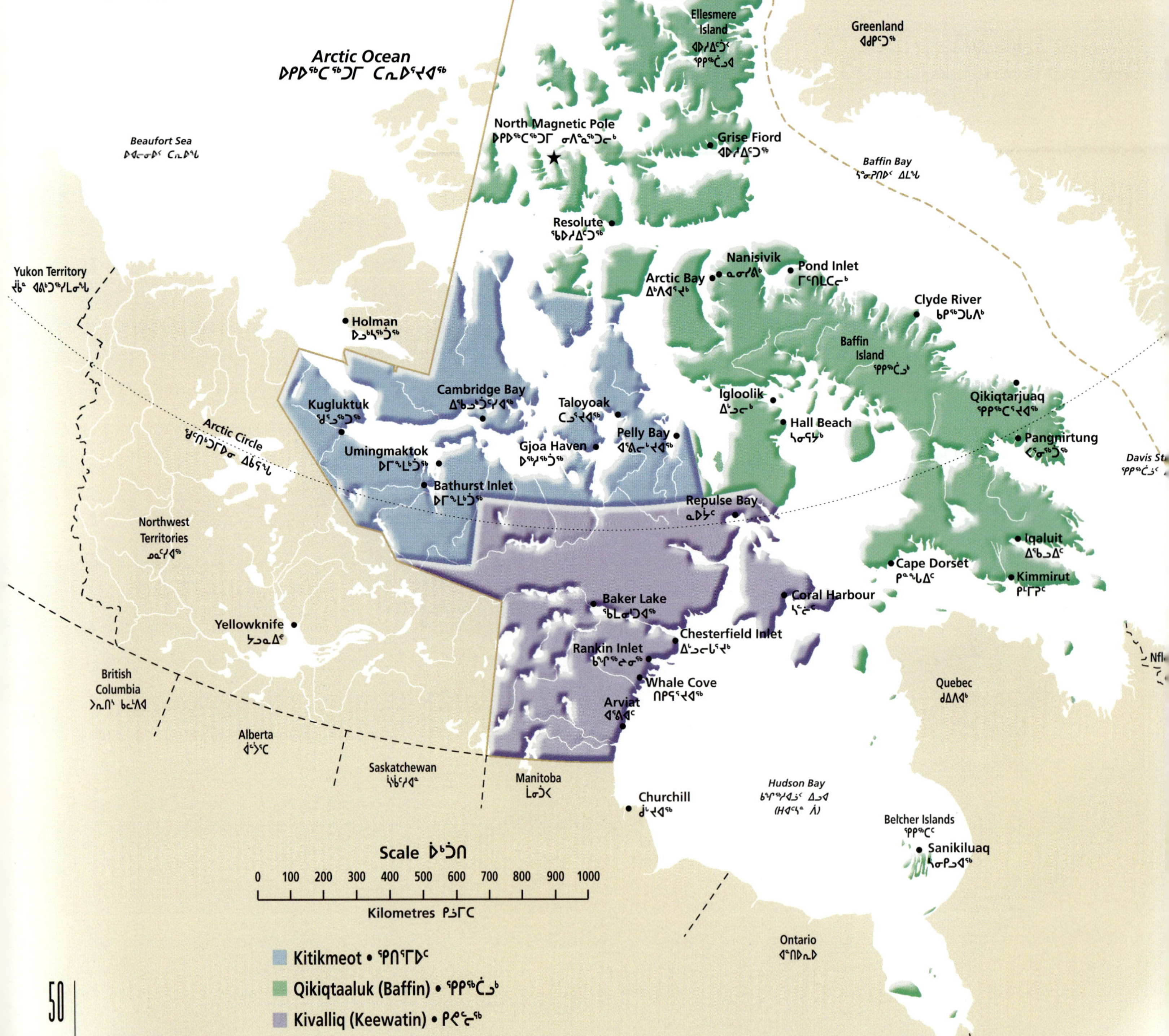

> **"The wildlife issue (Article 5) was very important. This is the article that relates to our lifestyle up here in Nunavut. We're so close to the wildlife."**
>
> **– David Aglukark, a co-chief negotiator for Inuit on the land claim**

Sharing in order to survive

Inuit have always turned to one another to help achieve a goal. When food was scarce, the men would get together and hunt as a team. It is through this connection to the land, to wildlife and to each other, that Inuit have survived for centuries. Today, however, where camp members once achieved goals through oneness, competitiveness now drives our society. The wage economy takes precedence over the traditional hunting lifestyle, and individuals compete with each other for jobs, education, business ventures and so on.

It is evident today that Inuit are still connected to their roots, though. When the opportunity arises, Inuit leave their communities and live out on the land for a time. It is because of this lifestyle and this recognition of the importance of our land and wildlife that Inuit have come together over many years to create the territory of Nunavut.

In the early 1970s, a group of young Inuit formed the Inuit Tapirisat of Canada (ITC) to represent all Inuit, and to voice concerns over the welfare of the land and wildlife as a growing number of mining, oil and gas companies and governments expressed interest in using the land. Once again Inuit, in a time of struggle, banded together, this time in the form of an interest group rather than nomadic encampments. They successfully negotiated a land claim agreement with one of the most powerful governments in the world, paving the way for the new territory of Nunavut.

Not only did the Nunavut Land Claims Agreement (NLCA) lead to the *Nunavut Act* — the legislation that created the new territory of Nunavut — it also gave the Inuit five lands and resources co-management bodies, and considerable control in areas normally handled by the federal government. The co-management bodies (or Institutions of Public Government, as they are also termed) are the Nunavut Wildlife Management Board (NWMB), the Nunavut Planning Commission (NPC), the Nunavut Impact Review Board (NIRB), the Nunavut Water Board (NWB), and the Nunavut Surface Rights Tribunal (NSRT). Under the direction of the Inuit in Nunavut, they oversee how the land and water are used, and how wildlife is managed and preserved in the Nunavut Settlement Area, the land mass traditionally occupied and used by Inuit, and defined in the NLCA.

ᐊᒥᖅᑳᖃᑦᑕᕐᓂᐅᑉ ᐊᓐᓇᐅᒪᒍᑕᐅᓂᖓ

ᐃᓄᐃᑦ ᐃᑲᔪᖅᑐᖃᐅᑎᓯᒪᑐᖃᖅᑐᑦ ᑐᕌᖅᑕᐅᔪᒥᒃ ᐊᑐᓕᕆᓐᓇᕆᒪᔾᔪᑎᖃᕐᓂᕐᒧᑦ. ᓂᕿᖃᓗᐊᓐᖏᓕᕐᓂᕋᖓᑦ, ᐊᖑᑎᑦ ᑲᑎᓪᓗᑎᒃ ᐊᖑᓇᓱᖃᑎᒌᒃᐸᓪᓚᐅᖅᑐᑦ. ᑕᒪᐅᓇᑎᒎᑦ ᐊᒃᑐᐊᓂᖃᕐᓂᕐᒧᑦ ᓄᓇᒧᑦ, ᐊᒻᒪᓗ ᐆᒪᔪᓄᑦ ᐃᖕᒥᖕᓄᓪᓗ ᖃᓂᓐᓂᕐᒧᑦ, ᐃᓄᐃᑦ ᑕᐃᑦᓯᒪᓂᕐᓂᑕᑎᑐᑦ ᐊᓐᓇᐅᒪᕙᒍᑎᖃᓚᐅᖅᑐᑦ. ᑕᒪᐅᓇ ᓄᓇᓕᖃᑎᒌᒃᑐᓂ ᐊᓐᓇᐅᒪᓂᖕᒋᑦ ᐊᑕᐅᓯᐅᓂᒃᑯᑦ ᐃᑲᔪᖅᑐᖅᑐᖅᐅᓪᓗᑎᒃ ᐱᕙᓪᓕᐅᖅᑎᓪᓗᒋᑦ, ᒫᓐᓇᓕ ᐃᒻᒫᖓᓗᐃᑦ ᐊᒃᓯᕈᕐᓂᖅᓴᐅᖃᑦᑕᕐᓂᒃᑯᑦ ᓵᓚᒃᓴᖃᖅᓂᕐᒥᒃ ᓯᕗᒻᒧᒍᑕᐅᓯᒪᓕᖅᒪᑦ ᐃᓅᓯᕆᔭᑦᑎᓐᓂ. ᐅᓪᓗᒥᐅᓕᖅᑐᖅ ᐃᓄᐃᑦ ᐊᔾᔨᐅᓐᖏᑦᑕᖓᓂᒃ ᐊᒃᓯᕈᕈᑎᖃᕈᓐᓇᐊᖃᓕᖅᑐᑦ. ᑮᓇᐅᔭᓕᐅᕐᓂᖅ ᓯᕗᓪᓕᐅᑎᓯᒪᓕᖅᒪᑦ ᐊᖑᓇᓱᒃᑲᖅᑕᕐᓂᕐᒥᑦ, ᐊᒻᒪᓗ ᑕᒪᐃᑕ ᐃᖅᑲᓇᐃᔭᖅᑖᕋᓱᐊᖅᑐᑦ ᓵᓚᒃᓴᖅᓴᕈᑎᒃ ᑭᓯᐊᓂᐅᓕᖅᑐᑦ. ᑕᒫᓇ ᐊᑐᖅᑕᐅᓕᖅᑯᓂ ᐃᓕᓐᓂᐊᖅᑲᑦᑕᕐᓂᕐᒧᑦ, ᓇᖕᒥᓂᖅ ᐱᓯᓇᓯᖅᑲᕐᓂᕐᒧᑦ ᐊᒻᒪᓗ ᐊᓯᖕᒋᓐᓄᑦ ᐊᔾᔨᐅᙱᖕᒋᑦᑐᓄᑦ.

ᖃᐅᔨᒪᓐᓇᖅᑐᖅᓯ ᐅᓪᓗᒥᐅᔪᖅ ᐃᓄᐃᑦ ᓱᓕ ᐊᑕᓯᒪᓂᖃᕐᒪᑕ ᐱᕆᐊᕝᕕᕆᓪᓗᐊᖅᑕᒥᖕᓄᑦ. ᐱᔪᓐᓇᖅᓯᒐᐃᒐᒥᒃ, ᐃᓄᐃᑦ ᓄᓇᓕᒡᔪᐊᓂᒃ ᕿᒪᐃᓪᓗᑎᒃ ᓄᓇᒦᕆᐊᖅᑐᖅᓯᒪᖃᑦᑕᖅᑕᕋᓚᑕ. ᑕᒪᓐᓇ ᐃᓅᓯᖓᔪᓂᖅ ᐱᔪᐃᑎᕆᑦᓗᒍ ᐊᒻᒪᓗ ᑕᒪᓐᓇ ᓄᓇᐅᑉ ᐊᑐᓪᓕᖓᓂᖓᑕ ᐆᒪᔪᐃᓪᓗ ᐊᑐᓪᓕᖓᓂᖏᑦ ᐃᓕᑕᕆᔭᐅᓯᒪᓂᖓᓄᑦ ᐃᓄᐃᑦ ᑲᑎᒍᓐᓇᓚᐅᖅᒪᑕ ᑕᒪᑐᒥᖓ ᐋᖅᑭᒃᓯᐃᓇᓱᒃᓗᑎᒃ ᓄᓇᕗᑖᕈᓐᓇᖅᓯᖕᓂᕐᒥᒃ. ᐊᒥᓱᓂᒃ ᐊᕐᕌᒍᓂᒃ ᑕᒪᓐᓇ ᐱᕙᓪᓕᐊᑎᑕᐅᓇᓱᒃᑐᖅ ᐃᓕᑕᕆᔭᐅᓪᓗᓂᓗ ᐊᑐᓪᓚᑦᑎᐊᕐᓂᖓ.

ᐊᕐᕌᒍᐃᑦ ᖃᓂᒋᔭᖓᓂ 1970-ᒥ, ᖃᑦᓯᐅᓚᐃᑦ ᒪᒃᑯᒃᑐᑦ ᐃᓄᐃᑦ ᐱᒋᐊᖅᑎᑎᓚᐅᖅᑐᑦ ᐃᓄᐃᑦ ᑕᐱᕇᑦᓴᑦ ᑲᓇᑕᒥᒃ ᑭᒡᓕᖅᑐᐃᖁᑦᑐᕐᒥᑦ ᐃᓄᓕᒫᓂᒃ. ᓂᐱᒋᔭᐅᖁᑦᑐᕆᓪᓗ ᐃᓱᒫᓗᑎᒋᔭᐅᔪᓄᑦ ᓄᓇᐅᑉ ᐊᒻᒪᓗ ᐆᒪᔪᐃᑦ ᐸᐸᑕᐅᒐᔭᖅᑕᐅᓂᖏᓐᓂᒃ ᑎᑭᐸᑦᑕᓕᐊᑦᑕᓕᖅᑎᑦᑐᒋᑦ ᐅᔭᕋᖕᓂᐊᖅᑎᑦ, ᐅᖅᓱᐊᓗᖕᓂᐊᖅᑎᑦ ᐊᒻᒪᓗ ᒐᓯᓕᕆᔩᑦ ᑲᒪᑦᐸᓂᐅᔭᓂᒃ ᐊᒻᒪᓗ ᒐᕙᒪᒋᔭᐅᔪᑦ ᐱᑦᓯᐊᑎᑎᓂᕐᒥᒃ ᓵᑉᐸᑦᓯᐊᓕᖅᑎᑦᑐᕐᒥᑦ ᐊᑐᐃᓂᖅᑲᒪᓕᑦᑐᑎᒃ ᓄᓇᒥᒃ ᐆᒪᔪᖕᒋᓐᓂᒡᓗ. ᑕᐃᒪᒃᑲᓐᓂᖅᓯᓕ, ᐃᓄᐃᑦ, ᐊᒃᓯᕈᕐᓇᖅᑐᖅᑲᓕᕐᖓᑦ ᑲᑎᓪᓗᑎᒃ ᐃᑲᔪᖅᑕᐅᑎᒥᐊᓚᐅᖅᑐᑦ. ᑕᐃᒪᓐᓇᓕ ᑕᐱᕇᒃᑐᓂ ᑕᐃᑦᓯᒪᓂᑑᓐᓂᕐᑦᑐᖅ ᓈᑉᐸᓕᐊᑦᑕᖅᑎᐅᑦᑐᑎᒃ ᓄᓇᖅᑲᑲᐃᓐᓇᖅᐱᖕᒥᖕᓄᑦ. ᓯᕗᒻᒧᑦ ᐃᖕᒋᖅᑦᑎᐊᓚᐅᖅᑐᑦ ᐊᖕᒋᖃᑎᒌᒍᑕᐅᓇᓯᐊᖅᑐᒥᒃ ᖄᖏᑦᑐᑎᒃ ᓄᓇᒥᒃ ᓇᖕᒥᓂᖅᑖᕐᓂᕐᒥᒃ. ᐊᐳᖅᑕᐅᓯᒪᓪᓗᑎᒃ ᓴᓐᖏᓂᖅᐸᐅᔪᒥᒃ ᒐᕙᒪᐅᔪᒥᒃ ᓯᓚᕐᔪᐊᓕᒫᒥ. ᓯᕗᓂᖑᑦ ᐸᕐᓇᒍᑕᐅᓪᓗᓂ ᓄᓇᕗᑖᕆᓯᓂᐊᖅᑐᖅ.

ᓄᓇᕗᒥ ᓄᓇᑖᕐᓂᖅ ᐊᖕᒋᕈᑕᐅᓂᖓ ᐱᒋᐊᕈᐃᓐᓚᐅᖅᓯᒪᔪᖅ ᓄᓇᕗᒥ ᒪᓕᒐᖕᔪᐊᖓᓂ — ᒪᓕᒐᒃᔪᐊᖅ ᓄᓇᕗᑖᕐᓂᕐᒥᒃ ᐱᔪᓐᓇᐅᑎᐅᔪᖅ — ᐊᒻᒪᓗ ᐱᔪᓐᓇᖅᑎᑎᓪᓗᓂ ᑕᓪᓕᒪᓂᒃ ᓄᓇᓕᓐᓂᕐᒧᑦ ᐊᒻᒪᓗ ᓱᓇᐅᐃᓐᓇᖅᑲᐅᑎᓂᒃ ᐊᐅᓚᑦᑎᔨᐅᖅᑲᑕᐅᔾᔪᓐᓇᕐᓂᕐᒥᒃ ᐃᓄᖕᓄᑦ. ᐊᒻᒪᓗ ᐊᖏᔪᒻᒪᕆᖕᒥ ᓄᓇᒥᒃ ᑲᓇᑕᐅᑉ ᒐᕙᒪᒃᑯᖓᓐᓄᑦ ᑲᒪᒋᔭᐅᓂᖃᖅᐸᓚᐅᖅᑐᒥᒃ.

Below: *In 1980, Peter Alareak, Michael Amaruq and Josephie Padlayat sought international support at the Inuit Circumpolar Conference in Nuuk, Greenland to ban oil, gas and mineral development until land claims were settled. Right: The NPC at work in Wager Bay, 1998. From left to right, Akalayok Qavavau, Jayko Alooloo, Louis Pilakapsi, John Crump and Richard Spaulding*

ᐊᑖᓂ: 1980ᒥ, ᐲᑕ ᐊᓚᕆᐊᖅ, ᒪᐃᑯ ᐊᒪᕈᖅ ᐊᒻᒪ ᔩᓯᐱ ᐸᑦᓛᔭ ᐃᑲᔪᖅᑐᖅᑕᐅᓂᖅ ᕿᓂᕐᓯᑦ ᐃᓄᐃᑦ ᓄᓇᕐᔪᐊᓕᒫᒥ ᐅᑭᐅᖅᑕᖅᑐᒥᐅᑕᑦ ᑲᑎᒪᕕᒃᔪᐊᖓᓂ ᓅᒃ, ᐊᑯᑭᑦᑐᓂᑦ ᒫᓐᓇ ᐅᖅᓱᐊᓗᒃᓯᐅᕐᓇᖅ, ᒐᓯᓯᐅᕐᓂᖅ ᐊᒻᒪ ᐅᔭᕋᖅᓯᐅᖅᓯᐅᕐᓂᖅ ᓅᖅᑲᖅᑎᖁᓪᓗᒍ ᑕᒪᓐᓇ ᓄᓇᑖᕈᓯᖕᓂᖅ ᐱᐊᓂᓚᐅᕐᑎᓐᓇᒍ.

ᑕᓯᖅᐱᐊᓂ: ᓄᓇᕗᑦ ᐸᕐᓇᐃᔩᑦ ᐱᓕᕆᓯᕗᑦ ᐅᐃᔪ ᐸᐃᒥᓐ, 1998. ᓴᐅᒥᖕᒐᓂ ᑕᓯᕝᕙᐊᓄ, ᐊᖃᓚᔪᖅ ᖃᕙᕙᐅ, ᔭᐃᑯ ᐋᓗᓘᕐ, ᓗᐃ ᐱᓚᑲᐹᓯ, ᔫᓐ ᑯᕌᑉ ᐊᒻᒪ ᕆᑦᓯᑦ ᔅᐹᑎᖕ

Arthur Boutilier

Rita Novalinga

“ᐆᒪᔪᓕᕆᓂᖅ (ᐃᓚᒍᑕᖓᓂᑦ 5) ᐱᒻᒪᕆᐊᓗᐅᕐᐳᖅ. ᐅᓇ ᐃᓚᒍᑕᐅᔪᖅ ᓇᓗᓇᐃᕐᓯᒪᕗᖅ ᐃᓅᓯᑦᑎᓐᓂ ᓄᓇᕗᒻᒥᑦ. ᖃᓂᒃᓴᒻᒪᕆᒃᑲᑦᑕ ᐆᒪᔫᑦ.”

– ᑕᐃᕕᑦ ᐊᒃᑰᑲᖅ, ᐃᒃᓯᕙᐅᑕᐅᖄᖅᑕᐅᔪᖅ ᐋᖅᑭᒃᓯᓂᑦ ᐃᓅᓐᓄᑦ ᓄᓇᑖᕐᓯᒍᓐᓂᒃᑯᑦ

FACTS on Nunavut
ᖃᐅᔨᒪᔭᒃᓴᑦ ᓄᓇᕘᔪᒥ

Size of Nunavut Territory: ᓄᓇᕗᑦ ᓄᓇᖁᑎᒋᔭᖓᑕ ᐊᖏᓂᖓ	1,994,000 square kilometres 1,994,000 ᓯᒃᑭᒃᑕᑦ ᑭᓗᒥᑕᐃᑦ
Population: ᐊᒥᖑᓂᖏᑦ	24,730 (number of Inuit: 20,480)* 24,730 (ᐃᓄᐃᑦ ᐊᒥᖑᓂᖏᑦ: 20,480)*
Capital of Nunavut: ᓄᓇᕗᒥ ᐊᖓᔪᖅᑳᖅᖃᕕᒃ	Iqaluit (population: 4,220)* ᐃᖃᓗᐃᑦ (ᐊᒥᖑᓂᖏᑦ: 4,220)*
Nunavut Day: ᓄᓇᕗᑦ ᐅᓪᓗᖓ	July 9 ᔫᓚᐃ 9

*Population statistics: 1996 Census of Canada
*ᐃᓄᐃᑦ ᐊᒥᖑᓂᖏᑦ: 1996-ᒥ ᓈᔾᔭᐃᔨᓂᑦ ᑲᓇᑕᒥ

Nunavut Tourism ᓄᓇᕗᑦ ᐳᓚᕆᐊᖅᑐᓕᕆᔨᑦ

Above and below: The NWMB's five-year study on wildlife species such as walrus and caribou will help in setting harvesting quotas. Far top right: James Taipana fishes with a traditional kakivak *on the Thelon River. Far bottom right: For Inuit, getting out on the land is like coming home*

ᖁᓛᓂ ᐊᒻᒪ ᐊᑖᓂ: ᓄᓇᕗᑦ ᐆᒪᔪᓕᕆᔨᖏᑦ ᑲᑎᒪᔨᖏ ᐊᕐᕌᒍᓄ ᑕᓪᓕᒪᓄ ᖃᐅᔨᓴᕐᓂ ᐆᒪᔪᓕᕆᓂᕐᒧ ᐊᐃᕕᕐᓂᑦ ᑐᒃᑐᓂᓪᓗ ᐃᑲᔪᕐᓂᐊᕐᐳᖅ ᐊᖑᔭᐅᔭᓐᓇᖅᑕᕐᓂᐊᕐᑐᓂᑦ. ᖁᓛᓂ ᑕᓕᕐᐱᐊᓂ: ᔭᐃᒻᔅ ᑕᐃᐸᓇ ᐃᖃᓗᒐᓱᒃᑐᖅ ᑲᑭᕙᖕᓂ ᐊᑐᕐᓗᓂ. ᐊᑖᓂ ᑕᓕᕐᐱᐊᓂ: ᐃᓄᖕᓄ, ᓄᓇᑦᑕᐃᓐᓇᒨᕐᓗᓂ ᓲᕐᓗ ᐊᖏᕐᕋᕐᓂᐅᒐᑦ

Nunavut Tourism ᓄᓇᕗᑦ ᐳᓚᕆᐊᖅᑐᓕᕆᔨᑦ

Nunavut's lands and resources co-management bodies

The NWMB, NPC, NIRB, NWB, and NSRT have Inuit members who are appointed according to region by Nunavut Tunngavik Incorporated (NTI). This ensures that each region within Nunavut has proper Inuit representation. The co-management bodies also have appointees from the federal and territorial governments, and these members may or may not be Inuit.

The NWMB is the main regulator of access to wildlife resources. With an eye to sustainable wildlife populations, it manages the way wildlife is used by Inuit and other residents in the Nunavut Settlement Area. The NWMB is unique because it works closely with Nunavut's three regional wildlife organizations and the territory's 27 local hunters and trappers organizations.

The NPC's mandate is to create land-use plans within the Nunavut Settlement Area. The land-use plans

ᐊᐅᓚᑦᑎᔨᐅᖃᑕᐅᓪᓗᑎᒃ ᑎᒥᖁᑎᒋᔭᐅᔪᑦ (ᐅᑉᐸᓘᓐᓃᓪᓚᑦ ᑭᒃᑯᒃᑖᓂ ᒐᕙᒪᓕᕆᔨᐅᖃᑕᐅᔪᑦ, ᑕᐃᒪᓐᓇᑦᑕᐅᖅ ᑕᐃᔭᐅᓂᖅᑲᓯᖅᑐᑦ) ᐃᓚᖅᑲᐅᖅᑐᖅ ᐅᑯᓂᖓ ᑎᒥᖁᑎᒋᔭᐅᔪᓂᒃ. ᐅᑯᐊ ᐃᓚᒋᔭᐅᓪᓗᑎᒃ: ᓄᓇᕗᒥ ᐆᒪᔪᓕᕆᔩᕐᔪᐊᑦ ᑲᑎᒪᔨᖏᑦ (NWMB), ᓄᓇᕗᒥ ᐸᕐᓇᐃᔩᑦ (NPC), ᓄᓇᕗᒥ ᐊᒃᑐᐃᓂᖅᑲᑦᑕᕐᓂᐅᔭᓄᑦ ᖃᐅᔨᓴᖅᑎᒃᑯᑦ ᑲᑎᒪᔨᖏᑦ (NIRB), ᓄᓇᕗᒥ ᐃᒪᓕᕆᔩᑦ ᑲᑎᒪᔨᕐᔪᐊᖏᑦ (NWB), ᐊᒻᒪᓗ ᓄᓇᕗᒥ ᓄᓇᐃᑦ ᖄᖏᓐᓄᑦ ᐃᓯᒪᖅᓯᕈᓐᓇᐅᑎᑖᕐᐸᓪᓕᐊᓪᓕᑦ (NSRT). ᐃᓄᐃᑦ ᓯᕗᓕᖅᑎᐅᓗᑎᒃ ᓄᓇᕗᒥ, ᖃᐅᔨᓴᖅᑎᐅᒐᔪᖅᑐᑦ ᖃᓄᖅ ᐊᐅᓚᑕᐅᑦᑎᐊᖅᑎᒋᖓᒪᖔᑕ ᓄᓇᐅᑉ ᐃᒪᐅᓪᓗ ᐊᑐᖅᑕᐅᓂᖓ. ᐊᒻᒪᓗ ᖃᓄᖅ ᐆᒪᔪᐃᑦ ᐊᐅᓚᑕᐅᑎᑦᑎᐊᕐᓂᖅᑲᕐᒪᖔᑕ ᐊᒻᒪᓗ ᐸᐸᑕᐅᕙᓪᓕᐊᓂᖏᑦ ᓄᓇᕗᑖᕈᑎᐅᓯᒪᔪᒥ. ᓄᓇᐅᑉ ᐊᖏᑎᒋᓂᖓ ᐊᑐᖅᑕᐅᒐᔪᓚᐅᕐᓂᖅᑲᕐᑐᓂ ᐃᓄᖕᓄᑦ, ᐊᒻᒪᓗ ᓇᓗᓇᐃᖅᑕᐅᓯᒪᓪᓗᓂ ᓄᓇᕗᑖᕈᑎᐅᑉ ᐊᖏᕈᑎᖓᓂ.

ᓄᓇᕗᑦ ᓄᓇᒥᒃ ᐊᒻᒪᓗ ᐊᑐᖅᑕᐅᒃᑲᓂᕈᓐᓇᖅᑐᑦ ᐊᐅᓚᓯᖅᑕᐅᓂᒃᑯᑦ ᑎᒥᖁᑕᐅᓂᖏᑦ

ᑕᒪᒃᑯᐊ ᑎᒥᖁᑎᐅᔪᑦ NWMB, NPC, NIRB, NWB, ᐊᒻᒪᓗ NSRT ᑕᒪᐃᑕ ᐃᓅᔪᓂᒃ ᑲᑎᒪᔨᖃᖅᑐᑦ ᑎᒃᑯᐊᖅᑕᐅᓪᓗᑎᒃ ᐊᕕᒃᑐᖅᓯᒪᓂᖕᒑᕐᓂᖏᑎᒍᑦ ᓄᓇᕗᑦ ᑐᓐᖓᕕᒃ ᑎᒥᖓᓐᓄᑦ (NTI). ᑕᒪᓐᓇ ᓈᒪᔪᓂᒃ ᑲᑎᒪᔨᖅᑲᐅᖅᑎᑎᒍᑕᐅᔪᖅ ᐊᕕᒃᑐᖅᓯᒪᔪᒃᑖᓂᑦ ᑲᑎᒪᔨᖅᑲᕈᓐᓇᖅᑲᑦᑕᖁᑦᑐᒥᑦ ᐃᓄᖕᓂᒃ ᓈᒻᒪᒃᑐᓂᒃ ᐃᓚᖅᑲᐅᑦᑎᐊᖅᑐᓂᒃ. ᑕᒪᒃᑯᐊ ᐊᐅᓚᑦᑎᔨᐅᖃᑕᐅᓂᐅᔪᑦ ᐃᓚᖃᐅᕐᒥᔪᑦ ᑎᒃᑯᐊᖅᑕᐅᓯᒪᔪᓂᒃ ᑲᓇᑕᐅᑉ ᒐᕙᒪᒃᑯᖓᓐᓂᑦ ᐊᒻᒪᓗ ᓄᓇᑦᓯᐊᑉ ᒐᕙᒪᒃᑯᖓᓐᓂᑦ. ᐊᒻᒪᓗ ᑖᒃᑯᐊ ᑲᑎᒪᔨᐅᔪᑦ ᐃᓚᖏᑦ ᐃᓅᔪᑦ ᐃᓚᖏᑦᑐ ᐊᓯᒥᔭᐅᔪᑦ.

ᓄᓇᕗᒥ ᐆᒪᔪᓕᕆᔩᕐᔪᐊᑦ ᑲᑎᒪᔨᖏᑦ (NWMB) ᓇᓗᓇᐃᖅᓯᔨᐅᔪᑦ ᐱᔭᐅᔪᓐᓇᖅᑲᑦᑕᕐᓂᖏᓐᓂᒃ ᐆᒪᔪᐃᑦ ᐊᑐᖅᑕᐅᒃᑲᓂᕈᓐᓇᖅᑐᓪᓗ. ᖃᐅᔨᓴᓇᔭᐅᓪᓗᓂ ᓯᕗᓂᕐᒧᑦ ᐊᑐᖅᑕᐅᖏᓐᓇᕈᓐᓇᕐᓂᐊᕐᓂᖏᑦ ᓯᓇᑐᐃᓐᓇᐃᑦ ᓄᖑᑕᐅᑦᑕᐃᓕᓂᒃᑯᑦ ᖃᐅᔨᓴᖅᑎᐅᓗᑎᒃ, ᐊᐅᓚᑦᑎᔨᐅᔪᑦ ᖃᓄᖅ ᐆᒪᔪᐃᑦ ᐱᓇᓱᒃᑕᐅᖃᑦᑕᒪᖔᑕ ᐃᓅᓐᓄᑦ. ᐊᒻᒪᓗ ᐊᓯᖏᓐᓄᑦ ᓄᓇᒥᓴᖅᑐᓄᑦ ᓄᓇᕗᒥ ᓄᓇᖏᓐᓂᒃ ᐊᖏᕈᑎᓯᒪᓂᐅᔪᓂ. ᓄᓇᕗᒥ ᐆᒪᔪᓕᕆᔩᕐᔪᐊᑦ ᑲᑎᒪᔨᖏᑦ (NWMB) ᐊᔾᔨᒋᔭᐅᙱᑦᑐᖅ ᐃᖅᑲᓇᐃᔭᖅᑎᖃᕐᔫᖑᒻᒪᑦ ᖃᓂᒋᓪᓗᒋᑦ ᐊᓯᖏᑦ ᓄᓇᕗᒥ ᐱᖓᓱᔪᑦ ᐊᕕᒃᑐᖅᓯᒪᓂᖏᑦᑕ ᑎᒥᖁᑎᖏᓐᓂᒃ ᐊᒻᒪᓗ ᓄᓇᓕᖕᓂ 27-ᖑᔪᑦ ᐆᒪᔪᕐᓂᐊᖅᑎᑦ ᒥᑭᒋᐊᕐᓂᐊᖅᑎᓪᓗ ᑲᑎᒪᔨᖏᑦ.

give guidance and direction to mining, oil and gas companies, or any company or organization that wishes to use the land. The NPC is challenged by the distinct and differing lifestyles of Inuit throughout Nunavut's regions, so it has created six planning regions and allowed for community representation throughout Nunavut to better represent each region.

The NIRB examines project proposals for their cultural, socio-economic and environmental impacts on land, air and water, taking into consideration the effects on people and wildlife within the Nunavut Settlement Area. Not only does NIRB use recognized scientific methods, it also uses Inuit traditional knowledge when reviewing proposals for possible impacts.

The NWB manages the use and regulation of water in the Nunavut Settlement Area. This includes all lakes, rivers and coastal waters. NWB also uses traditional Inuit knowledge as well as proven technical skills to determine whether water-use applications should proceed to development.

In Nunavut, there are three Regional Inuit Associations (RIAs) — the Kivalliq Inuit Association, the Kitikmeot Inuit Association and the Qikiqtani Inuit Association (for the Baffin Region). Part of their role involves working with NTI in implementing the land claim and managing Inuit-owned land. If a developer wants to use Inuit land, but the developer and the RIA don't agree on conditions for accessing the land, then the matter is settled by the NSRT. This tribunal can require developers to pay a fee, based on impact and determined by the NSRT, before they use Inuit land.

In Inuit hands now

The creation of these co-management bodies through the implementation of the Nunavut Land Claims Agreement puts the future well-being of our land and wildlife in the hands of Inuit. With our history of survival, strength, unity, and our love for the environment, Inuit can be assured that, like that morning years ago when I walked out of the tent and saw not only the geese flying over, but also saw the sheer beauty of the land, future generations will know this same experience.

Nunavut Tourism ᓄᓇᕗᑦ ᐳᓚᕋᑦᑕᓕᕆᔨᖏᑦ

Brian Aglukark heads the Iqaluit regional office of the Nunavut Planning Commission, working as a liaison officer and mapping co-ordinator. Aglukark, who hails from Arviat, goes out on the land to hunt whenever he can.

Nunavut Tourism ᓄᓇᕗᑦ ᐳᓚᕋᑦᑕᓕᕆᔨᖏᑦ

ᓄᓇᕗᒻᒥ ᐸᕐᓇᐃᓯᑦ (NPC) ᐊᑐᐊᓗᓐᓴᖅᑕᑦ ᓴᓇᓂᕐᒥᒃ ᓄᓇᐅᑉ ᐊᑐᖅᑕᐅᓂᐊᕐᓂᖅᑕᓐᓄᑦ ᐸᕐᓇᐃᓂᕐᒥᒃ ᓄᓇᕗᑖᕐᓯᓐᓴᐅᔭᑉ ᐃᓗᐊᓂ. ᓄᓇᒧᑦ ᐊᑐᖅᑕᐅᓂᐊᕐᓂᖏᑦ ᐸᕐᓇᒍᑕᐅᓯᒪᔪᑦ ᓯᕗᓪᓕᖅᑎᐅᒍᑕᐅᓯᖅᑐᑦ ᒪᑯᓄᐊ ᐅᔭᖃᖕᓂᐊᖅᑎᓄᑦ, ᐅᖅᓯᐊᓗᓪᓗᓯᓄᑦ ᐊᒻᒪᓗ ᓴᓯᓪᓗᓯᓄᑦ ᑳᒃᐸᓂᒋᔭᐅᔪᓄᑦ. ᖃᓄᐃᓐᓇᕐᓘᓐᓪᓗ ᑭᓇᐅᓐᓇᒃᑯᑦ ᑲᑐᔾᔨᔨᐅᔪᑦ ᑎᒥᐅᔪᓪᓗ ᐊᑐᐃᔪᒪᔪᑦ ᓄᓇᒥᒃ. ᓄᓇᕗᒻᒥ ᐸᕐᓇᐃᓯᑦ (NPC) ᐊᒃᓯᕿᕿᑎᖅᑲᖅᑐᑦ ᐃᓄᐃᑦ ᓇᒥᑐᐃᓐᓈᖅᑐᑦ ᓄᓇᕗᒻᒥ ᐊᔾᔨᙱᓐᓂᖏᓐᓄᑦ ᐃᓅᖁᕐᓂᖏᓐᓅᓪᓗ. ᑕᒪᓐᓇ ᐊᐳᖅᑕᐅᖁᓪᓗᒍ, ᓄᓇᕗᒻᒥ ᐸᕐᓇᐃᓯᑦ (NPC) ᐋᖅᑭᒃᓯᓯᒪᔪᑦ ᐸᕐᓇᐃᔨᐅᔪᓐᓇᖅᑐᓂᒃ ᐊᑕᐅᓯᕐᒥᒃ ᐊᕕᓂᓪᓗᒥᒃ ᐊᕕᒃᑐᖅᓯᒪᓂᐅᔭᓂᒃ ᓄᓇᕗᓖᒥ. ᐊᕕᒃᑐᖅᓯᒪᔪᑦ ᐃᓚᐅᖃᑕᐅᑎᐊᕈᓐᓇᖁᓪᓗᒋᑦ.

ᑖᒃᑯᐊ ᓄᓇᕗᒻᒥ ᐊᒃᑐᐃᓂᖅᑲᖅᑕᕐᓂᐅᔪᓄᑦ ᖃᐅᔨᓴᖅᑎᒃᑯᑦ ᑲᑎᒪᔨᖏᑦ (NIRB) ᖁᒥᕐᕿᕙᒃᑐᑦ ᐱᕙᓪᓕᐊᑎᑕᐅᔪᒪᔪᑦ ᑐᒃᓯᕋᕿᑎᖏᓐᓂᒃ. ᒪᑯᓂᖓ ᐊᒃᑐᐃᓂᖅᑲᕆᓴᕐᒪᖔᑕ ᐃᓪᓗᒃᑯᓯᒥᒃ, ᐃᓅᓯᖅ ᑮᓇᐅᔭᓕᐅᕐᓂᕐᓗ ᐊᒻᒪᓗ ᐊᕙᑎᐅᑉ ᐊᒃᑐᖅᑕᐅᓚᐅᕐᓂᖓ. ᒪᑯᐊ ᐊᒃᑐᖅᑕᐅᓚᐅᕐᓂᖏᑦ ᓇᓗᓇᐃᔭᖅᑕᐅᓪᓗᑎᒃ ᓄᓇ, ᓯᓚ ᐊᒻᒪᓗ ᐃᒪᖅ, ᐃᓚᒋᔭᐅᒋᓪᓗᓂ ᖃᓄᖅ ᐃᓕᖓᓂᖅᑲᕆᓴᕐᒪᖔᑕ ᐃᓄᖕᓄᑦ ᐆᒪᔪᓄᓪᓗ ᐊᖏᕿᑕᐅᓯᒪᔪᒥ ᓄᓇᑖᕐᓯᐅᔪᒥ. ᐊᑐᖃᑦᑕᖅᑎᓪᓗᒋᑦ ᓄᓇᕗᒻᒥ ᐊᒃᑐᐃᓂᖅᑲᖅᑕᕐᓂᐅᔪᓄᑦ ᖃᐅᔨᓴᖅᑎᒃᑯᑦ ᑲᑎᒪᔨᖏᑦ (NIRB) ᐃᓕᑕᕐᓴᐅᓯᒪᔪᓂᒃ ᖃᐅᔨᒪᔨᕐᔪᐊᓄᑦ ᒪᓕᒋᐊᖅᑲᖅᑕᖅᑕᕐᓂᖏᓐᓂ ᒪᓕᒃᑕᐅᑐᐃᓐᓇᐅᔪᓐᖏᑦᑐᑦ ᑭᓯᐊᓂᓕ ᐃᓄᐃᑦᑕᐅᖅ ᖃᐅᔨᒪᑐᖃᕐᓂᖏᓐᓂᒃ. ᑕᒪᒃᑯᐊ ᖁᒥᕐᕿᔭᐅᓕᖅᑎᓪᓗᒋᑦ ᑐᒃᓯᕋᕿᑕᐅᔪᑦ, ᖃᓄᐃᓐᓇᖅ ᐅᔾᔨᕆᔭᐅᑎᐊᖅᓯᒪᖁᓪᓗᒋᑦ ᐊᒃᑐᐃᓂᕆᔪᐃᓐᓇᕆᐊᖅᑲᖅᑕᖏᑦ.

ᓄᓇᕗᒻᒥ ᐃᒪᓕᕆᔨᑦ ᑲᑎᒪᔨᕐᔪᐊᖏᑦ (NWB) ᐊᐅᓚᑦᑎᔪᑦ ᐃᒪᐃᑦ ᐊᑐᖅᑕᐅᓂᖏᓐᓂᒃ ᓱᓕᓂᕐᓴᐅᓂᖏᓐᓂᓪᓗ ᓄᓇᕗᑖᖅᓯᒪᓂᕐᒥ. ᑕᒪᒃᑯᐊ ᑲᒪᒋᔭᐅᓂᖅᑲᓪᓗᒃᑖᖅᑐᑦ ᐃᒪᓖᑦ ᑕᓰᑦ, ᑰᑦ ᐊᒻᒪᓗ ᓯᓈᔭᐃᑦ. ᐃᒪᓕᕆᔨᒃᑯᑦ ᖃᐅᔨᒪᓂᖅᑐᖅᑕᐅᔪᓂᒃ ᐃᓄᖕᓄᑦ ᐊᑐᖅᐸᒃᑐᑦ ᐊᒻᒪᓗ ᖃᐅᔨᒪᔨᕐᔪᐊᓄᑦ ᖃᐅᔨᒪᔭᐅᔪᓂᒃ. ᑐᒃᓯᕋᕿᑕᐅᔪᑦ ᐃᒪᕐᒥᒃ ᐊᑐᕿᒪᔾᔪᑎᑦ ᑲᔪᓯᑎᐊᕿᓐᓇᖅᑎᑕᐅᒪᖔᑕ ᐃᓱᒪᓕᐅᖅᑎᑐᓪᓗᑎᒃ.

ᓄᓇᕗᒻᒥ ᐱᖓᓱᓂᒃ ᐊᕕᒃᑐᖅᓯᒪᔪᓂ ᑲᑐᔾᔨᖃᑐᖅᑐᖅ ᑲᑎᒪᔨᓂᖅᑐᓂᒃ ᐃᓄᖕᓄᑦ (RIAs) — ᑭᕙᓪᓕᕐᒥ ᐃᓄᐃᑦ ᑲᑐᔾᔨᖃᑎᒌᖏᑦ, ᕿᑎᕐᒥᐅᑦ ᐃᓄᐃᑦ ᑲᑐᔾᔨᖃᑎᒌᖏᑦ ᐊᒻᒪᓗ ᕿᑭᖅᑕᓂ ᐃᓄᐃᑦ ᑲᑐᔾᔨᖃᑎᒌᖏᑦ. ᐃᓚᖓᑦ ᐃᖅᑲᓇᐃᔮᓂᓴᖓᑦ ᓄᓇᕗᑦ ᑐᓐᖓᕕᒃᑯᓐᓂᒃ ᐃᖅᑲᓇᐃᔭᖃᑎᖃᕐᓂᖅ. ᑕᒪᓐᓇ ᓄᓇᕗᑖᕿᑕᐅᔪᖅ ᓯᕗᓪᓕᒃᑎᑕᐅᓂᖓᓂᒃ ᐊᒻᒪᓗ ᐊᐅᓚᑦᑎᓪᓗᑎᒃ ᐃᓅᖕᓄᑦ ᓇᖕᒥᓂᓐᓴᐅᔪᓂᒃ ᓄᓇᓂᒃ. ᓴᓇᕖᑦᔪᐊᓕᐅᔪᑦ ᐊᑐᕈᒪᓗᓴᖅᐸᑦ ᐃᓅᖕᓄᑦ ᓇᖕᒥᓂᓐᓴᐅᔪᒥᒃ ᓄᓇᒥᒃ, ᑭᓯᐊᓂᓕ ᓴᓇᕖᑦᔪᐊᓕᒃ ᐊᒻᒪᓗ ᐊᕕᒃᑐᖅᓯᒪᔪᓂ ᑎᒥᖁᑎᒋᔭᐅᔪᖅ ᐃᓅᖕᓄᑦ ᐊᖏᖃᑎᒌᒍᓐᓇᖏᑉᐸᑎᒃ ᒪᓕᒃᑕᐅᒋᐊᓖᑦ ᓄᓇ ᐊᑐᖅᑕᐅᓚᐅᖅᑎᓪᓗᒍ, ᑕᒪᓐᓇ ᑲᒪᒋᔭᐅᓂᖅᑲᖅᑐᖅ ᓄᓇᕗᒻᒥ ᓄᓇᐃᑦ ᖄᖏᓐᓄᑦ ᐃᓱᒪᖅᓱᕐᓇᐅᑎᑖᕐᐸᓪᓚᐊᓪᓚᑦ NSRT-ᑯᓐᓄᑦ. ᑖᒃᑯᐊ ᑐᓂᓯᒍᓐᓇᖅᑐᑦ ᓄᓇᒧᑦ ᐃᓯᕈᓐᓇᐅᑎᓂᒃ ᐊᒻᒪᓗ ᐃᓄᐃᑦ ᓄᓇᖓᓐᓂᒃ ᐊᑐᕈᓐᓇᕐᓂᕐᒥᒃ, ᐊᑮᑐᐊᕈᑎᒃ ᐊᑭᓕᓐᓂᐊᖅᑕᐅᔪᓂᒃ.

ᐃᓄᖕᓄᑦ ᑎᒍᒥᐊᖅᑕᐅᓕᖅᑐᖅ

ᐱᕐᕈᖅᑎᑕᐅᓂᖏᑦ ᑕᒪᒃᑯᐊ ᐊᐅᓚᑦᓯᓂᖅᑕᐅᓪᓗᑎᒃ ᑎᒥᐅᔪᑦ ᓚᓐᓂᒃᑯᑦ ᓄᓇᕗᑖᕐᓂᕐᒧᑦ ᐊᖏᖅᑎᕿᔪᑕᐅᔪᒥᒃ ᓯᕗᓂᕐᒧᑦ ᑎᒍᒥᐊᖅᑕᐅᔪᑕᐅᓚᖅᑐᑦ ᑲᒪᒋᔭᐅᑦᑎᐊᖃᓱᕐᓂᕐᓚᓂᒃ ᓄᓇᐃᑦ ᐆᒪᔪᐃᓪᓗ ᐃᓄᖕᓄᑦ. ᓯᕗᓂᐅᔪᒥ ᐊᓐᓇᐅᒪᔪᓐᓇᖅᐸᓪᓚᐅᕐᓂᕐᒥᒃ, ᓴᙱᓂᕐᒥᒃ, ᐊᑕᐅᓯᐅᓂᕐᒥᒃ, ᐊᒻᒪᓗ ᐊᒃᑐᐊᓂᖅᑎᐊᕐᓂᕐᒥᒃ ᐊᕙᑎᒧᑦ, ᐃᓄᐃᑦ ᖁᓚᖁᔭᐅᓐᖏᑦᑐᑦ, ᑕᐃᑦᓯᒪᓂᑐᑦ ᐅᐸᖓ ᐊᓪᓗᖓ ᑐᐱᓐᓂᒃ ᑕᑯᔭᓐᓇᓚᐅᖅᑲ ᑲᖑᕐᓂᒃ ᖁᓪᓕᑎᓐᓂ ᑎᖏᔪᓂᒃ, ᐃᓚᒃ ᑖᒃᑯᐊᑐᐊᖑᓐᖏᑦᑑᓗᐊᖅ ᑕᑯᖃᓐᓂᖅᑑᓪᓗᑎᒃ. ᑕᐃᒪᓐᓇᑎᑦᑕᐅᖅ ᑭᖑᐴᒃᓴᑦ ᑕᑯᔭᒃᓴᖅᑯᓪᓗᒋᑦ ᐊᑐᖅᑯᓪᓗᒋᓪᓗ ᐅᐸᒍᑦ ᐊᑐᐊᓂᒃᓯᒪᔾᔪᑎᓐᓂᒃ.

ᐳᕋᐃᐊᓐ ᐊᒡᓘᒃᑲᖅ (Brian Aglukark) ᐊᖓᔪᖅᑳᖑᔪᖅ ᐊᕕᒃᑐᖅᓯᒪᔪᓂ ᐃᖅᑲᓇᐃᔮᕕᖓᓂ ᐃᖃᓗᖕᓂ ᓄᓇᕗᒻᒥ ᐸᕐᓇᐃᔨᓂ (NPC). ᐃᖅᑲᓇᐃᔮᓚᒃ ᓄᓇᓕᖕᓂ ᖃᐅᔨᒪᖃᑦᑕᐅᑎᓪᓗᓯᐅᑦᑐᓂ ᐊᒻᒪᓗ ᓄᓇᙳᐊᓕᓐᓂᕐᒥᒃ ᐊᐅᓚᑦᑎᔨᐅᑦᑐᓂ. ᐊᒡᓘᒃᑲᖅ, ᐊᕝᕕᐊᒥᖔᖅᓯᒪᔪᖅ, ᓄᓇᐃᓐᓇᒧᑦ ᐊᖑᓇᓱᒋᐊᖅᐸᒃᑐᖅ ᖃᖓᑐᐃᓐᓇᖅ.

ᓯᕗᓂᒃᓴᑦᑎᓐᓂ ᓴᐳᔾᔨᓯᕗᒍᑦ
Safeguarding our future

Nunavut Surface Rights Tribunal
ᓄᓇᕗᒻᒥ ᓄᓇᒧᑦ ᐱᔪᓐᓇᐅᑎᓕᕆᔩᑦ

P.O. Box 1419, Iqaluit, NT XOA 0H0
Telephone / ᐅᖄᓚᐅᑎᖓ: (867) 979-1555 Fax / ᓱᒃᑲᔪᒃᑯ: (867) 979-1528

The NSRT issues land entry orders and mediates any disputes involving surface rights. The NSRT also determines fair compensation from developers wishing access to Inuit lands and for any resulting loss of wildlife. This is done with the involvement of other Institutions of Public Government of Nunavut.

ᓄᓇᕗᒻᒥ ᓄᓇᒧᑦ ᐱᔪᓐᓇᐅᑎᓕᕆᔩᑦ ᑐᓂᓯᕙᒃᐳᑦ ᓄᓇᓕᕆᔪᒪᔪᓄᑦ ᐊᒻᒪᓗ ᐋᖅᑭᒃᓯᐃᔨᐅᓪᓗᑎᒃ ᐊᑲᐅᙱᓕᐅᕈᑎᓂ ᓄᓇᐅᑉ ᖄᖓᓃᑦᑐᓂᑦ. ᐊᒻᒪᑦᑕᐅᖅ ᓄᓇᕗᑦ ᓄᓇᐅᑉ ᖄᖓᓄᑦ ᐱᔪᓐᓇᐅᑎᖏᓄᑦ ᐃᖅᑲᖅᑐᐃᔾᔪᑎᖓ ᕿᓇᐅᔭᖅᑖᕈᑎᖃᖅᐸᒃᐳᑦ ᓈᒻᒪᓈᖅᓯᒪᓕᓯᒃᑐᓂᑦ ᓄᓇᓕᕆᔨᐅᕙᒃᑐᓂᑦ ᐊᑐᐃᓐᓇᖅᑲᖁᒪᔪᓂ ᐃᓄᐃᑦ ᓄᓇᖁᑎᖏᓐᓂ ᐊᒻᒪᓗ ᓂᕐᔪᑎᓂ ᐊᓯᐅᑎᑦᑎᑦᑕᖅᑳᓂᕐᑯᖕᒪ. ᐅᓇ ᐱᓕᕆᓂᐅᓰᖕᖑᔪᖅ ᐱᖃᑎᖃᖅᓱᑎᒃ ᐱᓕᕆᕝᕕᐅᔪᓂᑦ ᒐᕙᒪᓕᕆᓂᒃᑯ ᓄᓇᕗᒻᒥ.

Nunavut Wildlife Management Board
ᓄᓇᕗᑦ ᐅᒪᔪᓕᕆᔨᕐᔪᐊᑦ ᑲᑎᒪᔨᖏ

P.O. Box 1379, Iqaluit, NT XOA 0E0
Telephone / ᐅᖄᓚᐅᑎᖓ: (867) 979-6962 Fax / ᓱᒃᑲᔪᒃᑯ: (867) 979-7785
Web site / ᖃᕆᓴᐅᔭᒃᑯ: www.nunanet.com/~nwmb

The NWMB is responsible for maintaining and protecting the territorial wildlife for the residents of Nunavut. This involves managing wildlife consistent with the principles of conservation, sustainability and ecosystemic integrity.

ᓄᓇᕗᒃ ᐅᒪᔪᓕᕆᔨᕐᔪᐊᑦ ᑲᑎᒪᔨᖏ ᑲᒪᔨᐅᒍᑦ ᐊᐅᓚᑦᑎᓂᕐᒥ ᐊᒻᒪ ᓴᐳᔾᔨᓯᒪᓂᕐᒥ ᐅᒪᔪᓂ ᓄᓇᖃᖅᑐᓄᑦ ᓄᓇᕗᒻᒥᓐ. ᑕᒪᓐᓇ ᐱᓕᕆᓂᖅᑲᕆᒐᒃ ᐅᒪᔪᓂ ᑲᒪᔨᐅᓂᕐᒥᓐ ᒪᓕᒃᑐᓐᓇᖅ ᐊᓯᐅᑎᑦᑎᑦᑕᐃᓕᓂᕐᒍᑦ, ᐊᑐᒃᑲᓐᓂᕈᓐᓇᕐᓂᒃᑯ ᐊᒻᒪ ᐊᕙᑎᓕᕆᓂᒃᑯ.

ᑲᒪᒋᔭᒃᓴᓂ ᑲᒪᑦᑎᐊᕐᓂᐅᔪᖅ ᐊᐅᓪᓚᑦᑎᓂᐅᔪᖅᑐ ᓄᓇᕗᒻᒥ ᓄᓇᒥᐅᑕᐃᑦ ᐊᑐᖅᑐᒃᓴᓕᕆᓂᖅ ᐱᓕᕆᑦᑎᐊᕐᓂᖃᕆᐊᖃᓪᓚᕆᖕᒪ ᐱᓕᕆᐊᕆᓪᓚᖅᑖᕐᓂᒃᑯ, ᐱᓇᓯᐊᕙᒻᒪᕆᐅᓂᒃᑯ ᐊᒻᒪ ᑲᑐᔾᔨᖃᑎᒌᖕᓂᒃᑯ ᑲᑐᔾᔨᖃᑎᒌᖕᒋᓐᓄᑦ. ᐱᓕᕆᖃᑎᒌᖕᓂᖅ ᐱᓕᕆᐊᒃᓴᓂ, ᑲᑐᔾᔨᖃᑎᒌᖕᒍᔪ ᐃᖕᒥᖕᓄ ᐃᑲᔪᖃᑦᑕᐅᑎᒍᑦ ᑕᒪᓐᓇ ᓄᓇ, ᐃᒪᖅ ᐊᒻᒪ ᐆᒪᔪᑦ ᑖᒪᓃᑦᑐ ᓄᓇᕗᒻᒥ, ᐱᓕᕆᐊᖕᒍᐃᓐᓇᖅᑯᑦᑐᒋ, ᓱᕈᒃᑕᐅᖁᓇᒋ ᐊᒻᒪᓗ ᐊᑐᕐᑕᐅᒃᑲᓂᕈᓐᓇᖅᑯᑦᑐᒋ ᑭᖑᕚᕆᓂᐊᕐᑕᑦᑎᓐᓄᑦ.

The responsible care and management of Nunavut's natural resources requires the dedication, commitment and cooperative spirit of many organizations. Working together, these organizations are helping to ensure that the land, water and wildlife that comprise the new territory of Nunavut will remain vibrant, unspoiled and sustainable for generations to come.

Nunavut Planning Commission
ᓄᓇᕗᑦᒥ ᐸᕐᓇᐃᔩᑦ

P.O. Box 12, Taloyoak, NT XOE 1B0
Telephone / ᐅᖄᓚᐅᑎᖓ: (867) 561-6896 Fax / ᓱᒃᑲᔪᒃᑯ: (867) 561-6897
Web site / ᖃᕆᓴᐅᔭᒃᑯ: www.npc.nunavut.ca

NPC is responsible for protecting, preserving and monitoring the state of land and wildlife, while ensuring that sustainable development is carried out that will benefit the local economies.

ᓄᓇᕗᑦᒥ ᐸᕐᓇᐃᔩᑦ ᐱᓕᕆᔨᐅᕗᑦ ᓴᐳᔾᔨᔨᐅᓂᕐᒥ, ᐊᓯᐅᑎᑦᑎᑦᑕᐃᓕᓂᕐᒥ ᐊᒻᒪ ᖃᐅᔨᓴᕐᑎᐅᓂᕐᒥ ᓄᓇᒥᓐ ᐊᒻᒪ ᐆᒪᔪᓂᑦ, ᑕᒪᓐᓇ ᐱᓕᕆᓂᖅ ᐱᕙᓪᓕᐊᓂᕐᒧ ᐊᑐᕐᑕᐅᕙᓪᓕᐊᑎᓪᓗᒍ ᓄᓇᓕᖕᓂ ᐱᕙᓪᓕᐊᓂᐅᔪᖅ ᐊᑳᐅᓈᑐᒃᑰᕐᑎᒐᓯᒃᓗᒍ.

Nunavut Planning Commission ᓄᓇᕗᑦᒥ ᐸᕐᓇᐃᔩᑦ NUNAVUNMI PARNAIYIIT

Nunavut Impact Review Board
ᓄᓇᕘᒥ ᐊᑦᑎᓕᕆᓂᕐᒨᑦ ᑲᑎᒪᐄᑦ

P.O. Box 2379, Cambridge Bay, NT XOC 0E0
Telephone / ᐅᖄᓚᐅᑎᖓ: (867) 983-2593 Fax / ᓱᒃᑲᔪᒃᑯ: (867) 983-2594
Web site / ᖃᕆᓴᐅᔭᒃᑯ: www.ipg.nunavut.ca/nirbpg.htm

Using traditional Inuit knowledge and scientific methods, the NIRB is responsible for assessing the ecosystemic and socio-economic impact of project development.

ᐊᑐᕐᓗᑎᒃ ᐃᓄᐃᑦ ᖃᐅᔨᒪᓂᕆᔭᖏᓐᓂ ᐊᒻᒪᓗ ᖃᓪᓗᓈᑦ ᖃᐅᔨᓴᕐᓂᕆᔭᖓᓂ, ᓄᓇᕗᑦ ᐊᑦᑎᓕᕆᓂᕐᒨᑦ ᑲᑎᒪᔩ ᑲᒪᔩ- ᐅᕗᑦ ᖃᐅᔨᓴᕐᑎᐅᓂᕐᒥ ᐊᑦᑎᒋᔭᒥᓐ ᐊᒻᒪ ᐃᓅᖃᑎᒌᓂᒃᑯ ᐱᕙᓪᓕᐊᓂᕐᒥ ᑕᒪᒃᑯᐊ ᖃᓄᖅ ᐊᒃᑐᐃᓂᖃᕋᔭᒃᓴᖕᒋᓐᓂ ᐱᓕᕆᐊᒃᓴᑦ ᐱᕙᓪᓕᐊᓂᐅᔪᑦ.

ᓄᓇᕗᑦ ᐊᑦᑎᓕᕆᓂᕐᒨᑦ ᑲᑎᒪᐄᑦ
NUNAVUT IMPACT REVIEW BOARD
NUNAVUTMI KANOGILIVALIANIKOT ELITTOHAIYEOPLOTIK KATIMAYIIT

Nunavut Water Board
ᓄᓇᕗᒻᒥ ᐃᒪᓕᕆᔨᖕᒋᑦᑕ ᑲᑎᒪᔩᕐᔪᐊᖕᒋᑦ

P.O. Box 119, Gjoa Haven, NT XOE 1J0
Telephone / ᐅᖄᓚᐅᑎᖓ: (867) 360-6338
Fax / ᓱᒃᑲᔪᒃᑯ: (867) 360-6369
Web site / ᖃᕆᓴᐅᔭᒃᑯ: www.ipg.nunavut.ca/nwb

The mandate of the NWB is to ensure the responsible use, management and preservation of Nunavut's inland freshwater.

ᓄᓇᕗᑦ ᐃᒪᓕᕆᔨᖕᒋᑦᑕ ᑲᑎᒪᔩᕐᔪᐊᖕᒋᑦ ᐱᓕᕆᐊᖃᕐᓯᒃᐳᑦ ᓇᒻᒪᓈᕐᓯᒪᔪᒥᓐ ᐊᑐᕐᑕᐅ- ᑎᑦᑎᓂᕐᒥᓐ, ᐊᐅᓪᓚᑦᑎᓂᕐᒥᓐ ᐊᒻᒪ ᓱᕋᒃᑕᐅᑎᑦᑕᐃᓕᑎᑦᑎᓂᕐᒥ ᓄᓇᕗᑦ ᑕᓯᖕᒋᓐᓂᑦ.

NUNAVUT WATER BOARD

Build a career in the new Nunavut
ᐃᖅᑲᓇᐃᔮᒃᓭᑦᓚᕆᖕᓅᖕᒐᔪᒥᓐ ᐱᓕᕆᕚᑦᓯᐊᕆ ᓄᓇᕗᒻᒥᑦ
Havavialukkluni nutaami Nunavutmi

Nunavut has arrived. And with it come many exciting career opportunities for qualified people.

Nunavut Arctic College – the Inuit college – has the programs you need to succeed. Courses offered at our Keewatin, Kitikmeot and Nunatta Campuses can help you prepare for the many employment opportunities Nunavut will offer.

Choose from the many quality courses and programs we have available, including: Teaching • Computers • Environmental Technology • Management and Administration • Social Work • A&D Counseling • Interpreting and Translating • Inuit Language and Culture • Fine Arts and Crafts • Adult Basic Education • Literacy Programs • and many more...

At Nunavut Arctic College, our goal is to help you reach yours. Find out more: contact Nunavut's own college, today!

ᓄᓇᕗᑦ ᑕᑯᐸᑐᓯᕗᖅ! ᑕᑯᐸᓃᓯᕐᓂᖕᒐᓄᑦᑐ ᐱᕕᒃᓴᖅᑕᖅᑲᒪᓂᓯᒍᖅ ᐃᖅᑲᓇᐃᔮᒃᓴᓂᑦ ᐃᓕᑦᑎᓯᒪᔪᓄᑦ ᐃᓄᖕᓄᑦ.

ᓯᓚᑦᑐᖅᓴᕐᕕᒃ – ᐃᓄᐃᑦ ᓯᓚᑦᑐᖅᓴᕐᕕᖓᑦ – ᐃᓕᓐᓂᐊᕐᕕᒃᓴᖅᑲᐅᔪᑦ ᐃᓕᖕᓂᑦ ᐃᑲᔪᕐᓇᖅᑐᓂᑦ ᐊᓂᒍᐃᑦᑎᐊᕐᓂᕐᒧᑦ. ᐃᓕᓐᓂᐊᕐᕕᒃᓴᑦ ᐊᑐᐃᓐᓇᐅᑎᑕᐅᔪᑦ ᑭᕙᓪᓕᕐᒥ, ᕿᑎᕐᒥᐅᓂᑦ ᐊᒻᒪ ᓄᓇᑦᑕ ᓯᓚᑦᑐᖅᓴᕐᕕᖓᓂ, ᐃᑲᔪᕐᓇᖅᐳᑦ ᐃᖅᑲᓇᐃᔮᒃᓴᓄᑦ ᐸᕐᓇᒃᑎᑦᑐᑎᑦ ᐃᖅᑲᓇᐃᔮᒃᓴᑦ ᓴᖅᑭᓐᓂᐊᓕᕐᑎᑦᑐᒋ ᓄᓇᕗᒻᒥ.

ᓂᕈᐊᓚᐅᕈ ᐃᓕᓐᓂᐊᕐᕕᒃᓴᓂᑦ ᐊᑐᐃᓐᓇᐅᑎᑦᑎᓐᓂᑦ ᐅᑯᐊ ᐱᖃᓯᐅᑎᓯᒪᑎᑦᑐᒋᑦ: ᐃᓕᓐᓂᐊᕐᑎᑦᑎᔨᐅᓂᖅ • ᖃᕆᑕᐅᔭᓕᕆᓂᖅ • ᐊᕙᑎᓕᕆᓂᕐᒧᑦ ᐱᓕᕆᐊᒃᓴᓂᑦ • ᐊᐅᓚᑦᑎᔨᐅᓂᕐᒧᑦ • ᐃᓄᓕᕆᓂᕐᒧᑦ • ᐃᓅᓯᓕᕆᓂᕐᖑᕐᓂ • ᑐᓵᔨᐅᓂᕐᒧᑦ • ᐃᓄᐃᑦ ᐅᖃᐅᓯᖓᓐᓂᑦ ᐃᓕᖁᓯᖓᓐᓂᓪᓗ • ᓴᓇᙳᐊᒐᓕᕆᓂᕐᒧᑦ • ᐃᓐᓇᕐᓄᑦ ᖁᑉᐸᕆᐅᖅᓴᓂᕐᒧᑦ • ᐅᖃᓕᒪᓕᐅᖅᓴᓂᕐᒧᑦ • ᐊᒻᒪ ᐊᓯᖏᓐᓄᑦ ᐅᓄᒻᒪᕆᒃᑐᓄᑦ...

ᓯᓚᑦᑐᖅᓴᕐᕕᖕᒥ, ᐱᓇᓱᐊᕈᖅᐳᒍ ᐃᓕᔅᓯᓐᓂ ᐊᓂᒍᐃᑦᑎᐊᑎᑦᑎᓂᕐᒥᓐ. ᖃᐅᔨᒋᐊᒃᑲᓐᓂᓕ, ᐅᑦᑐᒥ ᐅᖃᓚᐅᑎᑦ ᓯᓚᑦᑐᖅᓴᕐᕕᖑᒻᒪ!

Nunavut taya tikittogaalok. Ovalo tikinnami amigaitonik allianaktonik havakhaniotiok Havakvikhanik kinanot ayoitonot inuknot.

Nunavutmi Okioktaktomi Elihakvikyoat – okoa Inuit elihakvikyoangit – pikaliktot Sekogotinik elvit ayoikhaotikhaknik ayoigiakni. Elihaotit sekogotit noiyut Okononga Kivallikmeonot, Kitikmeonot, ovalo Nunata Sekogviit, tabkoa ekayuk-Niagahi opalongaiyagiakni amigaitonot havaakhanot Nunavutmi.

Kanogitot elvit oktugomayatit oktoingialgit ayoikhakvikhat ovalo sekogotit Ovagut angmaktavut hapkoat: Sekootitiinik • Kaggitaoyat • Nunalikiot Sekogotait • Atanionik ovalo Afisilikinik • Olasilikinik • Angayaknaktolikiot Ekayutit • Okaktit ovalo Numiktitiginik • Inuit Okaohilikiot ovalo Elitkohilikiot • Hanaoyaknit & Mikhoknit • Eniknigit Elihakviit • Kablonatot Okayukhaknit • ovalo Amigaitot elihaotit...

Talavani Nunavut Okioktaktomi Elihakvikyoani, ovagut hivonivut eliffingnik Ekayuknahoakniagapta havalakiyaffingnik. Honanik naonaitiagomakpan, hivayaklogit Nunavutkot elihakvikyoanga, oblomi!

Keewatin Campus
Bag 002
Rankin Inlet, NT
X0C 0G0
Tel.: (867) 645-5500
Fax: (867) 645-2387

Kitikmeot Campus
Box 54
Cambridge Bay, NT
X0E 0C0
Tel.: (867) 983-7232
Fax: (867) 983-2404

Nunatta Campus
Box 600
Iqaluit, NT
X0A 0H0
Tel.: (867) 979-7222
Fax: (867) 979-4579
For program information, call (867) 979-7222, or e-mail: pdominix@nac.nu.ca

ᓯᓚᑦᑐᖅᓴᕐᕕᒃ
NUNAVUTMI ILIHAGIAKPAALIVIK
Nunavut Arctic College

NUNAVUT ᓄᓇᕗᑦ

Nunavut is an idea born of the people, nurtured by the people and now celebrated by the people of the Canadian North. I am very proud and pleased to be a part of this remarkable story.

The creation of Nunavut is a dream that has been accomplished through the cooperation of the federal and territorial and Inuit governments. Canada is working in meaningful partnership with Aboriginal people to build stronger communities and a stronger nation.

Much has been achieved, but much remains to be done. We will work together to advance the great legacy of the many people who have spent years making Nunavut a reality. We hold them in great honour.

I am pleased to be a part of the birth of Nunavut and to continue my role in this historic enterprise.

Les résidants du Nord canadien ont fait naître l'idée du Nunavut, l'ont fait grandir et en célèbrent maintenant la concrétisation. J'éprouve une grande fierté et une grande joie à l'idée d'être associée à cette belle aventure.

La création du Nunavut est un rêve qui s'est réalisé grâce à la collaboration du gouvernement fédéral, du gouvernement territorial et des autorités inuites. Le Canada travaille en partenariat avec la population autochtone à édifier des collectivités et une nation plus fortes.

Même si de nombreux objectifs ont été atteints, il reste encore beaucoup de travail à effectuer. Nous unirons nos efforts pour faire fructifier le riche héritage de tous ceux et celles qui ont consacré de nombreuses années à la création du Nunavut. Nous les tenons en haute estime.

Je suis ravie de participer à la naissance du Nunavut et de continuer à jouer mon rôle dans cette entreprise historique.

ᐃᓱᒪᒋᔭᐅᖅᖄᖅᓯᒪᔪᖅ ᓄᓇᕗᑦ ᐃᓄᖕᒋᓐᓂᒃ, ᐱᕈᐃᔭᐅᓯᒪᓪᓗᓂ ᖁᕕᐊᓲᑕᐅᓪᓗᓂᓗ ᑖᒃᑯᓄᖓ ᑲᓇᑕᒥ ᐃᓄᖕᓂᓄᑦ. ᐅᐱᑦᑐᐊᓘᔪᖓ ᖁᕕᐊᕐᕗᖓᓗ ᐱᖅᑲᑕᐅᓚᒪ ᐅᓂᒃᑳᓚᐅᖅᑕᐅᑦᑎᐊᖅᓯᒪᔪᒥᒃ.

ᐱᖑᖅᑎᑕᐅᓂᖓ ᓄᓇᕗᑦ ᐃᓱᒪᑦᑎᐊᕙᓘᔪᖅ ᐋᖅᑭᒃᓱᖅᑕᐅᓯᒪᔪᖅ ᐃᑲᔪᖅᑎᖃᖅᑐᓂᒃ ᒐᕙᒪᑐᖃᖅᑯᓐᓂᒃ ᓄᓇᓯᐊᒥᓗ ᐃᓄᐃᓪᓗ ᒐᕙᒪᖏᓐᓂᒃ. ᑲᓇᑕ ᓄᓇᖃᖅᑳᖅᑐᓂᒃ ᐃᖅᑲᓇᐃᔭᖃᑎᖃᑦᑎᐊᕐᓂᖓᓂᒃ ᓄᓇᓕᖃᖁᓪᓗᒋᑦ ᓴᖏᓂᖅᓴᓂᒃ ᓄᓇᖅᑲᑎᒌᓂᓪᓗ.

ᑎᑭᑕᐅᓯᒪᔪᓗᓚᐅᓕᖅᑐᑦ, ᑭᓯᐊᓂ ᓱᓕ ᑎᑭᑕᒃᓴᐅᔪᑦ ᐅᓄᖅᑑᔪᑦ. ᐱᓇᓱᐊᖃᑎᒌᖕᓂᐊᖅᐳᒍᑦ ᓯᕗᓗᐊᒃᑎᖁᓪᓗᒍ ᐅᓄᖅᑐᓄᑦ ᐃᓄᐃᑦ ᐊᖐᒍᓚᕆᓗᖕᓂᒃ ᐊᒃᓱᕈᖅᓯᒪᓪᓗᑎᒃ ᓄᓇᕗᑦ ᓴᓇᔭᐅᓇᓱᐊᖅᓯᒪᓂᖓ ᐱᑦᓚᓐᖑᖁᓪᓗᒍ. ᐃᓱᒪᒥᓪᒪᓐᒃᑕᕗᑦ ᐊᖏᔪᐊᓗᖕᒥᒃ.

ᖁᕕᐊᓱᒃᑐᖓ ᓄᓇᕗᑦ ᐃᓂᔭᐅᑎᓪᓗᒍ ᑲᔪᓯᓪᓗᖓᓗ ᑎᒥᐅᔪᖅ ᓇᓗᓇᐃᒃᑯᑕᖅᑖᕐᓂᐊᕐᓂᖓᓄᑦ.

Jane Stewart, P.C., M.P.
Minister of Indian Affairs and Northern Development

Jane Stewart, c. p., députée,
ministre des Affaires indiennes et du Nord canadien

ᔭᐃᓐ ᔅᑏᐅᑦ, ᒪᓕᒐᓕᐅᖅᑎᕐᔪᐊᖅ ᒐᕙᒪᐅᑉ
ᒪᓕᒐᓕᐅᖅᑎᖏᓐᓂᒃ ᒥᓂᔅᑕᐅᔪᖅ ᒐᕙᒪᒃᑯᖏᓐᓂ
ᐅᑭᐅᖅᑕᖅᑐᒥᓗ ᐱᕙᓪᓕᐊᔪᓂᒃ

Canada

MESSAGE FROM THE GOVERNMENT OF MANITOBA

On behalf of the people and Government of Manitoba, I am very pleased to extend my congratulations to the people of Nunavut.

April 1, 1999 will forever be a milestone in Canadian history. It defines the day when a dream became a reality. Partnerships between all Canadians have made it possible for tremendous progress to be made over the last few years as we moved towards the creation of Nunavut. Of course, nowhere is the spirit of pride and achievement greater than in Inuit people themselves.

Manitobans have enjoyed a long, historic and valuable relationship with you. We are proud that our two governments recently signed a Memorandum of Understanding to encourage further co-operation and development. It reaffirms our province's commitment to work alongside you, the people of the eastern Arctic, as you prepare to meet the challenges, rewards and tremendous potential that is synonymous with the birth of Nunavut. We look forward to being your partner in the coming years as you shape your destiny and a new path for the future.

May we continue to develop closer partnerships from which all may find greater strength, prosperity, and new opportunities. Congratulations once again!

Premier Gary Filmon

ᒥᓇᖅ ᒪᓂᑑᐸᐅᑉ ᒐᕙᒪᖓᓂᑦ ᐱᔪᖅ

ᐃᓄᖕᒥᓐᓂᑦ ᐊᒻᒪᓗ ᒐᕙᒪᖕᒐᓐᓂᑦ ᒫᓂᑑᐸᐅᑉ, ᖁᕕᐊᓱᒻᒪᕆᑉᐳᖓ ᐅᐱᒍᓱᓐᓂᕐᓂᑦ ᓄᓇᕗᒻᒥᐅᑉ ᐃᓄᖕᒥᓐᓄᑦ.

ᐊᐃᕆᓕ 1, 1999 ᐃᓱᒃᖕᖏᑦᑐᒧᑦ ᐊᐅᓚᕈᔾᔪᐅᓂᐊᕐᑐᖅ ᑲᓇᑕᐅᑉ ᐃᖅᑲᓇᕐᓂᕆᓯᒪᔪᓕᒫᖕᒥᓐᓂᑦ. ᓴᖅᑭᑎᑦᓯᕐᓗᓂ ᐅᑉᓗᖕᒐᓂᑦ ᐃᓱᒪᒋᔭᐅᒃᑦᑕᕐᓚᐅᕐᑐᑦ ᓱᕐᓗ ᓯᓐᓇᕐᑑᒪᑦᑎᒍᑦ ᐱᐅᓯᐅᓂᐊᓕᕐᓗᓂ. ᑲᓇᑕᒥᐅᓕᒫᑦ ᐃᑲᔪᖅᑎᒌᓐᓂᖕᒋᑦ ᐱᒍᓐᓇᕐᑎᑦᓯᓚᕿᕗᖅ ᐱᕚᓕᐊᓂᕆᓯᒪᓪᒪᕆᒃᑦᑕᓂᐅᓚᐅᕐᑐᒥᒃ ᐅᑭᐅᑦ ᖃᑦᓯᑦ ᓇᑎᓪᓗᒋᑦ ᓄᓇᕗᑦ ᓄᐃᑕᐅᕚᓪᓕᐊᓕᕐᑎᓗᒍ. ᐅᐱᓐᓇᕐᓂ, ᑖᓐᓇᕐᑕᒐ ᐃᓄᐃᑦ ᐱᔪᓂᖕᒐ ᐊᒻᒪᓗ ᐱᒍᓐᓇᕐᓂᖕᒐ ᓴᖅᑭᕐᐳᖅ.

ᒫᓂᑑᐸᒥᐅᑦ ᐊᑯᓃᕐᑐᒥᒃ ᐃᓕᑦᓯᓐᓂᒃ ᐃᓅᖅᑎᖅᑲᕐᓇᕆᐊᒥᓂᒃ ᐊᒻᒪᓗ ᐱᓇᓱᐊᖅᑎᖅᑲᕐᓇᕆᐊᒥᓂᒃ ᓇᑯᕐᓴᕐᐳᑦ. ᐅᐱᒍᓱᑉᐳᒍᑦ ᑕᒪᕐᒥᒃ ᒪᕐᕉ ᒐᒪᕚᕆᔭᕗᒃ ᓴᐃᓂᖅᑲᒻᒥᐅᓚᐅᕐᒪᑎᒃ ᑐᑭᓯᒪᐅᑎᒥᒃ ᑲᔪᓯᑎᑦᓯᕐᓂᕐᒧᑦ ᐱᓇᓱᐊᖅᑎᕆᓐᓂᕐᒥᒃ ᐊᒻᒪᓗ ᐱᕚᓪᓕᐊᕐᑎᑦᓯᖅᑎᕆᓐᓂᕐᒥᒃ. ᖃᐅᔨᑎᑦᓯᒥᐊᓪᓚᕐᑐᖅ ᒐᕙᒪᕗᑦᑕ ᐱᓇᓱᐊᖅᑎᖅᑲᕐᒪᓪᓚᕆᓐᓂᖕᒐᓂᒃ ᐃᓕᑦᓯᓐᓂᒃ, ᐅᐊᓕᓂᐅᑉ ᐃᓄᖕᒥᓐᓂᒃ, ᐊᑐᐃᓐᓇᕈᕐᑎᓕᕐᑎᓗᓯ ᐱᔪᒥᑎᒋᓂᕐᒥᒃ, ᐱᒍᓐᓇᕐᔪᓂᐊᕐᑕᓯ ᐊᒻᒪᓗ ᓱᓇᑐᐃᒻᓇᐃᑦ ᐱᒍᓐᓇᕐᓂᐊᕐᑕᓯ ᓄᓇᕗᑦ ᐃᓅᓕᕐᓂᖕᒐᓄᑦ. ᐅᓇᒻᒥᓱᑉᐳᒍᑦ ᐱᓇᓱᐊᖅᑎᖅᑲᓂᐊᕐᓂᑦᑎᓐᓂᒃ ᐃᓕᒃᓯᓐᓂᒃ ᐊᕿᐅᐃᑦ ᑎᑭᓂᐊᕐᑐᓂᑦ ᐋᖅᑭᕐᓱᐃᑎᓪᓗᓯ ᐃᓅᓯᕆᓂᐊᕐᑕᓲᓯᓂᒃ ᐊᒻᒪᓗ ᓄᑖᖅ ᐊᕐᑯᕐᑎᒃ ᐊᑐᓂᐊᓕᕐᑕᓴᓯ ᓱᕗᓂᑦᓴᖏᓐᓂᒃ.

ᑲᔪᓯᓚᐅᕐᑕ ᐱᕚᓪᓕᐊᕐᑎᑦᓯᕐᓂᕐᒧᑦ ᐱᓇᓱᐊᖅᑎᕆᓐᓂᕐᒧᑦ ᐊᒻᒪᓗ ᓲᖕᒍᓂᖅᓴᐅᒍᑎᒋᓂᐊᕐᓗᒍ, ᐱᑕᖅᑲᕐᓇᐅᑎᒋᓗᒍ, ᐊᒻᒪᓗ ᓄᑖᓄᑦ ᐱᒍᓐᓇᐅᑎᒋᒍᓐᓇᕐᓂᐊᕐᑕᓯ. ᐅᐱᓐᓇᕐᐳᓯ ᐃᓘᓐᓇᓯ!

ᐊᖕᒐᔪᖅᖄᕐᒪᕆᖕᒐ ᑭᐊᕆ ᕕᐅᓚᓐ
ᒫᓂᑑᐸᐅᑦ

Manitoba

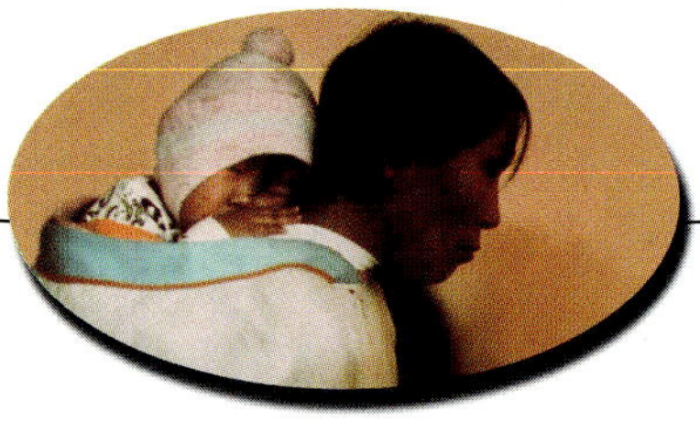

LIVING WITH CHANGE
ᐃᓅᓂᖅ ᐊᓯᖕᒍᖅᐸᓪᓕᐊᔪᒥ

Love of family, appreciation of the seasons, respect for another's isuma*:*
such cornerstones of Inuit society have triumphed
over recent drastic changes,
and will continue to survive uncompromised

ᐃᓚᒌᑦᑎᐊᕐᓂᖅ, ᓯᓚᐅᑉ ᐊᓯᔾᔨᖅᐸᓪᓕᐊᓂᖓᓂᒃ ᒪᓕᒡᓂᖅ, ᐃᓱᒪᒋᔭᐅᔪᓂᒃ ᑲᒪᑦᑎᐊᕐᓂᖅ: ᑕᒪᒃᑯᐊ ᐃᓅᓪᓗᑕ ᐃᓕᖅᑯᓯᕆᔭᕗᑦ ᐃᓅᓯᕗᑦ ᓰᓐᓂᖅᐸᓪᓕᐊᑎᓪᓗᒋᑦ, ᐊᒻᒪᓗ ᓯᕗᓂᕐᒧᑦ ᐊᑐᐃᓐᓇᓪᓚᖓᔭᕗᑦ ᓱᕋᖕᖏᓪᓗᑕ

Wilkinson/NWT Archives; oval inset: Nunavut Tourism

By Rachel Attituq Qitsualik

While the landscapes and wildlife bespeak Nunavut's magnificence, it is the territory's longtime inhabitants — the Inuit — who are the land's manifestation of warmth and humanity. Though an ancient people, Inuit today live in modern homes, surf the Internet, and argue fine legal points over coffee and donuts. Yet lying just under the surface of their industrialized existence thrives a millennial culture and tradition.

Prior to the large-scale movement of Inuit to permanent settlements in the 1950s, Inuit society existed much as it had since time immemorial. A superb example of ingenuity, adaptability, and perseverance in one of the world's most unforgiving environments, Inuit life in the pre-settlement era focused upon a cycle of activities coinciding with the availability of wildlife, and the changing seasons.

Nunavut Tourism

Nunavut Tourism

ᓀᑦᓯ ᐊᑏᑦᑐᖅ ᕿᑦᓯᐊᓚᒃ

ᓄᓇᐅᑉ ᑕᐅᑦᑐᖓ ᓇᒥᑐᐃᓐᓇᖅ ᐊᔾᔨᒋᔭᐅᓂᖃᓐᖏᑎᓪᓗᒍ ᐊᒻᒪᓗ ᐆᒪᔪᖁᑎᖏᑦ ᑕᑯᔭᐅᔪᒪᒐᔪᒃᑐᑎᒃ, ᓄᓇᒥᐅᑕᖏᑦ ᐃᓄᐃᑦ ᑕᑯᔭᖅᑐᖅᑕᐅᒐᔪᙱᖅᐸᐅᔪᑦ. ᐃᓕᖅᑯᓯᒋᑦ ᓄᓇᑖᕆᖃᑦᑕᐅᒐᓗᐊᖅᑎᓪᓗᒍ, ᐅᓪᓗᒥ ᐃᓗᕋᖅᑐᖅᑐᒍᑦ ᓄᑕᐅᓕᖅᑐᓂᒃ ᑕᐃᑦᓯᒪᓂᑎᒫᖓᑦᑐᖅ, ᖃᕆᑕᐅᔭᓂᒃᑯᑦ ᐊᑐᖅᐸᒃᑐᑦ ᐊᒻᒪᓗ ᓂᕆᕕᖕᓂ ᓂᕆᔭᖅᑐᖅᐸᒃᑐᑦ ᓯᓇᒍᐃᓐᓇᕐᓂᓪᓗ ᑮᓇᐅᔭᓂᒃ ᐊᑭᖏᓐᓂᒃ ᐅᔾᔨᖅᑐᖅᐸᒃᑐᑦ ᓂᐅᕕᖅᐸᒃᑐᑦ. ᑭᓯᐊᓂᓕ ᐅᔾᔨᕐᓇᖅᑐᖅ ᐃᓄᐃᑦ ᓯᓚ ᐊᑐᕐᒪᑕ ᐃᓕᖅᑯᓯᑐᖃᕆᓪᓚᐅᖅᑕᒥᖕᓂᒃ.

ᓯᕗᓂᐊᒍᑦ ᐃᓄᐃᑦ ᓄᑦᑎᖅᑎᑕᐅᓚᐅᓐᖏᑎᓪᓗᒋᑦ ᐃᓄᒋᐊᒃᑐᓄᑦ 1950 ᐊᑐᓕᖅᑎᓪᓗᒍ, ᐃᓄᐃᑦ ᐃᓕᖅᑯᓯᖓᑦ ᖃᖓᓕᕚᖅ ᐊᓯᔾᔨᓚᐅᓐᖏᑦᑐᖅ. ᐊᓈᓐᓇᒪᑦᑕᓚᐅᖅᑐᑦ ᓯᓚᕐᔪᐊᒥ ᐊᔪᕐᓇᕐᓂᖅᐸᐅᔪᒥ ᐊᒻᒪᓗ ᓯᓚᖃᖅᑐᒥ ᐅᑐᓇᐊᓇᖅᑐᒥᒃ ᖃᓄᐃᓐᓇᕐᓗ ᑲᐱᐊᓇᖅᑐᖃᖅᑐᒥ. ᐆᒪᔪᓂᒃ ᐊᖑᓇᓱᒃᓗᑎᒃ ᒪᓕᒃᑕᖅᓗᑎᒃ ᐊᐅᓚᓂᖏᓐᓂᒃ ᐊᒻᒪᓗ ᐊᑐᐃᓐᓇᐅᓂᖏᓐᓂᒃ ᐱᕝᕕᒃᓴᐅᓂᖏᓐᓂᒃ ᒪᓕᒃᓗᑎᒃ.

Left: Baker Lake Christmas party, 1956. Community gatherings are still a hallmark of Inuit society. Above: New games and old – Iqaluit's Nicki Eejeesiak at bat, Kugluktuk's June Klengenberg absorbed in a string game

ᓴᐅᒥᐊᓂ: ᖃᒪᓂᑦᑐᐊᕐᒥ ᖁᕕᐊᓯᕝᕕᒃᓯᐅᕐᓂᖅ, 1956. ᓄᓇᓕᖕᓂ ᑲᑎᖃᑎᒌᖕᓂᖅ ᓯᓚ ᓇᓗᓇᐃᒃᑯᑎᐅᒍᖅ ᐃᓅᖃᑎᒌᖕᓂᕐᒧ. ᖁᓚᓂ: ᓄᑖᑦ ᐱᖑᐊᕈᓰ ᐊᒻᒪ ᓄᑕᐅᖏᑦᑐᑦ – ᐃᖃᓗᖕᒥᐅᑕᖅ ᓂᑭ ᐃᔩᓯᐊᖅ ᐊᓇᐅᓯᓚᒫᔪᖅ, ᖁᓪᓗᒃᑑᕐᒥᐅᑕᖅ ᔫᓐ ᑲᓚᖕᒐᖕᐳᒡ ᐊᔭᕋᕐᑐᖅ

Fleming/NWT Archives

Leadership by consensus

Traditionally, leadership was flexible, and based largely upon consensus. For example, if several families were living in the same camp for a period, the best caribou hunter might be consulted in planning the next caribou hunt. If a berry-picking or fishing expedition was being planned, the woman with the most experience might be consulted. The leadership that did exist tended to be temporary and based upon required skills alone.

Ultimate cultural authority rested with the elders. Not only were elders held in high regard, but they also represented a vast wealth of traditional — and vital — knowledge. Without a written language, Inuit preserved their culture through oral history. Consequently, they excelled at storytelling. Adults and children alike once snuggled together, in the light of the *qulliq* (seal-oil lamp), to eagerly await stories. Such stories contained important themes and knowledge that served to educate the younger people.

Respect and family

The heart of Inuit society was the family, a unit based upon mutual respect. If there is a single characteristic that typifies Inuit culture, it is the concept known as isuma. As with so many concepts unique to Inuit, isuma is difficult for non-Inuit to grasp. It refers to the innermost thoughts and feelings a person has — their mindset. A fundamental tenet of Inuit society was the sacred nature of isuma: that another's mind was not to be intruded upon.

Young children were thought not to have fully developed isuma, and were consequently considered exempt from adult responsibilities. Misbehaving children were not scolded or punished — the parents instead distracted or ignored them. This was not casual indifference, but rather the belief that the child was simply not old enough to be taught how to behave.

This dynamic of respect runs throughout Inuit society and lies at its very core. Its influence can be seen in the unwillingness of Inuit to offer opinions as to what others may be thinking, or in the quiet contemplation of Inuit during a meeting or general discussion.

Wilkinson/NWT Archives

ᐃᓚᒌᓐᓂᖅ ᐃᖅᑲᒥᑦᑎᐊᕐᓱᖕᓂᕐᒧ

ᐃᓄᐃᑦ ᐃᓕᖅᑯᓯᖓᒍᑦ ᐃᓚᒌᑦᑎᐊᕐᓂᖅ ᐃᖅᑲᒥᑦᑎᐊᕐᓱᖕᓂᕐᒧ ᐃᓅᓯᐅᓚᐅᖅᑐᖅ. ᐃᓄᐃᑦ ᐃᓕᖅᑯᑎᖓᑎᒍᑦ ᐃᓱᒪᒋᔭᐅᔪᑦ ᐃᒃᐱᒋᔭᐅᑦᑎᐊᖅᑕᓚᐅᖅᑐᑦ. ᖃᓪᓗᓈᑎᑐᑦ ᐅᓂᒃᑳᐅᓯᓇᓱᒡᒍᒧ ᑐᑭᓯᓇᑦᑎᐊᙱᓐᑑᒐᓗᐊᖅ ᐃᓕᖅᑯᓯᓐᖏᓪᓗᒍ, ᑭᓯᐊᓂᓕ ᐊᔾᔨᒋᔭᐅᓚᐅᙱᑦᑐᑦ ᓇᒥᑐᐃᓐᓇᕐᒥ ᐃᓱᒪᒋᔭᐅᔪᑦ ᑲᒪᒋᔭᐅᑦᑎᐊᕐᓂᖏᑦ. ᓇᖏᓐᓂᖅ ᐃᓱᒪᒋᔭᐅᔪᑦ ᐃᓱᒪᖅᓯᕈᑕᐅᓪᓗᑎᒃ ᐊᑐᖅᑕᐅᕙᓚᐅᖅᑐᑦ.

ᓄᑕᕋᐃᑦ ᐃᓱᒪᒃᑲᕋᓗᐊᖅᓱᑎᒃ ᓱᓕ ᐱᕈᖅᓯᒪᙱᓪᒪᑕ, ᐃᓈᖅᑎᑐᑦ ᓱᓕᓂᑎᑕᐅᓯᓚᐅᙱᑦᑐᑦ. ᐱᑦᑎᐊᙱᒃᑳᖓᑕ ᐅᖃᕐᒥᑎᑦ ᓱᐊᒃᑕᐅᑦᑕᓚᐅᙱᑦᑐᑦ — ᐊᖓᔪᖅᑳᖏᓐᓄᑦ ᓴᐃᒻᒪᖅᓴᖅᑕᐅᓗᑎᒃ ᐱᑦᑎᐊᖅᑎᑕᐅᓇᓱᒃᖢᑎᒃ. ᐃᓱᒪᒃᑦᑎᐊᓕᖅᐸᑦ ᑭᓯᐊᓂ ᐃᓕᓐᓇᖅᓂᖏᑦ ᒪᓕᒃᑕᐅᓪᓗᑎᒃ ᖃᓄᖅ ᐃᓅᓯᖃᕆᐊᒃᓴᖏᑦ ᐃᓕᑎᑕᐅᓪᓗᑎᒃ.

ᑕᒪᓐᓇ ᐃᖅᑲᒥᑦᑎᐊᕐᓱᖕᓂᖅ ᐊᓯᓂᒃ ᐃᓄᐃᑦ ᐃᓅᓯᓕᕆᙱᓐᓂ ᐊᑐᐃᓐᓇᖅᑕᑦᑕᐅᓯᓐᓂᖅᑐᖅ ᐊᒻᒪᓗ ᐊᔾᔨᒋᔭᐅᓇᓂ ᓇᒥᑐᐃᓐᓇᖅ. ᓄᓇᕗᒻᒥᑦ ᑎᑭᓛᖅᑐᒥᑦ ᑕᑯᔪᖃᖅᐸᒃᑐᑦ ᐃᓄᐃᑦ ᐊᐃᐸᐅᑎᙱᑦᑐᓂᒃ ᐅᖃᖅᑐᖃᖅᑎᓪᓗᒍ ᐊᒻᒪᓗ ᓯᙱᑐᑎᔭᐅᓇᓂ ᐊᓯᒥᖕᓄᑦ ᑲᒪᒋᔭᐅᙱᓐᓇᓯᒋᔭᐅᓗᓂ. ᐱᓗᐊᖅᑐᒥᒃ ᑲᑎᒪᔪᖃᖅᑎᓪᓗᒍ ᐃᓄᐃᖕᓂᒃ.

ᓯᕗᓕᖅᑎᐅᓂᖅ ᐊᖏᖃᑎᒌᖕᓂᒃᑯᑦ

ᑕᐃᑦᓱᒪᓂᓪᓚᑦᑐᖅ, ᐊᖓᔪᖅᑳᖑᓂᖅ ᑕᒪᒃᑭᓄᑦ ᐋᖅᑭᒃᓱᒪᔪᑦᑕᓪᓚᑦᑐᖅ. ᔫᓯ ᐅᓇ ᐆᒃᑑᑎᒥᓪᓗ, ᐃᓄᐃᑦ ᓄᓇᖕᒥᐅᑕᐅᓂᖅᐸᑕ, ᐊᖑᓇᓱᒃᑎᐅᔪᑦ ᐊᔪᙱᓐᓂᖅᐸᐅᔪᑦ ᑐᒃᑐᓕᐊᕐᓂᐊᖅᐸᑕ ᓯᕗᓕᖅᑎᐅᓪᓗᑎᒃ. ᐊᒻᒪᑦᑕᐅᖅ ᐊᕐᓇᓂ, ᐃᖅᑲᒃᓯᐅᖅᑲᑎᒌᖕᓂᐊᖅᐸᑕ ᐸᐅᕐᖓᖅᓯᐅᕐᓂᐊᖅᐸᑕᓘᓐᓃᑦ ᒪᓕᒃᑕᐅᓂᐊᖅᑐᒥᒃ ᓯᕗᓪᓕᐅᔪᖅᑲᕐᓗᓂ. ᐊᔪᙱᓐᓂᖓᑦ ᒪᓕᒃᑕᐅᓗᓂ ᐊᒻᒪᓗ ᐃᓅᓯᒃᑖᓐᖓᓂᐅᙱᑦᑑᓪᓗᐊᖅ ᓈᓚᒃᑕᐅᓂᐊᕐᓗᓂ. ᖃᐅᔨᒪᑦᑎᐊᕐᓂᖓ ᓯᓇᔪᖃᖅᐊᖃᖅᑎᓪᓗᒍ ᑐᕌᖓᕕᒋᔭᐅᓂᐊᕐᓗᓂ.

ᐃᓯᒪᑦᒪᖅᑐᓂᕐᓗ ᐃᓐᓄᖅᑲᓄᑦ ᐊᑐᖅᑕᐅᑦᑕᐅᖅᑐᖅ. ᐃᓐᓄᖅᑲᐃᑦ ᐅᐱᒋᔾᔪᐃᓐᓇᐅᓂᒃᑯᑦ ᐱᕙᓪᓕᐅᖅᑎᑕᐅᙱᑦᑐᑦ ᑭᓯᐊᓂᓪᓗ ᖃᐅᔨᒪᔫᑎᒃ ᓯᓚᑐᓯᒥᒃ ᐊᒻᒪᓗ ᐃᓅᓯᒧᑦ ᖃᐅᔨᒪᔫᓯᐊᖃᖅᑐᓂᒃ ᓄᐊᑦᑎᕈᑎᒃ. ᐃᓄᐃᑦ ᑎᑎᕋᕐᑎᖃᓪᓚᐅᙱᑦᑎᓪᓗᒋᑦ ᓴᓇᑐᐃᓐᓇᐃᑦ ᐃᓕᑕᐅᓯᒪᔪᑦ ᐅᖃᐅᓯᕆᔭᐅᓂᒃᑯᑦ ᐃᓕᑕᐅᕙᓪᓚᐅᖅᑐᑦ.

Above: Community has always been key – Pangnirtung residents, 1936.
Left: Hunting ptarmigan and warming hands, Pond Inlet, early 1950s
ᖁᓛᓂ: ᓄᓇᓖᑦ ᐱᒻᒪᕆᐅᖃᑦᑕᐃᓐᓇᕐᐳᑦ - ᐸᖕᓂᖅᑑᖅᒥᐅᑕᑦ, 1936. ᓴᐅᒥᐊᓂ: ᐊᕿᒡᒋᖃᓱᒃᑐᑦ ᐊᒻᒪ ᐊᖖᐃᔾᔨᕐᓯᕐᑐᖅ, ᒥᑦᑎᒪᑕᓕᒃ, 1950 ᐱᒋᐊᕐᓯᒪᓕᕐᑎᓪᓗᒍ

"I remember looking around the room at all the faces of all the people who played some role in it over the years. And I thought of some of the people who weren't present . . . of how many people it had taken for this to be achieved."

– Chief federal negotiator Tom Molloy, on the signing of the final agreement in Iqaluit, May 1993

Each family spent much of the year travelling, setting up camps wherever food was available, before moving on when it became scarce. While immediate family formed the basic unit, extended families were very important and would gather together with others when the seasons and availability of food permitted. These were times of great joy and feasting — times for stories, singing, drumming, eating, playing, and chatting.

Tremendous love for children

The parents bore primary responsibility for providing food, clothing, and shelter for the other members. Here, there was true gender equality. While the husband was the primary provider of food staples, such as large animals, the wife played an equally vital role as food preparer, seamstress, care-giver, and maintainer of heat and fire. As well, all family members contributed wherever they could, with older children looking after younger ones.

Inuit love their children. This seems like a truism, but it's reinforced by a great degree of open and very physical affection that is showered upon young children: from mothers carrying their babies in their *amautit* (baby-carrying parkas), to the "aaaaahs" and cooing that seem to arise every time Inuit with young children meet friends and relatives. Childhood is traditionally a wonderful time for Inuit. Children's young wants and needs are tolerated more than in most southern Canadian children. Everybody wants to cuddle and *kunik* (kiss) them.

The love of children is also reflected in Inuit customary adoption practices. Inuit families with an abundance of children may allow a family member or close friend to adopt one of their children — perhaps the greatest gift of all. The child is usually raised knowing her birth mother, who often plays an active role in the raising of the child. Such generosity, consideration, and empathy are hallmarks of Inuit culture.

ᐅᓂᒃᑳᖅᑐᐊᒃᑯᓪᓘᓐᓇᓚᑦ ᐃᓕᑎᑕᐅᓪᓗᑎᒃ. ᐃᓐᓇᐃᑦ ᓄᑕᖅᑲᓪᓗ ᖁᓪᓕᑐᐃᓐᓇᕐᒧᑦ ᖃᐅᒻᒪᖅᑯᑎᖃᖅᑐᑎᒃ ᐅᓂᒃᑳᖅᑐᐊᓂᒃ ᑐᓴᕐᓇᖅᑐᓂᒃ ᐅᓂᒃᑳᖅᑐᖃᖅᑎᓪᓗᒍ. ᐅᓂᒃᑳᖅᑐᐊᑐᐃᓐᓇᐅᓐᖏᑦᑐᓂᒃ ᐃᓕᒍᑎᒃᓴᐅᔪᓂᒃ ᐊᒻᒪᓗ ᖃᐅᔨᖃᑦᑕᐅᑎᓪᓗᑎᒃ ᖃᓄᖅ ᐃᓱᒪᒻᒪᕆᒃᑳᕐᒥᒃ ᐱᓗᐊᖅᑐᒥᒃ ᒪᒃᑯᒃᑐᓄᑦ ᐊᑐᖅᑕᐅᔪᒃᓴᓂᒃ.

ᐃᓄᐃᑦ ᓄᓇᓕᒫᖅᑲᖅᑕᓚᐅᖅᑐᑦ ᐊᒥᔫᓐᖏᓪᓗᑎᒃ ᐃᓚᖏᑦ. ᐆᒪᔪᖅᓯᐅᖅᓗᑎᒃ ᓇᒧᑐᐃᓐᓇᖅ ᐊᕐᖁᑉ ᖃᓄᐃᓐᓂᖓ ᒪᓕᒃᓗᓂᕐᔪᒃ ᓄᓇᖃᕆᐊᖅᑐᖅᓗᑎᒃ. ᐆᒪᔪᖃᓐᖏᓕᕐᖓᑦ ᐊᓯᐊᓄᑦ ᓅᑉᐸᒃᓗᑎᒃ. ᓄᓇᒥ ᐊᓕᐊᓇᐃᒍᓯᒃᓗᑎᒃ ᐃᓚᒌᑦ ᐃᓅᖃᑎᒌᒍᓐᓇᕐᒪᑕ. ᓂᕆᓵᖅᐊᕐᓇᐅᓕᕐᖓᑦ ᓂᕆᖃᑎᒌᒃᓗᑎᒃ, ᕿᓚᐅᔾᔭᖅᓗᑎᒃ, ᐱᖑᐊᖅᓗᑎᒃ ᐊᒻᒪᓗ ᐅᖃᓪᓚᓐᓴᖃᑎᒌᒃᓗᑎᒃ.

ᓄᑕᖅᑲᐃᑦ ᓇᓪᓕᒋᔭᐅᓂᖏᑦ

ᐊᖓᔪᖄᖑᔭᐅᔪᑦ ᑲᒪᔾᔪᑦᑕᓗᐅᖅᑐᑦ ᕿᑐᕐᖏᕐᒥᖕᓂᒃ. ᓂᕿᒃᓴᖅᓯᐅᖅᑎᑐᓪᓗᑎᒃ, ᐋᓐᓂᖅᑲᖅᑎᑎᓪᓗᑎᒃ ᐊᒻᒪᓗ ᐃᓂᒃᓴᖅᑎᑎᓪᓗᑎᒃ ᓄᑕᖅᑲᒥᓂᒃ. ᐊᖑᑎᑦ ᐊᕐᓇᐃᓪᓗ ᐊᔾᔨᒋᖕᒥᒃ ᐊᒃᓯᑭᕐᓂᖃᓗᖅᑐᒃ ᐃᓅᖅᑎᒋᑦ ᑲᒪᒋᔭᐅᑎᐊᖁᓪᓗᒋᑦ. ᐊᖑᑎᑦ ᐊᖏᔪᓂᒃ ᐆᒪᔪᖅᓯᐅᖅᑎᓪᓗᒋᑦ, ᐊᕐᓇᐃᑦ ᑲᒪᒋᐊᖃᓗᖅᑐᑦ ᓂᕿᒃᓴᓇᔪᐅᔪᓂᒃ ᐊᒻᒪᓗ ᐊᓐᓄᕌᒃᓴᓇᔪᐅᔪᓂᒃ. ᓄᑕᖅᑲᐃᑦ ᐃᑲᔪᖅᑎᐅᑎᓪᓗᒋᑦ, ᐃᓗ ᓈᒻᒪᑦᑎᐊᖅᑲᓗᐊᖅᒪᖔᑦ ᑭᓇᑐᐃᓐᓇᕐᒧᑦ ᐊᔪᓐᖏᑦᑐᒧᑦ ᑲᒪᒋᔭᐅᔪᓐᓇᓚᐅᖅᑐᖅ. ᓄᑕᖅᑲᐃᑦ ᐃᑲᔪᕐᓂᒃᑯᑦ ᖁᕐᖏᐊᕐᓂᒃᑯᓪᓗ ᐃᓛᒃᐸᓪᓚᐊᑎᑕᐅᓪᓗᑎᒃ.

ᐃᓄᐃᑦ ᓇᓪᓕᒍᓯᒻᒪᕆᒃᑐᑦ ᓄᑕᖅᑲᒥᖕᓂᒃ. ᑕᒪᓐᓇ ᐅᖃᕆᐊᖅᑲᖅᑑᔭᓐᖏᑦᑑᓗᐊᖅ ᑭᓯᐊᓂᓕ ᓯᓕᔪᖅ. ᐃᓄᐃᑦ ᓄᓇᖕᒐᓐᓄᑦ ᑎᑭᑦᑐᑦ ᑕᑯᔪᓐᓇᖅᐸᒃᑐᑦ ᓄᑕᖅᑲᐃᑦ ᐊᖃᖅᑕᐅᓂᖕᖏᓐᓂᒃ ᐊᒻᒪᓗ ᓇᓪᓕᒋᔭᐅᓂᖕᖏᓐᓂᒃ. ᓄᑕᕋᓛᑦ ᐊᒫᖅᑕᐅᑦᑎᒃ ᑯᓂᒃᑕᑉᐸᒃᓗᑎᒃ ᐊᒻᒪᓗ ᓇᓪᓕᒋᔭᐅᑦᑎᐊᖅᓗᑎᒃ ᓇᒥᑐᐃᓐᓇᖅ ᐃᓚᒥᖕᓄᑦ ᐱᓐᓇᓱᐅᑦᓗᑎᒃ. ᓄᑕᕋᐅᓪᓗᓂ ᖁᕕᐊᓇᖅᑐᖅ ᐱᕈᖅᐸᓪᓕᐊᓪᓗᓂ ᐃᓄᐃᑦ ᐃᓪᓚᖅᑯᓯᖏᓐᓂ. ᖃᓪᓗᓈᑦ ᓄᑕᖄᖕᖏᑎᑦ ᐱᕈᐃᔭᐅᑦᑕᐅᖕᖏᒻᒪᑕ ᐃᓱᒪᖅᓱᕐᓂᖅᓴᐅᓪᓗᑎᒃ. ᓇᓪᓕᒋᔭᐅᓂᖕᖏᓐᓂᒃ ᖃᐅᔨᒪᑎᑕᐅᑦᑎᐊᖅᓗᑎᒃ ᐃᕿᑕᐅᓪᓗᑎᒃ ᑯᓂᒃᑕᐅᓪᓗᑎᓪᓗ.

Nunatsiaq News

Nunavut Tourism

Top: Snug in her kamiit *(sealskin boots), Alukie Mike of Iqaluit learns sewing as part of an elder-led school program. Right: Inuit society required older children to look after younger ones, but left lots of time for play. Left to right: Martha Qappik, Adina Tagarlik Duffy, Amy Suniq Duffy and Janet Paniyuk, Coral Harbour, 1988*

ᖁᓛᓂ: ᑲᒥᒃᓯᒪᓪᓗᓂ ᐅᖁᔫᔭᓂ (ᕿᓯᖑᓂ), ᐊᓗᑭ ᒪᐃᒃ ᐃᖃᓗᖕᒥᐅᑕᖅ ᒥᖅᓱᖅᓂᖅ ᐃᓕᓐᓂᐊᖅᑐᖅ ᑕᒪᓐᓇ ᐃᓐᓇᑐᖅᑲᕐᓄ ᐃᓕᓐᓂᐊᕐᑎᔪᑕᐅᓪᓗᓂ ᐃᓕᓐᓂᐊᕐᕕᖕᒥ. ᑕᓕᖅᐱᐊᓂ: ᐃᓄᐃᑦ ᕿᑐᕐᖓᕐᖏᓐᓂ ᐊᖓᔪᒃᖠᕐᓂ ᐃᑲᔪᕐᑕᐅᖃᑦᑕᓇᐊᖃᕈᕐᐳᑦ ᐸᐃᓇᔾᔨᓪᓗᒋ, ᑭᓯᐊᓂᓕ ᐱᖑᐊᕈᓐᓇᐃᓐᓇᕐᐸᒃᖢᑎᒃ. ᓴᐅᒥᐊᓂᑦ ᑕᓕᕐᐱᐊᓄᑦ: ᒫᑕ ᖃᐱᒃ, ᐋᑏᓇ ᑕᖄᓕᒃ ᑕᕕ, ᐃᒥ ᓯᓂᖅ ᑕᕕ ᐊᒻᒪ ᔮᓇᑦ ᐸᓂᔪᒃ, ᓴᓪᓖᑦ, 1988

“ᐃᖅᑲᐅᒪᔪᖓ ᕿᒥᕿᐊᕐᔪᖓ ᑮᓇᕐᓂᑦ ᑕᑯᓂ ᐱᓕᕆᖃᑕᐅᓯᒪᔪᓂᑦ ᐊᕐᖁᒍᓯᓂ. ᐊᒻᒪ ᐃᖅᑲᐅᒪᒋᓪᓗᖓ ᐃᓄᖕᓂ ᑕᑯᓃᖏᑦᑐᓂᑦ. . .
ᐃᓯᒪᓪᓗᖓ ᐃᓅᓯᖕᓂ ᑭᓯᐊᓂ ᐊᑐᕐᓗᑎᒃ ᑕᒪᓇ ᓴᖅᑭᑦᑐᖅ.”

– ᐊᖓᔪᖅᑳᖅ ᒪᕋᒍᖅᑯᓐᓂ ᐋᔩᕐᑎᓄᑦ, ᑖᒻ ᒪᓗᐊᐃ, ᐊᑎᓕᐅᕐᓂᖅᑕᕐᑎᓪᓗᒍ ᑲᖑᓪᓕᕐᐹᒥᓐ ᐊᖏᕈᑎᒥᓐ ᐃᖃᓗᖕᓂ, ᒪᐃ 1993

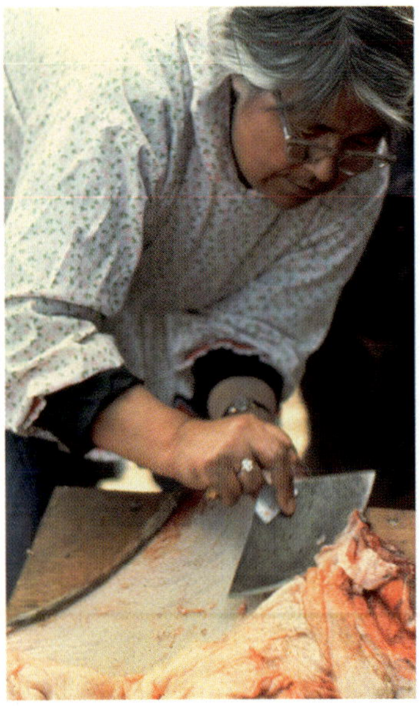
Nunavut Tourism ᓄᓇᕗᑦ ᐳᓚᕋᑦᑐᓕᕆᔨᒃᑯᑦ

Drastic changes

Today, the complexity of everyday life increases with an unprecedented rapidity. Although one of the elements that has enabled Inuit to survive the rigors of life in the Arctic has been their incredible ability to adapt, the speed and degree of change in our society has taken its toll on the people and culture. The most dramatic and pervasive changes have perhaps occurred as a result of the wage economy. Whereas Inuit in pre-settlement days were always fully "employed" in the day-to-day business of survival, the modern unemployment rate in some communities can now exceed 60 per cent. This problem stems from past errors and cross-cultural difficulties, and it has had a devastating impact on a great number of Inuit families. The acquisition of southern skills has been slow. The strain that this places on Inuit society remains one of the indelible legacies of the imposition of a community lifestyle.

As well, the relationship between youth and elders has undergone considerable change. Inuit youth are today educated in classrooms, watch WWF wrestling and the latest sitcoms, and listen to the Spice Girls and Marilyn Manson. Their grasp of the Inuktitut language has faded, and has limited their ability to communicate with their elders, who are the source of traditional knowledge. It is an unfortunate fact that much of the information needed to thrive in the modern world can be found not through elders, but through texts, CD-ROMs and the Internet. While elders continue to play an important and respected role in Inuit society, that role is now endangered.

Nunatsiaq News ᓄᓇᑦᓯᐊᕐᒥ ᐱᕙᓪᓕᐊᔪᑦ

Inuit values prevail

Despite the massive changes that have at times threatened to overwhelm Inuit society, Inuit have endured without compromising their basic values. While many things have changed in their society, Inuit continue to relish time spent talking with friends and relatives, exchanging a bit of gossip, or hearing about recent

ᓄᑕᖅᐃᑦ ᐱᓐᓇᓱᐳᓂᖏᑦ ᑕᑯᓱᐳᔮᓐᓇᕐᒥᔮᑦ ᐃᓄᐃᑦ ᐃᓕᖅᑯᓯᖏᑕ ᒪᓕᒃᑕᐅᑦᑕᕐᓂᖏᑦ ᑎᒍᐊᖅᑳᑦᑕᕐᓂᒃᑯᑦ. ᐃᓕᒌᑦ ᓄᑕᖄᕆᐅᓗᐊᖅᑐᑦ ᑎᒍᐊᖅᑕᐅᑎᑎᒍᓐᓇᖅᑐᑦ ᕿᑐᕐᖓᕐᒥᖕᓂᒃ ᐃᓚᒥᓄᑦ. ᑕᒪᓐᓇ ᐃᓄᐃᑦ ᐃᓕᖅᑯᓯᖓᑎᒍᑦ ᐊᑲᐅᑦᑕᓚᐅᖅᑐᖅ, ᓄᑕᕋᓱᐅᔭᖅ ᐋᓇᒥᓂᒃ ᖃᐅᔨᒪᐃᓐᓇᖅᑎᑕᐅᓪᓗᓂ, ᐊᓯᐊᓄᑦ ᐊᐅᓪᓚᖅᑎᑕᐅᕆᐊᖃᕐᓂᖏᓪᓗᓂ ᖃᓪᓗᓈᑦ ᐃᓪᓕᖅᑯᓯᖓᑎᑐᑦ. ᑕᒪᓐᓇ ᐃᓅᓪᓚᓇᒃᑎᑐᑦ ᐃᓕᖅᑯ-ᓯᒪᓇᒃ.

ᐊᓯᔾᔨᒪᓂᖕᓂᖅ

ᐅᓪᓗᒥᐅᔪᕐᓕ, ᐊᓯᔾᔨᖅᓯᒻᒪᓇᒃᑐᖅ ᐃᓄᐃᑦ ᐃᓅᓯᓇᓲᖏᑦ ᑕᐃᑦᓯᒪᑎᑐᑦ ᐱᔭᓐᓕᖅᑐᑦ. ᐃᓕᖅᑯᓯᑐᖃᐃᑦ ᐊᑐᖅᑕᐅᔭᓐᓕᖅᐸᓪᓕᐊᑎᓪᓗᒋᑦ ᓱᓇᑐᐃᓐᓇᐃᑦ ᓄᑖᕐᑯᑦ ᐊᐅᓚᑕᐅᕙᓪᓕᐊᑎᓪᓗᒋᑦ. ᐃᓄᐃᑦ ᐊᓐᓇᐅᒪᔭᓐᓇᓚᐅᕈᑎᖏᑦ ᖃᓄᐃᓐᓇᖅ ᐊᓯᔾᔨᖅᐸᓪᓕᐊᔪᓂᒃ ᒪᓕᒃᓱᖅᑎᒃ ᐊᓯᔾᔨᖃᑕᐅᓪᓗᑎᒃ ᐱᔭᓐᓇᖅᐸᓪᓚᐅᕐᓂᖏᑦ. ᑭᓯᐊᓂᓕ ᐅᓪᓗᒥ ᐊᑭᓖᓯᒪᔪᑦ ᐃᓅᓯᕐᒥᖕᓄᑦ ᐊᒃᑐᖅᑕᐅᓯᒪᓂᖅᖃᖅᑯᑦ. ᐃᓄᐃᑦ ᐊᓯᔾᔨᖅᑎᑕᐅᓗᓂ ᐊᒻᒪ ᐃᓕᖅᑯᓯᖏᑦ ᐊᔾᔨᖅᑎᑕᐅᓗᓂ ᑕᒪᓐᓇ ᐊᒃᓯᑫᓐᓇᖅᑐᒃᑯᑦ ᑐᐊᕕᓗᐊᖅᑐᒃᑯᑦ ᓱᓇᑐᐃᓐᓇᐃᑦ ᐃᓕᖅᑯᓯᕐᒥᓂᒃ ᐊᑐᖓᖅᑕᐅᓂᖏᓐᓂᒃ ᐊᐅᓚᑦᑎᓂᕐᒥᑦ ᐱᓱᐊᕆᑕᐅᔪᑦ ᐅᑦᑐᒥ ᑮᓇᐅᔭᑎᒍᑦ ᑭᓯᐊᓂ ᓯᓇᑐᐃᓐᓇᐃᑦ ᐃᓐᖏᕐᓂᖅᑲᖅᑐᖓ. ᐃᓄᐃᑦ ᓯᓚ ᐃᓄᕕᐊᒃᑐᓂ ᓄᓇᖃᓪᓚᐅᖏᓐᓂᑦᑐᑦ ᑕᒪᐃᑦ ᐅᑦᑐᒥᑎᒎᖏᑦᑐᖅ ᓯᓚᑦᓯᓇᐊᒃᓴᖅᑲᐅᕙᖅᑐᑦ, ᐅᑦᑐᒥᓕ ᓛᓇᐅᔪᖅ ᓇᐸᖏᑕᓘᓪᓗ ᐊᒥᓲᓂᖅᓴ-ᐅᓂᖏᑦ ᓯᓚᓇᐊᒃᓴᖃᖏᑦᑐᑦ ᓇᖏᓂᖅ ᕿᓇᐅᔭᓕᐅᕿᓇᕐᓂᖏᒃ ᐃᓅᔪᖏᑦᓴᒥᒃ. ᑕᒪᓐᓇ ᑕᐃᑦᓯᒪᓂᒥᑦ ᐊᐅᓚᑕᐅᔪᑦ ᐊᑲᐅᖏᑦᑐᖅᑯᑦ.

ᐃᖏᕐᕿᑎᑕᐅᕙᓪᓕᐊᕐᓂᖏᑦ ᐱᓪᓗᒋᑦ ᑕᐃᒪᐃ-ᓯᒪᓪᖅᑐᖅ ᐊᒻᒪ ᑕᒻᒪᖅᑐᒃᑯᑦ ᒪᓪᓕᒃᑕᐅᓂᑯᑦ ᐊᒃᑐᐃᖓᑕ ᐅᓪᓗᒥᒧᑦ ᓯᓚ. ᖃᓪᓗᓈᑦ ᓄᓇᖓᓐᓂ ᐊᔭᖏᔾᔭᑕᐅᔭᖅᑐᑦ ᓱᒃᑲᐃᑦᑐᒥᒃ ᐃᓕᑕᐅᔭᕐᓂᖅᓯᐊᓗᖃᑕᐅᔭᖅᑐᑦ ᐃᓅᓯᖏᓐᓄᑦ ᐊᒃᓯᑭᑦᑎᓕᓯᒪᔪᖅ ᓄᓇᓕᖕᓂ ᐃᓅᓯᖃᓐᓇᖅᑲᓂᖅᓯᐊᕐᓂᕐᒥᒃ.

ᐊᒻᒪᓗᑦᑕᐅᖅ, ᒪᒃᑯᑦᑐᐃᑦ ᐃᓐᓇᐅᖅᑲᓂᒃ ᐅᓂᒃᑳᕆᔭᐅᖏᒃᑐᑦ ᐊᔾᔨᐅᖏᑦᑐᑦ ᐊᔾᔨᖏᓐᓂᖏᑦᑐᖅ. ᐃᓄᐃᑦ ᒪᒃᑯᑦᑐᖏᑦ ᐃᓕᓐᓂᐊᖅᑎᑕᐅᓯᒪᓪᓚᑦ ᐃᓕᓐᓂᐊᕕᖕᓂ. ᖁᕕᐊᕈᓐᓇᖅᓱᑎᒃ WWF-ᒥᒃ ᐊᒻᒪ ᐊᓯᖏᓐᓂᒃ ᐃᓄᒃᑐᑦ ᐃᓕᖅᑯᓯᖃᖅᖢᒍᑦ ᐊᔾᔨᓯᖃᖏᑦᑐᓂᒃ. ᓈᓚᒍᓐᓇᖅᑐᑦ ᐃᖏᖅᑎᐅᔪᓂᒃ Spice Girls ᐊᒻᒪ Marilyn Manson-ᒥᒃ. ᐃᓄᐃᑦ ᐅᖃᐅᓯᖅᑲᖓᓂᒃ ᐊᑐᕿᓪᓚᖅᐸᓪᓕᐊᔪᑦ ᐊᒻᒪ ᐃᓐᓇᐅᖃᐃᑦ ᒪᒃᑯᑦᑐᐃᓪᓗ ᖃᓂᑉᐸᓪᓚᐅᕐᓂᖏᑦ ᔭᒐᐃᔭᐅᕙᓪᓕᐊᔪᑦ. ᐃᓕᖏᕕᒃᓴᐅᔪᓪ ᑭᖑᕙᓪᓗᑦ ᐱᑖᕋᔭᐅᕙᓐᖏᓪᓕᖅᑲᑕ. ᒪᓕᒃᑲᐅᓚᐅᓗᐊᖅ ᐊᔪᓐᖏ-ᓐᓂᕋᔭᐅᕆᐊᓖᑦ ᐅᓪᓗᒥᒧᑦ ᐊᑐᖅᑕᐅᔪᒃᓯᐃᑦ ᐃᓕᑕᑦᑕᓪᓕᖅᑲᑕ ᐃᓐᓇᐅᖅᑯᒍᓐᓇᖏᑦᑐᖅ ᑭᓯᐊᓂᓪᓚ ᐅᖅᑲᓖᓪᓚᐅᒃᑯᑦ, ᖃᕆᑕᐅᔭᒃᑯᑦ (CD-ROM) ᐊᒻᒪ ᐱᑐᒃᓯᒪᓂᒃᑯᑦ ᖃᕆᑕᐅᔭᒃᑯᑦ. ᐃᓐᓇᐅᖅᑲᐃᑦ ᐃᓂᖃᕐᕿᓗᐊᖅᑎᓪᓗᒋᑦ ᓱᓕ ᐃᓄᐃᑦ ᐃᓅᓯᖏᓐᓂ, ᑕᒪᓐᓇ ᓵᓚᒋᔭᐅᓯᒪᕙᓪᓕᐊᔪᖅ ᐃᒃᐱᒋᔭᐅᑦᑎᐊᕐᓂᖓ.

ᐃᓄᐃᑦ ᓇᖕᒥᓂᖏᑦ ᐊᓐᓇᐅᒪᔪᑦ

ᑕᐃᒪᐃᑦᑐᒃᑲᓗᐊᖅᑎᓪᓗᒍ ᓱᓇᑐᐃᓐᓇᐃᑦ ᐃᓕᖅᑯ-ᓯᒥᑎᑦ ᑕᐃᒪᐃᖑᓐᓂᖅᑎᓪᓗᒋᑦ, ᐃᓄᐃᑦ ᐃᓕᖅᑯᓯᖓᑦ ᐱᕙᓪᓕᐊᔪᖅ ᓱᓕ, ᐊᔾᔨᒋᔭᐅᖏᑦᑐᖅ ᐊᒻᒪ ᓴᒃᑯᑕᐅᓪᓚᖓᓂ. ᐊᒥᓱᑦ ᓱᓇᑐᐃᓐᓇᐃᑦ ᐃᓅᓯᕙᒥ ᐊᓯᔾᔨᖅᑯᖅᑲᐅᑎᓪᓗᒋᑦ ᐃᓄᐃᑦ ᑐᖁᓪᓚᐃᓐᓇᖅᑐᑦ ᐃᓚᒌᔭᒥᖕᓄᑦ, ᖃᓄᐃᒻᒪᖕᒫᖅᒥᒃ ᓇᓗᓇᐃᔭᖅᑐᑎᒃ, ᐅᖃᖃᑎᒌᒃᑐᑎᒃ, ᖃᓄᖅᑐᓐᓂᑦ ᖃᓄᐃᑦᑐᖃᓪᓚᕆᖕᒫᑦ ᓄᓇᒥᔭᒥᖕᓂ ᑐᓴᖃᑦᑕ-ᐅᑎᓪᓗᑎᒃ. ᖃᓄᖅ ᐃᓅᖃᒥᑦ ᐃᓯᒪᖕᒪᖔᑕ ᖃᓄᖅᑐᖅ ᐊᔾᔨᖕᒋᔭᐅᖃᖅᑎᖃᓐᒪᖔᑕ ᐅᐱᒋᔭᐅᖕᒋᓐᓇᐅᔪᖅᑐᖏᑦ ᖃᖕᒐᑐᐃᓐᓇᖅ.

Above: Preparing a sealskin with an ulu *(woman's knife). Left: Whalers brought variations on square dancing – now considered "traditional" Inuit dance – in the 1800s. From left, Soloman Atagoyuk, Pauloosie Pudloo, Joanasie Nowdlak, and Annie Aningmiuq of Rankin Inlet*

ᖁᓛᓂ: ᕿᓯᓕᕆᔪᖅ ᐅᓗᒧᓐ. ᓴᐅᒥᐊᓂ: ᐊᕐᕙᖕᓂᐊᖅᑏ ᒧᒥᕈᓯᕐᓂ ᓇᓴᓚᐅᕐᓯᒪᔫᑦ ᐊᔾᔨᖏᖕᒋᑦᑐᓂ – ᒫᓐᓇ ᐃᓯᒪᕆᔭᐅᓕᕐᑐᖅ ᐃᓄᒃᑎᑐᑦ ᒧᓇᕈᓯᕐᒥᓐ – 1800ᖏᓐᓂᑦ. ᓴᐅᒥᐊᓂ, ᓵᓚᒻ ᐊᑕᒍᔪᒃ, ᐸᐅᓗᓯ ᐸᓪᓗᖅ, ᔪᐊᓇᓯ ᓇᐅᓪᓚᖅ, ᐊᒻᒪ ᐋᓂ ᐊᓂᖕᒥᐅᖅ ᑲᖏᕐᓕᓂᕐᒥᐅᑕᑦ

events in town. Sensitivity to the feelings and rights of others remains a fundamental Inuit trait.

The Inuit of Nunavut today revel in an increasingly official recognition of their culture. Customary adoption, for example, has been recognized by the territorial government, and Inuit are learning to identify and guard their rights. On the community level, one may still find children playing through the extended daylight of an arctic summer, long after southern children have been put to bed. Still, one may find a man, woman, or youth chatting pleasantly over tea with some elder they had approached for advice, eyes respectfully lowered, as in tradition. Still, one may see families joyfully laughing together as they pack for a camping trip out on the land, ever to Inuit what the backyard is to southerners. Still, one may watch a husky patiently waiting as his master harnesses him, preparing him and his pack mates for this season's hunting trip.

Even today, Inuit enjoy a special sense of time dictated, as of old, by elemental needs: the love of family, feasts, the pleasures brought with the seasons, and especially Nunavut — the

Nunatsiaq News ᓄᓇᑦᓯᐊᖅ ᓂᐅᔅ

land itself. For these reasons, despite their modernity, their ancestors would recognize in them the spirit and freedom that once they lived.

Pijariiqpunga.

Rachel Attituq Qitsualik is a freelance writer, her career in Inuit issues spanning approximately 25 years. Raised in a traditional lifestyle in Pond Inlet, she has witnessed the full transition of her culture into modernity.

Editor's note: *The word "pijariiqpunga" has no English equivalent. In traditional Inuit culture, each speaker is allowed his or her own isuma. Others won't interrupt until a speaker indicates that they've said all they needed to. There is no time limit: a speaker can sit in silence for quite a while, yet no one will speak until he or she ends with "pijariiqpunga." It means that they're finished, and someone else can have a turn to speak.*

ᓄᓇᕗᒥ ᐃᓄᐃᑦ ᒫᓐᓇᐅᔪᖅ ᐊᓕᐊᓇᐃᒍᓱᒍᓐᓇᖅᑐᑦ ᐃᓕᑕᕆᔭᐅᕙᓪᓕᐊᓂᖏᓐᓂᒃ ᐃᓕᖅᑯᓯᖏᓐᓂᒃ ᓇᖕᒥᓂᕆᔭᖏᓐᓂᒃ. ᐲᕐᓗ ᐅᓇ ᐆᒃᑑᑎᒋᓗᒍ ᐃᓄᒃᑎᑐᑦ ᑎᒍᐊᖃᑦᑕᕐᓂᖅ ᓄᑦᖅᑲᓂᒃ, ᐃᓕᑕᕆᔭᐅᓯᒪᓕᖅᑐᖅ ᓄᓇᑦᓯᐊᑉ ᑲᕙᒪᒃᑯᖓᓐᓄᑦ. ᐊᒻᒪᓗ ᐃᓄᐃᑦ ᓇᖕᒥᓂᕆᔭᒥᖕᓂᒃ ᐸᐸᑦᓯᒍᓐᓇᕆᐊᒃᓴᖅ ᐃᓕᑦᑖᖅᓯᕙᓪᓕᖅᑐᑦ. ᓄᓇᓕᐅᔪᓂ, ᓄᑕᕋᐃᑦ ᐃᓯᒪᖅᓯᓯᖅᑐᑦ ᓯᕿᓪᓚᓐᓇᖅᑎᓪᓗᒍ ᐊᓕᐅᓐᓇᖅᓗᑎᒃ. ᖃᓪᓗᓈᑦ ᓄᓇᖓᓂ ᓄᑕᖅᑲᖏᑦ ᐃᓐᓇᖅᓯᒪᑐᖃᓪᓚᖅᓵᑎᓪᓗᒋᑦ. ᐃᓐᓇᑐᖄᓪᓕ ᑏᑐᖃᑎᒌᒃᑐᑦ ᑕᑯᔭᐅᔭᓐᓇᕐᒥᔭᑦ. ᐊᐱᕆᔭᖅᑐᕈᒪᒍᑎᒃ ᑐᕌᖓᓯᒃᑎᑕᐅᓪᓗᑎᒃ ᐅᖃᐅᓯᖃᕈᒪᒍᑎᒃ ᐃᓅᓯᕆᔭᒥᖕᓂᒃ ᐊᔭᓪᓚᖅᑕᒥᖕᓂᒃ. ᖃᐅᔨᒪᒐᒥᒃ ᐃᑲᔪᖅᑕᐅᓂᐊᕐᒥᒃ. ᐃᓕᖅᑯᓯᑐᖃᒥᒃ ᐊᑐᕐᓗᑎᓗᒋᓪᓚᑦ ᐃᓐᓇᑐᖃᕐᔪᑦ ᐅᖃᐅᔾᔭᖅᑕᐅᒍᑎᒃ ᐃᔾᔨᓗᐊᓇᐊᖃᖕᖏᓐᓂᕐᒥᒃ ᐅᖃᖅᑎᓪᓗᒍ, ᑕᒪᓐᓇ ᐃᓕᑕᐅᓯᒪᔪᖅ ᑭᓇᑐᐃᓐᓇᓘᑦ. ᐃᓚᖏᑦ ᑕᑯᔭᐅᔭᓐᓇᕐᒥᔭᑦ ᐸᕐᓇᖅᑎᒌᒃᑐᑦ ᐅᐱᕐᖔᒥ ᕿᒨᒃᓯᕐᓗᑎᒃ ᐊᐅᓪᓚᕐᓂᐊᕐᒥᒃ. ᐊᓃᓇᔭᑦ ᕿᒻᒥᒥᖕᓂᒃ, ᕿᒨᒃᓯᒃᑯᑦ ᒪᖅᑲᐃᓐᓂᐊᕐᒪᑕ.

ᐅᓪᓗᒥᓘᓐᓃᑦ, ᐃᓄᐃᑦ ᓯᕿᕐᖑᔭᒥᒃ ᐊᑐᓐᖏᓪᓗᑎᒃ ᐱᔭᓐᓇᖅᐸᒃᑐᑦ — ᑕᐃᑦᓯᒪᑎᑐᖃᖅᑎᑐᑦ — ᐊᑐᓇᐊᖃᖅᑕᒥᓂᒃ ᐊᑐᐊᓚᖃᖅᓗᑎᒃ: ᐃᓅᖓᑎᒌᑦᑎᐊᕐᓂᕐᒥᒃ, ᓂᕆᑲᓪᔪᐊᖓᑎᒌᖕᓂᕐᒥᒃ, ᐊᕐᕿᒍᒥᒃ ᒪᓕᖕᓂᕐᒥᒃ, ᐊᒻᒪᓗ ᐅᐱᒋᔭᐅᑦᑎᐊᕆᑎᖃᕐᓂᖅ ᓄᓇᕗᑦ —ᓇᖕᒥᓂᕆᔭᑦᑎᓐᓂᒃ. ᑕᐃᒪᓐᓇᖃᐃ ᐱᔾᔪᑎᒋᓗᒍ, ᓯᕗᓕᑦᑎᓐᓄᑦ ᑕᑯᔭᐅᓇᔭᕈᑦᑕ ᐃᓕᑕᕆᔭᐅᓇᔭᖅᑐᒍᑦ.

ᐱᔭᕇᖅᐳᖓ.

Arthur Boutilier ᐋᑕ ᐳᑎᓕᐅ

ᓈᓯ ᐋᑏᑦᑐᖅ ᕿᑦᓯᐊᓗᒃ ᓇᖕᒥᓂᖅ ᑎᑎᕋᖅᑎᐅᔪᖅ, ᐃᖃᓇᐃᔭᑐᖃᖅᓯᒪᔪᖅ ᐃᓄᖕᓂᒃ ᐃᑲᔪᖅᑐᐃᔪᓂᒃ ᐊᕐᕌᒍᓂᒃ 25-ᓂᒃ ᒥᑦᓯᒪᑕᓕᖕᒥᐅᑕᖅ ᐱᕈᓗᐅᖅᑐᖅ ᐃᓄᒃᑐᑦ, ᑕᑯᓯᒪᓪᓗᓂᓗ ᐃᓕᖅᑯᓯᖓᑕ ᐊᓯᔾᔨᖅᐸᓪᓕᐊᓂᖓᓂᒃ ᐱᒋᐊᕐᕕᖓᓂᑦ ᐱᓯᐊᓄᑦ.

ᐋᖅᑭᒃᓯᐃᔨᐅᔪᑉ ᑐᓴᕈᔭᖓ: *ᐅᖃᐅᓯᖅ "ᐱᔭᕇᖅᐳᖓ" ᖃᓪᓗᓈᑎᑐᑦ ᐊᔾᔨᖃᖕᖏᑦᑐᖅ. ᐃᓄᐃᑦ ᐃᓕᖅᑯᓯᖓᑦ, ᐃᓄᒃ ᐅᖃᓕᒃᑳᖓᑦ ᐱᔭᕇᕐᓂᖅᓯᖅᑐᖅ. ᐊᓯᒥᓄᑦ ᐅᓚᕕᔅᑕᐅᓇᓂ ᐅᖃᕆᐊᖃᖅᑐᒍ ᑭᓇᑐᐃᓐᓇᒃᑯᑦ ᓂᐸᐃᖅᓯᒪᓯᒪᓪᓚᑦ. ᓇᐃᑦᑐᒥᒃ ᑕᑭᔪᒥᒃ ᐅᖃᕈᓐᓇᖅᑐᖅ: ᓂᓪᓕᖏᑕᐃᓐᓇᖅᐸᓪᓗᓂᓘᓐᓇᓚᑦ, ᐱᔭᕇᕈᓂ ᐃᓯᓕᔾᔪᑎᖃᕐᓂᐊᕐᒪᑦ ᐅᖃᓗᓂ "ᐱᔭᕇᖅᐳᖓ." ᑕᐃᒪ ᐱᔭᕇᖅᐸᑕ, ᐊᓯᖓᑦᑕᐅᖅ ᐅᖃᕈᓐᓇᖅᓯᓪᓗᓂ.*

Top: "Arctic Elvis" Jimmy Ekho draws fans in communities across Nunavut. Above and below: In town and out – an iglu *near Pond Inlet and first light on Iqaluit's main drag*
ᖁᓛᓂ: "ᐅᑭᐅᖅᑕᖅᑐᖅᒥ ᐃᐊᕕᔅ" ᔨᒥ ᐃᖁ ᑐᓵᔨᖅᑐᖅᑕᐅᖃᑦᑕᖅᑐᖅ ᐅᑭᐅᖅᑕᖅᑐᓕᒫᒥ. ᖁᓛᓂ ᐊᒻᒪ ᐊᑖᓂ: ᓄᓇᓕᖕᓂ ᓯᓚᑖᓂᓗ – ᐃᒡᓗᕕᒡᔪ ᒥᑦᑎᒪᑕᓕᒃ ᖃᓂᒋᔮᓂ ᐊᒻᒪᓗ ᖃᐅᒪᒃᐸᓕᐊᓕᕐᑎᓪᓗᒍ ᐃᖃᓗᐃᑦ ᐊᑐᓇᐊᖕᒐᓂ

Nunatsiaq News ᓄᓇᑦᓯᐊᖅ ᓂᐅᔅ

THE WORLD'S MOST COMPLETE AND AUTHORITATIVE GUIDE TO TRAVELLING IN CANADA'S ARCTI

The Nunavut Handbook

1999 Commemorative Edition

Celebrate the New Territory

On April 1, 1999, Nunavut officially became Canada's newest territory. Join the celebration with this special edition of *The Nunavut Handbook*. Updated and expanded, the 454-page guidebook includes 20 pages of beautiful color photos, entire new sections on the new government, plus all the latest information you need to know about visiting this extraordinary land.

Essential Reading for Every Arctic Traveller

The world's only guidebook to Canada's historic new territory, *The Nunavut Handbook* contains 100 information-filled chapters on accommodations, transportation, preparation, attractions, outfitters, weather, national and territorial parks and much more, including a chapter on every community.

Successor to the highly acclaimed 1998 Nunavut Handbook

Praise for the 1998 Edition

"This massively detailed travel guide, the product of no fewer than 45 expert contributors, has everything a visitor could ever want to know about this extraordinary land and its resourceful and ambitious Inuit people."

– *Essentially America*

"The 1998 Nunavut Handbook:... *an amazingly complete and handy directory and guidebook for the venturesome or for those who simply want to visit one of Earth's few remaining pristine wildernesses."*

– *The Globe and Mail*

"Bigger, better and completely updated, The Nunavut Handbook *is a nicely packaged guide to the people and the wildlife of Canada's Eastern Arctic, one of the last great untouched wilderness areas on our shrinking planet."*

– *USA Today*

VISIT OUR WEB SITE!

See the award-winning interactive version of *The Nunavut Handbook* on the Internet at www.arctic-travel.com
Order your special-edition copy of *The Nunavut Handbook*, 1999 Commemorative Edition, today!
Call 1 800-263-1452, or 613-727-5466, and ask for Inga. Have a credit card handy.
You can also write to *The Nunavut Handbook*, 16 Concourse Gate, Suite 200, Nepean, ON Canada K2E 7S8.

The Inuit Tapirisat of Canada

ᐃᓄᐃᑦ ᑕᐱᕇᓴᑦ ᑲᓇᑕᒥ

Promoting the rights and culture of Canada's Inuit - Yesterday, Today, and Tomorrow.

ᑲᓇᑕᒥᐅᑦ ᐃᓄᐃᑦ ᐱᔪᓐᓇᕐᓂᕆᔭᖏᓐᓂᑦ ᐃᓕᖅᑯᓯᑐᖃᖏᓐᓂᓪᓗ ᓯᕗᒻᒧᐊᖅᑎᕆᓂᖅ - ᐃᑉᐸᒃᓴᖅ, ᐅᑉᓗᒥ, ᐊᒻᒪᓗ ᖃᐅᒃᐸᑦ.

Ippaksak...

Yesterday

Twenty-seven years ago the Inuit Tapirisat of Canada was created to voice nationally the interests of Canada's 41,000 Inuit in Labrador, Nunavik, Nunavut and Inuvialuit.

An early call from this national voice was for the creation of an Inuit Territory called Nunavut. Indeed, it was a vision from the Inuk soul...but to many it seemed an impossible dream.

Qaupat...

Today

Twenty-seven years later, on April 1, 1999, the dream of creating Nunavut became real and the Inuit Tapirisat of Canada continues to carry the voice of Inuit nationally.

Nunavut is a monument to the patience of our people, the skill of our negotiators and the vision of our leaders. Now the real work begins.

Uhlumi...

Tomorrow

Twenty-seven years into the future, we will look back to the creation of Nunavut as the beginning of a partnership between Canada and Nunavut Inuit based on the recognition of our rights, our history and our living culture.

Then, as today and yesterday, the Inuit Tapirisat of Canada will continue to ensure that the promise represented by Nunavut is fulfilled.

Ippaksak...

ᐃᑉᐸᒃᓴᖅ

ᐊᕐᕌᒍᑦ 27-ᖑᓚᐅᖅᑐᑦ ᐃᓄᐃᑦ ᑕᐱᕇᓴᑦ ᑲᓇᑕᒥ ᐋᖅᑭᒃᑕᐅᓚᐅᖅᐳᑦ ᓂᐱᒋᔭᐅᔪᒃᓴᐅᓪᓗᑎᑦ ᑲᓇᑕᒥ ᐃᓄᖕᓄᑦ ᒐᐸᑐᐊᒥᐅᓄᑦ, ᓄᓇᕕᖕᒥᐅᓄᑦ, ᓄᓇᕗᒻᒥᐅᓄᑦ, ᐊᒻᒪᓗ ᐃᓄᕕᐊᓗᖕᒥᐅᓄᑦ.

ᑕᒪᒃᑯᓇᓐᖑᑦ ᑲᓇᑕᒥᐅᓄᑦ ᓂᐱᓂᑦ ᐃᓄᖕᓄᑦ ᓄᓇᒋᔭᐅᔪᒃᓴᒥᑦ ᐋᖅᑭᒃᓯᔪᒪᓕᓚᐅᖅᐳᑦ ᓄᓇᕘᓂᖅᑕᐅᔪᒥᑦ. ᓇᓗᓇᓐᖏᓪᖅ ᐃᓄᐃᑦ ᑕᕐᓂᖓᓐᓂᓐᖔᕐᓯᒪᓂᖓᓂᑦ...ᐊᒥᓱᓄᑦ ᓴᐱᕐᓇᖅᓯᔪᓚᐅᕐᓗᐊᖅᑎᓪᓗᒍ.

Qaupat...

ᐅᓪᓗᒥ

27 ᐊᕐᕋᒍᑦ ᓈᓯᒪᓕᖅᑎᓪᓗᒋᑦ, ᐄᐱᕆ 1, 1999-ᒥᑦ, ᓄᓇᕗᒻᒥᑦ ᐋᖅᑭᒃᓯᔪᒪᓂᐅᓚᐅᕐᓯᒪᔪᖅ ᐋᖅᑭᒻᒪᑎᓚᐅᖅᐳᖅ ᐊᒻᒪᓗ ᐃᓄᐃᑦ ᑕᐱᕇᓴᑦ ᑲᓇᑕᒥ ᓯᓚ ᐃᓄᖕᓂᑦ ᓂᐱᖃᖅᑎᑦᑎᕗᑦ ᑲᓇᑕᓕᒫᒥ.

ᓄᓇᕗᑦ ᓇᓗᓇᐃᕈᑕᐅᕗᖅ ᐃᓄᐃᑦ ᕿᓄᐃᑦᑑᓂᖏᓐᓄᑦ, ᐋᕐᖃᑎᕆᒃᑎᕗᑦ ᐊᔪᓐᖏᓐᓂᖃᕐᓂᖏᓐᓄᑦ ᐊᒻᒪᓗ ᓯᕗᓕᐅᖅᑎᕗᑦ ᓴᖅᑲᖅᑲᕐᓂᖏᓐᓄᑦ. ᒫᓐᓇ ᑕᐃᒪ ᐱᓕᕆᐊᒃᓴᓪᓚᑦᑖᑦ ᐱᓕᕆᐊᖑᔪᓐᓇᕐᓯᕗᑦ.

Uhlumi...

ᖃᐅᒃᐸᑦ

ᐊᕐᕋᒎᓂᐊᖅᑐᓂᑦ 27-ᓂᑦ, ᓄᓇᕗᑦ ᐋᖅᑭᓚᐅᕐᓂᖓᓂᑦ ᖃᐅᔨᓵᖅᐳᒍᑦ ᐃᓚᒌᓯᒋᐊᕈᑕᐅᓚᐅᕐᓂᖓᓄᑦ ᑲᓇᑕᒥᐅᓄᑦ ᐃᓄᖕᓄᓪᓗ ᓄᓇᕗᑦᒥᐅᓄᑦ ᐱᔪᓐᓇᕐᓂᓴᑦᑎᓐᓂ, ᐃᓅᓯᑦᑎᓐᓂ, ᐊᒻᒪ ᐃᓕᖅᑯᓯᑐᖃᓪᓚᑦᑖᑦᑎᓐᓂ ᑐᓐᖓᕕᖃᕐᓗᑕ.

ᑕᐃᔅᓱᒪᓂ, ᐅᑉᓗᑦᑕᐅᖅ ᐅᑉᓗᒥ ᐃᑉᐸᒃᓴᕐᓗ, ᐃᓄᐃᑦ ᑕᐱᕇᓴᑦ ᑲᓇᑕᒥ ᖃᐅᔨᓴᐃᓐᓇᕐᓂᐊᖅᐳᑦ ᓄᓇᕗᒻᒥᑦ ᓱᓕᓂᐊᕐᓂᖅᓯᒪᔪᑦ ᐋᖅᑭᓪᓚᑦᑖᖅᑐᐊᕐᒪᖔᑕ.

ᐃᓄᐃᑦ ᑕᐱᕇᓴᑦ ᑲᓇᑕᒥ
Inuit Tapiriiksat Kanatami
Inuit Tapirisat of Canada.

Suite 510, 170 Laurier Ave. W., Ottawa, Ontario K1P 5V5
Tel: (613) 238-8181 Fax: (613) 234-1991

Well done, Nunavut!
ᐱᓕᕆᑦᑎᐊᖅᐳᓯ, ᓄᓇᕗᑦ!
Nunasi Corporation became a part of the Nunavut dream in 1978. The journey has been long and at times difficult, but we have always been proud to be a part of this great vision.
After April 1, 1999, Nunasi will continue to provide training, create jobs and establish profitable enterprises for our shareholders: the Inuit of Nunavut.
To all the brave, bold and honourable people who had the vision to foresee this day, we say, "Well done."
ᓄᓇᓯ ᑯᐊᐳᕇᓴ ᐃᓚᐅᖃᑕᐅᓯᒪᒐᖅ ᓄᓇᕗᑦᑖᕋᓱᖕᓂᕐᒧᓐ 1978ᒥ. ᐱᓕᕆᓂᐅᔪᖅ ᐊᑯᓂᐋᓗᒃ ᐱᓕᕆᐊᖑᔪᓯᒪᒐᖅ ᐃᑖᓐᓂᑦᓗ ᐊᔪᕐᓇᓚᐅᕐᐸᒃᓗᓂ, ᑭᓯᐊᓂᓕ ᐱᒃᑯᓕᓯᒪᒻᒪᕆᒃᐳᒍ ᐃᓚᒋᔭᐅᓂᑦᑎᓐᓂ ᑕᒪᑐᒥᙶ ᑕᐅᑐᙵᐊᖅᑕᐅᓯᒪᔪᒥᓐ.
ᐄᐳᕈ 1, 1999 ᐊᓂᒍᖅᐸᑦ, ᓄᓇᓯ ᐃᓕᓐᓂᐊᖅᑎᑦᑎᖃᑦᑕᐃᓐᓇᕐᓂᐊᖅᑐᑦ, ᐃᖅᑲᓇᐃᔮᒃᓴᓂ ᓴᖅᑭᑦᑎᕙᓪᓗᑎᒃ ᐊᒻᒪᓗ ᓴᖅᑭᑦᑎᒻᒪᕆᒃᓗᑎᒃ ᑮᓇᐅᔭᓕᐅᕈᑕᐅᔪᓐᓇᖅᑐᓂ ᐱᓕᕆᐊᓂᑦ ᓇᖕᒥᓂᖃᖅᑎᕆᔭᑦᑎᓐᓄᑦ: ᐃᓄᐃᑦ ᓄᓇᕗᒻᒥᐅᑕᑦ.
ᐊᔪᙱᒻᒪᕆᒃᓯᒪᔫᑦ, ᐊᒃᓱᕈᖅᓯᒪᔫᑦ ᐅᐱᓐᓇᖅᑐᓅᓪᓗ ᐃᓄᖕᓄ ᓯᕗᓂᑦᑎᓐᓂ ᑕᐅᑐᙵᐊᖅᑲᑦᑕᖅᓯᒪᔪᓂ ᐅᓪᓗᒥᒥᓐ, ᐅᖃᖅᐳᒍᑦ, "ᐱᓕᕆᑦᑎᐊᖅᐳᓯ ᐊᒃᓯᐊᓗᒃ."
NUNASI CORPORATION ᓄᓇᓯ ᑯᐊᐳᕇᓴᓐ
260, 5022-49TH STREET, YELLOWKNIFE, NT X1A 3R7
TEL. / ᐅᖄᓚᐅᑎ: (867) 920-4587 • FAX / ᓱᒃᑲᔪᒃᑯᑦ: (867) 920-4592

OUR LANGUAGE, OUR SELVES
ᐅᖃᓪᓚᐅᓯᕋᑦ, ᐅᕙᒍᑦ

Parents, with the help of schools and government, will be key to making Inuktitut a living, working language in the generations ahead

ᐊᖓᔪᖅᑳᕆᔭᑦ ᐃᑲᔪᖅᑎᖃᕐᓗᑎᒃ ᐃᓕᓐᓂᐊᕐᕕᖕᓂᑦ ᒐᕙᒪᒃᑯᓐᓂᓪᓗ ᐱᓗᐊᑕᒪᕆᐅᓂᐊᖅᐳᑦ ᐅᐱᒍᓱᖕᓂᖃᕐᓂᕐᒥᒃ
ᐅᖃᐅᓯᕐᒥᖕᓂᒃ ᐊᒻᒪᓗ ᐊᑐᕈᓯᒍᒥᒍᓱᒃᑎᑦᑎᓗᑎᒃ ᑭᖑᕚᕆᓂᐊᖅᑕᑦᓂᓈᑦ

NWT Dept. of Information/NWT Archives; oval inset: Nunavut Tourism

By Alexina Kublu and Mick Mallon

Is there a Canadian culture? Is there an Inuit culture? An Inuktitut word for "way of life" is *inuusiq*. Based on the word for person, *inuk*, it means something like "the way of being a person." Is there a connection between the language I speak and the person I am? Let us tell you a story.

Some years ago, Kublu applied for a job with an Inuit organization in Ottawa, and dashed off the usual résumé. On checking it over, however, she thought, "But this is an Inuit organization. If the person who reads this résumé is a traditional Inuk, what will he think of it, and of me?"

So she translated it into Inuktitut . . . and it sounded arrogant, boastful, and cold, cold, cold. Then she sat down and wrote a résumé directly in Inuktitut. It came out fine, until she translated it into English. The English version was vague, unfocused, even wimpy!

In fact, studies have suggested that many fluently bilingual people shift their personalities (or shall we say their cultures?) as they shift language. So there is a connection.

Wilkinson/NWT Archives ᐅᐃᐅᑭᓐᓴᓐ / ᓄᓇᑦᓯᐊᕐᒥ ᐸᐸᑕᕐᕕᒃ

ᐊᓕᒃᓯᓈ ᑯᑉᓗ ᐅᒻᒪ ᒥᒃ ᒫᓚᓐ

ᑲᓇᑕᒥᐅᓄᑦ ᐃᓕᖅᑯᓯᐅᓂᖅᑕᐅᔪᖃᕈᓐᓇᖅᐸ? ᐃᓄᐃᓐᓄᑦ ᐃᓕᖅᑯᓯᐅᓂᖅᑕᐅᔪᖃᕈᓐᓇᖅᐸ? "ᐃᓅᓯᖅ" ᐃᓄᐃᓐᓄᑦ ᐊᑐᖅᑕᐅᓚᐅᔫᖑᔪᖅ ᐃᓅᑉ ᐱᐅᓯᖓᓂᒃ ᐅᖃᐅᓯᖃᖅᐳᑎᒃ. ᑖᓐᓇ ᑐᙵᓂᖃᕐᒪᑦ ᐅᖃᐅᓯᕐᒥᒃ "ᐃᓄᒃ"ᒥᒃ. ᑭᓇᐅᓂᕋ ᐅᖃᓪᓚᒍᓯᕋ ᐊᒃᑐᐊᖃᑦᑕᐅᑎᓂᖃᖅᐹᒃ? ᐅᓂᒃᑲᐅᓯᓇᓚᐅᕆᓚᒍᑦ.

ᐊᕐᕌᒍᓗᓴᐅᓕᖅᐳᑦ ᑯᑉᓗ ᑎᑎᕋᓚᐅᖅᑎᓪᓗ ᐃᖅᑲᓇᐃᔭᖅᑎᙳᕈᕋᓱᖕᓂᕐᒧᑦ ᐃᓄᐃᑦ ᑎᒥᖁᑎᖓᓐᓂᑦ ᐃᓪᓚᖓᓄᑦ ᐋᑐᕚᒥ ᐊᒻᒪᓗ ᐃᓐᒥᓂᒃ ᐅᖃᐅᓯᕆᓯᒪᔪᒥᒃ ᓇᒃᓯᐅᔾᔨᖃᓯᐅᔾᔨᓪᓗᓂ. ᕿᒥᕐᕈᒃᑲᓐᓂᓕᕐᒥᐅᒃ ᐃᓱᒪᓕᓚᐅᖅᐳᖅ, "ᐅᓇᓕ ᐃᓄᐃᓐᓄᑦ ᑎᒥᖁᑎᖃᔪᖅ. ᑖᔅᓯᒥᖓ ᑎᑎᕋᖅᓯᒪᔪᒥᒃ ᐅᖃᓕᒫᖅᑐᖅ ᐃᓄᓪᓚᕆᐅᒍᓂ ᖃᓄᖅ ᐃᓱᒪᒋᓕᕋᔭᖅᐹᖓᒋᐊᖅ."

ᐃᓄᒃᑎᑐᖕᒍᓕᖅᑎᕐᓗᓂᐅᓪᓗ... ᑭᓯᐊᓂ ᑖᓐᓇ ᑎᑎᕋᖅᑲᐅᔪᓂ ᐅᖃᓕᒫᒃᑲᓐᓂᕐᒥᐅᒃ ᐃᓐᒥᓂᒃ ᐱᐅᑎᑦᑐᐊᓘᔭᖅᓗᓂ ᐊᓯᒥᒃ ᐃᖅᑲᐅᓯᖕᓂᖅᑯᖅᔾᔨᑦᑎᐊᖅᓗᓂᓗ, ᐃᓄᕈᓗᐃᓐᓇᐅᖅᑯᔨᑎᓯᒪᑦᑎᐊᖅᓗᓂᓗ. ᑖᓐᓇ ᖁᔭᓈᖅᓗᓂᐅᒃ ᐃᓄᒃᑎᒡᒐᖅ ᑎᑎᕋᖅᓗᓂ. ᑖᓐᓇ ᖃᓄᐃᖅᑯᔾᔨᑦᑎᐊᖅᓗᓂ ᖃᓪᓗᓈᑐᖅᑎᓪᓗᐅᖅᑳᖅᑲᓂᒃ. ᖃᓪᓗᓈᑐᖅᑎᓯᒪᔪᙵ ᖃᓯᙳᖅᑯᔾᔨᓪᓗᓂ, ᑐᕿᖓᓂᖃᑦᑎᐊᖅᑯᔾᔨᕐᔪᓂᓗ, ᐃᖕᒥᓂᓗ ᓱᓇᐅᒃᓴᖅᑯᔾᔭᓇᓂ.

Left: Alex Ajagutianaq of Sanikiluaq teaches syllabics to young Inuit, 1971. Right: Department of Northern Affairs teacher Maxine Sutherland instructs children in Apex, outside Frobisher Bay, 1956. The teachers and the curriculum changed greatly in 15 short years – the old-style syllabics on the blackboard, left, admonish the children to obey their parents – and education and language instruction in Nunavut continue to evolve

ᓴᐅᒥᐊᓂ: ᐊᓕᒃᓯ ᐊᔭᒍᑕᐃᓈᖅ ᓴᓂᑭᓗᐊᕐᒥᐅᑕᖅ ᐃᓕᓐᓂᐊᕐᑎᑎᔪᖅ ᐃᐅᐋᓂ ᓄᑕᕋᕐᓄᑦ ᐃᓄᖕᓄ, 1971. ᑕᓕᕐᐱᐊᓂ: ᐃᓄᓕᕆᓂᖏᑦᑐᖃᕐᒃᑯ ᐃᓕᓴᐃᔨᖅᑯᑎᖓ ᒫᒃᓯᓐ ᓵᑕᓚᓐ ᐃᓕᓐᓂᐊᕐᑎᑎᔪᖅ ᓂᐊᖁᓐᖑᒧᑦ ᓱᑭᓯᙱᓐᓂ, ᒃᐱᐊᓗᐅᑎᑦ ᓯᓚᑎᑦᑎᐊᖓᓂ, 1956. ᐃᓕᓴᐃᔨ ᐊᒻᒪ ᐃᓕᓐᓂᐊᕈᑏ ᐊᓯᙳᖅᓯᒪᓪᓚᕐᒃᐳᑦ ᐊᕐᕌᒍᑦ 15 ᐃᓗᐊᓂ – ᐃᓄᒃᑎᑐᑦ ᑎᑎᖃᐅᓯᐊᓂᖅ, ᓴᐅᒥᐊᓂ, ᑎᑎᖃᐅᓯᖅᑳᕐᐳᖅ ᐊᖓᔪᖅᑳᖏᓐᓂᑦ ᑐᓵᓚᓐᖅᑕᖁᔨᓯᒪᓪᓗᓂ – ᐊᒻᒪ ᐃᓕᓐᓂᐊᕐᓂᓕᕆᓂᖅ ᐅᖃᐅᓯᓕᕆᓂᕐᓗ ᐱᕚᓪᓕᐊᖏᓐᓇᕐᐳᖅ

"Tagak Curley, the president of Inuit Tapirisat of Canada, immediately exclaimed that the new territory would naturally be called 'Nunavut.'"

– ITC legal advisor Peter Cumming, recalling the moment in June 1974 when, on the steps of the Tuktoyaktuk school, the broad goal for Inuit land claims in the Arctic narrowed to the creation of a new separate territory called "Nunavut"

For an Inuk like Kublu, language and culture are inextricably entwined in the perception of who she is, to herself and to others. In the eyes of older people in the community, she is a child who has tapped into the mysterious powers of the *qallunaat* (white people), but who still depends on her elders for so many answers about daily life in the past.

To her colleagues at the college where Kublu works, she is, we hope, an equal, with a professional competence extending beyond her particular role as instructor of interpretation and translation. To her students, she is a role model, one who has attained a balance between two worlds. To herself . . . well, she knows she can never be the kind of Inuk her elders were, but, with all due respect, she doesn't want to be. And she never could be a *qallunaaq* (white person).

The language of Inuit, Inuktitut, has changed in the last century, but it is still the same. In a good portion of the circumpolar world, it is alive and well. Kublu can communicate quite successfully with Greenlanders, for example, and if parachuted into Point Barrow in northern Alaska, which is much further away, she would be able to do the same after about a week or so.

The culture of Inuit has changed more than Inuktitut has, but most of those changes are on the outside. Kublu does not lead the same life her parents did, but in her approach to life, her system of values, her appreciation of the world around her, she is closer to them than to her qallunaat colleagues.

ᐊᒡᓛᑦ, ᖃᐅᔨᓴᖅᑕᐅᖃᑦᑕᖅᓯᒪᔪᑎᒍᑦ ᖃᐅᔨᒪᓇᖅᓯᓯᒪᔭᖅ ᒪᕐᖀᖕᓂᒃ ᐅᖃᐅᓰᖕᓂᒃ ᐊᑐᕆᓐᓇᑦᑎᐊᖅᑐᑦ ᐅᔾᔨᕐᓇᖅᑕᕐᒪᑕ ᐊᓯᐊᓂᒃ ᐅᖃᐅᓯᕐᒥᒃ ᐊᑐᓕᖕᖏᒥᒃ ᖃᓄᐃᓕᐅᕈᓯᕐᒥᒃ (ᐃᓛᒃ ᐃᓕᖅᑯᓯᕐᒥᓂᒃ) ᐊᓯᔾᔨᖅᓯᔫᖕᒍᓄᑦ. ᑕᕝᕙᓇ ᓄᓇᐃᖅᑕᐅᓯᒪᔪᖅ ᑖᒃᑯᐊ ᐊᒃᑐᐊᖃᑦᑕᐅᑎᓂᖃᖅᐳᒃ.

ᑯᐸᓗᒧᑦ, ᐅᖃᐅᓯᖓ ᐃᓕᖅᑯᓯᖓ ᖃᑎᙵᓚᓂᑯᒧᑦ ᓂᒥᖃᑦᑕᐅᑎᓯᒪᖅᑰᔾᔫᒃ ᑭᓇᐅᖅᑰᔾᓂᖓᔪᒥᓂᒃ ᐃᖕᒥᓄᑦ ᐊᓯᒥᓅᓗ. ᐃᓐᓇᕐᓅᓕ ᐃᓕᖕᒐᒍᑦ ᑕᐅᑐᒃᑕᐅᖕᒪᑦ ᓄᑕᖃᑯᓗᒃᑎᑐᑦ ᖃᓪᓗᓈᑦ ᐊᔪᙱᓐᓂᖓᔪᖕᒋᑕ ᐃᓕᖕᒐᓂᒃ ᐱᓯᒪᑦᑎᒐᓗᐊᖅᐳᓂ ᑭᓯᐊᓂ ᐃᓐᓇᕐᓄᑦ ᓈᓚᓐᓂᐅᔪᓐᓇᐊᖃᖃᑦᑕᖅᑐᖅ ᐃᓄᒃᓯᐅᑎᓪᓚᖕᓂᒃ ᑐᑭᓯᔪᒪᔭᖃᓕᖕᒐᒥ.

ᐃᖅᑲᓇᐃᔭᖅᑎᒥᓪᓕ ᓄᓇᕗᑦ ᓯᓚᑦᑐᖅᓴᕐᕕᐊᓂ ᐃᓱᒪᒋᔭᐅᖅᑯᓇᖁᔪᐊᖅᐳᖅ ᓇᓚᒧᕆᔭᐅᑐᐃᓐᓇᕐᓇᐊᒃᓴᖅ ᐃᖅᑲᓇᐃᔮᕐᒥᒍᑦ ᐊᔪᙱᓐᓂᖓᔪᕐᒥᑦ ᐅᖓᑖᒃᑯᔾᔨᓯᒪᓪᓗᑎᒃ ᐃᓕᓴᐃᔨᐅᓂᕐᒥᒃ ᑐᓵᔨᒃᓴᓄᑦ/ᑐᑭᓕᐅᕆᔨᒃᓴᓄᑦ. ᐃᓕᓐᓂᐊᖅᑎᑕᒥᓄᓪᓕ ᐊᔾᔨᒥᒋᔭᖃᖅᑐᖅᓯᒪᒐᓗᐊᖅᑐᖅ ᓇᔭᐅᑉᐳᖅ ᐃᓕᖅᑯᓯᖕᖓᓂᒃ ᒪᕐᖀᖕᓂᒃ ᐊᑐᖅᑎᑎᑉᐹᒃᓗᓂ. ᐃᖕᒥᓅᓕ... ᖃᐅᔨᒪᒐᒥ ᐃᓐᓇᓴᒥᑐᑦ ᐃᓅᑦᓯᓇᐅᑎᕆᔭᓐᖏᑦᑕᓇᐊᒃᓴᖅ, ᑭᓯᐊᓂᓕ ᖃᓄᐃᒃᓴᙱᑦᑐᖅ ᑕᐃᒪᐃᙱᑦᑲᓗᐊᕆᓂ. ᖃᐅᔨᒪᓪᓗᓂᓗ ᖃᓪᓗᓈᖑᓕᐅᖅᓯᒪᔾᔮᙱᓐᓂᖓᓂᒃ.

ᐃᓄᐃᑦ ᐅᖃᐅᓯᖏᑦ ᐊᓯᔾᔨᖅᐸᓪᓕᖅᓯᒪᔭᖅ ᑖᒃᑯᓇᓂ ᐊᕿᕗᒍᓂ Hᐊᓐᓇᓚᐅᓕᖅᑐᓂ, ᑭᓯᐊᓂᓗ ᐃᓕᖕᒐᒍᑦ ᓱᖁᑉᓯᒪᓗᐊᕿᓗᙱᒃᑭᓪᓗᓂ. ᓱᖁᑉᓯᒪᓗᐊᙱᑦᑐᖅ ᐊᑐᖅᑕᐅᑦᑎᐊᖅᐸᒃᑐᓂ. ᑯᐸᓗ ᐅᖃᖅᑎᖃᒃᑲᓗᐊᕿᓗᒃᐸᙱᑦᑐᖅ ᐊᑯᑭᑦᑐᕐᒥᐅᓂᒃ. ᐊᓚᔅᑳᒧᓗ ᑲᑕᐃᔭᐅᓇᔭᕈᓂ ᐅᖓᓯᒋᓐᓂᖅᓴᐅᓗᐊᖅᑎᓪᓗᒍ ᐅᖃᐅᓯᖓᓂᒃ ᓱᖏᐅᑎᔾᔨᕕᒍᓂᐅᒃ ᐅᖃᖅᑎᕆᔦᓐᓇᖅᓯᓇᔭᕐᒥᔭᖏᑦ.

ᐃᓄᐃᑦᑕ ᐃᓕᖅᑯᓯᖏᑦᑕ ᐊᓯᔾᔨᖅᐹᓪᓕᖅᓯᒪᓂᖓ ᓴᖅᑭᔮᖅᓂᖅᓴᐅᒐᖅ ᐅᖃᐅᓯᖏᑦᑕ ᐊᓯᔾᔨᖅᐹᓪᓕᖅᓯᒪᓂᖓᓂᑦ. ᑕᒪᓐᓇᓕ ᐊᓯᔾᔨᖅᐹᓪᓕᖅᓯᒪᓂᖅ ᖄᖏᓐᓇᑯᐊᒎᖓᔪᖅ. ᑯᐸᓗ ᐊᖓᔪᖅᑳᓇᓄᑦᑕᒥ ᐃᓅᓯᓇᓚᐅᖅᑕᖏᓐᓂᒃ ᐊᑐᙱᓪᓚᖅ, ᑭᓯᐊᓂᓕ ᐃᓅᓯᖏᑦᑎᒍᑦ, ᐱᒻᒪᕆᐅᔪᖅᑯᑎᖏᑦᑎᒍᓪᓗ, ᐊᕙᑎᒥᓴᕐᒥᓂᒡᓗ ᐅᐱᒋᔭᖃᕐᓂᖓᔭᕐᒥᒍᑦ ᐊᕐᓚᖅᑳᖅᓂᖓ ᖃᓂᒋᓂᖅᓴᓇᐸᐃᑦ ᐃᓕᓴᐃᔨᐅᖅᑎᑦᑎᔪᒥᓂᐅᓂᑦ ᖃᓪᓗᓈᐅᓪᓗᒍᔪᓂᑦ.

Mabel Angulalik, Bessie Omilgoetok and Frank Analok of Cambridge Bay play a game of nugluktaq. *Communication between elders and youth will be key to survival of the Inuit language and culture*

ᒪᐃᐳᑦ ᐊᖑᓕᓕᒃ, ᐸᓯ ᐅᒥᐊᒍᐃᑐᒃ ᐊᒻᒪ ᕗᕌᓐᒃ ᐊᓇᓗᒃ ᐃᖃᓗᒃᑑᑦᑎᐊᕐᒥ ᓄᒡᓗᒃᑕᖅᑐᑦ. ᐅᖃᓪᓚᖃᑎᒌᖃᑦᑕᕐᓂᖅ ᐃᓐᓇᑐᖃᓪᓗ ᓱᕈᓯᓪᓗ ᐅᖃᐅᓯᕐᒥ ᐊᑐᕐᑎᕐᓂᓐᓇᕈᓐᓇᕐᐳᑦ ᐃᓕᖅᑯᓯᕐᒥᓪᓗ

Nunavut Tourism ᓄᓇᕗᑦ ᐳᓚᕋᖅᑐᓕᕆᓂᖅ

Nunatsiaq News ᓄᓇᑦᓯᐊᕐᒥ ᐱᕐᕈᓐᓇᕐᓂᖏᑦ

Peter Ittinuar, Nunavut's first Inuk member of Parliament and a former director of the Inuit Cultural Institute (ICI), consults the ICI's Inuktitut Dictionary. The ICI developed a standardized orthography for Inuktitut, and is now working on a northern encyclopedia

ᐲᑕ ᐃᑎᓐᓄᐊᕐ, ᓄᓇᕗᒻᒥᐅᑕᖅ ᓯᕗᓪᓕᖅᐹᖑᓚᐅᕐᐳᖅ ᐃᓅᓪᓗᓂ ᒪᓕᒐᓕᕆᔩᒻᒪᕆᐅᖃᑕᐅᓗᓂ ᒪᓕᒐᓕᕆᕝᕕᒃᔪᐊᒥ ᐊᒻᒪᓗ ᐊᐅᓚᑦᑎᔨᐅᓚᐅᕆᓪᓗᓂ ᐃᓄᒻᒪᕆᓕᕆᔩᑯᓐᓄ, ᕿᒥᕐᕈᔪᖅ ᐃᓄᒻᒪᕆᓕᕆᔩᑦ ᑐᑭᓕᐅᕆᑎᖓᓂ (ᑐᑭᓯᐅᕆᑎᒥ). ᐃᓄᒻᒪᕆᓕᕆᔩᑦ ᐃᓄᒃᑎᑐᑦ ᑎᑎᕋᐅᓯᕐᒥ ᐋᖅᑭᒃᓱᐃᓚᐅᕐᐳᑦ, ᒫᓐᓇ ᐱᓕᕆᐊᖃᓕᖅᑐᖅ ᐅᑭᐅᖅᑕᖅᑐᕐᒥ ᖃᐅᔨᒋᐊᕈᑕᐅᓂᐊᖅᑐᒥ

The nature of the Inuktitut language

In English, and in most other European languages, a sentence is a string of beads. Each bead is a tiny little word, and the beads are strung together to make meaning.

> I am happy to be here.
> *Je suis content d'être ici.*
> *Yo estoy contento de estar aquí.*

But in Inuktitut the words are like Lego™ blocks, intricate pieces locked together to produce a nugget of meaning.

> *quviasuktunga tamaaniinnama*
> (happy + I here + in + be + because I)

How about this word, produced at random: *Pariliarumaniralauqsimanngittunga*, "I never said I wanted to go to Paris."

These words are produced by a grammatical system that is much more regular than anything in English. Inuit students like studying grammar. They get pleasure out of seeing the logical flow of something they always took for granted. The grammar is not only precise, it is complex.

In Inuktitut, there are several hundred basic verb endings, as well as variations depending on the sound system. Take, for example, the verb root *malik* — "follow."

> *maliktunga* — "I follow"
> *malikkassik* — "because you two follow"
> *malikkit* — "follow them!"
> *malikkuttikkuk* — "if we two followed those two"
> *malingmangaakku* — "whether I followed her"

A simpler example of Inuktitut word-building is *ui*, a husband. An *uiviniq* is a former husband. ("Would he have to be dead to be called a uiviniq?" Mallon once asked one of his co-teachers. She paused thoughtfully for a moment and replied, "It would depend on what he had done.")

A *uiksaq* is a potential husband, a "fiancé." And, with complete logic, a

ᐃᓄᐃᑦ ᐅᖃᐅᓯᖓᑦᑕ ᐋᖅᑭᐅᒪᓂᖓ

ᖃᓪᓗᓈᑎᑐᑦ ᐅᖃᐅᓯᓪᓗ ᖃᓪᓗᓈᑏᖓᐸᒃᑐᑎᑐᑦ ᐅᖃᖅᑕᐅᔪᑦ ᓴᐸᖓᓕᕆᔪᑎᑐᑦ ᐋᖅᑭᐅᒪᓂᖃᖅᐳᑦ ᑭᖑᓕᕇᒃᓱᖅᓯᒪᑎᑦᑎᐊᖅᓱᑎᒃ. ᓱᕐᓗ ᓴᐸᖓᑯᓗᒃ ᐃᓛᒃᑯᑦ ᐅᖃᐅᓯᓪᓗᓂ ᑖᒃᑯᐊᓗ ᓄᐃᑦᑐᖅᑕᐅᓪᓗᑎᒃ ᑐᑭᖃᖅᑐᒥᒃ ᐅᖃᓇᐊᒌᖓᒥᒃ.

> *Je suis content d'être ici.*
> *Yo estoy contento de estar aquí.*
> I am happy to be here.

ᐊᐃ ᐋᒻ ᕼᐋᐱ ᑐ ᐲ ᕼᐃᐅ.
ᐅᐸᕖᖓ ᖁᕕᐊᓯᒃ ᐃᓐᓇᒪ ᒫᓂ.

ᑭᓯᐊᓂᓕ ᐃᓄᐃᑦ ᐅᖃᐅᓯᖓᑦᑕ ᐋᖅᑭᐅᒪᓂᖓ ᓱᕐᓗ ᓄᑦᑕᒃᑲᑦ ᓴᓇᔭᒃᓴᖁᑎᒥᑎᓲᖓᔪᑦ ™Lego-ᓂᖅᑕᐅᔪᑎᑦ ᑖᒃᑯᐊ ᐃᖕᒥᓄᑦ ᐃᕕᖅᑕᒃᓴᐅᑎᑦᐊᖅᓱᑎᒃ ᑐᑭᓯᓇᖅᓯᑎᓯᒪᔪᒥᒃ ᐊᖅᑭᓯᒋᐊᕌᖓᒥᒃ. ᖁᕕᐊᓯᒃᑐᖓ ᑕᒫᓂᓐᓇᒪ.

ᐅᓇᓕᑭᐊᖅ: ᐃᖃᓗᖕᒥᐅᑕᐅᓂᖅᐸᓕᕐᓂᑰᓇᔭᕋᓯᒥᓚᐅᖅᓯᒪᖖᒋᓴᕋᓗᐊᖅᐳᖓ. ᐊᑕᐅᓯᐊᑰᒐᓗᐊᕋᒥ ᑐᑭᖃᓕᖅᑎᓯᒪᑎᑦᐊᓐᓂᓪᓗᓂ.

ᑖᒃᑯᐊ ᐃᓄᒃᑎᑐᑦ ᐅᖃᖅᓯᒪᔪᑦ ᑐᑭᓇᓯᑎᑕᒃᓴᐅᔭᓐᓇᖅᑐᑦ ᐅᖃᐅᓯᓕᓐᓂᒃᑯᑦ ᕿᒥᕐᕈᓪᓗᒋᑦ ᐋᖅᑭᐅᒪᒥᖅᑐᑦ ᖃᓪᓗᓈᑦ ᐅᖃᐅᓯᖓᓂᒃ ᐋᖅᑭᐅᒪᑦᑎᐊᖅᓯᒪᓂᖅᑲᖅᓂᖅᓴᒻᒪᕆᐅᔪᒥᒃ. ᐅᔾᔨᕆᖅᑳᖅᑐᑦ ᐃᓄᐃᑦ ᐃᓕᓐᓂᐊᖅᑐᑦ ᐊᓕᐊᓇᐃᖏᔭᖅᖃᖅᑕᖅᑐᑦ ᐅᖃᐅᓯᒥ ᐋᖅᑭᐅᒪᓂᖓᓂᒃ ᐃᓕᓐᓂᐊᓇᐊᒃᓴᖅ. ᖁᕕᐊᒋᔭᖃᕈᖕᒍᖕᒪᑕ ᕿᒥᕐᕈᔭᓇᐊᒃᓴᖅ ᐅᖃᐅᓯᒥᖕᓂᒃ ᐋᖅᑭᓯᓇᖅᑲᖅᑎᐊᖅᑐᖅᓯᐊᓇᐊᒃᓴᖅ ᓯᕗᓂᐊᒎᑦ ᐃᓯᒪᒋᓪᓚᖖᓇᒎ ᐅᖃᓪᖃᖅᑕᑐᐃᓐᓇᓚᐅᖅᑕᕋᓗᐊᕐᒥᖕᓂᒃ. ᐅᖃᐅᓯᐅᑉ ᐋᖅᑭᐅᒪᓂᖓ ᐅᖅᑲᐅᑎᔪᒥᒃ ᓇᓗᐅᑖᖅᑕᐃᓯᒪᓪᓚᑖᑐᐃᓐᓈᖖᒋᓪᓚᖅ ᑭᓯᐊᓂᓕ ᐃᓚᖖᒍᑦ ᐱᔭᕆᐊᑐᓂᖅᑲᖅᐸᖅ.

ᐃᓄᐃᑦ ᐅᖃᐅᓯᖓᑦᑎᒍᑦ ᖃᓄᐃᓐᓂᖁᓂᖅ ᓇᓗᓇᐃᖅᓯᓯᒪᓕᑎᐊᖃᑦᑕᖅᐳᖅ ᑭᓇ ᖃᓄᐃᓕᐅᕆᖕᒪᖕᒫᑦ, ᖃᔭᐅᖕᒪᖕᒫᑕ ᖃᓄᐃᓕᐅᕆᔪᑦ ᑭᓇᒍᓪᓘᓐᓂᑦ ᑭᓯᒍᓪᓘᓐᓂᑦ ᖃᓄᐃᓕᐅᕆᖕᒪᖕᒫᑦ ᐊᒻᒪᓗ ᑳᒃᑯᐊ ᐅᖃᐅᓯᐅᑉ ᐅᐃᒍᐊ ᐊᑐᖅᑕᐅᔪᖅ ᐊᓯᔾᔨᖅᐸᒃᑲᓂ ᐃᓚᓕᐅᑎᔪᒍᑦ ᐃᕕᖅᑎᑎᑦᑐᓇᑎᐊᕐᑯᓪᓗᒍ. ᐅᓇ ᐆᒃᑑᑎᓕᓪᓗᒍ "ᒪᓕᒃ."

ᒪᓕᒃᑐᖓ ᑖᓯᒪᓂ ᓇᓗᓇᐃᖅᓯᓯᒪᔪᖅ ᑭᓇ ᒪᓕᖕᒪᖕᒫᑦ ᖃᓄᐃᓕᓂᔪᓗ ᐃᓄᒍᓂᖕᒐᓂᒃ

ᒪᓕᒃᑲᔅᓯᒃ ᑖᓯᒪᓂ ᓇᓗᓇᐃᖅᓯᓯᒪᔪᖅ ᑭᓇ ᒪᓕᖕᒪᖕᒫᑦ ᐃᓄᒎᓂᖕᒐᓂᓪᓗ ᑭᓇᓗ ᒪᓕᒃᑕᐅᖕᒪᖕᒫᑦ ᒪᓕᒃᑕᐅᔫᓪᓗ ᖃᔭᐅᖕᒪᖕᒫᑎᒃ.

ᑖᓐᓇᑕᐃᓐᓇᖅ ᑐᑭᖃᕆᓐᓇᒐᖅ ᒪᓕᒍᒃ ᖃᔭᐅᓂᖕᓂᖏᓐᓂᒃ ᐅᖃᓪᓚᕝᕕᐅᓂᖕᓂᖏᓐᓗ. ᑳᒃᑯᓇᓂ ᐅᖃᖅᑕᐅᔫᑉ ᐃᓚᖓ ᑭᓯᐊᓂ ᑐᓴᓚᐅᕐᓗᑎᑦ ᖃᐅᓇᖅᓯᓇᔭᖅᑐᖅ ᓇᓕᐊᒃ ᐊᑐᖅᑕᐅᒐᓗᐊᕐᒪᖕᒫᑦ.

ᒪᓕᒃᑭᑦ ᑖᓯᒪᓂᓕ ᓇᓗᓇᐃᖅᓯᓯᒪᔫᖅ ᑎᓕᓯᒪᓂᕐᒥᒃ ᑭᓇᓗ ᑎᓕᔭᐅᖕᒪᖕᒫᑦ ᑎᓕᔭᐅᔪᕐᓗ ᐃᓄᒎᓂᖕᒐᓂᒃ ᒪᓕᕆᐊᖃᖅᑕᖕᓕᓪᓗ ᐊᒥᓲᓂᖕᒋᓐᓂᒃ.

ᒪᓕᒃᑯᑦᑎᒃᑯᒃ ᑖᓯᒪᓂ ᓇᓗᓇᐃᖅᓯᓯᒪᔪᖅ ᒪᓕᒃᑐᓪᓗ ᒪᓕᒃᑕᐅᓂᐊᖅᑐᓪᓗ ᐊᒥᓲᓂᖕᒋᓐᓂᒃ. ᐃᓯᒪᒋᔭᕆᐊᖃᖅᑕᒍᑦ ᐊᒥᓲᓂᕿᐃᓂᖅ ᐊᑐᓕᖅᑲᑦᑕᕿᑎᒍᑦ ᒪᕿᐃᓐᓇᐅᔭᖕᓕᑐᐊᕌᖓᑕ.

ᒪᓕᖕᒪᖕᒫᒃᑯᑦ ᑖᓯᒪᓂ ᓇᓗᓇᐃᖅᓯᓯᒪᔪᖅ ᑭᓇ ᒪᓕᖕᒪᖕᒫᑦ ᑭᓇᓗ ᒪᓕᒃᑕᐅᖕᒪᖕᒫᑦ ᑳᓇᓗ ᐅᖃᓪᓚᒃᑐᖅ ᓇᓗᓇᐃᖅᓯᑦᑐᓂ ᓇᓗᓕᐅᖅᑲᓂᕐᒥᓂᒃ.

ᐃᒪᓐᓕᑦᑐᓕ ᐅᓇ ᐅᖃᐅᓯᒃᑯᑦ ᐊᔪᕐᓇᖖᒋᓐᓇᖅᓴᐅᒐᖅ "ᐅᐃ", ᐅᐸᓂ ᐅᖃᐅᓯᕐᒥ "ᐅᐃᕕᓂᖅ" ᓇᓗᓇᐃᖅᓯᒪᒐᖅ ᑳᓇ ᐅᖃᐅᓯᐅᔪᖅ ᐅᐃᒥᔭᐅᔭᓕᕐᓂᖕᒪᓂᒃ. (ᒥᑭ ᑐᑭᓯᐹᓪᓕᒃᑲᓂᕋᓯᒃᓯᓂ ᐃᓕᓴᐃᖅᑎᒥᔭᒥᓄᑦ ᐊᐱᕆᓚᐅᖅᓯᒪᖕᒪᑦ, "ᑖᓇ

uiksaviniq is a former potential husband, or an ex-fiancé. In fact, Inuktitut could be described as a more precise and analytical instrument for defining things than English is, for all its literary richness. When Quebec linguist Louis-Jacques Dorais analysed words for imported items in Nunavik (arctic Quebec), he found that less than six per cent of the new words were borrowed from English, whereas 76 per cent were descriptive expressions (the others were modifications of traditional words). Furthermore, of the descriptive words, nearly half described the new item by its function, rather than by its appearance — a pretty sophisticated approach to word definition. For instance, the Inuktitut word for computer is *qarasaujaq* — "something that works like a brain" — while *qulimiguulik*, meaning "that which has something going through the space above itself," is Inuktitut for helicopter.

Standardization?

Inuktitut has a long, rich history as an oral language, but its writing systems are fairly new.

Even though there are some seven or so major dialect groupings of Inuktitut in Nunavut, Inuit from across their territory understand one another. In the western Kitikmeot Region, the dialect is known as Inuinnaqtun and is written in roman orthography, just as it is in Labrador, the Canadian western Arctic, Alaska, and in Greenland, where a tradition of literacy based on the roman alphabet goes back centuries.

In the rest of Nunavut, however, Inuktitut is written in syllabics, a

						ᓈᓃᑦ Naaniit Finals
ᐃ	i	ᐅ	u	ᐊ	a	H
ᐱ	pi	ᐳ	pu	ᐸ	pa	ᑉ
ᑎ	ti	ᑐ	tu	ᑕ	ta	ᑦ
ᑭ	ki	ᑯ	ku	ᑲ	ka	ᒃ
ᒋ	gi	ᒍ	gu	ᒐ	ga	ᒡ
ᒥ	mi	ᒧ	mu	ᒪ	ma	ᒻ
ᓂ	ni	ᓄ	nu	ᓇ	na	ᓐ
ᓯ	si	ᓱ	su	ᓴ	sa	ᔅ
ᓕ	li	ᓗ	lu	ᓚ	la	ᓪ
ᔨ	ji	ᔪ	ju	ᔭ	ja	ᔾ
ᕕ	vi	ᕗ	vu	ᕙ	va	ᕝ
ᕆ	ri	ᕈ	ru	ᕋ	ra	ᕐ
ᕿ	qi	ᖁ	qu	ᖃ	qa	ᖅ
ᖏ	ngi	ᖑ	ngu	ᖓ	nga	ᖕ
ᖠ	&i	ᖢ	&u	ᖤ	&a	ᖦ

Englishman and Anglican missionary Edmund Peck, or Uqammak ("the one who speaks well"), translated the Bible into Inuktitut and in 1894 established Baffin Island's first permanent church mission near Pangnirtung, teaching syllabics to Inuit
ᐃᖕᓚᓐᒥᐅᑕᖅ ᐊᒻᒪ ᐋᖕᓕᑲᓐᑯ ᐊᔪᕆᖅᓯᐃᔨᖕᒐ ᐊᑉᒪᓐ ᐸᒃ, ᐅᖃᒻᒪᖅᐅᓂᕋᖅᑕᐅᔪᕕᓂᖅ, ᐃᓄᒃᑎᑑᓕᕆᓚᐅᖅᓯᒪᔪᖅ ᔫᑎᐅᑉ ᐅᖃᐅᓯᖕᒋᓐᓂ ᐊᒻᒪ 1894ᒥ ᓴᖅᑭᑎᓚᐅᖅᓯᒪᔪᖅ ᕿᑭᖅᑖᓗᖕᒥ ᑐᔪᐊᖅᕕᖕᒥ ᐸᖕᓂᖅᑑ ᖃᓂᒋᔭᖕᒐᓂ, ᐃᓕᓐᓂᐊᖅᑎᑦᑎᓪᓗᓂ ᐃᐅᐊᓂ ᐃᓄᖕᓄ

ᐊᖕᒍᑦ ᑐᖁᖕᒐᓕᕆᐊᖄᖅᐸ ᐅᐃᕕᓂᐅᓂᕋᖅᑕᐅᓂᐊᕈᓂ? ᑖᓐᓇ ᑭᐅᔪᖅ ᐃᓯᒪᒃᓴᖅᓯᐅᕐᕌᓚᐅᖅᓯᓂ ᑭᐅᕚᖅᐳᖅ, "ᐱᑦᑎᐊᖖᒋᓐᓂᑰᒍᓂᖃᐃ ᐃ."

ᑖᔅᓱᒪᓂᓕ "ᐅᐃᒃᓴᖅ" ᓇᓗᓇᐃᖅᓯᓯᒪᔪᖅ ᑖᓐᓇ ᓱᓕ ᐅᐃᒋᔭᐅᓚᖖᒋᑦᑐᖅ, ᐅᖃᐅᓯ ᒪᓕᒃᓗᒍ ᑐᑭᓯᓇᓯᓯᒪᔪᖅ "ᐅᐃᒃᓴᕕᓂᖅ" ᐅᐃᑳᕆᔭᐅᖖᒋᓐᓂᑰᓂᖕᒐᓂᒃ. ᐊᓚᓚᑦ, ᑖᓐᓇ ᐃᓄᐃᑦ ᐅᖃᐅᓯᖓᑦ ᐅᖃᐅᑕᐅᔪᓐᓇᖅᐳᖅ ᐅᖃᐅᓯᖅᑳᕐᓂᐊᕐᓗᓂ ᓇᓗᓇᐃᖅᓯᓯᒪᑦᑎᐊᕈᓐᓇᕐᓂᖅᓴᐅᓂᖕᒐᓂᒃ ᖃᒥᕐᕈᑎᑦᑎᑦᑎᐊᖅᓯᒪᓂᖅᑕᓴᐅᓂᖕᒐᓂᒃ ᐅᖃᐅᓯᕆᔭᐅᔪᒥᒃ ᖃᓪᓗᓈᑦ ᐅᖃᐅᓯᖕᒐᓐᓂᐅᖕᒐᓂᑦ, ᖃᓪᓗᓈᑎᑑᖕᒐᓂᒃ ᑎᑎᕋᖅᓯᒪᔪᖃᐅᖅᑐᓪᓚᒪᕆᐊᓘᓚᐅᕐᓗᐊᖅᑎᓪᓗᒍ. ᑖᓐᓇ ᐅᖃᐅᓯᓕᕆᔩ ᑯᐃᐹᒃᒥᐅᑕᖅ ᓗᐃ ᔮᒃ ᑐᕇ ᖄᒥᕐᕈᓪᓗᓂ ᐅᖃᐅᓯᖅ ᐊᑐᖅᑕᐅᔪᓂᒃ ᐃᓄᖕᓄᑦ ᓄᓇᕕᖕᒥᐅᓄᑦ ᐱᒋᔭᐅᖕᒋᓐᓇᖕᒋᑦᑐᑦ ᑕᐃᒎᓯᖅᑕᓇᔾᖕᒋᓐᓂᒃ, ᖃᐅᔨᓕᓚᐅᖅᐳᖅ ᑖᒃᑯᐊ 6ᐳᓴᑐᐃᓐᓇᖕᒋᑦ ᐅᕙᓘᓐᓕᑦ ᕼᐊᓐᓇᓚᒃᐅᐸᑕ 6ᖕᒋᓐᓇᐃᑦ ᖃᓪᓗᓈᑦ ᐅᖃᐅᓯᖕᒐᓐᓂᖕᒌᖕᒐᔪᑦ. ᑳᒃᑯᐊᓕ 76ᐳᓴᑦ ᐅᕙᓘᓐᓕᑦ ᕼᐊᓐᓇᓚᐅᒃᐸᑕ 76ᖕᒋᑦ ᑕᐃᒎᓯᖅᑕᓕᐅᖅᑕᐅᓯᒪᔪᑦ ᑖᔅᓱᒪ ᑕᐅᑦᑕᐊ ᐊᑑᑖᓅᓕᑦ ᐊᑐᖅᓱᒍ, ᑳᒃᑯᐊᓕ 12ᐳᓴᖕᒋᑦ ᐅᖃᐅᓯᑐᖃᖅ ᐊᑐᖅᑕᐅᖄᑦᑕᖅᐸᕇᖅᑐᖅ ᑖᔅᓱᒧᖓ ᑕᑯᔭᐅᓕᑕᐃᓐᓇᖅᑐᒧᑦ ᐊᑐᖅᑕᐅᓕᖕᒌᖅᓱᓂ. ᑳᒃᑯᓇᓂ ᑕᐅᑦᑐᐊᓄᓪᓗ ᐊᑑᑖᓄᓪᓗ ᑕᐃᒎᓯᖅᑕᓕᐅᖅᑕᐅᔪᑦ ᓈᑉᐸᓪᓗᐊᓃᓚᐅᖅᐳᖅ – ᐃᓯᒪᒃᓴᖅᓯᐅᕆᔾᔪᑕᐅᑦᑎᐊᖅᐸᖕᓂᖕᒋᓐᓂᒃ ᑕᐃᒎᓯᖅᑕᖅᑖᕆᑎᑦ ᓇᓗᓇᕈᓐᓃᖅᓯᒪᔪᖅ. ᐅᑯᐊ ᐆᒃᑑᑎᒋᓪᓗᒋᑦ "ᖃᕋᓴᐅᔭᖅ," ᑖᓐᓇᒎᖅ ᐅᖃᐅᓯᐅᔪᖅ ᖃᕋᓴᖅᑎᑑᖕᒐᔪᖅ ᖃᕋᓴᓪᓚᕇᖕᒐᓂ, ᐅᓇᓕ "ᖁᓕᒥᒎᓕᒃ" ᑕᐅᑐᖅᑯᓕᖅᑎᑦᑎᓇᖅᐳᖅ ᑖᓐᓇ ᐅᖃᐅᓯᐅᔪᖅ ᖁᓕᒥᒎᑦ ᐃᖕᒋᕐᕋᔪᖅᑯᑎᖃᕐᓂᖕᒐᓂᒃ.

ᐊᔾᔨᒌᓕᖅᑎᑦᑎᓂᖅ

ᐃᓄᐃᑦ ᐅᖃᐅᓯᖓᑦ ᑲᔪᓰᓐᓇᕆᓐᓇᖅᑎᑕᐅᓂᖅᑲᖅᓯᒪᔪᖅ ᑐᓴᐅᒪᑎᑦᑎᕙᖕᓂᒃᑯᐃᓐᓴᖅ ᐅᖃᐅᔾᔨᕙᒃᓯᑎᒃ ᑭᓯᐊᓂᓕ ᑎᑎᕋᖅᐸᒍᓯᖕᒐᑦ ᓄᑖᐸᔫᔭᖅ ᓱᓕ.

ᐅᖃᐅᓯᖅᑲᖅᑲᑎᒌᒃᑐᑦ ᑲᑎᖅᓱᖕᒍᐊᕋᔭᕈᑎᒍᑦ 7ᐸᓗᓂᕋᕈᓐᓇᖅᐸᒐᑦ ᓄᓇᕗᒻᒥ ᑭᓯᐊᓂ ᐅᖃᐅᓯᕐᒥᒃ ᐊᑕᐅᓯᕐᒥᒃ ᐊᑐᕋᒥᒃ ᑐᑭᓯᐊᖃᑦᑕᐅᑎᔪᓐᓇᖅᐸᒃᐳᑦ. ᐅᐊᓕᓂᕐᒥ ᕿᑎᕐᒥᐅᓂ ᐅᖃᐅᓯᖅᑎᒃ "ᐃᓄᐃᓐᓇᖅᑐᓐ"ᖑᓂᖅᐸᐃᖅ ᐃᓅᔨᖕᒐᔪᑎᑐᑦ/ᖃᓪᓗᓈᑦ ᑎᑎᖅᑲᖁᑎᖕᒋᓐᓂᒃ ᐊᑐᖅᓱᑎᒃ ᑎᑎᕋᖅᐸᒃᐳᑦ. ᓄᓇᕗᑦ ᓯᓚᑖᓂ ᐃᓄᐃᑦ ᑕᐃᒫᒃ ᑎᑎᕋᖅᐸᒃᑭᐳᑦ ᓛᐸᑐᐊᕆᒥ, ᐅᐊᓕᓂᕐᒥᐅᓂ, ᐊᓛᔅᑲᒥ ᐊᑯᑭᑦᑐᕐᒥᐅᓄᓗ. ᐊᑯᑭᑦᑐᕐᒥᐅᑦ 200 ᐊᕐᕌᒍᑦ

“ᑕᒫᖅ ᒨᓕ, ᐊᖓᔪᖅᑳ ᐃᓄᐃᑦ ᑕᐱᕐᓂᐅᔅᓯᑦᑯᓐᓄ, ᐅᖃᖅᑐᑎᒋᔪᖅ ᓄᑖᖅ ᓄᓇ ᐃᒪᕐᒨᕐᓂᐊᓕᕐᑐᖅ ᐊᑎᖅᑲᖅᓴᕐᓂᖓᓂᑦ ‘ᓄᓇᕗᑦ.’”

– ᐃᓄᐃᑦ ᑕᐱᕇᒃᓯᑦᑯ ᒪᓕᒐᓕᐅᕆᓂᖓ ᐋᑕ ᑲᒥᖕ, ᐃᖅᑲᐅᒪᔪᖅ ᔫᓂ 1974-ᒥ, ᑕᓱᕝᕙᐊᑉ ᐃᓕᓐᓂᐊᕐᕕᖓᑕ ᒪᔪᕐᑐᑎᖏᓐᓂᑦ, ᐃᓄᐃᑦ ᓄᓇᑖᕐᓯᖕᓂᐅᓴᖓ ᑕᒪᐃᑎᒍᑦ ᑕᐅᑐᒃᑕᐅᓂᐅᔪᖅ ᒥᑭᓪᓕᕆᐊᕐᑐᖅ ᓴᖅᑭᑦᑎᓂᕐᒧᓐ ᐃᒻᒥᒃᑰᓕᖓᔪᒥ ᑕᐃᔭᐅᔪᒃᓯᒪ “ᓄᓇᕗᑦ”

phonetic form of writing that was developed by Rev. James Evans for the Cree, adapted for the Inuit in the latter part of the 1800s by the Anglican missionaries John Horden and E. A. Watkins, and brought to the Arctic by their colleague, Edmund Peck. A standardized dual orthography for both roman and syllabics was established in the late 1970s by the Inuit Cultural Institute. Time has revealed one or two minor problems with the system, but on the whole it is accurate, learnable and logical. It has gained acceptance in the east, but westerners have been much less receptive, preferring to use an older roman style of spelling.

Standardization of the language, however, is a different matter. It is much more controversial. People who have pride in their language feel very strongly about their dialect. (This certainly comes across in college language courses, where students react immediately to anything they interpret as an attack on the autonomy of their own dialect.) Luckily, however, it can be argued that there is no need to standardize the basic core of the language. Experience over the last 30 years has shown that sophisticated Inuit across Nunavut can readily communicate with each other, either at formal conferences or in informal social situations. They make automatic minor adaptations to adjust to each other's patterns. Where standardization is necessary is in the development of technical terms, and that is usually not such an emotional issue.

Survival is a far more serious issue than standardization.

The survival of Inuktitut

The century that is passing has not been kind to the minority languages of the world, particularly the aboriginal languages (and cultures) of North America. A few years ago it was reported that, given the statistics, one would expect only Cree and Inuktitut to have a chance of surviving another 100 years in Canada. That opinion, however, is no grounds for complacency.

ᐅᖓᑖᓄᑦ ᐅᖃᐅᓯᕐᒥᖕᓂᒃ ᑎᑎᕋᖅᐸᒃᓯᒪᓂᑰᓕᖅᐳᑦ.

ᓄᓇᕗᒻᒥᐅᓕ ᐃᓕᖓᓂ ᑎᑎᕋᐅᓯᕐᒥᒃ ᖃᓂᐅᔫᖅᐸᐃᓚᔭᐅᖃᑦᑕᖅᑐᒥᒃ ᐊᑐᖅᓱᑎᒃ ᑎᑎᕋᖅᐸᒃᐳᑦ. ᑖᓇ ᑎᑎᕋᐅᓯᖅ ᐊᑐᖅᑕᐅᓕᐊᖕᒐᓚᐅᖅᓯᒪᔪᖅ ᐊᔪᖅᓯᐃᔾᔪᖅ ᔭᐃᒥᓯ ᐃᕙᓐᔅ ᐊᓪᓚᓄᑦ/ᐅᓇᓕᖏᓐᓄᑦ ᑯᓂᒍᓂᖅᑕᐅᔪᓄᑦ ᑎᑎᕋᐅᓯᖁᑎᓕᐊᖑᓪᓗᓂ. ᐊᕐᕌᒍᑦ ᕼᐊᓐᓇᓕᖕᒋᓐᓂᐅᓕᖅᐳᖅ ᑖᓇ ᑎᑎᕋᐅᓯᓕᐊᖑᓂᖓ ᐃᓄᖕᓄᑦ ᐊᑐᖅᑕᐅᔭᓐᓇᖅᓯᑎᑕᐅᓚᐅᖅᑎᓪᓗᒍ ᑳᒃᑯᖕᓄᖓ ᐊᔪᖅᓯᐃᔩᖕᓄᒃ ᔫᓐ ᕼᐅᐊᑕᓐ ᐊᒻᒪ ᐃ.ᐊ. ᒁᑭᓐᔪᓪᓗ. (ᐃᐊᑯᒪᓐ ᐱᐊᒃ) ᐅᖃᒻᒪᐅᓪᓚ ᑕᒪᐅᖕᒐᐅᑎᓂᑯᕆᓯᒪᕖ. ᐃᓄᒻᒪᕆᓕᕆᔨᒃᑯᑦ 1970ᑦ ᐊᑐᖅᑎᓪᓗᒋᑦ ᐋᖅᑭᒃᓯᓕᓚᐅᖅᓯᒪᔪᑦ ᑎᑎᕋᐅᔾᔪᖓᓂᒃ ᐊᑐᖅᑕᐅᖃᑦᑕᖅᑐᒃᑮᖓᓂᒃ ᑕᒪᐃᓐᓄᑦ, ᑖᒃᑯᐊᓗ ᖃᓂᐅᔮᖅᐸᐃᑎᑦ ᖃᓕᐅᔮᖅᐸᐃᑎᑐᓗ ᑕᐃᔭᐅᖃᑦᑎᓚᐅᖅᓱᑎᒃ. ᑕᐃᒪᖓᓕᑦ ᐊᑐᖅᑕᐅᑎᑕᐅᓕᓚᐅᖅᑎᓪᓗᒋᒃ ᓈᒻᒪᑎᐊᖅᑐᒪᓕᐊᓅᖕᒋᓐᓂᖓ ᓇᓗᓇᐹᓕᖅᓯᒪᒐᓗᐊᖅᐳᖅ ᑭᓯᐊᓂᓗᑦᑕᐅᖅ ᓇᓗᓇᖕᒋᒃᑭᒍᖅ ᐅᖃᖅᑕᓲᖅᑐᓄᑦ ᑎᑎᕋᕈᑎᒋᔭᐅᑎᐊᓗᒃᓴᐅᓂᖓᓂᒃ, ᐃᓕᑕᒃᓴᐅᓂᖓᓂᖕᒎ, ᐊᒻᒪᓗ ᐋᖅᑭᐅᒪᓂᖓᒃ ᑐᑭᖃᖅᑐᖅᑎᒃ. ᑲᓇᖕᓇᖅᓯᐊᓂ ᖃᓂᐅᔮᖅᐸᐃᑎᑦ ᑎᑎᕋᖅᐸᓕᖅᐸᒋᕐᓂᑯᓂ ᐊᑐᖅᑕᐅᔭᓇᐊᒃᓯᖅ ᖃᓄᐃᓯᔭᐅᖕᒋᒃᑲᔪᐊᖅᑎᓪᓗᒍ ᐅᐊᓕᓂᕐᒥᐅᓄᑦ ᑐᖕᒐᓯᒃᑎᑕᐅᓗᐊᖅᓯᒪᖕᒋᓪᓚᖅ ᑎᑎᕋᐅᓯᑐᖃᓕᖅᓯᒪᔭᕐᒥᒃ ᐊᑐᕆᒧᓯᖓᓖᖅᐸᒃᑲᒥᒃ ᖃᓪᓗᓈᑦ ᑎᑎᖅᑲᖁᑎᖕᓂᒃ ᐊᑐᖅᓱᑎᒃ.

ᐅᖃᐅᓯᐅᑉ ᐊᔪᕈᓐᓃᖅᑎᖅᑕᐅᓂᖓᓗ ᑎᑎᕋᐅᓯᐅᑉ ᐊᔪᕈᓐᓃᖅᑎᖅᑕᐅᓂᖓᓗ ᑖᓐᓇᑦᑕᐃᓐᓇᐅᖕᒋᓪᓚᖅ. ᐅᖃᐅᓯᒥᒃ ᐊᔪᕈᓐᓃᖅᑎᓇᓱᖕᓂᖅ ᐊᑭᖃᖅᑐᖅᑕᐅᔭᓇᕐᓂᖅᓴᐅᒐᖅ. ᐃᓄᐃᑦ ᐅᖃᐅᓯᖕᒐᓂᒃ ᐱᓪᓚᕆᐅᑎᔾᔨᓂᓪᓚᑦ ᐅᖃᐅᓯᖅᑕᓚᔅᓯᒪᖕᓂᒃ ᐃᑉᐱᕆᔭᖃᕐᕙᐊᔾᔪᖕᒍᒐᑦ. (ᑖᓐᓇ ᐅᔾᔨᕐᓇᖅᑐᒪᓚᐅᖃᑦᑕᖅᐳᖅ ᓯᓚᑦᑐᖅᓴᕐᕕᖕᒥ ᐃᓄᐃᑦ ᐅᖃᐅᓯᖓᓐᓂᒃ ᐃᓕᓐᓂᐊᖅᑎᓪᓗᒋᑦ, ᐃᓕᓐᓂᐊᖅᑎᑦ ᐃᓕᖕᒋᑦ ᐸᓯᔪᒃᓯᕋᕕᒃᑕᕐᒪᑕ ᐊᒃᓱᕉᓯᓯᕋᐃᑉᐸᒃᓱᑎᓪᓗ ᐅᖃᐅᓯᖅᓯᖅᑎᒃ ᐊᓯᔾᔨᖅᑕᐅᓇᓯᓚᓯᕆᓕᖃᖓᒥᔾᔪᒃ.) ᐃᓄᒃᑎᑐᑦ ᐅᖃᓪᓚᒃᐸᒃᑐᓕᕐᖃᕐᒍᐃᑦ ᐊᔾᔨᒋᔭᐅᖕᒋᑦᑐᑦ ᐃᓚᖓᓂᒃ ᐊᑐᖅᓯᓇᓱᒃᑲᓐᓂᕐᓂᖅᓴᐅᓂᒥᒃ ᐊᔾᔨᖅᑐᖅᑕᕆᓪᓗ ᐃᓄᐃᑦ ᐅᖃᐅᓯᖏᑦ 30ᐸᖑᓕᖅᑐᓂᒃ ᐃᓄᐃᑦ ᐅᖃᐅᓯᕐᒥᖕᓂᒃ ᖃᐅᔨᒪᑦᑎᐊᖅᑐᑦ ᐅᖃᖃᑎᖃᕐᒃᑲᖅᐸᖕᒋᒪᑕ ᑲᑎᖃᑎᖃᕐᓂᖏᓐᓂ ᑲᑎᒪᓂᖅᑎᒍᓐᓈᓕᑦ ᐅᕙᓐᓈᓕᑦ ᖁᕕᐊᓱᓐᓂᕐᒧᑦ ᖃᑎᖃᑎᖃᕈᑎᖃᕐᓂᖓᓂ. ᐅᖃᐅᓯᖅᑕᓴᒥᖓᓂᒃ ᐊᔾᔨᖅᓯᐊᕐᔪᒃᐸᒃᐳᑦ ᐊᔾᔨᖏᐸᓗᒃᑐᒥᒃ ᑲᑎᙵᔪᑦ ᐅᖃᓪᓚᑐᓯᖅᑯᑦᑐᑎᑦ. ᐊᔾᔨᓕᖅᑎᑦᑎᑐᖅᑕᐃᓂᖅ ᐅᕙᓐᓈᓕᑦ ᐊᑕᐅᓯᕐᒥᒃ ᑕᐃᔫᓯᖅᑕᖅᑎᑦᑎᓴᓇᐊᒃᓯᖅ ᐱᑕᖃᕐᓂᖅᓴᐅᔭᓇᐊᖅᑕᖅᐸᒃᐳᖅ ᒪᑯᓂᖓ ᖃᑦᑐᓈᑎᑐᒻᒪᓇᐊᑐᒃ ᐅᖃᖅᓯᒪᔪᓄᑦ, ᑭᓯᐊᓂᑐ ᑕᒪᓐᓇ ᐃᒃᐱᒍᓱᒍᑎᖃᐅᕝᕙᐊᖕᒋᓐᓂᖅᓴᐅᕙᒃᐳᖅ.

Nortext

ᐅᖃᐅᓯᐅᑉ ᐊᔪᕈᓐᓃᖅᑎᖅᑕᐅᓂᖓᓗ ᑎᑎᕋᐅᓯᐅᑉ ᐊᔪᕈᓐᓃᖅᑎᖅᑕᐅᓂᖓᓗ ... ᐅᖃᐅᓯᖅ ᐱᑕᖃᐃᓐᓇᕐᓂᒃᓴᖓ ᐱᓪᓚᕆᐅᓂᖅᓴᐅᒐᖅ ᐊᔾᔨᖓᓂᖓᒃ ᐊᔪᕈᓐᓃᖅᑎᖅᑕᐅᖃᑦᑕᖓᓂᖅᓴᓂᖓᓂᑦ.

ᐃᓄᐃᑦ ᐅᖃᐅᓯᖓᑦᑕ ᐱᑕᖃᐃᓐᓇᕐᓂᒃᓴᖓ

ᑖᓇ 1ᕼᐊᓐᓇᓚᒥᒃ ᐊᕐᕌᒍᓂᒃ ᐊᓂᒍᐃᓕᖅᑐᖅ ᐃᑲᔪᐊᓐᓄᑯᓗᒃᓯᓯᒪᙱᓚᖅ ᓄᓇᕐᔪᐊᕐᒥᐅᑦ ᖃᔅᓰᓐᓂᐅᓂᖅᓴᓄᑦ ᐅᖃᐅᓯᖃᖅᑐᖅᑎᒥᓯᖏᓐᓄᑦ, ᐱᔪᐊᖅᑐᒥᒃ ᒥᐊᓕᒐᐃᑦᑐ ᑲᓇᑕᒥᐅᑕᐃᑦᑐ ᓄᓇᖃᖅᑳᖅᑐᖅᑯᑎᖏᑦ ᐅᖃᐅᓯᖅᑯᑎᖏᓐᓄᑦ ᐊᓪᓚᑦ ᐃᓕᖅᑯᓯᖅᑯᑎᖏᓐᓄᑦ. ᑕᐃᔅᓯᒪᓂᐊᖅᑰᓕᖅᐳᖅ ᐅᖃᖅᑐᖅᑲᓚᐅᖅᑎᓪᓗᒍ ᑲᓇᑕᒥᐅᖅ ᑯᕆᑦ (ᐊᓪᓚ/ᐅᓇᓕᖏᑦ) ᐃᓄᐃᓪᓗ ᐅᖃᐅᓯᖏᑦ ᐱᑕᖃᐃᓐᓇᖅᑐᖏᓐᓂᐊᖅᓯᒪᓕᖅᓯᒪᔪᑦ ᐊᕐᕌᒍᓄᑦ ᕼᐊᓐᓇᓚᒃᑲᓂᕐᓄᑦ. ᑕᒪᓐᓇ ᑕᐃᒫᒃ ᐃᓱᒪᓕᖅᓯᒪᓂᐅᓂᖅ ᐅᒃᐱᓇᓱᐃᑐᐃᓐᓇᕐᓂᐅᓐᓇᐊᖅᑎᑦᑕᖅ.

Jose Kusugak headed the Inuit Cultural Institute's efforts to standardize written Inuktitut between 1974 and 1977.

Jose Kusugak headed the Inuit Cultural Institute's efforts to standardize written Inuktitut between 1974 and 1977. Seated beside Kusugak is Eric Anoee

ᔫᓯ ᑯᓯᒐᖅ ᓯᕗᓕᐅᖅᑎᐅᓚᐅᖅᓯᒪᔪᖅ ᐃᓄᒻᒪᕆᓕᕆᔨᒃᑯ ᐱᓕᕆᐊᕆᓚᐅᖅᑕᖓᓂ ᑎᑎᕋᐅᓯᖅ ᐃᓄᒃᑎᑐᑦ 1974ᒧ 1977ᒧ ᐊᑯᓐᓂᖓᓂ. ᓴᓂᑦᑎᐊᖓᓂ ᐃᒃᓯᕚᖅᑐᖅ ᑯᓯᒐᐅᑉ ᐃᐅᓂᒃ ᐊᓄᐃ

Nunavut Tourism ᓄᓇᕗᑦ ᐳᓚᕋᖅᑐᓕᕆᔨᑦ

Today, very few native children in western Nunavut speak, or even understand, their native language. And it is the children who count. Visit a community and listen to the children playing. It doesn't matter how much Inuktitut is spoken in the store by adults shopping, or in the kitchens among elders visiting. What language are the children using? The first sign of decay is when the children play in English. The second is when the parents speak in Inuktitut and the children reply in English. The third is when the language of the home is English, except for the elders in the corner, a generation cut off from their grandchildren.

Linguists use a term to express the effort to revive a dying language: "salvage linguistics." The situation along the central Arctic coast of Nunavut — the communities of Cambridge Bay, Kugluktuk, Umingmaktok and Bathurst Inlet — can today be realistically described as one of salvage. There is a race against time, as a small group of Inuit teachers there work to preserve and transmit their language before it is too late.

Will they solve the problem? Or to put it more broadly: can institutions such as government and education save a language on their own? No.

Commitment in the home

The essential element is commitment in the home: commitment by parents. Institutions can't legislate that. What they can do is encourage and support it. But the essential element will come from the people. The essential element will be a pride in the language, and a determination to use it.

Two factors chip away at the stronghold of a minority language such as Inuktitut. One is that by the time parents realize its use is disappearing, it is already too late.

The second factor is the overwhelming power of English, a power felt today across the world. It's not just that English is the language of Shakespeare, and Ernest Hemingway, and Margaret Atwood. It is also the language of Coca-Cola, and the Apollo program, and Bill Gates, and Michael Jackson, and Disney World. English is the language of power, and of glitter. Parents use English to link their children to the source of power.

continued on page 79

Below: After 31 years of broadcasting, Iqaluit's Jonah Kelly signed off from CBC North radio in 1997. Inuktitut language programming has been essential to the survival of the language

ᐋᑖᓂ: 31 ᐊᕐᕌᒍ ᓈᓚᐅᑎᒃᑯ ᐅᖃᕐᑎᐅᓂᑯ ᔫᓇ ᑮᓕ ᓄᖅᑲᓚᐅᕐᓯᒪᔪᖅ ᓯᐲᓰᑯ ᓈᓚᐅᑎᓕᕆᓂᖓᓂ 1997ᒥ. ᐃᓄᒃᑎᑐᑦ ᐅᖃᐅᓯᒃᖁᑦ ᓈᓚᐅᓯᕆᓂᖅ ᐊᑐᕐᓂᖅᖢᖅᐳᖅ ᐃᓄᐃᑦ ᐅᖃᐅᓯᖓᓂ ᓵᖅᑭᔮᖅᑎᑦᑏᓐᓇᕐᓂᒥ

Nunatsiaq News ᓄᓇᑦᓯᐊᕐᒥ ᐱᕙᓪᓕᐊᔪᑦ

ᐅᓪᓗᒥᐅᓕᖅᑐᖅ ᓄᑕᖅᑲᑦ ᖃᓲᓇᑯᓗᐃᑦ ᓄᓇᕗᑦ ᐅᐊᓕᓂᐊᓂ ᐅᖃᕈᓐᓇᖅᐳᑦ ᐅᑯᐊᓘᓐᓃᑦ ᑐᑭᓯᐊᕗᑦ ᐅᖃᐅᓯᕐᖓᐅᑎᒋᓇᔭᖅᑕᕋᓗᐊᕐᒥᖕᓂᒃ ᐃᓄᐃᑦ ᐅᖃᐅᓯᖓᓐᓂᒃ. ᐃᓄᐃᑦ ᐅᖃᐅᓯᖓᑦ ᐱᑕᖃᐃᓐᓇᕐᓂᐊᖅᐸᑦ ᓄᑕᖅᑲᑦ ᐱᒻᒪᕆᒃᔪᐊᕿᓘᒍᑦ. ᓄᓇᓕᖕᓄᐊᕈᑦ ᓄᑕᖅᑲᑦ ᐱᙳᐊᖑᔭᖅᑎᓪᓗᒋᑦ ᓈᓚᒃᑭᑦ. ᓯᕐᑯᑕᐅᓗᐊᑰᕝᖏᓐᓂᖅᓴᐅᕗᖅ ᐃᓐᓇᐃᑦ ᐃᓄᒃᑎᑐᑦ ᐅᖃᓪᓚᖅᑕᐅᑎᔪᑦ ᓂᐅᕖᕐᕕᖕᒥᓯ-ᐅᖅᑎᓪᓗᒋᑦ ᐅᕙᓘᓐᓇᓪᓚᑦ ᐅᓪᓚᖅᑕᐅᑎᓯᒪᓪᓗᑎᒃ ᐃᓄᒃᑎᑐᑦ ᐅᖃᓪᓗᓇᒃᓴᖅᑕᐅᑎᒃᐸᑕ. ᓇᓚᐊᖕᓂᓪᓚ ᐊᑐᖅᑐᑎᒃ ᓄᑕᖅᑲᑦ ᐅᖃᓪᓚᑲᑕᒃᐸᑦ? ᐅᖃᐅᓯᐅᑉ ᐱᑕᖃᕐᓚᕿᓯᓚᐊᓚᕐᓂᖕᒋᓂᒃ ᓵᖅᑮᔭᖅᑳᖅᔭᖅᐳᖅ ᓄᑕᖅᑲᑦ ᐱᙳᐊᑐᐃᓐᓇᖅᑐᑎᒃ ᖃᓪᓗᓇᐅᔭᖅᐸᒃᐸᑕ. ᐱᑕᖃᕐᓕᖅᐸᓪᓕᐊᓂᐅᑉ ᓇᓗᓇᐃᖅᑕᐅᓯᒪᓂᖓᓂ ᑐᓪᓕᓇᔭᐅᒐᖅ ᐊᖓᔪᖅᑳᓇᔭᑦ ᐃᓄᒃᑎᑐᑦ ᐅᖃᓪᓚᒃᑎᓪᓗᒋᑦ ᓄᑕᖅᑲᒥᓄᑦ ᖃᓪᓗᓈᑐᑦ ᑭᐅᔭ-ᐅᖅᑕᓖᕈᑎᒃ. ᐱᖓᔪᖓᓂᖓᑦ ᐊᖏᕐᕋᒥ ᕿᑐᕐᖓᓇᓐᑦ ᖃᓪᓗᓇᐅᔭᖅᑕᐅᑎᓪᓗᑎᒃ ᓂᖏᐅᒃᑯᖏᑦ ᐃᑦᑐᒃᑯᖏᑦ ᐃᓄᒃᑎᑐᑦ ᐃᖏᕐᖕᓄᑦ ᐃᓄᒃᑎᑐᑦ ᐅᖃᓕᖅᑕᖅᑐᑐᐊᖑᒃᐸᑕ.

ᐅᖃᐅᓯᓕᕆᓂᐅᑉ ᐅᖃᐅᓯᖅᑯᑎᖃᖅᐳᑦ ᐅᖃᐅᓯᖅ ᐊᑐᖅᑕᐅᔾᔭᓐᓂᖅᐸᓪᓕᐊᓕᖅᑐᖅ ᓵᖅᑭᑎᑕᐅᒃᑲᓐᓂᕋᓱᒃᑐᒍ ᑕᐃᔭᐅᕙᒃᐳᓂ "ᐱᑕᖃᕈᓐᓂᓕᖅᑑ-ᒪᓗᐊᖅ ᓵᖅᑭᑎᑕᐅᒃᑲᓐᓂᕋᓱᒃᑐᖅ." ᓄᓇᓖᑦ ᐃᖃᓗᒃᑑᑦᑎᐊᕐᒥᓗ, ᖁᕐᓗᖅᑐᒥᓗ, ᐅᒥᖕᒪᒃᑑᕐᒥᓗ, ᑭᖕᖓᐅᖕᒥᓗ ᐅᖃᐅᓯᕆᔭᒃᓴᐅᕙᑦ ᐱᑕᖃᕈᓐᓃᓕᖅᑐᒥᒃ ᓵᖅᑭᑦᑎᒃᑲᓐᓂᕋᓱᖕᓂᕐᕋᓗᑦ. ᑕᐅᕝᓂ ᐃᓚᓐᓂᐊᖅᑎᑦᑎᕚᓪᓗ ᑐᐊᕕᐊᓇᔭᓇᐊᖅᑲᕐᓂᒃᓲᖅᑐᒃᑲᓐᓂᓯᒪᑦ ᐅᖃᐅᓯᖅᑎᒃ ᐱᑕᖃᐃᓐᓇᕐᓂᐊᖅᑎᓐᓇᓱᒃᓗᓂᔪᒃ ᓄᑕᖅᑲᓄᑦ ᑐᓐᓂᖅᑯᑎᒋᕙᒃᓗᓂᔪᒃ ᑭᖑᕚᓗᐊᓚᐅᕐᓂᖕᒥᓂᒃ.

ᑕᐃᒃᑯᐊ ᐃᓕᓐᓂᐊᖅᑎᑦᑎᔨᑦ ᑕᒪᑐᒥᖓ ᓈᒻᒪᑦᑎᐊᙵᕐᓂᐅᔪᒥᒃ ᐋᖅᑭᒃᓯᔫᓐᓇᖅᒎᖅᐸᑦ? ᐅᑉᐸ-ᔫᓐᓚᑦ ᑎᒥᐅᔪᑦ ᔩᓱ ᒐᕙᒪᐅᔪᑦ ᐅᑉᐸᔫᓐᓚᑦ ᐃᓕᓐᓂᐊᕐᕕᐅᔪᑦ ᒪᑭᒪᑎᑦᑎᔪᓐᓇᖅᒍᖅᐸᑦ ᐅᖃᐅ-ᓯᕐᒥᒃ? ᐋᒃᑲᐅᖅᒎᖅᑐᖅ.

ᐊᖏᕐᕋᒥ ᐃᓄᒃᑎᑐᑦ ᐅᖃᓪᓚᖅᑕᕈᒪᓂᖅ

ᐃᓄᐃᑦ ᐅᖃᐅᓯᖓᑦ ᐱᑕᖃᕐᓃᕐᓂᐊᖏᓐᓇᑦᑖ ᑖᓇ ᐱᑕᖃᐃᓐᓇᕐᓂᐊᖅᑐᖃᒃᓴᖅᑕᖅᐳᖅ ᐊᖏᕐᕋᒥ ᐱᑕᖃ-ᐃᓐᓇᖅᑐᕐᓂᖅ: ᐱᓗᐊᖅᑐᒥ ᐊᖓᔪᖅᑳᖓᔪᑦ ᐱᑕᖃᖅᑐᕐᓂᖓᔪᖓᑦ. ᑎᒥᒋᔭᐅᔪᓄᑦ ᑕᒪᓐᓇ ᐊᑐᖅᑕᐅᔭᓇᐊᖐᖅᑐᕋᓐᖏᑕᖓᑦ. ᐃᑲᔪᖅᑐᐃᑐᐃᓐᓇᕈᓐᓇᖅᐳᑦ. ᑕᒪᓐᓇ ᐱᑕᖃ-ᐃᓐᓇᖅᑐᕐᓂᖅ ᐃᓄᖕᓂᖕᖓᖕᖓᔪᓇᐊᖅᑲᖅᐳᖅ. ᑕᒪᓐᓇ ᐱᑕᖃᐃᓐᓇᖅᑐᕐᓂᖅ ᑐᙵᓂᖅᑲᕐᓂᐊᖅᐳᖅ ᐅᖃᐅᓯᕐᒥᒃ ᐅᐱᒋᔭᖅᑲᕐᓂᕐᒥᒃ ᐊᑐᖅᑐᑦᔪᒪᓂᕐᒥᓪᓗ.

ᒪᕿᓪᓗᐊᑕᐅᕝᕕ ᐃᓄᐃᑦ ᐅᖃᐅᓯᖓᓐᓂᒃ ᓄᖑᕐ-ᐃᕗᐅᓪᓗᑎᒃ. ᓯᕗᓪᓖᖅ, ᐊᖓᔪᖅᑳᖓᔪᑦ ᐅᔾᔨᕆ-ᓯᓚᑕᐃᓐᓇᖃᓗᐊᕐᓗᑎᒃ ᐱᑕᖃᕐᓃᖅᐸᓪᓕᐊᓂᖓᓂᒃ ᑭᖑᕚᓗᐊᓕᓐᓂᕐᓗᑎᒃᓗ.

ᑐᓪᓕᐊᓕ ᐅᓇᐅᒐᖅ, ᖃᓪᓗᓈᑦ ᐅᖃᐅᓯᖓᑦ ᓵᙱᔪᒪᓇᐊᔪᓂᖓ. ᐅᖃᕐᓗᐊᖅᑕᕆᑕᐅᔪᓐᓇᕐᓂᖓ-ᓅᙱᑦᑐᖅ ᑭᓯᐊᓂ ᐊᑐᖅᑕᐅᕙᙱᓐᓂᖓᓄᑦ ᓯᓚᕐᔪᐊᒥ ᐊᖓᔪᖅᑳᕐᔪᐊᒡᒍᑕᐅᔪᑦ ᐃᖏᕐᖓᓄᑦ ᐅᖃᖅᑎᕆᒍᒪᔭᕐᖓᒥᒃ. ᑖᓐᓇᓗ ᐅᖃᐅᓯᖅ ᐊᑐᖅᑕᐅᕙᙱᓐᓇᓄᑦ ᐱᔪᒥᓭᓇᔾᔭᑕᓪᓗᓂ, ᔩᕐᓗ ᑕᓚᕖᓯᓂ ᑕᕐᓇᔭᒐᕐᓂᓗ. ᐊᖓᔪᖅᑳᖑᔪᑦ

ᑲᔪᓯᔪᖅ ᒫᒃᐱᒐᖅ 79

INUIT ART: The New Reality
ᐃᓄᐃᑦ ᓴᓇᙳᐊᒐᖏᑦ: ᖃᓄᐃᓕᕐᓂᖓ ᓄᑖᖅ

By Terry Ryan

Inuit *art* is alive and well.

Inuit *production* and presentation of art, in its many manifestations, is both exciting and problematic. This is neither new, nor necessarily alarming — simply an ongoing reality for this significant element of Nunavut's culture and economy.

Our present-day conception of contemporary Inuit art can be traced back exactly 50 years, when success was unexpectedly attained with the Canadian Handicraft Guild's 1949 exhibition in Montreal. This was both rewarding and exciting, coinciding as it did with a slow awakening of national pride in all things Canadian. The name of James Houston will be familiar to many as a major figure in recognizing, encouraging and promoting contemporary Inuit art. Houston's work in Cape Dorset with artists such as Osoetuk Ipeelie and Kenojuak Ashevak allowed the Canadian government to provide that early stimulus that was, in retrospect, so very crucial to the introduction of Inuit art to a worldwide audience.

However, early attempts to persuade the major art institutions of the esthetic importance of Inuit art were maligned somewhat by government officials' determination to create an "industry." There were, after all, few economic alternatives in these remote arctic settlements. A successful cottage industry has been sustained to be sure, producing items ranging from outdoor clothing to miniature tools, sculpture and graphic arts, jewelry, tapestries and pottery. From this diverse effort has developed some wonderfully unique individual examples of the human ability to express the esthetic, and to express it in a voice that speaks to all nations with directness and honesty. The result is the existence today of major collections of Inuit art in many distinguished public and private holdings throughout the world.

The pace of change in the Arctic over the past 50 years has been so marked, so accelerated, and so all-encompassing, that change in artistic expression has been inevitable. For the arts to remain truly valid and maintain support, a new "eye" must be evident. From an era when the arctic lifestyle allowed time for true introspection and pride of craft, Inuit art as we know it today has been

ᑎᑎᕋᖅᑐᖅ ᑎᐊᕆ ᕋᐃᐊᓐ

ᐃᓄᐃᑦ ᓴᓇᙳᐊᒐᖏᑦ ᐆᒪᑎᑕᐅᑦᑎᐊᖅᑐᑦ ᐊᒻᒪᓗ ᐃᖏᕋᑦᑎᐊᖅᑐᑦ.

ᐃᓄᐃᑦ ᓴᓇᕙᖕᓂᖏᑦ ᐊᒻᒪᓗ ᑕᑯᒃᓴᐅᑎᑎᓂᖏᑦ ᓴᓇᙳᐊᒐᓂᒃ, ᖃᓄᐃᑦᑐᑐᐃᓐᓇᕐᓂᒃ ᓴᓇᓯᒪᔪᓂᒃ, ᐊᓕᐊᓇᐃᓐᓂᖃᖅᑐᖅ ᐊᔪᕐᓇᕈᑎᖃᖅᐸᒃᖢᓂᓗ. ᑕᒪᓐᓇ ᐱᒋᐊᓕᖅᓯᒪᐃᓐᓇᕆᐊᖕᖏᑦᑐᖅ, ᐊᒻᒪᓗ ᑕᒪᐃᑎᒍᑦ ᐃᓯᒫᑎᒃᓴᐅᓐᖏᑦᑐᓂ. ᑕᐃᒪᐃᓐᖏᓐᓇᖅᑐᑐᐃᓐᓇᖅ ᑕᒪᑐᒨᖓ ᐊᑐᑦᓯᓇᒋᔭᐅᔪᒧᑦ ᕿᓇᐅᔭᓕᐅᕐᓂᕐᒧᑦ ᐅᑭᐅᖅᑕᖅᑐᒥ ᐃᓕᖏᔭᐅᓂᖓᓄᑦ ᐃᓕᖅᑯᓯᒧᑦ.

ᐅᓪᓗᒥᐅᔪᖅ ᑐᑭᓯᓂᓴᑦᑎᒍᑦ ᐃᓄᖕᓄᑦ ᓴᓇᙳᐊᓇᔭᐅᓯᖅᑐᓂᒃ ᐱᒋᐊᓚᐅᖅᓯᒪᔪᖅ ᐊᕐᕌᒍᓂ 50-ᓂᒃ ᐊᑐᓕᖅᑐᓂ. ᓂᕆᐅᖕᓇᖕᖏᑦᑐᒃᑯᑦ ᖃᐅᔨᒪᔭᐅᓯᑳᓪᓚᖓᓂᖃᓚᐅᖅᑎᓪᓗᒋᑦ ᒫᓐᑐᕆᐊᓪᒥ ᑕᑯᔭᒃᓴᖅᑎᑎᑦᑎᓪᓗᒋᑦ ᑲᓇᑕᒥ ᓴᓇᙳᐊᖅᑎᑦ ᑲᑐᔾᔨᖏᑦ (Canadian Handicraft Guild) 1949-ᒥ. ᑕᒪᓐᓇ ᖁᕕᐊᓇᓪᓚᐅᖅᑐᖅ ᐊᑕᐅᑦᑎᒃᑰᖅᑕᐅᑎᓪᓗᒍ ᑲᓇᑕᓕᒫᒥ ᓇᒥᓂᖅ ᐃᓚᒋᔭᐅᕙᓪᓕᐊᓂᖓᒃ ᖃᐅᔨᓯᖅᑎᓪᓗᒋᑦ. ᐊᑎᖓ ᔮᒃ ᕼᐅᔅᑕᓐ ᓴᐅᒥᒃ (James Houston) ᐊᒥᒍᓄᑦ ᖃᐅᔨᒪᔪᐅᑲᔪᖅᑐᖅ ᐊᒃᓯᕈᑎᖃᓪᓚᐅᖅᑐᖅᓗ ᐃᓄᐃᑦ ᓴᓇᐅᒐᖕᖏᓐᓂᒃ ᐃᓕᑕᕆᔭᐅᓂᖕᖏᓐᓂᒃ, ᐊᖕᒐᔪᖅᑕᐅᓂᖕᖏᓐᓂᒃ ᐊᒻᒪᓗ ᐊᔪᖅᑕᐅᓂᖕᖏᓐᓂᒃ. ᓴᐅᒥᐅᑉ ᑭᖕᖓᓂ ᐊᒃᓯᕈᕐᓂᕆᓚᐅᖅᑕᖏᑦ ᓴᓇᖅᑎᖅᑯᓂ ᓴᓇᐅᒐᖅᑎᓂ ᐲᓗ ᐅᓯᐃᑦᑐᖅ ᐊᐃᐱᓕ ᐊᒻᒪᓗ ᕿᓐᓄᐊᕐᔪᐊᖅ ᐋᓯᕙᖅ ᐱᔪᓐᓇᖅᑎᑎᓚᐅᖅᑐᑦ ᑲᓇᑕᐅᑉ ᒐᕙᒪᒃᑯᖕᖓᓂᒃ ᐊᔪᐅᒃᓯᓐᖓᓐᖏᓐᓂᒃ ᓴᓇᙳᐊᒐᕐᓂᒥᒃ. ᑭᖑᓪᓕᒍᑦ ᑕᑯᓗᒍ, ᐃᓄᐃᑦ ᓴᓇᙳᐊᒐᖏᑦ ᓇᓗᓐᖏᓕᖅᑕᐅᒍᑎᖓᓐᓂᒃ ᓯᓚᕐᔪᐊᓕᒫᒧᑦ ᐱᒋᐊᕐᓂᖅᑲᖅᑕᐅᖅᑕᖅ ᑕᒪᑐᒥᖓ ᐊᒃᓯᕈᖅᑲᖅᑕᐅᕐᓂᖓᓄᑦ.

ᑭᓯᐊᓂᓕ, ᐱᒋᐊᓕᕚᖅᑎᓪᓗᒋᑦ ᐊᖏᔫᔪᓂ ᓴᓇᙳᐊᖅᑐᓕᕆᔩᑦ ᐊᔪᕐᓇᖅᓯᐅᔾᔭᖅᐸᓪᓚᐅᖅᑐᑦ ᐃᓕᑕᕆᑎᑎᓂᕐᒥᒃ ᓴᓇᙳᐊᒐᐃᑦ ᐱᐅᓯᑕᐅᓂᖏᑦ ᐊᑐᕐᓂᖕᖏᓐᓄᑦ. ᒐᕙᒪᒃᑯᑦ ᐊᒃᓯᕐᓂᖅᓴᐅᕙᓪᓚᐅᖅᑎᓪᓗᒋᑦ ᐋᖅᑮᓂᕐᒥᒃ "ᓴᓇᙳᐊᖅᑐᓕᕆᓂᕐᒥᒃ." ᑕᐃᑦᓯᒪᓂᐅᓪᓚᐅᖅᑐᖅ ᓱᖃᐃᒻᒪ, ᐊᒥᒨᖕᖏᑦᑐᓂᒃ ᑭᓯᐊᓂ ᖃᓄᔭᓪᓗᕐᕕᖃᓪᓗᓯᑕ ᐃᓄᑭᓐᓂᖅᓴᐅᔪᓂ, ᐅᐸᒃᓴᕿᓐᓇᖕᖏᑦᑐᓂ ᐅᑭᐅᖅᑕᖅᑐᒥᐅᓂᒃ ᓄᓇᓕᖕᓂᒃ. ᓴᓇᙳᐊᕐᕕᖃᖅᐸᑦ ᐃᖏᕋᑐᐊᖅᐸᑦ ᐃᓯᒪᕆᔭᐅᑦᑕᓪᓚᐅᖅᑐᖅ ᐃᖖᒍᓕᓗᐊᖅ, ᓴᓇᓯᒪᔪᓂᒃ ᐊᓄᕌᓂᒃ ᓯᓚᒥᓯᐅᑎᓂᑦ ᒪᐅᖓ ᓴᓇᙳᐊᖓᓄᑦ ᒥᑭᑐᓄᑦ ᐱᐅᓴᐅᑎᖃᓗᖕᓄᑦ ᑎᑎᖃᐅᔭᖅᓯᒪᔪᓄᑦ, ᓄᕕᒃᓴᔭᖃᓗᖕᓄᑦ ᔭᕿᐅᔭᓂᓗ

Nunavut Tourism

Wilkinson/NWT Archives

Inuit artists such as Simon Pewatoalook, above, continue to capture the world's imagination – just as they did in 1960, when this cameraman, right, documented the making of a model kayak in Pelly Bay

ᐃᓄᐃᑦ ᓴᓇᙳᐊᖅᑏ ᐆᑐᓇᖅ ᓴᐃᒪᓐ ᐱᐅᕖᑦᑐᐊᓗᒃᑐ, ᖁᖓᓂ, ᓯᓚ ᐃᓯᒪᓯᔪᐅᙳᐊᕐᑐᓂᑦ ᓴᖅᑭᑦᑎᖃᑦᑕᕐᐳᑦ – ᑕᐃᒪᖕᓇ 1960, ᐅᓇ ᐊᔾᔨᓕᐅᕆᔨ, ᑕᓕᖅᐱᐊᓂ, ᐊᔾᔨᓕᐅᕐᑎᓪᓗᒍ ᖃᔭᙳᐊᓕᐅᕐᑐᒥ ᐊᕐᕕᓕᒡᔪᐊᕐᒥ

transformed by a modern lifestyle and monetary economy full of frustrations and financial pressures. We may note a lessening of the Inuit artist's initial motivation — the desire to present with honesty and unique vision all that was so different from our own perplexing society. The wellspring of Inuit art today derives both from a recognition of the past and a reaction to the present.

As I write today in the offices of Dorset Fine Arts, amid Toronto's skyscrapers, I think of my work and life with the artists of Cape Dorset in the early '60s, and reflect on how greatly a day in the life of both artist and buyer has changed. The North was then a distant, inaccessible place, and to an Inuk the South was truly a mystery. In many respects that isolation allowed the Inuit artist to live unencumbered, with few outside influences and pressures. The informality of association between artist and buyer was wonderful in retrospect. That relationship has been transformed to meet the dictates of a new era.

But these transformations do not necessarily support dire predictions of Inuit art's premature demise: concerns that inventories of product are too high and that marketing efforts are wanting. More importantly, Inuit *art* flourishes. Each generation has had its world-renowned champions, and the current generation is no exception. The contemporary art "industry" of Canada's Arctic will remain vital as long as there are Inuit artists proud of their heritage and determined to express honestly their ever-changing culture. Their voices, though different from their elders, are no less worthy of our admiration and respect.

Inuit art, so admired over the past half-century, will undoubtedly continue to change. There is an onus on Nunavut's elected leaders, beginning in 1999 and for the next half-century, to support the artistic expression of Inuit culture and the new Nunavut. There is an onus, too, on the Inuit artist to be not merely a repetitive chronicler of times past, but a witness to and active participant in this exciting new era.

Toronto artist Terry Ryan first sailed to the Arctic in 1956, and settled in Cape Dorset in 1960. He is general manager of the West Baffin Eskimo Co-operative and Dorset Fine Arts in Toronto.

ᓴᓇᓯᒪᔪᑦ. ᑕᒪᒃᑯᓇᖕᒑᑦ ᑕᑯᕐᓂᖅᑐᓂᒃ ᓄᐃᔭᖅᓯᒪᔭᖅ ᐃᓅᑉ ᓴᓇᔨᒃᑲᐅᓂᖓᓂᖕᒎᖅᑐᒥᒃ, ᓇᒥᑐᐃᓐᓇᖅ ᑐᑭᓯᔭᐅᔪᓐᓇᖅᑐᒥᒃ ᐃᓚᑦᑕᕐᓇᖅᑐᒃᑯᑦ ᓯᓚᔪᒃᑯᓪᓗ. ᑕᐃᒪᓐᓇ ᐱᔪᑎᖃᖅᑐᖅ ᐊᒥᓱᓂᒃ ᑲᑎᖅᓱᖅᓯᒪᔪᖃᓚᕐᒪᑦ ᐃᓄᐃᑦ ᓴᓇᔾᔪᑎᖏᓐᓂᒃ ᓈᒻᒥᓂᕐᓇᔾᔭᐅᔪᓂᒃ ᐊᒻᒪᓗ ᑭᒃᑯᒃᑖᓄᑦ ᑕᑯᔭᖅᑐᖅᕕᐅᒍᓐᓇᖅᑐᓂ ᓯᓚᕐᔪᐊᓕᒫᒥ.

ᐅᑭᐅᖅᑕᖅᑐᒥ ᐊᓯᔾᔨᖅᐸᓪᓚᐊᓂᖕᒋᑦ ᓱᓇᑐᐃᓐᓇᐃᑦ ᓱᑲᔫᒪᓇᐊᓚᖅᑐᖅ ᐊᕐᕌᒍᔪᓂ 50-ᓂ. ᑕᒪᓐᓇ ᐊᓯᔾᔨᕐᓂᕐᒥᒃᑕᐅᖅ ᓴᓇᙳᐊᓗᓇᔪᐅᓂᒃᑯᑦ ᒪᓕᒃᓴᖅᑕᐅᓯᒪᖕᒥᔪᖅ ᓴᓇᙳᐊᖅᐸᖕᓂᖅ ᐊᒃᑐᖅᑕᐅᒥᓪᓗᓂ. ᓴᓇᙳᐊᖅᐸᖕᓂᖅ ᑐᑭᒃᑎᐊᖅᓱᖅᐸᑦ ᐃᑲᔪᖅᑕᐅᓂᖅᑲᖅᓱᖅᐸᓪᓗ, ᓅᑦᑎᒃ "ᐃᔨᒋᓱᖃᓇᐊᓚᒃ" ᐅᔾᔨᕐᓇᖅᑐᒃᑯᑦ. ᑕᐃᑦᓱᒪᓂ ᐃᓄᐃᑦ ᐱᕙᒃᓴᖃᑦᑎᐊᖅᑕᓗᐅᖅᑎᓪᓗᒋᑦ ᐃᓱᒪᒋᑦᑎᐊᖅᓯᒪᔪᒃᑯᑦ ᑐᐊᕕᓐᖏᑦᑐᒃᑯᑦ ᐊᒻᒪᓗ ᐅᐃᒪᔮᖅᑎᑕᐅᓚᐅᖏᒻᒥᒃ ᓴᓇᙳᐊᖅᐸᖕᓂᖏᒃ. ᐅᓪᓗᒥᐅᔪᖅ ᓴᓇᙳᐊᓗᓇᔪᐅᔪᑦ ᐃᓅᖕᓄᑦ ᒫᓐᓇᐅᔪᖅ ᓅᑕᖕᒍᔪᒃᑯᑦ ᐊᒃᑐᖅᑕᐅᓯᒪᓕᕐᒪᑦᑕᐅᖅ ᕿᓇᐅᔭᓕᐅᕆᐊᖃᕐᓂᕐᒥᒃ ᓯᓇᒍᐃᓐᓇᕐᓂᒃ ᐊᔪᕐᓇᕈᑕᐅᕙᒃᑐᓂᒃ. ᑕᑯᓐᓇᖅᑐᒍᑦ ᑕᐃᑦᓱᒪᓂ ᐃᓄᐃᑦ ᓴᓇᙳᐊᕈᑎᔪᒪᔪᑎᕆᓂᖅᑕᐅᖅᑐᒥᒃ — ᑕᑯᔭᒃᓴᖅᑎᑎᒍᒪᓂᕐᒥᒃ ᓯᓇᑐᐃᓐᓇᕐᓂᒃ ᓯᓚᔪᒃᑯᑦ ᐊᒻᒪᓗ ᒪᑐᐃᖓᒐᑎᒃᑐᒃᑯᑦ ᓯᓇᑐᐃᓐᓇᕐᓂᒃ ᐅᓪᓗᒥᐅᓕᖅᑐᖅ ᐊᔾᔨᒋᖕᖏᑦᑐᒥᒃ ᓯᓚᒪᔾᔪᖕᒐᑦ ᑕᒃᑯᓴᓕᖅᑐᓂᒃ. ᐅᓪᓗᒥ ᐅᔪᖅ ᐱᒋᐊᕐᕕᖕᒑᑦ ᐃᓄᐃᑦ ᓴᓇᖕᒍᐊᕐᓂᖏᑕ ᐃᑎᓂᖅᓯᒪᔪᖅ ᐃᓚᑦᑎᓂᕐᒥᒃ ᑕᐃᑦᓱᒪᓂᐅᓚᖅᑐᓂᒃ ᐊᒻᒪᓗ ᐅᓪᓗᒥᐅᔪᖅ ᖃᓄᐃᓕᓂᕐᒥᒃ.

ᐅᓪᓗᒥᐅᔪᖅ ᑎᑎᕋᖅᑎᓪᓗᖓ ᑎᑎᖅᑲᖁᕕᖕᒑᓂ Dorset Fine Arts, ᕿᒥᕐᕈᐊᓇᖅᓱᖕᒑ ᑐᕌᓐᑐᑉ ᐃᓄᒋᐊᒃᑐᑦ ᐃᒡᓗᔫᖕᓂᒃ, 1960 ᐊᑐᓕᖅᑎᓪᓗᒍ ᐃᓱᒪᒐᔪᒃᑐᖕᒐ ᖃᓄᖅ ᐊᓯᔾᔨᖅᓯᒪᖕᒪᖔᑦ ᓴᓇᙳᐊᖅᑎᑦ ᓂᐅᕕᖅᑎᓪᓗ ᐃᓅᓯᖕᒑᑦ ᐱᓯᒪᓕᕐᓂᖕᒐᓂᒃ. ᐅᑭᐅᖅᑕᖅᑐᖅ ᑕᐃᑦᓱᒪᓂ ᐅᖕᒐᓯᒃᑦᑐᑦᑕᓗᐅᖅᑐᖅ, ᐅᐸᒃᓴᖅᐃᓐᓇᓂ, ᐊᒻᒪᓗ ᐃᓅᖕᒧᑦ ᖃᑦᓗᓈᑦ ᓄᓇᖕᒑᑦ ᐋᖑᔭᐊᕐᓇᖅᑲᓚᐅᖅᓱᓂ. ᐊᒥᓱᓂᒃ ᑎᑭᐊᖅᐃᓐᓇᓐᖕᒋᖅ ᑕᐃᑦᓱᒪᓂ ᐃᓄᐃᑦ ᓴᓇᙳᐊᖅᑎᑦ ᐃᓅᔦᖕᓇᓐᖕᒋᖅᑐᑎᒃ ᐃᓄᐃᑦ ᓴᓇᖕᒍᐊᖅᑎᑦ ᐃᓅᔦᖕᓇᖅᐸᒃᑎᑦ...

ᑐᕌᓐᑐᒥᐅᑕᖅ ᑎᐊᕆ ᕋᐃᐊᓐ ᓯᕗᓪᓕᖅᐹᖑᓪᓗᓂ ᐅᑭᐅᖅᑕᖅᑐᒧᐊᖅᓯᒪᔪᖅ 1956ᒥ, ᑭᙵᓂᓪᓗ ᓄᓇᑖᖅᓱᓂ 1960ᒥ. ᐊᖓᔪᖅᑳᖑᔪᖅ ᐱᖓᓇᐅᑉ ᑯᐊᒑᖕᓂᑦ ᐊᒻᒪᓗ ᑭᙵᒥ ᑎᑎᖅᐅᔾᔨᐊᕐᓂᒃ ᑐᕌᓐᑐᒥ.

The Pangnirtung Tapestry Studio at the Uqqurmiut Centre for Arts and Crafts: an Inuit art form less than 30 years old drawing on millennia-old threads of Inuit culture

ᐸᖕᓂᖅᑑᒥ ᐊᑭᓐᓇᕐᒥᐅᑕᓕᐅᕐᕖ ᐅᖅᑯᕐᒥᐅᑦ ᓴᓇᙳᐊᕕᖕᒑ: ᐃᓄᐃᑦ ᓴᖅᑭᑦᑎᒍᑦ ᐊᑐᓕᕐᑐᕕᓂᖓ 30 ᐊᕐᕌᒍ ᐊᑐᕐᓯᑎ ᐊᑐᕐᑐᑲᓐᓂᕐᓗᖕᒥ ᐱᓕᕆᔾᔪᑎᒥᓐ

Nunavut Tourism ᓄᓇᕗᑦ ᐳᓚᕋᖅᑐᓕᕆᔨᑦ

continued from page 76

Education

However, many people believe that Inuktitut will be a source of strength to Nunavut. So what else can the institutions do to ensure its survival and growth?

Education comes to mind immediately. Research and development in Inuktitut curriculum began soon after the birth of the NWT Department of Education in 1970, and has continued. A training program for Inuit teachers teaching in Inuktitut was started in the early 1980s.

But there is still room for improvement. While a fully developed curriculum for high schools is lacking, even more crucial is the need to develop skills in second-language instruction, and to ensure that there is funding for Inuktitut second-language curriculum and materials. It is not only that the situation in the central Arctic is critical, and that the handful of dedicated Inuit teachers there need skilled technical support.

Inuit Broadcasting Corporation ᐃᓄᐃᑦ ᑕᑯᓐᓇᒐᒃᓴᓕᐅᕐᑎᖏᑦ

Even children in eastern Nunavut, in communities such as the territory's capital, Iqaluit, need an Inuktitut second-language emphasis in their language classes. This is especially true for children in cross-cultural families. In the vital area of adult education, there is a demand for classes in first-language literacy training, and in second-language training.

Nunavut Tourism ᓄᓇᕗᑦ ᐳᓛᖅᑐᓕᕆᔩᑦ

ᐃᓚᖓ ᒪᒃᐱᒐᐅᑉ 76

ᑖᔅᓱᒥᖓ ᐅᖃᐅᓯᕐᒥᒃ ᐊᑐᖅᑎᑦᑎᕙᒃᐸᑦ ᓄᑕᖅᑲᑎᒃ ᐃᓚᒋᔭᐅᖃᑕᐅᖁᓪᓗᓂᔾᔪᒃ ᑖᔅᓱᒥᖓ ᐅᖃᐅᓯᕐᒥᒃ ᓴᙱᓂᓕᐊᓗᖕᒥᒃ.

ᐃᓕᓐᓂᐊᕐᓂᓕᕆᓂᖅ

ᐃᓄᐃᑦ ᐊᒥᓱᐊᓗᐃᑦ ᐃᓱᒪᒋᔭᖃᕐᒪᑕ ᐃᓄᐃᑦ ᐅᖃᐅᓯᖓᑦ ᐱᒡᒍᒃᑎᑦᑎᕚᓪᓕᕈᑕᐅᔪᓐᓇᓂᐊᒃᓴᖓᓂᒃ ᓄᓇᕗᒃᑯᓪᓕᕈᑦᑕ. ᑕᐃᒪᓕ ᑎᒥᐅᔪᑦ ᖃᓄᐃᓕᒃᑲᓂᕋᓐᓇᖅᓯᔭᖅᑰᖅᐸᑦ ᐃᓄᐃᑦ ᐅᖃᐅᓯᖓᑦ ᐱᑕᖃᐃᓐᓇᖅᑎᓐᓂᐊᖁᓯᒡᓗᓂᔾᔪᒃ ᐱᕈᖅᐸᓪᓕᐊᑎᓐᓇᓱᖕᓂᐊᕐᓗᓂᔾᔪᓪᓗ?

ᐃᓕᓐᓂᐊᖅᑐᓕᕆᓂᖅ ᐃᓱᒪᒋᔭᐅᖓᓗᐅᑕᐅᔭᑉᐸᖅ. ᖃᐅᔨᓴᖅᐸᓪᓕᐊᓂᕐᓗ ᓴᖅᑭᑎᑦᑎᕙᓪᓕᐊᓕᕐᓂᕐᓗ ᐃᓄᒃᑎᑑᖓᔪᓂᒃ ᐃᓕᓐᓂᐊᕈᑎᑕᖅᑎᓇᓱᒃᖢᑎᒃ ᐱᒋᐊᓕᓚᐅᖅᓯᒪᕗᖅ ᓄᓇᑦᑎᐊᑉ ᐃᓕᓐᓂᐊᖅᑐᓂᕆᓂᓕᕆᔨᒃᑯᖏᑦ ᐱᒋᐊᖅᑎᑕᐅᑎᓪᓗᒋᑦ 1970ᒥ ᑕᐃᒪᙵᓪᓗ ᑲᔪᓯᑎᑕᐅᓪᓗᓂ. ᐃᓄᒃᑎᑐᑦ ᐃᓕᓐᓂᐊᖅᑎᑦᑎᖃᑦᑕᖅᑐᒃᓴᓂᒃ ᐃᓕᓐᓂᐊᖅᑎᔾᔭᓄᑦ ᐃᓕᓐᓂᐊᕐᕖᒃᑲᖅᓯᒪᓕᖅᐳᖅ 1980ᑦ ᐱᒋᐊᓕᕿᖅᓯᒪᑎᓪᓗᒋᑦ.

ᐱᐅᓯᕚᓪᓕᕐᓂᖅᑕᖃᕐᓇᖅᐳᖅ ᓱᓕ. ᐊᒃᑐᕌᑎᕆᔭᐅᔭᓇᐊᖅᑲᖅᑰᓕᓚᑦ ᐃᓅᓚᓗᐊᑦ ᐃᓄᒃᑐᑦ ᐅᖃᕐᓇᐃᓪᓕᓂᑰᓯᒪᔭᑦ ᐅᖃᓄᐅᖅᓴᔭᑎᒃᓴᕆᓐᓄᑦ ᐃᓕᓐᓂᐊᕈᑎᑕᖃᓇᐊᖃᓪᓚᑦ, ᕿᓇᐅᔭᖅᑕᖅᑎᑕᐅᔭᓇᐊᓕᒃ ᐃᓄᒃᑎᑐᑦ ᐅᖃᓄᐅᖅᓴᔭᑎᓄᑦ ᐃᓕᓐᓂᐊᖅᑕᔪᒃᓴᓂᒃ ᐋᖅᑭᒃᓯᖅᑕᐅᔪᖃᕈᓇᖅᑯᓪᓗᒍ ᐃᓕᓐᓂᐊᕈᑎᒃᓴᓕᐅᖅᑐᖃᕈᓇᖅᑯᓪᓗᒍ. ᐅᐊᓕᓂᕐᒥᐅᑐᐊᖅ ᕿᙵᓪᓚᑦᑎᔫᖕᒋᓕᕐᓚᑕ ᐅᖃᐅᓯᖅᑎᒃ ᓴᓚᐃᓇᔭᖅᑲᔅᓇᐊᒃᓴᒥᖕᓂᒃ ᐃᓕᓐᐊᖅᑎᑦᓲᕐᑎᖕᒋᑦ ᐃᑲᔪᖅᑕᐅᓂᖃᒻᒪᕆᐊᖃᕐᒪᑕ ᖃᓄᖅ ᓴᓚᐃᑦᑕᐃᓕᑎᑦᑎᓂᐊᕐᓗᑎᒃ ᐱᓕᕆᔪᓐᓇᖃᑦᑕᕋᔭᕐᒪᖔᑕ. ᒦᓂᑦᑕᐅᖅ ᑲᓇᖕᓇᖅᐸᓯᖕᒥ ᔩᕐᓗ ᐃᖃᓗᖕᓂ ᓄᑖᖅᑲᑦ ᐃᓄᒃᑎᑐᑦ ᐅᖃᓄᐅᖅᓴᑎᑕᐅᑉᓗᑎᒃ ᐃᓕᓐᓂᐊᖃᑦᑕᓂᐊᖃᕐᒥᔪᑦ. ᑕᒪᓐᓇ ᐅᖃᓄᐅᖅᓴᔭᓂᐊᖃᓂᖅ ᐱᓪᓗᐊᑕᕐᓂᖅᓴᐅᖅᑰᔨᖕᒪᑦ ᐃᓚᖅᑯᓯᖃᖃᑎᖏᓐᒋᑦᑐᖕᓂᒃ/ᐅᖃᐅᓯᖃᖃᑎᖏᓐᒋᑦᑐᖕᓂᒃ ᐊᖓᔪᖅᑳᖕᓂ. ᐃᓐᓇᐅᓂᖅᓴᓄᑦ ᐃᓕᓐᓂᐊᕐᕕᒋᔭᐅᔪᓄᑦ ᐱᑕᖃᓇᐊᖅᑯᔾᔭᖕᒪᑦ ᐃᓄᒃᑎᑐᑦ ᐅᖃᐅᓯᖕᒪᐅᑎᓃᑦ ᐅᖃᓄᐅᖅᓴᓗᐊᖅᑯᑎᒃ ᑎᑎᕋᓇᐅᖅᓯᑎᑕᐅᑲᑕᓇᐊᖃᓪᓚᑦ ᐊᒻᒪᓗ ᐊᓯᖕᒋᑦ ᐃᓄᒃᑎᑐᑦ ᐅᖃᓄᐅᖅᓯᑎᑕᐅᕙᒋᐊᖃᖅᑯᑎᒃ.

ᒐᕙᒪᒃᑯᑦ

ᐃᓄᐃᑦ ᐅᖃᐅᓯᖓᑦ ᓄᓇᕗᒻᒥ ᐃᓚᒋᔭᐅᓂᐊᖅᐳᖅ ᐅᖃᐅᓯᐅᓗᐊᑕᓴᐅᓂᐊᕐᓗᓂ (ᖃᓪᓗᓈᑎᑐᓪᓗ ᐅᐃᕖᑎᑐᓪᓗ ᐅᖃᐅᓯᐅᓗᐊᑕᐅᖃᑕᐅᓂᐊᕐᒥᔫᒃ).

The Inuktitut-speaking characters of IBC's popular Takuginai *and the Internet, above, now perform the educational role once undertaken by missionaries such as the Rev. Don Whitbread, seen here with a Pond Inlet student in 1954*

ᐃᓄᒃᑎᑐᑦ ᐅᖃᕈᓐᓇᖅᑐᑦ ᐃᓄᖕᒍᐊᑦ ᑕᑯᓇᐃᒥ ᐃᓄᐃᑦ ᑕᑯᓐᓇᒐᒃᓴᓕᐅᕐᑎᓄᑦ ᓴᖅᑭᑕᐅᓯᒪᔪᖅ ᐊᒻᒪᓗ ᖃᕆᓴᐅᔾᔪᑦ ᖁᓖᓂ ᐊᑐᖅᑕᐅᓕᕐᐳᑦ ᐃᓕᓐᓂᐊᖅᑎᑕᐅᑎᑕᐅᓯᒪᒃᖢᑎᒃ ᑕᒪᓐᓇ ᐱᒋᐊᖅᑕᐅᓚᐅᖅᓯᒪᓪᓗᓂ ᐊᔪᕆᖅᓯᐃᔨ ᑖᓐ ᐅᐃᑦᐳᕆᑦ, ᑕᑯᔭᐅᔪᖅ ᒥᑦᑎᒪᑕᓕᖕᒥ ᐃᓕᓐᓂᐊᖅᑎᒥ ᐱᖃᑎᖃᕐᓗᓂ 1954ᒥ

Government

Inuktitut will be one of Nunavut's three official languages (English and French are the other two). What's more, Inuktitut is to be the working language of the government. For those who believe in the importance of the language, this is a laudable objective. But there will be obstacles along the way.

In the central Arctic, where many younger Inuit are much more comfortable working in English, will there be an exception to the rule of using Inuktitut, or some compromise permitted?

A second complication is that for years to come, certain specialized positions will need to be filled by skilled southerners until such skills are acquired by residents of Nunavut. If Inuktitut is to be the working language, then there must be Inuktitut instruction for non-Inuit.

Nunavut Tourism ᓄᓇᕗᑦ ᐳᓚᕋᖅᑐᓕᕆᔨᑦ

ᐅᔾᔨᕆᓴᐅᓂᖅᓴᐅᓪᓗᐊᖅᐳᕐᓕ ᐃᓄᐃᑦ ᐅᖃᐅᓯᖓᑦ ᓄᓇᕗᒃᑯᑦ ᒐᕙᒪᒃᑯᖏᑦᑕ ᐅᖃᐅᓯᓪᓗᐊᑕᕆᓂᐊᕐᒪᔾᔪᒃ. ᑕᒪᒃᑯᓄᖓ ᐅᑉᐱᕈᓱᒋᖃᖅᑐᓄᑦ ᐅᖃᐅᓯᐅᑉ ᐱᒻᒪᕆᐅᓂᖓᓂᒃ ᑐᓴᖅᐸᒍ ᑕᒪᓐᓇ ᐸᑦᑕᒃᑐᕈᔾᔨᔪᒥᓇᖅᐳᖅ. ᑭᓯᐊᓂᓗ ᐊᒻᒪᐊᖅᑯᑎᑕᖃᐅᖃᑦᑕᕐᓂᐊᖅᐳᖅ ᐊᑐᓕᖅᑎᑕᐅᓇᓱᒃᑎᓪᓗᒍ.

ᐅᐊᓕᓂᕐᒥ ᐅᓄᖅᑐᑦ ᒪᒃᑯᒃᑐᑦ ᐃᓗᐊᓃᓴᖃᕐᓂᖅᓴᐅᖓᒪᑕ ᖃᓪᓗᓇᐅᓴᖃᑦᑕᕆᐊᒃᓴᖅ ᓴᓇᕝᕕᖓᒥᖕᓂ, ᑖᒃᑯᐊ ᐃᓱᒪᒋᔭᐅᓇᔭᖅᐸᑦ ᑕᒪᓐᓇ ᐃᖅᑲᓇᐃᔭᕐᕕᖕᒥ ᐃᓄᒃᑎᑐ ᐅᖃᓪᓚᑦᑕᕆᐊᒃᓴᖅ ᐊᑐᓕᖅᑎᑕᐅᓇᓕᖅᑎᓪᓗᒍ ᐅᐸᓗᓐᓂᑦ ᖃᓄᖅᑑᕈᑕᐅᓂᐊᖅᐸ ᖃᓄᕐᑎᐊᕇᓗᒃ ᐋᖅᑭᒃᓯᒪᑎᑕᐅᔪᓐᓇᕐᓂᐊᕐᒪᖔᑦ?

ᐊᒻᕕᐊᖅᑯᑕᐅᓂᐊᖅᑐᑦ ᑐᓕᕆᖅᑰᕐᔭᖓᑦ ᐅᓇᐅᒐᖅ, ᐃᖅᑲᓇᐃᔮᑦ ᐃᓇᖏᑦ ᐊᑯᓂᐸᓗᑭᓗᒃ ᓯᓕ ᖃᓪᓗᓈᓂᖖᑖᖅᓯᒪᔪᑦ ᐃᖅᑲᓇᐃᔮᖑᔪᕆᐊᖃᕐᓂᐊᖅᑯᕐᒪᑕ ᐃᓄᒃᑑᕈᓐᓇᖅᑐᓂᒃ ᐃᓕᓯᒪᔪᕐᑲᓕᓚᐅᖅᑎᓐᓇᒍ ᓄᓇᕗᒻᒥ. ᐃᓄᐃᑦ ᐅᖃᐅᓯᖓᑦ ᐃᖅᑲᓇᐃᔭᕐᕕᖕᒥ ᐅᖃᐅᓯᓪᓗᐊᑕᕆᓴᐅᓂᐊᖅᐸᑦ ᐃᓄᒃᑎᑐᑦ ᐅᖃᕆᐅᓴᑎᑕᐅᖃᑦᑕᕆᐊᖃᕐᓂᐊᖅᐳᑦ ᐃᓄᒃᑐᑦ ᐅᖃᕈᓐᓃᖏᑦᑐᑦ.

ᑕᒪᓐᓇ ᐱᔭᕆᐊᑭᑦᑐᑯᓗᒃᔫᙱᑦᑐᖅ. ᖃᓪᓗᓇᐅᔭᖅᐸᒃᑐᑦ ᒐᕙᒪᒃᑯᓄᑦ ᐃᖅᑲᓇᐃᔭᖅᑎᖁᑎᒋᔭᐅᔪᑦ ᐅᐃᕖᑎᑐᑦ ᐃᓕᑦᑎᓪᓚᑦᑕᕐᒪᑕ. ᐅᐃᕖᓪᓗ ᐅᖃᐅᓯᖓᑦ ᐃᓕᑦᑎᕐᓂᕐᓂᖅᓴᐅᓂᖅᑕᐅᓪᓗᓂ ᐃᓄᐃᑦ ᐅᖃᐅᓯᖓᓐᓂᐅᖓᓂᑦ.

Nunatsiaq News ᓄᓇᑦᓯᐊᖅ ᐱᐅᓕᑦ

The first Anik satellite brought television to Nunavut in 1972, and the first live broadcasts to the Arctic a year later. Inuktitut will have to be used in everyday life, above, to preserve the language and the Inuit culture it nourishes

ᓯᕗᓪᓕᖅᐹ ᐊᓂᒃ ᖁᒻᒧᒃᑎᑕᐅᓯᒪᔪᖅ ᓴᖅᑭᑦᑎᓯᒪᕗᖅ ᑕᓚᕖᓴᒥᓐ ᓄᓇᕗᒻᒧ 1972ᒥ, ᐊᒻᒪᓗ ᓯᕗᓪᓕᖅᐹᖅ ᓴᖅᑮᔭᐅᑎᒋᔪᓂ ᐊᑐᕐᐸᓪᓕᐊᔪᓂ ᑕᑯᔅᓴᐅᔪᓐᓇᕐᓯᓚᐅᕐᐳᑦ ᐊᕐᕌᒍ ᐊᓂᒍᖓᓐᓇᕐᑎᓪᓗᒍ. ᐃᓄᒃᑎᑐᑦ ᐊᑐᖃᑦᑕᐊᖃᕐᓂᐊᕐᑐᖅ ᖃᐅᑕᒫᑦ ᐃᓅᓯᒃᑯ, ᖁᓛᓂ, ᑕᒪᓐᓇ ᐅᖃᐅᓯᖅ ᐊᓯᐅᖁᓇᒍ ᐊᒻᒪᓗ ᐃᓄᐃᑦ ᐃᓕᖁᓯᖏ ᐱᕙᓪᓕᐊᕐᖓᓐᓇᖁᓪᓗᒋᑦ

Verb Root	Person	Place
titiraq-	*titiraqti*	*titirarvik*
write	clerk	office
niuviq-	*niuviqti*	*niuvirvik*
trade	trader	store
ilinniaq-	*ilinniaqti*	*ilinniarvik*
learn	student	school
mumiq-	*mumiqti*	*mumirvik*
dance	dancer	dance hall

This won't be easy. Thirty-odd years of French instruction in the Canadian federal government have had mixed results at best.

One possible compromise is an increased Inuktitut flavor in the workplace, combined with a well-thought-out language training program. Inuktitut expressions would increasingly be used in the office. A growing number of non-Inuit staff would be able to communicate at a very basic level before having to fall back on English to develop their ideas, and some would eventually be able to function in the language.

Language and culture tomorrow

So here we stand, on the threshold of the new century, facing a future that holds promise and challenges. Would we have the courage to accept the offer of a glimpse of Nunavut in 2099? Would such a glimpse show us homes where Inuktitut continues to be spoken, offices where it is in common use, a lively cultural scene with literature and music expressing our way of life? In our present situation there is indeed the promise of such a future. Let us hope and work for the strength and commitment to attain it.

Alexina Kublu is an Inuk who teaches interpreters and translators at Nunavut Arctic College in Iqaluit. Mick Mallon, also from Iqaluit, is a qallunaaq who teaches Inuktitut as a Second Language.

ᐃᒻᒪᖄ ᐃᒫᒃ ᐋᖅᑭᐅᒪᓂᖅᑲᖅᑐᓕᐅᕈᓐᓇᖅᐳᑦ ᐃᓄᐃᑦ ᐅᖃᐅᓯᖓᑦ ᐃᖅᑲᓇᐃᔭᖅᑎᓄᑦ ᐃᓄᒃᑎᑐᑦ ᐊᔪᕐᓂᖅᐸᐹᖅᑐᓄᑦ ᐊᑐᖅᑕᐅᓂᖅᓴᐅᖃᑦᑕᓕᖁᔭᖅᐸᑦ ᑑᓵᔭᐅᓂᖅᓴᐅᕙᓕᕐᓗᓂ ᐊᒻᒪ ᐅᖃᓐᓇᖅᐸᕐᓃᖕᖏᑦᑐᑦ ᐋᖅᑭᒪᓂᖃᑦᑎᐊᖅᑐᒥᒃ ᐃᓕᓐᓂᐊᓚᒃᓴᓕᕈᔭᐅᓇᔭᕈᑎᒃ. ᐃᓄᒃᑎᑐᑦ ᓂᓪᓕᖅᑐᖃᐅᖅᑕᕐᓂᖅᓴᐅᓇᔭᖅᐳᖅ ᑖᒃᑯᐊ ᐊᔪᕈᓐᓕᖅᐸᓪᓕᐊᔭᐅᔪᑦ ᐊᑐᖅᑕᐅᑦᑕᕐᓂᖅᓴᐅᓇᓱᒡᓗᑎᒃ. ᐅᓄᖅᓯᕙᓪᓕᐊᓇᔭᖅᐳᑦ ᐃᓄᒃᑐᑦ ᐅᖃᕈᓐᖏᓚᐅᖅᑑᒐᓗᐊᑦ ᐃᓄᒃᑐᑦ ᐅᖃᖁᓯᖕᓂᖅᓴᐅᖃᑦᑕᓕᕐᓗᑎᒃ ᖃᓪᓗᓇᐅᔭᙵᖃᓕᓗᐅᖅᑲᖁᑎᒃ ᐃᓚᖏᓪᓗᓐᓇᓚᑦ ᐃᓄᒃᑎᑐᑦ ᐅᖃᒪᔭᖃᑦᑕᓕᕆᓐᓇᓯᓇᔭᖅᓗᑎᒃ.

ᐅᖃᐅᓯᕐᓗ ᐃᓕᖅᑯᓯᕐᓗ ᓯᕗᓂᑦᑎᓐᓂ

ᑕᕝᕙ ᒫᓐᓇᒃᑯᑦ ᒫᓕᒃᐳᒍᑦ ᓯᕗᓂᒃᓴᕗᑦ ᐊᒡᓕᖅᑐᖅᑐᖅ ᐃᓱᒪᒃᓴᖅᓯᐅᕈᑎᒋᓪᓗᑎᒍᑦ. ᒪᕿᓪᓗᐊᑕᐅᒃ ᓯᕗᓂᒃᓴᑦᑎᓐᓂ ᓄᑖᖑᓪᓗᑎᒃ ᐱᒻᒪᕆᐅᓪᓗᑎᒃᓗ. ᓄᑖᒥᒃ ᓄᓇᕐᖃᕐᓂᐊᓕᖅ. ᐊᕐᕌᒍᓪᓗ ᕼᐊᓐᓇᓚᐅᔪᑦ ᐱᒋᐊᕐᓂᐊᓕᕐᒪᑕ. ᓯᕗᓂᒃᓴᕗᑦ ᒫᓐᓇᒃ ᐃᓱᒪᒋᓪᓗᑎᒍᑦ ᓂᕆᐅᓐᓇᖅᑐᖁᑎᖃᕈᑎᒐᑦᑎᒍᑦ ᐃᓚᖕᒐᒍᓪᓗ ᑯᒃᓴᓰᓐᓇᖅᑐᖅᑕᖃᐅᕆᓪᓗᓂ. ᑕᐅᑐᙵᐊᖅᑕᖃᖅᑎᓪᓗᑕ ᓄᓇᕗᑦ ᖃᓄᐃᓕᖓᓕᖁᔭᕆᖕᒫᑦ 2099ᒥ ᑕᑯᑎᑕᐅᔪᒪᓇᔭᖅᑰᖅᐱᑕ ᖃᓄᐃᑦᑑᓪᓚᑖᖁᔭᕆᖕᒫᑦ? ᑕᑯᑎᑕᐅᓇᔭᕈᑦᑕ ᑕᑯᓇᔭᖅᑰᖅᐱᑕ ᐊᖏᕐᖁᓇᔭᐅᔪᓂ ᐃᓄᒃᑎᑐᑦ ᐅᖃᓪᓗᓐᓴᒃᑕᒃᑐᓂᒃ, ᑎᑎᖅᑲᕕᖕᓂᓗ ᐅᖃᐅᓯᓪᓗᐊᑕᕆᔭᐅᓗᓂ, ᐃᓕᖅᑯᓯᕆᔭᓇᔭᖅᐸ ᐊᑐᖅᑎᑕᐅᓗᓂ ᐅᖃᓕᒫᒐᕐᓂ ᑎᑕᐅᓯᕐᓂᓗ ᐃᒃᐱᒋᔭᑦᑎᓐᓂᒃ ᓴᖅᑭᑎᑦᑎᔪᓐᓇᕐᓗᒍ ᐃᓅᓯᕆᔭᑦᑕ ᒥᒃᓵᓄᑦ?. ᒫᓐᓇᒃᑯᑦ ᑕᐃᒪᐃᓕᖓᓕᔪᒥᓇᖅᑐᒥᒃ ᓯᕗᓂᒃᓴᖅᐳᖑᑦ. ᓂᕆᐅᓯᔭᕐᑦᑎᐊᓚᐅᖅᑕ ᐊᒃᓱᕈᕈᑎᒋᑦᑎᐊᓚᐅᕐᓚᒍᑦ ᓴᙱᓂᖅᑲᖅᑎᑕᐅᔪᒪᓪᓗᑕ ᐱᑕᖃᖁᔨᓂᖃᑦᑎᐊᕐᓗᑕᓗ ᑖᓐᓇ ᓂᕆᐅᒋᔭᒐᑦ ᑕᐃᒪᓐᓇᐅᔪᓐᓇᕐᓂᐊᖁᓪᓗᒍ.

ᐊᓕᒃᓯᓇ ᑯᑉᓗ ᐃᓕᓐᓂᐊᖅᑎᑦᑎᔨᐅᒐᖅ ᐅᖃᐅᓯᓕᕆᓂᕐᒥᒃ ᐃᓕᖅᑯᓯᕆᓂᕐᒥᓗ ᐃᓕᓐᓂᐊᖅᑕᐅᕙᒃᑐᓂᒃ ᓄᓇᕗᑦ ᓯᓚᑦᑐᖅᓴᕐᕖᐊᓂ ᐃᖃᓗᖕᓂ. ᒥᑭ ᒫᓚᓐ ᐃᖃᓗᖕᒥᐅᑕᐅᑎᒐᖅ ᐃᓄᒃᑐᑦ ᐅᖃᐅᓯᖓᑎᑦᑎᔨᐅᖃᑦᑕᖅᐳᖅ ᐃᓄᒃᑐᑦ ᐅᖃᐅᓯᖏᓐᓂᑦᑐᓄᑦ.

Graduates of Iqaluit's Inukshuk High School, light the qulliq *(seal-oil lamp). Nunavut will need more graduates, and more graduates to choose post-secondary education*
ᐊᓂᒍᐃᔪᑦ ᐃᖃᓗᐃᑦ ᐃᓄᒃᓱᒃ ᐃᓕᓐᓂᐊᕐᕕᐊᓘᐊᓂ, ᖁᓪᓕᕐᒥ ᐃᑯᒪᐃᔪᒃ. ᓄᓇᕗᑦ ᐃᓕᓐᓂᐊᕐᓂᕐᒥ ᐊᓂᒍᐃᔪᓂ ᓴᖅᑭᖏᕕᐅᒃᑲᓐᓂᕆᐊᖃᕐᓂᐊᕐᑐᑦ, ᐊᒻᒪ ᖁᑦᑎᖕᓂᖕᓴᒥᓐ ᐃᓕᓐᓂᐊᕈᒪᔪᓂᑦ

ᐅᖃᓯᐅᑉ ᑐᖕᖓᓂᐊ	ᐃᓄᒃ	ᐃᓂ
ᑎᑎᕋᖅ- ᐅᕋᐃᑦ	ᑎᑎᕋᖅᑎ ᑯᓘᒃ	ᑎᑎᕋᕖᒃ ᐋᕕᔅ
ᓂᐅᕕᖅ- ᑐᓃᑦ	ᓂᐅᕕᖅᑎ ᑐᓃᑐᕐ	ᓂᐅᕕᕖᒃ ᔅᑑᕐ
ᐃᓕᓐᓂᐊᖅ- ᓘᓐ	ᐃᓕᓐᓂᐊᖅᑎ ᔅᑑᑕᓐᑦ	ᐃᓕᓐᓂᐊᕖᒃ ᔅᑯᓪ
ᒧᒥᖅ- ᑖᓐᔅ	ᒧᒥᖅᑎ ᑖᓐᓴᕐ	ᒧᒥᕖᒃ ᑖᓐᔅ ᕼᐋᓪ

To the People of Nunavut...

Levi Barnabas
M.L.A. High Arctic

Goo Arlooktoo
M.L.A. Baffin South

Tommy Enuaraq
M.L.A. Baffin Central

Charles Dent
M.L.A. Yellowknife Frame Lake

THE PREMIER OF THE NORTHWEST TERRITORIES

HON. JAMES ANTOINE
M.L.A. NAHENDEH

April 1, 1999

On this historic occasion, my colleagues and I wish the people of Nunavut all the best for their future. Our prayers and good wishes are with you.

Today is your first in your new territory. Years of negotiation, planning and consultation have gone into making this day a reality. You have the opportunity to build your government from the ground up, to design your own programs and services to meet your needs, and to set your own priorities.

Your neighbours in the Northwest Territories have followed your progress with anticipation. Today we applaud your achievements and look forward to your accomplishments in the future.

The people of Nunavut and the NWT know the challenges that face the North in the future. I know that we can meet these challenges together, as partners and as friends.

Sincerely,

Jim Antoine

LEGISLATIVE ASSEMBLY
YELLOWKNIFE, NT
CANADA X1A 2L9
Telephone (867) 669-2311
Facsimile (867) 873-0385

Roy Erasmus
M.L.A. Yellowknife North

Steven Kakfwi
M.L.A. Sahtu

Mark Evaloarjuk
M.L.A. Amittuq

Kelvin Ng
M.L.A. Kitikmeot

Samuel Gargan
M.L.A. Deh Cho

Kevin O'Brien
M.L.A. Kivallivik

Floyd Roland
M.L.A. Inuvik

Seamus Henry
M.L.A. Yellowknife South

Jane Groenewegen
M.L.A. Hay River

Edward Picco
M.L.A. Iqaluit

Manitok Thompson
M.L.A. Aivilik

David Krutko
M.L.A. Mackenzie Delta

Don Morin
M.L.A. Tu Nedhe

John Ningark
M.L.A. Natilikmiot

Michael Miltenberger
M.L.A. Thebacha

Jake Ootes
M.L.A. Yellowknife Centre

James Rabesca
M.L.A. North Slave

Vince Steen
M.L.A. Nunakput

John Todd
M.L.A. Keewatin Central

ᓄᓇᕗᑦ ᐃᓄᒃᑯᓐᓂᑦ...

ᓂᕋᐃ ᐸᓇᐸᐢ
ᒪᓕᒐᓕᐅᕐᑎ ᖁᑦᑎᒃᑐᕐᒥᐅ

ᒍ ᐋᕐᓗᒃᑐ
ᒪᓕᒐᓕᐅᕐᑎ ᕿᑭᖅᑖᓗᐸ ᓂᒋᐊᓄᑦ

ᑖᒥ ᐃᓄᐊᕋᖅ
ᒪᓕᒐᓕᐅᕐᑎ ᕿᑭᖅᑖᓗᐸ ᕿᑎᐊᓄᑦ

ᔅᓯ ᑎᐊᓐᑦ
ᒪᓕᒐᓕᐅᕐᑎ ᔭᓗᓇᐃᑦ ᑲᓛᒃ ᓚᐃᒃᒧᓐ

ᕈᐊᐃ ᐃᕌᓯᔅ
ᒪᓕᒐᓕᐅᕐᑎ ᔭᓗᓇᐃᑦ ᐅᐊᖕᓇᖓᓄᑦ

ᓯᑏᕙᓐ ᑳᒃᑲᐃ
ᒪᓕᒐᓕᐅᕐᑎ ᔅᑑᒧᓐ

ᖁᓚ ᐃᑦᑐᓗᐊᕐᔪᒃ
ᒪᓕᒐᓕᐅᕐᑎ ᐊᒥᑦᑐᕐᒧᑦ

ᑭᐊᕕᓐ ᐅ
ᒪᓕᒐᓕᐅᕐᑎ ᕿᑎᕐᒥᐅᑦᓄᑦ

ᓴᒥᐅᑦ ᒫᓚᓐ
ᒪᓕᒐᓕᐅᕐᑎ ᑕ ᐹᒧᓐ

ᑭᐊᕕᓐ ᐅᑦᑐᕋᐃᐊᓐ
ᒪᓕᒐᓕᐅᕐᑎ ᑭᐸᓪᓚᕕᒃᒧᓐ

ᖁᓗᐊᐃᑦ ᐹᓛᓐᑦ
ᒪᓕᒐᓕᐅᕐᑎ ᐃᓅᕕᖕᒧᓐ

ᐹᒥᔅ ᕼᐊᓐᓇ
ᒪᓕᒐᓕᐅᕐᑎ ᔭᓗᓇᐃᑦ ᓂᒋᐊᓄᑦ

ᔭᐃᓐ ᒍᕈᓇᕕᓚᓐ
ᒪᓕᒐᓕᐅᕐᑎ ᕼᐊᐃ ᕆᕗᒧᓐ

ᐋᑐᐊᖅ ᐋᒍ
ᒪᓕᒐᓕᐅᕐᑎ ᐃᖃᓗᖕᓄᑦ

ᒪᓅᓯᐅ ᑖᐅᔪᐃ
ᒪᓕᒐᓕᐅᕐᑎ ᐊᐃᕕᓕᒃᒧᓐ

ᑕᐃᕕᑦ ᑯᕆᑯ
ᒪᓕᒐᓕᐅᕐᑎ ᒪᒃᑫᓐᓯ ᑎᐊᑕᒧᓐ

ᑖᓐ ᒍᓚᓐ
ᒪᓕᒐᓕᐅᕐᑎ ᑑ ᓂᑎᒧᓐ

ᔮᓐ ᓂᖕᖓᒃ
ᒪᓕᒐᓕᐅᕐᑎ ᓇᑦᑎᓕᒃᒥᐅᓄᑦ

ᒪᐃᑯᑦ ᒥᐊᑦᓐᐳᒍ
ᒪᓕᒐᓕᐅᕐᑎ ᑕᑉᐸᔅᓵᒧᓐ

ᔭᐃᒃ ᐆᑦᔅ
ᒪᓕᒐᓕᐅᕐᑎ ᔭᓗᓇᐃᑦ ᕿᑎᐊᓄᑦ

ᔭᐃᓪᔅ ᕋᐱᒃ
ᒪᓕᒐᓕᐅᕐᑎ ᓄᐊᑦ ᓯᓚᐃᕕᒧᓐ

ᕕᓐᔅ ᓯᑏᓐ
ᒪᓕᒐᓕᐅᕐᑎ ᓄᓇᒃᐳᑦᒧᓐ

ᔭᓐ ᑖᑦ
ᒪᓕᒐᓕᐅᕐᑎ ᕿᑫᓪᓗᖅ ᕿᑎᐊᓄᑦ

THE PREMIER OF THE NORTHWEST TERRITORIES

ᔭᐃᒥᓯ ᐋᓐᑐᐊᓐ
ᒪᓕᒐᓕᐅᕐᑎ ᓇᕼᐊᓐᓂᒧᓐ

ᐄᐳᕈ 1, 1999

ᐅᑦᑐᒥ ᐱᓕᒪᓇᐅᑎᑦᑐᒍ, ᐱᓕᕆᖃᑎᒋᔭᒃᑕᒃᑲᓗ ᐅᕙᖕᓕᓗ ᐃᓅᖕᓂ ᓄᓇᕗᒥ ᓂᕈᐅᖕᓂᖃᑦᑎᐊᕐᓂᕐᒥ ᓂᕈᐅᑦᑎᐊᕐᑯᕙᒍᑦ ᐊᑲᐅᔪᒥᓐ ᓯᕗᓂᒃᓴᒥᓐ. ᑐᒃᓯᐊᕐᓂᑦᑎᒍ ᐊᒻᒪ ᐃᓯᒪᕕᒋᕙᑦᑎᒋᑦ.

ᐅᑦᑐᒥ ᓯᕗᓪᓕᕐᐹᖑᔪᖕᒪᓐ ᓄᓇᒥᓕᕐᑕᔅᓯᓐᓂ. ᐊᕐᖁᒍᓚᔅᖕᓂ ᐋᔩᕈᑎᑦ, ᐋᖅᑭᒃᓯᐃᓃᑦ ᐊᒻᒪᓗ ᐅᖃᓕᒫᖅᑎᖅᖅᓃ ᐊᓂᒍᕐᐳᑦ ᐅᓇ ᐅᑦᑐᖅ ᓵᖅᑭᒻᒪᓇᒃᑎᑦᑐᒍ. ᐱᕕᖃᓕᕐᐳᔪ ᕼᐅᒪᔅᓯᓐᓂ ᐊᒻᒪᓗ ᐱᓕᕆᐊᒃᓴᔅᓯᓐᓂ ᐋᖅᑭᒃᓯᐃᓅᓐ ᐱᒋᐊᕐᓂᖅᑕᓂᑦ ᑕᑉᐸᐅᖕᖓ, ᐋᖅᑭᒃᓯᐃᒍᓐᓇᕐᓯᑦᑐᓯ ᐱᓕᕆᐊᒃᓴᔅᓯᓐᓂ ᐊᒻᒪ ᐱᔾᔪᑎᖃᐅᑎᒃᓴᔅᓯᓐᓂᑦ ᑕᒪᓐᓇ ᐊᑐᕈᒪᔭᔅᓯ ᑐᕌᖓᓇᓱᒃᑐᓯᐅᒃ. ᑕᐅᑐᐃᓐᓇᕐᐳᑦ. ᐅᑦᑐᒥ ᓯᕗᓂᓯᓐᓂ ᓂᕈᐅᒃᐳᒍᑦ ᓯᕗᓂᔅᓯᓐᓂ ᖃᓂᒋᔭᔅᓯᓐᓂ ᓄᓇᖃᕐᑐᑦ ᓄᓇᑦᓯᐊᕐᒥ ᐱᓕᕆᓂᓯᓐᓂ ᐊᒻᒪᓗ ᓵᖅᑭᑎᒻᒪᓇᒃᑎᑦᑐᓯᐅᒃ ᐱᒃᑯᕆᐅᑎᒋᑦ ᐱᓇᓱᒃᑕᔪ ᐋᓐᓂᖃᖅᑎᐊᕐᒍᑦᑐᒍ.

ᐃᓄᐃᑦ ᓄᓇᕗᒥ ᐊᒻᒪᓗ ᓄᓇᑦᓯᐊᕐᒥ ᖃᐅᔨᒪᔪᑦ ᐱᓇᓱᒋᐊᖃᖅᓯᐊᕐᑕᕐᓂᓐᓂᑦ ᐱᓇᓱᖕᓂᐊᕐᑕᔪ ᐊᑐᕐᓇᕐᓂᐊᕐᑎᒍᑦ, ᑲᑐᔾᔨᖃᑎᒌᖕᓂᒃᑯᑦ ᐊᒻᒪ ᓯᕗᓂᒃᓴᒧᓐ. ᖃᐅᔨᒪᒍᖕᓚ ᑲᑐᔾᔨᓗᑕ ᑕᒪᓐᓇ ᐊᑐᕐᓇᕐᓂᐊᕐᑎᒍᑦ, ᑲᑐᔾᔨᖃᑎᒌᖕᓂᒃᑯᑦ ᐱᖃᓐᓇᕇᖕᓂᒃᑯᑦ.

ᐃᓚᓐᓇᕆᔭᐃ,

ᔩᒻ ᐋᓐᑐᐊᓐ

LEGISLATIVE ASSEMBLY
YELLOWKNIFE, NT
CANADA X1A 2L9
Telephone (867) 669-2311
Facsimile (867) 873-0385

ᐊᖓᔪᖅᑳᒪᓂᐅᑉ ᐅᖃᐅᓯᖏᑦ

MOT DU PRÉSIDENT

CHAIRMAN'S MESSAGE

ᑲᑎᕕᒃ ᓄᓇᓕᓕᒫᑦ ᑲᕙᒪᖓᑕ ᑲᑎᒪᔨᖏᓐᓂ ᐱᒍᑦᔨᓗᖓ, ᐅᖃᕈᒪᔪᖓ ᐅᐱᒍᓱᑦᔨᓂᕗᓐᓂᒃ ᐃᓅᓐᓂ ᐱᕋᖅᑎᓯᖃᑕᐅᓯᒪᔪᓂᒃ ᓄᓇᕗᒥᒃ. ᓂᕆᐅᑉᐳᒍᑦ ᐱᓇᓱᖃᑎᒌᖃᑦᑕᓂᐊᖅᓂᑎᓐᓂ ᓯᕗᓂᑦᓴᑎᓐᓂ.

ᔮᓂ ᐋᑕᒥ
ᐊᖓᔪᖅᑳᖓ

Au nom du Conseil de l'Administration régionale Kativik, j'aimerais féliciter tous ceux et celles qui ont participé à la création du Nunavut. Nous nous réjouissons à la perspective de travailler en collaboration avec votre région.

Le président,
Johnny N. Adams

On behalf of the Council of the Kativik Regional Government, I would like to congratulate everyone who has contributed to the creation of Nunavut. We look forward to future co-operation between our two regions.

Johnny N. Adams
Chairman

ᑲᑎᕕᒃ ᓄᓇᓕᓕᒫᑦ ᑲᕙᒪᖓ
Administration régionale KATIVIK Regional Government

ᑐᓴᒐᒃᓴᖅ ᓴᒃᑯ ᐱᕈᒃᓴᐃᖕᕕᒃ ᑯᐊᐳᕇᓴᖕᑯ ᑲᑎᒪᔨᖏᓐᓂᑦ

A Message from the Sakku Investments Corporation Board of Directors

ᐄᐳᕆ 1, 1999ᒥ, ᐊᕐᖀᒍᓄ ᐊᕿᑎ ᐅᖓᑖᓂ ᐋᔾᔭᑲᑖᓪᓚᓚᐅᕐᓱᑎ, ᓄᓇᕗᒻᒥ ᐃᒻᒥᒃᑰᕐᑐᖅ ᐊᕕᒃᓯᒪᓂᒃᑯ ᓴᕿᑦᑕᓇᓚᐄᖕᒪᓐ. ᑖᒃᑯᐊ ᐊᕐᖀᒍ ᐃᓗᐊᓂ, ᐃᓄᐃᑦ ᑭᖕᒐᕐᑐᐃᔾᔨᑦ ᐱᖓᓱᓂ ᐊᕕᒃᓯᒪᓂᑰᕐᑐᑦ ᐊᒃᓱᕈᕐᕋᑦᑕᓚᐅᕐᐳᑦ ᓴᖅᑭᑦᑎᒐᓱᒃᓱᑎᒃ ᐊᖏᓛᒥᓐ ᓄᓇᑖᕐᓂᕐᔪᓐ ᐊᖏᕈᑎᒥ ᑲᓇᑕᒥᓐ.

ᑭᖕᒐᕐᑐᐃᓪᓗᑎᒃ ᐃᓄᖕᓂ ᑭᕙᓪᓕᕐᒥᐅᑕᕐᓂ, ᓴᒃᑯ ᐱᕈᒃᓴᐃᖕᕕᒃ ᑯᐊᐳᕇᓴᖕᑯ ᐃᓕᓴᕐᓯᕙᓪᒪᖕᒪᑕ ᓯᕗᓕᐅᕐᑎᑦᑕ ᐊᒃᓱᕈᕐᓂᕋᖅᑦᑕᓚᐅᕐᑕᖏᓐᓂᑦ, ᐊᒻᒪᓗ ᐱᑯᒋᕙᓪᓗᑎᒍ ᐃᓄᐃᑦ ᓄᓇᕗᒻᒥ.

ᓴᒃᑯ ᐸᐸᑦᑎᔨᑦ ᑯᐊᐳᕇᓴᖕᑯ ᐱᓇᓱᒃᐳᑦ ᐃᓅᐊᕐᑐᒃᑰᕐᑐᒥᓐ ᐱᕙᓪᓕᐊᓕᓇᓂᒃᒥᓐ ᑭᕙᓪᓕᐅᒃ ᐃᓗᐊᓂ. ᓯᕗᓂᒃᓴᕗᑦ ᐱᕕᖅᑲᖅᑎᑦᑎᓚᐄᕗᑦ ᐃᖅᑲᓇᐃᔭᒃᓴᓂᑦ ᒐᕙᒪᒃᑯᓐᓂ ᐊᒻᒪᓗ ᐃᒻᒥᒍᕐᑐᓂᑦ ᐃᓄᖕᓄᑦ. ᑐᓐᖓᓱᒃᑎᑦᑎᕗᒍᑦ ᑭᒃᑯᓕᒫᓂᑦ ᐃᓚᐅᕐᑯᔨᑦᑐᑕ ᑕᒫᓂ ᐊᑐᕐᓂᐊᓕᕐᑐᒥᓐ.

ᐅᑯᓄᖓᓕ ᓂᕈᐊᕐᑕᐅᓵᕐᑐᕕᓂᕐᓄᑦ ᑭᖕᒐᕐᑐᐃᔭᐅᓂᐊᕐᑐᓄᑦ ᒪᓕᒐᓕᐅᕐᕕᐅᓂᐊᓕᕐᑐᒥ ᓄᓇᕗᒻᒥ, ᐱᒃᑯᓕᕐᑲᑎᕐᑲᕈᒪᒋᕗᒍᑦ, ᐊᒻᒪᓗ ᓯᕗᓂᑦᑎᓐᓂ ᐱᓕᕆᕐᑲᑎᒋᔪᒪᓪᓗᑎᒍ.

On April 1, 1999, after more than 20 years of negotiations, the territory of Nunavut will become a reality. Over this period of time, Inuit representatives from all three regions of Nunavut have devoted much of their effort to bring about the largest land claims settlement in Canadian history.

On behalf of the people of the Kivalliq Region, Sakku Investments Corporation wishes to recognize the efforts of our leaders, and we congratulate the people of Nunavut.

Sakku Investments Corporation is dedicated to building a healthy and viable economy for the Kivalliq Region. The future will provide many opportunities for jobs in government and the private sector for Inuit. We invite everyone to participate in this new era.

To the newly elected representatives in the legislative assembly of Nunavut, we offer our congratulations, and we look forward to working with you in the future.

ᔫ ᖃᓗᔾᔭᖅ, ᐃᓯᒪᑕᖅ Joe Kaludjak, President
ᓴᒃᑯ ᐱᕈᒃᓴᐃᖕᕕᒃ ᑯᐊᐳᕇᓴᖕ Sakku Investments Corporation

Sakku Investments Corporation
ᓴᒃᑯ ᐱᕈᒃᓴᐃᖕᕕᒃ ᑯᐊᐳᕇᓴᖕ

Our new territory, Nunavut,

gives an opportunity for all residents to participate fully in a public government and create a responsible system close to the people. The new territorial government will be able to react positively to the unique needs and requirements of the people of Nunavut while respecting and incorporating Inuit values and traditional ways.

Choosing Inuktitut to be one of the working languages of the new territory will enable unilingual Inuit to participate more actively in the process and ensure the future of our language.

The eyes of the world are on Nunavut and the success story it has become. We can all be proud of our accomplishments to date.

I welcome the chance to work with the residents of Nunavut as we are presented with many new challenges and opportunities. Let us all rise to the occasion together.

ᓄᓇᑖᕆᓂᐊᓕᕐᑕᕗᑦ, ᓄᓇᕗᑦ,

ᓄᓇᑖᕆᓂᐊᓕᕐᑕᕗᑦ, ᓄᓇᕗᑦ, ᐱᕕᖃᕐᑎᑦᑎᓕᕐᒪᓐ ᓄᓇᖃᕐᑐᓕᒫᓂᑦ ᒐᕙᒪᐅᓂᐊᕐᑐᒥᓐ ᐋᖅᑭᒃᓯᐅᖃᑕᐅᓂᕐᒥ ᐊᒻᒪᓗ ᐱᓕᕆᓂᖃᕐᓗᑎᒃ ᐃᓄᙵ ᐊᒃᑐᐊᔪᓂᑦ. ᓄᑖᖅ ᐊᕕᒃᑐᕐᓯᒪᓂᒃᑯ ᒐᕙᒪᐅᓂᐊᓕᕐᑐᑦ ᐱᓕᕆᔾᓇᕐᓂᐊᕐᐳᑦ ᐃᓄᐃᑦ ᐱᔪᓇᐊᖃᕐᑕᕐᒋᓐᓂᑦ ᐊᑐᓇᐊᖃᕐᑕᕐᒋᑦᑎᒍᓪᓗ ᓄᓇᕗᒥ ᑕᒪᒃᑯᐊ ᐃᓄᙵᓐ ᐱᒻᒪᕆᐅᔪᑦ ᐃᓅᓯᕐᒧᓐ ᐃᓕᖁᓯᕐᒨᓗ ᐃᓯᒪᒋᔭᐅᓗᑎᒃ.

ᐃᓄᒃᑎᑐᑦ ᐅᖃᐅᓯᖅ ᐊᑐᕐᑕᐅᖃᑕᐅᓂᐊᕐᑎᓪᓗᒍ ᐃᖅᑲᓇᐃᔭᕐᓂᒃᑯ ᐃᓄᒃᑎᑐᑐᐃᓐᓇ ᐅᖃᓪᓚᒃᑐᓂᑦ ᐃᓚᐅᑎᑦᑎᑦᑎᐊᓂᐊᕐᑐᑦ ᐱᓕᕆᓂᒃᑯ ᐊᒻᒪᓗ ᐅᖃᐅᓯᖅ ᓯᕗᓂᑦᑎᓐᓄ ᐋᖅᑭᒃᓯᒪᑎᑕᐅᓗᓂ.

ᓄᓇᕐᔪᐊᓕᒫᒥᐅᑕᑦ ᑕᐅᑐᙵᑕ ᓄᓇᕘᒥᓐ ᐊᒻᒪᓗ ᑕᒪᓐᓇ ᐊᓂᒍᐃᑦᑎᐊᕐᓂᖓ ᑕᐅᑐᒃᑕᐅᒋᓪᓗᓂ. ᐅᕙᑦᑎᓐᓂ ᐱᒃᑯᒋᔾᓇᒻᒪᕆᒃᐳᒍᑦ ᐱᓕᕆᐊᕆᔭᑦᑎᓐᓂ ᒫᓐᓇᒧᓐ. ᑐᓐᖓᓱᒃᑎᑦᑎᕗᖓ ᐱᕕᖃᕐᓂᕐᒥᓐ ᐱᓕᕆᖃᑎᒋᙳᓂᒃᑯ ᐊᒃᓯᕈᕐᓇᕐᑐᓂ ᐱᓕᕆᐊᒃᓴᖃᕐᑎᓪᓗᑕ ᐱᕕᓴᓂᓪᓗ. ᐊᑏ ᑕᒪᑦᑕ ᑕᒪᑐᒥᖓ ᖁᕙᕆᐊᕐᕕᖃᓗᑦᑕ ᐊᑕᐅᑦᑎᒃᑯᑦ.

Nancy Karetak-Lindell ᓈᓐᓯ ᖃᕆᑕᖅ-ᓕᓐᑎᐅ

Member of Parliament ᑲᓇᑕᒥ ᒪᓕᒐᓕᐅᖅᑎᐅᖃᑕᐅᔪᖅ

1 800 531-4982

HUNTERS AND HIGH FINANCE
ᐊᖑᓇᓱᒃᑏᑦ ᐊᒻᒪᓗ ᐊᑭᑐᔪᑦ

Nunavut must develop a thriving, modern economy to support the political and cultural aspirations of its people. Understanding today's economy and how the challenge will be met requires a look back — way back

ᓄᓇᕗᑦ ᐃᒪᐃᒋᐊᓕᒃ ᓯᕗᒻᒧᐊᖅᑎᑎᓗᓂ ᐃᖏᕐᕋᑦᑎᐊᖅᑐᒥᒃ, ᓄᑖᖑᖅᑐᒥᒃ ᑮᓇᐅᔭᓕᕆᓂᕐᒥᒃ ᐃᑲᔪᖅᑕᐅᖁᓪᓗᒋᑦ ᐃᓄᐃᑦ ᒐᕙᒪᓕᕆᓂᖏᑦ ᐊᒻᒪᓗ ᐃᓕᖅᑯᓯᑎᒍᑦ ᐸᐸᑦᑐᒪᔭᖏᑦ. ᐅᓪᓗᒥᐅᔪᖅ ᑐᑭᓯᒪᔭᐅᓂᖓ ᑮᓇᐅᔭᐃᑦ ᐃᖏᕋᖅᑲᓂᖏᓐᓂᒃ ᐊᒻᒪᓗ ᖃᓄᖅ ᑕᒪᓐᓇ ᐊᐳᖅᑕᐅᑦᑎᐊᕈᓐᓇᕐᒪᖔᑦ ᑭᖑᒧᑦ ᕿᒥᕐᕈᑕᐅᒋᐊᓕᒃ - ᑭᖑᒻᒧᒻᒪᕆᒃ

Wilkinson/NWT Archives; oval inset: Nunavut Tourism

By Kenn Harper

The social and economic unit for pre-contact Inuit was the camp, which usually meant the extended family. Each camp was held together by a strong-willed individual: a camp boss. Complex rules determined the sharing of the game, for sharing was important for survival. Alliances were formed through hunting partnerships and strategic marriages of children — the improvident hunter survived, but barely, and often on the largesse of an extended family.

Wider trade relationships also existed. Meteoric iron was traded from group to group. Driftwood, and later wood from the wrecks of exploration and whaling ships, was a valuable commodity for coastal dwellers trading with Inuit farther inland. In the southern Keewatin (now Kivalliq), both trade and skirmishes occurred with Chipewyan and Cree from the subarctic forest, while Inuit of the western Kitikmeot traded with Dene of the Mackenzie Valley.

Whalers and traders

The seasonal arrival of whalers from Europe and America, beginning in the early 1800s, brought with it a different kind of trade, and radical changes to the lives of many coastal Inuit. The Europeans brought foreign objects — guns, bullets, tea, cloth — that made life easier, yet which also brought a dependence on the white man's return.

Arctic Co-operatives Ltd. ᐃᓚᖓᑦ

ᑎᑎᕋᖅᑐᖅ ᑭᓐ ᕼᐋᐳᕐ

ᐃᓕᖅᑯᓯᒧᑦ ᐃᓅᓯᒧᓪᓗ ᓱᓇᑕᖃᕐᓇᕐᓂᕐᒧᓪᓗ ᑐᙵᓂᓇᔭᐅᓚᐅᖅᑐᖅ ᐃᓄᐃᑦ ᐃᓅᓯᖕᒋᓐᓂ ᖃᓪᓗᓈᑦ ᑎᑭᓚᐅᙱᑎᓪᓗᒋᑦ ᓱᓕ ᐅᓇᐅᓚᐅᖅᑐᖅ ᓄᓇᖅᑲᑎᒌᖕᒍᔪᑦ ᐃᓚᒌᖕᓂᖕᒋᑦ. ᓄᓇᖅᑲᑎᒌᒃᑐᐃᑦ ᐊᐅᓚᑕᐅᓪᓗᑎᒃ ᐱᓯᑎᒧᑦ: ᓄᓇᓕᐅᔪᒥ ᐃᓯᒪᑕᕐᒧᑦ. ᒪᓕᒃᓗᑎᒃ ᓴᓇᕐᑲᑎᒌᖕᓂᕐᒥᒃ ᐊᒥᖅᑳᕐᑲᑎᒌᖕᓂᕐᒥᓪᓗ ᐱᑕᖑᔪᔪᓂᒃ, ᑕᒪᓐᓇ ᐊᑐᒪᓇᓚᐅᖅᑐᖅ ᐃᓄᐃᑦ ᐊᓐᓇᐅᒪᔪᓐᓇᕐᓂᖏᓐᓄᑦ. ᑕᐱᓅᒃᓗᑎᒃ ᐊᖑᓇᓯᖃᑎᒌᑦ ᐊᒻᒪᓗ ᓄᑕᖅᑲᖏᑦ ᓄᓕᐊᓇᕐᑯᔭᐅᔪᓂᒃ ᐅᐃᒋᖁᔭᐅᔪᓂᒃ ᑲᑎᖃᑕᖅᑎᓪᓗᒋᑦ. ᑖᒃᑯᐊ ᒪᖃᐃᒍᓇᕐᑎᐊᓐᖏᑦᑐᑦ ᐃᑲᔪᖅᑕᐅᓂᒃᑯᑦ ᐃᓅᕙᓚᐅᖅᑐᑦ, ᐄᑭᓘᓗᐊᖅ, ᐊᒻᒪᓗ ᐱᔭᓐᓇᖃᑦᑕᖅᑕᒥᖕᓂᑦ ᐃᓚᒥᖕᓂᑦ.

ᓂᐅᕕᖃᑦᑕᐅᑎᔪᑦ ᐅᖓᓯᖕᓂᖅᓴᒧᑦ ᐱᑕᖃᓚᐅᕐᒥᔪᑦ. ᓴᕕᒃᓴᖅ ᓯᑎᔪᖅ ᐊᑐᖅᑕᐅᕙᓚᐅᖅᑐᖅ ᐃᓚᒌᓄᑦ ᐊᔾᔨᒌᖑᖏᑦᑐᓄᑦ. ᕿᔪᐃᑦ, ᐊᒻᒪᓗ ᑭᖑᓂᐊᒍᑦ ᓇᒡᕚᖅᑕᐃᑦ ᕿᔪᐃᑦ ᕿᓂᖅᑎᕝᕕᓂᕐᓂᑦ ᐊᒻᒪᓗ ᐊᕐᕕᓂᐊᖅᑐᓂᑦ, ᐊᑐᖅᑕᐅᒪᓂᒃᐸᓚᐅᖅᑐᖅ. ᐃᓄᖕᓄᑦ ᐊᑐᖅᑕᐅᓗᓂ ᑕᓇᐅᕐᒥᐅᑕᓄᑦ ᓂᐅᕕᕆᑕᐅᑦᑕᖅᓗᓂ ᐃᓄᖕᓂᑦ ᓄᓇᐃᓐᓇᕐᒥᐅᑕᓂᑦ. ᑭᕙᓪᓕᐅᑉ ᐱᖓᓐᓇᖓᓂ, ᓂᐅᕕᖃᑎᖃᖅᐸᓚᐅᖅᑐᑦ ᐅᓇᑕᖃᑦᑕᖅᓱᑎᒡᓗ ᐅᓇᓕᖕᓂᒃ (Chipewyan) ᐊᒻᒪᓗ ᐃᖅᑭᓕᕐᓂᒃ (Cree) ᐅᑭᐅᖅᑕᖅᑐᑉ ᖃᓂᒋᔭᖓᓂᒥᐅᓂᒃ ᓇᐸᖅᑐᓕᖕᒥ. ᐊᒻᒪᓗ ᐃᓄᐃᑦ ᐅᐊᓕᓂᕐᒥ ᕿᑎᕐᒥᐅᑦ ᓂᐅᕕᖃᑦᑕᐅᑎᕚᒃᑎᓪᓗᒋᑦ ᐃᖅᑭᓕᕐᓂᒃ ᐅᐊᓕᓂᐅᑉ ᓇᖅᓴᖓᓂ (Mackenzie Valley).

ᐊᕐᕕᕐᓂᐊᖅᑎᑦ ᓂᐅᕕᖅᑎᓪᓗ

ᐊᕐᕌᒍᑉ ᐃᓚᖓᓂ ᑎᑭᑦᑕᕐᓂᖏᑦ ᒪᓕᒃᓗᒋᑦ ᐊᕐᕕᕐᓂᐊᖅᑎᑦ ᑕᓇᐅᑉ ᐊᑭᐊᓂᑦ ᐊᒻᒪᓗ ᐊᒥᐊᓕᒃᑳᓂᑦ, ᐱᒋᐊᓚᐅᖅᑐᑦ 1800ᓂ, ᐊᒻᒪᓗ ᐊᔾᔨᒋᔭᐅᓐᖏᑦᑐᒥᒃ ᓂᐅᕕᖃᑦᑎᓕᓴᓕᖅᓗᑎᒃ. ᑕᒪᓐᓇ ᐊᒃᓯᐊᓗᒃ ᐊᓯᔾᔨᕈᑕᐅᓚᐅᖅᑐᖅ ᐃᓅᓯᖓᔭᐅᔪᓄᑦ ᑕᓇᐅᕐᒥᐅᑕᐅᔪᓄᑦ ᐃᓄᖕᓄᑦ. ᑕᓇᐅᑉ ᐊᑭᐊᓂᒥᐅᑦ ᑎᑭᑉᐸᓕᐊᔪᑦ ᓄᑖᓂᒃ ᓱᓇᒃᑯᑎᓂᒃ ᑎᑭᑎᑎᓚᐅᕐᓂᖏᑦ ᐱᔾᔪᑕᐅᓪᓗᓂ – ᖁᑭᐅᑎᓂᒃ, ᖃᔪᓂᒃ, ᑏᒥᒃ, ᓄᕕᒃᓴᔭᓂᒃ – ᐃᓅᓯᕐᒧᑦ ᐃᑲᔪᕈᑕᐅᓪᓗᑎᒃ ᐊᔪᕐᓇᖕᖏᓐᓂᖅᓴᕈᖅᑕᐅᓪᓗᓂ. ᑭᓯᐊᓂᓕ ᖃᓪᓗᓈᓄᑦ ᐃᑲᔪᖅᑕᐅᕆᐊᖃᓕᕐᓂᕐᒥᒃ ᓄᐃᑐᑎᖃᓚᐅᕐᒪᑦ ᐅᑎᖃᑦᑕᓇᐊᖃᓕᖅᑎᓪᓗᒋᑦ ᐅᑕᖅᑭᔪᐃᕙᒃᓗᑎᒃ.

ᑭᖑᓂᖓᒍᑦ ᑎᑭᓴᖅᑕᐅᔪᓄᑦ ᐅᑭᐅᖅᑕᖅᑐᒥ ᐃᓅᓯᖓᔪᐃᓯᒪᓕᖅᑐᖅ. ᑕᒪᓐᓇᓗ ᐃᑲᔫᓯᐊᓂᖓᖃᕐᓂᖅ ᐱᕙᓪᓕᐊᓪᓗᓂ ᐊᕐᕕᕐᓂᐊᖅᑎᑦ ᓄᓇᓕᖃᓕᖅᑎᓪᓗᒋᑦ ᓄᓇᓕᒋᔭᐅᔪᓂ ᓵᕐᓗ ᐸᕐᓂᖅᑰᕐᒥᑎᑐᑦ. ᐊᒥᓱᑦ ᐃᓄᐃᑦ ᕿᒪᐃᓚᐅᖅᑐᑦ ᓄᓇᒋᔭᖅᑲᕐᒥᖕᓂᒃ ᐊᒻᒪᓗ

The evolution of Nunavut commerce – the Apex Hudson's Bay Co. store in June 1955, left, and Co-op manager Isaac Gullage presiding over the grand opening of Igloolik's newest supermarket, December 1998

ᐊᓯᖏᕐᑯᕐᐸᓪᓕᐊᓂᖅ ᐱᕙᓪᓕᐊᓂᐅᔪᖅ ᓄᓇᕗᒻᒥ – ᓂᐊᖁᓐᖑᐹ ᓂᐅᕕᕐᕕᕕᓂᖓ ᔫᓐ 1955, ᓴᐅᒥᐊᓂ, ᑯᐊᐸᒃᑯ ᐊᖓᔪᖅᑳᖓ ᐊᐃᓴᒃ ᒐᓚᔾ ᑲᒪᔨᐅᒐᖅ ᐃᒡᓗᓕᖕᒥ ᓄᑖᖑᓛᒥ ᓂᕿᑖᖅᕕᐊᕐᑲᑦᑕᕐᓂᐊᕐᑐᒥᓐ, ᑎᓯᐱᓂ 1998

> "We stressed that we're in a very high-cost area. In other agreements, a cap is placed on resource royalty provisions when the standard of living of an aboriginal group becomes equal to the general population of Canada. In our situation . . . there's no cap."
>
> – Paul Okalik, an assistant chief negotiator for Inuit on the land claim

Wilkinson/NWT Archives ᐅᐊᑭᓐᓴᓐ/ᓄᓇᑦᓯᐊᕐᒥ ᑉᐸᑕᓪᓗᐊ

The Hudson's Bay Co.

Dependence on imports has been a hallmark of northern life ever since. Dependence increased when whalers established permanent shore stations in communities such as Pangnirtung. Many Inuit abandoned traditional camp life and congregated near the shore stations as paid labor. This was a cashless society, and Inuit were paid in trade goods. To this day in the Baffin Region (Qikiqtaaluk), the Inuktitut word for Saturday is *sivataaqvik* — the time when you get your biscuits.

It was once again a mixed blessing for the Inuit that independent traders quickly filled the void when bowhead stocks declined in the late 1800s. The traders expected the Inuit to hunt, and to trade the results of that hunt with them, usually for the same motley assortment of trade goods that the whalers had provided. The object of the hunt was traditional game — seal for their skins, walrus for their hides and tusks, narwhal for their tusks — and the Inuit kept the meat. The traders discouraged Inuit from living in large communities: effective hunting was best done over a wide geographic area. Inuit middlemen arose to trade with those Inuit who were far removed from trading posts. Among these were Stephen Angulaalik in the Kitikmeot, Kanaaka in southern Baffin, and Ilatnaaq in the northern Keewatin.

The reign of the independent traders was short. In the early 1900s, the Hudson's Bay Co. (HBC) established its own posts throughout the Arctic, indenturing men to hunt exclusively for them for five-year periods. By the 1930s, when fur prices on world markets were high, the trapping of white foxes brought relative affluence to many Inuit.

During these years, a number of initiatives were introduced, usually by the HBC, to help some Inuit become more self-sufficient. There was boatbuilding in Kimmirut and southern Hudson Bay, and fox-farming in Pangnirtung. But the Inuit who benefited from these efforts were few: they were the *Kabloonamiut* — the settlement Inuit, as the anthropologist Vallee called them. Most Inuit still lived in camps, and the Inuit of the camps lived hard lives indeed.

continued on page 93

ᑲᑎᑦᑕᓕᖅᑐᑎᒃ ᓄᓇᖁᑎᓕᔾᔪᑦ ᖃᓂᒋᔭᖕᒋᓐᓂ ᐃᖅᑲᓇᐃᔭᖅᑎᐅᓪᓗᑎᒃ. ᑕᐃᒪᓐᓇ ᕿᓇᐅᔭᓪᓚᖕᒥᒃ ᐊᑐᖅᑐᖅᑳᖅᑕᓐᖏᒃᑲᓗᐊᖅᑎᓪᓗᒍ, ᐃᓄᐃᑦ ᐊᑭᓕᖅᑕᐅᓂᓪᓗᐅᖅᑐᑦ ᓂᐅᕕᖅᑕᐅᔪᓐᓇᖅᑐᒃᑯᑦ. ᐅᓪᓗᒥᒧᑦ ᑎᑭᓪᓗᒍ ᕿᑰᑖᓗᖕᒥ, ᐃᓄᒃᑎᑐᑦ ᑕᐃᔭᐅᑦᑕᖅᑐᖅ ᓯᕙᑖᖅᕕᐅᑉ ᐅᓪᓗᖓ (Saturday) ᐊᑎᖅᑲᓕᖅᑎᑕᐅᔪᖅ ᓯᕙᑖᖅᕕᖕᒥᒃ — ᐅᓪᓗ ᑕᐃᔭᐅᓪᓗᓂ ᐅᓪᓗᓐᓂᔭᐅᓪᓗᓂ ᐱᕝᕕᒃᓴᓐᓂᔭᐅᓪᓗᓂ ᑐᓂᔭᐅᓂᐊᕐᓂᕐᒥᒃ ᓯᕙᓂᒃ.

ᑕᐃᒪᒃᑳᓂᖅ ᓱᓕ ᐊᑲᐅᔪᒥᒃ ᐊᑲᐅᓐᖏᑦᑐᒥᓪᓗ ᐱᑕᖅᑲᓕᖅᑐᖅ ᐃᓄᖕᓄᑦ ᓇᖕᒥᓂᖓᑦ ᓂᐅᕕᖅᑏᑦ ᑎᑭᑦᑕᓕᖅᑎᓪᓗᒋᑦ ᐊᕐᕖᑦ ᓄᖑᑉᐸᓪᓚᓕᖅᑎᓪᓗᒋᑦ ᖃᓂᒋᔭᖕᖓᓂ 1800. ᓂᐅᕕᖅᑎᐅᔪᑦ ᓂᓐᐅᓚᐅᖅᑐᑦ ᐃᓄᐃᑦ ᐊᖑᓇᓱᒃᑲᑦᑕᕐᓂᐊᕐᓂᖏᓐᓂᒃ, ᐊᒻᒪᓗ ᓂᐅᕕᐅᑎᖅᑲᕐᓗᑎᒃ ᐱᑕᖅᑕᒥᖕᓄᑦ, ᓱᓪᓗᐊᕕᐅᕈᓐᖏᑦᑐᓄᑦ ᓂᐅᕕᐊᒃᓴᓐᓴᐅᔪᓄᑦ ᓂᐅᕕᐊᒃᓴᓐᓴᐅᕙᓚᐅᖅᑐᓄᑦ ᐊᕐᕕᕐᓂᐊᖅᑎᓄᑦ. ᐱᓇᓱᒃᑕᐅᔪᑦ ᐱᑕᖅᑕᐅᔪᖅᑲᕐᓂᒃ ᒪᑯᓂᖓᓇᑦᓯᕐᓂᒃ ᐊᒥᖏᓐᓄᑦ, ᐊᐃᕖᑦ ᕿᓯᖏᓐᓄᑦ ᐊᒻᒪᓗ ᑑᒑᖏᓐᓄᑦ, ᕿᕐᓂᖅᑐᓄᑦ ᕿᓚᓗᒐᕐᓄᑦ ᑑᒑᖏᓐᓄᑦ-ᐊᒻᒪᓗ ᐃᓄᐃᑦ ᓂᕿᖏᓐᓂᒃ ᐱᓯᒪᕙᒃᑎᓪᓗᒋᑦ. ᓂᐅᕕᖅᑎᐅᔪᑦ ᓄᓇᖃᓪᓚᒃᑎᑎᓂᕐᒥᒃ ᐃᓄᖕᓂᒃ ᓄᖅᑲᖅᑎᑎᓯᒪᓚᐅᖅᑐᑦ: ᐱᓇᓱᖕᓂᖅ ᓄᓇᐅᑉ ᐊᖏᓛᖑᒍᑦ ᐱᔪᓐᓇᕝᕚᖅᑎᑕᐅᓪᓗᓂ. ᐃᓄᐃᑦᑕᐅᖅ ᓂᐅᕕᖅᑎᐅᔪᑦ ᐱᑕᖅᑲᓕᓚᐅᖅᑐᑦ ᓂᐅᕕᖅᑎᐅᓪᓗᑎᒃ ᐃᓄᖕᓄᑦ ᐅᖓᓯᒃᑐᒦᑦᑐᓄᑦ. ᐃᓚᖏᔭᐅᓚᐅᖅᑐᑦ ᐅᑯᐊ ᓯᑏᕕᓐ ᐊᖑᓖᓚᒃ ᕿᑎᕐᒥᐅᓂ, ᑲᓈᑲ ᕿᑭᖅᑖᓘ ᐱᖓᖕᓇᖓᓂ, ᐊᒻᒪᓗ ᐃᓚᑦᓈᖅ ᑭᕙᓪᓕᐅᑉ ᓂᒋᖓᓂ.

ᓂᐅᕕᕐᕕᒃ Hudson Bay Company

ᓂᐅᕕᖅᑎᐅᑦᑕᖅᑐᑦ ᓇᖕᒥᓂᖓᑦ ᐊᑯᓂᐅᓗᐊᖅᑐᒥᒃ ᐃᖏᕐᕋᓚᐅᓐᖏᑦᑐᑦ. ᐱᒋᐊᓕᖅᑎᓪᓗᒋᑦ 1900, ᕼᐊᑦᓴᓐ ᐹ ᓂᐅᕕᕐᕖᖕᓂᒃ ᓇᖕᒥᓂᕆᔪᕐᒥᖕᓂᒃ ᐱᑕᖅᑲᓕᖅᑎᑎᓚᐅᖅᑐᑦ ᐅᑭᐅᖅᑕᖅᑐᒥ ᓇᒥᑐᐃᓐᓇᖅ. ᐊᖑᓇᓱᒃᑎᓂᒃ ᐱᓕᕆᔾᔪᑎᓕᖅᑐᑎᒃ ᐊᖑᓇᓱᒃᑎᐅᕆᐊᖅᑐᓂᒃ ᓇᖕᒥᓂᑐᐃᓐᓇᕐᒥᖕᓄᑦ ᑕᓪᓕᒪᐅᔪᓂ ᐊᕐᕌᒍᓂ ᒪᓕᒃᑐᓂ. ᑎᑭᑎᓪᓗᒍ 1930-ᖑᔪᑦ ᐊᕐᕌᒍᐃᑦ, ᒥᖅᑯᖏᑦ ᐊᑭᖏᑦ ᐳᖅᑐᑎᓪᓗᒋᑦ ᓱᓕ, ᑎᓴᒥᓂᐊᖅᓯᐅᕐᓂᖅ ᒥᑭᕆᐊᒃᑯᑦ ᐊᔪᖅᓴᓐᖏᓕᕈ-ᑕᐅᓚᐅᕐᒪᑦ ᐊᒥᓱᓄᑦ ᐃᓄᖕᓄᑦ.

ᑕᒪᒃᑯᓇᓕ ᐊᕐᕌᒍᔪᓂ, ᖃᑦᓯᓪᓚᖕᓂᒃ ᓴᓇᔭᐅᑎ-ᐊᖅᑐᖅᑲᓚᐅᖅᑐᖅ, ᐱᓗᐊᖅᑐᒥᒃ ᓂᐅᕕᖅᑎᒃᑯᓐᓄᑦ ᐃᓄᐃᑦ ᓇᖕᒥᓂᖅ ᓇᖏᖅᓯᒍᓐᓇᕐᖁᓪᓗᒋᑦ. ᐅᒥᐊᓂᒃ ᓴᓈᕝᕕᒃᓴᖅᑲᐅᖅᑎᑕᐅᓪᓗᑎᒃ ᑭᒻᒥᕈᒻᒥ ᐊᒻᒪᓗ ᕼᐊᑦᓴ ᐹ ᐱᖓᖕᓇᖕᖓᓂ. ᐊᒻᒪᓗ ᑎᓴᒥᓂᐊᓕᓐᓂᕐᒥᒃ ᐱᓕᕆᕝᕕᖃᕐᓗᓂ ᐸᖕᓂᖅᑑᒥ. ᑕᐃᒃᑯᐊ ᐃᓄᐃᑦ ᐃᑲᔪᖅᑐᐅᓂᖃᖅᑐᑦ ᑕᒪᑐᒪᖕᖓᑦ ᓱᓕᓐᓂᐊᓕᔭᐅᔪᓄᑦ ᐊᒥᓱᐃᓐᖏᑦᑐᕈᓗᐊᓚᐅᖅᑐᑦ: ᑕᐃᒃᑯᐊᖑᓚᐅᖅᑐᑦ ᖃᓪᓗᓈᒥᐅᑦ - ᓄᓇᓕᖕᓈᑦᑐᐃᑦ ᐃᓄᐃᑦ, ᐃᓅᓯᕐᒧᑦ ᖃᐅᔨᓴᖅᑎᐅᔪᖅ Vallee, ᑕᐃᒪᓐᓇ ᑕᐃᓚ-ᐅᖅᑕᖏᑦ. ᐊᒥᓱᑦ ᐃᓄᐃᑦ ᓱᓕ ᓄᓇᓕᖅᑲᖅᓯᒪᔪᑎᒃ ᓄᓇᐃᓐᓇᕐᒥ ᐃᓅᓚᐅᖅᑐᑦ, ᐊᒻᒪᓗ ᓲᕐᖃᐃᒻᒪ-ᐅᓚᐅᖅ ᐃᓄᐃᑦ ᐊᔪᖅᓴᒻᒪᓐᒃᐸᓚᐅᖅᑐᑦ ᐊᒃᓱᕈᖅᑐᒥᒃ ᐃᓅᓯᖃᖅᓯᒪᔪᖅᑎᒃ.

ᑲᔪᓯᔪᖅ ᒪᒃᐱᒐᖅ 93

Above: Charlie Sagiaktuk backs up a water truck outside Frobisher Bay (Iqaluit), 1955. Many Inuit were trained and employed early on to assist in the building of the modern Nunavut economy, but traditional skills survive in the subsistence economy. Right: As a gesture of respect for the land, a north Baffin hunter takes blood from a ring seal's stomach, early 1950s

ᖁᓛᓂ: ᓵᓕ ᓵᒋᐊᕐᑐᖅ ᐃᒥᕐᑕᐅᑎᒥ ᑲᖑᕐᐱᐊᕐᑎᑦᑎᔪᖅ ᕗᕉᐱᓯ ᐸᐃᒥᓐ (ᐃᖃᓗᐃᑦ), 1955. ᐊᒥᓱᑦ ᐃᓄᐃᑦ ᐃᓕᓐᓂᐊᕐᑎᑕᐅᓯᒪᕗᑦ ᐃᖅᑲᓇᐃᔭᕐᑎᑕᐅᓪᓗᑎᒡᓗ ᐃᑲᔪᕐᓂᐊᕐᒪᑕ ᐱᕙᓪᓕᐊᓂᕐᒥᓐ ᓄᓇᕗᒻᒥ, ᑭᓯᐊᓂ ᐃᓕᖁᓯᑐᖃᑦ ᐊᑐᕐᐸᑦ ᓱᓕ ᐊᑐᒃᑲᓂᕈᓐᓇᕐᑐᓕᓐᓂᕐᒍᓐ.
ᑕᓕᖅᐱᐊᓂ: ᓄᓇᒥᓐ ᐃᒃᐱᒍᓱᒍᓐ, ᐊᖑᓇᓱᒃᑎ ᕿᑭᖅᑖᓗᒥ ᐅᐊᖕᓇᖓᓂ ᓇᑦᑎᕐᑕᖓᑕ ᐊᐅᖓᓂ ᒥᓗᒃᑐᖅ, 1950 ᐱᒋᐊᓕᕐᓯᒪᑎᓪᓗᒍ

Wilkinson/NWT Archives ᐅᐊᑭᓐᓴᓐ/ᓄᓇᑦᓯᐊᕐᒥ ᑉᐸᑕᓪᓗᐊ

Wilkinson/NWT Archives

The Subsistence Economy
ᐊᖑᓇᓱᖕᓂᒃᑯᑦ ᐆᒪᔾᔪᑎᖃᕐᓂᖓ

By Larry Simpson

Picture an Inuit hunter on the land or sea ice observing a caribou herd or a seal at a breathing hole. The hunter naturally relates their well-being to his own, both in the short term and in the longer term.

Now picture a white-shirted man watching the big board at a stock exchange, forever aware of the impacts of such things as currency devaluations or commodity market fluctuations on the other side of the world, and the impact of these on his own fortunes. Are these realities opposites? Perhaps not. Can one participate in both worlds? Ideally, yes. The wired world is here to stay, but, hopefully, so too is the direct and sustainable relationship between Inuit and the natural world.

The subsistence economy is not typically measured in Gross National Product, yet the dollar value of the subsistence economy is astounding. Consider that the replacement-cost value of country food harvested in Nunavut is estimated at a minimum of $30 million, or at least equal to the cost of food imports from Southern Canada. Consider, too, that country food is generally much more nutritious.

Then there is the value of byproducts of the hunt that help to drive Nunavut's arts and crafts industry. There is caribou antler for carvings, narwhal and walrus ivory for carvings and jewelry, and sealskins for murals and small garments and toys. While Nunavut's arts and crafts industry is currently in a slump, it is nevertheless worth many millions of dollars per year to Inuit.

We must consider, too, that clothing made from animal skins has both a replacement value and a survival value — nothing has yet surpassed the insulating efficiency of caribou clothing.

Finally, there is also an important cash-economy element to the subsistence economy. Cash revenues are earned from the subsistence economy by selling sealskins within and between communities as the byproduct of the seal hunt, and by selling arctic char, caribou, or whatever has been hunted. Some of that money is needed to buy gas, hunting equipment and supplies to finance the cost of future hunts. Of 500 pounds of frozen arctic char piled on a *qamutik* (a sled pulled by a dogteam or snowmobile), the hunter may sell 100 pounds of the fish for, say, $1.75 per pound. This $175 will cover the cost of harvesting the other 400 pounds. But that 400 pounds of fish has a replacement value — or real value — of $2,000 as food on the table (hamburger or chicken at the local Inuit

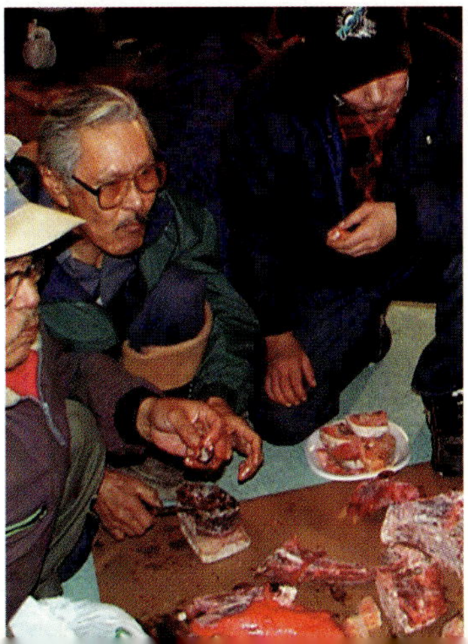

Nunatsiaq News

ᑎᑎᕋᖅᑐᖅ ᓛᕆ ᓯᒻᓴᓐ

ᑕᐅᑐᖕᒍᐊᕐᓗᒍ ᒪᖃᐃᑎ ᐃᓄᒃ ᓄᓇᒥ ᓯᑯᒥᓐᓃᑦ ᑐᒃᑐᓕᐊᖅᓯᒪᔪᖅ ᓇᑎᖅᓯᐅᖅᑐᖅᓈᓂᑦ ᐊᒡᓗᒥ. ᒪᖃᐃᑎ ᐃᓱᒪᒋᔭᓕᒃ ᐊᖑᓇᓱᒃᑕᓂ ᐱᐅᑐᐊᖅᐸᑦ ᓇᖕᒥᓂᕐᒥᓪ ᓂᕆᐅ-ᒋᓪᓗᓂᐅ ᐊᑲᐅᓂᖅᑳᓂᐊᕐᓂᖓ. ᑕᒪᐃᓐᓂ ᐊᑯᓂᒧᑦ ᖃᓂᑦᑐᒧᓪᓗ.

ᑕᐃᒪᓕ ᑕᐅᑐᖕᒍᐊᕐᓗᒍ ᐊᖑᑦ ᖄᖅᑐᒥᒃ ᐅᐱᓂᕈᖅᓯᒪᔪᖅ ᕿᒥᕐᕈᔪᖅ ᕼᓇᐅᔭᓕᐅᖅᑕᐅᔪᑦ ᓄᐊᑕᐅᖿᑎᖏᑕ ᑕᑯᓇᕐᕕᒃᓴᐅᖿᑎᖏᓐᓂᒃ. ᐅᔾᔨᕆᔭᖅᖢᓂ ᕼᓇᐅᔭᐃᑦ ᖁᒻᒧᒃᐸᓪᓕᐊᓂᖏᑦ ᐊᒻᒪᓗ ᑲᑕᒃᐸᓪᓕᐊᓂᖏᑦ, ᓯᓚᕐᔪᐊᒥ ᐊᑭᐊᓃᑦᑐᑦ ᑕᓇᐅᕙ. ᐊᒻᒪᓗ ᖃᓄᖅ ᐃᓅᓯᖓᓄᑦ ᐊᒃᑐᖅᑕᐅᓂᖃᕆᔭᕆᖕᒫᑦ. ᑖᒃᑯᐊ ᐃᓅᓯᕆᔭᐅᔪᒃ ᐊᔾᔨᒌᓐᖏᓗᐊᕐᓂᖃᖅᐸᒃ? ᐃᒻᒪᖃ ᐋᒃᑲ. ᑕᒪᒃᑭᖕᓂ ᐃᓅᔪᖃᕈᓐᓇᖅᐸ? ᐊᑲᐅᓂᖅᓴᐅᔪᖅ, ᐃᖑᓇᔭᖅᐸᑦ. ᐅᓪᓗᒥᐅᔪᖅ ᐅᐊᔭᓕᒃᑯᑦ ᑭᓯᐊᓂ ᓱᓇᑐᐃᓐᓇᐃᑦ ᐃᖏᕋᕋᓕᒪᑕ. ᐊᒻᒪᑦᑕᐅᖅ ᐃᓄᐃᑦ ᐆᒪᔾᔪᑎᖃᕐᓂᖓᑦ ᐊᖑᓇᓱᖕᓂᒃᑯᑦ ᓄᓇᒋᔭᒥᖕᓂ.

ᐊᖑᓇᓱᖕᓂᒃᑯᑦ ᐆᒪᔾᔪᑎᖃᕐᓂᖅ ᖃᐅᔨᓴᖅᑕ-ᐅᔭᓐᓇᖏᑦᑐᖅ ᑲᓇᑕᐅᑉ ᑮᓇᐅᔭᖁᑎᓗᒃᑖᖏᑎᑐᑦ ᓇᓗᓇᐃᔭᖅᑕᐅᓂᖓᑎᑐᑦ, ᑭᓯᐊᓂᓕ ᐊᑭᖃᖅᓯᒪᓂᖏᑦ ᓂᐅᕕᐊᒃᓴᐅᓇᔭᖅᐸᑕ ᓂᕿᖏᔭᐅᔪᑦ ᐊᖑᓇᓱᖕᓂᒃᑯᑦ ᐊᑭᑐᔫᓇᔭᕐᒪᑕ. ᐊᑭᓕᖅᑕᐅᕆᐊᖃᖅᓯᖅᐸᑕ ᓂᕿᕆᔭ-ᐅᓗᒃᑖᖅᑐᑦ ᓂᕿᑐᐃᓐᓇᕆᔭᐅᔪᑦ ᓄᓇᕗᒥ ᖃᓂᒋᔭᖕᒐᓂ ᐃᒪᓐᓇ ᐊᑭᖃᖅᑰᖅᓴᔭᖅᑐᑦ $30 ᒥᓕᐊᓐᓂᒃ. ᐅᕙᓐᓂᑦ ᓇᓕᒧᒐᔭᖅᑐᑦ ᐊᑭᓕᔭ-ᐅᓇᔭᖅᑐᓂᒃ ᑲᓇᑕᐅᑉ ᓄᓇᖁᑎᒋᓐᓂᖓᓖᖅᑐᓂᒃ ᖃᓐᓄᓈᑦ ᓄᓇᖓᓐᓂᑦ. ᐊᒻᒪᑦᑕᐅᖅ, ᐃᓱᒪᒋᔭ-ᐅᔭᕆᐊᓕᒃ ᓄᓇᒥᐅᑕᐃᑦ ᓂᕿᖏᔭᐅᔪᑦ ᓂᕿᑦᑎᐊᕙᐅᓂᖅᓴᐅᓂᖏᑦ ᓂᐅᕕᖅᑕᐅᔪᓂᑦ.

ᓱᓇᑐᐃᓐᓇᕐᓂᒃ ᐊᑐᕈᑎᖃᕐᓂᖓᔭᖏᑦ ᐊᖑᓇ-ᓱᒃᓗᑎᒃ ᐱᕆᔭᐅᓱᖅᑐᑦ ᓄᓇᕗᒥ ᓴᓇᐅᓯᕐᓂᕐᒧᑦ ᐊᒻᒪᓗ ᐊᖏᖕᒧᑦ ᓴᓇᓯᒪᔪᓂᒃ ᐃᓚᒋᔭᖅᐸᖕᓂᖓᓂᒃ ᐃᑲᔪᖅᑐᐃᓂᖃᕐᓂᖅᑕᖅᓯᒪᔪᖅ. ᑐᒃᑐᐃᑦ ᓇᔪᖏᑦ ᓴᖑᒐᖅᑕᐅᕙᒃᑐᑦ, ᕿᓚᓗᒐᕐᓂᑦ ᐊᐃᕖᑦ ᑑᒑᖏᑦ ᓴᖑᒐᓕᐅᖅᑕᐅᓪᓗᑎᒃ ᐱᐅᓴᐃᑦᑐᖅᑕᐅᓪᓗᑎᒃ, ᓇᑦᓰᑦ ᐊᒻᒪᓗ ᐊᐃᕖᑦ ᑑᒑᖏᑦ ᓴᖑᒐᓕᐅᖅᑕᐅᓪᓗᑎᒃ ᐱᐅᓴᐃᑦᑐᖅᑕᐅᓪᓗᑎᒃ. ᓇᑦᓰᑦ ᐊᒥᖏᑦ ᐊᑐᖅᑕᐅᓪᓗᑎᒃ ᓂᐊᖁᐊᓄᑦ ᒥᑭᔪᓄᑦ ᐱᖁᐊᓄᑦ. ᒫᓐᓇᐅᔪᖅ ᓄᓇᕗᑦ ᓴᓇᖕᖑᐊᖅᓯᓂᖅᑕ ᐊᑭᑦᑎᐊᖏᑦᑕ ᑲᑖᒃᓯᒪᔫᓪᓗᐊᑦ, ᑭᓯᐊᓂᓕ ᐊᒥᓱᒻᒪᕆᖕᓂᒃ ᒥᓕᐊᓐᓂᒃ ᕿᓇᐅᔭᓂᒃ ᑐᕋᖕᖓᓂᖅᖢᑦ ᐊᕐᕌᒍᒥ ᐊᑕᐅᓯᕐᒥ ᐃᓄᖕᓄᑦ.

ᐃᖅᑲᐅᒪᔭᐅᕆᐊᖅᑲᖅᒥᔪᖅ, ᐊᒻᒪ ᓯᓚ, ᐊᓐᓄᕋᑦ ᓴᓇᔭᐅᕙᒃᑐᑦ ᐆᒪᔪᐃᑦ ᐊᒥᖏᓐᓂᑦ ᐃᓇᖏᖅᑕ-ᐅᒃᐸᑕ ᐊᑭᑐᓗᔭᖅᒥᔪᑦ ᐊᒻᒪᓗ ᐊᑲᐅᔾᔪᑎᖃᖅᖢᑎᒃ ᐊᓇᐅᒪᔾᔪᓐᓇᕐᓂᖏᑦ. ᐊᔾᔨᖃᖕᖏᓪᓚᑦ ᑐᒃᑐᐃᑦ ᐊᒥᖏᑦ ᐅᖅᑯᓂᖓᓂᒃ ᐊᑐᖅᑕᐅᔭᓐᓇᖅᑐᒥᒃ ᐊᓐᓄᕋᓕᐅᕈᑎᒋᔭᐅᓗᓂ.

ᑭᖑᓪᓕᖓᓪᓗᒥᒃ, ᐆᒪᔾᔪᑎᒃᑕᕐᓂᕐᒧᑦ ᑐᑭᖃᕐᒥᔪᖅ ᕿᓇᐅᔭᒃᑲᑦᑕᕈᓐᓇᕐᓂᕐᒧᑦ. ᐊᖑᓇᓱᖕᓂᒃᑯᑦ ᕿᓇᐅᔭᓕᐅᕈᑕᐅᓯᒪᔪᑦ ᓇᑦᓯᑦ ᐊᒥᖕᓂᑦ ᓂᐅᕕᐊᒃᓴᐅᓂᖕᒋᑎᒍᑦ ᓄᓇᓕᖕᓂ ᐱᔭᐅᔪᓂᒃ ᐊᖑᓇᓱᖕᓂᒃᑯᑦ. ᐊᒻᒪᓗ ᐃᖃᓗᒃᐲᑦ ᓂᐅᕕᐊᒃᓴᐅᑉᓐᓂᖕᒋᓈᓐᓄᑦ, ᑐᒃᑐᐃᑦ ᐊᓯᖕᒋᓈᓂᓪᓗ ᓂᕿᕆᓴ-ᐅᑉᐸᒃᑐᓂᒃ. ᐃᓚᖕᒐᑕ ᕿᓇᐅᔭᓕᐅᖅᑕᐅᔪᑦ ᐅᖅᑕᐅᑦᑕᖅᑕᐅᑦᑐᑦ ᖓᓭᒥᒃ ᓂᐅᕕᖅᓂᕐᒧᑦ, ᐊᖑᓇᓱᒍᑎᓄᑦ ᐊᒻᒪᓗ ᑕᖁᐊᓄᑦ ᓯᕗᓂᖕᒥ ᐊᖑᓇᓱᒃᓗᓂ ᐅᖅᑕᐅᑖᖅᑐᓄᑦ. 500 ᐸᐅᓐᓂᒃ ᐅᖁᒪᐃᓐᓂᖅᑐᒥᒃ ᐃᖃᓗᒃᑐᖃᖅᐸᑦ ᐊᒻᒪᓗ ᐅᓯᔭᐅᓗᑎᒃ ᖃᒧᓯᒃᑯᑦ ᓂᐅᓂᐊᖅᑕᐅᓗᑎᒃ (ᕿᒻᒥᒃᑯᑦ ᖃᒧᑕᐅᔭᒃᑯᓐᓂᑦ), ᒪᖃᐃᑎ ᓂᐅᕕᐊᒃᓴ-ᕈᓐᓇᖅᓴᖅᑐᖅ 100 ᐸᐅᓐᓂᒃ ᐅᖁᒪᐃᓐᓂᓕᖕᓂᒃ, ᐃᒪᓐᓇᖃᐃ ᐊᑭᖃᖅᑎᑕᐅᖕᒍᐊᕐᓗᑎᒃ $1.75-ᓂᒃ ᐊᑕᐅᓯᕐᒧᑦ ᐸᐅᓐᒧᑦ. ᑖᒪᓐᓇ ᕿᓇᐅᔭᓕᐊᕆᔭᐅᔪᖅ $175 ᐊᑭᓖᒍᑕᐅᒍᓐᓇᖅᓴᖅᑐᖅ ᐊᓯᖏᓐᓂᒃ

Above: Jacob Sissennark tests the edge of a traditional bone-tipped harpoon near Pelly Bay, 1960. Left: Jimmy Koomarjuk, centre, and others enjoy a recent country-food feast. Feasting on traditional foods remains a cornerstone of Inuit society

ᖁᓛᓂ: ᔭᐃᑯᑉ ᓯᓯᓐᓇᖅ ᖃᐅᔨᓴᖅᑐᖅ ᑐᕌᒥ ᓴᓇᓯᒪᔪᒥᓐ ᓴᒃᑯᒥᓐ ᐊᖏᓚᒡᔪᐊᑉ ᖃᓂᒋᔮᓂ, 1960. ᓴᐅᒥᐊᓂ ᔨᒥ ᑯᒫᖅᔪᒃ, ᕿᑎᐊᓂ, ᐊᒻᒪ ᐊᓯᖏ ᓂᕆᔪᑦ ᓂᕆᕕᒡᔪᐊᖅᓇᒥ ᐃᓄᐃᑦ ᓂᕿᖏᓂ. ᓂᕆᕕᒡᔪᐊᖅᓂᖅ ᓯᓚ ᐃᓅᖃᑎᒌᒍᑕᐅᑯᖅ

Co-op or Northern store would cost the hunter at least $5 per pound). Recognition of this fundamental reality is one reason the Nunavut Land Claims Agreement (NLCA) created Nunavut's resource-management bodies. The NLCA and territorial government help provide for outpost camps, hunter-support programs, elder and youth conferences, income reform and more, ensuring that subsistence uses of wildlife will always take priority over commercial or tourist quotas when conservation is required.

The importance of maintaining the subsistence economy is nowhere more tragically obvious than in the decline in the early 1970s of the eastern Arctic seal hunt, and the dire social effects of its collapse. What many of the animal-rights activists responsible for the market's decline choose not to see is that the subsistence economy represents a relationship of man with the natural world that has spun a complex web of cultural beliefs, values, and attitudes that can sustain ecosystems that include man. The subsistence economy is the tie that binds Inuit to the natural world, and all over the world it has been shown that "to use is to protect."

The subsistence economy has become a rare treasure. Hunting is about food on the table, but it is also about respect for the land, and building and maintaining ties with kin groups and with fellow residents. The subsistence economy is also the wellspring of traditional knowledge, or IQ (*Inuit Qaujimajatuqangit*): once dismissed as the outdated opposite of good western science, it is now recognized as having value for aboriginal and non-aboriginal people alike in our attempt to understand how life interrelates on the tundra or in the sea.

Nunavut will never see Ford plants and other big manufacturers. Yet the new territory may remain one of the few places on Earth where people successfully straddle tradition and innovation, "the land" and the Internet.

Larry Simpson of Iqaluit is a sector development specialist, renewable resources, with the Department of Sustainable Development, government of Nunavut.

Terry Pearce ᑎᕆ ᐱᐅᔅ

ᐅᓯᔭᒃᓵᓂᒃ ᐱᓇᓱᒃᑕᐅᔪᓂᒃ ᐅᖁᒪᐃᓐᓂᓕᖕᓂᒃ 400 ᐸᐅᓐᖄᓐᓂᕐᓂᒃ ᓱᓕ. ᑭᓯᐊᓂᓕ 400 ᐸᐅᓐᖑᔪᑦ ᐃᓇᖏᖅᑕᐅᓇᔭᖅᐸᑦ ᐃᖃᓗᐃᑦ ᐊᑭᓪᓚᖕᒐᑦ ᐃᒪᐃᒃᑲᔭᖅᑐᖅ $2,000-ᓂᒃ ᓂᕿᒃᓵᖑᔭᐅᓇᔭᖅᑐᓂᒃ. ᓵᖑᔪᒥ ᓂᕿᒋᔭᐅᒍᓂ ᑕᐃᒪᓐᓇ ᐊᑭᓪᓚᖑᔭᖃᔭᖅᑐᖅ (Hᐋᓪᐳᒐ ᐊᕿᒡᒋᐅᔭᕐᓈᓂᑦ ᑯᐊᐸᒥᑦ ᓂᐅᕕᖅᑕᐅᓇᔭᖅᑐᖅ ᐊᑭᓖᔭᐅᑦᑕᕋᔭᖅᑐᖅ ᒪᖃᐃᑎᒧᑦ ᓂᐅᕕᖅᑕᐅᒍᓂ ᐃᒪᓐᓇ $5-ᓂᒃ ᐸᐅᓐᖓᑦ ᐊᑕᐅᓯᕐᒧᑦ). ᑕᒪᓐᓇ ᐃᓕᑕᕆᔭᐅᓂᖃᕐᓂᖓ ᐱᙳᑎᒋᓪᓗᒍ ᓄᓇᕗᑖᕆᑦ ᐊᖏᕈᑕᓗᐅᖅᑐᖅ ᑐᓐᖓᓂᖁᔭᐅᖓᒪᑦ ᐋᖅᑭᒍᑕᐅᓪᓗᓂ ᐊᐅᓚᑦᑎᔾᔪᐅᖃᑕᐅᒐᔭᖅᑐᓂᒃ ᑎᒥᖁᑎᐅᔪᓂᒃ. ᓄᓇᕗᒥ ᐊᖏᕈᑕᓗᐅᖅᑐᖅ ᐊᒻᒪᓗ ᒐᕙᒪᒋᔭᐅᔪᖅ ᐃᑲᔪᐃᒐᔪᖅ ᓄᓇᓕᒑᖅᑐᓂᒃ, ᒪᖃᐃᑎᑦ ᐃᑲᔪᖅᑕᐅᕙᖕᓂᖏᓐᓂᒃ, ᐃᓄᒃᑯᐃᑦ ᒪᒃᑯᒃᑐᐃᓪᓗ ᑲᑎᒪᔪᓐᓇᖅᑕᕐᓂᖏᓐᓂᒃ, ᑮᓇᐅᔭᓕᐅᖅᑕᐅᕙᒃᑐᑦ ᐊᓯᐦᑖᕆᐊᖅᑕᐅᓂᖏᓐᓂᒃ, ᐊᒻᒪᓗ ᐊᒥᓱᓂᒃ ᐊᓯᖏᓐᓂᒃ. ᑲᒪᒋᔭᐅᑦᑎᐊᖅᑐᒃᑯᑦ ᒪᖃᐃᑦᑐᓂᒃ ᐊᐅᓚᓐᓂᖅᑲᕐᓂᖅ ᑕᒪᒃᑯᐊ ᓯᕗᓕᐅᑎᔭᐅᖏᓐᓇᖅᑎᓪᓗᒋᑦ ᐆᒪᔪᖅᓯᐅᕐᓂᐅᔪᑦ ᐸᐸᑕᐅᒋᐊᖃᖅᑐᖃᓕᖅᖢᑦ. ᓯᕗᓕᐅᑎᔭᐅᓗᓂ ᑮᓇᐅᔭᓕᐅᕐᓂᕐᒧᑦ ᐅᕙᓐᓃᑦ ᐳᓚᕋᖅᑎᔪᑦ ᐱᔭᐅᔪᓐᓇᖅᑎᑕᐅᓂᖏᓐᖓᑦ.

ᐊᖑᓇᓱᖕᓂᒃᑯᑦ ᐱᓇᓱᒍᓐᓇᕐᕕᖕᓂᕐᓂᖅ ᐊᐅᓪᓚᕆᓂᖓ ᓇᓗᓇᐃᖅᑕᐅᔪᓐᓇᖅᑐᖅ ᓇᑦᑦᔨᑦ ᕿᓯᖏᑕ ᐊᑭᖏᑕ ᑲᑕᓚᐅᖅᑎᓪᓗᒋᑦ 1970ᑦ ᐊᐅᓪᓚᖅᑎᓪᓗᒋᑦ ᕿᑭᖅᑖᑉ ᒥᒃᓵᓐᓂ. ᐃᓅᓯᕐᒧᑦ ᐊᑕᓂᖅᑲᕐᓂᖓ ᖃᐅᔨᔭᐅᓚᐅᖅᑐᖅ. ᐊᒥᓱᑦ ᐆᒪᔪᓂᒃ ᓯᕐᓈᖅᑎᑦ ᑐᑭᓯᒪᓐᖏᓪᒪᑕ ᑲᑦᑎᑎᓚᐅᕐᓂᕐᒥᖕᓂᒃ ᓇᑦᔫᑦ ᕿᓯᖏᑕ ᐊᑭᖏᓐᓂᒃ ᐃᓅᓯᖏᓐᓂᓪᓗ ᐊᔪᖅᓴᖅᑎᑎᓚᐅᕐᓂᖏᓐᓂᒃ ᐃᓄᖕᓄᑦ. ᐃᓄᐃᑦ ᐊᒃᑐᐃᓂᖃᑎᐊᖅᑎᓪᓗᒋᑦ ᐊᕙᑎᒥᖕᓄᑦ ᒪᓕᒃᑕᖅᖢᑎᒃ ᐃᓕᖅᑯᓯᕐᒥᖕᓂᒃ ᐊᒻᒪᓗ ᐸᐸᑦᓯᔪᓐᓇᑦᑎᐊᖅᖢᑎᒃ ᐆᒪᔪᓂᒃ ᐊᑐᓇᐊᖃᖅᐸᒃᑕᕐᒥᖕᓂᒃ. ᐃᓄᐃᑦ ᐃᓕᒋᔭᐅᓪᓗᑎᒃ ᐸᐸᑕᐅᔭᕆᐊᖃᖅᖢᖏᑦ. ᐊᖑᓇᓱᑦᖃᓲᖅ ᐊᐅᑐᐊᒍᑕᐅᖕᒪᑦ ᐃᓅᖅᓅᑦ ᐊᕙᑎᒥᖕᓅᑦ, ᐊᒻᒪᓗ ᓇᒥᑐᐃᓐᓈᖅ ᓯᓚᕐᔪᐊᒥ ᑐᑭᖃᖅᑐᖅ "ᐊᑐᖅᑕᐅᑦᑎᐊᖅᐸᑦ ᐸᐸᑕᐅᓂᖃᖅᑐᖅ."

ᐊᖑᓇᓱᖕᓂᒃᑯᑦ ᐆᒪᔾᔪᑎᖃᕐᓂᖅ ᐊᑐᖅᑕᒐᔪᓐᖏᓕᕐᒪᑦ. ᐊᖑᓇᓱᒃᐸᕐᓂᖅ ᓂᕿᖃᕈᑕᐅᑦᑕᕐᒪᑦ, ᐊᒻᒪᓗ ᑐᑭᖃᓪᓗᓂ ᓄᓇᒥᒃ ᑲᒪᑦᑎᐊᕐᓂᕐᒥᒃ, ᐊᒻᒪᓗ ᐃᓅᓯᖃᕈᑎᑦᑎᐊᕐᓂᕐᒥᒃ ᐃᓚᖁᑎᒋᔭᒥᒃ ᐊᒻᒪᓗ ᓄᓇᓕᖁᑎᒋᔭᒥᒃ. ᐊᖑᓇᓱᒃᑲᑦᑕᕐᓂᒃᑯᑦ ᐆᒪᔾᔪᑎᖃᕐᓂᖅ ᖃᐅᔨᒪᔭᐅᑐᖃᖅᑐᓂᒃ ᐃᓕᑦᑎᔾᔪᐅᒍᓐᓇᕐᒥᔪᖅ: ᑕᐃᑦᓱᒪᓂ ᐃᓄᐃᑦ ᖃᐅᔨᒪᔭᑐᖃᖏᑦ ᖃᐅᔨᒪᔭᐅᑦᑕᕆᒪᓗᐊᓐᖏᑦᑐᑦ ᐊᑐᓐᖏᓐᓇᓱᒋᔭᐅᓪᓗᑎᒃ. ᒫᓐᓇᐅᔪᖅ ᐃᓕᑕᕆᔭᐅᓯᒪᓕᖅᑐᖅ ᓄᓇᖅᑲᖅᑳᖅᑐᓄᑐᐃᓐᓇᐅᓐᖏᑦᑐᖅ ᑭᓯᐊᓂᓕ ᓄᓇᖅᑲᖅᑳᖅᑑᓐᖏᑦᑐᓄᓪᓗ ᐊᑐᕈᓐᓇᕐᓂᖓ. ᖃᓄᖅ ᐃᓅᓯᖅ ᐃᓕᖓᓂᖅᒪᖔᑦ ᓄᓇᐃᓐᓇᕐᒥ ᑕᕆᐅᒥᓈᑦ.

ᓄᓇᕗᑦ ᓴᓇᕕᒡᔪᐊᕐᕕᓕᖕᓂᒃ ᓄᓇᒃᑰᔫᕈᑎᓕᐅᑎᓛᖕᓂᒃ ᐱᑕᖅᖃᖅᓯᒪᓂᐊᓐᖏᑦᑐᖅ ᐊᒻᒪᓗ ᐊᓯᖏᓐᓂᒃ ᐃᖅᑲᓇᐃᔭᕐᕕᒡᔪᐊᓂᒃ ᓴᓇᕕᖕᓂᒃ ᓱᓇᑐᐃᓐᓇᓂᒃ. ᑭᓯᐊᓂᓕ ᑳᓐᓇᑐᐊᖑᑐᐃᓐᓇᕆᐊᓕᒃ ᓯᓚᕐᔪᐊᒥ ᐃᓄᖏᓐᓂᒃ ᒪᕐᕿᖕᓂᒃ ᐱᔪᓐᓇᖅᑐᓂᒃ ᐊᑐᖅᑕᐅᑐᖅᖢᑐᓂᒃ ᓄᑖᓂᓪᓗ, "ᓄᓇᒥᒃ" ᐃᓐᑐᓂᑦᒥᓪᓗ.

ᓚᐊᕆ ᓯᒻᓴᓐ ᐃᖃᓗᖕᒥᐅᑕᖅ ᖃᐅᔨᒪᔨᐅᔪᖅ ᐱᕙᓪᓕᐊᑎᑎᓂᕐᒥᒃ ᐆᒪᔪᓕᕆᔨᒃᑯᓂ ᒐᕙᒪᖏᓐᓂ ᓄᓇᕗᒻᒥ.

Nunatsiaq News

The subsistence economy includes furs and skins for use at home and for sale abroad. Left: A polar bear skin is stretched in Pond Inlet. Above: Sarah Kunuk and Christina Choinard of Iqaluit enjoy the latest from Nunavut's growing sealskin fashion industry
ᐊᐅᒃᑲᓂᕈᓐᓇᕐᑐᑦ ᐃᓚᖃᕐᐳᑦ ᐊᒥᕐᓂᑦ ᕿᓯᖕᓄᓗ ᐊᐅᑦᑕᐅᕙᒃᓗᑎᒃ ᐊᖏᕐᖁᒥᓐ ᐊᒻᒪ ᓂᐅᕐᕿᑎᒃᓴᐅᓪᓗᑎ. ᓴᐅᒥᐊᓂ: ᓇᓄᕐᖅ ᐸᓂᕐᓯᕐᑐᖅ ᒥᑦᑎᒪᑕᓕᖕᒥ. ᖁᓛᓂ: ᓵᕋ ᑯᓄᒃ ᐊᒻᒪ ᑯᕆᔅᑏᓇ ᓯᐃᓇᕐ ᖁᕕᐊᓰᑎᖃᕐᐳᑦ ᐱᕈᕐᐸᓪᓕᐊᔪᒥ ᕿᓯᓕᕆᓂᕐᒥᓐ ᓄᓇᕗᒻᒥ

“ᐅᖃᖃᑦᑕᕐᓯᒪᕗᒍᑦ ᐊᑭᑐᔪᒦᓐᓂᑦᑎᓐᓂ. ᐊᓯᖏᓐᓂ ᐊᖏᕈᑎᓂᑦ, ᓇᓗᓇᐃᕐᓯᓯᒪᖃᑦᑕᕐᒪᑕ ᐋᖅᑭᒃᓯᓯᒪᔪᓂᑦ ᑮᓇᐅᔾᔭᐅᕈᑎᓄᑦ ᕿᑐᕐᖏᐅᕐᓂᐅᔪᓂ ᐃᓅᓯᖓᓂᖅ ᓄᓇᖃᖅᑳᖅᑐ ᐱᓕᕆᖃᑎᒌ ᓇᓕᒧᒃᓯᐅᑎᓯᒪᓕᕈᑎ ᑲᓇᑕᒥᐅᓄᑦ. ᐅᕙᑦᑎᒍᑦ. . . ᑕᐃᒪᐃᙱᓚᑦ.”

– ᐹᓪ ᐅᑲᓕᖅ, ᐃᑲᔪᖅᑎ ᐋᕐᕌᒍᒥ ᐃᓅᓄᑦ ᓄᓇᑖᕐᓯᓐᓂᕐᒧᓐ

continued from page 90

Government looks northward

The late 1940s and early 1950s saw the arrival of the Canadian and U.S. military in Nunavut. The military brought with it wage labor and increased dependence on southern goods when it created airbases in communities such as Iqaluit (Frobisher Bay), and numerous Distant Early Warning (DEW) Line stations across the North, but by 1950, in the barren lands of the Keewatin, Inuit were starving. Caribou migration patterns had shifted, moving Canadian writer Farley Mowat to write on the plight of “the people of the deer.” This situation, coupled with an increasing interest in non-renewable northern resources, finally turned the attention of non-military southern officials northward. First came northern service officers to administer welfare, then school teachers. In the 1960s, Inuit were urged to abandon their traditional camps and move into settlements. Dependence on outsiders and the wage economy became firmly entrenched throughout Nunavut, though this sometimes brought its own miseries, as when animal-rights activists destroyed the northern sealskin industry in the early 1970s.

In the two generations since Inuit left the land, government influence has become all-pervasive in the Inuit economy. Some argue that a general sapping of individual initiative has taken place, and that only now, with

Nunavut's Wage vs. Non-Wage Economy
ᓄᓇᕗᒻᒥ ᑮᓇᐅᔭᓕᐅᕐᓂᒃᑯᑦ ᑮᓇᐅᔭᓕᐅᙱᓐᓂᒃᑯᓪᓗ ᐊᓐᓇᐅᒪᔾᔪᑎᑦ

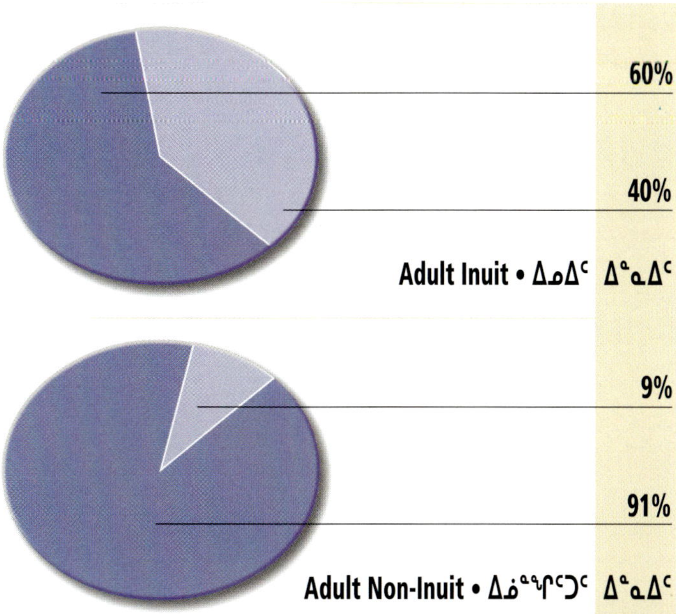

People who participate in labor force (wage economy)
ᐃᓄᐃᑦ ᐃᓚᐅᔪᑦ ᐃᖅᑲᓇᐃᔭᖅᑐᓂ (ᑮᓇᐅᔭᓕᐅᕐᓂᒃᑯᑦ ᐊᓐᓇᐅᒪᔾᔪᑎᑦ)

People who do not participate in labor force (non-wage economy)
ᐃᓄᐃᑦ ᐃᓚᐅᙱᑦᑐᑦ ᐃᖅᑲᓇᐃᔭᖅᑐᓂ (ᑮᓇᐅᔭᓕᐅᙱᓐᓂᒃᑯᑦ ᐊᓐᓇᐅᒪᔾᔪᑎᑦ)

Population of Nunavut • ᓄᓇᕗᒥ ᖃᑦᓯᐅᓂᖏᑦ:	24,730
Inuit • ᐃᓄᐃᑦ:	20,480
Non-Inuit • ᐃᓅᙱᑦᑐᑦ:	4,250

Sources: 1996 Census of Canada, 1994 GNWT Labour Force Survey
ᑐᓴᕈᑏᑦ: 1996ᒥ ᑲᓇᑕᓖᒥ ᖃᐅᔨᓴᕐᓂᖅ, 1994 ᓄᓇᑦᓯᐊᑉ ᒐᕙᒪᖏᑦᑕ ᐃᖅᑲᓇᐃᔭᕐᑐᓂ ᖃᐅᔨᓴᕐᓂᖅ

Nunavut Tourism ᓄᓇᕗᑦ ᐳᓛᕆᐅᖅᑐᓕᕆᔨᑦ

Offloading arctic char at a Gjoa Haven test fishery
ᐅᓯᖏᖅᓰᔾᔪᖅ ᐃᖃᓗᖕᒥᓐ ᐅᕐᓱᖅᑑᑉ ᐃᖃᓗᓕᕆᐊᕐᕕᐊᓂᑦ

ᐃᓚᖓ ᒫᐱᕗᐅᑉ 90

ᒐᕙᒪᑦ ᐅᑭᐅᖅᑕᖅᑐᒧᑦ ᕿᕕᐊᖅᐳᑦ

ᐊᑐᓕᖅᑐᖅᑎᓪᓗᒋᑦ 1940 ᐊᒻᒪᓗ ᐱᒋᐊᕐᓂᖓᓂ 1950 ᑲᓇᑕᒥᖕᓘᖅᑐᓂᑦ ᐊᒥᐊᓕᒃᑲᓂᒡᓗ ᐅᓇᑕᖅᑐᒃᓴᖏᑦ ᓄᓇᕗᒧᑦ ᑎᑭᓪᓗᖅᑐᑦ. ᐅᓇᑕᖅᑐᒃᑲᐃᑦ ᐃᖅᑲᓇᐃᔭᕈᓐᓇᕐᓂᕐᒥᒃ ᐊᑭᓕᖅᑕᐅᓂᒃᑯᑦ ᑎᑭᓴᐃᕗᑦ. ᐊᒻᒪᓗ ᐊᑐᖅᐸᓪᓕᐊᓂᕐᒥᒃ ᖃᓪᓗᓈᖅᑕᓂᒃ ᒥᑦᑕᕐᕕᖃᓕᖅᑎᓪᓗᒋᑦ ᓲᕐᓗ ᒪᑯᓇᓂ ᐃᖃᓗᖕᓂ (Frobisher Bay), ᐊᒻᒪᓗ ᐊᒥᓱᓂ ᑎᐅᓚᐃᓐᓂ (DEW) Line-ᓂ. ᑕᒻᒪᑯᐊ ᐱᑕᖃᓗᒃᑖᖅᐸᓪᓕᐊᓪᓗᑎᒃ ᐅᑭᐅᖅᑕᖅᑐᓕᒻᒥ ᓇᒥᓕᒻᒦᖅ. ᑭᓯᐊᓂᓕ ᐊᕐᕌᒍᐃᑦ 1950 ᐊᑐᓕᖅᑎᓪᓗᒋᑦ, ᓄᓇᐃᓐᓇᒥᐅᑕᐃᑦ ᑭᕙᓪᓕᕐᒥ ᐱᕐᓕᓕᓚᐅᖅᑐᑦ. ᑐᒃᑐᐃᑦ ᐃᑳᖅᑕᕐᓂᖏᑦ ᐊᓯᔾᔨᕐᓂᖅᑎᓪᓗᒋᑦ, ᑲᓇᑕᒥ ᑎᑎᕋᖅᑎᐅᔪᖅ ᕚᓕ ᒧᐊᑦ (Farley Mowat) ᑎᑎᕋᓇᐊᓚᐅᖅᑐᖅ ᑲᐱᐊᓇᖅᑐᒃᑰᕐᓂᖏᓐᓂᒃ “ᐃᓄᒋᔭᐅᔪᓂᒃ ᑐᒃᑐᓄᑦ.” ᑕᒪᓐᓇ ᐊᔪᖅᓴᓕᕈᑎᐅᓂᑯ, ᐃᓚᖃᖅᑐᓂ ᐃᓄᐃᑦ ᓄᓇᖓᓐᓂ ᐊᑐᖅᑕᐅᒃᑲᓐᓂᕈᓐᓇᙱᑦᑐᓂᒃ ᐱᔪᒪᓂᕐᓕᐊᓂᖅ, ᐱᒋᐊᖕᕕᐅᓚᐅᖅᑐᖅ ᐅᓇᑕᖅᑐᒃᓴᐅᙱᑦᑐᓂᒃ ᐃᓱᒋᓕᕐᓕᐊᓕᓂᕐᒥᒃ ᐊᖓᔪᖅᖠᓴᔪᓄᑦ ᐅᑭᐅᖅᑕᖅᑐᒧᑦ. ᓯᕗᓪᓕᖏᑦᑐᒥᒃ ᑎᑭᐸᓪᓕᐊᔪᑦ ᐃᓚᖃᓚᐅᖅᑐᑦ ᒪᑯᓂᖓ ᐃᓄᓕᕆᔨᓂᒃ ᐊᐅᓚᑦᑎᔨᐅᕆᐊᖅᑐᖅᑐᓂᒃ ᐊᔪᖅᓴᖅᑐᓕᕆᓂᕐᒥᒃ, ᐃᓕᓐᓂᐊᖅᑎᑎᔨᓪᓗ ᑎᑭᐸᓪᓕᐊᓪᓗᑎᒃ. ᑕᐃᒪ 1960 ᐊᑐᓕᖅᑎᓪᓗᒍ ᐃᓄᐃᑦ ᐅᖃᐅᔾᔭᖅᑕᐅᓚᐅᖅᑐᑦ ᓄᓇᓕᒃᑎᒥᙶᕐᓂᒃ ᕿᒪᐃᖁᓪᓗᑎᒋᑦ ᐊᒻᒪᓗ ᓅᓪᓗᑎᒃ ᓄᓇᓕᙵᓄᑦ. ᐃᑲᔪᖅᑕᐅᒋᐊᖃᕐᓂᖅ ᓯᓚᑎᒥᐅᓄᑦ ᐊᒻᒪᓗ ᑮᓇᐅᔭᒧᑐᐃᓐᓇᖅ ᐃᖏᕐᕋᓯᓐᓂᖅ ᐊᑦᑕᑎᒋᔭᐅᑦᓚᓇᓕᓚᐅᖅᐳᖅ ᓄᓇᕗᒥ. ᑕᒪᓇᓕᑦᑕᐅᖅ ᐃᓐᒥᒃᑯᑦ ᐊᒃᓯᕈᕐᓇᕈᑎᖃᕐᓇᖅᑐᐊᖅᑐᖅ ᓲᕐᓗ ᐆᒪᔪᓂᒃ ᓯᕐᓈᖅᐲᑦ ᓄᖅᑲᖅᑎᑎᓚᐅᖅᑎᓪᓗᒋᑦ ᓇᑦᓯᖅᓯᐅᕐᓂᕐᒥᒃ ᐊᑭᖏᓐᓂᒃ ᑲᑕᒃᑎᑎᓪᓗᑎᒃ ᐱᒋᐊᓕᖖᖅᑐᓂ 1970-ᓂ.

ᒪᕿᔪᓂ ᓯᕗᓂᖃᕐᕕᐅᔪᓂ ᐃᓄᐃᑦ ᓄᓇᒥᔾᔪᒥᖕᓂᒃ ᕿᒪᐃᓯᒪᓂᖃᖅᑎᓪᓗᒋᑦ, ᒐᕙᒪᓄᑦ ᐊᑐᖅᑕᐅᓂᖅ ᐃᓅᓯᓗᒃᑖᒧᑦ ᑐᓐᖓᕕᐅᓕᖅᐳᖅ ᐃᓄᐃᑦ ᑮᓇᐅᔭᓕᐅᕐᕕᖏᑎᒍᑦ. ᐊᒥᓱᓪᓗᐊᓪᓚᑦ ᐅᖃᖅᓯᒪᖅᑐᑦ ᑕᒪᑐᒥᖓ ᓇᖏᓂᖅ ᓇᖏᖅᓯᒪᒍᓐᓇᕐᓂᖅ ᐃᓇᖏᖅᑕᐅᓚᐅᕐᓂᖓᓂᒎᖅ ᐱᑕᖃᓕᖅᑎᑕᐅᓗᓂ. ᒫᓐᓇᐅᔪᑮᖅ ᑭᓯᐊᓂ, ᓄᓇᕗᖃᓕᕈᑎ ᐃᓄᐃᑦ ᐊᒻᒪᓗ ᓇᖏᓂᖃᓕᕈᑎ ᓄᓇᑏᖅᑕᒥᖕᓂᒃ, ᐃᓄᐃᑦ ᐅᑎᕋᔭᕋᓯᕆᔭᐅᔪᑦ ᐃᖏᒥᖕᓂᒃ ᐃᖏᕋᑎᑎᒍᓐᓇᕐᓂᕐᒥᒃ ᐊᐅᓚᑦᑎᓚᐅᖅᑕᒥᖕᓄᑦ.

ᐃᓄᐃᑦ ᐱᓇᓱᖕᓂᕆᓯᒪᔭᖏᑦ ᐱᒋᐊᑐᐃᓐᓇᓚᐅᙱᑦᑐᑦ ᓄᓇᕗᑖᕋᓯᖕᓂᑐᐃᓐᓈᒃᑯᑦ. ᓯᕗᓂᒥ ᐃᓅᖕᓄᑦ ᐊᐅᓚᑕᐅᒍᓐᓇᖅᑐᒃᑯᑦ ᐃᓛᒃ. ᐱᒋᐊᓕᖖᖅᑐᓂ 1950-ᓂ ᐊᒻᒪᓗ 1960-ᓂ, ᒐᕙᒪᐃᑦ

Nunatsiaq News ᓄᓇᑦᓯᐊᖅ ᓂᐅᔅ

Creation of a decentralized territorial government will bring construction jobs like Pauloosie Akavak's, left, and other more lasting benefits to many Nunavut communities
ᓴᖅᑭᑦᑎᓂᖅ ᒐᕙᒪᒥᓐ ᓄᓇᕕᒻᒧ ᐃᓗᓕᐅᕐᓂᕐᒥ ᓴᖅᑭᑦᑎᓂᐅᒐᖅ ᐆᑐᓇᖅ ᐸᐅᓗᓯ ᐋᑲᕚᒃᑐᑦ, ᓴᐅᒥᐊᓂ, ᐊᒻᒪᓗ ᐊᓯᙱᓐᓂᑦ ᓴᖅᑮᔪᙱᓐᓇᕈᓐᓇᕐᑐᓂᑦ ᓄᓇᕗᑦ ᓄᓇᓕᙱᓐᓂᑦ

the settlement of land claims and the establishment of a de facto Inuit territory, are Inuit in a position to regain their lost independence.

Inuit efforts at taking control of their own economic future did not begin with the creation of Nunavut. In the 1950s and 1960s, government encouraged the formation of local co-operatives. Despite — or because of — massive infusions of government money over the intervening decades, most have been only marginally successful.

Today almost every community has a Northern store (the modern take on the HBC trading posts of yesterday), and most have a co-op and other private enterprises. Both federal and territorial governments have provided incentives for northern businesses, and the incentives have been greater for Inuit-owned businesses or those training and employing Inuit.

The modern Nunavut community provides jobs: in government, municipal services, teaching and nursing, clerking, transportation, maintenance, and in entrepreneurial pursuits. It provides a subsistence living in hunting and trapping. For some it provides a good living as artists, or as wage laborers in seasonal construction. And in each community, professional-level jobs are increasingly held by Inuit. But for most Inuit, life has become a tenuous mix of wage labor and hunting. Family and extended family partnerships — often invisible to the outsider — ensure that the hunter has access to cash for machinery and gas, and the wage laborer has access to country food and skins for clothing. But with few exceptions, the small communities remain heavily dependent on government dollars.

Prospects

Nearly half of Nunavut residents are under the age of 20, whereas this group represents just 27 per cent of Canadians as a whole, meaning that job creation cannot hope to keep up. Unemployment is high. So is disillusionment, as evidenced by high rates of suicide and substance abuse. The education system has not succeeded in graduating Inuit professionals — doctors, nurses, lawyers, accountants — and so non-Inuit, some of whom become committed

ᐃᑲᔪᕐᓯᓚᐅᖅᑐᑦ ᓴᓇᔨᐅᓂᙱᓐᓂᒃ ᑯᐊᐸᓖᑦ ᓄᓇᓕᕐᓂ. ᑖᐃᒪᐃᒃᑲᓗᐊᖅᑎᓪᓗᒍ — ᐃᒻᒪᖄ ᐱᔾᔪᑕᐅᓪᓗᓂ — ᐊᙳᔪᓂᒃ ᑮᓇᐅᔭᓂᒃ ᐃᑲᔪᕈᑎᖃᖅᓯᒪᑎᑕᐅᓂᒃᑯᑦ ᐊᕐᖁᔪᓂ ᖄᖏᖅᓯᒪᔪᓂ, ᐱᓪᓗᐊᕈᑕᐅᓯᒪᙱᑦᑐᑦ ᐃᓚᑐᐃᓐᓇᖕᒐᒍᑦ ᐃᖏᕐᖃᑦᑎᐊᖅᓯᒪᓂᖃᖅᑐᑦ.

ᐅᓪᓗᒥᓕ ᑕᒪᕐᒥᒃᓴᐃᑦ ᓄᓇᓖᑦ ᓂᐅᕕᕐᕕᖃᖅᑐᑦ Hᐊᑦᓴᓐ ᐋᒥᒃ (ᒪᓕᒐᖃᖅᑐᑎᒃ ᑕᐃᒃᑯᓂᖓ ᓂᐅᕕᖅᑎᐅᕙᓚᐅᖅᑐᕕᓂᕐᓂᒃ ᓯᕗᓂᕐᒥᐅᓚᐅᖅᑐᓂ), ᐊᒻᒪᓗᑦᑕᐅᖅ ᐊᒥᓱᑦ ᑯᐊᐸᖃᖅᑐᑦ ᐊᓯᙱᓐᓂᓪᓗ ᓇᒻᒥᓂᖃᔪᐅᔪᓂᒃ ᐱᓇᓱᒻᕕᖃᖅᑐᑎᒃ. ᑕᒪᒃᑭᖕᓂᒃ ᑲᓇᑕᐅᑉ ᒐᕙᒪᒃᑯᖏᑦ ᐊᒻᒪᓗ ᓄᓇᑦᓯᐊᑉ ᒐᕙᒪᒃᑯᖏᑉ ᐅᑭᐅᖅᑕᖅᑐᒥᐅᓂᒃ ᐱᓯᓇᓯᓕᕐᓂᒃ ᐱᓕᒻᒪᒃᓴᕈᑎᖅᑲᖅᑎᑎᓯᒪᔪᒃ. ᐊᒻᒪᓗ ᐃᑲᔪᖅᑕᐅᒍᑎᑦ ᐱᑕᖅᑲᕐᓂᖅᓴᐅᓪᓗᑎᒃ ᐃᓄᐃᑦ ᓇᒻᒥᓂᕆᔭᐅᔪᑦ ᑕᐃᒃᑯᐊᓪᓘᓐᓃᑦ ᐱᓕᒻᒪᒃᓴᕐᕕᖃᖅᑐᓄᑦ ᐊᒻᒪᓗ ᐃᖅᑲᓇᐃᔭᕐᕕᖃᖅᑎᑎᔪᓄᑦ ᐃᓄᖕᓂᒃ.

ᐅᓪᓗᒥᐅᓕᖅᑐᖅ ᐊᑐᖅᑕᐅᔪᒃᑯᑦ ᕿᓇᐅᔭᓕᕆᐅᔪᒃᑯᑦ ᓄᓇᕗᒥ ᓄᓇᓖᑦ ᐱᑕᖅᑲᖅᑎᑎᔪᑦ ᐃᖅᑲᓇᐃᔭᕐᕕᖕᓂᒃ: ᒐᕙᒪᓂ, ᓄᓇᓕᕐᓂ ᐱᔭᑦᑎᕈᑎᐅᔪᓂ, ᐃᓕᓐᓂᐊᖅᑎᑎᓂᕐᓂ ᐊᒻᒪᓗ ᒧᓇᖅᓯᐅᓂᒃᑯᑦ, ᐊᓪᓚᒃᑎᐅᓂᒃᑯᑦ, ᐃᖏᕐᕋᑦᑕᐅᑦᓯᓇᓂᒃᑯᑦ, ᓴᓗᒻᒪᖅᓴᐃᔨᐅᓂᒃᑯᑦ, ᐊᒻᒪᓗ ᐊᓯᖏᑎᒍᑦ ᕿᓇᐅᔭᓕᐅᕐᑲᓯᖕᓂᒃᑯᑦ. ᓯᓚᓇᐃᕕᖃᖅᒥᔪᖅ ᒪᖃᐃᑎᐅᓂᒃᑯᑦ/ᐊᖑᓇᓱᒃᑎᐅᓂᒃᑯᑦ ᑎᓴᒐᓂᐊᖅᓯᐅᕐᓂᒃᑯᓪᓗ. ᐃᓚᖏᓐᓄᑦᑐᖅ ᕿᓇᐅᔭᓕᐅᑎᐊᖅᑐᖃᕈᓐᓇᖅᑐᑦ ᐊᓐᓇᐅᒪᓇᑎᐊᖅᑐᒃᑯᑦ ᓴᓇᙳᐊᖅᑎᐅᓂᒃᑯᑦ. ᐅᐸᔫᓐᓇᓕᑦ ᐊᕐᕋᒍᐃ ᐃᓚᖓᓂ ᒪᓕᒃᓗᑎᒃ ᐃᓗᓕᐅᖅᑎᐅᓂᒃᑯᑦ. ᑕᒪᐃᓐᓂᒃᓴᒃ ᓄᓇᓕᐅᔪᓂ, ᐃᓕᓯᒪᔪᑦ ᕿᓇᐅᔭᓕᐅᕈᑎᓕᒫᖅ ᐃᓄᖕᓄᑦ ᐱᑕᖅᑲᐸᓪᓕᐊᔪᑦ. ᑭᓯᐊᓂᓕ, ᐊᒥᓱᓄᑦ ᐃᓄᖕᓄᑦ, ᐃᓕᖅᑯᓯᖅ ᑲᑎᓯᒪᔪᒃᑯᑦ ᑭᓯᐊᓂ ᐃᖏᕐᖑᑕᐅᔪᖅ ᑕᑎᕆᓐᓇᖅᑕᐅᒍᓐᓇᖏᑦᑐᒃᑯᑦ ᑲᑐᑎᓯᒪᔪᒃᑯᑦ ᕿᓇᐅᔭᓕᐅᕐᓂᕐᒥᒃ ᐊᒻᒪᓗ ᐊᖑᓇᓱᖕᓂᕐᒥᒃ. ᐃᓚᕆᑦ ᐊᒻᒪᓗ ᐃᓚᕆᑦ ᐃᑲᔪᖃᑎᒌᖕᓂᖅᑲᖅᑐᑦ ᑕᐱᓈᒃᓗᑎᒃ — ᓯᓚᑎᒥᐅᓂᑦ ᐅᔾᔨᕆᔭᐅᒍᓐᓇᖏᑦᑐᑦ — ᐱᑕᖅᑲᖅᑎᑦᑎᒍᓐᓇᖅᓯᓂᕐᒥᒃ

ᐊᖑᓇᓯᒃᑎ ᐊᒥᐊᒃᑯᖃᓐᖏᑦᑐᒃᑯᑦ ᐅᖅᓯᐊᓗᖅᑲᕐᒪᖔᑦ ᐊᒻᒪᓗ ᐃᖏᕐᖁᐅᑎᓂᒃ ᓯᕗᒻᒧᒍᑕᐅᓂᖅᑲᖅᐸᒃᑐᑦ. ᐊᒻᒪᓗᑦᑕᐅᖅ ᑕᐃᒃᑯᐊ ᐊᖑᓇᓯᑦᑎᐅᖏᑦᑐᑦ ᓂᕿᖅᑲᖅᑎᑕᐅᑦᑕᖅᓗᑎᒃ ᐃᑲᔪᖅᑕᒥᖕᓄᑦ ᓂᕿᒻᒪᖕᓂᒃ ᐊᒻᒪᓗ ᐊᓄᕿᒃᓴᐅᓇᔭᖅᑐᓂᒃ ᐱᑎᑕᐅᕙᒃᓗᑎᒃ. ᐊᒥᔫᙱᑦᑐᑦ ᖃᑦᔫᓐᓇᑯᓗᐃᑦ ᓇᖕᒥᓂᖅ ᕿᓇᐅᔭᓕᐅᖅᐸᒃᑲᓗᐊᖅᑎᓪᓗᒋᑦ, ᓄᓇᓕᖕᒥᐅᑕᐃᑦ ᐃᓄᑭᓐᓂᖅᓴᓂ ᐃᑲᔪᖅᑕᐅᓂᒃᑯᑦ ᑭᓯᐊᓂ ᒐᕙᒪᒃᑯᑦ ᐊᓐᓇᐅᒪᒍᑎᖅᑲᓯᖅᑐᑦ.

ᓯᕗᓂᕐᒥ ᐱᒍᓐᓇᐅᑕᐅᒍᓐᓇᖅᑐᑦ

ᖃᓂᒋᔭᖓᓂ ᓇᑉᐸᖓᑕ ᓄᓇᕗᒥ ᐃᓄᖁᑎᒋᔭᐅᔪᑦ ᐅᑭᐅᓖᑦ 20-ᓂᒃ ᐊᑖᓂᒻᒪᑕ, ᐊᒻᒪᓗ ᑖᒃᑯᐊ ᐃᓚᒋᔭᐅᑐᐃᓐᓇᖁᓗᐊᖅᑎᓪᓗᒋᑦ 27 ᐳᓴᑎᒋᔭᐅᓪᓗᑎᒃ ᑲᓇᑕᒥᐅᑕᓖᒫᓂᑦ, ᑐᑭᓕᒃ ᐃᖅᑲᓇᐃᔭᖅᑎᑎᓂᖅ ᐊᖑᒻᒪᑎᒍᓐᓇᖏᓐᓂᖓᓂᒃ ᓂᓄᐅᕝᕕᒃᓴᖃᓐᖏᑦᑐᖅ ᑕᒪᓐᓇ.

ᐃᖅᑲᓇᐃᔮᖃᓐᖏᑦᑐᑦ ᐳᖅᑐᓗᐊᖅᑐᑦ. ᐊᒻᒪᓗᑦᑕᐅᖅ ᖁᓚᓕᕐᓂᖅ, ᑕᒪᓐᓇᓗ ᑕᑯᔭᐅᔪᓐᓇᖅᑐᖅ ᐊᒥᔫᓗᐊᖅᑐᑦ ᐃᖕᒥᓂᒃᑕᑦᓯᙱᑎᒍᑦ ᐊᒻᒪᓗ ᓂᐅᖅᑐᖅᔪᖓᖅᑐᓂᒃ ᐊᑐᖅᑲᑦᑕᕐᓂᖅ. ᐃᓕᓐᓂᐊᖅᑐᓕᕆᔨᐅᔪᑦ ᓯᓕ ᐱᔪᓐᓇᖅᑐᓂᒃ ᐃᓕᓐᓂᐊᕐᓂᕐᒥᖕᓂᒃ ᐃᓕᓯᒪᔪᑦ ᓯᓚᓐᓇᐊᖕᒋᖓᑦ ᐃᓕᖅᑲᖅᑎᑕᐅᔪᑎᒃ ᐱᑕᖅᑲᖅᑎᑦᑎᖕᓇᙱᒪᑕ. ᒪᑯᓂᖓ — ᔫᒃᑖᓂᒃ, ᓘᓐᓇᖅᓯᓂᒃ, ᒪᓕᒐᓕᕆᔨᓂᒃ, ᕿᓇᐅᔭᓕᕆᔨᐅᔪᓐᓃᓪᓗ — ᐊᒻᒪᓗ ᑕᐃᒪ ᓄᓇᖅᑲᖅᑳᖅᑎᐅᙱᑦᑐᓄᑦ, ᐃᓚᖏᑦ ᐊᖏᖅᑲᑕᖅᓗᐊᖅᑐᑦ ᓄᓇᕗᒥ, ᑕᒪᒃᑯᓂᖓ ᑕᒪᐃᓐᓂᒃᑲᓴ ᓯᓚᓇᐊᖅᓯᒪᔪᑦ ᐃᖅᑲᓇᐃᔮᓇᔭᐅᔪᓂ.

to making Nunavut their long-term home, hold almost all of these jobs.

The myth that all Inuit are natural artists has also been dispelled, to the dismay of many who relied on the selling of soapstone carvings for their livelihood. Many warehouses are today filled with unsalable Inuit art and craft items. Governments and Inuit organizations are addressing this dilemma, and a strategy is being developed to support a true art market.

Mining has always been important in Nunavut. From the fool's gold that tricked English explorer Martin Frobisher in the 16th century, to the Kitikmeot copper that supplied Inuit with weapons and tools, to the mica mines of Kimmirut at the turn of the present century, minerals have been sporadically exploited by both Inuit and non-Inuit. Modern mining in Nunavut began in Rankin Inlet in the 1950s with a nickel mine. Many believe that Inuit in the Keewatin acquired their well-known entrepreneurial streak from their experience working at the mine. Nanisivik, a lead and zinc mine in operation since 1974, is the longest-running mine in Nunavut. Nanisivik has often been called a failure because it never achieved the goal of 60 per cent Inuit employment. Yet it is a major success story because of its consistent achievement of 20 to 25 per cent Inuit employment at a time when no other employers, including the federal and territorial governments, could claim statistics anywhere close. Mining today holds great promise for Nunavut.

Tourism, often cited as a panacea for Nunavut's economic woes, is not. Despite unparalleled physical beauty and exotic wildlife, high airfares and poorly developed infrastructure

Fleming/NWT Archives ᕙᓚᒥᖕ/ᓄᓇᕐᓯᐊᕐᒥ ᐸᐸᑕᐅᔪ

ᖃᐅᔨᒪᔭᐅᓇᓯᒋᓂᑯ ᑕᒪᐃᑕ ᐃᓄᐃᑦ ᓴᓇᕐᖑᐊᕈᓐᓇᕐᑎᐅᓂᖏᑦ ᐅᐱᓇᔭᐅᓐᖏᓕᕐᒥᖕᒪᑦ, ᐊᒥᓱᑦ ᓴᓇᕐᖑᐊᖅᑎᐅᓂᒃᑯᑦ ᑮᓇᐅᔾᔭᒃᓴᕈᑎᖃᖅᐸ- ᓚᐅᕋᓗᐊᖅᑐᑎᒃ ᑲᑕᒍᑎᖃᖅᓯᒪᓪᓚᑦᑕᐅᖅ. ᐊᒥᓱᑦ ᓯᕐᓗᐊᖑᔪᑦ ᑕᑳᖅᑐᑦ ᓴᓇᕐᖑᐊᒐᖅᑕᐅᓂᑰᔪᓂᒃ ᓂᐅᕕᖅᑕᐅᔪᓐᓇᓐᖏᑦᑐᓂᒃ ᐊᒡᒐᖑᓪᓗ ᓴᓇᐅᒐᖅᓯ- ᒪᔪᓂᒃ. ᒐᕙᒪᐃᑦ ᐃᓄᐃᓪᓗ ᑕᒪᑐᒥᖓ ᕵᖓᓇᓱᒃᑲᓗᐊᖅᑐᑦ ᐊᔪᕐᓇᕈᑕᐅᓱᖅᑐᒥᒃ, ᐊᒻᒪᓗ ᓯᕗᓂᕐᒧᑦ ᐋᖅᑭᒃᑕᐅᓯᒪᓇᓱᒃᑐᓕᒃ ᐱᕙᓪᓕᐊᑎᑕ- ᐅᖁᓪᓗᒍ ᓱᓕᔪᒃᑯᑦ ᐃᓄᐃᑦ ᓴᓇᐅᒐᖏᓐᓂᒃ ᓂᐅᕕᖅᑕᐅᕙᒍᑎᐅᒍᓐᖅᑐᒃᑯᑦ.

ᐅᔭᕋᖕᓂᐊᕐᓂᖅ ᐊᑐᕐᓂᖃᓪᓚᕆᒃᑐᖅ ᓄᓇᕗᒥ. ᑕᐃᒃᑯᐊ ᒎᓪᒪᓇᐅᓐᖏᑦᑐᐃᓐᓇᖅᓯᐅᑎᒥᓂᖅ ᓴᓪᓗᕿᑕᐅᒍ- ᑕᐅᓪᓗᑎᒃ ᖃᓪᓗᓈᓄᑦ ᐊᑭᐊᒥᐅᓄᑦ ᒫᑎᓐ ᕗᕌᐱᓯᒥᒃ 16-ᖑᔪᒥ ᕼᐊᓐᑕᓪᓚᐅᔪᑦ ᐊᕐᕋᒍᕐᓯᔾᔨᕐᓂ. ᑕᒪᒃᑯᓄᖓᓗ ᑲᓇᔾᔪᑦ ᐊᑐᖅᑕᐅᕙᒃᑐᓄᑦ ᕿᑎᕐᒥᐅᓄᑦ ᓴᓇᕈᑎᒋᔭᐅᓪᓗᑎᒃ ᓯᒋᐊᕈᑕᐅᓪᓗᑎᓪᓗ. ᐅᔭᕋᖕᓂᐊᖅᑕᐅᔪᓄᓪᓗ ᒪᐃᑲᒥᒃ ᑭᒻᒥᕈᒻᒥ ᖃᖓᕕᖑᔪᓯᒪᔪᒥ ᖃᓪᓗᓈᖃᓪᓚᕕᖕᓂᕐᒥ. ᐅᔭᖅᑲᐃᑦ ᐊᑐᖅᑕᐅᑐᖃᖅᓯᒪᔪᑦ ᐃᓄᖕᓄᑦ ᖃᓪᓗᓈᓄᓪᓗ. ᓄᑖᖑᔪᒃᑯᑦ ᐅᔭᕋᖕᓂᐊᕐᓂᖅ ᐱᒋᐊᓚᐅᖅᑐᖅ ᓄᓇᕗᒥ ᑲᖏᖅᖢᓂᕐᒥ 1950ᑦ ᐱᒋᐊᓕᖅᑎᓪᓗᒋᑦ ᐊᒻᒪᓗ ᓂᑲᓪ. ᐊᒥᓱᑦ ᐃᓯᒪᔪᑦ ᓇᒻᒥᓂᖃᖅᑲᔪᖕᓂᖏᑦᑕ ᐃᓄᒃᑎᖏᑦᑕ ᑭᐸᓪᓕᐅᑉ ᑕᐃᑲᖕᖓ ᐱᒋᐊᓚᐅᖃᓯᒋᔭᐅᓪᓗᓂ. ᐃᖅᑲᐃ- ᔭᖃᑦᑕᖅᓂᒃᑯᑦ ᐅᔭᕋᖕᓂᐊᕐᕕᖕᓂ. ᓇᓂᓯᕕᒃ, ᐋᖅᑭᒃᓴᒥᒃ ᐊᒻᒪᓗ ᔨᖕᒃᒥᒃ ᐅᔭᕋᖕᓂᐊᕐᕕᐅᔪᖅ ᐱᒋᐊᓚᐅᖅᑐᖅ 1974-ᖑᑎᓪᓗᒍ. ᐊᒻᒪᓗ ᐊᑯᓂᐅᓂᖅᐸᐅᔪᒥᒃ ᐃᖏᕐᕋᓯᒪᔪᖅ ᐅᔭᕋᖕ- ᓂᐊᕐᕕᖕᓂ. ᓇᓂᓯᕕᒃ ᐃᑲᔪᕐᓗᐊᓐᖏᓐᓂᖏᑦᑐᑦ ᑕᐃᔭᐅᓯᒪᔪᖅ 60 ᐳᓴᓐᑎᒧᑦ ᑎᑭᓯᒪᓐᖏᓐᓂᖕᒐ ᐃᖅᑲᐃᔭᖅᑎᑎᓂᖅ ᐃᓄᖕᓂᒃ. ᑭᓯᐊᓂᓕ ᐊᑲᐅᒋᔭᐅᓯᒪᖕᒥᔪᖅ 20-ᒥᑦ 25-ᒧᑦ ᐳᓴᓐᑎᒧᑦ ᐃᓄᖕᓂᒃ ᐃᖅᑲᐃᔭᖅᑎᑎᓯᒪᓂᖕᖓᓐᓂᒃ ᐅᓪᓗᕆᔭᒥ ᐱᑕᖃᓐᖏᑎᓪᓗᒍ ᑕᐃᒪᓐᓇᑎᑐᑦ ᐃᑲᔪᖅᑎᕆᔪᒥᒃ. ᐃᓚᐅᓪᓗᑎᒃ ᑲᓇᑕᐅᑉ ᒐᕙᒪᖓ ᐊᒻᒪᓗ ᓄᓇᑦᓯᐊᑉ ᒐᕙᒪᖓ. ᐅᓪᓗᒥᓕ ᐅᔭᕋᖕᓂᐊᕐᓂᖅ ᓂᕆᐅᓐᓇᑦᑎᐊᕐᕕᖅᑐᖅ ᓄᓇᕗᒥ.

Same waters, different visitors. Seen here circa 1908, the last of the old arctic whaling ships, the Active, *above, has yielded Nunavut's waters to modern cruise ships and tourists, below. These passengers explore Kekerten, site of one of the whalers' most important stations*

ᐃᒪᖅ ᑖᓐᓇᑕᐃᓐᓇᖅ, ᐊᔾᔨᒋᖕᒋᑕᖕᒋ ᐳᓛᖅᑏ. ᐅᓇ 1908ᓕᖅᓴᖅ, ᕿᖑᓪᓕᖅᐹᖑᖃᑕᐅᔪᖅ ᐊᕐᕕᖕᓂᐊᖅᑏ ᐅᒥᐊᖕᒋᓐᓂ, ᐊᑎᓕᒃ Active-ᒥ (ᐋᒃᑎᕝ), ᖁᓛᓂ, ᒪᓂᒻᒪᐃᓯᒪᓕᖅᐳᑦ ᐅᑭᐅᖅᑕᖅᑰ ᐃᒪᖕᒐᓂ ᐊᓯᖕᒋᓐᓄᑦ ᐅᒥᐊᖅᔪᐊᓄᑦ ᐳᓚᖅᑏᓄᓪᓗ, ᐊᑖᓂ. ᐅᑯᐊ ᐃᑭᒪᔪᕕᓃᑦ ᕿᒥᕿᒡᔪᑦ ᕿᑭᖅᑕᓂ, ᑖᓇ ᐅᐸᒃᑕᐅᒐᔪᓚᐅᖅᑐᕕᓂᖅ ᐊᕐᕕᖕᓂᐊᖅᑎᓄᑦ

Food Costs ᓂᕿᑦ ᐊᑭᑐᓂᖏᑦ

	Toronto ᑐᕌᓐᑐᒥ	Iqaluit ᐃᖃᓗᖕᓂ
2 litres of 2% milk 2 ᓖᑕ 2ᐳᓴ ᐃᒻᒧᒃ	$2.79	$5.71
1 dozen large eggs 1 ᑑᖅᓯᒪᔪᑦ ᒪᓐᓃᑦ	$1.65	$2.95
1 loaf white bread ᐊᑕᐅᓯᖅ ᐸᓚᐅᒐᖅ ᖃᑯᖅᑐᖅ	$0.89	$2.59
Bucket of KFC chicken KFC ᑑᖅ ᐊᑕᐅᓯᖅ ᐊᕿᒋᖅ	$21.99	$43.99

conspire to slow growth. Tourism today remains only a small piece in the puzzle of northern economic development.

A major part of putting the puzzle together will be the Nunavut Land Claims Agreement (NLCA). When Inuit set out to settle their land claims with the federal government, it was not enough for them to have some Inuit land, and to trade ownership of the rest of the land for cash compensation. There had to be incentives for Inuit ownership of businesses, and Inuit employment.

Article 24 of the Nunavut final agreement compels the federal and territorial governments to adopt policies that maximize the involvement of Inuit in Nunavut business, through outright Inuit ownership, Inuit majority ownership, joint ventures with non-Inuit firms, and employment. Questions remain about how Article 24 should be applied, but its very existence has led to a radical change in the way business operates in Nunavut, and a very obvious increase in Inuit involvement in business at all levels. Meanwhile, Article 23 of the settlement calls for training to work toward the goal of a representative public service in which 85 per cent of civil servants will be Inuit.

A unique phenomenon in the evolution of northern business is the rise of the "birthright corporation." Nunasi Corporation, headquartered —

ᐳᓚᕋᖅᑐᓕᕆᓂᖅ, ᐃᓯᒪᒋᔭᐅᓚᐅᖅᑲᓗᐊᖅᑐᖅ ᐃᑲᔪᕐᓂᐊᖅᓯᒋᔭᐅᓪᓗᓂ ᓯᓇᑐᐃᓐᓇᕐᓂᒃ ᓄᓇᕗᑖᕈᑎᒥᓪᓗᓂᒃ (NCLA). ᐃᓄᐃᑦ ᐋᖅᑭᖅᑎᖅᑲᓚᐅᖅᑎᓪᓗᒋᑦ ᓄᓇᕗᑖᖅᓯᖕᓂᕐᒧᑦ ᑲᓇᑕᐅᑉ ᒐᕙᒪᒃᑯᑎᖏᓐᒍᑦ, ᓄᓇᑖᑐᐃᓐᓇᕐᓂᕐᒥᒃ ᓈᒻᒪᒋᔭᖅᑲᓚᐅᓐᖏᒻᒪᑕ. ᐊᒻᒪᓗ ᑭᐳᑕᐅᓗᓂ ᓄᓇᒋᔭᐅᔪᖅ ᑮᓇᐅᔭᑖᖅᑎᑕᐅᓂᕐᒧᑦ. ᐱᑕᖃᕆᐊᖃᓚᐅᕐᒪᑦ ᐃᑲᔪᖅᑕᐅᒍᑎᓂᒃ ᐃᓄᐃᑦ ᓄᓇᕗᒥ ᓇᖕᒥᓂᖅ ᐱᓯᓇᓯᖃᕐᑯᓪᓗᒋᑦ, ᐃᓄᖕᓄᑦ ᓇᖕᒥᓂᕆᔭᖃᕐᓂᒃᑯᑦ ᐃᓄᑐᐃᓐᓇᕐᓄᑦ, ᐃᓄᖕᓄᑦ ᐊᒥᓱᓂᖅᓴᓄᑦ ᓇᖕᒥᓂᖃᖅᑎᑕᐅᓂᖏᓐᓄᑦ, ᑕᐱᖃᕐᓂᒃᑯᑦ ᓄᓇᖃᖅᑲᖅᑎᐅᖏᑦᑐᒃᑯᑦ, ᐊᒻᒪᓗ ᐃᖅᑲᓇᐃᔭᖅᑎᑕᐅᓂᒃᑯᑦ. ᐊᐱᕆᔭᐅᒍᑎᑦ ᖃᓄᖅ ᐃᓚᖓ 24 ᐊᑐᖅᑕᐅᓂᐊᕐᓂᖓᓄᑦ, ᐱᑕᖃᕐᓂᖓ ᐊᓯᔾᔨᕈᑕᐅᓪᓚᑲᒃᓯᒪᖕᒪᑦ ᖃᓄᖅ ᓄᓇᕗᒥ ᐱᓯᓇᓯᒋᔭᐅᔪᑦ ᐊᐅᓚᑕᐅᖃᒃᑕᕐᓂᖕᖏᓐᓄᑦ. ᑕᑯᔭᐅᔪᓐᓇᖅᑐᒃᑯᓪᓗ ᐱᓯᓪᓗᐊᑎᑎᓂᖓᑦ ᐃᓄᐃᑦ ᐃᓚᖃᑕᐅᓕᕐᓂᖏᓐᓂᒃ ᐱᓯᓇᓯᖅᑲᖅᑐᒃᑯᑦ ᐅᔾᔨᕐᓇᒻᒪᕆᖕᒥᔪᖅ. ᑕᐃᒪᓂᑦᑕᐅᖅ ᓯᓚ, ᐃᓚᖓ 23-ᒥ ᓄᓇᕗᑖᕈᑎᒥ ᑐᕌᒃᓴᖅᑲᖅᒥᔪᖅ ᐱᓕᒻᒪᒃᓴᖅᑎᑎᓂᕐᒥᒃ ᑭᒃᑯᒃᑖᓄᑦ ᐃᖅᑲᓇᐃᔭᖅᑎᒃᓴᓂᒃ 85 ᐳᓴᓐᑎᖏᑦ ᑭᕙᓪᓕᖅᑐᐃᔪᑦ ᐃᓅᕈᓪᓗᒋᑦ.

ᐊᔾᔨᒋᔭᐅᓐᖏᑦᑐᖅ ᐱᕙᓪᓕᐊᑎᑕᐅᓂᖓᓂ ᐅᑭᐅᖅᑕᖅᑐᒥ ᐱᓯᓇᓯᖅᑲᖅᑐᓂ ᐱᕈᖅᐸᓪᓕᐊᓂᖓ "ᓇᖕᒥᓂᓕᖕᓄᑦ ᑯᐊᐳᕆᐃᓇᐅᔪᑦ." ᓄᓇᓯ ᑯᐊᐳᕇᓴᓐ, ᐊᖓᔪᖅᑳᖃᕐᕕᓕᒃ — ᓇᐃᓐᓂᐊᖅᑐᒥᖅᑲᐃ - ᔭᓇᐃᒥ, ᓇᖕᒥᓂᖃᖅᑐᖅ ᑭᒃᑯᒃᑖᓄᑦ ᐃᓄᖕᓄᑦ. ᓄᓇᕗᒥ ᐱᖓᓱᐃᔪᓂ ᐊᕕᒃᑐᖅᓯᒪᓂᖏᓐᓂ ᓇᖕᒥᓂᓖᑦ ᑮᓇᐅᔭᓕᕆᓂᕐᒧᑦ ᐱᕙᓪᓕᐊᑎᑎᔨᐅᔪᓂᒃ. ᓇᖕᒥᓂᓴᐅᔪᖅ ᐃᓄᐃᑦ ᑕᐃᒃᑳᓐᑐᑦ ᐊᕕᒃᑐᖅᓯᒪᔪᒥ ᐃᑲᔪᖅᑕᐅᕐᑯᓪᓗᒋᑦ. ᑲᑐᔾᔨᔾᔨᖕᒋᓈᑦ ᐊᕕᒃᑐᖅᓯᒪᔪᓂ ᑮᓇᐅᔭᓕᐅᖅᑎᐅᒍᑎᖅᑲᖅᐳᑦ. ᑕᒃᑯᐊ ᑯᐊᐳᕇᓴᒋᔭᐅᔪᑦ ᓇᖕᒥᓂᓴᐅᔪᑦ ᓴᓐᖏᔪᑦ ᐱᓯᓇᓯᑐᐃᓐᓇᐅᓐᖏᒻᒪᑕ: ᐃᓚᖃᕐᓯᖕᒍᔪᑦ ᐃᓅᓯᕐᒥᒃ ᐃᑲᔫᑎᒃᓴᓂᒃ, ᐊᒥᓱᑦ ᓇᖕᒥᓂᓴᐅᔪᑦ ᐱᓯᓇᓯᓛᑦ, ᑕᒪᕐᒥᒃ ᐃᓄᖕᓄᑦ ᓇᖕᒥᓂᓴᐅᔪᑦ ᐊᓯᖏᓐᓄᓪᓗ, ᖁᕝᕙᐊᒋᓴᖅᓯᖑᓐᖏᑦᑐᑦ ᐃᓯᒪᑕᐅᓂᖏᓐᓂᒃ ᓇᖕᒥᓂᓴᐅᔪᑦ ᑯᐊᐳᕇᓴᖕᑯᔪᑦ. ᐅᑭᐅᖅᑕᖅᑐᒥ ᓱᕐᓗ ᐃᓇᖏᖅᓯᓗᐊᖅᓯᒪᑎᓪᓗᒋᑦ ᐱᓯᓇᓯᖅᑲᖅᑐᓂᒃ ᓇᖕᒥᓂᖅᑲᖅᑐᓂᒃ.

Nunatsiaq News

Nunavut Tourism

With only 21 kilometres of inter-community roadway, Nunavut towns and hamlets still rely heavily on an annual "sealift," left, when open waters allow economical sea-borne delivery of bulk goods and heavy equipment (like that maintained by Jonah Evaloardjuk, above)

21 ᑭᓛᒥᑕᒃᑐᐃᓐᓇᕐᒥ ᑕᑭᓂᖅᑲᖅᓗᓂ ᐊᖅᑯᑎ, ᓄᓇᕗᑦ ᓄᓇᓖᑦ ᐊᒻᒪ ᕼᐋᒻᓚᑦᖏ ᓯᓚ ᐅᒥᐊᕐᔪᐊᓂ ᐊᑐᒻᒪᓂᒃᐳᑦ ᐱᖁᑎᑖᕐᓂᖅᒧᑦ ᓴᐅᒥᐊᓂ, ᓯᑯᐃᖅᑎᓪᓗᒍ ᐊᕐᖏᔪᓂ ᐱᖁᑎᓂ ᑎᑭᐅᔾᔨᕙᒃᑕᖅᒪᑕ ᓄᓇᓯᐅᑎᓂᓪᓗ ᐅᖁᒪᐃᑦᑐᓂ (ᐆᑐᓇᖅ ᑲᒪᒋᔭᐅᔪᑎᑐᑦ ᔫᓇ ᐃᕙᓗᐊᖅᔫ, ᖁᓛᓂ)

one hopes temporarily — in Yellowknife, is owned by all the Inuit of Nunavut. Each of Nunavut's three regions has its own economic development corporation, owned beneficially for all the Inuit of that region by the regional Inuit political organization as its economic-development arm. These birthright corporations are more than just powerful and diversified businesses: they generally contain a component of social-development agency as well, though many private businesses, both Inuit and non-Inuit owned, complain of the dominance of the birthright corporations in the competition for northern business.

While the capital and the regional centres in Nunavut are thriving, life remains tough in most Nunavut communities. For this reason, the Nunavut Implementation Commission (NIC) recommended a decentralized model for Nunavut's government, allowing the economic boost of the creation of the government to be shared with the maximum number of citizens. It was a noble recommendation, and it was endorsed by the federal and territorial governments, and Nunavut Tunngavik Incorporated (NTI), which administers the implementation of the NLCA for Inuit. It will take determination and political will to ensure its success, but the people of Nunavut deserve no less.

With the dawn of Nunavut, most of its citizens remain oblivious to the extent of their dependence on the continued largesse of the federal taxpayer. But the situation is improving. With the leadership of the Inuit political organizations and governments, and the partnerships being fostered between Inuit and non-Inuit business, growth is being encouraged in every sector of the northern economy, be it mining, transportation, renewable resource development, or tourism. Determined Nunavut leaders will have to be, like camp "bosses" of centuries past, strong-willed individuals, willing to draw on traditional Inuit values and skills, as well as the talents and energies of relative newcomers, to create a thriving Nunavut.

Businessman Kenn Harper of Iqaluit is also a historian, linguist and author who has lived 30 years in the Arctic.

ᐊᖓᔪᖅᑮᒃᑯᐱᒃ ᐊᒻᒪ ᐃᓄᒋᐊᖕᓂᖅᓴᐃᑦ ᓄᓇᕗᒥ ᐱᕐᕈᖅᐸᓪᓕᐊᑦᑎᐊᕋᓱᐊᖅᑎᓪᓗᒋᑦ, ᐊᓯᕐᖅᓴᕋᑕ ᓱᓕ ᐊᒥᓱᑦ ᓄᓇᓕᐅᔭᐅᔪᑦ ᓄᓇᕗᒥ. ᑕᐃᒪᓐᓇ ᐱᔾᔪᑎᒋᓪᓗᒍ ᓄᓇᕗᑦ ᒪᓕᒃᓴᓕᕆᔨᖏᑦ (NIC) ᐱᒋᐊᖅᑎᑎᕈᔾᔭᓚᐅᖅᑐᑦ ᐊᖓᔪᖅᑮᒃᑯᐱᖓ ᓯᐊᒻᒪᒃᓯᓂᖅᓴᐅᕙᓪᓗᒍ ᐱᒃᓴᖅᑐᓂᖓ ᓄᓇᓕᖕᒥᐅᓂᖅᓴᐅᓗᓂ. ᑮᓇᐅᔮᐃᑦ ᐱᕈᖅᐸᓪᓕᐊᒐᔭᕐᓂᖏᑦ ᓯᐊᒻᒪᒃᓯᒪᓂᖅᓴᐅᕙᓪᓗᒋᑦ ᓇᒧᒃᑖᑦ ᐃᓄᒃᖅᑐᓂ. ᑕᒪᓐᓇ ᐅᐱᓐᓇᕋᓗᐊᖅᑐᖅ ᐱᒋᐊᖅᑕᐅᕙᔭᐅᔪᖅ, ᐊᒻᒪ ᐃᑲᔪᖅᑕᐅᓂᖅᖃᕈᓂ ᑲᓇᑕᐅᑉ ᒪᓕᒐᖓᓐᓄᑦ ᓄᓇᑦᓯᐊᑉ ᒪᓕᒐᖏᓐᓄᓪᓗ. ᐊᒻᒪ ᑐᕌᖓᐱᒃᑯᓐᓄᑦ. ᑖᒃᑯᐊ ᐊᐅᓪᓚᑎᑦᔨᐅᑎᓪᓗᒋᑦ ᐊᖏᕐᖁᑎᑐᖃᕐᒥᒃ ᓯᕗᓂᒃᑎᑎᓂᕐᒥᒃ ᐃᓄᖕᓄᑦ ᑭᒡᒐᖅᑐᖅᓱᑎᒃ. ᒪᓕᒐᓕᕆᓂᕐᒥᒃ ᐊᒃᓯᑭᑭᑎᖃᕐᓗᑎᒃ ᓯᕗᓪᓕᕆᐊᖃᖃᔭᖅᑐᑦ, ᑭᓯᐊᓂᓕ ᓄᓇᕗᒥᐅᑕᐃᑦ ᐱᐅᔪᒥᒃ ᓂᕆᐅᒋᔭᒃᓴᖃᕆᐊᖃᕋᑕ.

ᓄᓇᕗᑦ ᐱᖁᔪᖅᐸᓪᓕᐊᑎᓪᓗᒍ, ᐊᒥᓱᑦ ᐃᓅᖁᑎᔭᖏᑦ ᖃᐅᔨᒪᓗᐊᕐᖓᒻᒪᑕ ᑲᓇᑕᒥᐅᕗᑦ ᑖᒃᓴᖏᓐᓄᑦ ᐊᑭᓕᖅᑕᐅᖃᑦᑕᖅᑐᒃᑯᑦ ᐃᑲᔪᖅᑕᐃᓂᖃᕐᓂᕐᒥᖓᓂᒃ. ᑭᓯᐊᓂᓕ ᑕᒪᓐᓇ ᐋᖅᑭᒃᐸᓪᓕᐊᔫᓗᐊᖅ. ᓯᕗᓕᖅᑎᖏᑎᒍᑦ ᑎᒥᖁᑎᐅᔪᓂ ᐊᒻᒪ ᒪᓕᒋᔭᐅᔪᓂ, ᐊᒻᒪ ᑕᐱᓐᖒᑎᒍᑦ ᐃᓄᖕᓄᑦ ᓄᓇᖃᖅᑳᖓᕆᑦᑐᓄᓐᓄ, ᐱᕈᖅᐸᓪᓕᐊᓂᖅ ᒥᐊᓂᕆᔭᐅᑎᐊᖅᑐᖅ ᐅᑭᐅᖅᑕᖅᑐᑉ ᑮᓇᐅᔭᖏᑕ ᐃᖏᕐᕋᓂᕆᔭᖏᓐᓂ. ᐅᔭᕋᖕᓂᐊᕐᓂᒃᑯᑦ, ᐃᖏᕐᕋᑕᖅᑐᓕᕆᓂᒃᑯᑦ, ᐊᑐᖅᑕᐅᒃᑲᓂᕈᓐᓇᖅᑐᒃᑯᑦ, ᐅᓪᓚᕐᓈᓕᑦ ᐸᓕᖅᑐᓕᕆᓂᒃᑯᑦ. ᓯᕗᒻᒧᒨᒪᔪᖅ ᓯᕗᓕᖅᑏᑦ ᐃᒪᐃᒋᐊᖃᓪᓚᖓᔪᑦ, ᓲᕐᓗ ᓄᓇᓕᐅᓪᓚᐅᖅᑐᓂ "ᐃᓯᒪᑕᐅᔪᑎᑦ ᐱᓯᑎᑦ" ᑕᐃᑦᓯᒪᓂ ᑕᐃᒪᐃᖃᑦᑕᓚᐅᖅᑐᑎᑦ. ᐃᓯᒪᒃᑎᐊᕐᓗᑎᒃ, ᓴᓐᖏᔪᒥᒃ ᐃᓅᓯᒃᓴᕐᓗᑎᒃ, ᑐᖓᓂᖅᑐᓂᒃ ᐃᓄᐃᑦ ᐃᓕᖅᑯᓯᓪᓕᓐᖓᓂᒃ ᐊᒻᒪ ᐊᔪᙱᓐᓂᑎᒃ ᒪᓕᒡᓗᒋᑦ ᐊᒻᒪ ᐆᒪᐅᓂᐅᔪᑦ ᑎᑭᓖᖅᑐᓂ, ᓄᓇᕗᑦ ᐱᕚᑎᐊᖅᑐᒃᑯᑦ ᓴᓇᔪᐸᒃᓴᒃᑯᓪᓗᒍ.

ᓈᒥᓂᓕᒃ ᑭᓐ ᕼᐊᕐᐳ ᐃᖃᓗᖕᒥᐅᑕᐅᔪᖅ ᓯᕗᓂᓕᕆᔨᐅᖕᒥᔪᖅ, ᐅᖃᐅᓯᓕᕆᔨᐅᓪᓗᓂ ᐅᖃᓖᒪᓕᐅᖅᑎᐅᓪᓗᓂᓗ 30-ᓂᒃ ᐊᕐᕌᒍᓂᒃ ᐅᑭᐅᖅᑕᖅᑐᒥᐅᑕᐅᓯᒪᔪᖅ.

Nunavut Tourism ᓄᓇᕗᑦ ᐳᓛᖅᑐᓕᕆᓂᖅ

This 1980 flight over Nunavik (northern Quebec) was typical of arctic air travel of the time (among the passengers, Zebedee Nungak, centre, long-time president of Makivik Corporation). The Iqaluit airport, above, now managed by Qikiqtaaluk Corporation, an Inuit birthright organization, shows how much air travel has developed since, but continually improving infrastructure will be key to a healthy Nunavut economy

ᐅᓇ 1980ᒥ ᖃᖓᑕᔪᐅᓂᒍ ᓄᓇᕕᒃ ᖁᓖᒍ ᑕᒪᓐᓇᓗ ᐊᑐᖅᑕᐅᕙᒃᑐᓂ ᓄᒃᑕᖅᑐᓂ (ᐃᑭᒪᖕᑲᑕᐅᔪᖅ ᔨᐱᑎ ᓅᖕᒐᖅ, ᕿᑎᐊᓂ, ᒪᑭᕕᒃᑯᑦ ᐊᖓᔪᖅᑳᒃᑯᑖᕕᓂᖓᖅ). ᐃᖃᓗᐃᑦ ᒥᕚᖓ, ᖁᓛᓂ, ᒫᓐᓇ ᐊᐅᓚᑕᐅᔪᖅ ᕿᑭᖅᑖᓗᒃ ᑯᐊᐳᕇᓴᓐᑯᓐᓄ, ᐃᓄᐃᑦ ᓄᓇᖃᖅᑳᖅᑐᑦ ᑲᑐᔾᔨᖃᑎᒌᖕᒃᑎᖓᑦ, ᓇᓗᓇᐃᕐᓯᕗᖅ ᖃᖓᑕᖃᑦᑕᕐᓂᖅ ᐅᑭᐅᖅᑕᖅᑐᒥ ᖃᓄᐃᓯᒪᓕᕐᓂᖓᓂ ᑕᐃᒪᓐᖓᓂ, ᐊᒻᒪ ᐱᕚᓪᓕᐊᖕᒋᓐᓇᕐᓗᓂ ᐃᑲᔫᒪᓇᓕᖁᓪᓗᓂᓗ ᐅᑭᐅᖅᑕᖅᑐᒥ ᐱᕚᓪᓕᐊᓂᐅᔪᒥᓐ

Getting Here,
shouldn't be an adventure.
No matter where you're flying across the North, getting here shouldn't be an adventure. Fly Canadian North and fly our northern airline with unmatched service and a friendly northern attitude.
We have the routes and connections you need to get you wherever you want to go in the North... all year round.
For more information and reservations call your travel agent or Canadian North.
Canadian NORTH
A member of the NorTerra Group of Companies
Your North – Your Airline
ᐅᑭᐅᖅᑕᖅᑐᒥ ᓄᓇᑉᓯᖕᓂ - ᖃᖕᒐᑕᔫᖅᑯᑎᓯ
ILIPSI NUNAPSI - ILIPSI TINGMIVIKSI
Canadian NORTH
Winnipeg
Thompson
Churchill
Arviat
Whale Cove
Rankin Inlet
Baker Lake
Chesterfield Inlet
Coral Harbour
Repulse Bay
Cape Dorset
Iqaluit
Pangnirtung
Broughton Island
Ottawa
Calgary
Edmonton
Fort Smith
Hay River
Lutsel K'e
Yellowknife
Wha Ti
Fort Simpson
Rae Lakes
Tulita
Deline
Norman Wells
Fort Good Hope
Fort McPherson
Cambridge Bay
Paulatuk
Inuvik
Tuktoyaktuk
Sachs Harbour
Resolute
Canadian North
Canadian North Future Routes
Canadian Airlines
Air Tindi
North Wright Air
Aklak Air
Calm Air
Kenn Borek Air
Map courtesy of Northern Transportation Company Limited, Hay River, NT

PHOTO BY: MIKE BEEDELL

A celebration of Inuit accomplishment

ᓇᓪᓕᐅᓐᓂᖅᓯᐅᖅᓂᖅ ᐃᓄᐃᑦ ᓴᖅᑭᑎᑕᖕᒐᓂᑦ

Shell Canada congratulates and applauds the Inuit for their determination and vision in creating the new territory of Nunavut. As the guardians of a major portion of our great nation, the citizens of Nunavut have been entrusted with many new challenging opportunities.

In the spirit of co-operation and partnership, Shell Canada looks forward to forging a special relationship with the people of Nunavut. As one of Canada's leading energy companies and a supplier of petroleum products in the North for more than 35 years, we recognize the wisdom of incorporating the traditional knowledge of Inuit elders into future resource development. At Shell Canada, we value safeguarding Nunavut's environment and wildlife, while preserving the values and culture of the Inuit.

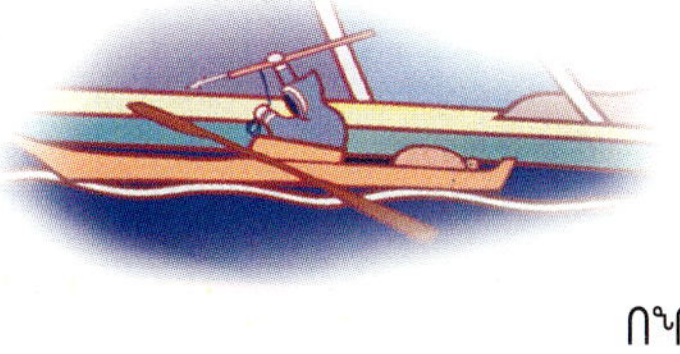

ᓯᐅᓪ ᑲᓇᑕ ᐱᒃᑯᒋᔭᖅᑲᒻᒪᕆᒃᐳᑦ ᐸᑦᑕᒃᑐᐃᓪᓗᑎᒡᓗ ᐃᓄᐃᑦ ᐃᓐᓇᖏᓐᓂ ᐱᓕᕆᐊᖅᑭᓯᐃᓐᓇᖅᑎᓪᓗᒋ ᓯᕗᓂᒃᓴᒥᖕᓂ ᓴᖅᑭᑦᑎᒐᓯᒃᑎᓪᓗᒋᑦ ᓄᑖᒥᓐ ᐊᕕᒃᑐᖅᓯᒪᓂᑎᒍᑦ ᓄᓇᕗᒻᒥ. ᐸᐸᑦᑎᔨᐅᒻᒪᕆᒃᑎᓪᓗᒋ ᐊᖏᔪᒥᓐ ᓄᓇᑦᑕ ᐃᓚᖓᓂᑦ, ᓄᓇᕗᒻᒥᐅᑕᑦ ᓴᖅᑭᑦᑎᕝᕕᐅᓚᖅᐳᑦ ᐱᕕᒃᓴᓂ ᓄᑖᓂᑦ.

ᑲᑐᔾᔨᖃᑎᒌᖕᓂᖅᑎᒍ ᐊᒻᒪ ᐱᓕᕆᖃᑎᒌᖕᓂᒃᑯ, ᓯᐅᓪ ᑲᓇᑕ ᓂᕆᐅᒃᐳᑦ ᐱᓕᕆᖃᑎᖃᕐᓂᒃᓴᒥᓐ ᓄᓇᕗᒻᒥᐅᓂᑦ. ᓯᕗᓕᐅᖅᑎᐅᖃᑕᐅᑎᓪᓗᒋᑦ ᑲᓇᑕᒥᓐ ᐊᐅᓚᔾᔪ-ᑎᖏᓐᓄᑦ ᐊᒻᒪᓗ ᐅᖅᓱᐊᓗᖕᒥ ᐱᔦᑦᑎᖃᐅᑎᖃᖅᑎᓪᓗᒋ ᐅᑭᐅᖅᑕᖅᑐᕐᒥ ᐊᕐᕌᒍᑦ 35 ᐅᖓᑖᓄᑦ, ᑐᑭᓯᐅᒪᒐᔪᒍᑦ ᐃᓄᐃᑦ ᖃᐅᔨᒪᔾᔪᖏ ᓴᖅᑮᔭᓇᐊᖅᑲᓂᖏᓐᓂᑦ ᓯᕗᓂᒃᓴᒧᓐ ᐱᕙᓪᓕᐊᓂᐊᖅᓂᖑᓐ ᐋᖅᑭᒃᓯᐃᓂᐊᖅᓗᓂ. ᓯᐅᓪ ᑲᓇᑕᐅᑎᓪᓗᑕ, ᓄᓇᕗᑦ ᐊᕙᑎᖓᓂᑦ ᐆᒪᔪᖏᓐᓂᓪᓗ ᓴᐳᔾᔨᓯᒪᕆᐊᖃᕐᓂᖅᑎᓐᓂ, ᑕᒪᓐᓇ ᐃᓕᖅᑯᓯᖅ ᐃᒃᐱᒋᖕᒥᓗᒍᓗ.

Shell Canada Limited

A *Public* GOVERNMENT
ᑭᒃᑯᑐᐃᓐᓇᕐᓄᑦ ᒐᕙᒪ

A largely Inuit public service, a decentralized government, a special relationship with Nunavut's land claim agreement — these are some of the reasons Nunavut will have a government with a twist

ᐊᒥᓲᓪᓗᑎᒃ ᐃᓄᐃᑦ ᐱᓱᑦᑎᖅᑐᓂ ᑭᒃᑯᓗᒃᑖᓄᑦ, ᓴᓐᖏᓂᕆᔭᐅᔪᓂᒃ ᐊᔪᓐᖏᖅᔪᑕᐅᔪᓂᒡᓗ ᓅᓯᒪᔪᖅᖃᕐᓂᖅ, ᐃᓛᒃᑯᑦ ᓴᓇᖃᑎᖃᕐᓂᕐᒥᒃ ᓄᓇᕗᑖᕈᑎᐅᔪᒥᒃ ᐊᖏᕈᓯᒥᒃ — ᑕᒪᒃᑯᐊ ᐃᓚᖏᑦ ᐱᔾᔪᑕᐅᔪᑦ ᓄᓇᕗᑦ ᒐᕙᒪᒥᓂᐊᕐᑕᖓ ᐊᔾᔨᒋᔭᐅᖏᑦᑐᒥᒃ ᒐᕙᒪᐅᓂᖓᓄᑦ

FCA/Arcop Architects in Joint Venture; oval inset: Mike Beedell ᐊᖑᒪᔫᑦ ᐃᓗᐊᓂ: ᒪᐃᒃ ᐱᑐᐅᑦ

By Mike Vlessides

Take 28 communities, spread them over almost two million of the most formidable square kilometres on the Earth's surface, top it off with the daunting task of implementing a new government, and you've got a recipe that would scare off most would-be public servants. Yet this is exactly the task facing the people of Nunavut as April 1, 1999 dawns.

For Inuit, however, a people long renowned for their adaptability, the creation of Nunavut and the administrative government it requires has been well conceived, and owes its roots to more than two decades of vision and dedication.

The government of Nunavut is a public government, not an ethnic form of self-government. Negotiators working on a land claims agreement for Nunavut decided early on to opt for a public government, a pragmatic decision that would aid them in their quest to achieve a territory. Thomas Suluk, one of several former chief negotiators, recalls that the people originally wanted an Inuit government. But negotiators urged them to "eliminate this nativeness, this separateness, because it doesn't have a snowball's chance in hell of making it." By supporting a public government, "we can get the same thing."

Nick Newbery

ᑎᑎᕋᖅᑐᖅ ᒪᐃᒃ ᕝᓚᓯᑎᔅ

ᓴᓂᕝᕙᐃᒍᑲᑦ 28-ᓂᒃ ᓄᓇᓕᖕᓂᒃ, ᓯᐊᒻᒪᒃᑐᒋᑦ ᐅᖓᑖᓂ ᒥᕐᕈᒃ ᒥᓕᐊᓐᓄᑦ ᑭᓗᒦᑕᓄᑦ ᓯᒃᑭᑕᓄᑦ ᓯᓚᕐᔪᐊᑉ ᖄᖓᓄᑦ ᓄᓇᕐᑯᑎᖓᓄᑦ, ᓄᓇ ᑲᐱᐊᓇᖅᑐᖅᑳᖅᐸᒃᑎᓪᓗᒍ ᐊᒻᒪᓗ ᐃᓚᒍᒍ ᒐᕙᒪᒥᒃ ᑲᔪᓯᑦᓯᒋᐊᖃᕐᓂᕐᒥᒃ, ᑕᐃᒪᓗ ᑲᑉᐱᐊᒋᔭᐅᓕᕋᔭᖅᑐᖅ ᑭᓇᑐᐃᓐᓇᕐᒧᑦ ᒐᕙᒪᓄᑦ ᐱᓯᑦᑎᖅᑎᐅᒍᒪᒐᔭᖅᑐᒧᑦ. ᑭᓯᐊᓂᓕ ᑕᐃᒪᓐᓇᑦᑎᐊᖅ ᓴᓇᔭᒃᓴᐅᔪᑦ ᐱᑕᖃᓕᖅᑐᑦ ᓄᓇᕗᒥᐅᓄᑦ ᑲᒪᒋᔭᐅᒥᐊᓕᕐᓂᒃ ᑎᑭᓕᖅᑎᓕᖅᑎᓪᓗᒍ ᐄᐳᓗ 1, 1999.

ᐃᓄᖕᓄᓕ ᑭᓯᐊᓂ, ᖃᐅᔨᒪᔭᐅᑦᑎᐊᖅᑐᑦ ᐊᔪᓐᖏᑦᑐᕐᓂᕐᖏᓐᓄᑦ, ᓄᓇᕗᑦ ᑲᔪᓯᑎᑕᐅᓂᖓ ᐊᒻᒪᓗ ᒐᕙᒪᖓᑕ ᐊᐅᓚᑦᑎᓲᕖᐅᔭᕈᑎᖓ ᐸᕐᓇᒃᑕᐅᑦᑎᐊᖅᓯᒪᓕᕐᒪᑎᒃ. ᐊᒻᒪᓗ ᐋᒻᖏᑦ ᐱᒋᐊᖅᓯᒪᔪᑎᖏᑦ ᓯᕗᓂᐊᒍᑦ ᐋᖅᑭᒃᓱᖅᑕᐅᓂᒃᑯᑦ ᐊᒃᓱᕈᕈᑕᐅᓂᒃᑯᑦ ᐃᖏᕋᓕᖅᑎᑕᐅᓯᒪᔪᑦ ᓯᕗᓂᕐᒧᑦ ᐃᓱᒋᑦᑎᐊᕐᓂᕐᒧᑦ ᐃᓱᒪᓕᐅᑦᑎᐊᕈᑎᒧᑦᑐ.

ᑲᕙᒪᒋᔭᐅᔪᖅ ᓄᓇᕗᒥ ᑭᒃᑯᑐᐃᓐᓇᕐᓄᑦ ᑲᕙᒪᒋᔭᐅᔪᖅ, ᐃᒪᐃᓐᖏᓪᓗᓂ ᖃᓄᐃᓐᓂᖓᓂᒃ ᒪᓕᒃᑐᓂ ᐃᓄᕐᑯᑎᖃᕐᓂᖓᓂᒃ ᑲᕙᒪᐅᓐᖏᑦᑐᖅ. ᐊᖏᖅᑲᑎᒌᒐᓯᐊᖅᑎᑦ ᓯᓚᓇᐊᖃᓚᐅᖅᑐᑦ ᓄᓇᕗᑖᕐᓂᕐᒧᑦ ᐊᖏᖅᑲᑎᒌᒍᑎᕖᓂᕐᒥᒃ ᓂᕈᐊᓚᐅᕐᒪᑕ ᐱᒋᐊᕐᓂᖓᓂ ᑭᒃᑯᑐᐃᓐᓇᕐᓄᑦ ᑲᕙᒪᖅᑲᕐᓂᕐᒥᒃ. ᐃᓱᒪᓕᐅᖅᑐᕕᓕᑦ ᐃᓱᒪᑦᑎᐊᖅᑐᑎᒃ ᓄᓇᕗᑖᕋᓯᐊᕈᑎᒃᓴᒥᒃ. ᑖᒪᓯ ᓱᓗᒃ, ᐊᖏᖅᑲᑎᒋᓯᒪᔪᐊᖅᑐᓂ ᐊᖓᔪᖅᑳᖑᖅᑲᑕᐅᔪᖅ ᓯᕗᓕᖅᑎᐅᓪᓗᓂ, ᐃᖅᑲᐅᒪᓪᓗᐊᖅᑐᖅ ᐃᓄᐃᑦ ᓯᕗᓪᓕᕐᒥᒃ ᐱᔪᒪᓪᓗᕋᓗᐊᕐᒪᑕ ᐃᓄᖕᓂᒃ ᑲᕙᒪᓕᓐᓂᐊᕈᑎᔪᓂᒃ. ᑭᓯᐊᓂᓕ ᐊᖏᖅᑲᑎᒋᓯᒪᔪᖅᑎᐅᔪᓄᑦ ᐊᔭᐅᖅᑕᐅᓪᓗᐅᖅᑐᑦ ᓵᒃᑯᐃᖁᓪᓗᒋᑦ "ᑕᒪᑐᒥᖓ ᓇᓗᓪᓗᑎᒃ ᐱᓇᓱᐊᖅᑕᖓᓐᓂᒃ, ᑕᒪᑐᒥᖓ ᐊᕕᓯᒪᓂᐅᒍᑎᒥᒃ, ᐱᔭᐅᒍᓐᓇᖅᓯᐅᕐᓂᖓ ᐊᔪᕐᓇᕐᓂᖅᓵᐅᓚᔭᖅᑎᓪᓗᒍ ᐊᐳᑎᐅᑉ ᒪᕐᖑᓚᔭᓐᖏᓐᓂᖓᓂᒃ ᐃᑯᒪᒥᑦ." ᐃᑲᔪᖅᑕᐅᑎᓪᓗᒍ ᑭᒃᑯᑐᐃᓐᓇᕐᓄᑦ ᑲᕙᒪᖅᑲᕐᓂᕐᒥᒃ, "ᑕᐃᒪᓐᓇ ᓯᓚ ᐱᔪᓐᓇᖅᓯᖅᑕ."

The new legislative assembly building in downtown Iqaluit (as seen in the architect's rendering, left, and above) – a government for the people, of the people. Before, the eastern and central Arctic was governed from afar. The capital of the NWT, Yellowknife, is as far from Iqaluit as Vancouver is from Thunder Bay

ᓄᑖᖅ ᒪᓕᒐᓕᐅᕐᕕᒃᓴᖅ ᐃᒡᓗᕐᔪᐊ (ᑎᑎᕋᐅᔭᖅᑕᐅᓯᒪᔪᖅ, ᓴᐅᒥᖕᒥ ᐊᒻᒪ ᖁᓛᓂ) – ᑲᕙᒪ ᐃᓄᖕᓄᑦ, ᐃᓄᖕᓂ ᐊᐅᓚᑕᐅᓗᓂ. ᓯᕗᓂᐊᒍᑦ, ᐅᐊᖕᓇᒥᐅᑕᑦ ᕿᑎᕐᒥᐅᑕᓪᓗ ᑲᕙᒪᓕᓐᓂᕕᐅᖃᑦᑕᐅᖅᑐᑦ ᐅᖓᓯᒃᑐᒻᒪᕆᐊᓗᖕᒥ. ᓄᓇᑦᓯᐊᑉ ᐊᖓᔪᖅᑳᖅᑲᕕᐊ, ᔭᓗᓇᐃᑦ, ᐅᖓᓯᒃᐳᖅ ᐃᖃᓗᖕᓂ ᕚᓐᑰᕙᒥᓐ ᑕᓐᑐ ᐸᐃᑎᑐ ᐅᖓᓯᖕᓂᖃᖅᑐᖅ

The government and the NLCA

The Nunavut territory comprises the area that roughly corresponds with traditional and contemporary Inuit use, along with the northern portions of the High Arctic islands and the islands of Ungava Bay, Hudson Bay, and James Bay that are not part of adjacent provinces. Like any bureaucratic body, the government of Nunavut will be responsible for the operation and administration of the new territory. It will be following the recommendations set out in *Footprints 2*, a report prepared by the Nunavut Implementation Commission (NIC), the agency created under federal statute to advise on the design of the new government of Nunavut.

The job of governing will be done in a form both complementary to, and unique from, that which represents the rich political history of Canada. Like all other Canadians, Nunavut residents will enjoy a public government and have their rights and responsibilities ultimately determined by the *Canadian Charter of Rights and Freedoms*.

But unlike other provinces and territories in Canada, Nunavut has a public government and land claim agreement that are linked on several key issues. For example, the Nunavut Land Claims Agreement (NLCA) specifies that the number of Inuit employed in the public service be directly proportional to the number of Inuit in Nunavut society. This figure is set at 50 per cent for April 1, 1999, and will slowly increase to 85 per cent to reflect the fact that Inuit comprise the overwhelming majority of Nunavut residents.

Also unique to the government of Nunavut as a result of the land claim agreement is its ability to make decisions in certain areas of jurisdiction reserved for the federal government in Canada's other territories. For example, along with federal government representatives, Inuit also hold representative positions on institutions of public government that were created by the land claim agreement. As a result, Inuit appointees and Nunavut government representatives

ᑲᕙᒪ ᐊᒻᒪᓗ ᓄᓇᕗᑖᕐᓂᕐᒧᑦ ᐊᖏᕐᖃᑎᒌᒍᑎᖃᓂᖅ

ᓄᓇᕗᑦ ᓄᓇᖑᐊᑎᖓ ᐃᒪᐃᓪᓗᖓᔪᖅ ᐱᑕᖃᖅᑐᓂ ᐃᓗᓕᐊᓂ ᓄᓇᒥᒃ ᖃᓂᒋᔮᖓᓂ ᐊᑐᖅᑕᐅᕙᓪᓚᐅᖅᑐᒥᒃ ᓯᕗᓪᓕᓄᑦ ᐊᒻᒪᓗ ᒫᓐᓇᐅᓂᖅᓴᖏᑦ ᐊᑐᖅᑕᐅᕙᒃᓯᒪᔪᓂᒃ. ᑲᓇᖕᓇᖓᓂ ᕿᑭᖅᑕᐃᑦ ᖁᑦᓯᒃᑐᒥ ᐅᑭᐅᖅᑕᖅᑐᒥ ᐊᒻᒪᓗ ᕿᑭᖅᑕᖏᓐᓂ ᐅᖓᕚᕙ, ᕼᐅᑦᓴᓐ ᐲ, ᐊᒻᒪᓗ ᓰᕿᓂᕐᒥᐅᑦ ᐃᓚᒋᔭᐅᖕᖏᑐᐊᖅᐸᑕ ᐊᕕᒃᑐᖅᓯᒪᔪᓂ ᐊᑭᖏᓐᓂ. ᐊᓯᖏᑎᑐᑦ ᑲᕙᒪᓕᕆᔨᐅᔪᑦ ᑎᒥᖏᑎᑐᑦ, ᓄᓇᕗᑦ ᑲᕙᒫᖓᑦ ᑲᒪᒋᔭᖃᓚᖓᔪᖅ ᐊᐅᓚᑕᐅᓂᖓᓂᒃ ᓅᑦ ᓄᓇᕗᑖᕐᓇᔪᐅᔾ. ᒪᓕᒐᔪᖅᑐᖅ ᐱᕆᐊᖅᑕᐅᖁᔭᐅᔪᓂᒃ ᐅᖃᓖᒪᓕᐊᖑᓚᐅᖅᑐᒥ *Footprints 2*, ᒪᒃᐱᖅᓗᐊᖑᓚᐅᖅᑐᖅ ᓄᓇᕗᑦ ᑲᕙᒪᒃᓴᓕᕆᔨᖏᓐᓄᑦ.

ᑎᒥᖑᑎᒋᔭᐅᔪᑦ ᐱᕆᐊᖅᑎᑕᐅᓚᐅᖅᑐᑦ ᑲᓇᑕᐅᑉ ᑲᕙᒪᒃᑯᖓᑕ ᒪᓕᒐᖏᓐᓂᒃ ᒪᓕᒃᖢᑎᒃ ᐋᖅᑭᒃᓯᐃᔨᐅᖁᓪᓗᒋᑦ ᓄᓇᕗᑦ ᑲᕙᒥᓇᔭᖅᑕᖓᓂᒃ.

ᐱᓇᓱᒃᑕᐅᓚᖓᔪᑦ ᑲᕙᒪᓕᕆᓂᓕᑦ ᐃᓚᖃᖅᓯᔭᖅᑐᑦ, ᐊᒻᒪᓗ ᐊᔾᔨᒌᙱᑦᑕᖃᖅᓯᔭᖅᓗᑎᒃ ᑕᒪᕐᒥᒃ, ᑲᓇᑕᒃᑯᑦ ᐊᑐᖅᑕᐅᓯᒪᔪᖅᑲᒃᑯᑦ ᑲᕙᒪᓕᕆᓂᐅᔪᖅᑲᖅᑐᓂᒃ. ᑲᓇᑕᓕᒫᒥᑎᑐᑦ, ᓄᓇᕗᒥᐅᑦ ᑲᕙᒪᖃᓚᖓᔪᑦ ᑭᒃᑯᐃᓐᓈᓄᑦ. ᐊᒻᒪᓗ ᐱᔪᓐᓇᐅᑎᖏᑦ ᑲᒪᒋᐊᖃᖅᑕᖏᓪᓗ ᒪᓕᒋᐊᖃᕈᑎᖏᑦ ᐋᖅᑭᒃᑕᐅᓯᒪᓪᓗᑎᒃ ᑲᓇᑕᒥᐅᑦ ᓴᐳᑎᔭᐅᓯᒪᓂᖏᑦ ᐱᔪᓐᓇᐅᑎᖃᕐᓇᖅᑐᖏᓐᓄᓪᓗ ᒪᓕᒐᖓᓂᒃ.

ᐊᔾᔨᒌᙱᑦᑐᒥᒃ ᐊᓯᖏᓐᓂᑦ ᐊᕕᒃᑐᖅᓯᒪᔪᓂ ᑲᓇᑕᒥ, ᓄᓇᕗᑦ ᑭᒃᑯᓕᒫᓄᑦ ᑲᕙᒪᖃᖅᑐᖅ. ᐊᒻᒪᓗ ᓄᓇᕗᑖᕐᓂᕐᒧᑦ ᐊᖏᕐᖃᑎᒌᒍᑕᐅᔪᖅ ᐊᒃᑐᐊᓂᖃᖅᑕᐅᔪᖅ ᐱᓪᓚᕆᐅᔪᓂᒃ. ᓲᕐᓗ ᐅᓇ ᐆᒃᑰᑎᒋᓗᒍ, ᓄᓇᕗᒧᑦ ᐊᖏᕐᖃᑎᒌᒍᑎᕕᓂᖅ ᓇᓗᓇᐃᖅᓯᓯᒪᔪᖅ ᖃᑦᓯᐅᓂᖏᓐᓂᒃ ᐃᓄᐃᑦ ᐃᖅᑲᓇᐃᔭᖅᑎᑦ ᐱᕋᑦᑎᖅᑐᑦ ᒪᓕᒃᑲᖅᓂᖏᓐᓂᒃ ᐃᓄᐃᑦ ᖃᑦᓯᐅᓂᖏᓐᓂᒃ ᓄᓇᕗᒥ. ᑕᒫᓇ ᐋᖅᑭᒃᑕᐅᓯᒪᔪᖅ ᓇᑉᐸᖏᓐᓂᒃ ᐄᐳᕈ 1, 1999-ᒧᑦ, ᐊᒻᒪᓗ ᓱᒃᑲᐃᑦᑐᒥᒃ 85 ᐳᓴᓐᑎᒧᑦ. ᑕᒫᓇ ᒪᓕᑲᔭᖅᑐᖅ ᐃᓄᐃᑦ ᐊᒥᓲᓂᖅᓴᐅᓂᖏᓐᓂᒃ ᓄᓇᕗᒥᐅᑕᓂ.

ᐊᒻᒪᓗᑦᑕᐅᖅ ᐊᔾᔨᒌᙱᓪᓕᒻᒥᔪᖅ ᐊᓯᖏᓐᓂᑦ ᐱᕆᐊᖅᑎᑕᐅᒍᑕᐅᓯᒪᔪᖅ ᓄᓇᕗᑦ ᐊᖏᕐᖃᑎᒌᒍᑎᕕᓂᖓᒍᑦ ᓇᖏᓂᖅ ᐃᓯᒪᓕᐅᕈᓐᓇᕐᓂᖓᒍᑦ ᑲᓇᑕᐅᑉ ᑲᕙᒪᖓᑕ ᐊᐅᓚᑕᐅᒍᓐᓇᖅᑐᖅᑲᐅᓚᐅᖅᑐᓂᒃ. ᐊᓯᖏᓐᓂ ᑲᓇᑕᐅᑉ ᓄᓇᖑᐊᑎᖏᑦ ᐊᕕᒃᑐᖅᓯᒪᓂᖏᓐᓂ. ᑕᐃᒪᓐᓇ ᐱᔾᔪᑎᒋᓗᒍ, ᐃᓄᐃᑦ ᑎᒃᑯᐊᖅᑕᐅᓯᒪᔪᑦ ᐊᒻᒪᓗ ᓄᓇᕗᒧᑦ ᐱᓯᑎᖅᑎᐅᔪᑦ ᐃᒃᓯᕙᖅᑕᐅᓚᖓᔪᑦ ᐊᐅᓚᑦᑎᔨᐅᓪᓗᑎᒃ ᑎᒥᖁᑎᒋᔭᐅᔪᓂ. ᒪᑯᓂᖓ ᑎᒥᐅᔪᓂ ᓄᓇᕗᒥ ᐆᒪᔪᓕᕆᔪᓯᔪᐊᑦ ᑲᑎᒪᔨᖏᓐᓂ, ᓄᓇᕗᒥ ᐸᓐᓇᐃᔩᑦ, ᐊᒃᑐᐃᓂᖅᑲᑦᑕᓂᐅᔭᓄᑦ ᖃᐅᔨᓴᖅᑎᒃᑯᑦ ᑲᑎᒪᔨᖏᓐᓂ, ᓄᓇᕗᒥ ᐃᒪᓕᕆᔨᑦ ᑲᑎᒪᔩᔭᐊᖏᓐᓂ ᐊᒻᒪᓗ ᓄᓇᕗᒥ ᓄᓇᐃᑦ ᖄᖏᓐᓄᑦ ᐃᓯᒪᖅᓯᕈᓇᐅᑎᑖᕐᐸᓪᓚᐊᓪᓚᑦ ᑲᑎᒪᔨᖏᓐᓂ.

ᐱᓴᖅᑐᓂᖅᑎᓪᓗᒋᑦ ᓄᓇᕗᒥ ᓲᕐᓗ ᐊᓐᑎᐅᓇᐅᑉ ᒪᓕᒐᓕᐅᕐᕕᖓᓂ, ᓄᓇᕗᑦ ᑲᕙᒪᖓᑦ ᐊᕕᒃᑐᖅᓯᒪᔪᓂ ᑲᕙᒪᐅᓇᔭᖅᑐᖅ ᐊᔾᔨᒋᐅᙱᑦᑐᓂᖅᑲᖅᑐᒥᒃ.

Nunatsiaq News ᓄᓇᑦᓯᐊᕐᒥ ᐱᕐᓕᐊᑦ

In 1997, NIC executive director Simon Awa tallied the votes that spelled 'no' for a groundbreaking gender-even legislature. Former Nunavut Tunngavik Incorporated executive director Alex Campbell, among others, felt disappointed: "I didn't think we did a proper campaign to get people really interested and knowing the issues"

1977ᒥ, ᓄᓇᕗᑦ ᐸᕐᓇᐃᔩᑦ ᑲᑎᒪᔨᖏᑦᑕ ᐊᐅᓚᑦᑎᔨᖓ ᓴᐃᒪᓐ ᐊᕙ ᓇᐃᓴᐃᓚᐅᕐᕗᖅ ᓂᕈᐊᕈᑕᐅᔪᓂ 'ᐋᒃᑳ'-ᑐᓂ ᓂᕈᐊᕐᓂᖅᑳᖅᑎᓪᓗᒋ ᐊᕐᓇᓪᓗ ᐊᖑᑏᓪᓗ ᓇᓗᒧᕿᔾᔪᐅᖕᒪᖔ ᑲᑎᒪᕖᒃᔭᐊᕐᓴᒥᓐ. ᓄᓇᕗᑦ ᑐᓐᖓᕕᒃᑯ ᑎᒥᖓᑕ ᐊᐅᓚᑦᑎᔩᕙᓂᖓ ᐊᓕᒃᔅ ᑳᒻᐹᓪ, ᐊᓯᖏᓪᓗ, ᐊᐃᑦᑖᕿᓯᓚᐅᕐᐳᑦ: "ᒪᓂᓴᐅᓯᐅᑦᑎᐅᖅᑰᓚᐅᖏᓐᓇᑦᑕ ᐃᓄᖕᓂ ᑕᒪᑐᒥᖓ ᐃᓱᒪᒋᔭᖃᓪᑎᑲᓯᒃᑲᑎᒍᑦ ᐊᒻᒪ ᑐᑭᓯᑎᐊᓂᖏᓪᓗᑎᒍᑦ"

> **"Political control is always a better exercise closer to the people than far away."**
>
> – Jack Stagg, chief federal negotiator of the Nunavut political accord

sit side by side on such administrative bodies as the Nunavut Wildlife Management Board, Nunavut Planning Commission, Nunavut Impact Review Board, the Nunavut Water Board and the Nunavut Surface Rights Tribunal.

With powers approaching that of the Ontario legislative assembly, the government of Nunavut will be a territorial government with a twist.

Consensus politics, and elections

Nunavut will have no political parties at the territorial level. Instead, the legislative assembly of the new territory will operate on the basis of consensus politics. Like the aboriginal decision-making system it mimics, the legislative assembly's decisions will be made according to the consensus of the majority of its members rather than political party lines. Political parties exist in Nunavut only for the purposes of supporting candidates running in federal elections.

A few weeks ago, Nunavut elected its first 19-member legislative assembly. (A groundbreaking proposal to elect an equal number of women and men to Nunavut's legislative assembly was defeated in a 1997 Nunavut-wide plebiscite.) The members of the legislative assembly (MLAs) hold a secret ballot to elect a speaker, who oversees operation of the assembly. Also elected in a secret vote by the MLAs is the premier of Nunavut, as well as the executive (cabinet). The regular sittings of the assembly will be open to the public.

Nunavut's government has 10 departments, each headed by a minister; MLAs without ministerial portfolios will perform the role of the opposition. Territorial elections will be held every five years by popular vote. Federally, Nunavut is represented by one member of Parliament, and one senator.

While the government of the Northwest Territories conducts its daily business in English, the government of Nunavut will be dominated by Inuktitut, the language of the Inuit. Other official languages are English and French. Additionally, Nunavut will bear its own flag and coat of arms, as well as other symbols that distinguish it as a government and territory.

ᐊᖏᖅᑲᑎᒌᖕᓂᒃᑯᑦ ᒐᕙᒪᓕᕆᓂᖅ, ᐊᒻᒪᓗ ᓂᕈᐊᕐᓂᖅ

ᓄᓇᕗᑦ ᒐᕙᒪᓕᕆᓂᖏᑦ ᐊᐅᓚᑕᐅᔾᔭᖕᖏᑦᑐᑦ ᐃᓕᖁᕐᑐᓂᒃ ᒐᕙᒪᓕᕆᔨᖅᑲᕐᓂᒃᑯᑦ ᐊᖏᒃᑐᖅᓯᒪᔪᓂ. ᑭᓯᐊᓂᓕ, ᒪᓕᒐᓕᐅᕐᕕᒃ ᓄᑖᒥ ᐊᐅᓚᑕᐅᓚᖓᔪᖅ ᐊᖏᖅᑲᑎᒌᖕᓂᒃᑯᑦ. ᓄᓇᖃᖅᑳᖅᑐᑦ ᐃᓯᒪᓕᐅᕈᑎᒋᕙᓪᓗᐅᖅᑕᖓᑎᑦ ᐊᔾᔨᖓᓂᒃ ᒪᓕᒃᖢᓂ, ᒪᓕᒐᓕᐅᕐᕕᖕᒥ ᐃᓯᒪᓕᐅᖅᑕᐅᔪᑦ ᐋᖅᑭᒃᑕᐅᓇᔭᖅᑐᑦ ᒪᓕᒡᓗᑎᒃ ᐊᒥᓲᓂᖅᓴᐅᔪᑦ ᒪᓕᒐᓕᐅᕐᕕᖕᒥ ᐃᓯᒪᕆᔭᖏᓐᓂᒃ. ᐃᓚᒃᑯᑦ ᒐᕙᒪᖃᕐᓂᖅ ᓄᓇᕗᒥ ᐊᑐᖅᑕᐅᕙᒃᑐᖅ ᑭᓯᐊᓂ ᓂᕈᐊᖅᑕᐅᕐᑯᓪᓗᒋᑦ ᑲᓇᑕᐅᑉ ᒐᕙᒪᒃᑯᖏᑕ ᓂᕈᐊᒐᒃᓴᓕᐅᔭᖏᓐᓂᒃ.

ᐱᓇᓱᐊᕈᓯᐅᓚᐅᖅᑐᒥ ᖃᖏᖅᑐᒥ, ᓄᓇᕗᒥᐅᑦ ᓂᕈᐊᓚᐅᖅᑐᑦ ᓯᕗᓪᓕᖅᐹᖅᑐᒥᒃ 19-ᓂᒃ ᐃᓂᓕᖕᓂᒃ ᒪᓕᒐᓕᐅᖅᑎᓂ ᑲᑎᒪᔨᒃᓴᐅᔪᓂᒃ. (ᐊᑐᕐᑕᐅᔪᒪᔪᒥᓐ ᒪᓕᒐᓕᐅᕐᑎᖅᑲᕈᒪᓂᖅ ᓇᓕᒨᒃᑯᑎᒃ ᐊᕐᓇᓪᓗ ᐊᖑᑎᓪᓗ ᓂᕈᐊᕐᓂᒃᑯ ᓴᖅᑭᑕᐅᓂᖁ ᐹᓚᐅᓚᐅᕐᐳᖅ 1997-ᒥ ᓄᓇᕗᓕᒫᒥ ᓂᕈᐊᕐᓂᒃᑯᑦ) ᐃᓚᒋᔭᐅᔪᑦ ᒪᓕᒐᓕᐅᖅᑎᓂ ᑭᒃᑯᒃᑖᓄᑦ ᖃᐅᔨᓴᐅᒋᐊᖃᕈᓐᖏᑦᑐᒃᑯᑦ ᓂᕈᐊᖅᓯᓇᔭᖅᑐᑦ ᐅᖃᖅᑎᒥᒃ, ᐊᐅᓚᑦᑎᔨᐅᓇᔭᖅᑐᒥᒃ ᑲᑎᒪᕕᖕᒥᒃ. ᓂᕈᐊᖃᑦᑕᕐᒥᐅᑦ ᑭᒃᑯᒃᑖᓄᑦ ᑕᑯᔭᐅᕆᐊᖃᖕᖏᑦᑐᒃᑯᑦ ᐊᖓᔪᖅᑳᖅᔪᐊᕐᒥᒃ, ᐊᒻᒪᓗ ᐊᐅᓚᑎᔨᓂᒃ. ᒪᓕᒐᓕᐅᖅᑎᑦ ᑲᑎᒪᖃᑦᑕᕐᓂᖏᑦ ᒪᑐᐃᖓᖃᑦᑕᕐᓂᐊᕐᑐᑦ ᑭᒃᑯᐃᓐᓇᕐᓄ.

ᓄᓇᕗᑦ ᒐᕙᒪᖓ ᐊᖏᒃᑐᖅᓯᒪᔪᖅ ᖁᓕᓄᑦ, ᓯᕗᓕᐅᖅᑕᐅᓪᓗᓂ ᒥᓂᔅᑕᒧᑦ, ᒪᓕᒐᓕᐅᖅᑎᑦ ᒥᓂᔅᑕᐃᑦ ᑲᒪᒋᔭᓐᓇᖅᑲᖅᑕᖏᓐᓂᒃ ᐱᑕᖃᙱᑦᑐᑦ ᐊᐃᕙᕈᐅᓇᔭᖅᑐᑦ. ᓂᕈᐊᕐᓇᖅ ᐊᕐᕌᒍᑦ ᑕᓪᓕᒪ ᖄᖏᕐᖂᖓᑕ ᐱᓇᔭᖅᑐᑦ ᓂᕈᐊᖅᑐᖅᑲᕐᓗᓂ ᓂᕈᐊᒐᒃᓴᐅᔪᓂᒃ. ᑲᓇᑕᐅᑉ ᒐᕙᒪᒃᑯᖓᒍᑦ, ᐊᑕᐅᓯᕐᒥᒃ ᑲᑎᒪᔨᖅᑲᖅᓴᖅᑐᑦ, ᐊᒻᒪᓗ ᐊᑕᐅᓯᕐᒥᒃ ᑲᓇᑕᒥ ᒪᓕᒐᓕᐅᖅᑕᐅᔪᓂ ᖃᐅᔨᓴᖅᑎᒥᒃ.

ᓄᓇᑦᓯᐊᑉ ᒐᕙᒪᖓ ᖃᓪᓗᓈᑎᑐᑦ ᐃᖅᑲᓇᐃᔭᖅᓴᖅᑎᓪᓗᒋᑦ, ᓄᓇᕗᑦ ᒐᕙᒪᖓ ᐊᑐᖅᓴᖅᑐᖅ ᐃᓄᒃᑎᑐᒻᒥᒃ. ᐊᓯᖏᑦᑕᐅᖅ ᐃᓚᑕᓅᔪᓯᒪᔪᑦ ᐅᖃᐅᓯᑦ ᐃᓚᖃᖅᓴᖅᑐᑦ ᖃᓪᓗᓈᑎᑐᑦ ᐊᒻᒪᓗ ᐅᐃᕖᖅᑎᑐᑦ. ᐊᒻᒪᓗᑦᑕᐅᖅ, ᓄᓇᕗᑦ ᓇᖏᓂᖅ ᓴᐃᒻᒪᑎᖅᑲᖅᓴᖅᑐᖅ ᓇᖏᓂᖅᓗ ᓇᓗᓇᐃᒃᑯᑕᖅᑲᖅᓗᓂ. ᐊᒻᒪᓗᑦᑕᐅᖅ ᐊᓯᖏᓐᓂᒃ ᓇᓗᓇᐃᒃᑯᑕᓂᒃ ᐃᓕᖁᕐᑯᑦ ᒐᕙᒪᐅᓂᖓᓂᒃ ᐊᕕᒃᑐᖅᓯᒪᓂᐅᓂᖓᓂᒃᓗ ᐃᓚᑕᓄᓴᐅᒍᑎᓂᒃ.

Nunavut Implementation Commissioner Meeka Kilabuk shows off some early suggestions for a Nunavut territorial flag. The contest was open to all Canadian citizens, but the Chief Herald of Canada had the last word
ᓄᓇᕗᑦ ᐸᕐᓇᐃᔭᐅ ᑲᒥᓯᓇᐅᖅᑕᐅᔪᖅ ᒦᑲ ᕿᓚᐸᒃ ᑕᑯᖅᓱᐃᔪᑦ ᓴᐃᒪᑎᒃᓱᒫ ᑕᖅᓴᒃᓴᐅᑎᑕᐅᓚᓱᒃᑐᓂ ᓄᓇᕗᒻᒧ. ᑕᒪᓐᓇ ᓵᓚᒃᓴᖅᓯᕐᓂ ᑭᒃᑯᓕᒫᓄ ᒪᑐᐃᖕᖖᕿᑎᑕᐅᓚᐅᖅᓯᒪᔪᖅ ᑲᓇᑕᒥᐅᑕᕐᓄ, ᑭᓯᐊᓂᓕ ᐊᖓᔪᖅᑳᖅ ᓴᐃᒪᑎᓄᑦ ᐅᖃᖅᑕᖓ ᐱᒻᒪᕆᐅᓚᐅᖏᕗᖅ

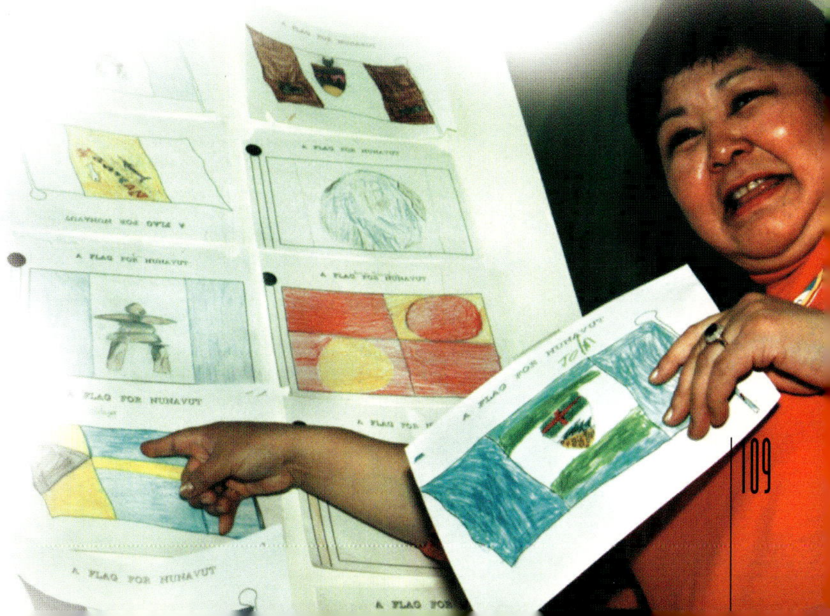

“ᒪᓕᒐᓕᕆᓂᒃᑯ ᐱᓕᕆᓂᖅ ᐊᑲᐅᓂᖅᓴᐅᕙᓪᓚᐅᔾᒪᓐ ᑲᓂᒃᓴᕐᓂᕐᓴᐅᓪᓗᓂ ᐃᓄᖕᓂ ᐅᖓᓯᒃᑐᒥᐅᕙᑦᑐᖅ.”

- ᔭᒃ ᓵᓐᓴ, ᐊᖓᔪᖅᑳᖅ ᒐᕙᒪᒃᑯᖏᓐᓂ ᐋᔩᑎᓄᑦ ᓄᓇᕗᑦ ᒪᓕᒐᓕᕆᓂᕐᒥᓄᑦ

Government of Nunavut
ᓄᓇᕗᑦ ᒐᕙᒪᖓᑦ

Legislative Assembly
ᒪᓕᒐᓕᐅᖅᑏ

Department of Executive and Intergovernmental Affairs
ᐊᐅᓚᑦᓯᔨᑦ ᐊᒻᒪᓗ ᒐᕙᒪᐅᖃᑎᒌᑦ ᐃᓚᐅᕝᕕᖓᑦ

Department of Finance and Administration
ᑮᓇᐅᔭᓕᕆᓂᕐᒧᑦ ᐊᐅᓚᑦᓯᓂᕐᒧᓪᓗ ᐃᓚᐅᕝᕕᖓᑦ

Department of Human Resources
ᐃᖅᑲᓇᐃᔭᖅᑐᓕᕆᔨᒃᑯᑦ ᐃᓚᐅᕝᕕᖓᑦ

Department of Justice
ᐃᖅᑲᖅᑐᐃᕕᓕᕆᔨᒃᑯᑦ ᐃᓚᐅᕝᕕᖓᑦ

Department of Public Works, Telecommunications and Technical Services
ᓴᓇᔪᓕᕆᔨᒃᑯᓐᓂ, ᑐᓴᐅᒪᖃᑦᑕᐅᑎᓕᕆᔨᒃᑯᓐᓂ ᐊᒻᒪᓗ ᓯᓇᕐᕿᑎᓕᕆᔨᓂ ᐃᓚᐅᕝᕕᖓᑦ

Department of Sustainable Development
ᐱᕙᓪᓕᐊᔪᓕᕆᔨᒃᑯᑦ ᐊᑐᖅᑕᐅᒃᑲᓐᓂᕈᓐᓇᖅᑐᓂᒃ ᐃᓚᐅᕝᕕᖓᑦ

Department of Health and Social Services
ᐋᓐᓂᐊᕐᓇᖏᑦᑐᓕᕆᔨᒃᑯᑦ ᐃᓄᓕᕆᔨᒃᑯᓪᓗ ᐃᓚᐅᕝᕕᖓᑦ

Department of Education
ᐃᓕᓐᓂᐊᖅᑐᓕᕆᔨᒃᑯᑦ ᐃᓚᐅᕝᕕᖓᑦ

Department of Culture, Language, Elders and Youth
ᐃᓕᖅᑯᓯᓕᕆᔨᒃᑯᑦ, ᐅᖃᐅᓯᓕᕆᔨᒃᑯᑦ, ᐃᓐᓇᑐᖃᓕᕆᔨᒃᑯᑦ ᐊᒻᒪᓗ ᒫᒃᑯᒃᑐᑦ ᐃᓚᐅᕝᕕᖓᑦ

Department of Community Government, Housing and Transportation
ᓄᓇᓖᓐᓂ ᒐᕙᒪᓕᕆᔨᒃᑯᑦ, ᐃᒡᓗᓕᕆᔨᒃᑯᑦ ᐊᒻᒪᓗ ᐃᖏᕐᕋᑦᑕᖅᑐᓕᕆᔨᒃᑯᑦ ᐃᓚᐅᕝᕕᖓᑦ

Boards, Commissions, Corporations and Agencies
ᑲᑎᒪᔩᑦ, ᑲᒥᓵᑦ, ᑯᐊᐳᕇᓴᑦ ᐊᒻᒪᓗ ᐃᖅᑲᓇᐃᔭᕝᕕᑦ

Nunavut Boards of Education
ᓄᓇᕗᒥ ᐃᓕᓐᓂᐊᖅᑐᓕᕆᔨᒃᑯᑦ ᑲᑎᒪᔨᖏᑦ

Nunavut Arctic College
ᓄᓇᕗᒥ ᐅᑭᐅᖅᑕᖅᑐᒥ ᓯᓚᑦᑐᖅᓴᕐᕕᒃ

Nunavut Boards of Health
ᓄᓇᕗᒥ ᐋᓐᓂᐊᕐᓇᖏᑦᑐᓕᕆᓂᕐᒧᑦ ᑲᑎᒪᔩᑦ

Nunavut Business Credit Corporation
ᓄᓇᕗᒥ ᓇᖕᒥᓂᖅᑲᖅᑐᓄᑦ ᐊᑐᖅᑐᐊᖅᑐᓕᕆᕝᕕᒃ ᑯᐊᐳᕇᓴᓐ

Nunavut Development Corporation
ᓄᓇᕗᒥ ᐱᕙᓪᓕᐊᑎᑦᑎᓂᕐᒧᑦ ᑯᐊᐳᕇᓴ

Nunavut Legal Services Board
ᓄᓇᕗᒥ ᒪᓕᒐᓕᕆᔨᓄᑦ ᑲᑎᒪᔨᖏᑦ

Nunavut Liquor Commission
ᓄᓇᕗᒥ ᐃᒥᐊᓗᓕᕆᔨᒃᑯᑦ ᑲᒥᓵᖓᑦ

Nunavut Liquor Licencing Board
ᓄᓇᕗᒥ ᐃᒥᐊᓗᓕᕆᓂᕐᒧᑦ ᓚᐃᓴᓐᓯᓕᕆᔨᖏᑕ ᑲᑎᒪᔨᖏᑦ

Sport Nunavut
ᐱᖕᖑᐊᖅᑐᓕᕆᔨᒃᑯᑦ ᓄᓇᕗᒥ

Power Corporation
ᐆᒻᒥᖅᑯᑎᓕᕆᓂᕐᒧᑦ ᑯᐊᐳᕇᓴ

Workers' Compensation Board
ᐱᓕᕆᔨᑦ ᐋᓐᓂᖅᑐᑦ ᐊᑭᓕᖅᑕᐅᓂᖓᓄᑦ ᑲᑎᒪᔩᑦ

Decentralization

Reflecting the diverse nature of the regions it represents, the government of Nunavut will be decentralized, with approximately 700 required headquarters positions divided among Iqaluit, the capital of Nunavut, and 10 other communities — Igloolik, Rankin Inlet, Cambridge Bay, Cape Dorset, Arviat, Gjoa Haven, Kugluktuk, Pangnirtung, Baker Lake, and Pond Inlet. The government's core machinery functions, including the Department of Executive and Intergovernmental Affairs, the Department of Finance and Administration, the Department of Human Resources, and the Department of Justice, will be situated in Iqaluit, along with the ministerial, policy and planning, financial administration, and personnel-related functions of the government of Nunavut's other departments.

One of the ultimate goals of decentralizing the government is to give Nunavut's three regions decision-making authority, and extend

continued on page 112

ᓴᓐᖏᓂᕆᓴᐅᔪᓂᒃ ᐊᔪᓐᖏᓐᓂᕆᓴᐅᔪᓂᓪᓗ ᓄᑎᕆᕙᓪᓕᐊᓂᖅ

ᒪᓕᒡᓗᓂ ᐊᔾᔨᒋᖕᒋᓂ ᐊᔾᔨᒌᙱᑦᑐᓂᒃ ᐊᕕᒃᑐᖅᓯᒪᔪᓂᒃ, ᓄᓇᕗᑦ ᒐᕙᒪᖓᑦ ᓴᓐᖏᓂᕆᓴᐅᔪᓂᒃ ᐱᔪᓐᓇᐅᑎᓂᒡᓗ ᓄᑎᕆᕙᓪᓕᐊᓂᖅᓯᒪᓇᔭᖅᑐᖅ. ᐱᑕᖃᕐᓂᐊᖅᑐᑦ ᐊᖓᔪᖅᑳᒃᑯᕕᖕᒥ 700ᖏᓐᓄᖑᕋᑦ ᐃᖅᑲᓇᐃᔭᒃᓴᐃᑦ ᐊᕕᒃᑕᐅᓯᒪᓗᑎᒃ ᒪᑯᓄᖓ ᐃᖃᓗᖕᓄᑦ, ᐊᖓᔪᖅᑳᒃᑯᕕᐅᔪᖅ ᓄᓇᕗᒥ, ᐊᒻᒪᓗ ᖁᓕᓄᑦ ᓄᓇᓕᐅᔪᓄᑦ. ᐅᑯᐊᖑᔪᑦ — ᐃᒡᓗᓕᒃ, ᑲᖏᖅᖠᓂᖅ, ᐃᖃᓗᒃᑑᑎᐊᖅ, ᑭᙵᐃᑦ, ᐊᕐᕕᐊᑦ, ᐅᖅᓱᖅᑑᖅ, ᖁᕐᓗᖅᑑᖅ, ᐸᖕᓂᖅᑑᖅ, ᖃᒪᓂ'ᑐᐊᖅ, ᐊᒻᒪᓗ ᒥᑦᑎᒪᑕᓕᒃ. ᒐᕙᒪᐃᑦ ᓯᓕᓇᒋᐊᖃᖅᑕᖏᑦ, ᐃᓚᒋᔭᐅᓪᓗᓂ ᐊᖓᔪᖅᑳᒃᑯᕕᒃ ᐊᒻᒪᓗ ᒐᕙᒪᖃᑎᒌᑦ ᐃᖅᑲᓇᐃᔭᖃᑎᒌᖕᓂᖏᑦ, ᑮᓇᐅᔭᓕᕆᔨᒃᑯᑦ ᐊᐅᓚᑦᑎᔨᒃᑯᓪᓗ, ᐃᖅᑲᓇᐃᔭᖅᑐᓕᕆᔨᒃᑯᑦ, ᐊᒻᒪᓗ ᐃᖅᑲᖅᑐᐃᕝᕕᓕᕆᔨᒃᑯᑦ. ᑖᒃᑯᐊᓕ ᐃᓂᖃᕐᓂᐊᖅᑐᑦ ᐃᖃᓗᖕᓂ, ᐊᒻᒪᓗ ᒥᓂᔅᑕᓕᕆᔨᒃᑯᑦ, ᐸᓇᐃᔨᑦ ᐊᑐᐊᒐᓕᐅᖅᑏᓪᓗ ᑮᓇᐅᔭᓕᕆᔨᓪᓗ, ᐊᒻᒪᓗ ᐃᖅᑲᓇᐃᔭᖅᑐᓕᕆᔨᐅᓂᖏᑦ ᓄᓇᕗᑦ ᒐᕙᒪᖓᑕ ᐊᓯᖏᓐᓂ ᐊᕕᒃᑐᖅᓯᒪᓂᖏᓐᓂ.

ᐊᑕᐅᓯᖅ ᓯᕗᓂᕐᒧᑦ ᑐᕌᖅᑕᐅᔪᖅ ᐱᒃᓴᖅᑐ-ᓂᕐᒥᒃ ᓄᑎᕆᖅᑎᑦᑐᕐᒥᑦ ᓄᓇᕗᒧᑦ ᓄᑎᓂᖅ ᐱᖓᓱᖏᓐᓄᑦ ᐊᕕᒃᑐᖅᓯᒪᓂᖏᓐᓄᑦ ᐃᓱᒪᓕᐅ-ᕈᓐᓇᕐᓂᕐᒥᒃ ᐊᐅᓚᑦᑎᒍᓐᓇᕐᓂᕐᒥᒃ. ᐊᒻᒪᓗ ᐃᖅᑲᓇᐃᔮᒃᓴᐅᔪᓂᒃ ᓅᑎᕆᓗᑎᒃ ᐊᒥᓱᓄᑦ ᓄᓇᓖᓄᑦ. ᐊᕕᒃᑐᖅᓯᒪᔪᓂ ᒐᕙᒪᓕᕆᕝᕕᑦ ᒪᑯᓇᓈᓐᓇᔭᖅᑐᑦ ᐃᒡᓗᓕᖕᒥ (ᕿᑭᖅᑖᓘᑉ ᐊᕕᒃᑐᖅᓯᒪᕝᕕᖓᓂ), ᑲᖏᖅᖠᓂᕐᒥ (ᑭᕙᓪᓕᐅᑉ

ᑲᔪᓯᔪᖅ ᒫᒃᐱᒐᖅ 112

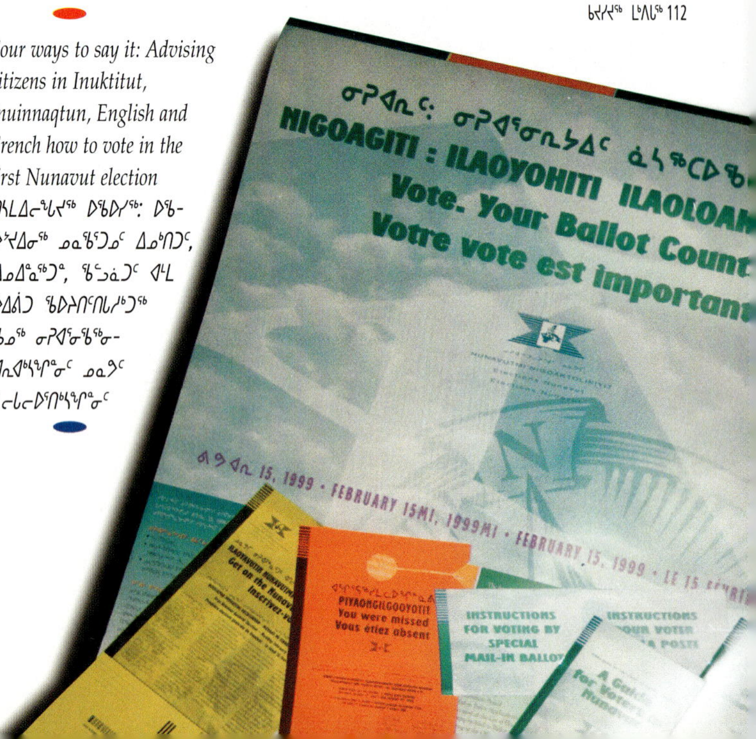

Four ways to say it: Advising citizens in Inuktitut, Inuinnaqtun, English and French how to vote in the first Nunavut election

ᑎᓴᒪᐃᓕᖓᔪᖅ ᐅᖃᐅᓯᖅ: ᐅᖃ-ᐅᔾᔨᐃᓂᖅ ᓄᓇᖃᖅᑐᓄᑦ ᐃᓄᒃᑎᑐᑦ, ᐃᓄᐃᓐᓇᖅᑐᓐ, ᖃᓪᓗᓈᑐᑦ ᐊᒻᒪ ᐅᐃᕖᑐ ᖃᐅᔨᑎᑦᑎᑲᓯᒃᑐᖅ ᖃᓄᖅ ᓂᕈᐊᕐᓂᖅᑲᖅᓂ-ᐊᕆᐊᒃᓴᖏᓐᓂᑦ ᓄᓇᕗᑦ ᒪᓕᒐᓕᐅᕐᑎᒃᓴᖏᓐᓂᑦ

The First MLAs
ᓯᕗᓪᓕᖅᐹᑦ ᒪᓕᒐᓕᐅᖅᑏ

By Marion Soublière

Clear, crisp winter weather and years of pent-up enthusiasm produced an extremely high voter turnout in Nunavut's historic first election Feb. 15, 1999. Eighty-eight per cent of Nunavut's 12,210 eligible electors cast ballots.

In the ridings of Baker Lake, Cambridge Bay and Iqaluit Centre, voter turnout even surpassed 100 per cent. That's because more voters showed up at the polls than appeared on the official voters list.

The people of Nunavut chose 19 political representatives to send to Nunavut's first legislative assembly: 15 Inuit and four non-Inuit. Only one of the new members of the legislative assembly (MLAs) is a woman — Manitok Thompson, one of the most vocal opponents of the gender parity proposal that would have introduced equal numbers of men and women into Nunavut's legislature. The proposal was defeated in a Nunavut-wide plebiscite in May 1997.

Among the new territory's first MLAs are businessmen, former politicians, hunters, an airport maintenance worker, and Nunavut's first Inuk lawyer.

The newly elected MLAs were to be sworn in on April 1, 1999 in Iqaluit. Nunavut's former Interim Commissioner, Jack Anawak, who has also served as the area's federal member of Parliament, won in the riding of Rankin Inlet North. He was widely expected to be selected premier. The man considered his main opponent before the election, former NWT deputy premier Goo Arlooktoo, failed to win in the riding of South Baffin.

Election results were still considered unofficial as this publication was going to press. One re-count was under way for the riding of Kugluktuk, where only six votes stood between the winner, Donald Havioyak, and runner-up Ida Ayalik-McWilliam.

The MLAs

(Number of registered voters indicated after each riding.)

Rankin Inlet North - 508: **Jack Anawak**
Rankin Inlet South (including Whale Cove) - 607: **Manitok Thompson**
Arviat - 820: **Kevin O'Brien**
Nanulik (Chesterfield Inlet, Coral Harbour) - 554: **James Arvaluk**
Baker Lake - 698: **Glenn McLean**
Amittuq (Hall Beach, Igloolik) - 893: **Enoki Irqittuq**
Akulliq (Pelly Bay, Repulse Bay) - 532: **Ovide Alakannuark**
Nattilik (Taloyoak, Gjoa Haven) - 817: **Uriash Puqiqnak**
Kugluktuk - 649: **Donald Havioyak**
Cambridge Bay (including Umingmaktok, Bathurst Inlet) - 584: **Kelvin Ng**
Quttiktuq (Grise Fiord, Resolute, Nanisivik, Arctic Bay) - 656: **Levi Barnabas**
Tunnuniq (Pond Inlet) - 544: **Jobie Nutarak**
Uqqumiut (Clyde River, Qikiqtarjuaq) - 652: **David Iqaqrialu**
Pangnirtung - 689: **Peter Kilabuk**
Iqaluit Centre - 415: **Hunter Akat Tootoo**
Iqaluit East - 688: **Ed Picco**
Iqaluit West - 806: **Paul Okalik**
South Baffin (Kimmirut, Cape Dorset) - 764: **Olayuk Akesuk**
Hudson Bay (Sanikiluaq) - 343: **Peter Kattuk**

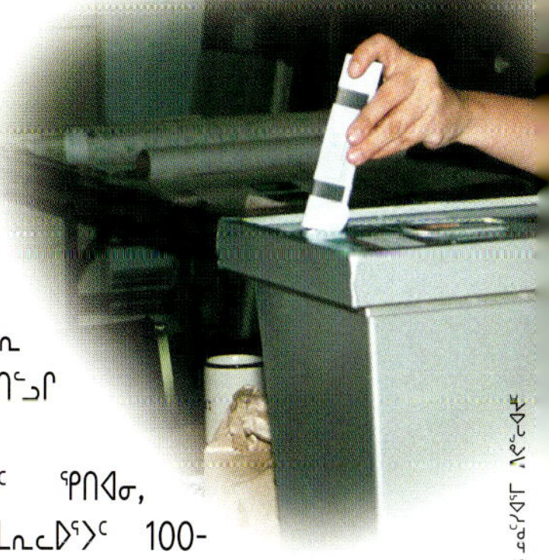
Nunatsiaq News ᓄᓇᑦᓯᐊᕐᒥ ᐱᕙᓪᓕᐊᔪᑦ

ᑎᑎᕋᖅᑐᖅ ᒥᐊᕆᐊᓐ ᓲᑉᓕᐃ

ᓯᓪᕿᑦᑎᐊᕐᑐᖅ, ᐅᑭᐅᑉ ᓯᓚᖓ ᐊᒻᒪᓗ ᐊᕐᕋᒍᒐᓴᓂ ᐅᑕᕿᓂᐅᔪᖅ ᓴᖅᑭᑎᓂᐅᓚᐅᕐᐳᖅ ᓂᕈᐊᕆᐊᕐᑐᕐᑐᓂ ᐊᒥᓱᒻᒪᕆᖕᓂ ᓄᓇᕗᑦ ᓯᕗᓪᓕᖅᐹᖕᖓᓂ ᓂᕈᐊᕐᓂᖅᑕᖅᑎᓪᓗᒋᑦ ᕖᕝᕗᐊᕆ 15, 1999ᒥ. 88-ᐳᓴᓐᑦ ᓂᕈᐊᕆᐊᕐᑐᓚᐅᕐᑐᑦ 12,210-ᖑᑎᓪᓗᒋ ᓂᕈᐊᕈᓐᓇᕐᑐᑦ ᓄᓇᕗᒻᒥ.

ᖃᒪᓂᑦᑐᐊᕐᒥ, ᐃᖃᓗᒃᑑᑦᑎᐊᕐᒥ ᐊᒻᒪᓗ ᐃᖃᓗᐃᑦ ᕿᑎᐊᓂ, ᓂᕈᐊᕆᐊᕐᑐᕐᑐᑦ ᓂᕈᐊᕈᓐᓇᕐᑐᑦ ᓇᐃᓴᕐᑕᐅᓯᒪᔪᑎᒍ ᖄᖏᐅᑎᒻᒪᕆᓚᐅᕐᐳᑦ 100-ᐳᓴᓐᑦᒥᓐ. ᓲᖃᐃᒻᒪ ᓂᕈᐊᕆᐊᕐᑐᕐᑐᑦ ᐅᓄᕐᓂᖅᓴᐅᓚᐅᕐᑐᑦ ᑎᑎᕋᕐᑕᐅᓯᒪᔪᓂᑦ ᓂᕈᐊᖅᐱᐅᔪᓂᑦ.

ᐃᓄᐃᑦ ᓄᓇᕗᒻᒥᐅᑦ ᓂᕈᐊᓚᐅᕐᐳᑦ 19ᓂ ᒪᓕᒐᓕᕆᓂᒃᑯᑦ ᑮᓪᓗᕐᑐᐃᓂᐊᕐᑐᓂ ᓯᕗᓪᓕᖅᐹᒥ ᒪᓕᒐᓕᐅᖅᐱᐅᓂᐊᕐᑐᒥᓐ ᓄᓇᕗᒻᒥ: 15 ᐃᓅᓪᓚᓐ ᐊᒻᒪ ᑎᓴᒪᓐ ᐃᓅᓪᓚᓇᐅᖏᑦᑐᑦ, ᐃᓚᐅᓪᓗᓂ ᐊᑕᐅᓯᖅ ᐱᐊᓪᓈᒻᒥᐅᑕᐱᓂᖅ. ᐊᑕᐅᓯᑐᐊᑯᓗᒃ ᐃᓚᒋᔭᐅᓪᓚᕐᑐᖅ ᒪᓕᒐᓕᕆᔨᒃᓴᒥ ᐊᕐᓇᐅᒐᖅ – ᒪᓂᑦᑐᖅ ᑖᒻᓴᓐ, ᑖᓐᓇ ᓂᐱᖄᕐᖑᖅᑕᐅᓂᖁ ᐱᐅᒃᓴᖏᓗᓂ ᐊᕐᓇᓂᓪᓗ ᐊᖑᑎᓂᓪᓗ ᓇᓚᒃᑭᖁᔨᓂᖁᒥ ᓄᓇᕗᑦ ᒪᓕᒐᓕᐅᖅᐱᕆᓂᐊᕐᑕᖓᓄᑦ. ᑕᒪᓐᓇ ᓴᖅᑕᐅᑎᓪᓗᒍ ᒪᐃ 1997ᒥ ᓂᕈᐊᕐᓂᒃᑯ ᓵᓚᐅᓚᐅᕐᓯᒪᔪᖅ.

ᓂᕈᐊᕐᑕᐅᔪᓕᓐ ᓄᑖᒥ ᐃᒻᒥᒃᑯᕐᑐᒥ ᐊᐱᒃᓯᒪᓂᒃᑯ ᓇᖕᒥᓂᖅ ᐱᔅᓂᖅᑲᑎᐅᔪᑦ, ᒪᓕᒐᓕᕆᔨᐱᓃᑦ, ᐊᖑᓇᓯᑦᑏ, ᒥᕝᕕᖕᒥ ᐃᖅᑲᓇᐃᔭᕐᑎ, ᐊᒻᒪᓗ ᓄᓇᕗᑦᒥ ᐃᓄᒃ ᓯᕗᓪᓕᖅᐹᖑᓪᓗ ᐃᖅᑲᖅᑐᐃᔨ.

ᑖᒃᑯᐊ ᒪᓕᒐᓕᐅᕐᑎᐅᓂᐊᓕᕐᑐᑦ ᐊᖏᕐᑎᑕᐅᓂᐊᓚᐅᕐᑐᑦ ᐱᓕᕆᐊᕆᓂᐊᕐᑕᕐᒥᖓᓄ ᐄᐳᕈ 1, 1999ᒥ ᐃᖃᓗᖕᓂ. ᓄᓇᕗᑦᑐ ᑲᒥᓯᓇᐅᑲᐃᓐᓇᓚᐅᕐᑐᖅ, ᔮᒃ ᐊᓇᕈᐊᖅ, ᑖᓐᓇ ᒪᓕᒐᓕᐅᖅᐱᓪᔪᐊᕐᒥ ᓯᕗᓕᐅᕐᑎᓚᐅᕐᑐᖅ ᓄᓇᕗᒻᒥ ᑮᓪᓗᕐᑐᐃᓪᓗᓂ, ᓵᓚᒃᓴᓚᐅᕐᐳᖅ ᑲᖏᕐᖠᓂᐅᑉ ᑲᓇᖕᓇᖓᓄᑦ. ᐃᓱᒪᒋᔭᐅᓚᐅᕐᑐᖅ ᓯᕗᓕᐅᕐᑎᐅᓂᕐᒧᖕᒐ ᐱᓇᓱᖕᓂᐊᓇᐊᒃᓴᖕᖓᓂ ᒎ ᐋᕐᓗᒃᑐ, ᑖᓐᓇ ᓯᕗᓕᐅᕐᑎᐅᑉ ᑐᓪᓕᖓᓚᐅᕐᑕᖓ ᓄᓇᑦᓯᐊᑉ ᒐᕙᒪᒃᑯᖕᒥᓂ, ᓂᕈᐊᕐᓇᐅᑉ ᓯᕗᓂᐊᒍᑦ ᐃᓱᒪᒋᔭᐅᓚᐅᕐᑐᕈᓗᐊᕐᕕ ᐊᓇᕈᐊᕐᓗ ᓯᕗᓕᐅᕐᑎᐅᓂᕐᒧᑦ ᐱᓇᓱᒃᑎᕆᓂᐊᕐᓇᐊᒃᓴᖕᖓᓂᑦ, ᓵᓚᐅᓚᐅᕐᐳᖅ ᓂᕈᐊᕐᑕᐅᖕᖏᕐᑐᓂ ᕿᑭᖅᑖᓗᑉ ᓂᒋᐊᓄ.

ᓂᕈᐊᕐᓂᐅᑉ ᖃᓄᐃᓐᓂᖓ ᓱᓕ ᐃᓱᒪᒃᓴᖅᓯᐅᕈᑕᐅᕐᓂᓚᐅᖕᒋᑦᑐᑦ ᐅᓇ ᐅᖃᓕᒫᒐᖅ ᓴᖅᑭᓐᓂᐊᓕᖅᑎᓪᓗᒍ. ᐊᑕᐅᓯᖅ ᓇᐃᓴᖅᑕᐅᒃᑲᓐᓂᖅᑐᖅ ᐅᑕᕿᔭᐅᔪᖅ ᑕᕝᕙ ᖁᕐᓗᖅᑑᒥ, ᐊᖅᕕᓂᓕᖕᓂ ᓯᕗᓪᓕᐅᔪᖅᑎᓪᓗᒍ ᐅᓇ ᑖᓄᑦ ᕼᐊᕕᐅᔭᒃ, ᓵᓚᖅᑲᐅᖅᑎᓪᓗᒍ ᐊᐃᑕ ᐊᔭᓕᒃ-ᒪᒃᕕᓕᐊᒻᒥ.

ᒪᓕᒐᓕᐅᖅᑎᐅᔪᑦ

(ᓂᕈᐊᖅᑎᐅᔪᑦ ᐊᑎᓕᐅᖅᓯᒪᔪᑦ ᓴᓂᐊᓂ ᑕᑯᒃᓴᐅᔪᑦ ᓂᕈᐊᖅᕕᖕᓂ.)

ᑲᖏᖅᖠᓂᖅ ᑲᓇᖕᓇᖅ - 508: **ᔮᒃ ᐊᓇᕈᐊᖅ**
ᑲᖏᖅᖠᓂᖅ ᐱᖓᖕᓇᖅ (ᐃᓚᒋᔭᐅᓪᓗᓂ ᑎᑭᕋᕐᔪᐊᖅ) - 607: **ᒪᓂᑦᑐᖅ ᑖᒻᓴᓐ**
ᐊᕐᕕᐊᑦ - 820: **ᑭᐊᕕᓐ ᐅᑉᕆᐊᓐ**
ᓇᓄᓕᒃ (ᐃᒡᓗᓕᒑᕐᔪᒃ, ᓴᓪᓖᑦ) - 554: **ᔩᒥᔅ ᐊᕐᕚᓗᒃ**
ᖃᒪᓂᑦᑐᐊᖅ - 698: **ᒋᓕᓐ ᒪᒃᓚᐃᓐ**
ᐊᒥᑦᑐᖅ (ᓴᓂᕋᔭᒃ, ᐃᒡᓗᓕᒃ) - 893: **ᐃᓄᑭ ᐃᖅᑭᑦᑐᖅ**
ᐊᑯᓪᓕᖅ (ᐊᕐᕕᓕᒡᔪᐊᖅ, ᓇᐅᔮᑦ) - 532: **ᐆᕕᑦ ᐊᓚᒃᑲᓐᓄᐊᖅ**
ᓇᑦᑎᓕᒃ (ᑕᓗᕐᔪᐊᖅ, ᐅᖅᓱᖅᑑᖅ) - 817: **ᔪᕋᐃᐊᔅ ᐳᕿᖅᓇᒃ**
ᖁᕐᓗᖅᑑᖅ - 649: **ᑖᓄ ᕼᐊᕕᐅᖅ**
ᐃᖃᓗᒃᑑᑦᑎᐊᖅ (ᐃᓚᒋᔭᐅᓪᓗᓂ ᐅᒥᖕᒪᒃᑑᖅ, Bathurst Inlet) - 584: **ᑭᐊᓪᕕᓐ ᐃᖕ**
ᖁᑦᑎᒃᑐᖅ (ᐊᐅᔪᐃᑦᑐᖅ, ᖃᐅᔪᐃᑦᑐᖅ, ᓇᓂᓯᕕᒃ, ᐃᒃᐱᐊᕐᔪᒃ) - 656: **ᓖᕖ ᐸᓇᐸᔅ**
ᑐᓄᓂᖅ (ᒥᑦᑎᒪᑕᓕᒃ) - 544: **ᔫᐱ ᓄᑕᖅ**
ᐅᖅᑯᒥᐅᑦ (ᑲᖏᖅᖢᒑᐱᒃ, ᕿᑭᖅᑕᕐᔪᐊᖅ) - 652: **ᑏᕕᑎ ᐃᒃᑲᖅᕆᐊᓗᒃ**
ᐸᖕᓂᖅᑑᖅ - 689: **ᐲᑕ ᕿᓚᐯᒃ**
ᐃᖃᓗᐃᑦ ᕿᑎᐊᓂ - 415: **ᕼᐊᓐᑐᕐ ᐊᑲᑦ ᑐᑐ**
ᐃᖃᓗᐃᑦ ᓂᒋᖅ - 688: **ᐃᑦ ᐲᑯ**
ᐃᖃᓗᐃᑦ ᐅᐊᖕᓇᖅ - 806: **ᐸᓪ ᐅᑲᓕᖅ**
ᕿᑭᖅᑖᓗᒃ ᐱᖓᖕᓇᖅ (ᑭᒻᒥᕈᑦ, ᑭᙵᐃᑦ) - 764: **ᐅᓚᔪᒃ ᐊᑭᓱᒃ**
ᕼᐊᑦᓱᓐ ᐹ (ᓴᓂᑭᓗᐊᖅ) - 343: **ᐲᑦᑐᖅ ᑲᑦᑐᒃ**

Nunatsiaq News ᓄᓇᑦᓯᐊᕐᒥ ᐱᕙᓪᓕᐊᔪᑦ

Election night in Iqaluit ᓂᕈᐊᕐᓇᐅᑉ ᐅᓐᓄᐊᒃᓴᓂ ᐃᖃᓗᓐᓂ

Nunatsiaq News

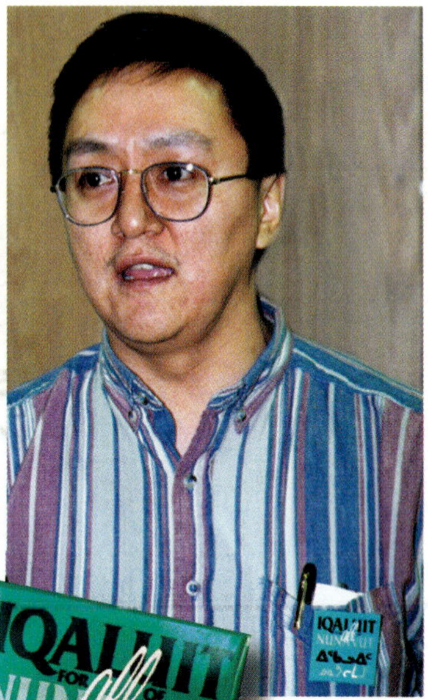

Nunatsiaq News

A journey into new terrain

continued from page 110

new jobs to as many areas as possible. Regional government centres will be located in Igloolik (Baffin Region), Rankin Inlet (Kivalliq Region), and Cambridge Bay (Kitikmeot Region). Decentralization will also help limit the changes associated with moving too many new people into one community.

Once the government of Nunavut is in place, it will receive the lion's share of funding for its operational and public-service costs from the federal government. This five-year formula financing agreement will account for approximately 95 per cent of Nunavut's governmental revenues; the remainder will be raised through taxation and the sale of goods and services. The 1999–2000 governmental budget is set at $620 million, $580 million of which has been allocated to cover the costs of programs and services. The rest is available to the incoming government to allocate as it sees fit. The federal monies are an unconditional grant.

In traditional Inuit fashion, the government of Nunavut will proceed deliberately into unknown terrain. The government will be implemented over three or four years, beginning with a core government of approximately 200 new headquarters public servants by April 1, 1999. With 1,700 GNWT employees converting over to the government of Nunavut, a total of 1,900 Nunavut government public servants are reporting to work as the territory gets under way.

On April 1, 1999, a dream that was first put forth on paper in 1976 becomes a reality. For the residents of Nunavut, the creation of their own government is the product of many generations of insight, wisdom, and the ability to adapt to a world in constant flux.

A former resident of Nunavut, magazine writer and editor Mike Vlessides of Canmore, Alberta has written extensively about the North, contributing to Up Here and Canadian Geographic magazines.

ᐃᓚᖓ ᒪᒃᐱᒐᐅᑉ 110

ᐊᕕᒃᑐᖅᓯᒪᕕᖓᓂ), ᐊᒻᒪ ᐃᖅᑲᓗᒃᑑᑦᑎᐊᕐᒥ (ᕿᑎᕐᒥᐅᑦ ᐊᕕᒃᑐᖅᓯᒪᕕᖓᓂ). ᐱᒃᓯᖅᑐᓂᕆᔭᐅᔪᑦ ᓅᑕᐅᓂᖓᑦ ᐃᑲᔪᐃᓇᔭᖅᑐ ᐊᒥᓲᓗᐊᖅᑐᑦ ᐃᓄᐃᑦ ᓅᑕᐅᒥᐊᖅᑲᓐᖏᓐᓂᖏᓐᓂᒃ ᐊᑕᐅᓯᕐᒧᑦ ᓄᓇᓕᖕᒧᑦ.

ᓄᓇᕗᑦ ᒐᕙᒪᖓᑦ ᐃᓂᖓᓕᓕᖅᐸᑦ, ᑮᓇᐅᔭᖅᑖᖅᐸᒃᑕᖏᑦ ᑕᒪᒃᑭᑲᓯᖏᑦ ᐊᐅᓚᔾᔪᑎᖏᑦ ᐱᔪᓇᔭᖅᑐᑦ ᑲᓇᑕᐅᑉ ᒐᕙᒪᖏᓐᓂᑦ. ᑮᓇᐅᔭᖅᑖᕈᑕᐅᓰᑦ ᐊᖏᕐᑲᑎᑮᒍᑕᐅᓯᒪᓪᓗᑎᒃ ᑕᓪᓚᒪᓄᑦ ᐊᕐᕌᒍᓄᑦ 95 ᐳᓴᓐᑎᖓᓄᑦ ᐊᑐᖅᑕᐅᕙᒃᑐᓂ ᐱᔪᓇᖓᔪᑦ ᓄᓇᕗᑦ ᒐᕙᒪᒃᑯᖓᓄᑦ. ᐊᓯᖏᓪᓚ ᐱᔪᑦᑕᕐᔭᖅᑐᑦ ᑖᒃᓯᓚᓂᒃᑯᑦ ᐊᒻᒪ ᓂᐅᕕᖅᑕᐅᕙᖕᓂᖏᑦ ᓂᐅᕕᐊᒃᓯᓂᒃ ᐊᒻᒪ ᐱᔨᑦᑎᖅᐸᑎᓂᒃ. ᐊᕐᕌᒍᒧᑦ ᑮᓇᐅᔭᒃᓯᖏᑦ 1999-2000-ᒧᑦ ᒐᕙᒪᐃᑦ ᑮᓇᐅᔭᒃᓴᓇᔭᖅᑕᖏᑦ ᐋᖅᑭᒃᑕᐅᓯᒪᔪᑦ $620 ᒥᓕᐊᓐᓄᑦ. $580 ᒥᓕᐊᓐ ᓴᓂᕐᕙᖅᑕᐅᓯᒪᔪᑦ ᐱᕙᓪᓕᐊᑎᑕᐅᔪᑦ ᐱᔨᑦᑎᕈᑕᐅᔪᓪᓗ ᐊᑭᓪᓕᖅᑕᐅᒍᓐᓇᖁᓪᓗᒋᑦ. ᐊᒥᐊᒃᑯᖓ ᒐᕙᒪᓄᑦ ᖃᓄᖅ ᐃᓱᒪᒋᔭᐅᔪᓄᑦ ᐊᑐᖅᑕᐅᕙᓕᔭᖅᑎᓪᓗᒋᑦ. ᑲᓇᑕᐅᑉ ᒐᕙᒪᒃᑯᖓᓂᕐᖔᖅᑐᑦ ᑐᓂᕆᓯᐅᔪᖅ ᒪᓕᒃᑕᐅᔪᒃᓴᓂᒃ ᐋᖅᑭᒃᓯᒪᒍᑎᖃᙱᓂ.

ᐃᖏᕐᕋᓂᖅ ᓄᑖᒃᑯᑦ ᐊᖅᑯᑎᒃᑯᑦ

ᐃᓄᐃᑦ ᐱᔪᓯᖓᑦ ᐊᑐᖅᑕᖅᑲᖓᑦ ᒪᓕᒃᓗᒍ, ᓄᓇᕗᑦ ᒐᕙᒪᖓᑦ ᐱᒋᐊᓕᖅᐳᖅᑐᖅ ᓄᑖᒧᑦ ᐊᖅᑯᑎᒃᑯᑦ ᐊᑐᖅᑕᐅᓯᒪᖏᑦᑐᒃᑯᑦ. ᒐᕙᒪᐅᔪᖅ ᐊᐅᓪᓚᖅᑎᑕᐅᓂᖓ ᐱᓪᓚᖓᔪᖅ ᐱᖓᓱᓂᑦ ᓯᑕᒪᓂᓗᓐᓃᑦ ᐊᕐᕌᒍᒃᑯᑦ, ᐱᒋᐊᕐᓂᖅᑳᕐᓗᓂ ᒐᕙᒪᕐᑯᑎᐅᓇᔭᖅᑐᒥᒃ 200-ᓂᒃ ᐊᖓᔪᖅᖄᒃᑯᕕᖓᒥ ᒐᕙᒪᓕᕆᔨᖅᑲᖅᓱᑎᒃ ᐄᐳᕆᓪ 1, 1999-ᒥ. ᓄᓇᑦᓯᐊᑉ ᒐᕙᒪᒃᑯᖏᓐᓄᑦ ᐃᖅᑲᓇᐃᔭᖅᑎᐅᔪᑦ 1,700-ᖑᔪᑦ ᓅᑕᐅᓇᔭᖅᑎᓪᓗᒋᑦ ᓄᓇᕗᑦ ᒐᕙᒪᖓᓄᑦ, ᑲᑎᓪᓗᒋᑦ 1,900-ᖑᔪᑦ ᓄᓇᕗᒥ ᐃᖅᑲᓇᐃᔭᖅᑎᔭᖅᑐᑦ ᐱᔨᑦᑎᖅᑎᑦ. ᑭᒡᒐᖅᑖᓄᑦ ᐱᔨᑦᑎᖅᑐᑦ ᐃᖅᑲᓇᐃᔭᓕᖅᑎᔭᖅᑐᑦ ᓄᓇᕗᑦ ᐃᖏᕐᕋᓕᖅᑎᑕᐅᑎᓪᓗᒍ.

ᑕᒡᕙᓂ ᐄᐳᕆ 1, 1999-ᒥ, ᑕᐅᑐᖑᒍᐊᖅᑕᐅᔪᑦ ᓯᕗᓪᓕᖅᐅᔪᒥ ᐋᖅᑭᒃᓱᖅᑕᐅᓚᐅᖅᑐᑦ ᐸᐃᑉᐸᒃᑯᑦ 1976-ᒥ ᐱᓪᓗᐊᕕᖕᖑᕈᕐᓛᖅᑐᑦ. ᓄᓇᕗᒥᐅᑕᓄᑦ, ᓇᖕᒥᓂᖅ ᒐᕙᒪᖃᓕᕐᓂᖓᑦ ᐊᒥᓱᓂᒃ ᐊᕐᕌᒍᓄᑦ ᐸᕐᓇᒃᑕᐅᓯᒪᔪᒥᒃ, ᓯᓚᑐᓂᖏᑦ ᐊᑐᖅᑕᐅᓪᓗᑎᒃ, ᐊᒻᒪ ᐊᓯᔾᔨᖅᐸᓪᓕᐊᔪᒧᑦ ᐊᓯᔾᔨᖅᑲᑕᐅᔪᓐᓇᕐᓂᖏᑦ ᒪᓕᒃᑕᓗᑎᒃ ᓄᐃᑎᑎᔪᑦ.

ᓄᓇᕗᒥᐅᑕᓚᐅᖅᑐᖅ, ᐅᖃᓕᒫᒐᓕᐅᖅᑎ ᐊᒻᒪ ᐋᖅᑭᒃᓱᐃᔨᐅᔪᖅ ᒪᐃᒃ ᕙᓖᓯᑦ Canmore-ᒥᐅᑕᖅ, ᐋᓪᐳᑕᒥ ᑎᑎᕋᖅᓯᒪᔪᖅ ᐊᒥᓱᓂᒃ ᐅᖃᓕᒫᒐᓕᐊᖑᓯᒪᔪᓂᒃ ᐅᑭᐅᖅᑕᖅᑐᒥᓇᔪᓂᒃ, ᐅᑯᓇᓂ Up Here ᐊᒻᒪ Canadian Geographic.

Top: Caribou forage for food outside Canada's newest territorial capital, Iqaluit. Former mayor Joe Kunuk, top right, urged voters to choose Iqaluit over Rankin Inlet, Nunavut's next largest community, during a 1995 plebiscite

ᖁᓛᓂ: ᑐᒃᑐ ᓂᕿᒃᓴᖅᓱᐃᖅᐳᑦ ᑲᓇᑕᐅᑉ ᓄᑖᖑᓛᖅ ᐃᒪᓐᑯᖅᑐᖅ ᓄᓇ ᐊᕕᒃᓯᒪᓂᖓ ᐊᖓᔪᖅᑳᖅᕕᖓᓂ, ᐃᖃᓗᐃᑦ. ᒪᐃᔭᐅᓂᒍ ᔫ ᑯᓄᒃ, ᖁᓛᓂ ᑕᓕᕐᐱᐊᓂ, ᑎᓕᐅᕆᔪᖅ ᐃᖃᓗᖕᓂ ᓂᕈᐊᕐᖁᔨᓪᓗᓂ ᑲᖏᕐᖠᓂᕐᒥᐅᖏᑦᑐᖅ, ᓄᓇᕗᑦ ᐊᖏᓂᕐᐹ ᑐᓪᓕᖓ ᓄᓇᓕᖓ, 1995ᒥ ᓂᕈᐊᕐᓇᖅᑕᖅᑎᓪᓗᒍ

Light up the skies . . . Nunavut has arrived!
THE NORTERRA GROUP OF COMPANIES
NorTerra Inc.
Canadian NORTH
northern transportation company limited
SRI HOMES
WBM

ᓄᓇᕗᑦ ᑲᒥᓵᒃᓴᖑᓂᑦ ᐸᕐᓇᐃᔨᑦ

TATJA KAMISINAGOLAKTOP TITIGAKVIA

OFFICE OF THE INTERIM COMMISSIONER OF NUNAVUT

BUREAU DU COMMISSAIRE INTÉRIMAIRE DU NUNAVUT

HIVONIKHAMOT OKAOTIT
A VISION FOR NUNAVUT
ÉNONCÉ DE VISION

Ovani opalogaiyalikmata Nunavutmik, ovagut hivonikhakot kavamakhat ona;

Inuit hivolikot itkaomalogit;

Kivgakhikvigivak-logit ovalo tohakpaklogit Inuit tamaita nunani;

Inuit kivgakhigomayut ekayukpaklogit nunavutmi;

Inuit piomayaitnik apigivaklogit ehomagiyaitnik;

Honanggokpalianiagait ovalo piotiginiagait inuit Nunavutmiot;

Inuit niamgiyaklakivaliavaklogit tamaita;

Nanminigipkaklogit inuit piotigiliktakhait inuit, elagiit, ovalo nunaliit;

Kavamaotiaklotik ehoak tomik ovalo inuknot anmaomavaklotik;

Pittiaktinnahoaklogit kavamat ovalo nutaatlo poimayaoyut atogahoaklogit ovalo;

Eliogaklogit nakoonikhait inuit ovalo nakootiaktot kavamakakvikhat.

In preparation for Nunavut, we are guided by a vision of a government that:

Places people first;

Represents and is accountable and fair to all its residents;

Is a servant of the people of Nunavut;

Seeks direction from the people;

Is shaped by and belongs to the people of Nunavut;

Offers programs and services in an integrated and holistic manner;

Promotes harmony amongst people;

Places ownership of well-being into the hands of individuals, families; and communities;

Conducts itself with integrity and openness;

Encourages excellence and welcomes creativity and;

Incorporates the best of Inuit and contemporary government systems.

En préparation pour le Nunavut, nous sommes guidés par la vision d'un gouvernement qui :

donne priorité aux gens;

est représentatif et juste, et est imputable à tous ses citoyens;

se met au service de tous les habitants du Nunavut;

demande au peuple de lui montrer sa voie;

est façonné par et appartient aux habitants du Nunavut;

offre des programmes et des services d'une manière intégrée et holistique;

favorise l'harmonie au sein du peuple;

permet aux individus, aux familles et aux communautés de s'approprier leur bien-être;

fait preuve d'intégrité et d'ouverture;

encourage l'excellence et accueille la créativité;

incorpore le meilleur des modèles de gouvernment inuit et comtemporain.

The Interim Commissioner of Nunavut,

Jack Anawak, was appointed on April 15, 1997, to set up the administrative framework for the government of Nunavut. From a small staff of five in June 1997, the Office of the Interim Commissioner grew into the organization that established the foundations of the new government.

Committed to informing the people of Nunavut of progress in the development of their government, and to seeking their views, the Interim Commissioner travelled to communities throughout Nunavut. Accompanied by designated Deputy Ministers, Assistant Deputy Ministers, and senior staff, the Interim Commissioner held many meetings and consultations with the people.

These pictures tell the story of how the making of the government was brought to the people.

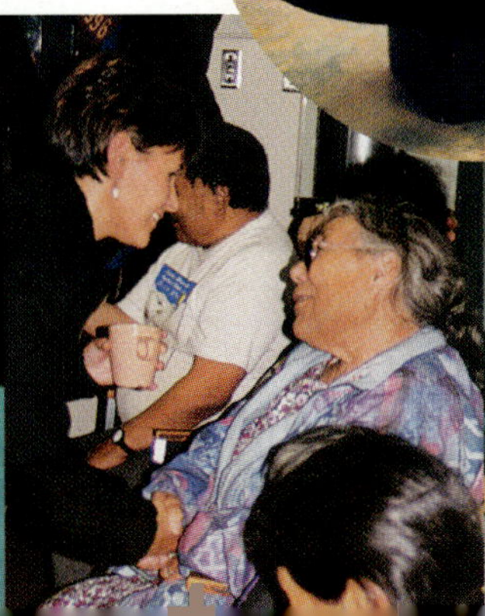

ᑲᒥᓯᓇᐅᑲᐃᓐᓇᖅᑐᖅ ᓄᓇᕗᒧᑦ, ᔮᒃ ᐊᓇᕈᐊᖅ, ᑎᒃᑯᐊᖅᑕ-

ᐅᓚᐅᖅᓯᒪᔪᖅ ᐊᐃᐳᕈ 15, 1997, ᐋᖅᑭᒃᓱᐃᕐᑯᔭᐅᓪᓗᓂ ᐊᐅᓚᔾᔪᑎᒋᓂᐊᖅᑕᕆᓐᓂᒃ ᓄᓇᕗᑦ ᒐᕙᒪᖏᑦᑕ.

ᐊᒥᓲᓐᖏᓚᐅᖅᑎᓪᓗᒋᑦ ᐃᖅᑲᓇᐃᔭᖅᑏᑦ ᑖᓕᒪᐅᓪᓗᑎᒃ ᔫᓂ 1997-ᖑᑎᓪᓗᒍ, ᑲᒥᓯᓇᐅᑲᐃᓐᓇᖅᑐᑉ

ᐊᓪᓚᕝᕙᐊ ᐱᕈᖅᐸᓪᓕᐊᒻᒪᕆᒃᑐᖅ ᑲᑐᔾᔨᖃᑎᒌᓐᖑᖅᑐᓂ ᐋᖅᑭᒃᓱᐃᔪᓂᒃ ᑐᓐᖓᕕᒃᓴᖏᓐᓂᒃ ᓄᑖᑉ ᒐᕙᒪᐅᓂᐊᖅᑐᑦ.

ᑐᑭᓯᒋᐊᖅᑎᒐᓱᐊᖅᑐᒋᑦ ᐃᓄᖏᑦ ᓄᓇᕗᑦ ᐱᕙᓪᓕᐊᓂᖏᓐᓄᑦ ᐋᖅᑭᒃᓱᖅᑕᐅᕙᓪᓕᐊᓂᖓᑕ ᒐᕙᒪᒃᓴᖅ ᐊᒻᒪᓗ ᑐᓴᕐᕕᒋᔪᒪᓪᓗᒋᑦ, ᑲᒥᓯᓇᐅᑲᐃᓐᓇᖅᑐᖅ ᐳᓚᕋᖃᑦᑕᓚᐅᖅᑐᖅ ᓄᓇᓖᑦ ᓄᓇᕗᒥ. ᒪᓕᒃᑕᐅᓪᓗᓂ ᒥᓂᔅᑕᐃᑦ ᑐᓪᓕᖏᓐᓄᑦ, ᒥᓂᔅᑕᐃᑦ ᑐᓪᓕᖏᑦᑕ ᑐᓪᓕᖏᓐᓄᑦ ᐊᒻᒪᓗ ᐊᖓᔪᖅᑲᐅᑎᓂᒃ ᐃᖅᑲᓇᐃᔭᖅᑎᓂᒃ, ᑲᒥᓯᓇᐅᑲᐃᓐᓇᖅᑐᖅ ᐊᒥᓱᓂᒃ ᑲᑎᒪᑎᑦᓯᓂᖃᖃᑦᑕᓚᐅᖅᑐᖅ ᐊᒻᒪᓗ ᑐᑭᓯᒋᐊᕐᑲᑎᖃᖅᑐᓂ ᐃᓄᖕᓂᑦ.

ᐅᑯᐊ ᐊᔾᔨᙳᐊᑦ ᑕᑯᒃᓴᐅᑎᑦᑎᔪᑦ ᖃᓄᖅ ᒐᕙᒪᒃᑯᑦ ᓴᖅᑭᓂᖏᓐᓂᒃ ᐃᓄᖕᓄᑦ.

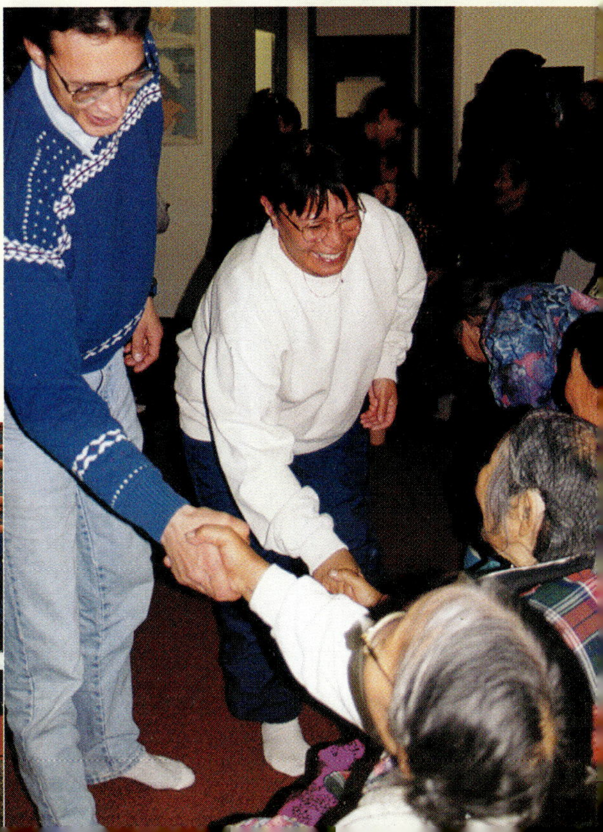

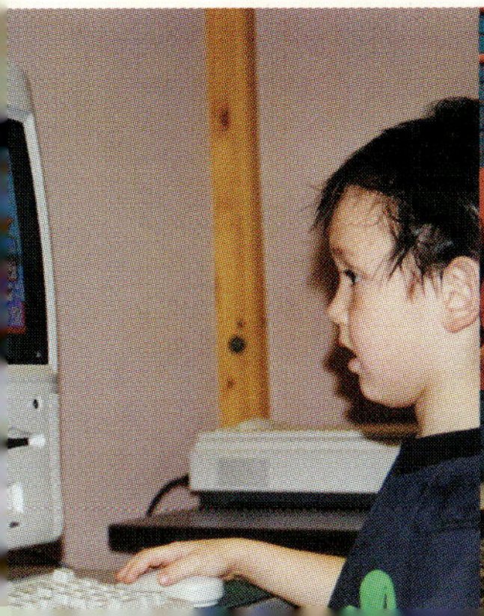

NUNAVUTMI KAMISINAGULAKTUK JACK ANAWAK, PIYAUHIYAYUK

APRIL 15-MI 1997, IHUAGHAITKUYAUPLUNI KAVAMAT HAVAKTIGHAINIK NUNAVUTMI. TALVUNA HAVALIHAAKHUTIK JUNE-MI 1997-GUTILLUGU TALIMAUHIMAYUT, TALVANGGA KAMISINAGULAKTUP TITIGAKVIA AKLIGAMI INIKTIGIVALIAYUT TUNGAVIGHAANIK KAVAMAUYUGHAT.

TUHAKTITIYUMAGAMIK NUNAVUTMIUNIK PIVALIAYUTAUYUTIGUT KAVAMAT KANUGIYUHIGHAITIGUT, INUITLU TUHAKVIGIYUMAPLUGIT, TAIMAITUMIK KAMISINAGULAKTUK NUNALAANUT PULAKTAKHIMAYUK NUNAVUTMI AULAUKATIKAKHUNI MINISITAGUYUGHAT TUKLIGHAINIK IKAYUKTIGIYAGHAINIKLU ATANGUYANIKLU PIKATIKAKHUNI NUNALIIT UPAKTAKHIMAYAIT. TALVUNA KAMISINAGULAKTUK NUNALIKNIK MIITIKATIKAKPAKTUK TUHAKTITINAHUAKHUNI, TUHAKVIGINAHUAKHUGILLU INUIT NUNALIIT UPAKTAKHIMAYAIT.

HAPKUA PIKSAT UNIPKAAGUYUT NAUNAIGUTAUNIAKTUT INUNGNUT KAVAMAT KANUGIJUHIGHAITIGUT.

Le commissaire intérimaire du Nunavut, M. Jack Anawak, fut nommé le 15 avril 1997

afin de mettre en place le cadre administratif du gouvernement du Nunavut. D'un groupe de cinq personnes à peine, en juin 1997, le Bureau du commissaire intérimaire est aujourd'hui devenu une organisation ayant jeté les bases du nouveau gouvernement.

Déterminé à informer les citoyens du Nunavut des progrès réalisés dans l'établissement de leur gouvernement, et pour recueillir leur opinion, le commissaire intérimaire s'est rendu dans les communautés, un peu partout au Nunavut. En compagnie des sous-ministres désignés, des sous-ministres adjoints et de certains hauts fonctionnaires, le commissaire intérimaire a organisé de nombreuses rencontres et consultations avec le public.

Ces photos racontent l'histoire de la création du nouveau gouvernement et la façon dont il fut présenté aux citoyens.

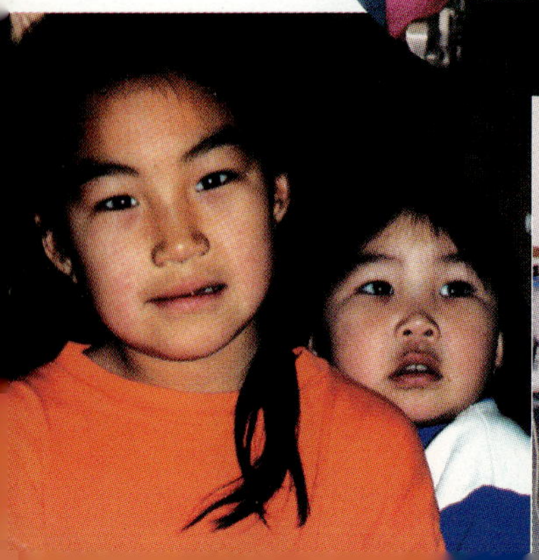

ᓄᓇᕗᑦ ᑲᓇᑕ • NUNAVUT CANADA • NUNAVUT KANATAMI

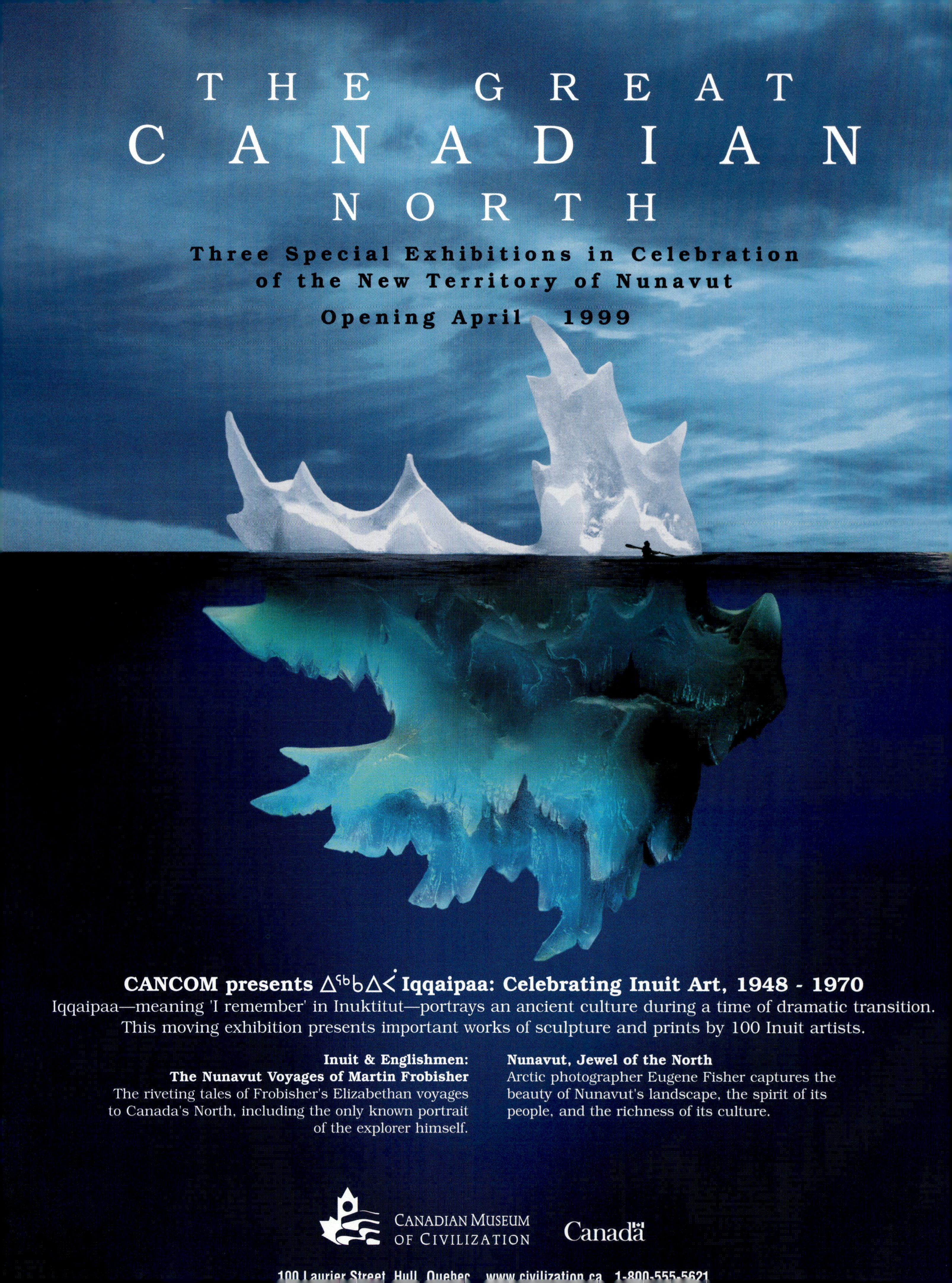
THE GREAT CANADIAN NORTH
Three Special Exhibitions in Celebration of the New Territory of Nunavut
Opening April 1999
CANCOM presents ᐃᖅᑲᐃᐹ Iqqaipaa: Celebrating Inuit Art, 1948 - 1970
Iqqaipaa—meaning 'I remember' in Inuktitut—portrays an ancient culture during a time of dramatic transition. This moving exhibition presents important works of sculpture and prints by 100 Inuit artists.
Inuit & Englishmen: The Nunavut Voyages of Martin Frobisher
The riveting tales of Frobisher's Elizabethan voyages to Canada's North, including the only known portrait of the explorer himself.
Nunavut, Jewel of the North
Arctic photographer Eugene Fisher captures the beauty of Nunavut's landscape, the spirit of its people, and the richness of its culture.
CANADIAN MUSEUM OF CIVILIZATION
Canada
100 Laurier Street, Hull, Quebec www.civilization.ca 1-800-555-5621

PARKS CANADA Welcomes our new Nunavut Territory
ᒥᕐᖑᐃᕐᓯᕙᓂᓇᐦᑯᑦ ᑲᓇᑕᒥ ᑐᙵᓱᒃᑎᑦᑎᔪᑦ ᓄᓇᕗᑦᑖᕐᑲᐅᒃᑎᓐᓂ

Experience the majestic splendor with a visit to our Canadian Arctic National Parks and National Historic Sites in Nunavut.

ᖃᐅᔩᓴᕈᐅᕈᐊᖅᑐᓚᐅᕈᑦ ᐱᐅᔫᒪᕆᖕᒥᒃ ᑕᑯᔭᓵᓕᖕᒥᑦ ᐳᓰᕆᐊᖑᑎᑦ ᑲᓇᑕᒥ ᐅᑭᐅᖅᑕᖅᑐᖅᑎᓐᓂ ᒥᕐᖑᐃᕐᓯᕙᖕᓂ ᐊᒻᒪ ᓄᓇᖏᔭᐅᕙᑦᑐᒥᓂᕐᓂᑦ ᑕᑯᔭᖅᑐᖑᑎᑦ ᓄᓇᕗᒻᒥᑦ.

Auyuittuq National Park

The oldest National Park in Nunavut is also one of the world's most scenic! Spectacular mountain ranges, towering peaks, giant glaciers. A hiker's dream, unspoiled and truly magnificent.

ᓄᓇᕗᒻᒥᑦ ᒥᕐᖑᐃᓯᕙᑐᖃᐅᓂᖅᐸᖅ

ᓯᓚᕐᔪᐊᕐᒥᑦ ᐱᐅᓂᑉᐸᖑᖃᑕᐅᔪᖅ ᑕᑯᒥᓇᕐᓂᖕᖑᓄᑦ. ᑕᑯᒥᓇᑦᑎᐊᖅᑐᑦ ᖃᖅᑲᖏᑦ ᐳᖅᑐᔫᑎᐊᓗᐃᑦ ᐊᒻᒪ ᐊᖏᔪᐊᓗᒃᒥᑦ ᐊᐅᔪᐃᑦᑐᓕᒃ. ᐱᔪᑦᑎᓄ ᐅᐸᒍᒥᓇᑦᑎᐊᖅᑐᖅ ᑳᔮᓇᑦᑎᐊᕐᓂᖑᓄ ᓄᓇᖑᑕᓗ ᓱᕐᕋᓯᒪᓪᓕᓐᓂᖑᓄᑦ.

Ellesmere Island National Park

Canada's most northern National Park. Teeming with arctic wildlife, historical sites and remnants of Paleo-Eskimo cultures. A park where cultural and natural heritage coexist in timeless beauty.

ᑲᓇᑕᒥ ᐅᑭᐅᕐᑕᖅᑐᑦ

ᖁᑎᖕᓂᐸᖑᓂᑦᑐᖅ ᐊᒻᒪ ᐃᓄᓂ ᓯᕗᓕᕙᓂᖕᓂᑦ ᐃᓅᖃᓂᒎᓗᓂ ᒥᕐᖑᐃᕐᓯᕙ ᐱᑕᖃᑦᑎᐊᖅᑐᖅ ᐃᓕᖁᓯᑐᖃᕕᓐᓂᖕᓂᑦ ᐱᐅᓯᑐᖃᕙᓂᖕᓂᓗ ᑕᑯᔪᒥᓇᕐᓂᖑ ᓄᖑᓂᐊᖏᑐᖅ.

Sirmilik National Park

Scheduled to open in the near future, Nunavut's newest National Park is home to an incredible abundance of bird species and marine wildlife. Jagged mountains and breathtaking glaciers provide a stunning backdrop to many historical Paleo-Eskimo and Whaling Era sites.

ᓯᕐᒥᓕᒃ ᒥᕐᖑᐃᕐᓲᕙᒃ

ᒪᑐᐃᓐᓛᓕᕈᕐᑐᖅ. ᓄᓇᕗᒥ ᓄᑖᖑᓗᖅ ᒥᕐᖑᐃᕐᓯᕙ ᓇᔪᑕᐅᕙᑐᖅ ᑎᒻᒥᐊᓄᑦ ᐊᒻᒪ ᐃᒪᖕᒥᐅᑕᖕᓄᑦ ᐅᒪᔪᓄᑦ ᐊᒥᓱᖕᒪᓇᖕᓄᑦ ᐳᑐᔩᑎᓂᑦ ᑭᖕᖓᖃᐅᕐᑐᖅ ᐊᒻᒪ ᓯᕐᒦᖃᓗᓂ ᑕᑯᐊ ᑕᑯᔪᒥᓇᖅᑐᕐᑯᑎᕆᕙᐃᑦ ᐱᑕᖃᑐᓂ ᐃᓄᐃᑦ ᓯᕗᓕᕙᓂᑦ ᓇᔪᕐᐸᑕᒥᓂᖕᖏᓂᒃ ᐊᒪ ᐊᕙᓚᕐᕕᐅᕙᑐᒥᓂᑦᓂ.

For more information on Nunavut's National Parks, National Historic Sites and Canadian Heritage Rivers, contact Parks Canada at (867) 473-8828.
ᖃᐅᔨᒋᐊᕐᓂᕈᕕᒪᒍᕕ ᓄᓇᕗᒥ ᒥᕐᖑᐃᕐᓯᕙᖕᓂ, ᓄᓇᖏᔭᐅᓂᑯᕕᓂᕐᓂ ᐊᒻᒪ ᑲᓇᑕᒥ ᑰᖕᓂ, ᐅᖃᓚᕕᒋᔪᓐᓇᕐᑕᑎᑦ ᑲᓇᑕᒥ ᒥᕐᖑᐃᕐᓯᕙᓂᓇᐦᑯᑦ ᐅᕙᓂ (867) 473-8828.

Superintendent, Nunavut National Parks • P.O. Box 353, Pangnirtung, NT X0A 0R0

Canadian Heritage Patrimoine Canadien
Parks Canada Parcs Canada

THE WORLD LOOKS NORTH

ᓄᓇᕐᔪᐊᖅ ᑕᐅᑐᓯᕗᖅ ᐅᑭᐅᖅᑕᖅᑐᕐᒥᓐ

Indigenous groups around the world are eager to learn more about Nunavut. Why? Because Nunavut's lesson — that aboriginal people can regain control of their world — offers a powerful measure of hope

ᓄᓇᖃᖅᑳᖅᑐᑦ ᓯᓚᕐᔪᐊᓕᒫᒥ ᐃᓕᑉᐸᓪᓕᐊᔪᒪᓂᖃᖅᑐᑦ ᓄᓇᕗᒥᒃ ᐱᔪᑎᖃᖅᑐᓂᒃ. ᓲᖅ? ᓄᓇᕗᒥ ᐃᓕᑕᐅᔪᖅ — ᓄᓇᖃᖅᑳᖅᑐᑦ ᐃᖕᒥᓂᒃ ᓯᓚᕐᔪᐊᒥᖕᓂᒃ ᐊᐅᓚᑦᑎᑯᓐᓇᕐᓂᖕᒐᑦ — ᓂᕆᐅᖕᓈᕐᐱᓪᓕᖕᒥᒃ ᐅᒃᑯᐃᑭᔾᔨᓂᖕᒐ ᑐᓴᖅᑕᐅᓪᓗᓂ

By Peter Jull

A dry red riverbed under a eucalyptus in the desert ranges of Central Australia seemed a strange place to be talking about the frustrations that had driven Inuit to push for creation of their own Nunavut government. However, it made perfect sense to the Pitjantjatjara elders seated in the riverbed to discuss their future. These Aborigines laughed with recognition to hear anecdotes from the Arctic about problems they knew too well, and then told their own.

That is the secret of indigenous internationalism. Problems that do not interest or seem important to governments at home often make good sense to people on the other side of the world. Greenlanders and Sami meeting in Copenhagen with Nunavut Inuit, Inuvialuit, Dene, and Métis in 1973 are generally thought to have started the world indigenous movement. Now there are such meetings every day, somewhere in the world.

ᑎᑎᕋᖅᑐᖅ ᐲᑕ ᔪᓪ

ᐅᖃᖅᑭᑦᑎᕆᓂᖅ ᐊᑖᓂ ᓇᐸᖅᑑᑉ ᓄᓇᐃᓐᓇᖓ ᐸᓂᖅᑐᒥ ᓯᐅᕋᐃᓐᓇᖓ Central Australia-ᒥ ᖃᓄᖅ ᐊᔾᔨᒋᔭᐅᓐᖏᑦᑐᒥᒃ ᑲᒪᓐᖅᑑᔭᖅᑐᖅ ᐅᖃᖅᑎᖃᖅᑎᓪᓗᑕ ᓲᖅ ᐃᓄᐃᑦ ᓄᓇᕗᑖᕋᓯᓐᖏᓐᒥᒃ ᐊᒃᓯᕆᓚᐅᕐᓂᕆᓐᓂᒃ. ᐊᒻᒪᓗ ᖃᓄᖅ ᐊᔪᕐᓇᕈᑎᖃᖅᐸᓚᐅᕐᓂᕐᒥᑦ. ᑭᓯᐊᓂᓕ, ᑐᑭᓯᑦᑎᐊᖑᔭᐅᖅᑐᖅ ᐅᑯᓄᖓ ᐃᓐᓇᕈᖃᖅᓴᐅᔪᓄᑦ ᐃᒃᓯᕚᖃᑕᐅᔪᓄᑦ Pitjantjatjara-ᖑᓂᖅᑕᐅᔪᓄᑦ. ᓯᕗᓂᖓᔪᒥᓂᒃ ᐃᒃᓯᕙᔪᑦ ᑰᕕᓂᐅᑉ ᓇᑎᖓᓂ ᐸᓂᖅᓯᒪᓕᖅᑐᒥ. ᑖᒃᑯᐊ ᓄᓇᖃᖅᑳᖅᑐᑦ ᐃᓛᖃᑕᐅᓚᐅᖅᑐᑦ ᑐᓴᕋᒥᒃ ᐅᑭᐅᖅᑕᖅᑐᒥᐅᓂᑦ ᖃᐅᔨᒪᕙᒥᒃ ᐊᔪᕐᓇᕆᑕᐅᓚᐅᖅᑐᓂᒃ ᐃᓕᑕᖅᓯᒪᕙᒥᒃ ᐊᑐᖅᓯᒪᒪᕙᒥᔾᔪᒃᑕᐅᖅ. ᐊᒻᒪᑦᑕᐅᖅ ᓈᒻᒥᓂᖅ ᐅᖃᐅᓯᖃᖅᐳᑎᒃ.

ᑕᒪᓐᓇ ᑭᒃᑯᒃᑖᓄᑦ ᖃᐅᔨᒪᔭᐅᓐᖏᑦᑐᖅ ᓄᓇᖃᖅᑳᖅᑐᑦ ᓯᓚᕐᔪᐊᓕᒫᓄᑦ ᑐᑭᓯᖃᑦᑕᖃᑎᒋᒃᐸᙵᓐᖏᑦ. ᐊᔪᕐᓇᖅᑐᓕᕆᔭᐅᔪᑦ ᐅᓐᓂᕐᓂᖓᓕᑦ ᐊᑐᓗᐊᕋᓯᒋᔭᐅᓐᖏᑦᑐᑦ ᐊᓐᖏᕋᕐᒥᖕᓂ, ᐃᓪᓚᖏᓐᓂᒃᑯᑦ ᑐᑭᓯᓇᕐᓂᖅᓵᐅᓯᖅᑐᑦ ᐊᓯᒥᙶᑦ ᐅᖓᓯᖕᓂᖅᓵᐅᔪᓂ ᓯᓚᕐᔪᐊᕐᒥ. ᐊᑯᑭᑦᑐᕐᒥᐅᑦ ᐊᒻᒪᓗ ᓵᒥᑦ ᑲᑎᒪᑦᑕᓚᐅᕐᓂᖕᒋᑦ Copenhagen-ᒥ ᓄᓇᕗᒥᐅᓂᒃ ᑲᑎᒪᖃᑎᖃᖅᖢᑎᒃ ᐊᒻᒪᓗ ᐃᓄᕕᐊᓗᐃᑦ, ᐃᖅᑭᓖᑦ, ᐃᖅᑭᓕᖕᒐᔪᓪᓗ 1973-ᒥ ᐃᓯᒪᒋᔭᐅᔪᑦ ᐱᒋᐊᕐᕕᐅᓇᓱᒋᔭᐅᓪᓗᑎᒃ ᓯᓚᕐᔪᐊᓕᒻᒥ ᐱᕙᓪᓕᐊᑎᑕᐅᓂᖓᑦ. ᑕᐃᒪᓐᓇ ᐅᓪᓗᑕᒫᑦ ᑲᑎᒪᖃᑦᑕᓕᖅᑐᑦ, ᓇᒥᑐᐃᓐᓇᖅ ᓯᓚᕐᔪᐊᓗᒃᑖᒥ.

ᓄᓇᕗᑦ ᓯᕗᓪᓕᕐᒥᒃ ᐋᖅᑭᒃᓯᐃᓯᒪᒍᑕᐅᔪᖅ ᐱᔾᔪᔭᕆᐊᖃᖅᑐᓂᒃ ᒪᓕᒃᖢᑎᒃ ᓇᒦᓐᖓᓂᒃ ᓄᓇᐅᑉ, ᐋᖅᑭᒃᓯᖅᑕᐅᓪᓗᓂ, ᓯᕗᓪᓕᖅᑕᐅᓪᓗᓂ, ᐊᒻᒪᓗ ᐱᔪᓐᓇᖅᓯᑎᑕᐅᓪᓗᓂ ᐃᓄᖕᓄᑦ ᑖᓕᓂᕐᒥᐅᑕᓄᑦ. ᑭᓯᐊᓂᑦᑕᐅᖅ, ᐊᓯᖏᓐᓄᑦ ᐃᓕᑕᕆᔭᐅᓯᒪᓂᖅᑲᖅᑐᖅ ᑐᑭᖃᖅᑎᑕᐅᓪᓗᓂᓗ.

ᑕᐃᑦᓯᒪᓂ ᑎᑭᓪᓚᖅᑐᖅ ᓄᓇᕗᒧᑦ ᐊᑎᓪᓗᒃ Leif Eriksen-ᒥᒃ ᐃᓯᒪᓚᐅᖅᓯᒪᑎᓪᓗᒍ "ᓱᓇᒨᓪᓗᓐᓂᓪᓚᑦ ᐱᐅᓂᖃᕐᖏᓪᒪᑦ ᐊᑐᕋᓂ" ᐊᕐᕋᒍᐃᑦ 1000-ᖑᔪᑦ ᑕᐃᑦᓯᒪᓂ ᖄᖓᒋᓯᒪᓕᖅᑐᓂ, ᐅᓂᒃᑳᑐᖃᐅᔪᓂ ᑎᑎᕋᖅᓯᒪᔪᓪᓚᑦᑐᖅ ᑕᒪᓐᓇ ᐅᖃᓚᐅᓂᖓᓚᐅᖅ. ᖃᓪᓗᓈᑦ ᑕᓇᐅᑉ ᐊᑭᐊᓂᕐᖓᓘᖅᑐᑦ ᐊᒻᒪᓗ ᑲᓇᑕᐅᑉ ᐱᖓᓲᓐᖓᓂᑦ ᖃᓄᑐᐃᓐᓇᖅ ᑕᒻᒪᖅᓱᑎᒃ ᖃᐅᔨᓯᒪᓂᖅᓯᒪᖓᒪᑕ. ᐅᓇᓗᓐᓂᓪᓚᑦ Eriksen ᐊᒻᒪᓗ ᑭᖑᕚᖏᑦ ᐃᓕᓚᐅᖅᑐᑦ ᓄᓇᕗᑦ ᐊᒻᒪᓗ ᐊᑯᑭᑦᑐᑉ ᑲᓇᖓᓐᖓ ᓴᓇᑐᐃᓐᓇᖅᑲᖅᓱᓂ ᐊᒃᓯᐃᓐᓂᕐᓂᒃ ᐊᑭᑐᓪᓗᑎᒃ ᓂᐅᕕᖅᑕᐅᒍᓐᓇᖅᑐᓂ ᖃᓪᓗᓈ ᓄᓇᖓᓐᓂ.

Below: *A sea of Danish flags greeted Canadian Inuit visiting west Greenland in 1958. Since then, the circumpolar world has changed vastly. Greenland Inuit gained more autonomy through a home rule government, and Nunavut becomes Canada's first largely aboriginal-run jurisdiction*

ᐊᑖᓂ: ᐃᒪᕐ ᓲᕐᓗ ᓴᐃᒪᑎᓄᑦ ᑐᓐᖓᓱᒃᑎᑦᑎᕗᑦ ᑲᓇᑕᒥᐅᓂ ᐃᓄᖕᓂ ᐳᓛᕐᑐᓂ ᐊᑯᑭᑦᑑ ᐱᖓᖕᓇᖓᓂ 1958ᒥ. ᑕᐃᒪᙵᓂ, ᓄᓇᕐᔪᐊᑉ ᐅᑭᐊᕐᑕᖅᑐᖓ ᐊᓯᖕᒍᕐᓯᒪᓕᕐᐳᖅ ᐊᖏᔪᒥᓐ. ᐊᑯᑭᑦᑐᑦ ᐃᓄᖏ ᐃᖕᒥᖕᓄ ᐱᓕᕆᓂᕐᓴ-ᐅᓕᓚᐅᕐᐳᑦ ᓇᖕᒥᓂ ᒐᕙᒪᖃᓕᕐᑎᓪᓗᒋ, ᐊᒻᒪ ᓄᓇᕗᑦ ᑲᓇᑕᒥ ᐊᖏᓂᕐᐹᖑᓪᓗᓂ ᓄᓇᖃᖅᑳᖅᑐᓂ ᐊᐅᓚᑕᐅᓂᐊᓕᕐᐳᖅ

Wilkinson/NWT Archives ᕕᐊᑭᓐᓴᓐ/ᓄᓇᑦᓯᐊᕐᒥ ᐸᐸᑕᐅᔪᑦ

Wilkinson/NWT Archives; oval inset: Mike Beedell ᕕᐊᑭᓐᓴᓐ/ᓄᓇᑦᓯᐊᕐᒥ ᐸᐸᑕᐅᔪᑦ; ᐊᖕᒪᓘᔾᔫ ᐃᓗᐊᓂ: ᒪᐃᒃ ᐱᑎᐅᓪ

"**Aboriginal peoples from all over the world . . . wanted to learn how we got through to the federal government in getting all these areas that no aboriginal group has ever gotten through negotiations.**"

– Paul Quassa, a chief negotiator for Inuit on the land claim

Nunavut is first and foremost a solution to particular needs in a particular region, designed, led, and achieved by the Inuit living there. However, it is also an important symbol and inspiration for others.

Since Leif Eriksen decided that Nunavut was "good for nothing" a thousand years ago, as the sagas say, Europeans from across the sea and from Southern Canada have been getting things wrong. Even Eriksen and his descendants figured out quickly that Nunavut and Northern Greenland were full of goods that brought high prices in Europe.

Nunavut in Canada

More recently, Canadians have thought of the North as a poor place needing the ideas and lifestyle of the South as much as material things. But something went wrong with this notion, too. Inuit were glad to have useful new goods, but had their own hopes and ways of doing things. Southern people seemed to be causing as many problems as they solved, and obviously had no understanding of northern needs or the importance of the land and sea to Inuit.

So Nunavut is not simply another piece of Canada getting its own flag and licence plates. It is a very different sort of place. It does not have the same ideas about using resources or buying land. It has a different language, and stories about how things are and should be which are totally unknown elsewhere in Canada. It has a government similar to provincial and territorial governments, but with a second 'constitution' in the form of the Nunavut Land Claims Agreement (NLCA) enshrining the result of special Inuit negotiations with Canada.

Inuit have persuaded the government of a powerful industrial state that it is time for a new approach. During the 1980s, premiers and delegations at constitutional conferences were intrigued by Nunavut and wanted information. Nunavut has

Nunatsiaq News ᓄᓇᑦᓯᐊᕐᒥ ᐱᑖᕐᓂᑦ

ᓄᓇᕗᑦ ᑲᓇᑕᒥ

ᖃᕆᐅᓂᖅᓴᓂ ᑲᓇᑕᒥᐅᑦ ᐃᓱᒪᒋᔭᖃᖅᓯᒪᓚᐅᑦ ᐅᑭᐅᖅᑕᖅᑐᒥᒃ ᐊᔪᖅᓴᖅᑐᓇᓯᒋᓪᓗᒋᑦ ᖃᓪᓗᓈ-ᓂᖏᖅᑐᓂᒃ ᐃᓱᒪᒋᔭᐅᔪᓂᒃ ᐊᒻᒪᓗ ᐃᓅᓯᖓ-ᑎᖏᓐᓂᒃ ᐱᑦᓯᓇᐊᖅᑕᐃᓕᔭᐅᓗᑎᒃ. ᑕᒪᓐᓇᑕᐅᖅ-ᑕᒻᒪᖅᓯᒪᓪᓚᕆᓚᐅᖅᑐᖅ. ᐃᓄᐃᑦ ᖁᕕᐊᓱᒃᑲᓐᓂᖅᐳᑎᒃ ᐊᑐᕐᓇᖅᑐᒥᖕᓂᒃ ᓴᓇᕐᕈᑎᓂᒃ, ᑭᓯᐊᓂᓕ ᓇᒥᓂᖅ ᐃᓱᒪᒋᔭᖃᕐᒥᖕᓂᒃ ᑐᕌᒐᖃᕐᒥᖕᓗ ᐃᓕᖅᑯᓯᖃᕐᒥ-ᔭᕆᖕᓂᓗ ᐊᑐᓪᓗᑎᒪᓂᕆᐊᓖᑦ. ᖃᓪᓗᓈᑦ ᐊᕙᑎᓕᐅᕐᓂᖅᓴᖏᓐᓂᒃ ᐃᒪᐃᑦᑐᔭᕆᓪᓚᑦ ᐊᔪᕐᓇᖅ-ᑎᓕᐅᕐᕕᖃᕐᓗᑎᒃ ᐃᑲᔪᖅᑕᐅᓚᐅᕐᓇᖏᓐᓂᒃ ᐃᓚᖓᒍᑦ. ᐊᒻᒪᓗ ᑐᑭᓯᓐᖏᒻᒪᑕ ᐅᑭᐅᖅᑕᖅᑐᒥᐅᑦ ᐱᔪᓐᓇᖅᑕᖏᓐᓂᒃ ᐅᑭᐅᖅᑕᖅᑐᒥ ᖃᐅᔨᒪᓐᖏᓪᓗᑎᒃ ᓄᓇᑉ ᐊᒻᒪᓗ ᑕᕆᐅᑉ ᐃᓄᖕᓄᑦ.

ᓄᓇᕗᑦ ᐃᓕᔭᐅᑎᐅᓇᐅᖏᑦᑐᖅ ᑲᓇᑕᒥ ᓇᒻᒥᓂᖅ ᑲᓐᓂᖅᑐᖅ ᓴᐃᒻᒪᑎᒥᒃ ᐊᒻᒪᓗ ᓴᐃᒻᒪᑎᒧᐊᖅᑕᒃ ᓄᓇᒦᑦᓯᖓᓂᖅ. ᐊᔾᔨᒋᖕᖏᑦᑐᖅ ᐊᒃᓱᕈᕐᓇᖅᑐᓂᒃ ᐅᖃᐅᓯᑦ, ᐊᒻᒪᓗ ᐅᓂᒃᑳᖅᑐᖅ ᖃᓄᐃᓐᓂᖓᓂᒃ ᐊᒻᒪᓗ ᑕᒪᓐᓇ ᓇᓗᓇᖅᑐᖅ ᑲᓇᑕᒥ ᓇᓗᓴᐅᔪᖅ. ᒐᕙᒪᖃᕐᒪᑦ ᐊᔾᔨᖓ-ᐅᓴᓕᒥᒃ ᐊᖏᒃᑐᖅᓯᒪᓂ ᐊᒻᒪᓗ ᓄᓇᓯᐊᖑᔪᓂ, ᐱᓯᐊᓂ ᑐᓪᓕᐊᓂᒃ "ᒪᓕᒐᖅᑕᖅ" ᐃᒪᓐᓇ ᐊᖏᕈᑎᓂᑦ ᑐᓂᔭᐅᒍᑦ ᓄᓇᕗᑦᒥᑦ. ᐃᓚᑕᖓ-ᐅᓯᒪᓪᓗᑎᒃ ᐊᖏᕈᑎᒋᔭᐅᓚᐅᖅᑐᖅ ᐃᓄᐃᑦ ᑲᓇᑕᒧᑦ ᐃᓴᖏᐅᖅᑐᑦ.

ᐃᓄᐃᑦ ᐊᔭᐅᖅᓯᒪᔪᑦ ᓴᖅᑭᑦᑎᒥᒃ ᒐᕙᒪ-ᔭᐅᔪᒥᒃ ᓴᓇᕐᕈᑎᓕᐅᕐᕕᐅᔪᑦ ᓴᓐᖏᓂᖃᖅᑐᑦ ᓄᑖᒥᒃ ᑐᕌᒐᖃᕐᓂᕐᒥᒃ. ᐊᑐᖅᑎᓪᓗᒋᑦ 1980-ᒥ, ᐊᖓᔪᖅᑳᕆᔭᐅᔪᑦ ᐊᒻᒪᓗ ᑎᓴᐅᑎᒋᔪᑦ ᑲᑎᒪᐃᓐᓇᖅᑐᑦ ᒪᓕᒐᖅ-ᐊᑦᑕᓂᖅ ᖃᐅᔨᒪᓂᖅᑖᕆᓯᒪᓕᕐᒪᑕ ᓄᓇᕗᑦ ᖃᐅᔨᒪᓂᖅ ᐊᒻᒪᓗ ᑐᑭᓯᒐᓱᐊᖅᑐᑎᒃ ᓇᓗᓇᐃ-ᕆᓂᖅ. ᓄᓇᕗᑦ ᓯᕗᓪᓕᕐᐹᖅ ᐅᐃᒪᔪᐊᕐᓂ ᓂᐱᖃᕈᓐᓇ. ᐊᒻᒪᓗ ᐊᔾᔨᖏᑦ ᓄᓇᖃᖅᑳᖅ-ᒥᐅᑦ ᐊᐳᖅᑐᖅᑕᐅᓯᒪᓕᕐᒪᑕ ᐊᔾᔨᖏᓐᓇᒥᒃᑕᕐᓂᖅ ᓚᓚᓐᓇᓂᒥᒃ ᐊᑐᐊᓂᓴᖅᑐᓂᒃ.

Mounties and maple leafs: the birth of Nunavut has strengthened Canadian sovereignty in the Arctic, an ongoing point of dispute. For a short time, Norway laid claim to Axel Heiberg and Ringnes islands in the High Arctic. The United States still doesn't recognize Canadian sovereignty of the Northwest Passage

ᐸᓖᓯ ᐊᒻᒪ ᒪᐃᑉᐳᓪ ᓕᕝ ᐸᓐᑭᒧᑦ ᐅᖃᐅᓯᖅ ᑎᓴᕐᕕᐅᔪᑦ, ᓄᓇᕗᑦ ᓴᖅᑭᑦᑐᖅ ᓵᓚᖃᕐᓇᖅᑎᑦᑎᔪᖅ ᑲᓇᑕᒥ ᐅᑭᐅᖅᑕᖅᑐᒥ ᑲᒪᓂᕆᔭᖅ, ᑕᒪᓐᓇ ᑕᐃᒪᖓᓪᓗ ᐊᑯᓂᖃᕋᓂ-ᐅᖃᖅᑕᐅᓯᒪᔪᖅ. ᕿᓚᒥᐅᔪᖅ, ᓄᐊᕗᐃ ᓄᓇᖃᖅᑎᕆᔭᖅ ᐋᓯᒃ ᕼᐊᐃᐸᒃ ᐊᒻᒪ ᕆᖕᓂᔅ ᕿᑭᖅᑕᓂ ᐅᑭᐅᖅᑕᖅᑐᒥ. ᐊᒥᐊᓕᑲ ᓯᓚ ᐃᓕᓴᕆᓯᒪᖏᑦᑐᖅ ᑲᓇᑕᒥᑦ ᐅᑭᐅᖅᑕᖅᑐᒥ ᑲᑕᒍᓴᐅᓂ ᑲᒪᔨᐅᓂᖓᓂ ᐊᑭᐊᓃᑦᑐᓴᖓᓂ

Right: In 1897, raising a British flag drew a cheer on Kekerten Island off Baffin Island's east coast, but on April 1, 1999, the world applauds as Nunavummiut *("people of Nunavut") unfurl their own flag. Below: 135,000 Inuit live in Alaska, Canada, Greenland and Chukotka, Russia*

ᑕᓕᕐᐱᐊᓂ: 1897ᒥ, ᐃᖕᓚᓐᒥᐅᑦ ᐊᐅᓚᔅᓯᓐᓂᖓ ᒪᑭᑎᑕᐅᑎᓪᓗᒍ ᕿᑭᖅᑕᓂ ᕿᑭᖅᑖᓗᒃ ᖃᓂᒋᔮᓂ ᖁᕝᕕᐊᓲᑕᐅᓚᐅᖅᓯᒪᕗᖅ, ᑭᓯᐊᓂᓕ ᐃᐳᕆ 1, 1999, ᓄᓇᕗᒻᒥᐅᑦ ᖁᕝᕕᐊᓱᒃᑎᖅᑲᓂᐊᖅᐳᑦ ᓄᓇᕗᒻᒥᐅᓂᑦ ᓴᐃᒪᑎᖕᒐ ᐋᕿᒃᑯᓂᔾᔪᑦ. ᐊᑖᓂ: 135,000 ᐃᓄᐃᑦ ᓄᓇᖃᖅᐳᖅ ᐋᓛᔅᑲᒥ, ᑲᓇᑕᒥ, ᐊᑯᑭᑦᑐᓂ, ᐊᒻᒪ ᓯᑰᑲ, ᐅᕆᓯᐊᒥ

Wakeham/NWT Archives ᖁᐃᕼᐊᒻ/ᓄᓇᑦᓯᐊᕐᒥ ᐸᐸᑕᐅᔪᑦ

gone about its business quietly, and has been attacked within Canada by some other aboriginal groups with different legal doctrines.

That will soon change. As soon as Nunavut is up and running it will be studied, visited, and admired by indigenous peoples across Canada. All indigenous peoples want something similar. They may argue about symbols and theory, but they want to govern their own lives and their own territory. What is different about Nunavut is that it is bigger than any other single indigenous region will be in Canada.

Nunavut abroad

Nunavut is no longer simply an Inuit idea, or merely an important idea for Canada. It is an important idea for the wider world.

For the circumpolar community, it is an end to paternalism and rule of white experts. It means the taking over of the Arctic by arctic peoples. There is nothing frightening about letting the people of a region take charge of their own problems. That shows that white people have matured in their understanding.

Nunavut also shows that democracy and human rights are fundamental rights of all people, and not something which they have to wait to buy when they have a million settlers in their territory or when oil wells in their hunting areas produce a billion dollars worth of export earnings.

There are many examples of Nunavut's importance abroad. At one 1994 conference in Canberra, Australia with world constitutional experts, some persons writing South Africa's new constitution wanted more information after a talk on Nunavut, and used the books and articles mentioned by the speaker. At another held in Brisbane, Australia in 1996, the New Zealand judge who was creating a whole new system of conservation for that country was delighted by the success of Inuit and remarked that Maori would make

ᑕᒪᓐᓇ ᕿᓚᒥᒃᑯᑦ ᐊᓯᔾᔨᓚᖓᔪᖅ. ᐃᖏᕐᕋᓱᑐᐊᖅᐸᑦ ᓄᓇᕗᑦ ᐃᓕᓐᓂᐊᖅᑕᐅᓇᔭᖅᑐᖅ, ᐳᓛᖅᑕᐅᒍᓂᒍ, ᐊᒻᒪᓗ ᐅᐱᒋᔭᐅᒍᓂ ᐊᒥᓱᓄᑦ ᓄᓇᖃᖅᑳᖅᑐᒥᐅᓄᑦ ᑲᓇᑕᓕᒫᒥ. ᑕᒪᕐᒥᓕᒫᑦ ᓄᓇᖃᖅᑳᖅᑐᒥᐅᑦ ᐊᑕᐅᓯᕐᒥᒃ ᐱᔪᒪᓂᖃᖅᑐᑦ. ᐊᐃᕙᐅᑎᔪᓐᓇᖅᑐᑦ ᐃᓱᒪᓕᐅᕈᑎᐅᔪᓂᒃ ᐊᒻᒪᓗ ᓇᓗᓇᐃᒃᑯᑕᓂᒃ ᐱᔾᔪᑎᖃᕐᓗᑎᒃ, ᑭᓯᐊᓂᓕ ᓇᖕᒥᓂᖅ ᒐᕙᒪᖃᕐᓂᒃᑯᑦ ᐊᐅᓚᓐᓂᖃᕈᒪᔪᑦ ᐊᒻᒪᓗ ᓄᓇᖁᑎᒋᔭᒥᖕᓂᒃ ᓇᖕᒥᓂᖅ ᐊᐅᓚᑦᑎᓗᑎᒃ. ᐅᓇᓕ ᐊᔾᔨᒋᓐᖏᓐᓂᕆᔭᐅᔪᖅ ᓄᓇᕗᒥ ᐊᖏᓛᖑᓂᖓ ᐊᓯᖏᓐᓂᑦ ᓄᓇᖃᖅᑳᖅᑐᓂᑦ ᐊᕕᒃᑐᖅᓯᒪᓂᕆᔭᐅᔪᓂ ᑲᓇᑕᒥ.

Nunavut's Circumpolar Neighborhood
ᓄᓇᕗᑦ ᐅᑭᐅᖅᑕᖅᑐᓕᒫᒥ ᓄᓇᓖᑲᑎᖏᑦ

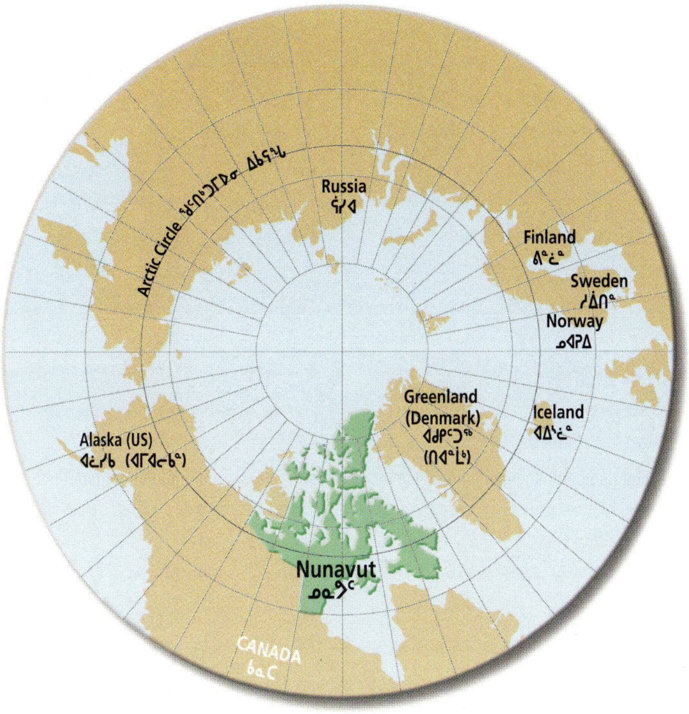

ᓄᓇᕗᑦ ᓯᓚᕐᔪᐊᓕᒫᒥ

ᓄᓇᕗᑦ ᐃᓄᑐᐃᓐᓇᕐᓗ ᐃᓱᒪᒋᔭᑐᐃᓐᓇᐅᓐᖏᓚᕐᒪᑦ. ᐅᑯᐊᓗᓐᓂᑦ ᐊᑐᖅᑐᑐᐊᖑᓐᖏᑦᑐᓂ ᑲᓇᑕᒥ. ᐊᑐᓚᐅᖅᑐᖅ ᓯᓚᕐᔪᐊᓕᒫᒥ.

ᓄᓇᓕᖅᑲᑎᒌᓄᑦ ᓯᓚᕐᔪᐊᓗᒃᑖᕐᒥ, ᐃᓱᒋᔭᐅᔪᖅ ᑲᒪᒋᔭᐅᑦᑕᓚᐅᕐᓂᖅ ᓱᕿᓯᖅᑎᑐᑦ ᐊᖓᔪᖅᑳᖅᑐᑎᑐᑦ ᐊᒻᒪᓗ ᖃᓪᓗᓈᑦ ᐃᓱᒪᑕᐅᑦᑕᕐᓂᖏᓐᓄᑦ. ᑐᑭᓕᒃ ᐅᑭᐅᖅᑕᖅᑐᖅ ᓇᖕᒥᓂᖅᐅᓕᕐᓂᐊᕐᓂᖏᓐᓂᒃ ᐅᑭᐅᖅᑕᖅᑐᒥᐅᓄᑦ. ᑕᒪᓐᓇ ᑲᐱᐊᓇᓐᖏᑦᑐᖅ ᓇᖕᒥᓂᖅ ᐃᓄᐃᑦ ᐊᕕᒃᑐᖅᓯᒪᔪᒥ ᐊᐅᓚᑦᑎᓕᑮᓐᓂᖏᓐᓂᒃ ᓱᓕᓇᐊᒥᖕᓂᒃ ᐊᔪᕐᓇᖅᑐᖅᑲᖅᐸᖕᓂᖏᓐᓂᖓᓐᓄ. ᑐᑭᓯᓐᓇᖅᑐᖅ ᖃᓪᓗᓈᖅ ᐱᑭᓕᑕᐃᓐᓇᕐᓂᖏᓐᓂᒃ ᑐᑭᓯᓂᕐᒥᒍᑦ.

ᓄᓇᕗᑦ ᑐᑭᖃᖅᑎᔪᖅ ᒐᕙᒪᑭᔪᒪᔭᒥᒃ ᓂᖓᐊᒌᓐᓇᕐᓂᕐᒥᒃ ᐊᒻᒪᓗ ᑭᒃᑯᓪᓗᒃᑖᔪᑦ ᐱᔪᓐᓇᐅᑎᐅᔪᑦ ᓇᖏᓂᖅᓴᐅᖕᒪᑕ ᑭᑐᓪᓗᒃᑖᓄᑦ. ᐊᒻᒪᓗ ᐅᑕᖅᑭᔭᐅᒋᐊᖅᑲᖁᓂ ᓂᐅᕕᖅᑕᐅᓇᓱᒋᐊᒃᓴᖅ ᒥᓕᐊᓐᓂᒃ ᐃᓄᖃᓕᑕᐃᓐᓇᕈᓂ ᓄᓇᖁᑎᒋᔭᒥᓂ. ᐅᕙᓗᐊᓪᓚᑦ ᐅᖅᓱᐊᓗᖕᓂᐊᖅᑐᖅᑲᓕᕈᑎᒃ ᐊᖑᓇᓱᒃᑲᒋᓱᖅᑕᒥᓂ ᐊᒻᒪᓗ ᑮᓇᐅᔭᖁᑎᒃᓴᐅᔪᓂᒃ ᐱᑕᖃᓕᕈᑎᒃ ᓄᓇᒋᔭᒥᓂᑦ ᐊᐅᓪᓚᖅᑎᑕᐅᓯᖅᑐᓂᒃ.

ᐊᒥᓱᓂᒃ ᐱᑕᓕᒃ ᑕᑯᔭᐅᔪᓐᓇᕈᑎᓂᒃ ᓄᓇᕗᑦ ᐅᐱᒋᔭᐅᓂᖓᓂᒃ ᐊᓯᒋᔭᑦᑎᓐᓂ. ᐊᑕᐅᓯᕐᒥ ᑲᑎᒪᕕᒃᔪᐊᕐᓂᖓᔪᒥ 1994-ᒥ Canberra, Australia-ᒥ ᓯᓚᕐᔪᐊᓕᒫᒥ ᖃᐅᔨᒪᔨᕐᔪᐊᓂᒃ ᒪᓕᒋᐊᕐᔪᐊᓕᓐᓂᑦᑐᒋᑦ, ᐃᓚᒋᔭᖏᑦ ᑎᑎᕋᖅᑐᑦ ᖃᐅᔾᔭᒃᑲᓂᕈᒪᓚᐅᖅᑐᑦ ᓄᓇᕗᒥ ᑲᒪᓕᕐᓂᖏᓐᓂᒃ. ᐋᕕᕆᑲᐅᑉ (South Africa) ᓄᑖᖅᒥᒃ ᒪᓕᒋᐊᖓᓂᒃ ᑎᑎᕋᖅᑎᕐᓗᒋᑦ ᐊᒻᒪᓗ ᐊᑐᕐᓗᑎᒃ ᐅᖃᓕᒫᒐᓕᐊᖑᓯᒪᔪᓂᒃ ᐅᖃᐅᓯᕆᔭᐅᔪᓂᒡᓗ ᐅᖃᕆᐊᖅᑐᖅᑎᑕᐅᔪᑦ. ᐊᒻᒪᑕᐅᖅ

Greg Coleman ᓗᓐᒐᓐ ᑯᓚᒪᓐ

Nunatsiaq News ᓄᓇᑦᓯᐊᖅ ᐱᕆᖃᑎᒋᔪᐃᑦ

Above: Forgotten waste outside Iqaluit – protecting the fragile arctic environment is a challenge for the new eight-country Arctic Council, whose founding chairman was Canadian Inuk Mary Simon. Right: Community-based Canadian Rangers, a civilian division of the military, are trained in search and rescue. Self-reliance is a must in the isolated North

ᖁᓛᓂ: ᐳᐃᒃᑐᒃ ᐊᒃᑕᑯᑦ ᐃᖃᓗᐃᑦ ᓯᓚᑎᐊᓂ – ᓴᐳᔾᔨᓯᒪᓂᖅ ᐅᑭᐅᖅᑕᖅᑐ ᐊᕙᓗᐊᓂ ᐊᒃᓯᕿᓇᕐᓂᐊᕐᐳᖅ ᑕᒪᒃᑯᓇᖓ ᑎᓴᒪᐅᔪᕐᑐᓄᑦ ᑲᑎᒪᔩᓄ ᐅᑭᐅᖅᑕᖅᑐᖅᓕᒫᒧᑦ, ᐊᒻᒪ ᑳᑯᓇᖓ ᐱᒋᐊᕐᑎᑦᑎᓂᑯᕗᖅ ᒥᐊᓕ ᓵᐃᒪᓐ ᑲᓇᑕᒥᐅᑕᖅ ᐃᓄᒃ. ᑕᓕᕐᐱᐊᓂ: ᓄᓇᓕᖕᓂ ᐅᓇᑕᕐᑐᒃᓴᓐᖑᐊᑦ, ᐅᓇᑕᕐᑐᒃᓯᑦ ᐱᓕᕆᔨᖏ, ᐃᓕᓐᓂᐊᕐᑎᑕᐅᕚᒃᐳᑦ ᐱᖑᓐᓇᕐᑐᓕᕆᓂᕐᒥ. ᐃᒻᒥᓂ ᐸᕐᑭᓂᖅ ᐅᑭᐅᖅᑕᖅᑐᕐᒥ ᐊᔪᕐᖏᓐᓂᐅᕆᐊᖃᒻᒪᕆᒃᐳᖅ

significant progress along similar lines. Others at that conference were shocked when I said that similar solutions might suit the Australian state of Queensland, but later that year the highest court cleared the way for Aboriginal land ownership across much of the state. Now the government, Aborigines, and environmentalists are looking at Nunavut as a model, while the Australian Parliament has recommended that Nunavut be studied by Australia's Torres Strait Islanders, where sea mammal-hunting people live in their traditional islands and demand self-government and sea rights. Also, the *Arctic Policy* of the Inuit Circumpolar Conference (ICC) — based heavily on lessons from Nunavut, Inuvialuit, and northern Quebec — is a valued and much-quoted document in some university research departments and indigenous organizations in the Southern Hemisphere.

In tropical swamps by the Gulf of Carpentaria in northern Australia, people living their ancient traditions are now working with Nunavut concepts and Inuit practices of co-managing fish, wildlife, and environments so they can educate governments and save their region from construction and development projects. Halfway around the world, Indians in the Amazon are increasingly aware of how Inuit and governments have, in the NLCA and creation of the territory of Nunavut, worked out generous and large-scale responses to social, cultural, and resource-management conflicts.

As a matter of fact, as I write this, Aborigines and various experts are gathering at a small town south of Darwin in northern Australia to plan their constitutional future. They are looking at national and territorial change, and their resource material includes a number of papers specifically about Nunavut, and others based on Nunavut experience. In 1992, when John Amagoalik visited Darwin to speak about Nunavut, many of these same people were present.

However, helpful people are not the only ones to spread news about Nunavut. Some crazy Americans put out books around the world saying that Nunavut is a plot by Prince Philip and the Queen — whose name appears on the cover of the NLCA along with Cape Dorset artist Kenojuak Ashevak's artwork — to

ᑲᑎᒪᓂᕆᔭᐅᔪᒥ Brisbane, Australia-ᒥ 1996-ᒥ ᐃᖅᑲᖅᑐᐃᔾᔪᔪᖅ New Zealand-ᒥ ᐃᖅᑲᓇᐃᔫᖃᖅᑐᒥᒃ ᓄᑖᕐᒥᒃ ᐊᐅᓚᓐᓂᕆᔭᐅᒍᑕᐅᓇᔭᖅᑐᒥᒃ ᑕᐃᑯᖓ ᓄᓇᖁᑎᖃᒥᓄᑦ ᐊᓕᐊᓇᐃᒋᔭᖃᓗᖅᑐᖅ ᐃᓄᐃᑦ ᓯᕗᒧᒃᓯᒪᓂᖏᓐᓂᒃ. ᓄᓇᖃᖅᑲᖁᑎᖏᓐᓂᒃ (Maori) ᓯᕗᒨᒍᑕᐅᓇᔭᕐᓂᐅᔪᓂᒃ ᐃᓯᒪᓗᐅᖅᑐᑦ ᐃᓄᐃᑦ ᐊᑐᖅᓯᒪᔭᖏᓐᓂᒃ ᐊᔾᔨᖃᕈᑎᒃ. ᐊᓯᖏᑦᑕᐅᖅ ᑲᑎᒪᖃᑕᐅᔪᑦ ᓂᕆᐅᓐᖏᓪᓗᑎᒃ ᖁᐊᖅᓵᓗᕐᒪᑕ ᐅᖃᕐᒪ ᑕᐃᒪᓐᓇᑦᑕᐅᖅ ᐋᖅᑭᒍᑕᐅᒍᓐᓇᕐᔪᕐᓂᖓᓂᒃ ᒍᒥᐅᑎᑭᖑᓗᓂᖑ-ᒥ ᓄᓇᖁᑎᖏᑕ ᐊᑉᑐᖅᓯᒪᓂᖓᓐᓂ Queensland-ᒥ. ᑭᖑᓂᐊᒍᑦ ᐊᕐᕌᒍᔪᒥ ᓯᓚ ᑖᑦᓯᒪᓂ ᐳᖅᑐᓂᖅᐸᐅᓪᓗᓂ ᐃᖅᑲᖅᑐᐃᔨᓕᕆᔨᐅᔪᑦ ᐋᖅᑭᒃᓯᐃᓚᐅᖅᑐᑦ ᓄᓇᖁᑎᖃᕐᓯᐅᔪᒥ ᓄᓇᖃᖅᑳᖅᑐᑦ ᓇᖕᒥᓂᖁᑎᖃᔪᓐᓇᖅᑕᖏᓐᓂᒃ ᓄᓇᖃᕆᓐᓇᕐᓂᖏᓐᓂᒃ. ᒫᓐᓇᐅᔪᕐᓕ, ᒐᕙᒪᒋᔭᐅᔪᖅ, ᓄᓇᖃᖅᑳᖅᑐᐃᑦ, ᐊᒻᒪᓗ ᐊᕙᑎᓕᕆᔨᐅᔪᑦ ᕿᒥᕐᕈᓕᖅᑐᑦ ᓄᓇᕗᑦ ᐊᔾᔨᓕᐅᖅᑕᐅᒍᓐᓇᕐᓂᖓᓂᒃ. Australia-ᒥ ᒪᓕᒐᓕᐅᕐᕕᖓᑦ ᐱᒋᐊᖅᑎᑎᕐᑯᔨᓚᐅᖅᑐᑦ ᓄᓇᕗᑦ ᐃᓕᓐᓂᐊᖅᑕᐅᕐᑯᓪᓗᒍ ᓄᓇᖃᖅᑳᖅᑐᖏᓐᓄᑦ (Torres Strait Islanders), ᐳᐃᔨᓂᒃ ᐱᓇᓱᒃᑎᐅᔪᓄᑦ ᐃᓕᖅᑯᓯᖅᑐᕐᒥᖕᓂᒃ ᓯᓚ ᐊᑐᖅᑐᓄᑦ ᕿᑭᖅᑕᓇᔪᒥᖕᓂ ᐊᒻᒪᓗ ᓇᖕᒥᓂᖅ ᒐᕙᒪᖁᑎᖃᕈᒪᔪᓄᑦ ᐊᒻᒪᓗ ᑕᕆᐅᒧᑦ ᐱᔪᓐᓇᐅᑎᖃᕈᒪᔪᓄᑦ. ᐊᒻᒪᓗᑦᑕᐅᖅ, ᐅᓇ ᐅᑭᐅᖅᑕᖅᑐᒥ ᐊᑐᐊᒐᓕᐊᖑᔪᖅ ᐅᑯᓇᖓ ᐋᖅᑭᒃᑕᐅᓯᒪᔪᖅ ᓯᓚᕐᔪᐊᓕᒫᒥ ᐃᓄᐃᑦ ᐱᔪᑎᒋᓪᓗᒋᑦ ᑲᑎᒪᕕᔾᔪᐊᖓᓂᑦ — ᑐᓐᖓᕕᖓ ᓄᓇᕗᒥ ᐃᓕᑕᐅᓯᒪᔪᓂᒃ, ᐃᓄᕕᐊᓗᖕᓂᑦ, ᐊᒻᒪᓗ ᑯᐃᐱᐊᒃ ᑕᕐᕋᖓᓂᑦ — ᐊᑐᖅᑕᐅᒐᔪᒃᑐᖅ ᐃᓕᑕᕆᔭᐅᓂᖃᑦᑎᐊᖅᓱᓂ ᓯᓚᑦᑐᖅᓴᕕᖕᓂ ᖃᐅᔨᓴᕕᖕᒋᓐᓂ ᐊᒻᒪᓗ ᓄᓇᖃᖅᑳᖅᑐᓄᑦ ᑎᒥᖁᑎᖏᔪᐊᓂ ᖃᓪᓗᓈᑦ ᓄᓇᖓᑕ ᒥᒃᓵᓐᓇᑦᑐᓄᑦ.

ᐅᖅᑰᔭᐊᓗᖕᒥ ᒪᓴᓕᐊᓗᖕᒥ ᖃᓂᒋᔭᖓᓂ Gulf of Carpentaria-ᒥ ᐅᐸᓗᑦᑐᒥ Australia ᑲᓇᖕᓇᖓᓂ, ᓄᓇᖃᖅᑖᖅᑐᑦ ᐃᓕᖅᑯᓯᑐᖃᒥᖕᒋᓂᒃ ᒪᓕᒃᓱᑎᒃ ᓴᓇᒍᑎᖃᐅᓕᖅᑐᑦ ᓄᓇᕗᒥ ᐃᓯᒪᒋᔭᐅᓯᒪᔪᓂᒃ ᐊᑐᖅᓱᑎᒃ. ᐃᓯᒪᒋᔭᐅᔪᑦ ᐊᑐᖅᑕᐅᒐᔪᒃᑐᓪᓗ ᐃᒪᓐᓇ ᓯᓚᓐᔪᐊᑕᐅᓪᓗᑎᒃ ᒪᑯᓄᖓ ᐊᐅᓚᑦᑎᖃᑕᐅᓂᕐᒥᒃ ᐃᖃᓗᒃᓯᐅᖅᑐᓕᕆᓂᕐᒥᒃ, ᐆᒪᔪᕐᓂᐊᖅᑐᓕᕆᓂᕐᒥᒃ, ᐊᒻᒪᓗ ᐊᕙᑎᓕᕆᓂᕐᒥᒃ. ᐃᓕᓐᓂᐊᖅᑎᑎᒍᓐᓇᖁᔭᖁᓪᓗᒋᑦ ᒐᕙᒪᒋᔭᒥᖕᓂᒃ ᖃᓄᖅ ᐸᐸᑦᓯᒍᓐᓇᖁᔭᕆᖕᒋᑦ ᓴᓇᕖᔭᐅᕕᐅᔪᓂᑦ ᐊᒻᒪᓗ ᐱᕙᓪᓕᐊᑎᑕᐅᔪᓂᒃ ᐊᖏᔪᓂᑦ. ᓯᓚᕐᔪᐊᕐᒥ ᓇᑉᐸᓪᓕᖅᓇᔭᖅᑕᖓᑕ ᐅᖓᓯᖕᓂᖓᑕ ᐊᑭᐊᓂ, ᐃᖅᑭᓖᑦ ᓄᓇᖃᖅᑳᖅᑐᖁᑎᖏᔪᐅᔪᑦ Amazon-ᒥ ᐅᔾᔨᕆᔭᖃᖅᐸᓪᓕᐊᓕᖅᑐᑦ ᖃᓄᖅ ᐃᓄᐃᑦ ᐊᒻᒪᓗ ᒐᕙᒪᐃᑦ ᓄᓇᕗᑖᕿᑎᒃᑯᑦ ᐊᖏᕿᑎᒋᔭᐅᔪᒃᑯᑦ ᐊᒻᒪᓗ ᐱᕐᖑᖅᑎᑕᐅᓂᖓᑎᒍᑦ, ᓴᓇᖃᑎᒌᒃᓯᒪᓂᖓᓂᒃ ᓯᕗᒨᒃᑕᐅᒐᓯᐊᖅᑐᓂᒃ. ᒪᑯᐊ ᐊᔪᕐᓇᕈᑕᐅᓯᖅᑐᑦ ᐃᓅᓯᓕᕆᓂᕐᒧᑦ, ᐃᓕᖅᑯᓯᓕᕆᓂᕐᒧᑦ, ᐊᒻᒪᓗ ᐊᐅᓚᑦᑎᖃᑎᒌᒍᓐᓇᕐᓂᕐᒧᑦ ᐊᑐᖅᑕᐅᒃᑲᓐᓂᕈᓐᓇᖅᑐᓂᒃ ᐃᖅᑲᓇᐃᔭᖃᑎᒌᒍᔾᔭᐅᓗᑎᒃ ᓯᕗᒨᒃᑎᑕᐅᓯᒪᓕᕐᒪᑕ. ᑕᒪᓐᓇᓗ ᐃᓕᕝᕕᐅᓯᒪᓕᖅᓱᓂ ᖃᓄᑎᒋ ᐊᑲᐅᔫᒃᑯᑦ ᐃᖏᕐᖁᓐᓇᖅᓴᖏᑎᖃᕐᓂᖓ.

ᑕᒪᓐᓇ ᑎᑎᕋᖅᑕᐅᓂᖓᓂ, ᓄᓇᖃᖅᑳᖅᑐᑦ ᐊᒻᒪᓗ ᖃᐅᔨᒪᔩᑦ ᐊᔾᔨᐅᖏᑦᑐᑦ ᑲᑎᒪᓪᓗᐅᖅᑐᖅ ᓄᓇᒋᔭᒥ ᒥᑭᑦᑑᔭᒥ ᐱᖓᖕᓇᖓᓂ Darwin-ᒥ Northern Australia-ᒥ ᓯᕗᓂᖓᑦ ᒪᓕᒐᖅᔭᐊᓕᓂᖏᓐᓂᒃ ᐸᕐᓇᐃᓂᐊᖅᓱᑎᒃ. ᕿᒥᕐᕈᔭᐃᑦ ᓄᓇᓖᒥᓄᑦ ᐊᒻᒪᓗ ᐊᕕᒃᑐᖅᓯᒪᔭᕐᑯᑎᒥᓄᑦ ᐊᓯᔾᔨᕈᑎᐅᓇᔭᖅᑐᓂᒃ. ᐊᒻᒪᓗ ᓇᓗᓇᐃᔭᕈᑎᖏᑕ ᐃᓚᒋᔭᖃᖅᑐᑦ ᓄᓇᕗᓕᕆᔭᓂᒃ ᐅᖃᓖᒪᒐᒃᓴᓂᒃ ᐊᒻᒪᓗ ᐊᓯᖏᑦᑕᐅᖅ ᓄᓇᕗᒥᒃ ᐱᔪᓐᓂᖅᓂᒃ. ᑕᐃᑲᓂ 1992-ᖑᓗᐅᖅᑎᓪᓗᒍ, ᔫᓐ ᐊᒪᕈᐊᓕᒃ ᐳᓚᕋᓗᐅᖅᑐᖅ Darwin, Australia-ᒧᑦ, ᐅᖃᓇᐊᖅᑐᖅᑎᑕᐅᓪᓗᓂ ᓄᓇᕗᒥᒃ ᐱᔾᔪᑎᖃᖅᓱᓂ, ᐊᒥᓱᑦ ᑖᒃᑯᐊ ᑕᐃᑲᓈᓗᐅᕐᒪᑕ ᑲᑎᒪᔪᓂ.

ᑭᓯᐊᓂᓕ, ᐃᑲᔪᕈᒪᔪᑦ ᑖᒃᑯᐊᑐᐊᖑᓐᖏᓪᒪᑕ ᓄᓇᕗᒥᒃ ᑐᓵᖅᑎᑎᒍᑎᖃᕈᒪᔪᑦ. ᐃᓚᖏᑦ ᐊᒥᐊᓕᒃᑲᒥᐅᑦ ᓇᓗᔪᑦ ᐅᖃᓖᒪᒐᓕᐅᓗᐅᖅᑕᖅᓯᒪᔪᒥᒃ ᓄᓇᕗᒧᖅ ᑯᐃᓐᒧᑦ ᐅᐃᖓᓄᑦ - ᐊᑎᖏᒃ ᑎᑎᖅᓯᒪᓪᓗᑎᒃ ᖃᖓᓂ ᐅᖃᓖᒪᐅᑉ ᐊᖏᖅᑲᑎᒌᒍᑎᕕᓂᐅᑉ ᐊᒻᒪᓗ ᑭᖓᐅᒥᐅᑦ ᓴᓇᙳᐊᖅᑎ ᕿᓐᓄᐊᖅᔭᐊᖅ ᐋᓯᕙᐅᑉ ᓴᓇᙳᐊᒐᖏᑦ — ᑎᑎᖅᓯᒪᖕᒪᑕᒎᖅ ᓄᓇᖁᑎᖏᔪᑦ ᐊᕕᒃᑕᐅᖁᓪᓗᒋᑦ ᐊᒻᒪᓗ ᓯᓇᑐᐃᓐᓇᖁᑎᖏᑦ ᑎᓪᓕᒃᑕᐅᖁᓪᓗᒋᑦ. ᑕᒃᑯᐊ ᐅᖃᓖᒪᒐᓕᐊᖑᓯᒪᔪᑦ ᑮᓇᐅᔭᓕᐅᕈᑕᐅᖕᒪᑕ!

“ᓄᓇᖃᖅᑳᖅᑐᑦ ᓄᓇᕐᔪᐊᓕᒫᒥ ᓇᓂᑐᐃᓐᓈᖅ . . . ᖃᐅᔨᒪᓪᓗᕐᐳᑦ ᖃᓄᐊᓘᒃ ᒐᕙᒪᑐᖃᒃᑯᑦ ᐱᙱᓯᒪᓇᓚᐅᕆᐊᒃᓴᑎᓐᓂᑦ ᓄᓇᒥᓐ ᐊᓯᒍᑦ ᓄᓇᖃᖅᑳᖅᑐᑦ ᑕᐃᒪᓐᓇ ᐱᔪᓐᓇᕐᐸᙱᑎᓪᓗᒋᑦ ᐋᖅᑭᑎᑦᓯᙵᓂᒃᑯᑦ.”

- ᐲᑦ ᔪᐊᓴ, ᐊᖓᔪᖄᖑᓪᓗᓂ ᐋᖅᑲᕆᑕᐅᓂᒃ ᐃᓄᖕᓄ ᓄᓇᑖᕋᓯᖕᓂᕐᒧᓐ

break up countries and steal their resources. Such stories apparently make money!

Even a former chief justice and a Northern Territory premier in Australia, people who should know better, find Nunavut threatening, and say so in speeches and press releases. They cannot imagine Aborigines and Torres Strait Islanders equal to whites or having their own respected place in the nation, it seems. Let us hope that Inuit and democratic feeling continue to upset such reactionary people all over the world.

Peter Ernerk ᐱᑕ ᐃᕐᓂᖅ

Still, it is not the specific lessons and details of Nunavut, but the grassroots discovery by isolated or powerless people of Nunavut's existence and the lesson it provides — that aboriginal people can regain control of their world — that is best of all. Former Inuit Tapirisat of Canada (ITC) leader Rosemarie Kuptana once mentioned my work to Aborigines in Alice Springs in the middle of Australia's outback, leading them to invite me to a meeting. Some had read notes I had written on Nunavut, and all present were aware of Inuit efforts to create the Nunavut land claim and territory. But that Nunavut is above all simply a symbol of hope was underscored in one memorable exchange. "Come on, sis!" one enthusiastic Aborigine shouted to a timid soul at this meeting. "Them Eskimo mob have done it!"

That is the most important message for downtrodden people anywhere: Inuit have made Nunavut. Others can take courage and do it, too.

Peter Jull worked in the NWT and Nunavut on and off from 1961, and was founding co-ordinator of the Nunavut Constitutional Forum. Today he writes and teaches on Nunavut and world indigenous issues at universities from his new home in Brisbane, Australia.

ᑕᐃᒃᑯᐊᓛᓐᓂᑦ ᐊᖓᔪᖄᖃᓂᕆᓪᓗᕐᑐᑦ ᓯᕗᓪᓕᖅᑎᐅᓚᐅᖅᑎᒃ ᐃᖅᑲᖅᑐᐃᔨᐅᓚᐅᖅᓯᒪᔪᖅ ᐊᑕᐅᓯᖅ Australia-ᒥ, ᐊᐃᑉᐸᖓᓗ ᐊᕕᒃᑐᖅᓯᒪᔪᒥ ᑲᓇᖕᓇᖓᓂ ᐊᖓᔪᖄᖃᓂᕆᔪᓪᓗᓂ, ᖃᐅᔨᒪᓂᖅᓴ-ᐅᔪᒃᓴᐅᒐᓗᐊᒃ ᓄᓇᕗᒥᒃ ᐊᑲᐅᒃᓴᙱᓯᒪᔪᒃ ᐅᓗᕆᐊᕆᓪᓗᓂᔾᔪᒃ. ᐊᒻᒪᓗ ᑕᐃᒪᓐᓇ ᑐᓴᖅᑎ-ᑎᓱᖅᐳᑎᒃ ᐅᖃᕆᐊᖅᑐᖅᑎᑕᐅᓚᐃᒐᒥᒃ ᑐᓴᕈᑎᒃᓴᓕ-ᕆᖏᒥᓪᓗ. ᐃᓱᒪᒋᔭᖃᕈᒪᙱᑦᑐᑦ ᓇᓕᔪᕆ-ᐊᒃᓴᖏᓐᓂᒃ ᓄᓇᖃᖅᑳᖅᑐᒥᐅᑦ (Aborigines) ᐊᒻᒪᓗ Torres Strait Islanders-ᒥᐅᑦ ᖃᓪᓗᓈᓄᑦ ᐅᑦᕙᓘᓐᓂᑦ ᐃᒪᓐᓇᖃᐃ ᐃᓂᖃᖁᔨᓇᑎᒃ ᓄᓇᖁᑎᕆᔭᒥᙵᓂᒃ ᐅᐱᕆᔭᐅᒍᑕᐅᓂᖃᕐᔭᖅᑐᓂᒃ. ᓂᕆᐅᖕᓂᖅᑕᓕ ᐃᓄᐃᑦ ᐊᒻᒪᓗ ᒐᕙᒪᕆᔪᒪᔭᒥᒃ ᓂᕈᐊᕈᓐᓇᕐᓂᖅ ᓇᒥᑐᐃᓐᓇᓕᒫᖅ ᓂᕐᖓᒍᑕᐅᑕ-ᕋᔭᕐᓂᖓᓐᓂᒃ ᓯᓚᕐᔪᐊᕐᒥᐅᑕᒃᑖᒥ.

ᑭᓯᐊᓂᓕ, ᑖᒃᑯᐊ ᐃᓕᒍᑎᑐᐃᓐᓇᐅᓐᖏᑦᑐᑦ ᓄᓇᕗᓕᓂᒃᑯᑦ, ᓇᖏᓂᖅᓴᐅᔪᓂᓪᓕ ᓄᓇᖃᖅᑳᖅᑐ-ᒥᐅᑦ ᐱᕙᓪᓕᐊᒍᓐᓇᕐᓂᖏᑦ ᐊᑐᖅᑐᑦ. ᐱᓗᐊᖅᑐᒥᒃ ᐱᒃᓴᖅᑐᓂᖃᕐᖏᑦᑐᓄᑦ ᑎᑭᑕᐅᓴᕋᐃᓐᖏᑦᑐᓄᑦ ᐃᓕᑉᑕᐅᔪᖅ ᐊᔾᔨᓕᐅᖅᑕᐅᒍᓐᓇᖅᓱᓂ — ᓄᓇᖃᖅᑳᖅᑐᑦ ᓇᖏᓂᖅ ᐊᐅᓚᓐᓂᖃᕆᓐᓇᕐᓂᖓᑦ — ᑖᓐᓇ ᐱᐅᓂᖅᐸᐅᔪᖅ. ᐃᓄᐃᑦ ᑕᐱᕇᒃᓴᒃᑯᓐᓂ ᓯᕗᓕᖅᑎᐅᖃᑕᐅᓚᐅᖅᑐᖅ ᕉᓯᒥᐊᕆ ᑯᑉᑖᓇ ᐅᖃᐅᓯᖃᓚᐅᖅᑐᖅ ᓴᓇᓯᒪᓂᕐᔭᓐᓂᒃ ᐱᔾᔪᑎᖃᖅᖢᓂ ᓄᓇᖃᖅᑳᖅᑐᓄᑦ ᑕᐃᑲᓂ Alice Springs-ᒥ ᕿᑎᖓᓂ Australia-ᒥ. ᑲᑎᒪᔪᓄᑦ ᖃᐃᖁᔭ-ᐅᑦᑕᕆᑎᓕᐅᖅᑕᖅ. ᐅᖃᓕᒫᖅᓯᒪᓚᐅᖅᑐᑎᒃ ᐃᓚᖏᑦ ᑎᑎᖅᖅᓯᒪᔭᓄᑦ ᓄᓇᕗᓪᓕᐊᕐᒥᒃ. ᑭᓯᐊᓂᓕ ᓄᓇᕗᑦ ᐃᓚᑕᓱᐅᓂᖃᕈᓐᓇᖅᓯᒪᓪᓗᓂ ᓂᕆᐅᖕᓂᕐᒥᒃ. ᐊᑕᐅᓯᖅ ᐅᖃᖅᑐᖅ ᐃᖅᑲᐅᒪᔭᖅ “ᐊᑏ ᓄᑳᖅ!”, ᑲᕐᕈᓯᒃᑐᒧᑦ ᑲᑎᒪᑎᓪᓗᒋᑦ. “ᑖᒃᑯᐊ ᐃᓄᐃᑦ ᐱᔮᕐᓯᒪᓕᖅᑕᖓᑦ!”

ᑕᒪᓐᓇ ᐊᑐᕐᓂᖅᐸᖑᔪᖅ ᑐᓴᖅᑕᐅᔪᒃᓴᓂ ᓇᒥᑐᐃᓐᓈᖅ ᐃᓄᖕᓄᑦ ᓵᓕᔭᐅᓯᒪᔪᓂ: ᐃᓄᐃᑦ ᓴᓇᓯᒪᔪᑦ ᓄᓇᕗᒥᒃ. ᐊᓯᖏᑦᑕᐅᖅ ᓴᙱᓂᖅᑲᖅᑐᓂᒃ ᓴᐱᙱᑦᑐᑎᒃ ᐱᔮᓐᓇᕐᒥᔪᑦᑕᐅᖅ.

ᐲᑕ ᔪᓪ ᐃᖅᑲᓇᐃᔭᖅᓯᒪᔪᖅ ᓄᓇᑦᓯᐊᒥ ᐊᒻᒪᓗ ᓄᓇᕗᒥ ᐱᒋᐊᖅᖢᓂ 1961-ᒥ, ᐊᒻᒪᓗ ᐃᓚᐅᖃᑕᐅᓚᐅᖅᖢᓂ ᓄᓇᕗᒥ ᒪᓕᒐᕐᔪᐊᓕᕆᓂᕐᒥᒃ ᑲᑎᒪᔩᒃᑯᓐᓂᒃ. ᐅᓪᓗᒥ ᑎᑎᕋᖅᑎᐅᔪᖅ ᐊᒻᒪᓗ ᐃᓕᓐᓂᐊᕐᕕᓐᓂ ᓄᓇᖃᖅᑳᖅᑐᓂᒃ ᐱᔾᔪᑎᓕᖕᓂᒃ ᐃᓕᓐᓂᐊᖅᑎᑦᑐᓂ ᐃᓕᓐᓂᐊᖅᑎᑦᑐᓂ ᐊᖏᕐᕋᒥᓂ Brisbane, Australia-ᒥ.

Nunatsiaq News ᓄᓇᑦᓯᐊᕐᒥ ᐱᑦᓚᑦᑐᑦ

Rosemarie Kuptana ᕈᓯᒥᐊᕆ ᑰᑦᑖᓇ

Top: An aboriginal dancer in impoverished Kovran, Russia. In early 1999, the ICC, with Canada's help, delivered aid to starving Russians. Above right: Rosemarie Kuptana. Right: Nunavut is a beacon of hope to Australian Aborigines and Torres Strait Islanders fighting for greater rights within their own country

ᖁᓖᓂ: ᓄᓇᖃᖅᑳᖅᑐᖅ ᒧᒥᖅᑎ ᑰᕚᕋ, ᕿᓯᐊᒥ. 1999 ᐱᒋᐊᓕᖅᑎᓪᓗᒍ, ᐃᓄᐃᑦ ᓄᓇᕐᔪᐊᓕᒦᒥ ᑲᑎᒪᔨᖏ, ᑲᓇᑕᒥᐅᓄᑦ ᐃᑲᔪᖅᑕᐅᓪᓗᑎ, ᐃᑲᔪᓪᓚᐅᕐᐳᑦ ᐱᖓᓕᖅᑐᓂᑦ ᐅᕿᓯᐊᕐᒥᐅᓂᑦ. ᖁᓖᓂ ᑕᓕᖅᐱᐊᓂ: ᕈᓯᒥᐊᕆ ᑯᑉᑖᓇ. ᑕᓕᖅᐱᐊᓂ: ᓄᓇᕗᑦ ᓯᕗᓂᒃᓴᒧᑦ ᓂᕆᐅᖕᓂᐅᕗᖅ ᐋᔅᑐᕌᓕᐊᐸ ᓄᓇᖃᖅᑳᖅᑐᖅᑯᑎᖏᓐᓄ ᐊᒻᒪᓗ ᑑᕋᔅ ᑕᓪᓗᕈᑎᐅᑉ ᕿᑭᖅᑕᖅᒥᐅᑕᖏᓐᓄ ᑖᒃᑯᐊ ᐱᔪᓐᓇᐅᑎᒥᖕᓂ ᐱᓇᓱᒃᑎᓪᓗᒋᑦ ᓄᓇᖏᓐᓂᑦ

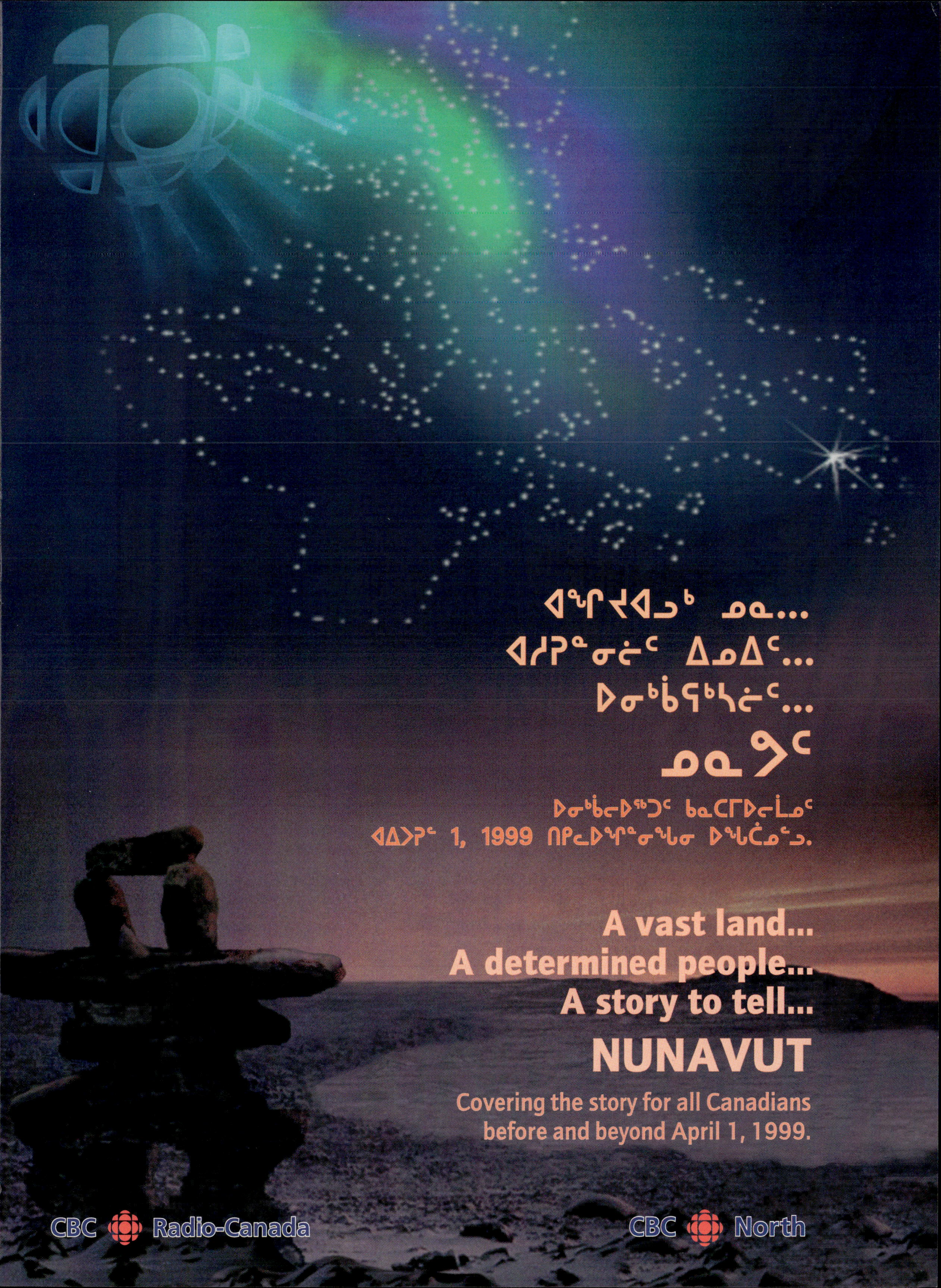

ᐊᖏᔪᐊᓗᒃ ᓄᓇ...
ᐊᓱᕈᓐᓂᓲᑦ ᐃᓄᐃᑦ...
ᐅᓂᒃᑳᑫᒃᓴᓲᑦ...
ᓄᓇᕗᑦ
ᐅᓂᒃᑳᓕᐅᖅᑐᑦ ᑲᓇᑕᒥᐅᓕᒫᓄᑦ
ᐊᐃᐳᕆᓪ 1, 1999 ᑎᑭᓪᓗᒍᓐᓂᖓᓂ ᐅᖓᑖᓄᓪᓗ.
A vast land...
A determined people...
A story to tell...
NUNAVUT
Covering the story for all Canadians
before and beyond April 1, 1999.
CBC Radio-Canada
CBC North

APRIL 1999 AVRIL
CANADA

Helping Nunavut build for the future

ᐃᑲᔪᕐᑏᑦ ᓄᓇᕗᒻᒥ ᐱᓕᕆᕙᓪᓕᐊᑎᓪᓗᒋ ᓯᕗᓂᒃᓴᒧᑉ

ᓄᐊᑦᕋᔅᑎᐅᑦ ᐱᒃᑯᒍᓲᑎᖃᕐᐳᑦ ᐃᓄᖕᓂ ᓄᓇᕗᒻᒥᐅᓂ ᐊᒻᒪᓗ ᓄᓇᑖᕐᓂᖏᓐᓂᑦ. ᓄᐊᑦᕋᔅᑎᐅᓪᒥ ᑐᑭᓯᐅᒪᒐᔪᒍ ᐱᒃᑯᓕᓯᒪᓂᕐᒥᓐ ᖁᕕᐊᒋᔭᖃᕐᓂᕐᒥᓪᓗ ᐱᓕᕆᐊᒥᓐ ᓴᖅᑭᑦᑎᓪᓗᓂ ᐊᒃᓱᕈᑕᐅᓂᖁᒥᓐ. ᐱᓕᕆᐊᕆᕝᕙᑕᒐᑦ ᑐᓴᐅᑎᓕᕆᓂᖅ ᖃᐅᔨᒪᔭᐅᖕᒪᓐ, ᑕᐃᒪᓕ ᓂᕆᐅᑦᑎᐊᕐᐳᒍ ᐱᓕᕆᖃᑎᖃᕈᒪᑎᓪᓗᑕ ᐃᓄᖕᓂ ᓄᓇᕗᒻᒥᐅᓂ ᐱᕈᕐᑎᑦᑎᕝᕕᓕᐊᓂᒃᑯ ᓯᕗᓂᑦᑎᓐᓂ. ᓄᐊᑦᕋᔅᑎᐅᓪᑯᓐᓂ ᑕᑎᕐᑲᓚᐅᓇᑦ, ᐱᒃᑯᓕᓯᒪᔪᑦ ᐅᑭᐅᕐᑕᖅᑐᒥᓐ ᐱᓕᕆᕙᕐᑲᕐᓂᖕᒋᓐᓂᑦ, ᐱᔭᑦᑎᕋᕐᑎᐅᑎᓪᓗᒋ ᓄᑖᖕᒍᓯᒪᓖᓂᑦ ᐱᓕᕆᔾᔪᑎᓂᑦ.

NorthwesTel congratulates the people of Nunavut on the birth of their new territory. At Northwestel, we understand the pride and sense of accomplishment that results from hard work and achieving your goals. With a solid history of providing full-service communications, we look forward to working in partnership with the people of Nunavut and building for the future. Look to Northwestel, a proudly northern company, providing today's finest high-tech communications solutions.

NorthwesTel

1-800-205-5003

WHAT'S IN A NAME?

ᐊᑎᖅ ᖃᓄᐃᕝᔪᑕᐅᖓᒪᓐ?

Names, as well as events, mark the road to Nunavut

ᐊᑏᑦ, ᐊᒻᒪ ᐱᓕᕆᓂᐅᔪᑦ, ᓇᓗᓇᐃᒃᑯᑕᐅᒍᑦ ᐊᖅᑯᑎᒧᓐ ᓄᓇᕗᒧᓐ

By Ann Meekitjuk Hanson

The technical translation of *nunavut* is simply "our land." The emotional, spiritual, deeper meaning of nunavut or *nunavun* is "our homeland." The unspoken meaning stresses "home." To some Inuit, with deeper knowledge of the language, when nunavut is spoken, the silent understanding means "we share in this together, unconditionally," and there is an intense gratitude.

We have gone through a lot in a short time. Among those who have left their mark on us are whalers, Christian ministers, traders, police, teachers, scientists, and southern politicians. Some of these people had good intentions, and our ancestors welcomed them because tradition and belief ruled them with good manners, kindness, and curiosity. Inuit today inherited both the good and bad effects of these influences.

I grew up knowing myself as an *Inuk* — simply translated, a human, breathing being. Later, I learned I was called an *Eskimo*. I never identified the word Eskimo as an insult. In fact, when I was travelling outside of Nunavut I would voluntarily and proudly offer the information, "I am an Eskimo." Today, I am back to Inuk.

ᑎᑎᕋᖅᑐᖅ ᐋᓐ ᒥᑭᔾᔪᒃ ᕼᐋᓐᓴᓐ

ᑐᑭᒋᔭᖓ ᑎᑎᕋᖅᑕᐅᓯᒪᓂᖓᒍᑦ ᓄᓇᕗᑦ ᑐᑭᑐᐃᓐᓇᓕᒃ "ᐅᕙᒍᑦ ᓄᓇᕗᑦ." ᐃᒃᐱᒋᓂᒃᑯᑦ, ᐃᓅᓯᒃᑯᑦ, ᑕᕐᓂᒃᑯᑦ ᑐᑭᖃᕐᓂᖅᓴᐅᔪᖅ ᓄᓇᕗᑦ ᐅᕝᕙᓐᓃᑦ ᓄᓇᕗᓐ "ᐅᕙᒍᑦ ᐊᖏᕐᕋᓛᓗ ᓄᓇᖁᑎᕆᔭᕗᑦ." ᑕᐃᒥᐊᖃᓐᖏᑦᑕᕗᑦ ᑐᑭᖃᖅᑐᖅ "ᐊᖏᕐᕋᓇᓚᑦᑎᔪ." ᐃᓄᖕᓄᑦ ᐃᓚᖏᓐᓄᑦ ᑐᑭᓯᓯᒪᓂᖃᕐᓂᖅᓴᐅᔪᓄᑦ ᐅᖃᐅᓯᕐᒥᒃ, ᐅᓇ ᐅᖃᐅᓯᖅ ᓄᓇᕗᑦ ᑕᐃᔭᐅᔭᕌᖓᑦ, ᐅᖃᖅᑕᐅᒋᐊᖃᓐᖏᑦᑐᒃᑯᑦ ᑐᑭᓯᓂᖃᕈᑕᐅᓯᖅᑐᖅ. ᐃᒪᓐᓇ "ᐅᓇ ᓄᓇ ᓄᓇᒥᔭᕗᑦ, ᐃᓯᒪᖅᓯᑎᐊᖅᑲᑕ" ᐊᒻᒪᓗ ᐊᒃᓯᐊᓗᒃ ᖁᔭᓕᓂᖃᖅᑐᖅ ᑐᑭᖓ.

ᐊᒃᓯᕿᓂᖃᖅᓯᒪᔪᒍᑦ ᐊᑯᓂᐅᓐᖏᑦᑑᓚᓗᐊᖑᔪᒥ. ᒪᑯᓄᖓᓗ ᐊᓯᔾᔨᖅᑕᐅᓯᒪᓪᓗᑕ ᑎᑭᑦᑐᓄᑦ ᐊᕐᕕᕐᓂᐊᖅᑎᓄᑦ, ᐊᔪᕐᓯᐃᔨᓄᑦ, ᓂᐅᕕᖅᑎᓄᑦ, ᐸᓖᓯᓄᑦ, ᐃᓕᓐᓂᐊᖅᑎᑎᔨᓄᑦ, ᖃᐅᔨᒪᔨᕐᔪᐊᓄᑦ, ᐊᒻᒪᓗ ᖃᓪᓗᓈᖖᒎᖅᑐᓄᑦ ᒐᕙᒪᓕᕆᔨᓄᑦ. ᐊᒥᓱᑦ ᑖᒃᑯᐊ ᐱᑦᑎᐊᕈᒪᓪᓗᑎᑦ ᐃᖅᑲᐃᔭᓚᐅᕐᓗᐊᖅᑐᑦ ᐊᒻᒪᓗ ᓯᕗᓪᓕᕆᔭᕗᑦ ᑐᕌᖓᓇᓚᐅᖅᓗᑎᒃ ᑎᑭᓕᖅᑐᓄᑦ. ᐃᓕᖅᑯᓯᕐᒥᓂᒃ ᐊᑐᖅᓗᑎᒃ ᑐᕌᖓᓯᒃᑎᑎᓚᐅᕐᒪᑕ, ᐱᑦᑎᐊᓇᐊᖅᑲᕐᓂᕐᒥᒃ ᐊᒻᒪᓗ ᑕᑯᔭᓇᐅᕐᓂᕐᒧᑦ. ᐃᓄᐃᑦ ᐅᓪᓗᒥᐅᔪᖅ ᑕᒪᒃᑭᖓᓂᒃ ᐱᐅᔪᓂᒃ ᐱᐅᓐᖏᑦᑐᓂᒃᓗ ᑭᖑᓂᖅᑎᑕᐅᓯᒪᓪᓚᖅᑐᑦ.

ᐱᕈᓚᐅᖅᑐᖓ ᖃᐅᔨᒪᓪᓗᖓ ᐃᓅᓪᓚ. ᑭᖑᓂᐊᒍᑦ ᐃᓕᑎᑕᐅᓪᓗᖓ ᑕᐃᔭᐅᕙᓪᓚ Eskimo-ᒥᒃ. ᐅᖃᐅᓯᐅᑉ ᐱᐅᓐᖏᓐᓂᖓᓂᒃ ᐃᓯᒪᕆᓚᐅᓐᖏᑦᑕᕋᓕ. ᓲᖃᐃᒻᒪᓕ, ᐊᐅᓪᓚᖅᓯᒪᓕᕋᐃᕙᓪᓚ ᓄᓇᕗᑦ ᓯᓚᑎᖓᓃᑦ ᐅᖃᖅᐸᓚᐅᖅᑐᖓ ᐊᓕᐊᓇᐃᒍᓯᒃᑯᖓ "Eskimo-ᖑᔪᖓ." ᐅᓪᓗᒥ, ᐅᑎᕐᒥᔪᖓ ᐃᓅᓂᕋᖅᑯᖓ.

ᑕᐃᑦᓯᒪᓂ, ᐃᓐᓇᑐᖃᐃᑦ ᐊᑎᖁᑦᑕᓚᐅᖅᑐᑦ ᐃᓅᓕᖅᑐᓂᒃ ᐃᓚᒋᔭᒥᖕᓂᒃ ᐅᕝᕙᓐᓃᑦ ᖃᓂᒋᔭᒥᖕᓂᒃ ᐃᓅᖕᓂᒃ ᐊᑎᖅᑲᕆᑦ, ᐊᒻᒪᓗ ᐊᒥᓯᑦ ᐊᑎᑐᖃᓇᔭᐅᔪᑦ — ᐃᒪᓐᓇᑐᑦ ᐊᓂᖅᒥᐅᖅ, ᐊᓐᓄᓚᑯᓗ, ᐊᓐᓄᕋᖅ, ᐊᓇᖅᑯᖅ, ᑭᒪᓗ, ᐊᐃᑏ, ᒫᑐ, ᖁᕕᐊᓇᑦᑐᑯᓗᒃ, ᒪᑭᕝᕕᒃ, ᔭᑕᐃ, ᐊᐃᐅᓛ, ᓲ,

"I hope Nunavut, and the Inuit, in some way formally recognize the work of their negotiators . . . these people made tremendous personal sacrifices over the years to participate in negotiations."

– Barry Dewar, a senior federal negotiator on the land claim

Traditionally, it was up to elders to name babies after relatives or favorite people, and many given names had long been used — names like Aniqmiuq, Annogakuluuk, Annogaq, Arnaquq, Kimalu, Aitii, Maatu, Quvianatukuluk, Makivik, Yutai, Aiuula, Suu, Yugayugausiq, Arnaguatsaaq, Angusimaajuq, Qiilabaq, Nuiijaut, Ikilluaq, and thousands more. When the missionaries came, some could not pronounce these ancient names properly. They gave our people names from the Bible — Joanasie, from John, Jamiesie (James), Olutie (Ruth), Miali (Mary), Salamonie (Solomon), Noah, Jonah, Ipeelie (Abel), Ilisapie (Elizabeth), and so on. Among ourselves, we always used our ancient names. So when I was baptized, I became Annie, but to my parents and elders, I was Lutaaq, Pilitaq, Palluq, or Inusiq.

To the Canadian government, however, I was Annie E7-121! In the early 1940s, Inuit had to be counted and identified for government records so that our parents or guardians could receive family allowance. E stood for east and W stood for west. We were given a small disc looped on a sturdy string, brown with black lettering. I only learned about last names when I went to school in Toronto in the early 1960s. My foster parents let me use their family name, so in Toronto I went by Annie Cotterill — E7-121 was not a very attractive name for a young girl! And when I came back home, I certainly did not want to be Miss E7-121 as a secretary in a government office, so I took my father's first name, Meekitjuk, as a surname.

I was not alone in disliking the number system. By the late 1960s, Simonie Michael, our first elected Inuk member of the Northwest Territories legislative assembly, stated that he no longer wanted to be known by his E7- number. Thus, Project Surname was created. Abe Okpik, a respected Inuk from the western Arctic, headed the project. Between 1968 and 1970, Abe visited every Inuit home and asked the families to choose a name. The head of the family picked a surname — often a relative's given name — and we were no longer known by numbers.

Place names, just like our own traditional names, are indigenous and meaningful. Kimmirut, or "heel," for the shape of a rock outcropping there, the community I am from, has always been Kimmirut. Until just a short time ago, however, it usually appeared as Lake Harbour on maps. Initiatives like the South Baffin Place Names Project are slowly returning Nunavut's communities to their names of old: Frobisher Bay officially became Iqaluit ("school of fish") in 1987, and in November 1998, Broughton Island became Qikiqtarjuaq ("big island").

But most importantly, there is the word nunavut. Now the same word, meaning our homeland, is being capitalized as Nunavut, to become a place name, a new *inuksuk* (directional beacon) for the world to see, and for us to share and to pass on to our children. What joy!

Ann Meekitjuk Hanson is a freelance writer living in Iqaluit.

ᔪᒐᔪᒐᐅᓯᖅ, ᐊᓐᓇᖅᑯᐊᒃᒍᖅ, ᐊᙳᓯᒫᔪᖅ, ᕿᓚᕝᕙᖅ, ᓄᐃᔭᐅᑦ, ᐃᑭᓪᓗᐊᖅ, ᐊᒻᒪᓗ ᐊᓯᖏᑦ ᐊᒥᓱᒻ ᓐᑦ. ᐊᔪᓕᖅᓯᐃᔩᑦ ᑎᑭᒻᒪᑕ, ᑕᒃᑯᓂᖓ ᐊᑎᖅᑲᕐᓂᒃ ᑕᐃᓯᑦᑎᐊᕈᓐᓇᓗᓐᖏᑦᑐᑦ. ᐅᑭᑦᑎᓐᓂᒃ ᐊᑦᑏᑦᑕᓗᖅᒪᑕ ᒪᒃᐱᖏᒥᖕᒐᖅᑐᒥᑦ (ᐃᔾᔪᔪᓂᑦ) — ᒪᑯᓂᖓ ᔪᐊᓇᓯ, John-ᒥᑦ, ᔩᒥᓯ, (James), ᐅᑎ (Ruth), ᒥᐊᓕ (Mary), ᓵᓗᒨᓂ (Solomon), ᓄᐊ, ᔫᓇ, ᐊᐃᐱᓕ (Abel), ᐃᓕᓴᐱ (Elizabeth), ᐊᒻᒪᓗ ᑕᐃᒪᓐᓇ ᐊᒥᓲᑦ ᓲᓕ. ᐅᕙᑦᑎᓐᓂ, ᐊᑎᑦᑲᕗᑦ ᐊᑐᖅᑕᓗᖅᑕᕗᑦ. ᐸᖅᑎᑕᐅᒐᒪ, Annie-ᖑᓕᐅᖅᓯᒪᔪᖓ, ᑭᓯᐊᓂᓕ ᐊᖓᔪᖅᑳᓐᓄᑦ ᐃᓄᑐᖅᑲᓄᓪᓗ, ᐊᑎᖃᓚᐅᖅᑐᖓᓕ ᓗᑖᖅ, ᐱᓕᑕᖅ, ᐸᓪᓗᖅ, ᐅᕝᕙᓃᑦ ᐃᓅᓯᖅ.

ᑲᓇᑕᐅᑉ ᒐᕙᒪᒃᑯᖓᓐᓄᓕ, ᑭᓯᐊᓂᓕ, Annie E7-121-ᖑᓚᐅᖅᓯᒪᔪᖓ! ᐊᕐᕌᒍᐃᑦ ᐱᒋᐊᓕᕠᖅᑎᓪᓗᒋᑦ 1940-ᓂ ᐃᓄᐃᑦ ᓈᓴᖅᑕᐅᒋᐊᖅᑲᓚᐅᕐᒪᑕ ᐊᒻᒪᓗ ᓇᓗᓇᐃᔭᖅᑕᐅᓗᑎᒃ ᒐᕙᒪᒃᑯᓐᓄᑦ ᑎᑎᕋᖅᓯᒪᕐᑯᑎᖏᓐᓄᑦ ᐊᖓᔪᖅᑳᕗᑦ ᑲᒪᔨᒋᔭᕗᓪᓕ ᓄᑕᕋᖅᓯᐅᑎᑖᖅᑕᕐᑯᓪᓗᒋᑦ. E ᑐᑭᖃᖅᑎᑕᐅᓪᓗᓂ ᑲᓇᖕᓇᖅ ᐊᒻᒪᓗ W ᐱᖓᖕᓇᖅ. ᑐᑭᖃᖅᑎᑕᐅᓪᓗᓂ ᐅᐊᓕᓂᕐᒧᑦ. ᒥᑭᔫᑲᓗᖕᓂᒃ ᐊᖕᒪᓗᑭᑖᖑᔪᓂᑦ ᑐᓂᔭᐅᓚᐅᖅᑐᒍᑦ ᐅᔭᒥᒃ-ᓴᑦᑎᓐᓂᒃ ᓴᕐᖏᔪᒥᒃ ᐱᑐᒍᑎᖃᖅᓱᑎᒃ ᓂᕈᖓ-ᑖᖑᓇᔭᖅᑐᒥᒃ, ᑲᔪᖅᓱᓂ ᕿᕐᓂᖅᑐᓂᒃ ᑎᑎᕋᖃᐅᖅᓱᓂ. ᖃᐅᔨᓕᑕᐃᓐᓇᓚᐅᖅᑐᖓ ᑭᖑᓪᓕᕐᒥᒃ ᐊᑎᖃᖅᐸᒃᑐᓂᒃ ᐊᐅᓪᓚᕐᓚ ᑐᕌᖅᑐᒧᑦ ᐱᒋᐊᓕᕠᖅᑎᓪᓗᒋᑦ ᐊᕐᕌᒍᑦ 1960-ᖑᔪᑦ. ᑎᒍᐊᖅᓯᒃᑲᒃ ᐊᒥᕐᒥᖕᓂᒃ ᐊᑐᖅᑎᑎᖕᒪᑎᒃ ᑕᐃᔭᐅᑦᑕᓚᐅᖅᑐᖓ, ᑐᕌᑐᒦᑎᓪᓗᖓ ᐃᒪᓐᓇ Annie Cotterill - E7-121 ᐊᑎᑎᐊᕚᐅᓐᖏᑦᑐᕈᓚᐅᕐᒪᑦ ᓂᕕᐊᖅᓯᐊᒧᑦ! ᐊᖏᕐᕋᓐᓄᑦ ᐅᑎᕐᒪ ᑕᐃᔭᐅᔪᓐᓇᓚᐅᓐᖏᓐᓇᒪ ᒐᕙᒪᒃᑯᓐᓂ ᐃᖅᑲᓇᐃᔭᖅᑎᐅᑎᓪᓗᖓ ᐃᒪᓐᓇ Miss - E7-121, ᑕᐃᒪᓕ ᐊᑖᑕᒪ ᐊᑎᖓᓂᒃ ᓯᕗᓪᓕᐅᔪᒥᒃ, ᒥᑭᔾᔪᖕᒥᒃ ᐊᑎᖃᓕᓚᐅᖅᐳᖓ ᑐᓪᓕᖕᓂᒃ ᐊᑎᖏᓕᖅᓱᒍ.

ᐃᓄᑐᐊᖑᓚᐅᓐᖏᑦᑐᖓ ᐱᐅᒃᓴᓐᖏᓐᓂᓐᓂ ᓈᓴᐅᑎᖃᖃᑦᑕᕐᓂᕐᒥᒃ. ᐊᑐᓕᑐᖃᖅᑎᓪᓗᒋᑦ 1960-ᖑᔪᑦ, ᓯᐃᒧᓂ ᒪᐃᑯ, ᓯᕗᓪᓖᓪᑐᔪᒥᒃ ᒪᓕᒐᓕᐅᖅᑎᓄᑦ ᓂᕈᐊᖅᑕᐅᓯᒪᔪᖅ ᐃᓅᓪᓗᓂ ᖃᐅᔨᒪᔭᐅᒍᒪᙱᓐᒪᒻᒪᑦ E7-ᓈᓴᐅᑎᒥᒍᑦ. ᑕᐃᒪᓐᓇ ᐊᑏᓂᕐᒧᑦ ᐱᕙᓪᓕᐊᑎᑕᐅᔪᖅ ᐱᒋᐊᖅᑎᑕᐅᓚᐅᖅᓯᒪᔪᖅ. ᐄᑉ ᐅᒃᐱᒃ, ᖃᐅᔨᒪᔭᐅᑦᑎᐊᖅᑐᖅ ᐅᐊᓕᓂᕐᒥᐅᑕᖅ, ᓯᕗᓕᖅᑎᐅᓚᐅᖅᑐᖅ ᐱᕙᓪᓕᐊᑎᑕᐅᔪᒥ. ᐱᒋᐊᓕᕠᖅᑎᓪᓗᒋᑦ 1968ᓗ 1970ᓗ ᐊᑯᓐᖓᓂ ᖑᔪᑦ, ᐅᒃᐱᒃ ᓇᒧᒃᑖᖅ ᐃᓄᐃᑦ ᐃᓪᓗᖏᓐᓄᐊᖅᓱᓂ ᐊᑎᓕᖅᑐᐃᓚᐅᖅᑐᖅ ᐊᐱᕆᑦᑕᖅᓱᓂᒋᑦ ᐃᓚᒌᑦ ᖃᓄᖅ ᐊᑎᖃᕈᒪᖕᒪᖖᒋᑕ. ᐃᓚᒌᓂ ᐊᖓᔪᖅᑲᕆᔭᐅᔪᖅ ᓂᕈᐊᖅᓱᓂ ᐊᑎᕆᔭᐅᓚᖕᒐᔪᒥᒃ-ᐊᒥᓱᐃᖅᓱᓂ ᐊᑎᕆᔭᐅᓪᓗᓂ ᐃᓚᒋᔭᐅᔪᑉ-ᐊᒻᒪᓗ ᑕᐃᒪ ᓈᓴᐅᑎᒃᑯᑦ ᓇᓗᓇᐃᖅᓯᒪᔭᐅᓂᓚᐅᖅᑐᒍᑦ.

ᓄᓇᓄᑦ ᐊᑎᖑᑎᕆᔭᐅᔪ, ᔫᓗ ᐊᑎᖅᑎᑎᑐᑦ, ᐊᑎᕆᔭᐅᖃᐅᔪᑦ ᐊᒻᒪᓗ ᑐᑭᖃᑦᑎᐊᖅᓱᑎᒃ. ᑭᒻᒥᕈᑦ, ᐅᕙᓃᑦ ᑭᖕᒥᒃ, ᐊᑎᕆᔭᐅᓯᒪᔪᖅ ᐅᔭᖅᑲᒥᒃ ᑭᖕᒥᒃᑎᑐᑦ ᑕᐅᑦᑐᓕᖕᒥᒃ ᐱᔾᔪᑎᖃᖅᓱᓂ. ᖃᖓᓕᕠᖑᓚᐅᖅᑐᕐᓕ ᖃᐅᔨᒪᔭᐅᑦᑕᓚᐅᖅᑐᖅ ᐃᒪᓐᓇ Lake Harbour ᓄᓇᕐᖑᐊᓂ. ᐱᓇᓱᒃᑕᐅᓯᒪᔪᑦ ᔫᕐᓗ ᕿᑭᖅᑖᑉ ᓄᓇᓂᒃ ᐊᑎᖃᖅᑎᖏᓐᓂᒃ ᑲᑎᖅᓯᐃᓂᖏᑕ ᐱᕙᓪᓕᐊᑎᑕᐅᓂᖓᑕ ᓱᒃᑲᐃᑦᑐᒥᒃ ᐅᑎᖅᑎᑎᕙᓪᓕᐊᓪᓗᐊᖅᑐᖅ ᐊᑎᖃᖅᑲᓂᒃ: Frobisher Bay ᐃᖃᓗᕐᖑᖅᓱᓂ 1987-ᒥ, ᐊᒻᒪᓗ ᓄᕕᐱᕆ 1998-ᒥ, Broughton Island ᕿᑭᖅᑕᕐᔪᐊᖑᓚᐅᖅᑐᖅ.

ᐊᑐᕐᓂᖅᐸᖑᔪᕐᓕ, ᑖᓐᓇ ᐅᖃᐅᓯᖅ ᓄᓇᕗᑦ (nunavut). ᑖᓐᓇᑕᐃᓐᓇᖅ ᓱᓕ ᐅᖃᐅᓯᖅ, ᑐᑭᖃᒃ ᐊᖏᕐᕋᓱᑦᑎᓐᓂ ᓄᓇᒥᒃ, ᐊᑎᓪᓚᑖᕐᖑᖅᑎᑕᐅᔪᖅ ᑎᑎᖅᑲᖓ ᓯᕗᓪᓕᑦᑐᖅ ᐊᖏᓪᓕᖅᑎᑕᐅᓪᓗᓂ Nunavut, ᒫᓐᓇ ᐊᑎᓱᐅᓪᓚᖅᓱᓂ ᓄᓇᒧᑦ, ᓄᑖᖑᓪᓗᓂ ᐃᓄᒃᓱᒃᑎᑐᑦ ᑭᒃᑯᓪᓚᑦᑖᓄᑦ ᑕᑯᔭᐅᔭᕐᓇᖅᑐᖅ, ᐊᒻᒪᓗ ᐅᕙᑦᑎᓐᓄᑦ ᑭᖑᕚᑦᑎᓐᓄᑦ ᑐᓂᔭᕐᓇᖅᓴᖅᑕᐳᑦ. ᐊᓕᐊᓇᐃ!

ᐋᓐ ᒥᑭᔪᒃ Hᐋᓐᓴᓐ ᐃᖃᓗᖕᒥᐅᑕᖅ ᓱᓕᓴᐊᖃᓯᖅᑐᖅ ᖃᓄᐃᓐᓇᖅ ᐃᓄᐃᑦ ᐃᓕᖅᑯᓯᖏᓐᓄᑦ ᑐᑦᑖᖓᔪᓂᒃ.

A government-issued E-number disk

ᒐᕙᒪᒃᑯᓐᓂ-ᐋᖅᑭᒃᑕᐅᓂᖅ ᓇᓗᓇᐃᒃᑯᑎ ᓇᐃᓴᐅᑎ

"ᓂᕆᐅᒃᐳᖓ ᓄᓇᕗᑦ, ᐊᒻᒪᓗ ᐃᓄᐃᑦ, ᓇᐅᒃᑯᒥᐊᖅ ᐃᓕᓴᖅᓯᓯᒪᓂᐊᕐᐳᑦ ᐋᔩᖅᑎᐅᓚᐅᖅᑐᓂᑦ. . . ᐅᑯᐊᓕ ᐃᖕᒥᖕᓂ ᐊᑐᕈᓐᓇᕐᑕᖏᓐᓂ ᓴᓂᕝᕙᐃᓪᓗᑎᒃ ᐊᕐᕌᒍᓄᓴᖕᓂ ᐋᔩᖃᑕᐅᖃᑦᑕᓚᐅᕐᐳᑦ."

- ᐱᐅᓕ ᑑᕗ, ᐊᖏᔪᒃᖠᖅ ᒐᕙᒪᑐᖃᒃᑯᓐᓂ ᐋᔩᖅᑎᐅᓂᒃ ᓄᓇᑖᕐᓯᓐᖓᓂᕐᒧᑦ

Nunavut ᓄᓇᕗᑦ

The Northern Sun... Rising on a Dream!

ᐅᑭᐅᖅᑕᖅᑑᑉ ᓯᕿᓂᖓ... ᓵᖅᑭᓕᕐᐳᖅ ᐃᓱᒪᒋᔭᐅᔪᑐᕐᑳᓗᖕᒍᓐ!

Canada Post Corporation celebrates with the people of Nunavut, as the sun rises on a dream that has become a reality.

With the birth of this new territory, Canada Post also marks the 10th anniversary of its own Northern Services Division. In the past 10 years, Northern Services has come a long way in improving the quality of postal services **for** Northerners **by** Northerners.

As a leading business in Nunavut, injecting over $13 million annually into the local economy, Canada Post is proud of the role it will continue to play in supporting the growth and evolution of Nunavut.

ᑲᓇᑕᒥ ᑎᑎᖅᑲᖅᓂᐊᕐᕕᓕᕆᔨᒃᑯᑦ ᓇᓪᓕᐅᓐᓂᕐᓯᐅᖅᑲᑕᐅᒐᑦ ᐃᓄᖕᓂ ᓄᓇᒐᒻᒦᑦᑐᓂ, ᓯᕿᓂᖅ ᓵᖅᑭᓕᕐᑎᓪᓗᒍ ᐃᓱᒪᒋᔭᐅᔪᑐᕐᑳᓗᖕᒍ ᓵᖅᑭᒻᒪᕆᒃᑐᒍᓐ.

ᓄᑖᖅ ᓄᓇ ᐃᒻᒥᒃᑰᖅᑐᖅ ᐊᕕᒃᓯᒪᓂᒃᑯ ᐱᒋᐊᓕᖅᑎᓪᓗᒍ, ᑲᓇᑕᒥ ᑎᑎᖅᑲᖅᓂᐊᕐᕕᓕᕆᔨᒃᑯ ᐊᒻᒪ ᓇᓪᓕᐅᓐᓂᕐᓯᐅᖅᑲᑕᐅᓕᕐᒪᑕ ᐊᕐᖂᒍᓂ ᖁᓕᓂ ᐅᑭᐅᖅᑕᖅᑐᖅᒥᓐ ᐱᔾᔪᑎᖃᖅᓂᖏᓐᓄᑦ. ᐊᕐᖂᒍᑦ ᖁᓕᓂ, ᐅᑭᐅᖅᑕᖅᑐᖅᒥ ᐱᔾᔪᑎᖃᕐᓂᐅᔪᖅ ᐊᐹᓐᖕᒐᑲᓪᓚᕈᓗᒍ ᐱᒋᐊᕐᓯᒪᒐᑦ ᐱᔾᔪᑎᖃᐅᑏ ᐱᐅᓯᕚᓪᓕᕐᑎᒐᓱᒃᑐᓂᔾᔭᒃ ᐅᑭᐅᖅᑕ-ᖅᑐᖅᒥᐅᓄᑦ ᐅᑭᐅᖅᑕᖅᑐᖅᒥᐅᓂᑦ.

ᓯᕗᓕᐅᕐᑎᐅᑎᓪᓗᒋ ᓇᖕᒥᓂᖅ ᐊᐅᓚᑕᐅᔪᓂᑦ ᓄᓇᕗᒻᒥ, ᐊᑐᖅᐸᒃᓗᑎᒃ $13-ᒥᓕᐊᓐᑖᓚᓂ ᐊᕐᖂᒍᑕᒫᓐ ᓄᓇᓕᖕᓄ ᑮᓇᐅᔭᓕᐅᕐᕈᑎᓂ, ᑲᓇᑕᒥ ᑎᑎᖅᑲᖅᓂᐊᕐᕕᓕᕆᔨᒃᑯᑦ ᐱᒃᑯᓕᒐᑦ ᐱᓕᕆᓂᕆᕐᑲᑦᑕᕐᑕᖕᖏᓐᓂᑦ ᐃᑲᔪᖅᑐᐃᕙᒃᑎᓪᓗᒋᑦ ᐱᕈᖅᐸᓪᓕᐊ-ᓂᐅᔪᒥᓐ ᐊᒻᒪ ᐋᖅᑭᒃᐸᓪᓕᐊᔪᒥᓐ ᓄᓇᕗᒻᒥ.

C O N G R A T U L A T I O N S ᐱ ᒃ ᑯ ᓈ ᓘ ᔭ ᓯ

CANADA POST POSTES CANADA